P9-CDB-817

THE
BEECHERS

Other Books by Milton Rugoff

Prudery and Passion: Sexuality in Victorian America
The Great Travelers (Editor)
The Penguin Book of World Folk Tales (Editor)
Donne's Imagery: A Study in Creative Sources

This family portrait is thought to have been taken at the studio of the famous photographer Mathew Brady in 1859. Standing, from the left: Thomas, William, Edward, Charles, Henry. Seated, from the left: Isabella, Catharine, Lyman, Mary, Harriet. Two members of the family were absent: James (left insert), who was a missionary in China, and George (right insert), who had died in 1843.

THE BEECHERS

❧

An American Family
in the Nineteenth Century

❧

MILTON RUGOFF

1817

HARPER & ROW, PUBLISHERS, New York

Cambridge, Hagerstown, Philadelphia, San Francisco,
London, Mexico City, São Paulo, Sydney

As always,
to Helen

THE BEECHERS. Copyright © 1981 by Milton Rugoff. All rights reserved. Printed in the United States of America. No part of this book may be used or reproduced in any manner whatsoever without written permission except in the case of brief quotations embodied in critical articles and reviews. For information address Harper & Row, Publishers, Inc., 10 East 53rd Street, New York, N.Y. 10022. Published simultaneously in Canada by Fitzhenry & Whiteside Limited, Toronto.

FIRST EDITION

Designer: C. Linda Dingler

Library of Congress Cataloging in Publication Data

Rugoff, Milton
  The Beechers: an American family in the nineteenth century.
  Bibliography: p.
  Includes index.
  1. Beecher family. I. Title.
CT274.B43R83 1981   973'.09'92 [B]   80-8696
ISBN 0-06-014859-4

81 82 83 84 85 10 9 8 7 6 5 4 3 2 1

95783

BELMONT COLLEGE LIBRARY

C T
274
.B43
R83
1981

Contents

III

Returning East

1850–1870

IV

Sunset of a Dynasty

1870–1900

Illustrations

Frontispiece: Family portrait (Photograph by Mathew Brady; Stowe-Day Foundation)

Acknowledgments

Anyone who writes about the Beechers is above all indebted to the many biographers and scholars who have written about various members of the family. I have tried to acknowledge my specific debts to them in my Notes on the Text and in the bibliography.

I profited greatly from the comments on the manuscript by Joseph S. Van Why, director of the Stowe-Day Foundation of Hartford, by Professor E. Bruce Kirkham, editor of a forthcoming collection of Harriet Beecher Stowe's letters, and Professor Clifford E. Clark, Jr., author of *Henry Ward Beecher: Spokesman of a Middle-Class America.*

I also had the exhilarating experience of receiving the generous praise and shrewd criticism of the late John Beecher, poet, teacher, and worthy descendant of the most bold-minded of his forebears. Another Beecher, Joseph Hooker, grandson of Isabella Beecher Hooker, was kind enough to give me special permission to quote from Isabella's diaries. Most generous was Alfred T. Abeles, husband of the late Margaret Beecher Abeles, who made available some sixty letters by James C. Beecher, James's wife Frances, and their children.

I am grateful to the Illinois College Library for allowing me to have a copy made of the manuscript *Life of Edward Beecher* by Charles Beecher.

I am glad of the opportunity to acknowledge the unstinting cooperation of the following: the Stowe-Day Foundation and especially Joseph S. Van Why, the director, Diana Royce, the head librarian, and Roberta Bradford, who helped in assembling the illustrations; the Research Libraries and the Berg Collection of the New York Public Library; the Schlesinger Library of Radcliffe College, and especially Elizabeth Shenton, assistant to the director; and the Archives and Manuscript division and the Beinecke Library of Yale University, all of whom made available to me many valuable letters and documents.

I cannot speak too warmly of the courtesy and kindness of the following institutions in answering queries or in furnishing copies and granting permission to quote from letters and other papers in their collections or for letting me use their facilities: Amherst College Library, Boston Public Library, Mugar Memorial Library of Boston University, Cincinnati Historical Society, Connecticut Historical Society, Greenburgh Library of Westchester County, N.Y., Houghton Library of Harvard University, Rutherford B. Hayes Library of Fremont, Ohio, Henry E. Huntington Library of San Marino, Cal., Indiana Historical Society, Library of Congress, Massachusetts Historical Society, Clements Library of the University of Michigan, Williston Memorial Library of Mount

Holyoke College, Library of Mechanics and Tradesmen, New York City, Mercantile Library, New York City, Museum of the City of New York, New-York Historical Society, New York State Library, First Congregational Church of Poughkeepsie, New York, Adriance Memorial Library of Poughkeepsie, Tioga County (N.Y.) Historical Society, Alderman Library of the University of Virginia, and the Yale University Art Gallery.

It is a pleasure to be able to thank Curtis Darrah and my daughter Kathy for their help in photographing the illustrations.

I am also much indebted to M. S. Wyeth, executive editor of Harper & Row, for his suggestions and encouragement. Finally, to my wife I owe more than words can express.

Milton Rugoff

New York, January 1981

Preface

I have tried in these pages to give an intimate picture of a segment of American life in the nineteenth century as it was lived by the members of a famous and influential family and, at the same time, to trace through them some of the changes in America's basic values in the nineteenth century.

The lives of the Reverend Lyman Beecher, his three wives, and his eleven surviving chidlren, reaching from the 1790s to 1900, from rural America to industrial America, illustrate in a hundred ways the transition from the last days of Puritanism to the beginning of the age of permissiveness. In two generations the Beechers emerged, along with many other Americans, from a God-centered, theology-ridden world concerned with the fate of man's eternal soul into a man-centered society occupied mainly with life on earth.

But the Beechers are not merely symbols—they are, as all who know them agree, a fascinating, not to say astonishing, family, vital, talented, passionate and marvelously articulate (they wrote well over one hundred books and an untold number of letters). Theodore Parker, a spiritual force himself, said of Lyman Beecher that he was "the father of more brains than any man in America." At least six of the clan achieved wide, and sometimes sensational, attention—Lyman, the father, as a leading preacher with a great store of flavorous opinions, Harriet Beecher Stowe as a truly gifted as well as immensely popular writer, Henry Ward Beecher as a spokesman for Victorian America, who nevertheless left a trail of scandal, Catharine as one of the three great pioneers in education and careers for women, Edward as an early midwestern college president and a close friend of an abolitionist martyr, and Isabella as a militant in the early campaigns for women's rights.

The Beechers were thus at or near the center of three or four of the major social movements of the nineteenth century—the decline of Puritanism and its displacement by a gospel of social service, the women's rights struggle, the antislavery ferment and the Civil War.

But their private lives were just as rich and diverse as their public activities. An old friend of theirs, Dr. Leonard Bacon of Yale, summed it up perfectly when he said: "This country is inhabited by saints, sinners and Beechers." Their trials and struggles, their defeats and victories, their dreams and their despairs, first in the small towns of New England and Long Island, then in Boston and early Cincinnati and in frontier villages of Ohio, Indiana and Illinois, eventually in Brooklyn, Maine and Florida and, for at least two members of the family, in Europe, constitute a family saga of a kind that has not been given the attention it deserves. Where a formal history is a tissue of generalizations, this book consists of particulars; where a history presents vast landscapes, this is a core sample.

"This country is inhabited by saints, sinners and Beechers."

DR. LEONARD BACON, about 1863

THE BEECHER FAMILY

Lyman Beecher (1775–1863) married (1799) Roxana Foote (1775–1816)

1. *Catharine* (1800–1878)

2. *William H.* (1802–1889) married (1832) Katherine Edes (?–1870)
   Six children: Agnes, Mary W., Lyman, Grace, Roxana, Robert E.

3. *Edward* (1803–1895) married (1829) Isabella Porter Jones (1807–1895)
   Eleven children: Edward, Henry H., Frederick W., George H.,
   Alfred, Isabella K., Ellen, Mary P., Eugene, Albert, Alice C.

4. *Mary F.* (1805–1900) married (1827) Thomas Clap Perkins (1798–1870)
   Four children: Frederick, Emily, Charles, Catherine

5. *Harriet* (February–March 1808)

6. *George* (1809–1843) married (1837) Sarah Buckingham (1817–1902)
   Two children: Catherine, George B.

7. *Harriet E.* (1811–1896) married (1836) Calvin Stowe (1802–1886)
   Seven children: Harriet B., Eliza, Henry, Frederick, Georgiana,
   Samuel, Charles

8. *Henry Ward* (1813–1887) married (1837) Eunice Bullard (1812–1897)
   Nine children: Harriet Eliza, unnamed son who died at birth,
   Henry B., George L., Katherine E., William C., Alfred,
   Arthur, Herbert

9. *Charles* (1815–1900) married (1840) Sarah Coffin (1815–1897)
   Six children: Frederick H., Charles M., Helen, Mary I., Essie,
   Hattie

Lyman Beecher married (1817) Harriet Porter (1790–1835)

10. *Frederick* (1818–1820)

11. *Isabella H.* (1822–1907) married (1841) John Hooker (1816–1901)
    Four children: Thomas, Mary, Alice, Edward

12. *Thomas K.* (1824–1900) married (1851) Olivia Day (1826–1853)
    married (1857) Julia Jones (1826–1905)
    Four adopted children from the Farrar family: Anna, Clara,
    Julia, May

13. *James C.* (1828–1886) married (1853) Ann Goodwin Morse (?–1863)
    married (1864) Frances Johnson (1832–1903)
    Three adopted children: Catherine E., Mary Frances, Margaret

Lyman Beecher married (1836) Lydia Beals Jackson (1789–1869)

I

THE
NEW ENGLAND
YEARS

1775-1832

1

LYMAN BEECHER

Belated Puritan

Once it soaked into the grain, the dye of Calvinism was nearly indelible. The Reverend Lyman Beecher loved his oldest daughter Catharine dearly, but when in 1822 her beloved, a professor at Yale College, was drowned at sea, Lyman would not relieve her of the dreadful fear, which was to haunt her endlessly, that the young man was doomed to eternal torment because he had died with his soul unprepared.

By the time Lyman Beecher was ordained in 1798, Puritanism—that is, the Calvinism of the Mathers—was almost dead. It had simply been too intense to be sustained in all its pristine rigor for more than a few generations.

There had been, to be sure, frenetic revivals and violent reawakenings throughout the eighteenth century. But a living faith does not require explosive revivals. And after every revival, including the Great Awakening ignited by Jonathan Edwards and George Whitefield in the 1740s, there was a greater backsliding than ever, a lapse once again into a more temperate faith or even resignation. An Edwards and a Whitefield brought a great bellows to the dying fire of Puritanism, but as soon as they rested from their labors the fire burned low once more.

Lyman Beecher was no Edwards or Whitefield, and in no way as awesome or austere as they, but he thought of himself as directly in the line of such great Puritan divines, and he carried on their work with utmost energy, totally unsuspecting that the world was passing him by. By the time he quit the pulpit he was a relict of a bygone age. But he lived and died convinced that he had done God's bidding in preparing men and women for the day of judgment.

Unlike an Edwards or a Mather, Beecher came not of a dynasty of clergymen but, at least on his father's side, of a line of blacksmiths—of yeomen, not gentlemen. His father, grandfather and great-grandfather had all set their anvils on the stump of the same great oak tree in the Connecticut town of New Haven. They were all physically powerful: Lyman Beecher said of his great-grandfather Joseph that he could pick up a barrel of cider and drink out of the bung hole, that his grandfather Nathaniel could lift a barrel of cider into a cart and that his father, David, could at least carry a full barrel into his cellar.

A sturdy man of middle height, David married five times—some nineteenth-century women's rights advocates would call that "serial polygamy"—and had twelve children. As a blacksmith, he was an essential craftsman (his hoes were said to have been among the best in New England) and his shop was a center of community life. In summer he also farmed, raising a fine grade of rye, "white as wheat."

But the most interesting fact about blacksmith David Beecher was that he was a man of reading and ideas, respected almost as much for his political and social opinions as for his ability to fashion a hoe or a horseshoe. He was part of that early America wherein a man might make his living by the sweat of his brow and the craft of his hands and still be one of the best read and most thoughtful men in the community. David Beecher regularly boarded Yale students and members of the Connecticut legislature (New Haven and Hartford were joint capitals of the state), in part because he liked to exchange ideas and opinions with them.

He prospered and at his death left between four thousand and five thousand dollars, a handsome sum in 1805. But, as his son Lyman summed it up, "In those days, six mahogany chairs in a shut-up parlor were considered magnificent; he never got beyond cherry."

One legacy he bestowed on his family was not quite so admirable. He was subject to what was called dyspepsia—probably aggravated by the highly spiced food the Beechers served in order to please their boarders—and it was on this that he blamed the fits of depression that sometimes overtook him. Such attacks became a kind of family malaise, reappearing in his son Lyman and in later generations of Beechers.

Lyman Beecher was born on October 12, 1775, the only child of his father's third and, it is said, best-beloved wife. His mother, who came of a genteel and respected family that included several clergymen, is described as a tall, fair and lovely woman. She died of consumption two days after his birth, and Lyman was turned over to the care of a childless aunt and uncle, the Lot Bentons, on a farm in nearby Guilford. His father soon remarried, but Lyman never returned home, except for visits and a sojourn or two; and his father clearly did not miss him. That Lyman Beecher never knew his mother and never had a home with his own parents does much to explain his deep attachment to his own children and his lifelong commitment to a large, closely knit family. At one time or another he gave every one of his eleven children—or at least their spiritual condition—as much attention as though each were an only child.

Lyman's uncle, Lot Benton, was a sturdy, independent New England yeoman, a classic New England type, thorny and cross-grained but not unkind. When Lyman would forget to blow out the candle before going to bed, the next night Uncle Lot would say, "Lyman, you shan't have no candle." But he never kept the threat. He had "good, quick, strong land," forty head of cattle, several score sheep and two horses; he made his own tools; he and his family grew oats, corn and flax, rotted, beat and bleached the flax, sheared their sheep and spun the wool, made their own cloth, sheets and shirting, baked bread, made butter and cheese out of the milk of their own cows, and cut and hauled their own wood. In their early married life the Bentons still ate out of wooden trenchers, but later, as a matter of status no less than convenience, they graduated to pewter, and finally to earthenware. In the evening they visited, chatted, ate apples, drank cider and told stories. For amusement Lyman and other boys hunted and fished in nearby woods, played checkers and attended "singing school." On Sunday nights the older boys went acourtin'.

One of Lyman's earliest memories in the world of the Bentons was of a night when a "blood-red arch" lit the sky. That made Stephen Benton, another uncle, declare, "Ah! We don't know at what time the day of judgment will come—at midnight or at cock-crowing," and little Lyman suddenly thought: It has come now. He began to cry and Annie, the adolescent girl who took care of him, put him to bed and distracted him not with fairy tales but with talk of a mysterious thing inside him called his soul.

Lyman grew up on the common country fare of the time: rye bread, milk and cheese, buckwheat cakes, salt pork, corned beef, Indian pudding, pie and cider. His duties were not light: he helped with plowing, hoeing corn, foddering and flax gathering. The climax of his farm labors came one spring when he had to plow a fifteen-acre plot three times over, using a crude, homemade plow hitched to a clumsy pair of oxen. In places the land was as steep as the side of a roof; several times he fell to daydreaming and allowed the plow to wander out of the furrow. As his son Henry later told the story, Lyman was "quick, nervous, restless; and to walk by the dull sides of slow-treading oxen all day long was a task beyond all endurance." So when Uncle Lot went out to the barn one morning and saw a saddle and a bridle lying in the middle of the yard, he was finally convinced that "Lyman would never be good for anything but to go to college." His father agreed. Ever afterward Lyman would say that it was oxen that sent him to college.

After that he worked in the summer and went to school in the winter, his father contributing to his support, but grudgingly.

The Bentons held family prayers daily and the Bible was read every morning; the only books in the house were a Bible and a psalm book. On Sunday, children were permitted to play after three stars became visible in the sky. Once, when Lyman wanted to play before the stars were out, a friend declared that God would put him in a fire and burn him "for-ever and ever." A lifetime later, Beecher recalled with undiminished viv-idness: "I understood what fire was, and what forever was. What emotion I had, thinking, No end! No end! It has been a sort of main-spring ever since." All his life, even during the most esoteric doctrinal disputes, he would retain this quite literal, this primitive sense of God's judgment.

Lyman spent the next two years in preparatory study with his uncle Williston, a parson. Of this uncle he later recalled mainly that he smoked his pipe incessantly, consuming, it was estimated, a ton of tobacco in his lifetime. He also learned from his uncle's dull and bumbling sermons what a sermon should not be. Then, at eighteen, he entered Yale.

New Haven, when Lyman arrived there, was a town of only a few thousand people; pigs roamed freely through the byways and geese had only lately lost that privilege. But any thought that the long reign of Puritanism had made it a place of rural innocence and exclusively God-fearing, law-abiding citizens must take into account the purpose of its new workhouse: The town regulations provided that any justice of the peace might commit to it any

rogues, vagabonds, sturdy beggars, lewd, idle, dissolute, profane and disorderly persons, all runaway stubborn Servants and children, Common Drunkards, Common Night walkers, Pilferers, all persons who neglect their callings, mis-spend their earnings and do not provide for their families, and all persons under distraction unfit to be at large.

Compassion was not exactly abundant: the dependent poor of the town were farmed out to the man who put in the lowest bid to feed and clothe them.

In 1793 Yale itself was little more than a high school in its facilities. Its science equipment consisted of a rusty orrery, a four-foot telescope, a decrepit air pump, a prism, and an elastic pump to demonstrate centrifu-gal force. But this sad array hardly mattered, since the school was devot-ed as much to divinity as to secular studies. And yet Yale was an educational center, sensitive to all the winds of doctrine. As a provincial school it was peculiarly susceptible to British and French ideas, especially those which, like skepticism and so-called infidelism, affected religious faith.

The rationalism of the Age of Enlightenment had contributed

mightily to the American as well as the French Revolution. Irreligious attitudes had filtered into the colonies not only through intellectual channels but coarsely, so to speak, through contact between New England militiamen and British regulars in the French and Indian Wars and between American and French soldiers in the Revolution. The Englishmen had unsettled Americans with their relaxed attitude toward religion and their uninhibited enjoyment of earthy pleasures. The French had proved even more distrubing with a "loose . . . atheism which neither believes nor disbelieves" and by their disdain for what they considered provincial piety.

There was, moreover, something quite contradictory between the freedom and independence fostered by the new republic and the tyrannous character of the Calvinist God. Nothing could have been more alien to the Puritan notion of sinful and puny man than the optimism and self-confidence of democracy. Unorthodox views were a commonplace among the guests at Thomas Jefferson's table, and Jefferson himself characterized the doctrines of Calvin and Athanasius as "the deliria of crazed imaginations"; Franklin was an avowed Deist; Burr a skeptic; and Ethan Allen, rough and ready hero of the Revolution, an enemy of revealed religion who offered his farm for sale in an effort to get out of "this holy state of Connecticut."

But it was Tom Paine, self-taught radical and more of a folk hero than an intellectual, who captured the imagination of the students. Thus there were two Tom Paine societies at Yale when Lyman Beecher entered the school. The president of the college, Ezra Stiles, was a keen-minded and urbane but rather pompous and pedantic little man. He went about in black clergyman's robes and a huge, whitish wig that in his later days, as one observer said, seemed to "extinguish" him.

Stiles was famous for his learning and his intense curiosity, a combination that led him into collecting all manner of scientific odds and ends. But it also betrayed him into an un-Calvinistic passion for the truth. This passion led him as a young tutor to treat deism seriously when that unsettling doctrine, with its vision of an indifferent God, first reached Puritan Yale. The only way "to conquer and demolish it," he announced, "is to come forth in the open field and dispute the matter on an even footing. . . . Truth, and this alone, being in fact our aim, open, frank and generous. . . ."

In time he returned to orthodoxy sufficiently to be made president of the college. And when the ideas of Godwin, Paine, Mary Wollstonecraft and other English radicals surfaced in America, he criticized their adherents as "deluded" and "self-opinionated deniers of the Lord." Yet he would not suppress their views.

But the students were marching to a different drummer. Who needed God if man armed with reason could manage for himself? By 1790 only four or five students were professing Christians, and leading members of the senior class had adopted such names as Voltaire, Rousseau and d'Alembert. The Moral Society of the college was forced to become a secret organization and it expelled any member who disclosed its proceedings. In their daily lives many students behaved like Parisian *bons vivants,* keeping wine and liquor in their rooms and indulging in profanity and other vices. Preachers who denounced all this as "the work of the devil" may well have taken the antics of undergraduates too seriously, but there is no doubt that in the early 1790s Yale—and Harvard too— was hardly a model of Christian morality and discipline.

As a freshman just come from the pious household of his aunt and uncle, Lyman Beecher was repelled by such behavior. He does admit that he played cards several times and swore off only when he fell into debt, so we may suspect more than a little of New England frugality in his avoidance of dissipation. Then, in his sophomore year, at a crucial point in Lyman's development, President Stiles died and the Reverend Timothy Dwight became president of the college. He immediately set about returning the school to Calvinistic dogma and Puritan living.

Dwight, a grandson actually and spiritually of Jonathan Edwards, and born only a few years after the peak of the Great Awakening, was an immensely active and versatile man. He was known for his travels throughout eastern America—which he recorded in huge books—and for his poems, epic in form and unreadability. With an intuitive awareness that democracy and individual liberty were among the natural enemies of a Puritan theocracy, he was implacable in his opposition to Jeffersonian republicanism. Striking at the roots of such attitudes, he declared: "Government, since the days of Mr. Locke, has extensively been supposed *to be founded upon the Social Compact.* No opinion is more groundless than this. . . . The foundation of all government is, undoubtedly, the will of God."

There is hardly a stranger story in American history than the way the iron creed of a very small sect, the Pilgrim Puritans, became the dominant code and source of the overall attitude toward life of most citizens of early America. The Puritans were fiercely independent, courageous and tough in the best sense. But their way of life was born of the needs of men and women who began as an embattled and fanatical minority, became wandering refugees and came to rest in a far-off wilderness where survival depended on loyalty and industry and on propitiating the God for whom they had suffered so much. Wringing their substance, as Harriet Beecher Stowe describes it in one of her New England novels, *Poganuc People,* out of the teeth and claws of reluctant nature, on a rocky and barren soil, under a harsh, forbidding sky, they made a God in their own image and a religion in the spirit of their disciplined lives.

At the daily level, Dwight revived all the terrors of Sin, lashing out triumphantly against pleasure, idleness and prodigality. His attacks against traffic with the "strange woman" would be echoed far into the nineteenth century by two generations of Beechers, first Lyman and later Henry Ward. Assailing "lewdness," Dwight saw the seeds of it in every form of art: "The numbers of the Poet, the delightful melody of Song, the fascination of the Chisel, the spell of the Pencil, have all been volunteered in the service of Satan, for the moral destruction of unhappy man."

Helpless to achieve salvation without God's grace, man was free only to bow, to agonize, and to submit. With divine assurance, "Old Pope Dwight," as he was popularly known, bestowed a fever of uncertainty on his subjects. As a practical evangelist he claimed to appeal to common sense, yet he contemptuously dismissed any intellectual efforts to comprehend God's purpose. He insisted that man was a free agent but that man's entire history showed that he was an incorrigibly rebellious and sinful creature. But students like Lyman Beecher, seeing such a challenging doctrine as a test of the soul, worshiped him.

Confronted by the rationalism of the skeptics, Dwight fought it with impassioned appeals to the students to join in the struggle of good against evil. With great flourishes of rhetoric and Biblical imagery he fulminated against the "infidels" as having "the malice . . . of the Dragon, the cruelty and rapacity of the Beast . . . the fraud and deceit of the false prophet." He convinced a generation of Lyman Beechers that there was no greater mission in life than to help weak and fallible men find their way to God. He handed on to them a view of this world as merely an antechamber to heaven and hell, of men as innately depraved since Adam's fall, and of Christ as having been sent by God to redeem mankind by his suffering and death.

In this tortuous system, those who came to God through the visionary experience called "conversion" were the Elect; they would be saved and would literally go to Heaven. It was the obligation of every Calvinist minister, as member of a church directly appointed by God, to make such "converts." A minister was not simply a church representative but an agent of God, and God was not an abstraction or an ethical force or the prime mover of a clockwork universe but a super-king, a lord who sat in judgment on every act and thought of corrupt man.

So it was that Dwight stirred Yale to a religious fervor that led to half a dozen revivals in the next twenty-five years.

Lyman took to the new president at once—"I was made for action," he said; "The Lord drove me, but I was ready"—and Dr. Dwight remained his lifelong ideal. "I loved him as my own soul," he said in a characteristic outburst, and added, with an equally typical bit of exaggeration, "and he loved me as a son."

It was in his junior year, while spending a weekend at home, that Lyman underwent conversion. As with his earliest fear of God's punishment, the stimulus was a minor incident of daily life. His stepmother, seeing a drunkard stumbling past, remarked that the passerby had once been under religious conviction; she immediately added the hope that he might escape hellfire. As soon as she had left the room, Lyman felt a strong impulse to pray.

I rose to pray and had not spoken five words before I was under as deep a conviction as ever I was in my life. The sinking of the shaft was instantaneous. I understood the law and my heart as well as I do now or shall in the Day of Judgment, I believe. The commandment came, sin revived, and I died, quick as a flash of lightning.

At just this point, a sermon by Dr. Dwight on the theme of "The harvest is past, the summer is ended, and we are not saved" plunged Lyman into despair. But Dwight, a veteran of harvesting souls as well as harrowing them, soon rescued the young man and sent him on his way to conversion. Theoretically, conversion began with a deep conviction of one's sinfulness, followed by repentance, and finally by full submission to God, a total and boundless commitment—a climax sometimes marked by a sudden blaze of light.

This concept is one of the paradoxes of Puritanism: it introduced an intensely emotional, almost mystical factor into the generally low-keyed Protestant experience. In Lyman's case it was characterized by a year of "sullen" moods and a fearful sense of being a hopeless sinner. Lacking guidance and relying on such books as Edwards's *Treatise on the Religious Affections,* he was repeatedly beset by doubts and hypochondria— one of the common side effects of American Calvinism. Light finally came, but by degrees, and he admitted that he could not describe the "clinical theology" of his experience. Indeed, he opposed the subjection of the religious emotions, especially by the young, to "the test of close metaphysical analysis." Later he asserted that he was converted in spite of such analyses. He would add that as a minister he himself had led many souls out of "the sloughs of high Calvinism." The image of the older Calvinism as a trackless bog out of which one must be led by some survivor is revealing. It was at the end of this agonizing period that he decided to become a minister, and in his senior year he added theology to the courses he was already taking in rhetoric, ethics, metaphysics and logic.

Meanwhile he was so hard pressed financially—and sufficiently a practical-minded New Englander—that he took over the college buttery.

He had the job of selling to students not only lemons, shoe black, cork-screws, soap and such, but also cider, strong beer, pipes and tobacco, none of which was provided by the college steward. He even arranged to have an English parson buy his wine supply for him. As a result, he was able to pay off his debts, buy himself a new suit and clear three hundred dollars—almost as much as his annual salary in his first years as a minis-ter. Ironically, scarcely fifteen years later he began a campaign against drinking that made the temperance movement a formidable force in the United States. Nor is it easy to see how he reconciled becoming a beer and tobacco agent only a year after his great religious experience.

Lyman Beecher was graduated in 1797. Although he probably took no note of it, there was a crucial shift in the proportion of the professions in his graduating class. Where Yale had once been made up overwhelm-ingly of young men preparing for the ministry, sixteen of the thirty-one members of the class of 1797 were studying to become lawyers, and only fifteen, ministers. For those who could read the omens, it was clear that the domination by clergymen, especially of the Congregational Church— the state religion of Connecticut—of American society was ending and that lawyers, considered in earlier days little better than pettifoggers, were about to take over political control.

Oblivious of such portents, Lyman spent a year in Yale Divinity School. Under the tutelage of Dr. Dwight he read the works of the lead-ing theologians of an older generation, Hopkins and Edwards, and wrote weekly pieces on such themes as "Is matter eternal?" "Is the Soul Imma-terial?" and "Was Moses Author of the Pentateuch?" Dwight was a leader in the struggle against Deism, and Lyman, relishing military met-aphors, reported that "the battle was hot, the crisis exciting." Revivals had languished during the Revolutionary period; now Dwight helped start them again. " . . . a new day was dawning as I came on the stage," Lyman reported, "and I was baptized into the revival spirit." That spirit was still in him almost sixty years later, when he wrote: "I soon found myself harnessed to the Chariot of Christ, whose wheels of fire have rolled onward, high and dreadful to his foes, and glorious to his friends. I could not stop."

Within a few years the same spirit would generate "camp-meeting" revivals, begun in Kentucky and Tennessee and spread through the "western" lands by so-called circuit riders. Had Beecher been a self-taught preacher instead of a graduate of Yale Divinity School, his ten-dency toward emotional appeals might well have led him into the overheated evangelism that dominated most camp meetings.

Beecher and his classmates spoke at revival meetings twice weekly in nearby New Haven. Lyman's fellow students thought his delivery too vehement as well as too flowery and metaphysical, and he himself later conceded that, inspired by Jonathan Edwards, he "tore a passion to tatters." But it gave him, at the very beginning of his career, a strong and perhaps exaggerated sense of his importance in the affairs of his congregation. And he would never lose his faith in the passionate sermon forcefully delivered.

Lyman now began visiting the home of General Andrew Ward, a patriarchal Revolutionary War veteran who lived at Nutplains, a two-hundred-acre farm on the Connecticut coast just outside Guilford. A descendant of Cavalier stock and an insatiable reader, General Ward had passed along his love of learning and fine engravings to his family. His daughter Roxana had married Eli Foote, a Tory lawyer and merchant known for his cultivated tastes, and she had borne him ten children. Because Foote had become an Episcopalian and General Ward had a leaning in that direction, the Wards joined the Episcopal Church. Just before his last child was born, Eli Foote died of yellow fever. General Ward soon brought his widowed daughter and her very sizable family to Nutplains and became both their father and their teacher.

Whenever the General returned from Hartford, where he served in the state legislature, there was a literary feast in the Ward home, for he brought back the latest books and periodicals. It was hardly surprising, then, that the entire circle in which the Foote girls moved should impress Lyman as one of "uncommon intelligence, vivacity, and wit." He thought Harriet, the eldest girl, as keen as could be—perhaps too keen—and Mary, the youngest, still in her early teens, the prettiest; but to Lyman Beecher, Roxana (she was named after her mother) was "the queen among those girls." "She," he said, "shone preeminent." With the impulsiveness that would always mark his responses, he was ardent from the very first, and she did not hold back.

The Foote clan had of course read *Sir Charles Grandison*, Samuel Richardson's immensely popular novel of a model of gentlemanly virtue and propriety, and young Roxana went so far as to say that she would not marry until she met a man like Sir Charles. In later years Lyman would smugly observe: "I presume she thought she had." It is more likely that Roxana Foote was attracted by the integrity of the blacksmith's son, the intensity of his spiritual commitment and his vitality.

Roxana Foote was a gentle and very talented young woman. Like any well brought up woman of the day, she was accomplished in all the household crafts, from cooking and making clothes to weaving, spinning and needlework. To illustrate feminine competence, Catharine Beecher would tell her students how her mother had in her reading come upon a plan for a "Russian stove," hired a man to make one and helped him build it. Aside from such practical talents, Roxana shared her grandfather's love of books (as soon as *Evelina*, by the much admired Fanny

Burney, arrived from England, a friend of Roxana's rode out on horseback to bring it to her). She had, moreover, a keen interest in history, scientific experiments and nature. Taught by a Haitian who had settled in Guilford, she spoke French fluently. She also sang, played the guitar, and painted miniature portraits on ivory that are still treasured by her descendants.

A sensitive woman, taught to be self-effacing, Roxana is said never to have spoken in the presence of strangers without blushing; and in her later role as a pastor's wife she never led the devotions in the women's weekly prayer meeting. Although she was brought up as an Episcopalian, her parents had come of a strictly Puritan line. Roxana said in later years that she could not remember the time when she had not turned to God in prayer. As the second oldest of ten children of a widowed mother, she had early learned to have children rely on her. Her family would come to think of her as angelic, by which they meant that she was patient, uncomplaining and unselfish. "She experienced resignation," her husband would say, "if anyone ever did . . . and if ever there was a perfect mind as respects submission, it was hers." He meant of course submission not only to God and her fate but also to him. But judging from her influence on her children, her submissiveness may have been more seeming than real.

Despite the intensity of his commitment to the church, Lyman continued to be subject to such violent alterations of despair and hope as might today be considered manic-depressive. Members of his family later insisted that the shifts in mood from exultation to depression and back again were not to be taken as a wavering from a steady, all-governing devotion. Still, such moods did not make him altogether easy to live with.

One episode illustrates strikingly how aggressive Lyman could be in his newfound role of champion of the faith. By contrast, the "submissive" Roxana seems admirably independent and clearheaded. Because she was not as demonstrative in her religious devotion as he, and was, after all, an Episcopalian—to a Calvinist a most unreliable creed—Lyman during their engagement became concerned over the state of her soul. Since she had never been converted by "supernatural agency" and had relied solely on her love of God and his goodness, her attitude seemed to Lyman a challenge to the function of the church. In his view, faith had to be of sterner stuff and the price of God's grace much more painful. Theirs was an immersion, a communion in Puritan anxieties in which all emotions, including the sexual, were sublimated into religious terms. So intense were his convictions that he went to Nutplains on one occasion determined to break off the engagement if Roxana did not agree with him. "I explained my views," he said, "and laid before her the great plan of redemption. As I went on, her bosom heaved, her heart melted, and mine melted too; and I never told her to her dying day what I came for."

His letters to her continue to be shot through with tormented descriptions of his doubts, fears and even tears. It was hardly surprising that her letters of this period—the summer of 1798—record a decline from her native faith and optimism into moments of despondency and guilt. In a remarkably expressive letter she asks for help in finding the "defects" in her prayers:

I am fully persuaded of the truth you have so much endeavored to impress upon me, that mankind are wholly depraved. I have long been sensible of my own inability to do right. But I never did, I do not now give up myself as lost. I feel, I cannot help feeling a hope so strong that ... helpless myself, I shall have help from God. This hope never leaves me. Ought I to encourage it or not? ... I trust to your friendship to point out the danger I am in. Spare me not because it is a delicate subject.

Her next letter was even more intensely agitated. He responded with several long letters tortuously analyzing her attitudes and prescribing various books for her to study. Plainly much of Roxana's increasing anguish, the sense of doom that repeatedly smothered her spurts of elation, was Lyman's doing. He knew that her family thought he was, as he later put it, "making her crazy." Realizing perhaps that in her loving trust she had no need of his tortured metaphysics, he writes: "The idea that you are a child of God and that I am needlessly and wickedly agitating and distressing you, fills me with anxiety."

But soon he was back again with his merciless challenges: if she loves God only because she thinks God is her benefactor it indicates a selfish heart. Her love, he insists, must be disinterested. At this point she began to show resistance, protesting that she loved God *because* he seemed to do only good: "Is it wickedness in me that I do not feel a willingness to be left to go in sin? ... when I pray for a new heart and a right spirit, must I be willing to be denied, and rejoice that my prayer is not heard? Could any real Christian rejoice if God should take from him the mercy bestowed?"

The climax of this trial by Calvinist fire came not with a question as to how much she loved him, but whether she was prepared to rejoice should God damn her for his own honor and glory. Shocked by the assumptions underlying his question, Roxana promptly pointed out that for her to be damned would mean that she had been truly wicked, and it was plainly inconceivable to her that God should find glory or honor in her wickedness and damnation.

At first stunned but then responding with characteristic impetuosity, Lyman cried, "Oh, Roxana, what a fool I've been!" His orthodoxy would never be quite the same again. Later, when converts in the midst of heated revival sessions would cry out that they were ready to be damned for the glory of God, the Reverend Lyman Beecher would sometimes shout: "Be damned, then, if you want to be!"

Nevertheless, when he delivered his first sermon after he was licensed to preach, he sought to distinguish between a true ground for confidence in one's salvation and a false basis such as a "spurious love of God." This warned Roxana as well as his other auditors that his tests for an acceptable love of God were still fearfully hard.

Later that month Lyman Beecher was invited to preach a trial sermon at the Presbyterian Church of East Hampton, Long Island. Riding his horse and carrying all his clothes in a small hair trunk, he went to New London, Connecticut, boarded a sloop and crossed Long Island Sound.

In 1798, East Hampton, with a population of only fifteen hundred, was a remote, quiet hamlet, an offshoot of rural New England. The main street, hardly more than two wheel ruts in a wide, grass-grown roadway, was lined with plain farmhouses, most of them unpainted and each with a woodpile next to the doorway and a barn close by. The street was so little used that flocks of geese constantly wandered about in it. At each end was a windmill. Around the town were dark forests overgrown with tangled vines, and everywhere were great flocks of wild fowl. Not far off was an endless beach of fine, snow-white sand bordering the sea. In their last years in East Hampton, a favorite activity of the older Beecher children was collecting the beach plums that grew thickly on the seaside dunes. Another game was to see who dared, like sanderlings, to run down closest to a retreating wave and rush back as the next wave came tumbling in.

Their father was equally fascinated by the sea. When he tells of a duck hunt at dawn, we get a moving glimpse of hidden sensibilities behind all his energy and exuberance.

'Twas a great deal earlier than I had supposed; but I kept on, and came down the east shore, where the surf is always foaming up on the beach . . . wave after wave, rolling and roaring, as high as your head; but now . . . for once it was still; you couldn't hear a sound except a little softly murmuring noise as the ripples came creeping up the beach; 'twas as still as stillness itself. . . . I laid down my gun and sat down to hear such a silence as I never did before. I forgot the ducks.

The remnants of various Indian tribes, demoralized by drink and poverty, lived on the edge of town. The church, the only one in the area, drew its congregation from half a dozen villages, including Amagansett, Three Mile Harbor, Springs, Fireplace, Wainscott, and the free blacks in an area that is still called Freetown. His parishioners came to church in huge, open nine-seater wagons drawn by a pair of horses; more than half of the inhabitants of those isolated villages made no other journey during their whole lives. There was not a store in town and all purchases were made from New York by way of a small schooner that ran once a week. In his *Travels in New England and New York,* Timothy Dwight said of East Hampton only that its inhabitants seemed to be peculiarly subject to "Hypochondria."

Soon word came that Lyman had been chosen as the next minister. His pay was to be three hundred dollars and, according to tradition, firewood. Ministers no longer received a share of stranded whales, but on at least one occasion Lyman worked off excess energy by joining the whaleboatmen in a chase.

But the response to the Reverend Beecher's spiritual message was not entirely favorable. It had been a surprise to him to find French skepticism rampant in Yale College, matrix of New England's clergy. Now it astonished him even more to find an "infidel club" composed of men of "talent, education and ... zeal" in the East Hampton area. They had even gone so far as to burn a Bible. "It was the age of French Infidelity," he wrote. "There was a leaven of skepticism all over the world." The church committee had declared that they wanted someone who could "stand his ground in argument and break the heads of these infidels." As always, opposition aroused Lyman. "The question was," he said, "Revivals or Infidelity," and he responded with cunning as well as vigor. "I did not attack infidelity directly," he said. "Not at all. That would have been cracking a whip behind a runaway team—made them run the faster. I always preached right to the conscience. Every sermon with my eye on the gun to hit somebody."

Having become the keeper of a holy mystery, he saw it as his duty to bring benighted souls in from outer darkness—to "convert" the natives. So he became a man with a mission, than which there is no more determined breed. He acted now—as he would all his life—as though it were the eleventh hour for all men and as though only he could save them. "Everything is at stake," he wrote to Roxana early in 1799. "Immortal souls are sleeping on the brink of hell. . . . A few days will fix their eternal state. Shall I hide the truth . . . labor to please the ear with smooth periods, and be the siren song to lure them down to hell?"

Such was the emotional tension aroused in young people by their religious obligations that they often suffered acute guilt at allowing an earthly love affair to overshadow their commitment to God. Lyman wrote: "Do I love God supremely? Am I willing to resign my dear Roxana? Is God my all in all?" Although such misgivings could hardly have reassured her concerning the depth of his feelings for her, she obviously understood and respected his dilemma. But Lyman was a passionate young man and the issue was not long in doubt. They were married in the fall of 1799 and Roxana joined him in East Hampton.

Before long, Lyman bought a two-story frame house and five acres, paying eight hundred dollars for them. He laid new pitch-pine floors, had a new fireplace built and he finished the back rooms and a small bedroom downstairs, spending three hundred dollars on these improvements. There was not a single carpet in town, so Roxana spun cotton and had it woven and then she sized it and painted it in oils with a border around it and flowers all over the center. When old Deacon Tallmadge came to the parlor door and saw the carpet, he stopped short. Beecher urged him to enter.

"Why, I can't," Tallmadge answered, " 'thout steppin' on it." Then, after admiring it for a while, he added, "D'ye think ye can have all that *and heaven too?*"

Early in February 1800, a revival fever stirred the town. It began before evening service on Sabbath: word came to the Reverend Beecher that two of his deacon's sons were "under conviction," meaning that they were experiencing the sudden religious excitement that preceded conversion. "Oh, how I went down there! . . ." Lyman recalled. "I spilled over. All the old folks waked up, and when I went home, after meeting, to Aunt Phebe's, the young people flowed together there . . . the work went on gloriously for six weeks and shook the whole town." He announced the results as though it were some kind of sports contest: "Eighty were converted." In all revivals this would be the measure of success—the number of those who declared themselves converted.

Driven by boundless zeal and nervous energy, Lyman preached or lectured seven or eight times a week throughout the winter in town and in nearby villages and as often as five times a week among the Indians and white people at Montauk Point. Barely able to make both ends meet, he also undertook to serve as principal of a local school, Clinton Academy, but he hated that work and barely mentions it in his memoirs.

All this was too much, both physically and spiritually, even for such a vital and dedicated young man, and after three years, and a bout of fever and ague in the winter of 1801–1802, he broke down. For weeks he was completely prostrated. After a while he was able to fish, hunt, and ride about the countryside and he began to regain vigor and spirit. Gradually he did more and more physical work, making turf fences, haying, hauling seaweed from Three Mile Harbor to mix with barnyard manure. But it was more than a year before he could resume his pastoral duties.

Once, after he had not preached for many months, an aging parishioner, Mr. Fithian, declared he would not pay his church taxes until Beecher preached again.

"What is the reason you ministers are so hungry for money?" he asked.

"I don't know," the young minister replied, "unless it is that we see our people growing covetous and going to hell, and want to get it away from them."

The inadequacy of his salary, now four hundred dollars a year, added sorely to his burdens. His situation became even more difficult after six children were born—Catharine in 1800, followed by William in 1802, Edward in 1803, Mary in 1805, a daughter who died at birth in 1808, and George in 1809. Unable to meet the expenses of even their relatively simple way of life, Lyman and Roxana decided to start a select girls' school. Besides day pupils, they took in five young girls as boarding students. Versatile Roxana taught English, French, drawing, painting and embroidery—an elegant curriculum for the girls of any community and especially one so remote. Roxana's sister Mary Foote helped with the teaching of English, and together, caught up in a rage that had swept Europe, they undertook a new school subject, chemistry. They used a textbook by the great Lavoisier and enthusiastically tried a variety of experiments. On the whole, the school was profitable.

Although younger than Roxana, Mary had already had a disastrous marital experience. A beautiful and, like her sister, a very sensitive young woman, she had married John Hubbard, a New Haven man who had become a planter in the West Indies, when she was eighteen. Innocently she had returned to the islands with him. To her horror she found that he already had a mulatto family. And life on a slave plantation, especially the relationship between white masters and black women, stunned and sickened her. Since such arrangements were widespread and completely accepted in the islands, her reaction simply baffled her husband. After a year she fled, returning home in deep despair. So when Lyman and Roxana opened their home to her, she came gladly and remained with them for many years. Although Harriet Beecher was only two years old when Mary died, she never forgot the stories she heard of Mary's experiences.

Now, in East Hampton everyone testified to Mary Foote's loveliness and charm. Catharine, the oldest child, said of her, "She was the poetry of my childhood." And a letter such as the following by Mary to her sister Esther is ample testimony to her sensitivity:

January, 1806

If I was gifted with any portion of genius, I might begin my letter with describing to you the loveliness of the night—a night in January—a night in East Hampton. I am sure, if a few more similar to this should occur, I should downright turn poet. . . .

I wish, dear Esther, you would write me all the news. We get no paper, and know no more of the affairs of the world than if we were not in it. Here we are so still, so quiet, so dull, so inactive, that we have forgotten but that the world goes on the same way. We have forgotten that there are wars, murders, and violence abroad in the earth; that there are society, and friendship, and intercourse, and social affection, and science, and pleasure, and life, and spirit, and gayety, and good-humor, alive still among the sons of earth. All here is the unvaried calm of a—frog-pond, without the music of it. We neither laugh nor cry, sing nor dance, nor moan, nor lament; but the man that took ten steps yesterday taketh the same today . . . and as standing water begins to turn green, so all the countenances you meet seem to have contracted the expression indicative of the unagitated state in which they live. I wish I could procure some nitrous oxyd ["laughing gas"] for them to inhale once a week. What do you suppose would be the effect? Suppose they would move a muscle in the face? Send me over a bottle. For my own part I am no better than an oyster, and as it is late will creep into my shell.

Besides Mary and the boarders, the household included a housekeeper and two bound servants, affectionate black girls named Zillah and Rachel, who took care of the children and the cooking.

Despite the Calvinist framework of the Beechers' lives, the atmosphere of the household was not strict. As Catharine, oldest of the children, recalled, "There was a free and easy way of living, more congenial to liberty and society than to conventional rules." Roxana was gentle and kind albeit detached; Catharine could not remember ever seeing her fondle and caress her little ones, as Lyman did.

In the end, discipline was left to Lyman—or perhaps assumed by him. He taught each of the children that obedience must be exact, prompt and cheerful. He enforced it, when necessary, with a quince switch and a severity that was remembered. If he succeeded, it was because the training was accompanied by unconcealed love and concern. Sometimes, especially after a demanding sermon, he relaxed by frolicking with the young ones. He would bring out an old violin and play lively airs he had learned at college. As soon, however, as the girls started to dance he would break off with a doleful screech of the strings.

He yielded unaccountably to prankish impulses. Once when some boys gathered at his window as he played his violin, he jerked up the sash, jumped out and chased them up and down the street, the boys gleefully making a game of it. Sometimes the combination of discipline and playfulness led him to strange, cruel tests of his children's trust in him: Catharine recalled that he had once held her out a garret window and swung her by her hands, and at another time had dipped her head into a tub of water to see what she would do.

Lyman was sometimes equally impetuous with Roxana. Soon after they were married, while they were riding together from Sag Harbor, they "reconnoitred," as Beecher recalled it, to find if there were any faults in each other that might cause trouble:

I told her I did not know as I had any faults—unless one: that I was passionate, quick, and quick over; but if she answered quick we might have trouble. Her face overspread with a glow of emotion, and tears flowed; and that single thing prevented the realization of the evil forever. If she saw I was touched, she never said a word—she appreciated the thing; she entered into my character entirely.

I scarcely ever saw her agitated to tears. Once, soon after we had moved into our new house, the two pigs did something that vexed me; I got angry and thrashed them. She came to the door and interposed. The fire hadn't gone out. I said quickly, "Go along in!" She started, but hadn't more than time to turn before I was at her side, and threw my arms around her neck and kissed her, and I told her I was sorry. Then she wept.

He added that that was the nearest to a quarrel they ever came. Lyman was, in short, not subtle and yet not simple. Moved by obscure forces, he passed from periods of boundless enthusiasm to a sick despondency. In his sermons, he was sometimes the solemn theologian, at other times the driving evangelist, and at still other times the country parson with a shrewd and homely humor. He was both the earnest reformer and the impulsive prankster; narrow in his religion, shallow in his social aware-ness, but sympathetic emotionally, and forever borne up by his nearly mystical faith in a grand millennium.

Brought up on a farm but trained as a Calvinist, he had a combina-tion of Puritan earnestness and Yankee humor that has been described as "New England doubleness." It is a duality found most strikingly in such public figures as Harriet Beecher Stowe, Henry David Thoreau, Emily Dickinson and, latterly, Robert Frost. The combination of qualities is of course different in each individual. But it is almost always marked by intense soul-searching or a high-minded concern with religious or spiri-tual matters side by side with a cross-grained, burr-like aspect, and a dry, sly humor.

In Lyman Beecher the combination was never so well displayed as when he illustrated some theological question or solemn relationship with an amusing image drawn from farm life. When he announced to his East Hampton congregation that he was starting a revival among them, they made him think, he said, of "hens in the night, when you carry a candle into the hen-roost, how they open first one eye and then the other, half asleep."

In time, purely religious matters proved not enough to absorb Ly-man's energies. So he turned to reform, but of individual morality rather than social inequity. When he heard that Aaron Burr had practiced pis-tol-shooting before prodding Alexander Hamilton into a duel and killing him, he was shocked. He was disturbed not only by what he considered the brutality and immorality of the act but also because Hamilton had been a principal in the Federalist party, which was the chief support of

YALE COLLEGE AS IT WAS THEN.

Yale College in the 1790s, at about the time Lyman Beecher was a student there.

Lyman Beecher in 1803, at East Hampton, Long Island, early in his first ministry.

The Litchfield, Connecticut, home of the Beechers from 1810 until they moved to Boston in 1826.

the established church in New England. He studied the subject on and off for six months and finally, in 1806, delivered a "Sermon on Dueling" to his East Hampton congregation. He repeated it before the synod of ministers, astonishing that august body with this departure from theological themes. "Dueling is a great national sin. . . . the whole land is covered with blood," he announced, and then went on to blast the myth that a duel was an "affair of honor": "A duelist may be a gambler, a prodigal, or fornicator, an adulterer, a drunkard and a murderer and not violate the laws of honor." Working himself up to a climax in the manner of an Edwards, he declared that "ten thousand plagues stand ready to execute His wrath; conflagration, tempest, earthquake, war, famine, and pestilence, wait His command only, to cleanse the land from blood." He proposed that societies be organized to stop all dueling. There was opposition from a few orthodox divines, who represented parishioners affiliated with "men of dueling principles," but the thirty-year-old newcomer was not in the least intimidated. "I rose and knocked away their arguments, and made them ludicrous," he wrote. " . . . Oh, I declare! If I did not switch 'em, and scorch 'em, and stamp on 'em. . . . It was the center of old fogyism, but I mowed it down, and carried the vote of the house."

The sermon was published with a "Recommendation" by several prominent clergymen, and over forty thousand copies were distributed. It was of little concern except to a handful of truculent "gentlemen," but it started Lyman Beecher on his way to a national reputation.

Growing impatient, and inspired by a meeting with a powerful revivalist pastor from Newark, Edward Griffin, Beecher mounted another revival. He concentrated on the doctrine of Election. "My object was to preach cut and thrust, hip and thigh, and not to ease off. I had been working a good part of a year with my heart burning, and they feeling nothing. Now I took hold without mittens." Never doubting the need for such a sense-pounding, heart-battering approach, or its long-term efficacy, he preached eight times on the same theme.

Besides making nearly one hundred converts, Beecher began in this series of sermons to set forth his view that men were "still entirely free and accountable for all the deeds done in the body." "There could be no justice in punishment" he declared, "no condescension, no wisdom, no mercy in the glorious Gospel, did not the government of God, though administered according to his pleasure, include and insure the accountable agency of man." The Lord, he said, would send to hell only those who were opposed to him, who voluntarily chose sin and rebellion, not poor, harmless animals or those who had done their best.

By allowing for free will and the possibility that men might achieve salvation through their own efforts, Beecher was, in a way, seeking to justify revivals and evangelism. It was a perceptible shift from the doctrine of predestination and the view of man as a helpless sinner subject to God's arbitrary will.

Such revivals were to become Lyman Beecher's principal instrument, his stock-in-trade. In them he was able to bring to bear all his talents and focus all his beliefs. This was indeed religion in action. A man of high physical potential—perhaps his heritage as a farm boy and a blacksmith's son—and strong convictions, he found in the intense sessions of a revival "campaign"—for that was what he considered it—a perfect outlet for his energies. Early aware that congregations soon grew bored by theological subtleties or Biblical exegesis, he regularly gave them the drama of revival. Among other advantages, the results were not deferred until the hereafter but were often evident within a month or two. It was not only a drama but a game, with the congregation as a team, Beecher as a coach, using all kinds of tactics and stratagems, and the score calculated in terms of awakened souls.

It could also be a most intimate doctor-and-patient relationship, with the preacher keeping a fever chart and giving spiritual prescriptions according to the patient's progress. Such a relationship is memorably illustrated in a passage in which Beecher, after a sermon at Springs, approaches a young man who has his head down:

I wanted to know if it was an arrow of the Almighty. I came along after sermon, and laid my hand upon his head. He lifted up his face, his eyes full of tears; I saw it was God. Then I went to the Northwest [another community], and the Lord was there; then to Ammigansett, and the Lord was there; and the flood was rolling all around.

For the congregation, too, it was a release. Inhibited in the expressing of sexual feeling, lacking such outlets as the theater and dancing, they experienced in revivals a shared excitement, emotions that might in the climax reach a moment of exaltation. It was the one activity in which the austerities of Calvinism, at least as practiced by Beecher, sanctioned emotional indulgence.

There was of course none of the hysteria that often marked the camp meeting revivals. In them, itinerant evangelists would gather a great crowd in some woodland grove and churn it into a frenzy. Day-and-night harangues stoked with threats of hell and damnation often aroused listeners to such a fever of excitement that they jerked about, shook, "babbled in tongues" and fell to the ground in fits. At the climax the preacher would often conjure up a vision of heavenly bliss for those who repented.

But in the more genteel communities of New England there was a certain opposition to the itinerant revivalists as disturbers of the peace and promoters of a rabid emotionalism.

Beecher's sermon on the doctrine of Election was published in 1808 and was widely circulated. It was such sermons that brought him to the attention of other congregations and, in 1810, gained him an invitation to preach a trial sermon at the Congregational Church of Litchfield, Connecticut. It came at just the right moment, for Beecher had already warned his East Hampton congregation that unless they would raise his salary by one hundred dollars annually—that is, to five hundred dollars—and pay his debts, amounting to five hundred dollars, he would leave. Even gentle Roxana was shocked that Christians who agreed that they needed a minister to help them escape hell and win heaven would not contribute as much to his support as they spent on tobacco and other luxuries. Although Lyman Beecher would never show much interest in money or property, he evidently found little reward and no dignity in penny-pinching or in the role of the poor and humble parson—especially when the parson had a household of a dozen souls. When he finally set a date for his departure, several parishioners made an attempt to hold him, but the effort was too little and too late.

So, at the invitation of Judge Tapping Reeve of Litchfield Law School, the Reverend Lyman Beecher delivered a sermon at the Litchfield Congregational Church. In a time of threat from skepticism, atheism and political change, he represented unshakable faith and social stability. The church promptly chose him as its minister. The salary was eight hundred dollars a year together with a load of wood from each parishioner. The wood was brought to the minister at an annual "woodspell"; to make it seem less like almsgiving, the minister would greet each visitor with hot flip, loaf cake and doughnuts. The flip was spicy homemade beer laced with rum and stirred with a hot poker to make it bubble—not exactly a temperance drink, especially as a minister's greeting to his congregation. The Beecher children later recalled woodspells more as festive occasions than as a matter of charity and economy.

The house the Reverend Beecher bought was a nondescript building, but it was well situated and set on an acre and a half of land. It had a large kitchen, a well room, a woodshed, two barns and a workshop; besides the living room there were three bedrooms downstairs and four small bedrooms upstairs. As in many such old houses, a regiment of rats was active in the walls at night and occasionally scurried across the floors, but in their reminiscences the children remembered even this as amusing. Outside was a row of quince trees, and nearby a young orchard. The new minister paid $1,350 for the house. It was to be his home for sixteen years, a time of monumental devotion, of increasing fame and genteel poverty, of hope and frustration.

2

A Parsonage in Litchfield

Never an ordinary New England town, Litchfield was now, as one resident put it, in its glory. It had a delightful setting, high in the Berkshire hills, surrounded by woods broken by meadows and pasturelands and abounding in streams, lakes and ponds. Its winters were long and rugged, with sleet storms and deep snow, but the other seasons were infinite variations on a theme of wild beauty. Its forests were rich in game and still dense enough so that wildcats could often be seen on ledges of rock to the north. Indian arrowheads were constantly being turned up by the plow and there were other mementos of the days when the Bantam Indians lit signal fires atop nearby Mount Tom to warn of the approach of their old enemies, the Mohawks.

Litchfield's wide streets were—and still are—lined with splendid trees and fine colonial homes—some of stately proportions—occupied by such well-known Connecticut families as the Tallmadges, Wolcotts, Seymours and Buells. It was a prosperous town with a solid base in grain mills, sawmills, forges, tanneries, fulling mills and sundry small factories and craftsmen's shops. A somewhat more exotic source of income was the Litchfield China Trading Company; it had brought wealth to more than one of the leading families. The town was still vital enough to attract new settlers. Located on the highroads between New York City and Boston as well as between Hartford and Albany, it was stirred by great four-horse coaches, horns blowing and whips cracking, that came through at regular intervals all day long. Attractive stores offered "ladies' fashionable shoes," the latest bonnets, and all kinds of fabrics—"Cambric, Muslins, Calicoes, Cassimeres, Baizes, and Tartan Plaid Bombazettes." For entertainment there might be a concert by the Jubal Society of the Episcopal Church, or "Miss Clinton, the young Columbian Vocalist from Boston," offering a "variety of fashionable and popular songs."

But even more remarkable was its level of culture and enlightenment. Less than forty miles from Yale College, it was a center of professional and other schools. Its law school, established in 1784 by Tapping Reeve, a distinguished lawyer and judge, was the first of its kind in

America and already famous. In its time it would graduate a thousand lawyers, including many governors, United States senators and cabinet members. The town itself had far more than the normal share of legislative leaders and government officials. Its "gentry" lived with dignity and decorum. It was, by the same token, a politically conservative town, so ardently Federalist that a director of the law school was at one point charged with seditious utterances against the administration.

In a way, Litchfield was already a living museum. Some of the older men, such as Colonel Benjamin Tallmadge, a hero of the Revolution, still clung to pre-Revolutionary styles, wearing powdered queue, cocked hat, silk stockings, white-topped boots, and breeches with buckles at the knee. Beecher himself, at this point a ruddy-faced, sturdy figure of about middle height (he was five foot seven), leaned more to the homespun side, eschewing queue and cocked hat but still wearing boots, buckled breeches, stock and cutaway coat. Not for him the newfangled tight trousers called pantaloons, or the shoes laced with thongs, which had appeared before the French Revolution. To him that was the garb of worldly men, Democrats and, doubtless, infidels.

Many years later, Harriet Beecher Stowe, while in Paris, met a French count who had been an émigré in America during the French Revolution and had studied law in Litchfield. Again and again this aristocrat recalled its society as "the most charming in the world."

Thus the circle the Beechers moved in was most gratifying for a minister fresh from a Long Island village. It helped to make Beecher's early years in Litchfield among the happiest in his life. In the family circle itself, Aunt Mary Foote still exercised her fine sensibilities and especially a taste for literature. Catharine never forgot how her reading aloud made Scott's poetry come alive.

There was also Uncle Samuel—another member of the Foote family—a far-venturing captain of a square-rigged clipper. After each of his voyages he would come among the Beechers like a figure of romance, bearing in his huge sea chest gifts from the Alhambra in Spain, Moorish slippers from North Africa, silver from South America, implements alleged to have come from the tombs of the Incas, and of course, vivid stories of his more exotic experiences.

Uncle Samuel spoke French and Spanish fluently and brought with him the latest works of contemporary authors—Scott's novels, the poetry of Byron and Moore, the essays of Irving. He also liked to debate theology with Beecher, and there he opened up new perspectives for the family with tales of Turks, Catholics, Moroccan Jews and other infidels. It was startling to hear him declare that such people were often as pious, honest and courageous as any Protestant. He had seen too much of the world to be persuaded that such parochial New Englanders as Lyman

Beecher could have a monopoly on religious truth.

From the law school came two distinguished jurists, Judge Reeve, a portly, patrician figure with silvery hair down to his shoulders and a gold-headed cane, and Judge John Gould—brother-in-law of Aaron Burr, who had himself attended the law school in Litchfield—the author of a textbook, *Gould on Pleading,* that was long considered the standard work in its field. The wives of both men were women of culture and wit. Mrs. Reeve—the Judge's second wife—an immensely fat and good-humored woman, became a constant visitor, often taking turns with Mrs. Beecher in reading aloud the popular, moralizing poetry of Hannah More or discussing with the Reverend Beecher the sad condition of the Hindus and how to go about converting them. Along with Sarah Pierce, head of the girls' academy, these women were not only well read in the classics but also lively conversationalists, and their influence on such impressionable Beecher girls as Catharine and, young as she may have been, Harriet was considerable. Sometimes students from the law school, attracted particularly by Aunt Mary, joined the circle. The students were by and large a lively lot and were even charged with "riotous" behavior on spring nights.

With a passion for exercise, Miss Pierce constantly urged her students to walk as much as possible. So on every pleasant evening her girls in their poke bonnets, high-waisted dresses and small, thin shoes, sometimes escorted by young men from the law school, could be seen strolling toward a favorite spot on Prospect Hill. It was such a scene that greeted twenty-two-year-old Edward Mansfield when he arrived in Litchfield in June 1823:

One of the first objects that struck my eyes ... was a long procession of school girls coming down North Street, walking under the lofty elms, and moving to the music of a flute and a flageolet. The girls were gayly dressed and evidently enjoying their evening parade, in this most balmy season of the year. ... That scene has never faded from my memory.

There were more than fifty law students, many of them from wealthy families, boarding in Litchfield, and Mansfield recalled going off to a neighboring village for a country supper and after ordering "turkey and oysters, served up with pickles and cake," setting "Black Caesar to play jigs on a cracked fiddle." He then adds:

But the grand occasions were ... when we got sleighs with fine horses, and buffalo robes, and foot-stoves, and invited the belles of Litchfield, who never hesitated to go, and set off to a distant village to have a supper and dance. I seldom danced ... but there were always some who did, and we had jolly times.

In later years many a married couple testified that their relationship had begun in those evening strolls along Litchfield's broad and shaded streets.

Like Samuel Foote, Judge Gould did not hesitate to challenge Beecher on points of orthodoxy. He even made a joke of the pitiless doctrine of total depravity, writing: "Tell Mr. Beecher I am improving in orthodoxy. I have got so far as this, that I believe in the total depravity of the whole French nation." Although he could hardly have unsettled Beecher, he may well have planted an alien seed or two in the minds of the older children.

In their first years in the town, both Lyman and Roxana were too busy to enjoy Litchfield society fully. Almost immediately Lyman began preaching toward a revival, lecturing as many as nine times a week. Such was his conviction that he became incensed when some of his parishioners thought they could assure their salvation by good works. Once he wrote his sister Esther that while he was absent nearly a dozen young people had "begun to hope." "I felt alarmed . . ." he said. "A few, no doubt, through excessive ignorance, mistook their first impressions for religion, and began to rejoice in *safety,* and not in God. . . ." With the untold cruelty of which the righteous are capable, he added, "The two Miss Candys have false hopes which I am now going over to destroy if I can."

Although it was a year or two before the revival caught on, it lasted for several years and was followed by another in 1816 and still another in 1825. They spread Beecher's reputation as an evangelist. Indeed, because Litchfield was a stronghold of orthodoxy without a trace of heresy and offered little challenge to such an activist as Beecher, he was soon invading neighboring communities to wage a kind of border warfare against the devil.

Meanwhile Roxana struggled with a multitude of family cares. In several letters to her sister-in-law Esther she lamented how little time she had for reading or other diversions:

Would now write you a long letter if it were it not for several vexing circumstances, such as the weather extremely cold, storm violent and no wood cut; Mr. Beecher gone; and Sabbath day, with company—a clergyman, a stranger; Catharine sick, George almost so; Rachel's finger cut off, and she crying and groaning with the pain. . . . So for reading, I average perhaps one page a week, besides what I do on Sundays. I expect to be obliged to be contented (if I can) with the stock of knowledge I already possess. . . . Mary has, I suppose, told you of the discovery that the fixed alkalies are metallic oxyds. I first saw the notice in the *Christian Observer.* I have since seen it in an *Edinburgh Review.* The former mentioned that the metals have been obtained by means of the galvanic battery. . . . I think this is all the knowledge I have obtained in the whole circle of arts and sciences of late; if you have been more fortunate, pray let me reap the benefit.

There is an intellectual curiosity here that is much like that of her father and her uncle Samuel, and a remarkable freedom from the old Puritan distrust of studies not connected with religion. But in the Beecher household sustaining such a freedom was beset with problems: a swarm of children and a husband who was evidently not the cultured Sir Charles Grandison she had dreamed of marrying.

A more strictly Puritan prohibition, the one against drinking, was, especially in fine society, no longer observed. In New England, almost as much as farther south, hard liquor was a staple of hospitality and a begetter of conviviality. The practice had begun among the upper classes and later spread to laboring men. Older people took elixirs laced with rum to stimulate the appetite, pregnant women were given rum in milk, crying babies were pacified with paregoric made of rum and opium, hard cider and ale were popular, and workers were often rewarded, like sailors, with a ration of rum.

Even at gatherings of preachers, drink flowed freely. At one ordination at a house in Plymouth, Beecher found the great sideboard covered with every kind of liquor, all of it supplied by the ministers' association, and everyone standing in line to get a drink. He adds:

There was a decanter of spirits also on the dinner table, to help digestion, and gentlemen partook of it through the afternoon and evening . . . and the sideboard, with the spillings of water, and sugar, and liquor, looked and smelled like the bar of a very active grog-shop. . . .

When they had all done drinking, and had taken pipes and tobacco, in less than fifteen minutes there was such a smoke you couldn't see. And the noise I cannot describe; it was the maximum of hilarity. . . . They were not old-fashioned Puritans.

Perhaps it was the country boy in Beecher, or a reflex action against any sort of self-indulgence, but he was outraged by the practice and he decided to fight it. Forgotten apparently was the money he had made from the sale of strong beer, wine and tobacco in his buttery job at Yale. He began by swearing not to attend such a gathering again. There had been a temperance movement, however feeble, in New England for some twenty years and the clergy was well aware of the problem. At the very next meeting of the Congregationalist ministers of Connecticut, a committee reported a disturbing increase in intemperance, but it declared that it "did not perceive that anything could be done."

"The blood started through my heart when I heard this," Beecher reported, "and I rose instanter and moved that a committee of three be immediately appointed to report at this meeting the ways and means of arresting the tide of intemperance." The committee was appointed—with Beecher as chairman. The next day it brought in a report recommending that parents should cease serving "ardent spirits" on their tables, that church members should not regard them as essential to hospitality, and that employers should stop giving them to their employees. The report, describing drink as a plague, a wasting consumption, a band of assassins, and a ravening beast of prey, was a triumph for the thirty-seven-year-old pastor. It was quickly adopted and a thousand copies were circulated.

Later, Beecher, after visiting a young married couple during his revival rounds and finding the husband drunk in bed and the wife in despair, delivered no less than six impassioned sermons against intemperance. He conjured up a harrowing vision of the degradation and ruin caused by the demon Drink and urged that liquor be legally banned. He opposed not only "ardent spirits" but even wine and beer, aligning himself with the extremist "Teetotalers."

The sermons were widely circulated not only in the United States but abroad. With the characteristic enthusiasm of his more optimistic periods, Beecher was convinced that he had routed the demon forever. It would, of course, take the American temperance movement another hundred years to achieve the goal of total prohibition.

Beecher was also scandalized by broadsides satirizing the Pilgrims and by young people who took advantage of innocent apple bees and corn huskings to indulge in drinking and dancing. So, as early as 1803, he called for the establishment of a Society for the Suppression of Vice and the Promotion of Good Morals. It was one of a succession of such societies, particularly in Boston and New York, that would climax late in the century in Anthony Comstock's notorious efforts to wipe out whatever he considered immoral.

Perhaps because Beecher as well as other resurgent Puritans saw that every tendency in the new republic was working against the old austerities, he began to crusade against all kinds of private lapses and public diversions: profanity, balls, circuses, strolling players, mail delivery and travel on the Sabbath ("We really broke up riding and working on the Sabbath," he boasted). All these were of course neither true nor formidable vices but only picayune offenses against the church's standards of behavior or what were to become middle-class notions of respectability. Recognizing how inconsequential these issues were, Beecher himself said: "Who can tell how great a matter a little fire may kindle?"

Despite Beecher's craving for authority, he never spoke out on any great moral, economic or political issue. At a time when the young republic was testing the basic values on which it had been founded, the Reverend Lyman Beecher, God's spokesman in Connecticut, ventured into the secular domain only to oppose dueling, intemperance, profanity and the like.

Although he spent much time in assaults on such minor lapses, Beecher regularly gave attention, almost automatically, to the grand set themes of the Puritan preachers—man's fallen state, the prevalence of sin, and the threat of damnation. And when he did so, he revealed a remarkable ability to adopt the sonorous periods, the apocalyptic tones and bone-chilling imagery—especially of an angry God—of his most eloquent forerunners. In a typical passage in "A Reformation of Morals Practicable and Desirable" (1812), he declared:

All the daring enterprise of our countrymen, emancipated from moral restraint, will become the desperate daring of unrestrained sin. . . . The hand that overturns our laws and altars is the hand of death unbarring the gates of Pandemonium and letting loose upon our land the crimes and miseries of hell. Even if the Most High should stand aloof and cast not a single ingredient into our cup of trembling, it would seem to be full of superlative woe. But he will not stand aloof. . . . The day of vengeance is in his heart; the day of judgment has come; the great earthquake that is to sink Babylon is shaking the nations, and the waves of the mighty commotion are dashing on every shore. . . .

Is this, then, a time to throw away the shield of faith, when his arrows are drunk with the blood of the slain; to cut from the anchor of hope, when the clouds are collecting, and the sea and the waves are roaring . . . and lightnings blazing in the heavens, and great hail is falling upon men, and every mountain, sea and island is fleeing in dismay from the face of an incensed God?

The style and the imagery were worthy of Edwards. And even if it did not arouse the fears and anxiety it might have inspired a century earlier, it is unlikely that Beecher's listeners recognized it as bombastic, overwrought and unfair to both God and man. The wrath of an angry God was one of the unfailing resources of any evangelist of the time.

When New England is described as a theocracy, what is meant is that the clergy—called the Standing Order—exercised political as well as religious and social influence, especially on the state level. Every householder was taxed to support the church. In the early days both law and custom had required everyone to attend both morning and afternoon Sunday services. If anyone failed to do so, the minister could be expected to call at the delinquent's home on Monday morning to get an explanation. And if any kind of sectarian meeting of Methodists or Baptists threatened, the minister might put on his cocked hat, take his gold-headed cane and march down the village street warning each household to stay away—and that would be that!

As an example of this tyrannical church power close to home, Lyman remembered that when his uncle Stephen Benton, "a cross-grained sort," refused to pay what amounted to a church tax, the authorities appropriated his heifer and sold it.

But well before Beecher came to Litchfield, various forces—the growth of Episcopalianism, Methodism and other sects, the rationalism of the Age of Reason, the promise of progress and the good life here on earth as against the far-off prospect of heavenly bliss, the entire thrust of democracy and Independence—had already begun to bring about a crucial reduction in that influence. As Beecher himself described it:

On election day they had a festival. All the clergy used to go, walk in the procession, smoke pipes, and drink. And, fact is, when they got together, they would talk over who should be governor, and who lieutenant governor, and who in the Upper House, and their counsels would prevail.

Finally, the lawyers, provoked by a Connecticut lieutenant governor who undertook a strict enforcement of Sunday laws and moral codes, put up their own candidate—a lawyer and a Federalist. "We have served the clergy long enough," they said. Making it a direct challenge to Congregationalism as the established religion, they recruited—Beecher claimed— "nearly all the minor sects, besides the Sabbath-breakers, rum-selling, tippling folk, infidels and ruff-scuff generally." Beecher's view was of course biased. The lawyers themselves had come a long way from their pre-Revolutionary status as pettifogging clerks: they had led in the founding of the Republic and they now dominated its governing bodies.

They won the election and, as Beecher, referring to their treatment of the clergy, declared: "They slung us out like a stone from a sling." In September 1818 the state of Connecticut officially disestablished religion, making church membership voluntary and ending the payment of the church tithe. At first the Reverend Beecher was heartbroken and inconsolable, but whether it was his native resilience or the need somehow to rationalize so overwhelming a defeat, he soon began to see the outcome as salutary for the clergy:

For several days I suffered what no tongue can tell *for the best thing that ever happened to the State of Connecticut*. It cut the churches loose from dependence on state support. It threw them wholly on their own resources and on God.

They say ministers have lost their influence; the fact is, they have gained. By voluntary efforts, societies, missions and revivals they exert a deeper influence than ever they could by queues, and shoe-buckles, and cocked hats, and gold-headed canes.

Talk as he might of how salutary this change would be for the church, Beecher simply did not realize the full implications for the clergy of the curtailment of its political influence.

Rarely did the larger political events of the period seem to affect the Beechers. Even the War of 1812 touched them only by accident. Forced to take in boarders, the Beechers decided to add a wing to the parsonage and pay for it with a tiny patrimony that Roxana had invested in her uncle Justin's business in New York. While they were in the midst of building, the business failed, mainly, it was felt, because of economic problems created by the war. Lyman would have been bankrupt had his congregation not come to his help.

Lyman also professed to see great dangers to freedom of speech and press in the government's treatment of those who opposed the war. He was further exercised by what he saw as a threat of military despotism, by rising taxes and damage to commerce. It was, in sum, "Mr. Madison's war"—disturbing but rather remote. In much the same vein, Roxana declared the war meant only a little more to her than one between "the Turks and Crim Tartars"; and it aroused her only insofar as it made everything more expensive. (When the postal tax was raised she expressed her disapproval by writing fewer letters.)

From all the dangers that the Reverend Beecher imagined he saw, the nation was at last saved, he averred, only by the intervention of God: ". . . when from impenetrable darkness the sun burst suddenly upon us and peace came, we said: 'Our soul is escaped as a bird out of the snare of the fowler. The snare is broken, and we are escaped.' " There is perhaps less concern here for "freedom of speech and press" than a clergyman's resentment at the increasing power of the government. He simply failed to see that Americans, having established a government based on reason and having conquered the wilderness and defeated Great Britain, were becoming surpassingly self-reliant. They could no longer be convinced that they were helpless sinners in the hands of an inscrutable, apparently merciless God.

The paradox here was that Beecher himself was full of hope, not because he shared the American optimism about what earthly man could accomplish but because he believed so implicitly that Christ's universal reign was imminent and that the ultimate reality was salvation.

Although chronologically a child of the American Revolution, Beecher denounced the French Revolution and referred to it with horror. Looking back at it in a sermon in 1814, he linked it with the "infidel philosophy" he had encountered at Yale and fought at East Hampton. Seeing it mainly in religious terms, he spoke of it as "a paroxysm of moral madness" spreading "contagion" and death, and, later, as "atheism sweeping with the besom of destruction." Nowhere is there any feeling for the plight of the disinherited, especially if they attempt to take their fate into their own hands—and thus presumably out of the hands of God. What did hell on earth matter when heaven was the goal.

Whether it was the waning of the Puritan influence or Lyman Beecher's craving for the familial warmth he had not known in his own childhood or Roxana's patrician background, the Beecher household was not austere. The larger parlor that occupied the ground floor was the scene of musical evenings with much singing and playing of piano and flute. And even the meetings of ministers there were, as we have seen, nothing if not convivial.

Roxana in particular radiated an atmosphere of serenity and repose. But in spite of her talents, lively intellectual interests and spiritual strength, she remains a figure in the background, characterized largely by such epithets as modest, submissive, pious and peace-giving. Having carried out the main function of her life, bearing nine children (one, the first Harriet, had died a month after birth) in seventeen years, she earned a reward not uncommon among mothers in those days—death from "consumption" at an early age. She was forty-one.

She had had symptoms of tuberculosis in the year before she died, but they had gone unrecognized. Then one night, only six weeks before her death, as Lyman was driving them back from a visit to a parishioner, the wind turned cold and brisk. "She told me then," Lyman reported, "that she did not expect to be with me long, and I saw that she was ripe for heaven. When we reached home, she was in a sort of chill. . . . " In a few days, she had all the symptoms of "galloping consumption."

Judging from all descriptions of her devout nature, there was no exaggeration in the picture of her last days as filled with such anticipations of heaven that she could hardly wait to get there. Indeed, we might today say that she succumbed so rapidly because she did little to fight the disease as the end approached. Roxana told her sobbing children—including Charles, whom she had borne only nine months before—that God would do more for them than she had done. Harriet, four years old at the time, recalled one striking image: Henry, too young to go to the funeral, frolicking kitten-like in his golden curls and little black frock. But a few days later, according to a family legend, Catharine found him digging in the yard. "I'm going to heaven," he said, "to find Ma."

Roxana's death was a heavy blow to Lyman. "There was no human mind in whose decisions he had greater confidence," Harriet wrote years later. "Both intellectually and morally he regarded her as the better and stronger portion of himself and I remember hearing him say that, after her death, his first sensation was a sort of terror like that of a child suddenly shut out alone in the dark." The pious resignation with which he had received her premonition that she was dying, and the exaltation of the words he later spoke over her body ("Roxana, you are now come unto Mount Zion, unto the city of the living God, the heavenly Jerusalem, and to an innumerable company of angels") did not help in the months that followed. "The whole year after her death was a year of great emptiness," he wrote, "as if there was not motive enough in the world to move me." Long afterward, in his old age, he would refer to her with undiminished sorrow.

His sense of loss was no greater than that of his children. Perhaps out of a feeling of guilt at the way she had been overworked, they made a legend out of her sensitivity, gentleness and purity, remembering only an angel who had never grown old—perfect mother, ideal woman. In time her deathbed wish, that they should all become missionaries, would have as much influence on them as all Lyman's relentless exhortations.

To help him cope with his motherless brood, his stepmother, Grand-mother Beecher, his father's fifth and last wife, and her daughter Esther—his half sister—reluctantly left their own home and moved into the house in Litchfield. Esther was a familiar New England type in her obsessive neatness and frugality, her anxieties and her capacity for self-sacrifice, but not so familiar in her wit, her intellectual gifts and her talent for storytelling. Grandmother Beecher ran closer to type: strict and puritanical but not unkind. The results of one of Esther's mottoes, "A place for everything and everything in its place," sometimes made the Reverend Beecher flee to the barn for relief. Another traditional rule, "Waste not, want not," led to a parsimony that was almost painful. But considering the meagerness of the Reverend Beecher's income and the size of his household, both her attitudes were understandable. The family loved her but everyone breathed a sigh of relief when her tour of duty was over.

It could not have been easy to cope with such a range of children—four teenagers, Catharine, William, Edward and Mary, three little ones, George, Harriet and Henry, and a baby, Charles. Reporting to Aunt Harriet Foote, Catharine wrote in February 1817:

Edward still continues at South Farms. William is in Mr. Collins' store, but boards at home. Mary goes to school to Miss Pierce, and George to Miss Collins. Henry is a very good boy, and we think him a remarkably interesting child. . . . . Charles is as fat as ever. . . . He can speak a few words to express his wants, but does not begin to talk.

Then, less than a year after Roxana's death, Lyman Beecher brought home a new wife. He was not acting precipitately: it was not unusual for a man to lose two or even three wives, each at a relatively young age, and remarry soon after each one died. In a rigidly monoga-mous society, it was also a way of repeatedly having another wife, each usually much younger than the one before. Roxana's death had been God's will, and the children needed a mother. Indeed, when Beecher had gone off to Boston that summer, the girls of Miss Pierce's school, not so innocent as they seemed, said, tittering, that he had gone "to buy him a wife."

But it turned out to be more than merely a practical arrangement. Within a few days of his meeting with Harriet Porter he was wooing her with all the impatience of a love-smitten eighteen-year-old and writing ardent letters to her almost every other day.

Harriet Porter was the beautiful and accomplished daughter of a leading Portland, Maine, family. Her father, Dr. Aaron Porter, was a prominent physician known for his courtly manners, and among her uncles were William King, first governor of Maine, Rufus King, United States senator from New York and twice minister to Great Britain, and Cyrus King, a congressman. Lyman Beecher at forty-two was a highly respected and widely known clergyman, but it is of some significance that this son of a blacksmith once again captured a wife from a patrician family. To the question of why this elegant young woman came to marry a poor minister with a little army of dependents, the answer must be that she was twenty-seven years old and thus on the brink of the most forlorn of early American conditions, spinsterhood, that Lyman Beecher as a man of God was an expert in heavenly if not in earthly matters ("He is to be considered a messenger from the court of Heaven," she wrote to Catharine), and that he was a passionate suitor who simply swept her off her feet. She had in fact already begun to pour her frustrated emotions into religious devotion when the Reverend Beecher appeared on the scene. In one of their first exchanges she lamented that her parents viewed God as truly benevolent. Her father, she wrote, has no doubt that he will be saved because he has always done the best he can and "Christ will do the rest," and her mother has suffered so much from sickness and discouragement that she is indifferent to her fate but believes that she has done nothing to merit "eternal displeasure." With an anxiety as great as Lyman's with his children, she concluded: "Oh, who shall bring them from their error or rescue them from remediless ruin?"

Her parents, noting the Reverend Beecher's poverty, his rustic ways and his large family, were keenly disappointed. Where Roxana, it was said, was a violet or an orchid, Harriet Porter was fine china. The impression made by the advent of the new mother was long afterward recorded by Harriet:

Never did mother-in-law [that is, stepmother] make a prettier or sweeter impression. . . . She seemed to us so fair, so delicate, so elegant that we were almost afraid to go near her. . . . She was peculiarly dainty and neat in all her ways and arrangements; and I remember I used to feel breezy, and rough, and rude in her presence. We felt a little in awe of her, as if she were a strange princess rather than our own mamma; but her voice was very sweet . . . and she took us up in her lap and let us play with her beautiful hands, which seemed wonderful things, made of pearl, and ornamented with strange rings.

As for the new Mrs. Beecher, she reported to her sister that she had never seen so many "rosy cheeks and laughing eyes" and that the house was one of "great cheerfulness and comfort." Fortunately she found Litchfield a compatible place for her, with more "piety, intelligence, and refinement" than she had seen anywhere. Judge Reeve in particular was "a distinguished man and a valuable Christian," and there was no sign, she noted, of poverty anywhere in the town.

In the house itself she found the dining room with its canvas carpet unattractive, but the large newly added parlor prettily furnished. The north room and the adjoining chamber were occupied by law students— not the most welcome tenants. A yard and garden yielded plenty of vegetables and cherries and an orchard supplied apples, cider and, as a substitute for butter, applesauce. Mrs. Beecher and her husband always took sweet apples and milk for the "nine o'clock supper." Everyone rose at break of day and said prayers before sunrise.

Mrs. Beecher described the children in generous terms: Catharine, the eldest, is at sixteen a fine-looking girl although not handsome. Mary, twelve years old, but large for her age, is very helpful. After Mary comes George, a big boy who takes care of the cow and learns well. Catharine and Mary look after the younger children, Harriet, Henry and baby Charles. Harriet and Henry are both affectionate and bright, and the way they always go hand in hand is most beguiling.

But the cordial atmosphere didn't last: after a while thirteen-year-old Mary was writing: "Mamma is not well, and don't laugh any more than she used to." Increasingly, especially after she had begun to bear her own children, Harriet Porter found the care of such a huge ménage, including its absentminded master, a trial and a drain. Gone were the order and ease she had known in the days of her growing up. And there was no end in sight.

In the year that he brought home his second wife, Lyman Beecher preached his most important sermon up to that time. Delivered in September 1817 at the ordination of a new pastor, Sereno Edwards Dwight, at the Park Street Church in Boston, it was directed, with all the passion he could command, against a great new threat—Unitarianism.

As early as the middle of the eighteenth century a score of Boston clergymen were entertaining Unitarian ideas, and in 1782 the congregation of King's Chapel in Boston officially adopted the Unitarian creed. Before long the name came to include persons of the most diverse shades of opinion, united only in their opposition to Calvinism. But the movement did not really gain strength until young William Ellery Channing came to the Federal Street Congregational Church in Boston in 1803. Revealing from the first an almost mystical vein, he eventually began to preach religion as a spiritual guide rather than a body of dogma and to protest against a fearful and servile view of God.

A slight figure of a man, with a sweet disposition and a nobility of character that led some of his followers to idolize him, he saw Christ as a great teacher, not a divine being, and the Bible as a great book rather than the inspired word of God. In the best-known expression of his views—one that thrust him into the leadership of the movement—a sermon delivered at an ordination in Baltimore in 1819, he defended the exercise of reason in matters of religion.

It was this rationalist and "liberal" approach that aroused Lyman's ire. "From the time Unitarianism began to show itself in this country," he recalled, "it was a fire in my bones." He had outlined his own theological position as early as his farewell sermon at East Hampton in 1810 and so he was well prepared when he joined issue with the enemy in Boston. "I had watched the whole progress of the Unitarian controversy, and read with eagerness every thing that came out on the subject. My mind had been heating, heating, heating. Now I had a chance to strike." To the Reverend Beecher the Unitarians' rejection of the godhead of Christ and their denial that Christ's sacrifice had alone saved mankind were heresies that led straight to hell. The sermon he delivered, "The Bible a Code of Laws," was a magisterial, tortuously argued effort to show that Scripture sets forth precisely and distinctly the laws of man's "moral government": total depravity, regeneration by special grace, atonement, justification by faith, and eternal punishment. If a man does not believe in these laws, it does not matter how "correct" his life is. If the heart is not involved, if the intention is not present, all obedience is "mere mechanical movements of the body." Calling for pure faith, he proclaimed that a Biblical law was a law regardless of its reasonableness and, even further, that a law might be a "mystery" and be nonetheless an object of faith.

However far New England society may seem to have traveled from the early forms of theocratic domination, such a sermon makes clear that for Lyman Beecher religion, as he saw it, was still the all in all, and that without it man was an empty shell. There is no mention anywhere of man's behavior with respect to other men, no connection made between the religious code and worldly matters, and no hint of the change of attitude toward religion that would come over many Americans, including all Lyman Beecher's own children, within the next half century.

If, indeed, Lyman Beecher's religion had been as narrow and rigid as his theology, he would have been only a sterile late-Puritan preacher and an unsympathetic human being. He was saved from both fates by his emotional responsiveness, his immense élan, and his capacity to convince people that such a faith as his was the way to bliss.

Beecher triumphantly described the sermon as hitting "every nail on the head." Of its effect he wrote: "Come to go out, the old men were all in a glorification talking and chatting. . . . The sensation all over the city was great. It was a perfect victory." The sermon was reprinted widely but it was a victory only as far as old men were concerned: for them Beecher was like "one of the old Puritan fathers risen from the dead." But time would show that it was little more than a rearguard action in the course of a steady retreat. In a letter to a fellow clergyman he resentfully acknowledged that the Unitarians through their great influence at Harvard were "corrupting the youth of the commonwealth" and "silently putting sentinels in all the churches, legislators in the halls, and judges on the bench, and scattering everywhere physicians, lawyers and merchants."

Only if we compare Beecher with such a preacher as Channing do we see how tradition-bound was his approach to his ministry. Perhaps the most liberated and high-minded thinker in church ranks, Channing was concerned from the outset not with theological doctrine but with the spiritual condition of man. A child of the Age of Reason, student of Rousseau, William Godwin and Mary Wollstonecraft, he believed in human perfectibility, which at once alienated him from the Calvinist view of man as fallen and incapable of saving himself. Insofar as Calvinism disdained reason, Channing thought its influence could be dreadful. He continued to preach the glory of God's word but of a God who was essentially merciful and found "real happiness in doing good, and in viewing with complacence obedient, virtuous, and happy children."

Unlike the Deists, Channing did not reject revelation, the miracles of Christ, or institutionalized religion, but he would have no part of such fearful doctrines as original sin. For him God was love, and religion was the "adoration of goodness." Seeing man as "a wonderful being" with an independent moral sense and infinitely improvable, he believed in education and social reform. Out of his profound faith in purely spiritual goals came his dislike of the "idolatry of wealth" and his opposition to slavery and war. It was such attitudes toward man and society that led to the social gospel that filtered into American religion in the half century after his death. But like Emerson and the Transcendentalists, he led to a thinning out of substance, a loss of the color and mystery and especially the fervor that make religion something more than a philosophical concept.

The difference between Channing and Beecher is pointed up even in their attitude toward Napoleon. Where Channing scored Napoleon for his blind egotism and lust for power, Beecher considered the Emperor a glorious fellow. Beecher met criticism of Napoleon's ruthlessness and lack of scruple with the assertion that the Bourbons had been "not a whit better morally, and imbecile to boot." Rather, he argued, that a wise and able bad man should rule than a stupid and weak bad man. Responding directly to Channing's attack on Napoleon, he said: "Why rein his character up by the strict rules of Christian perfection, when you never think of applying it to . . . any other ruler or general of the day?" He did express concern over the Emperor's soul, but that seems to have come as an afterthought. His daughter Harriet later dutifully explained this idolatry simply as an admiration for genius and especially executive genius, but it betrays more than a little of an older view of the absolute right of monarchs and a churchman's acceptance of submission to authority.

In his private life, Beecher was beset at intervals by nightmarish fears born of Calvinist dogma. Having evidently put out of mind the shock he had given Roxana Foote some twenty years earlier when he had tried to test her faith by asking whether she would still love God if he were to sacrifice her for his glory and honor, Beecher now subjected his second bride to a similar trial: a reading of Edwards's harrowing sermon "Sinners in the Hands of an Angry God." In it the dreadful fate that awaits the sinful is described again and again in such passages as:

If you cry to God to pity you, he will be so far from pitying you in your doleful case . . . that instead of that he'll only tread you under foot . . . he'll crush out your blood and make it fly, and it shall be sprinkled on his garments, so as to stain all his raiment. He shall not only hate you, but he will have you in the utmost contempt; no place shall be thought fit for you but under his feet, to be trodden down as the mire of the streets.

Like her predecessor, Harriet Porter reacted with revulsion to this vision of a perverse and tyrannical deity. Crying out, "Dr. Beecher, I shall not listen to another word of that slander on my Heavenly Father!" she left him in the middle of the reading. Once again a young woman had unhesitatingly identified a bloodcurdling view of God as the product of an overwrought imagination.

If the effect on Beecher was not shattering, it was surely one of the influences that led him to modify his more extreme views. He continued nonetheless to be racked by awful fears for the fate of "unprepared" souls. To his seventeen-year-old son William he wrote that although like most ministers he was successful in bringing the sons and daughters of other ministers to Christ,

my heart sinks within me at the thought that everyone of my own dear children are without God in the world, and without Christ, and without hope. I have no child prepared to die; and however cheering their prospects for time may be, how can I but weep . . . when I realize that their whole external existence is every moment liable to become an existence of unchangeable sinfulness and woe.

Working himself up into a paroxysm of morbid dread, he added:

My son, do not delay the work of preparation. . . . Time flies; sin hardens; procrastination deceives. . . . A family so numerous as ours is a broad mark for the arrows of Death. . . . To commit a child to the grave is trying, but to do it without one ray of hope concerning their future state . . . would overwhelm me beyond the power of endurance. . . . Let me not, if you should be prematurely cut down, be called to stand in despair by your dying bed, to weep without hope over your untimely grave.

This concern is repeated relentlessly in all his letters to his second son, Edward, then eighteen years old. In between warnings that he has no money to buy the young man a watch or even to pay for books that Edward needed, he exclaims:

If you ask why God passes you by, and does not by His grace counteract your voluntary stupidity [that is, inertia], I can not tell—oh, my son, I can not tell. But my heart is pained, is terrified at the thought that *you* should be left.

My heart overflows with grief and fear, and my eyes with tears while I write to you. *You must not continue stupid.*

A few months later he was again hounding the youth: "Oh, my dear son, *agonize* to enter in. You *must* go to heaven; you *must not* go to hell!" Such a passage points up two convictions that were basic in Lyman Beecher's faith: heaven is won with anguish—as though it otherwise would not be worthwhile—and hell and heaven are as real as fire and ice.

Such frantic fears were hardly uncommon among conscientious souls in the grip of Calvinism. Sometimes the fears alternated, as they did in Beecher, with an almost manic buoyancy, but at other times they led, as they also did in Beecher, to a breakdown.

Beecher had experienced such a collapse at the height of his revival efforts in East Hampton. Now in Litchfield, in his forty-sixth year, completely drained by a protracted revival (once, when a messenger from Hartford awakened him in the middle of the night to ask for his aid in a revival that had just begun, Beecher strode about shouting, "Wife! Wife! Revival in Hartford, and I am sent for!" and rushed off to Hartford), he fell into a deep depression. Among his symptoms were dyspepsia—the chronic complaint of Lyman and other Beechers—loss of voice, and an inability to study or work. For a time he tried such outdoor activities as hunting and fishing, which he loved, as well as a trip to Niagara Falls and Maine. These failed to help: "I am still under the rod of dyspepsia," he wrote, "and . . . cannot escape much pain and fear, and fog, and depression"; so he turned to hard physical labor. He took on eight acres next to his house, recruited a hired man, and bought a yoke of oxen, a plow and a horse cart. Throwing himself wholeheartedly, as always, into this new activity, he and his hired man cleared the east lot of alders and planted corn and potatoes. "I didn't study a sermon all that summer," he wrote. "There is some advantage in being an extempore speaker. Squire Langdon used to say that when he saw me out digging potatoes late Saturday night he expected a good sermon Sunday morning." The therapy worked: "Slowly but surely I got up."

Within a year he was engaged in a furious controversy with the Episcopalians—a controversy not so much over spiritual matters or doctrine as over their growing influence. Finding that they had acquired such control of a Hartford newspaper that it would not publish articles by Congregationalists, Beecher rushed around to garner support and subscriptions for a newspaper that would represent the Puritan view. The result, the *Connecticut Observer,* starting with 1,400 subscribers, was to Beecher "one of the grandest strokes of holy policy we have ever attempted for the Church of God."

So the Episcopalians were joined to the Unitarians, infidels, Deists, and Sabbath-breakers as enemies to be fought on every front. The Reverend Beecher had nothing but contempt for the Unitarian principle of "toleration." How mortified he would have been if he had lived to see his most famous child, Harriet, and his eldest, closest daughter, Catharine, converted to Episcopalianism, and his youngest daughter, Isabella, laid to rest by a Unitarian as well as a Congregational divine.

Despite the Reverend Beecher's morbid fears for their ultimate fate, his children were thriving. A letter from Edward, a scholarly young man who was soon to be valedictorian of his graduating class at Yale, reported that his sister Mary, seventeen, was about to replace her older sister, Catharine, as a teacher of music and drawing in a school in New London, brother George was qualifying to follow in his footsteps at Yale, eleven-year-old Harriet was reading everything she could lay her hands on, and of the two schoolboys, Henry and Charles, the former was "sprightly and active" and the latter "as honest and clumsy as ever."

Frederick, the first of Lyman's children by his second wife, had died in 1820 at the age of two, but as all early American graveyards testify, children dying in infancy—Lyman's father, David, had lost seven out of twelve children that way—was a common occurrence. And in any case, there were three more to come: Isabella, Thomas and James.

Catharine had grown into a competent, intelligent and ambitious young woman, devout and deeply attached to her father, but retaining a lively sense of humor. Her religious training had been calculated to provide her with an unshakable faith in God's wisdom, however inscrutable. But in her twenty-second year, life, in the form of unbearable tragedy, shook her faith to its roots.

3

CATHARINE

The Test of Faith

As the first of Lyman's children, born in East Hampton in September, 1800, Catharine occupied a special place in her father's heart. He saw her as literal evidence of the soul's immortality, part of the endless chain of life. She in turn identified with him to a remarkable degree, absorbing his beliefs and convictions.

Not at all inhibited by her pious upbringing, Catharine was a lively, high-spirited girl. Perhaps because her father was still a vigorous young man when she was a child, she remembered him as a kind of playmate, even though his play occasionally took the form of cruel tests of her faith in him.

As sometimes happens between a father and a first child who is a girl, he often treated her like a son. "He taught me to catch fish," she wrote, "and I was his constant companion, riding in his chaise . . . to the villages around, where he went to hold meetings." She hastens to add that as she grew older she began to "share with mother in his more elevated trains of thought."

Clever with words, Catharine helped maintain her authority as the oldest child by means of satiric little poems on household events. When rats made free with the room in which Catharine, Mary, Harriet and Isabella (Lyman's first surviving child by Harriet Porter) slept, Catharine came up with a long poem that began:

> One rat slipped on Miss Katy's shoes
> And danced about the room
> While with the tongs and candlestick
> Two others kept the tune.
>
> One rat jumped onto Harriet's bed
> And began to gnaw her nose.
> The other chose another extreme
> And nibbled Mary's toes—

All our impressions of her are of a carefree, vivacious girl utterly unprepared for the tragedy that would strike her a few years later. We get much the same picture of her as a student at Sarah Pierce's school for young ladies. One of the best of its kind, the school drew its students— and would do so for forty years—from some of the leading families of the region and from as far away as Florida, Canada and the Indies. All the Beecher girls attended it without charge because the Reverend Beecher served as its spiritual adviser—one of the few perquisites of a poor parson's position.

Miss Pierce, a luminary in Litchfield's enlightened society, was not too strict a taskmaster. Her "quiet relish for humor and fun," Catharine testified after she herself had become a well-known educator, "made her very lenient to me who never was any special credit to her as a pupil." Catharine claimed that aside from practicing the piano, dabbling in map drawing and painting, she did little at school but play. She was so "adroit" at "guessing" and what she euphemistically describes as exchanging answers with classmates that with "a few snatches at my books, I slipped through my recitations as a tolerably decent scholar." We learn from other sources that if she sailed through school with so little effort, she did so because she was, first of all, a very bright girl.

Although it had a full academic curriculum, a primary aim of Miss Pierce's academy, not unlike that of later "finishing schools," was to teach decorum, ladylike manners and "refined conversation"—in short, the social graces. With a growing middle class, especially in a prosperous town like Litchfield, the old-fashioned domestic skills such as spinning, weaving, and candlemaking seemed less important and far less admirable than piano playing and embroidery. Well-to-do Americans, particularly those who could afford servants or were influenced by European class consciousness, had begun to feel that well-bred young women should not work with their hands. If Miss Pierce's school did attempt to instill the genteel virtues, from Truth and Industry to Patience and Charity, it did so partly for moral and religious reasons but even more to help young women win the approval of the community. It was, in short, concerned as much with the goal—later called Victorian—of achieving social acceptance as with the Puritan need to please God and gain grace.

Mixing morality, religion, hygiene and diet, Miss Pierce would regularly interrogate her charges: "Have you prayed . . . ? Have you spoken any indecent word . . . ? Have you been neat in your person . . . ? Have you combed your hair with a fine tooth comb and cleaned your teeth every morning . . . ? Have you eaten any green fruit during the week . . . ?" It was the daily scholastic counterpart of the Sabbath catechism.

Roxana Foote Beecher died when Catharine was sixteen. Like all good Calvinist mothers, she died submissively and, so she said, willingly;

but the event, as we have seen, shook the Beecher household. Abruptly it thrust maturity on Catharine. As the oldest child she became Aunt Esther's chief assistant in the house, cutting and fitting all the children's clothing and, along with Mary, the next oldest daughter, helping in the kitchen.

At the same time she was drawn more than ever to her father, and he in turn stimulated her, she said, "to supply my mother's place." His appreciation obviously compensated for her new responsibilities. Indeed, when he brought home a new wife little more than a year later, Catharine's resentment outweighed her sense of relief. The letter of welcome she wrote to Harriet Porter says all the proper things but with an unmistakable lack of warmth. It opens: "The prospect of the connection to take place between my father and yourself, and the tender alliance so soon to subsist between you and this family, give me the liberty and pleasure of addressing you ... " and it closes with "we promise to make it our constant study to render you the affection, obedience, and all the kind offices which we should wish to pay our own mother were she now restored to us from the grave. . . . "

But her stepmother proved to be "a model of propriety and good taste." So Catharine, young and resilient, soon recovered her high spirits. She joined once again in the social life of the community, entering easily into friendships with young women and taking unchaperoned excursions with young men of the town. Her letters to her Philadelphia friend, Louisa Wait, are sprinkled with girlish outbursts. Speaking of a breathtaking view from a hillside in Massachusetts, she wrote: "I was right glad there was no gentleman with us for I should most assuredly have fallen in love in such a beautiful romantic spot." Her ebullience broke through even in her letters to her father, as when, during a stay in Boston, she wrote to him that she was "mad with Joy." That was a bit too much for the Reverend Beecher. "Should you return a Christian from your journey," he answered, "I should be 'mad with joy.' " Catharine was fully aware of her religious obligations, but where her father had spent his boyhood on Uncle Lot Benton's farm, she passed her girlhood in the lively world of Litchfield. Perhaps that explains her almost ingenuous view of the contradictions and cruelties of the Calvinist system. Many years later she wrote:

Up to the age of sixteen my conceptions ... of religion were about these: That God made me and all things ... that he knew all I thought and did; that because Adam and Eve disobeyed him once only, he drove them out of Eden, and then so arranged it that all their descendants would be born with wicked hearts, and that, though this did not seem either just or good, it was so; that I had such a wicked heart that I could not feel or act right in anything till I had a new one; that God only could give me a new heart; that if I died without it, I should go to a lake of fire and brimstone, and be burned alive in it forever; that Jesus Christ was very good and very sorry for us, and came to earth, and suffered and died to save us from this dreadful doom; that *revivals* were times when God and the Holy Spirit gave people new hearts; that, when revivals came, it was best to read the Bible, and pray, and go to meetings but that at other times it was of little use. . . . I could not feel or do anything that was right or acceptable to God, till my . . . depraved heart was renewed by special divine interposition. . . .

But this divine favor, she learned, was bestowed by God without reference to anything she might do. Ironically, the very innocence of the statement itself belies the whole notion of a child's depravity.

The years as chief helper in the Beecher household explain the confidence with which Catharine later wrote her very successful books on home management and "domestic economy." More immediately, her experience in taking care of the younger children encouraged her, at nineteen, to spend the next year and a half preparing to become a teacher. Partly because they were useful attainments for a woman teacher, she concentrated on piano playing, drawing and painting. Along with writing poetry—she leaned toward romantic ballads in the style of Scott—such accomplishments were also valuable for a marriageable young woman in Litchfield social circles.

It was in fact her poetry—published in the *Christian Spectator,* an evangelical magazine founded by her father—that brought her to the attention of a very eligible young man, Alexander Metcalf Fisher. And it was their common pleasure in playing the piano that helped draw them together.

It says much about this plain, rather angular, bright but as yet undistinguished young woman that she attracted so remarkable a man as Fisher. A mathematical genius, he was already, at the age of twenty-five, a full professor of mathematics and natural philosophy—later called physics—at Yale and was becoming known as a theoretician in the sciences. A typical story tells of his finding so many deficiencies in his arithmetic book that he had written his own textbook. (The manuscript, *A Practical Arithmetic,* is still in the Alexander Metcalf Fisher Collection at Yale.) He had mastered Latin, Greek and Hebrew at an early age, and during a year at Andover Theological Seminary, before he returned to Yale as a teacher, he had compiled a Hebrew grammar. No narrow scholar, he wrote verse and composed music.

He was also a devout young man and while passing through Litchfield he had twice in one day gone to hear the Reverend Beecher preach. Later he had come upon Catharine's poem in the *Christian Spectator.* Overcoming a native reticence (his portrait by no other than Samuel F. B. Morse shows a finely chiseled, sensitive, scholar's face), he made a point of visiting Litchfield again—and met Catharine. He escorted her to church, was invited to stay for dinner, and spent the evening playing the piano and singing songs with her. With the Reverend Beecher's complete approval he began to visit Catharine and when she went off to teach in New London, he wrote to her regularly.

Seeing in Fisher an ideal son-in-law, Lyman Beecher was pleased by the prospect. Fisher, too, was willing, but Catharine, outgoing and accustomed to an active social life, feared that Fisher would be emotionally and socially disappointing. "It always seemed to me," she wrote to her father from New London, "that devoted and exclusive attention to the abstract sciences almost infallibly will deaden the sensibilities of the heart and destroy social habits." Intellect was of cardinal importance, but in domestic life, she declared, "I could far better dispense with it than I could with a social disposition and an affectionate heart." She even went so far as to say that if she had to leave her father and home it would be little consolation to know that she was the wife of even "the greatest mathematician and philosopher in the country." Behind these lines lurks the influence, even if secondhand, of scores of Romantic novels and ballads. So, by the end of 1821, despite Fisher's "pretty letters," Catharine was threatening to break off their relationship. But this was simply a last stand: early in 1822 she capitulated completely and happily.

In no time Litchfield knew all about it: Horace Mann, then a law student in the town and later one of the law school's most celebrated graduates, was soon writing to Lydia Mann about the fashionable young woman of superior intellect to whom "Professor Fisher of New Haven has been *making love.*"

Catharine herself gave her friend Louisa Wait a surprisingly intimate, almost gushing account of the culmination of her love affair:

I wish you were lying beside me warm in bed, and I could tell you a mighty *interesting* tale but now I can barely give you the outline which you must fill up. Soon after you left here I received a *queer letter* from the Professor and I returned a queer answer, and our correspondence continued with an abundance of *spunk* on both sides until I refused to correspond any longer—this brought matters to a *crisis* as the doctors say—he proposed a personal interview to which I finally consented, and last Tuesday evening he arrived—and you cannot think what a long string of misunderstanding there was *all around,* but we finally both found out that we both loved each other . . . and we soon met on such terms as all lovers should meet, and I soon felt no doubt that I had gained the whole heart of one whose equal I never saw both as it represents intellect and all that is amiable and desirable in private character. I could not ask for more delicacy and tenderness. . . .

It is a letter not so much of a daughter of the Reverend Beecher as of a very warm and impressionable young woman in the age of Scott,

Byron and Moore, shamelessly romantic and untroubled by any Calvinist sense of guilt at the pleasures she is experiencing.

At the same time, Catharine faced another challenge—conversion. The Reverend Beecher found it intolerable that she should be about to go out into the world without having provided for her immortal soul. Conversion, as Lyman conceived it, was a spiritual crisis that had to be self-induced. It began with an acknowledgment that one had neglected God and with a conviction of one's sinfulness; and it had to be followed by repentance and finally, climactically, complete submission.

Catharine took the first step, solemnly resolving to put away pleasures and turn all her thoughts to religion. But she simply could not feel that she had been a lost sinner. Deeply concerned, Lyman wrote Edward in April 1821: "She feels so strongly her inability that she can not feel her guilt; and I have had much and assiduous labor with her on that point, and hope she is quiet."

But in March of 1822, Catharine was still asking Edward—who had just achieved conversion—how she could get herself to *feel*. His answer is a stunning example of how literal and simple the belief in heaven remained for such a youth; he describes the torment she will feel when all the members of her family are in heaven (he of course assumes this) and she is shut outside. "O how would the excuses which now paralyse your efforts disappear should you see the gates of glory close against you, excluding you from all you held dear on earth." His daughter's suffering was to Lyman Beecher a hopeful sign; to him torment seemed little enough to pay for escape from eternal punishment. Convinced that once Catharine was married her case would be hopeless, Lyman worked desperately on her. Almost triumphantly, he reported to Edward the condition to which he had reduced her: "Catharine has been sick three days, the first in acute distress. I had been addressing her conscience not twenty minutes before. She was seized with most agonizing pain. I hope it will be sanctified."

But it was all to no avail. Whether it was the age, or life in Litchfield, or a cool, commonsensical, anti-mystical strain in Catharine herself, or a combination of all of these, she remained conspicuously unconverted.

In the same letter in which Catharine had described to Louisa Wait the happy culmination of her affair with Alexander Fisher she lamented the fact that he would soon be leaving for a year in Europe to see what was being accomplished in scientific circles. In a later letter she described Fisher's parting visit, and added:

... it will seem a long time before I can hear from him ... He has recommendations to all the Universities in England and Scotland, and to most of the great scientific characters there and in France. . . . How much he will have to tell me and how happy we shall be when we meet again!

An Atlantic crossing by sailing ship in the 1820s was still sufficiently hazardous to make young Fisher's father, a Massachusetts farmer, caution him against undertaking it. Undiscouraged, Fisher departed on the packet *Albion* on April 1, 1822. But perhaps because of his father's warning, he was moved to leave a letter with the pilot notifying his parents that if he died while abroad, his friend Catharine Beecher should receive a legacy of two thousand dollars. Just three weeks later, on April 22, Fisher, along with twenty-one other cabin passengers, was drowned in the wreck of the *Albion* in a storm off the Irish coast.

It was not until June 1 that the Reverend Beecher, visiting in New Haven, heard the dreadful news. The following day he wrote this extraordinary letter to Catharine:

My dear Child,

On entering the city last evening, the first intelligence I met filled my heart with pain. It is all but certain that Professor Fisher is no more. . . .

Thus have perished our earthly hopes, plans and prospects. Thus the hopes of Yale College, and of our country, and, I may say, of Europe, which had begun to know his promise, are dashed. The waves of the Atlantic, commissioned by Heaven, have buried them all.

And now, my child, I must say that, though my heart in the beginning was set upon this connection, I have been kept from ever enjoying it by anticipation, even for an hour. The suspense in which my life has been held, the threatening of your life, with the impression of uncertainty about all things earthly taught me by the lesson of the last six years, have kept my anticipations in check, and prepared me, with less surprise and severity of disappointment, to meet this new scene of sorrow.

On that which will force itself on your pained heart with respect to the condition of his present existence in the eternal state, I can only say that many did and will indulge the hope that he was pious, though without such evidence as caused him to indulge hope. . . .

But on this subject we cannot remove the veil which God allows to rest upon it, and have no absolute resting-place but submission to his perfect administration.

And now, my dear child, what will you do? Will you turn at length to God, and set your affection on things above, or cling to the ship-wrecked hopes of earthly good? Will you send your thoughts to heaven and find peace, or to the cliffs, and winds, and waves of Ireland, to be afflicted, tossed with tempest, and not comforted?

Till I come, farewell. May God preserve you, and give me the joy of beholding life spring up from death.

In its uncompromising effort to turn Catharine's thoughts away from her boundless anguish and toward God, it began Lyman's year-long effort to save his daughter, in the only way he knew how, from a shattered spirit, a life of futile repining and, even worse, a failure to trust in God or seek solace in heaven.

But Catharine—in part because she was her father's daughter—was a strong-minded young woman. Beyond that, the circumstances simply refused to lend themselves to the prescribed Calvinist treatment. Among other things, Professor Fisher had been a devout young man of unimpeachable character, he had been conspicuously endowed with God-given talents, and he had been struck down without the slightest warning. But her father's letter, with its terrifying intimation that young Fisher may have been doomed to eternal perdition because he had died "unconverted," forced her to concern herself with her fiancé's ultimate fate. If anything, it aggravated her sense of the cruelty of the event and increased her misery immeasurably.

Many years later, Henry Ward Beecher remembered how as a boy of ten he had heard the news—only half comprehending its dreadful import—and from outside his father's study had seen the stricken figure of his oldest sister sitting with his father as he tried to comfort her. The tragedy, Henry Ward declared, had "broken up and destroyed all the religious teachings of her life. The doctrines she had learned did not sustain her."

The shock was traumatic. It was, she told Isabella years later, as though she had been "surrounded by the motion and constant noise of the ever whirling machinery and wheels of a great manufactory and all at once every sound and motion ceased and all was still as the grave—not a thread, not a circle or circumstance, for the eye or heart to rest upon."

Having had a more sympathetic response from her brother Edward, a senior at Yale who had just decided to become a minister, Catharine poured out her heart to him:

Oh, Edward, where is he now? Are the noble faculties of such a mind doomed to everlasting woe, or is he now with our dear mother in the mansions of the blessed? . . .

But when I think of the last sad moments of his short life—the horrors of darkness, the winds, the waves, and tempest, of his sufferings of mind when called to give up life and all its bright prospects, and be hurried alone, a disembodied spirit, into unknown eternal scenes, oh, how dreadful, how agonizing!

Could I but be assured that he was now forever safe, I would not repine. . . .

My dear brother, I am greatly afflicted. I know not where to look for comfort. The bright prospects that turned my thoughts away from heaven are all destroyed; and now that I have nowhere to go but to God, the heavens are closed against me, and my prayer is shut out. . . .

I feel no realizing sense of my sinfulness, no love to the Redeemer, nothing but that I am unhappy and need religion, but where or how to find it I know not.

As pious as her brother may have been, he was of a later generation than his father and would not shut the door to hope: "Mr. Fisher, I hope and believe is not lost. This is the belief of all who knew him. Let us think of him in a higher sphere of blessedness and happiness. . . . " Almost as important as his view of Fisher's fate was his remarkably mature advice—he was scarcely nineteen years old—on how Catharine should occupy herself:

. . . my dear Catharine, though your loss is great I cannot feel that your hopes are all blasted. . . . You have talent and influence, and cannot you consecrate them to the service of that Saviour who died for you, and live to do good? . . . There is no pleasure like that of doing good.

Meanwhile a delayed account of Fisher's last hours, given by the sole survivor of the wreck, added to her anguish. The man recalled that Fisher's face had been bloodied by a blow when the storm struck but he had been charged with reading one of the ship's compasses and had continued to the last to give the captain his course. At the very end he was seen standing in his stateroom door, his head bowed in "deep and anxious meditation."

Catharine's torment continued unabated. In another letter to Edward, in July 1822, she unburdens herself in lines filled with bitterness and despair:

When I have confessed my sins to God, there has always been a lurking feeling . . . that, as God has formed me with this perverted inclination, he was, as a merciful being, obligated to grant some counteracting aid. . . .

If all was consistent and right in the apprehension of my understanding there would be no such temptation to skepticism as I feel growing within me. . . . There have been moments when I have been so perplexed and darkened as to feel that no one could tell me what was truth from the Bible.

Neither her father's exhortations nor her brother's pleas could prevent her from crying out that like Job she cursed the day she was born and wondered why Christians were willing to bring immortal souls into such a dreadful world. "There is no help beneath the sun," she concludes, "and whether God will ever grant His aid He only knows."

In an accompanying letter to Edward, Lyman discussed Catharine's self-analysis with almost clinical detachment: "Catharine's letter will disclose the awfully interesting state of her mind. There is more *movement* than there ever existed before, more feeling, more interest, more anxiety; and she is now, you perceive, handling edge tools with powerful grasp."

A matter of the greatest personal loss to Catharine had been converted into a theological confrontation. Summing it up in a letter she left on

her father's writing table, Catharine described herself as a helpless creature in a frail bark rushing toward a precipice. "There is One standing
upon the shore," she concluded, "who . . . is all powerful to save; but He
regards me not. I struggle only to learn my own weakness, and supplicate
only to perceive how unavailing are my cries." The One was surely her
father as well as her God, and Beecher answered, consciously or not, as
though he were God. On the back of the letter he wrote:

It is many days, many years, I have stood on the bank unnoticed. I have called
and she refused; I stretched out my hand, and she would not regard. At length I
sunk the bark in which all her earthly treasure was contained, and, having removed the attraction that made her heedless, again I called, and still I call unheard. . . .

What shall I do? Yet a little longer will I wait, and if she accept my
proferred aid, then shall her feet be planted on a rock, and a new song be put
into her mouth. If she refuse, the stream will roll on, and the bark, the oar, and
the voyager be seen no more.

Whatever he felt as her father, speaking as God he could not help her
unless she submitted.

But Lyman Beecher loved his oldest daughter dearly and even
though his only advice to her in her extremity was to turn to God and
pray, at least once he did so with a moving sweetness. Jesus, he wrote,
"hears and pities [and] is altogether lovely." Yet in the same letter he
declares that because man is depraved and consults only his own selfish
heart, it is no wonder that God demands immediate spiritual obedience.
If you are calm, he warns, it is a "cold, sullen despondency, which pre-
vents feeling and paralyzes effort." When she continues to murmur and
repine, he asserts that God has convinced her that she is an "unholy,
selfish, proud, worldly, poor, disconsolate, and wretched being," but He
nevertheless offers to receive her, through Jesus, if she will only rely on
the Saviour for pardon, guidance and comfort.

Perhaps Beecher emphasized feeling and the exaltation of successful
conversion so vehemently because it was the only emotional affirmation
left in his religion after two centuries of emphasis on mankind's innate
depravity. For him the near ecstasy that often followed conversion was a
priceless experience. He was fond of telling of a parishioner at East
Hampton who, "converted after having lived through three or four revivals to the age of fifty, and having given up hope, used to exclaim for
several weeks after his change, 'Is it I! Am I the same man who used to
think it so hard to be converted, and my case so hopeless? Is it I—is it I?
Oh wonderful, wonderful!' "

Sadly in search of communion with others who had been close to
Fisher, but perhaps also as a puritanical penance, Catharine went, in

October 1822, to spend the winter with his family in Franklin, Massachusetts. But everything in his home—his portrait, his instrument, letters, books—combined to renew her grief. The ten-page letter she wrote to her father is a dramatic interior dialogue between a suffering self that knows it should not complain or give up faith in God's mercy and an outraged self that feels only an irreparable loss. Required to deny every natural impulse, Catharine whirled slowly round and round in a turmoil of unanswerable questions and anguished feeling. And we can only imagine what she thought when the local minister, with the best of intentions, preached a sermon praising young Fisher to the skies but concluding that "God may, and certainly will, do more good by his sudden . . . and alarming death than he could have done by his life."

Such a dehumanized logic surely shocked Catharine just as, long before, Lyman Beecher's conception of a God who might use cruelty to test one's faith had outraged both his first and second wife. It was a reduction to absurdity of what had been a fundamental piece of Calvinist wisdom: mankind's need for a faith that would help it bear the unbearable. In the end, the effort to embrace a God who had let her beloved be annihilated in the bloom of his youth and then condemned him to eternal torment because he died "unprepared" drove her almost to a breakdown.

It was during her stay at Fisher's home that Catharine learned from his diaries, correspondence and notebooks that he, too, had been deeply disturbed by an inability to achieve conversion and a state of grace. He had finally abandoned the study of divinity at Andover and for a few weeks had undergone a "delirium" verging on insanity. Through long sleepless nights he had filled notebooks with mad schemes for saving the world through science. Recovering, he had gone to Yale to pursue his career as a scientist. After that, he admitted, religion had been "more nearly than ever banished from my thoughts." After years of desperate efforts on Sabbath after Sabbath to devote himself to meditation and prayer, he finally gave up, resigning himself to an "inconceivable blindness of mind and hardness of heart."

Instead of being dismayed by this revelation, Catharine found support in it for her conviction that salvation must be possible—at least in part—through a blameless life, such as Fisher's, as well as through conversion. Her father, who had also read Fisher's diaries, argued that Fisher had blamed not God but himself. When she insisted that the only hope for her and "our whole wretched race" was in the thought that God is merciful and good and would reward those who sought him diligently, her father bluntly rejected such a view. She was trying, he said, to substitute a new version of God's character for what was a change in her own heart. That, he warned, "would cost her her soul." But Catharine had made up her mind: she declared that neither Lyman's nor Edward's arguments nor others, ten thousand times more powerful, would move her. "Consciousness would be that brow of iron that would resist them all."

With that decided, she was able at last to turn back to her work and to something like her old self, asserting that "the heart must have *something* to rest upon, and if it is not God, it will be the world."

That crisis in Catharine Beecher's religious life had a profound aftermath: Catharine herself would leave Calvinism behind; several of the Beechers, notably Henry Ward, would never forget how poorly their father's creed had served their eldest sister in her time of trial, and the books that Catharine published on religion and education would contribute measurably to undermining the old orthodoxy.

Inevitably the work Catharine turned to was teaching because, as she wrote, "There seems to be no very extensive sphere of usefulness for a single woman but that which can be found in the limits of a school room." Her father encouraged her in this resolve, more or less accepting the idea that Fisher's death was God's way of indicating that Catharine would serve in other directions than by becoming a wife and mother. He urged her, however, to start not "a commonplace, middling sort of school: but one of a higher order."

During her stay at the Fishers', Catharine had devoted herself to the study of her fiancé's scientific writings and notes and had read books on algebra, geometry, chemistry and "natural philosophy" to help her understand his work. Her rapid progress in these studies convinced her that her education had been sadly lacking, and it made her eager to continue her own intellectual development. Even more, it confirmed her belief that there was a great need for a school for girls that would make full use of their intellectual capacities. If Fisher had not died, it seems most unlikely that Catharine would have sought and achieved a career as an educator and an advocate of women's independence.

Because she had heard that Hartford lacked such a school she determined to start her work there. Using the money Fisher had left her and with her father soliciting his Hartford friends to send their children to her, she opened the Hartford Female Seminary in May 1823. It would remain a force in American education for more than sixty years.

The school began in a room above a harness shop at a busy point on Hartford's Main Street. It had seven pupils. Three years later, grown to almost one hundred students, it had to be moved to larger quarters in a church basement; still later it went into a new building of its own, with ten rooms and eight teachers. By the time Catharine left it in 1831 it ranked with Emma Willard's school in Troy, New York, and Zilpah P. Grant's in Ipswich, Massachusetts, as one of the outstanding academies for girls in the United States.

At the beginning, Catharine was fortunate enough to get help from Edward, who was conducting the Hartford Grammar School in order to finance his theological studies: among other things his coaching kept her a few lessons ahead of her Latin class. She and Mary, now eighteen years old, divided the teaching duties, hearing recitations in rhetoric, logic, natural philosophy, moral philosophy, chemistry, history, Latin and algebra. She was an excellent teacher, mild but firm, and always cheerful, so that many of her students admired her unreservedly. Occasionally she would relax completely and engage in a romp with her students at recess. But for the most part it was a wearing schedule. By the time the school moved into the church basement, Catharine had become more interested in the subjects taught than in the teaching itself. The daily routine in the noisy basement was, she found, exhausting and unrewarding:

Upon entering the school they commence . . . the business of keeping in order and quietness an assembly of youth, full of life and spirits and many of them ready to evade every rule. . . . To this distracting employment . . . was added the labour of hearing a succession of classes at the rate of one every eight, ten, or fifteen minutes. In attending to this, no time could be allowed to explain or illustrate. The teacher must endeavor to discover as quick as possible if the pupil could repeat a certain set of words; if so, nothing more could be expected.

By the time the duties of the day were over, the care of governing, the vexations of irregularities and mischief, the labour of hearing such a number and variety of lessons, and the sickness of heart occasioned by the feeling that nothing more could be attempted till the next day rose to witness the same round of duties.

The passage strikes notes that will seem all too familiar to many a teacher today. Even more interesting, it confutes any notion that discipline and respect for authority were bred in the bone in New England.

Although the school was a distinct success, Catharine, after four years of it, argued in an article in the *American Journal of Education* that the education of females was "irregular, superficial and deficient." She particularly decried the practice of learning by rote. Eventually, she predicted, there would be endowed institutions for girls, with regular courses of study, suitable facilities, and a system that would discourage students from starting and stopping at will. The community would then enjoy the "beneficial influence which refined and well educated women confer on society."

With some of her father's evangelical zeal, she urged the teachers in her school to build character and give moral and religious training rather than simply impart information. They must seek, above all, a "quickening of intellectual vigor."

Although she was now independent and a respected figure in Hartford society, Catharine maintained the closest ties with her family. At first she lived in a boardinghouse along with Edward, Mary and four-teen-year-old George, who was attending Edward's school. But once the seminary was solidly established she rented a house and shared it with Mary as well as with Harriet and Henry, who had come to Hartford to attend her school.

The communication between this Hartford "annex" and the main Beecher home in Litchfield and later in Boston was constant. At every opportunity Catharine fled back to the peace of her father's home, re-freshing herself at the deep well of his religious commitment. "You can-not imagine how much I enjoy this visit home," she wrote to Edward on one such occasion. "You know how happy it makes us to be with father. His society seems always to give a new impulse to the affection of the heart and to every intellectual power." Her emotional identification with him seemed almost as great as ever: ". . . I never hear anybody preach that makes me feel as father does; perhaps it may be because he is father. But I can not hear him without its making my face burn and my heart beat." Although she was socially active, her family and her school seemed to satisfy any need she may now have felt for deep personal attachments. Indeed, after breaking off a brief relationship with a suitor in Hartford in 1824, she seems never again to have seriously considered getting mar-ried and having children.

It was the example of her father that led her in 1826 to undertake a religious revival in her school and later in the community. In view of her own failure to achieve conversion and her agonizing effort to find conso-lation in religion after Fisher's death, it is doubtful that her motives in launching a revival were entirely or even mainly religious. She was sure-ly trying, as one of her biographers suggests, to use this powerful force—which she understood as only the eldest and closest of Lyman Beecher's daughters could understand it—to consolidate her position in the commu-nity. Clearly, much the same motives prompted her to become a member of Hartford's First Congregational Church, the wealthiest congregation in town. When she joined, she declared: "if I can not *be* a Christian I will try to be as near *like* one as I can." This was not said cynically but as a simple fact. There was much in her father's religion she still had not abandoned.

From the very first she urged religion on her students. In a talk to them in 1823 that showed how much Fisher's death was still with her, she said:

You can not now realize . . . how bereft, how lonely, how desolate is a heart that has no portion in heaven when the hopes of this world pass away . . . when the midnight pillow is bathed in tears of lonely bitterness, and the dawn of day brings no light to the soul.

This was of course a recommendation of religion not as a transforming experience but as a refuge from worldly disappointment. If her religion had not served her as well as it should, Calvinism, she knew, put the blame on her: she, not God, had proved inadequate. But the ache of loss has here been translated into a romantic vision of suffering youth. Outwardly she would recover from the horror of Fisher's death: inwardly there would be permanent scars.

At just this time the Reverend Beecher, now in Boston, started a revival as part of his campaign against the growing power of Unitarianism. It was therefore surprising that when he heard of his daughter's similar efforts, he did not approve of them. Such agitation and overheated reactions, he claimed, could be dangerous in young people. And when she invited him to help her, he rebuked her for presuming to draw him away from his all-important duties. In both of them there was an egoism, a streak of self-absorption hardly in keeping with their lofty motives.

Despite her father's failure to encourage her, Catharine Beecher's revival was very successful. It spread throughout Hartford and was taken up by all the local Congregational preachers. Significantly, she worked chiefly with the daughters of elite families, and she was rewarded by the contributions and support of grateful parents, especially those whose daughters she had brought to conversion.

In more than one way it was a curious role: she was the expert coach who had never been a successful player. And she worked—as she would work throughout her career—mostly with those who could support her efforts with money and prestige. She was not being hypocritical in either role; she simply borrowed her father's most powerful instrument to win the kind of backing she wanted.

After the revival she launched a campaign to raise five thousand dollars for a large new building for the school. At first the leading citizens rejected the plan as overly ambitious; so Catharine turned to their wives, and soon, magically, the money was forthcoming. The new building was opened in the fall of 1827. In scarcely more than four years she had become the director of a seminary with eight teachers, ten recitation rooms, a lecture room, and a study hall that could accommodate 150 pupils. It was a notable performance, the result of immense drive and vision.

As an educator Catharine anticipated modern methods in a dozen directions. The recitation hour, she insisted, should be used not to find out how much has been learned but to communicate by explanation and illustration. The various branches of study—geography, history, composition, the periods of literature—should be interrelated. She also stressed physical exercise—accompanied by music—to develop grace and good posture. She encouraged teachers to meet regularly with individual students in order to counsel and guide them, and she urged them to mingle with students after school. And in the best "progressive" tradition she solved a bright student's inability to memorize the propositions of geometry by explaining the reasoning behind them. The girl later became one of her most effective teachers of mathematics.

In 1829, when she was already thinking of giving up her responsibilities in the school, she published a little book, *Suggestions Respecting Improvements in Education*. It opened with the blunt charge that educational standards were low because anyone could become a teacher, teachers were poorly paid, and teaching was considered "a drudgery suited only to inferior minds." Among the desperate needs in school, she wrote, were schoolbooks prepared by experienced teachers, visual aids such as pictures, globes, maps and blackboards, and standards for testing. She called for small classes—she herself had only from six to ten pupils in her geometry and algebra classes and from ten to twenty in geography and grammar classes. Above all, there must be a "division of labor," with specialized teachers for each branch of knowledge instead of one teacher coping with as many as ten subjects. Most unexpected—and certainly unpuritanical—is her declaration that teachers have depended too much on authority and too little on affections. Even though women might lack the accurate knowledge and sound judgment of men, they had more access to such affections and could use them more effectively. Before long, she predicted, women would take exclusive charge of female schools. On the last page of the book, Catharine slipped in a discreet advertisement announcing that tuition at the Hartford Female Seminary was $12 per term—the fall term began November 18—and board was $2.50 per week.

Catharine now began to develop a "moral philosophy" to replace or, rather, to supplement the one with which she had grown up. Added to the torment of her effort to experience conversion was her failure to get help, in her time of trouble, from an apparently indifferent God. Once when Edward announced that he finally understood his "inward man," Catharine could only answer: "I wish I could catch my *inward woman* and give her such an inspection . . . but she is such a restless being that I cannot hold her still long enough to see her true form and outline." Whatever else she may have discovered about the God of Calvinism, she had found that in a crisis she had to rely on herself.

Also pulling her away from the religion of her ancestors was her association with the prosperous and professional families of Litchfield and Hartford. It was inevitable that something of their more worldly outlook should rub off on her. As Catharine's school drew students from farther and farther away, she became aware of the growing diversity of America's ethnic and regional types. It was simply unreasonable to ex-

pect all of them to be guided by the code of a single sect, however dominant it had once been. It was particularly awkward in dealing with the
increasing number of Episcopalians and Unitarians among whom Catharine looked for encouragement. She could hardly believe that such cultivated and well-rounded people were somehow outside the pale and
headed for damnation. In the book she would soon write on "moral philosophy," she observed that many of those opposed to the evangelical
cause were among "the learned, the intelligent, and the amiable; those
who are honestly believing that they are contributing to enlighten and
benefit mankind."

Although none of these influences had as yet undermined her confidence in the evangelical method, she had already shifted emphasis from
encouraging religious devotion to building moral character and from being answerable to God to being responsible to society. Where her father
had busied himself with·attacks on such "sins" as drinking, dueling and
breaking the Sabbath, Catharine organized a protest against the cruelty
of the Georgia legislature in driving the peaceful Cherokee Indians from
their reservations and out of the state. It was the first of the campaigns
for social causes for which Lyman Beecher's children were later to become famous. To some these campaigns would seem nobly humanitarian;
to others they were mostly a self-righteous interference in other people's
business.

It must have been Catharine's own inner crises that led her to begin
giving a course in "mental and moral philosophy." Even when she came
home to Boston, she brought her analytical exercises with her. "Catharine has been here," Hattie wrote to a friend in 1830, "and we have all
been thoroughly metaphysicated. . . . At breakfast we generally have the
last evening's argument hashed through and warmed over, indeed they
serve us with an occasional nibble through the whole day. One of Bishop
Butler's arguments lasted us for nearly three meals." She would descend
on her brothers in much the same way, so that they came to dread her
visits.

She finally put her conclusions in a book entitled *The Elements of
Mental and Moral Philosophy, Founded upon Experience, Reason and
the Bible.* She printed it at her own expense, but before publishing it she
sent it anonymously to various religious leaders and literary critics. She
thus aired her thoughts but avoided taking responsibility for them until
she saw how they were received. A few critics, she says, thought the book
dangerously unorthodox. It was in fact a bold work for a woman and she
was immensely proud of it. But when she carried fifty copies of it to her
new home in Cincinnati the following year, she "thought it prudent to
cut out the heretical pages." However, she not only sent a copy to one of
her father's Old School opponents, Archibald Alexander, but she wrote

that since she was passing through Philadelphia she would visit him to discuss the book. She added that she could not stop at a public house and therefore asked if she could stay at his home for a day or two. For the rest of a life filled with travel, she would use the same device for making herself an uninvited guest in the homes of locally prominent families.

In her book, her elaborate analysis of the workings of the human mind shows a fairly close study of eighteenth-century Scottish "Common Sense" philosophy. But she declares that this is only half the story, that the mind is unreliable and may be "disoriented" and make morally wrong decisions. Only God, as revealed in the Bible, she declares, can remedy this disorder. Except when it allows for a "natural goodness" in man, there is little in this textbookish exercise to remind us of the young woman who had written such challenging and rebellious letters after the death of Alexander Metcalf Fisher. It is sober, lofty, and relentlessly metaphysical.

The "heresy" was principally in the shift from a reliance on pure piety to achieving socially responsible behavior. In determining such behavior the family would obviously play a very important part. And since woman's most influential and acceptable role was in the family, Catharine would more and more aim at training women for that role.

Having published her views, Catharine decided that she herself must supervise the moral as well as the intellectual development of her charges. This called for some control of their behavior even outside school, and that led her to add boarding facilities instead of relying on private homes near the school. To parents it had seemed wiser to have their daughters living with private families than in a dormitory supervised by a woman—and an unmarried woman at that.

Catharine unhesitatingly undertook to raise twenty thousand dollars for this expansion. As so frequently in her educational schemes, she also had a personal motive: her sister Mary had married a Hartford lawyer, Thomas Perkins, in 1827, and having resigned from the school, left the rented house she had shared with Catharine. So a residence hall where both teachers and students could lodge would, among other things, give Catharine a place to live.

Catharine also decided that it would be impressive to have a leading woman educator head a department of "moral instruction." So she invited Zilpah Grant, an intensely religious woman who was associate superintendent at Mary Lyons' well-known Ipswich Academy, to join her. She even offered Miss Grant the post of associate principal at the quite handsome salary of one thousand dollars a year. But Zilpah Grant rejected her offer, finding something too worldly in Catharine's argument that the school attracted pupils from families of wealth and that such wealth should be put to evangelical uses. Catharine even induced her father to intercede. Using much the same approach, he wrote to Zilpah Grant that religion had long been "associated with poverty and ignorance, or, at best, with solid, strong, coarse, unpolished orthodoxy"; "taste and refinement" might not "convert the soul, but who can tell," he asked, "how many have been repelled by a want of them."

It was a transparent effort to use Miss Grant's piety to enlist the money and social prestige of affluent citizens in furthering Catharine's plans. Miss Grant rejected the proposal even more firmly than before, saying that she herself preferred straightforward to polished beliefs. In the end Catharine failed to raise the money she needed. It may well have been that her prospective patrons were not ready to have a school that was run by a woman assume the moral guidance normally supplied by the clergy. She would also always have trouble raising money because she opposed sectarianism and refused to bind her school to one denomination. Finally, there was the deep-rooted feeling that too much education would unfit a girl for her traditional role—that of homemaker.

Exhausted as well as humiliated, Catharine suffered the first of the nervous collapses she would undergo whenever one of her enterprises faltered or she lost interest in it. A few years later, addressing the graduating class of Massachusetts Normal School, she described her breakdown in terms much like those her father used and a remedy much like the one he favored:

I thought that if I exercised two hours a day and took eight hours of quiet sleep, and a proper time for meals, I might then work all the rest of the time without danger. And so I kept my mind under pressure of responsibility and mental effort for ten successive years. At the end of that time, without a day's warning of danger, I found the entire fountain of nervous energy exhausted. I could not read a page or write a line, or even listen to conversation without distress. The evil was irretrievable and I never again could assume the duties that wore me down, nor employ a tenth part of the time and faculties that could be profitably employed if full health were restored.

    . . . You must make up your minds that you not only will secure the requisite hours for sleep, and two hours exercise in the open air, but an hour or two every day in which you will have nothing to do but rest and amuse yourselves.

She never found a way of preventing a periodic failure of nerve. Hardly a year passed when she did not retreat for months at a time to some rest home for a "water cure" or other treatment.

While Catharine recuperated, her sister Hattie, who had herself been a star pupil and then a teacher in the school, took her place. Hoping to make up for the rebuff by Zilpah Grant, Harriet strove to bring students to conversion even after Catharine had abandoned that aim. For Catharine, being pious was no longer enough. Women must play a larger role. So she became convinced that her function was to train young women to achieve influence as well as independence by becoming teachers. But she also nursed, as always, a moral motive. "I see no other way in which our country can so surely be saved from the inroads of vice, infidelity [that is, religious infidelity] and error," she wrote to Mary Dutton in February 1830. "Let the leading females of this country become pious, refined and active and the salt is scattered through the land to purify and save."

Contrary to what is generally assumed, schoolteaching was still not thought suitable for a woman—certainly not as suitable as marriage— and men were still the principal teachers. But the growth of industry was beginning to draw heavily on the pool of available young men. And other changes were creating a need for more teachers: the coming of tax-supported schools, an expanding population, and the growth of a middle class in which women, increasingly idealized, were setting the social standards. Teaching, Catharine pointed out, "is a *profession*, offering influence, respectability, and independence," without requiring a woman "to outstep the prescribed boundaries of feminine modesty." Since she showed young women an alternative to becoming a household drudge or a spinster aunt, her advice would have had radical implications if she had not accepted another set of restrictions—Victorian notions of respectability, modesty and the properly feminine. The curious result was that this pioneer of new *careers* for women later became an opponent of new *rights* for women. Catharine was a strong-minded, shrewd and, basically, forward-looking educator, but she was also socially conservative. Beyond that, she lacked the rebellious spirit and the libertarian idealism of such women as Mary Wollstonecraft, Fanny Wright, Angelina Grimké, Elizabeth Cady Stanton and Margaret Fuller, to name only the major figures among those who sought the liberation of women as a sex. Her concern was not women's rights but women's self-improvement.

The most intimate glimpse of Catharine's Hartford circle comes from Angelina Grimké, daughter of a South Carolina planter, who had turned Quaker and would become a passionate abolitionist and a champion of women's rights. She visited Catharine in 1831, when the latter was living in the home of her married sister, Mary Beecher Perkins. Miss Grimké noted that Mrs. Perkins was very much "a lady" and that although she boarded twelve pupils as well as Catharine and Hattie Beecher, quiet and gentility reigned in her household. What impressed her most of all was that Catharine told her charges that they had "no right to spend their time in idleness, fashion and folly," but must prepare themselves to be useful members of the community. To a young woman who would give up plantation life for the sake of reforming society, Catharine's code, combining Puritan morality with the Protestant work ethic, must have seemed truly admirable.

But the most revealing moment occurred when Miss Grimké happened to read to Catharine a poem by a woman lamenting the death of her fiancé. Catharine was "convulsed by agitation." Regaining control of herself, she told the story of Fisher's death. She insisted, however, that it had been a blessing, changing her from an "uncommonly wild and thoughtless creature" without any concern for religion. In true Calvinist fashion, Catharine Beecher had managed to see tragedy and suffering as a blessing in disguise.

Although Catharine's social life in Hartford was most agreeable, with much horseback riding, excursions into the country with her students, weekly receptions for students, parents and friends, piano recitals and poetry readings, she again showed signs of a breakdown from mental as well as physical exhaustion. She was ready after eight years to leave behind the burdens of a school that had grown to well over one hundred students. Having reached a plateau in Hartford and more than ever convinced that she had a mission to shape the character of young women, she wanted to work in a larger arena.

The opportunity to do so came in 1832, when her father, partly out of frustration at his lack of success in Boston, turned to the West.

4

THE BOSTON YEARS

Just as in East Hampton in 1810 the Reverend Beecher had found that his annual salary of four hundred dollars—it had risen only one hundred dollars in ten years—could not possibly support his family, so in prosperous Litchfield in 1825 a salary of eight hundred dollars, which had not increased in sixteen years, appeared even more inadequate. His tastes were simple and he looked on his calling as a rich reward, but when his debts repeatedly amounted to two hundred dollars annually, even when he took in boarders, he again decided that he must move on.

So this preacher, one of the best known in the land, was, at the age of fifty, in debt and in pathetic need of a post that would allow him to live decently. In spite of his growing reputation, he could hardly look back with pride at his work in Litchfield. He would later recall how he had been forced to hold conferences in a dark and dirty schoolhouse lit with candles begged from neighbors and "stuck up on the side walls with old forks." "I cannot revert to the scene," he said, "without shuddering." After almost a thousand weeks of sermons he had, he realized, nothing new to say to his congregation and he later ruefully declared that he had spent sixteen of the best years of his life "at a dead lift."

Remembering how challenging had been his forays into Boston pulpits, he began to cast eyes toward the shining city to the north. Probably he had also heard rumors that the respected Hanover Street Church in Boston was considering making him an offer if he was available.

So it was hardly a coincidence that within a day after his resignation in January 1826, he was invited by the Boston church to be their minister—at a salary of two thousand dollars a year. Once again, as when he was called to Litchfield, he chose to see it as an act of Divine Providence. If it was such, it was somewhat equivocal, for Beecher was actually the church's second choice.

When the Beechers moved into Boston early in 1826, it had a population of fifty thousand and was growing rapidly, due mainly to the waves of Irish immigrants. Many older Bostonians could recall life in colonial days, and the city's principal means of transport remained the horse and the stagecoach. New York had long since passed Boston in population, business and energy, but Boston was still a major port, with goods coming in on great clipper ships from all over the world. Even more important, it was still the sacred city of the Pilgrims, the intellectual, cultural and religious hub of America, with many churches and schools, an important college, a library-museum and, by 1827, two theaters. It had, moreover, an upper class, an elite of well-to-do families who lived in patrician style, enjoying elegant homes, servants, fine clothes and such divertissements as balls and cardplaying. It was a city in other senses too, with all the temptations and perils of a mixed and changing community—what one student of Beecher has called, with perhaps a little exaggeration, "the Babylon of the rural Protestant imagination."

So the call to Boston was for Lyman Beecher a notable tribute. It was also, to such a militant Calvinist, a major challenge, for Boston was the center of Unitarian power. And it was a power, for in the years since Beecher's first visit to Boston to meet the challenge, a court decision, in 1820, had enabled the Unitarians to wrest control of over eighty Massachusetts churches from the Congregational orthodoxy.

Although Beecher had the stature, theological training and zeal to meet such a challenge, he was something of a curiosity in his new environment—the son of a line of blacksmiths, farm bred, single-minded, a bit quaint. Characteristically, he rode up to his new post—housed in an imposing new building on Hanover Street—in what one of his parishioners described as "a poor country chaise covered with white cotton cloth," and with horse, chaise and minister all equally unkempt. But when he began to preach in his "cut-and-thrust style," breaking all Boston rules of pulpit etiquette, the old horse and chaise were soon forgotten.

Compared to that of Unitarian ministers like Channing, Beecher's learning was all theological and his literacy strictly Biblical. He still used such rustic pronunciations as "creatur" and "natur" and his speech was sprinkled with homely expressions. When a flurry of attacks against him ruffled the religious press, he dismissed them with: "Oh, I don't mind because when I see the feathers fly, I know I've hit my bird." His son Thomas recalled how even in his late fifties, in Ohio, he kept a loaded gun by the door of his study, ready for the passenger pigeons that in the 1830s still came over in the millions. When he heard the roar of wings, he would rush out, have a shot at the birds and then return to his work.

On another occasion, when asked why he didn't strike back at an opponent who was attacking him viciously, he answered, "I threw a book at a skunk once and he had the best of it. I made up my mind never to try it again." He was often amusingly candid about his methods. When, after one of his sermons, young Hengy said that he had never heard his father preach so loud, Beecher exclaimed, "Oh, yes, the less I have to say the louder I holler."

The homespun quality appealed, of course, to his followers, but it prevented the more urbane Unitarians from taking him seriously. There was more than a little spiritual snobbery in their attitudes. Because there were rustic turns to his speech and he periodically launched attacks against what they had come to consider social amenities, they dismissed him as something of a "character," a bit comic, and could thereby ignore how genuine was his faith and how alive his spirit. Channing himself admitted that his "brogue or uncouth tones" made it difficult to give him the attention "to which, perhaps, his native good sense entitled him."

Canny in controversy and skillful in Biblical exegesis, he could nonetheless be completely careless in matters of money and dress. The stories of his absentmindedness were endless—of pushing three sets of spectacles in succession from his eyes up onto his head, walking into the wrong house and failing to realize it was not his own until he saw the strange faces there, getting off his horse at a camp meeting in the woods and forgetting about the poor beast for two days, forever mislaying money and notes, and so forth. One friend recalled seeing him rush down a street, completely preoccupied, eating an orange as though it were an apple, rind and all, with the juice spattering in all directions. Another remembered him hurrying along, carrying oysters tied in a handkerchief in one hand and a live lobster in the other, meeting two friends and getting into an animated discussion with them, totally unaware of the bizarre figure he cut or the amused stares of passersby.

His first wife never tired of telling of an incident that took place while he was on his way to church on a Sunday morning in the early Litchfield years. Coming to a trout stream and recalling that he had left a fishing pole under a nearby bridge, he skipped down the bank, got the pole and caught a trout. Hastily he slipped the fish into the tail pocket of his long minister's coat and rushed off to church. On going to the clothes closet for his coat the following Sunday, Roxana was aghast at what she smelled and found.

These were amusing eccentricities. Not so amusing were the racial prejudices he absorbed from his time and place. Such people as South Sea or Hawaiian islanders were looked upon as hopeless heathens, possibly without souls. When a bright Polynesian youth, Henry Obookiah, who had been brought to Connecticut by a New Haven ship captain, demonstrated that he could become a pious Christian, the local clergy were so pleased that they, including the Reverend Beecher, established the Cornwall Foreign Mission School. Its main aim was to give asylum to worthy pagans and even train them as missionaries.

Obookiah died, most inopportunely, the following year. Beecher, chosen to preach the funeral sermon, managed to interpret the young man's death as providential and a divine inspiration to other missionaries. The school did carry on for a few years, attracting "pagans" from Polynesia, China and Japan and from among those native-born aliens, Indians. Unfortunately, in 1823 an Indian, John Ridge, a former student, and Sarah Northrup, daughter of the school steward, fell in love and got married. Scandalized, the agents of the school, led by the Reverend Beecher, immediately banned all such marriages. But enemies of the institution and particularly the editor of the *American Eagle,* Isaiah Bunce of Litchfield, blamed the misguided zeal of Beecher and his associates for the "unnatural connection" and demanded that the girl be "publicly whipped, the Indian hung, and the mother drown'd."

The hostility grew into rage when it became known that Harriet Gold, a girl of good family, had secretly become engaged to a Cherokee, Elias Boudinot. Harriet was burned in effigy, called "lewd, disgusting and filthy," and some malevolent souls even hoped that she would die by her husband's "scalping knife." Bunce triumphantly denounced the mission authorities as the "adulterous offspring of mistaken piety" who had been "dandled in the lap of Mammon till that nuisance and monster at Cornwall had sprung from its loins." Beecher and his associates fell all over themselves in their effort to disassociate themselves from the affair, reviling the marriage as criminal and an insult to the community. (The couple, unrepentant, were married the following year.) And in 1826, the school, declaring that its function could now be carried on by missionaries abroad, closed down.

The entire episode was shot through with bigotry and white Protestant American elitism, and Lyman Beecher was its willing servant. The Puritans were the high priests of the one and only God, and woe unto the alien who failed to acknowledge their holy dominion or dared to claim one of their virgins. To Lyman Beecher, of course, it was all transparently simple—he was bringing light and hope to souls who might otherwise be damned for eternity.

No sooner had the Beechers settled in Boston than Lyman suffered, perhaps as a letdown after the crisis of leaving Litchfield, another severe attack of dyspepsia, an ailment that had distinct overtones of what we would call a failure of nerve. To ward off these attacks Beecher had resorted, in East Hampton and in Litchfield, to farm work; in Boston he sawed firewood for himself and sometimes for his neighbors, priding himself on both his energy and his skill. When he could not go outdoors he had a load of sand in his cellar which he shoveled from one side of the floor to the other. He also had parallel bars, a high bar and other "jimnastic" apparatus set up in his backyard, and visitors were sometimes astonished to come upon the reverend clergyman climbing ropes or whirling head over heels around a high bar.

And always there was the release afforded by his fiddle. He would play popular Scotch airs such as "Auld Lang Syne" and "Bonnie Doon" out of a yellowing old music book. A particular favorite with the youngsters was a contra dance with the impious title "Go to the Devil and Shake Yourself." Sometimes he would be carried away by the children's pleas that he do the "double shuffle," a dance he admitted he had learned on barn floors at corn huskings in his youth. Invariably the women of the house would put an end to these performances, not because they were unseemly but because he took off his shoes and ruined his socks.

The attack he suffered in Boston had its inevitable accompaniment—abysmal depression. His son William went so far as to write to Edward:

I spent a week in Boston at the installation. Father was quite unwell with dyspepsia. ... I never knew him more cast down. ... He took a chair, and turned it down before the fire and laid down. "Ah! William," said he, "I'm done over! I'm done over!" Mother told him he had often thought so before, and yet in two days had been nearly well again. "Yes; but I never was so low before. It's all over with me! ... but it is hard to see such a door of usefulness set open and not be able to enter."

Mrs. Beecher was right. By June she was writing:

I know not how a minister can desire anything better than to teach the Gospel in Boston. ... My husband's health is pretty good. He has some dyspepsia at times, but it always leaves him on the Sabbath.

We are at the North End, to which I first felt reluctant. Mr. Beecher is enthusiastic in regard to this situation. This soil was pressed by the feet of the Pilgrims, and watered by their tears, and consecrated by their prayers.

We then get a glimpse of how seriously she shared her husband's view that Boston had wandered far from the fold:

Here are their [the Pilgrims'] tombs, and here are their children who are to be brought back to the fold of Christ. Their wanderings and dispersions are lamentable ... but God will ... reclaim these churches; this dust and ruin shall live again.

By this time only the four youngest children were still at home: Henry, now thirteen, and Charles, eleven, and two that the second Mrs. Beecher had borne—Isabella, four years old, and Thomas, two. The three older girls, Catharine, Mary and Harriet, were living together in

Hartford, where Catharine's school was a flourishing three years old. Both Edward and George were at Yale and William was at Andover.

As Mrs. Beecher had foreseen, Lyman, having launched a revival, began to return to his lively self again. It was not only the most effective technique he had found for awakening an active interest in religion; it was also most rewarding to him personally, testifying to his powers of persuasion. Although he was now in his early fifties, he undertook it with undiminished ardor, as convinced as ever that the glorious triumph of the Church was not far off and that he was making a measurable contribution to it. He was doubtless aware that many whom he had converted in earlier revivals had lapsed into their former apathy, but he continued to see in each newly awakened soul evidence that he had a potent formula for bringing men to the active love of God.

As a modern editor of Beecher's *Autobiography* says, "In his image of himself, there was no place for failure." Essentially a buoyant spirit, he shared the early-nineteenth-century optimism that saw America as the hope of the world, the region in which it was most likely that a new society would be born. He was moved by something of the same millenarian spirit that inspired those who were launching utopias all over the United States. But where he looked forward to the Second Coming of Christ and the prospect of heaven hereafter, they dreamed—increasingly as the century wore on—of man himself establishing communities dedicated to love and social justice.

At first glance, Beecher's allowance of a measure of free agency to man under God might seem to be related to the late-eighteenth-century revolutions against absolute monarchs and the growing belief in everyman's right to a voice in his political and social fate. But there is no evidence of any egalitarian or anti-authoritarian ideas in Lyman Beecher's philosophy. He simply saw that without a degree of responsibility for their acts, some men became hopeless fatalists. In this he was merely adopting the down-to-earth approach of his old mentor at Yale, Dr. Dwight. In response to those who would allow man no ability to help himself, Dwight would ask what would happen if a farmer refused to plow, sow and reap lest such activity should imply a doubt of God's providence and his power to bring off the miracle of a harvest. Dwight's example may seem crude and unconvincing, but in rural Connecticut in 1800 it struck home.

In practice, Beecher made similar concessions, slyly accommodating dogma to the demands of the moment. In *Oldtown Folks*, Harriet Beecher Stowe describes the Reverend Avery, obviously modeled on her father, as cheerfully making little corrections in the doctrines of Edwards and Hopkins "in favor of some original-minded sheep who can't be got into the sheep-fold without some alteration in the paling. In these cases I have generally noticed that he will loosen a rail or tear off a picket, and let the sheep in, it being his impression, after all, that the sheep are worth more than the sheep-fold."

When his daughter Isabella was troubled by the view, held by her brother Edward, that God suffers as though he were human, Lyman conceded that God may pity us as a father pities his children, but how he does so and still retains his divine nature can no more be understood than how he governs the entire universe. There is no need, he assured Isabella, for you to trouble yourself on such a point.

The Reverend Beecher had learned that the passion with which he had first conducted revivals often lit fires that quickly burned out. It was a kind of instant faith, a forcing of the flower of religious feeling, and like some hothouse plants it did not survive in the atmosphere of daily life. So he now tended to exercise more control. So, too, when Catharine enthusiastically announced that she was launching a revival in her own school, he cautioned her against "the excitement and agitation of too much emotion which has rendered revivals so often fatal to the health of ministers and others."

Beecher started his Boston revival because he felt that the Old School Calvinist doctrine that man's fate was entirely in the hands of God made man a mere puppet. It was the aim of Beecher and the "New School" or New Haven churchmen, led by Beecher's friend Dr. Nathaniel W. Taylor, of the Yale Divinity School, to give back to man enough moral accountability for his own actions so that he could repent of his own free will. Beecher also realized, of course, that man needed "free agency" if revivals were to have any meaning and if ministers were to have the power to lead men to holy choices.

Beecher and Nathaniel Taylor first met in President Timothy Dwight's study at Yale early in the century. Taylor was already an assistant of Dwight's, while Beecher, some seven years younger, was only a rustic young pastor—Taylor thought he was a local farmer—from East Hampton, but they formed the deepest of bonds. Taylor, handsome and admired, went on to a prominent pastorate in New Haven and then returned to Yale Divinity School in the influential post of Dwight Professor of Didactic Theology.

Taylor and Beecher were both followers of Edwards, the great expounder of "New Light" Calvinism, but the problem for all Edwardeans was that Edwards had never resolved the question of where God's control of man's destiny ended and man's control began. Old School Calvinists claimed that Edwards's interpretations were contradictory, and irreverent souls summed it all up in a derisive rhyme:

> You will and you won't,
> You can and you can't,
> You'll be damned if you do,
> And damned if you don't.

But for the clergy it was a matter of vital importance. Even as a student Taylor had almost gone mad with brooding on his sinfulness and the origin of evil. Such questions continued to haunt him over the years. More clearly than Beecher, he came to realize that the doctrine of original sin and man's lack of power to make holy choices himself were no longer acceptable. After long soul-searching discussion and debate, he published his *Concio ad Clerum*. It declared in part that God had given man free will and that man had the freedom to choose God or take some other course. The tract stirred up endless controversy, with scores of passionate "Appeals," solemn "Replies" and hair-splitting "Rejoinders" on such utterly unanswerable questions as: If God is the author of all, did he not create evil and allow it to flourish? and: How can we allow free agency to man without diminishing God's power? Like tribal shamans, a tiny, self-selected group of priests cast a spell over their subjects with a flow of dark riddles and frightening visions.

Although Beecher occasionally deplored Taylor's more forthright utterances, he subscribed to "Taylorism" in principle and idolized Taylor personally. For all Beecher's independence of mind and manner, he was looked on, especially by their Old School antagonists, mainly as one who adopted Taylor's ideas.

On a few other issues, unremitting attacks by Unitarians did drive Beecher into denying the more extreme Calvinist positions. Chief and most vulnerable among these was infant damnation or, as Beecher euphemistically called it, infant salvation. As usual, once he had taken sides in a controversy he stated his position with dramatic overemphasis:

I am aware that Calvinists are represented as believing and teaching the monstrous doctrine that infants are damned, and that hell is doubtless paved with their bones. But, having . . . been conversant for thirty years with the most approved Calvinistic writers, and personally acquainted with many of the most distinguished Calvinistic divines . . . I must say that I have never seen or heard of any book which contained such a sentiment, nor a man, minister or layman, who believed or taught it.

But the doctrine of infant damnation was a logical result, however absurd, of belief in the inheritance of original sin. And so we find Beecher also hedging in his acceptance of that concept. Depravity, he said, was "wholly voluntary" in each individual. Yet somehow he managed to reconcile this view with the assumption that each man was doomed to sin— to repeat, in effect, Adam's fall. It was a tortuous attempt to shift the blame from an inherited guilt to man's weak nature.

Similarly, Beecher, following his teacher Dr. Dwight, modified the horror of "infant damnation" by saying that children sin only when they become old enough to make moral decisions. So childhood was not a state of innocence but merely a prelude to the moment when youth is faced with the realization of guilt. Hence the fierce pressure Beecher put upon his children to admit as soon as possible their rebelliousness against God and submit to Him lest they risk dying with all their sins upon them.

Beecher's rejection or at least alteration of these links in the Calvinist system—along with his kinship to Taylor—inevitably raised doubts among his more orthodox confreres concerning his reliability. The crucial challenge came in a long letter from an old friend, the Reverend Ebenezer Porter, president of Andover, a center of Old School dogma.

Porter warned Beecher, under the pretense of doing him a friendly favor, how close he was to falling into the pit of New School heresies. He taxed Beecher with exalting human agency while scanting dependence on God, with saying too little of man's total depravity and too much against infant damnation, with neglecting the Bible and, above all, with modifying the Gospel truth to render it more palatable, especially to critics. You are not a metaphysician but a "rhetorician and a popular reasoner," he wrote; your forte is "vivid argumentation and appeal from common sense and boundless stores of illustration." Stop, he concluded, before you cross the Rubicon.

Veteran campaigner and tactician, Beecher masked his mortification and marshaled a twenty-page reply. After expressing his boundless astonishment at the charges, he warned of the danger in suppressing disagreement. Proudly he cited passages from his published writings to counter the charges. He admitted only to a weakness for overstatement, saying, ". . . as to my hyperboles and metaphors, alas! I shall despair of ever reducing them to logical precision."

Beecher long afterward said that Porter had professed himself "relieved and satisfied" by Beecher's answer, but Beecher also confessed that the indictment, joined with other troubles, public and private, had occasioned "a year of darkness, bodily debility, and mental distress." "The Lord delivered me," he concluded, but the "wormwood and gall I have still in remembrance."

. . . Wars of words that left deep scars and did nothing for the cause of truth or the common weal. As seen from any later period, the entire debate between the two groups of Calvinists was a rattling of skeletons in abandoned closets. It was nonetheless acrimonious enough to lead in a few years to Beecher's being tried for nothing less than heresy.

It would be hard to say which side was more literal in its theology. Once, on a road outside Litchfield, Beecher met an Old School clergyman with whom he had agreed to exchange pulpits for the day. "Doctor Beecher," the other minister exclaimed, "I wish to call to your attention that before the creation of the world God arranged that you were to preach in my pulpit and I in yours on this particular Sabbath."

"Is that so?" Beecher replied. "Then I won't do it!" and abruptly turned his chaise and drove back to his own church.

While he disagreed with some of the views of the Old School Calvinists yet accepted the ministers themselves as fellow workers in the same cause, he saw the Unitarians simply as traitors. They were brilliant men who would leave the path to God so free of tests and trials as to make unnecessary all revivals and conversions. They were theologically undisciplined men who would tolerate all "free enquiry," no matter how dangerous.

For their part, some of the Unitarians found Beecher's evangelism unseemly and primitive. One of the severest judgments ever passed on Beecher came from Theodore Parker, passionate idealist and most radical of Unitarians. As a young man he had for a year or so attended the sermons of "the big gun of Calvinism" in his Hanover Street citadel. With the unsparing bluntness of a young rebel, he saw Beecher as well-meaning but the purveyor of an outworn, God-slandering dogma:

I went through one of his "protracted meetings". . . hearing the most frightful doctrines set forth in sermon, song and prayer. I greatly respected the talents, the zeal, and the enterprise of that able man, who certainly taught me much; but I came away with no confidence in his theology; the better I understood it, the more self-contradictory, unnatural and hateful did it seem. A year of his preaching about finished all my respect for the Calvinist scheme of theology.

Beecher's Boston revival was nevertheless surprisingly successful. When he finally held his first communion service, seventy converts came. He had been half aware that the sophisticated and refined followers of the leading Boston Unitarians looked upon him as something of a curiosity, an interloper from small-town New England. But the reaction to his revival efforts was, he claimed—exaggerating his effectiveness—almost violent:

There was an intense, malignant enragement for a time. Showers of lies were rained about us every day. The Unitarians, with all their principles of toleration, were as really a persecuting power while they had the ascendancy as ever existed. Wives and daughters were forbidden to attend our meetings; and the whole weight of political, literary, and social influence was turned against us, and the lash of ridicule laid on without stint. . . .

As for me, I cared for it all no more than for the wind. . . . I used to think as I walked the street, "If you could know any thing that was vile about me you would scream for joy; but you don't." All sorts of vile letters were written to me by abandoned people. . . . It was two years before the leaders of the Unitarians began to change their tactics and treat me gentlemanly.

Ironically, at the same time the Unitarians were deploring the intensity of Beecher's revivals, Beecher was criticizing the leading revivalist preacher of the period, Charles Grandison Finney, for even greater excesses. It was no accident that this took place during Beecher's first years in Boston; for that was a time when tumultuous revivals and intense pentecostal movements were sweeping America.

Ever since the early years of the century, circuit-riding evangelists had swung through the hinterland from Kentucky to Michigan. Everywhere they drew lonely, inhibited souls, disappointed with their daily lot, into the primitive psychological drama of the revival. Gathered in primeval groves, the crowds would be worked up to hysteria by hellfire-and-damnation sermons alternating with visions of heavenly salvation.

Out of much the same atmosphere sprang utopian religious movements, especially in the 1820s, ranging from the Shakers in upstate New York, the Separatists of Zoar in Ohio, and the Rappites in Indiana and Pennsylvania, to the beginnings of Mormonism and Joseph Smith's visions in western New York. Indeed, so many of these movements swept like brush fires through central New York that the region came to be known as "the burnt-over district." Whole towns were brought to conversion and backwoods prophets proclaimed the imminence of Doomsday or the Second Coming of Christ.

Finney was trained as a lawyer but was soon brought into the church by the waves of revivalism in upstate New York. Within a few years he had made a deep impression. A dominating figure, with heavy brows and intense gaze, his very presence overwhelmed those who met him. Mixing fearful threats, agonized pleas and an intimate, personalized style, he sent audiences into orgies of repentance. He preached from the church floor, scorning the pulpit, addressed individuals passionately and talked of God with an affecting familiarity. As soon as he began to press home his message, men and women swayed and cried out and even toppled from their seats as though stricken. "If I had a sword in my hand, I could not have cut them down as fast as they fell," he reported. Those so affected were called "the slain" and after one all-night meeting some of the converts had to be carried home. Even though he declared that salvation comes not alone from faith and God's grace but also through benevolence and good works, critics said his converts were mainly concerned with escaping hell.

Leading the opposition to Finney and his fellow evangelists was the aging Reverend Asahel Nettleton, a friend of Beecher's. He had long been a successful revivalist, but where he was subdued, Finney was bold;

where Nettleton set snares for sinners, Finney "rode them down in a cavalry charge." It was plainly a case of an ailing veteran resenting aggressive newcomers; bitterly he labeled them devils, aliens and ragamuffins. Eventually Nettleton persuaded Beecher that if unchecked, Finney and his imitators would justify the Unitarian charges that the methods of the entire New School revival movement were vulgar and violent.

So Beecher, although he had never seen or heard Finney, wrote to him and his allies, warning of the catastrophic dangers he saw in their practices. Not quite innocently, Nettleton sent a copy of the letter to a prominent clergyman, and soon it appeared in print. Beecher protested violently against the breach of confidence, but the damage had been done: the revivalists were split, with many ministers, especially in the western regions, siding with Finney, and accusing Beecher of having played into the hands of the Unitarians in their attacks on revivalism. Meanwhile Finney, having taken the provinces, moved on the capital.

Beecher and his associates met with Finney and his minions in what was supposedly an attempt at reconciliation. But with the belligerency that usually marked him in such a situation, Beecher ended—or so he claimed—with a warning:

Finney, I know your plan, and you know I do; you mean to come into Connecticut and carry a streak of fire to Boston. But if you attempt it, as the Lord liveth, I'll meet you at the State line, and call out all the artillerymen, and fight every inch of the way to Boston, and then I'll fight you there.

Beecher would always recall that statement with pride (in his *Memoirs*, Finney denied the story), as though it had been addressed not to a famous fellow Congregationalist but to some rogue or agent of the devil. But the meanest of Beecher's complaints against Finney was that he allowed women to express themselves publicly. "A greater evil, next to the loss of conscience and chastity, could not befall the female sex," he wrote. "No well educated female can put herself up, or be put up, to the point of public prayer, without the loss of some portion at least of that female delicacy, which is above all price." Even when she became a spokeswoman for education, his daughter Catharine never forgot that warning or forgave women who ignored it.

After a while, the squabble died of its own narrowness. Marked by jealousy and petty partisanship, mainly on the part of Nettleton but also of Beecher, it profited neither side nor the common cause. A settlement between the factions was reached in 1828. As Finney's reputation continued to grow and he conducted great revivals throughout Connecticut, a score of deacons urged Beecher to bring Finney to Boston. Beecher finally capitulated. Finney came, and preached and conquered: The excitement he generated in the very heart of the Unitarian domain was said to have been comparable to that of the Great Awakening.

Perhaps no one noticed, but the Reverend Lyman Beecher had been defeated on his own grounds and with his own weapons.

So there was a period in the 1820s when Lyman Beecher was engaged—to use his favorite metaphors—in skirmishes, rearguard actions or assaults on fellow churchmen on at least four fronts: on the Old School orthodoxy in an effort to make their Puritanism more tolerable; on the Episcopalians because they failed to require a saving faith in those they admitted to the communion; on the Unitarians for the denial of the Trinitarian godhead and man's sinfulness; and finally on the revivalists of the Finney kind because they were too fanatical and incendiary and because they unsettled the parishes which they invaded.

Thus to his Old School opponents at the one extreme he was a liberal and a heretic while to the perfervid Finneys at the other extreme he was a conservative. But the end result was that he spent an immense amount of time and energy in sterile controversy or jurisdictional disputes with other Protestant divines.

The reminiscences that Harriet Beecher Stowe contributed to her father's *Autobiography* (the entire family helped to prepare it) are colored and softened by the fact that her first mature view of her father came in Boston when he was at the peak of his career. Her recall, almost thirty years later, makes full use of her power as a novelist to shape scenes or characters as she wants us to see them.

In religious matters Harriet cherished tradition almost more than did any other of Lyman Beecher's children. "Within a stone's throw of our door," she writes, "was the old Copp Hill burying-ground, where rested the bones of the Puritan founders; and, though not a man ordinarily given to sentiment . . . we were never left to forget in any prayer of his that the bones of our fathers were before our door." So two centuries after the Pilgrims had arrived they still cast long shadows in New England, and Harriet, through her father's eyes, could see the Unitarians only as a negative force aimed at bringing Calvinism to an end. "When Dr. Beecher came to Boston," she wrote, "Calvinism or orthodoxy was the despised and persecuted form of faith. It was the dethroned royal family wandering like a permitted mendicant in the city where once it had held court, and Unitarianism reigned in its stead." But after every wave of "revolutionary enquiry," she asserts, people fall back exhausted into "the kindly arms of a positive belief"—a characterization of Beecher's Calvinism that Unitarians would have found quite unrecognizable. The weary and restless found, she says, a sympathetic ear and a firm faith in the Reverend Beecher. And he in turn was kept at a white heat of enthusiasm. Even his family prayers became "upheavings of passionate emotion."

Believing in spontaneity, the Reverend Beecher generally left the preparation of a sermon to an hour or so before he delivered it; then, after a swing or two with dumbbells to work off nervous excitement, he would scribble notes until the church bell began to toll. Soon he would come plunging down the stairs like a hurricane, and stuffing his notes into the crown of his hat and "hooking wife or daughter like a satchel on his arm," go racing breathlessly through the streets. At the church he would press his way down the crowded aisles and up the pulpit stairs. At least once he plunged into a sermon without the preliminary hymns and prayers.

Beecher's sermons, as Harriet reports, began with a plain statement addressed purely to the understanding, followed by citations from Scriptures as the word of God. He would then take up objections, usually in a sprightly and conversational tone. Last came the "application," for a sermon that did not induce action, he would say, was a sermon thrown away. His appeal at this point was direct and intense, punctuated by warnings and pleas: "Will you go to some solitary place tonight, and kneel down and pray? You are conscious you can do it. Will you do it?" He ended with the standard entreaties to go and sin no more.

In the *Autobiography* Harriet is the loyal daughter publicly paying tribute to her father as he had been in his prime. In private she was less flattering, admitting that as a girl she had often found his sermons unintelligible. Probably the truth was somewhere in between; as a law student in Litchfield in the mid-1820s reported, Beecher was at times movingly eloquent, at other times simply uninspired.

Not long after he had outfaced the Unitarian criticism of his revival practice, Beecher repeated his series of sermons on intemperance, thereby adding another group to those Bostonians who disapproved of him. He stirred up, he claimed, only the drinkers and vendors of drink all over the city. "There was," he declared, "a great ebullition of rage among a certain class." Undoubtedly there were rowdies in that "certain class," but democracy in the age of Jackson had also given rise to some rough-hewn citizens who simply resented such interference in their private affairs.

At the other end of the social scale, Unitarians who enjoyed such amenities as a few glasses of wine and even found spirits "beneficial" were equally alienated.

Soon, too, Beecher organized a Hanover Street Church Young Men's Association to counter the growing political influence of the Unitarians. Characteristically, the reforms it sought tended to curtail pleasures and personal liberties. The association saw to it that steamboat excursions to Nahant on Sundays—to some a heinous breach of the Sabbath—were stopped and that laws were passed against lotteries. New England found it easy to disapprove of such diversions because they were not only idle but cost money. The association did encourage popular lectures and the educational forums called lyceums. And Beecher's own love of music led him to encourage hymn singing and to bring to his church Lowell Mason, who would become the leading composer of church music in America. New England music, reflecting a history of persecution and exile, had been plaintive and mournful, wedded to the minor key. Now Beecher's enthusiasm and buoyant faith were credited, most of all by Mason himself, with fostering a bolder and livelier mode. Old hymns moved him deeply.

Whatever these activities added to Beecher's fame, they hardly contributed to his popularity. Thus when in 1830 the Hanover Street Church caught fire, the firemen who answered the alarm made no attempt to put out the blaze. Curiously, a merchant who had been allowed to rent a room in the church basement had, unbeknownst to anyone, stored jugs of liquor in it. So, as the church was engulfed in fire and the jugs of rum burst, the firemen shouted jokes about Beecher's "broken jug." The crowd that gathered, vastly amused by the spectacle of the liquor-loaded church of the leading temperance preacher going up in flames, began to chant:

> "While Beecher's church holds out to burn
> The vilest sinner may return. . . . "

But the Reverend Beecher was not so easily put out of face. The next day, as the church committee met glumly in Pierce's Bookstore, in skipped Beecher and, referring to the jug-shaped steeple, blithely announced, "Well, my jug's broke; just been to see it," and proceeded to encourage the members to build a new church.

By 1830, the edge of Beecher's excitement at coming to Boston had worn thin. Perhaps he also realized that, with the Unitarians and a cultivated elite on one side and an urban working class on the other, he was not cherished as much as he had expected to be. So the burning down of his church and the temporary dislocation of his congregation freed him to think of other fields to conquer.

By far the most challenging of these, in 1830, was "the West"— meaning mainly Kentucky, Tennessee, Ohio, Indiana and Illinois. The Ohio Valley was attracting all manner of settlers—New England farmers tired of struggling with a stony soil, working people fleeing from wage slavery in the mills and factories of the East, immigrants from the troubled areas of Europe. Even the President was a man from Tennessee.

And Henry Clay of Kentucky, Felix Grundy of Tennessee, Thomas Hart Benton of Missouri and their like were making western influence felt on the national scene. The tremendous increase in population throughout the region had within a few years made it a fertile new territory for evangelism. Just as Beecher shared the general optimism of the young republic but sought to focus it on salvation, so now he joined in the enthusiasm for the West, but as a great opportunity for the church rather than as a source of free land.

As early as July 1830, Beecher began talking of the West as the place where rival religions would decide the "moral destiny" and hopes of America. As far as he was concerned, the archrival among other religions was that age-old bogey of Protestant clergymen, Catholicism. Early in 1831 he began a series of lectures on the Roman Catholic menace, complete with paranoid warnings of Vatican plots against the United States. His daughter Harriet went so far as to say that his "great motive in going to Cincinnati was to oppose the influence of the Roman Catholic church in every way."

Once the dream came to him he was possessed by it. Forgotten was his violent opposition in other days to the families who were abandoning the hallowed New England earth for the uncertainties of the western wilderness. As all America had once been to Europeans, so now the West became for easterners the land of promise, nurturer of new beginnings, a place where everything was possible.

The moral destiny of our nation, and all our institutions and hopes, and the world's hopes, turns on the character of the West [he wrote to Catharine], and the competition now is for that preoccupancy in the education of the rising generation, in which Catholics and infidels have got the start on us.

I have thought seriously of going over to Cincinnati, the London of the West, to spend the remnant of my days in the great conflict, and in consecrating all my children to God in that region who are willing to go. If we gain the West, all is safe; if we lose it, all is lost.

In contemplating such a move Beecher was not a pioneer even in his own family circle: Uncle John Foote had settled in Cincinnati years before. So had General King, a cousin to Mrs. Beecher. And Uncle Samuel Foote, far-wandering sea captain, having married, had scouted the West—that is, mostly Ohio—for a place to settle and had enthusiastically reported that Cincinnati, "a beautiful city, right on the river," was his choice. When he came east for a visit in 1827, Uncle Samuel talked not of exotic peoples and strange customs in far-off places but of the attractions of the "Queen City" of the Ohio Valley. So Beecher was immensely flattered to learn that the trustees of the newly organized Lane Theological Seminary of Cincinnati were thinking of offering him the presidency of the school. The Reverend Franklin Y. Vail, who had been sent east to find a leader who could help establish the seminary, had reported to the trustees:

After much consultation, it appeared to be the common impression of those consulted that Dr. Beecher, of Boston, if he could be obtained, would be the best man. That, as he is the most prominent, popular, and powerful preacher in our nation, he would immediately give character, elevation, and success to our seminary, draw together young men from every part of our country, secure the confidence and co-operation of the ministers and churches both east and west of the Alleghany Mountains. . . .

After Vail had sounded him out, Beecher's reaction was characteristically exuberant:

There was not on earth a place *but that* I would have opened my ears to for a moment. But I had felt, and thought, and labored a great deal about raising up ministers, and the idea that I might be called to teach the best mode of preaching to the young ministry of the broad West flashed through my mind like lightning. I went home and ran in, and found Esther alone in the sitting room. I was in such a state of emotion and excitement I could not speak, and she was frightened. At last I told her. It was the greatest thought that ever entered my soul; it filled it, and displaced everything else.

When the official invitation came, it was reinforced by a pledge from Arthur Tappan, New York businessman and philanthropist, to put up at least twenty thousand dollars for the school if it could secure Dr. Beecher's services. Almost as encouraging was the fact that the chairman of the board of trustees, the Reverend Dr. Joshua Lacy Wilson, a most rigid Old School Calvinist, had given his blessing to the invitation.

Much as he might have wanted to accept, Beecher had an obligation he could not ignore: his Boston congregation had already begun to build a new church. So, very reluctantly, he declined. But he had caught the westering fever, and several events in the next two years strengthened the urge. First, Edward, who as pastor of the Park Street Church had been a great help to him in Boston, left late in 1830 to take up his duties as president of Illinois College, in Jacksonville, Illinois. Soon, too, the new church on Bowdoin Street was completed, freeing Beecher from any obligation to stay on.

Then, adding to the challenge, the Reverend Wilson, alerted by Old School colleagues in the East, belatedly began to look into Beecher's theological views—and was deeply disturbed. For he found that the man who was being counted on to win the West for dyed-in-the-wool Edwardean Calvinism held opinions that were, by his standards, little short of heretical. It agitated him even more to find that Beecher was a close friend and admirer of Dr. Nathaniel W. Taylor from that seedbed of New School heresies, the Yale Divinity School.

Wilson immediately declared his objections to the other trustees. But many leading Cincinnati citizens were highly pleased by the prospect of capturing so famous an eastern preacher for their outpost of religion and culture; so Wilson was defeated by a majority vote of the Lane trustees. But he had fired only the opening gun in what was to become a bitter struggle between New School and Old School factions.

Thus, when the secretary of the board of trustees at Lane wrote to Beecher, renewing the invitation, he declared that many ministers were neglecting their pastoral duties in order to hunt out heresies and defame their brethren. "Will you not come immediately?" he pleaded. "The armies of Israel need a leader." A few eminent New School adherents, seeing an opportunity to establish a western beachhead, added their encouragement.

Made wary, Beecher set out to reconnoiter Cincinnati. He took Catharine with him and they stayed for a month in Uncle Samuel Foote's house on the heights above the river. Our only record of the visit, a letter from Catharine to Harriet, overflows with enthusiasm about the beautiful location of the city and especially of Walnut Hills, the site of the seminary, "so elevated and cool that people have to come away to be sick and die." Reassuringly, she noted that the people were mostly from New England, including several old family acquaintances, not to mention uncles John and Samuel—"intelligent, sociable, free and hospitable." "I never saw a place," she added, "so capable of being rendered a Paradise." It was a report fit to make anyone caught in the humdrum of Boston or Hartford tingle with anticipation.

Not surprisingly, Catharine made sure to find parents who were eager to have just such a school as she was already planning. . . .

Because Beecher had stipulated that he be permitted to continue his work as a preacher, he was now offered the pastorate of the Second Presbyterian Church of Cincinnati. By the time he accepted the two posts in the spring of 1832, he was convinced that his decision was nothing less than a turning point in American church history:

The exigencies of our country demand seminaries. . . . And the question whether the first and leading seminary of the West shall be one which inculcates orthodoxy . . . is a question, in my view, of as great importance as was ever permitted a single human mind to decide. If I accept I consider the question settled that a revival seminary takes the lead. . . .

Beecher's insistence on a training school for revivals is worth noting: he knew that in that direction lay his strength, that appeals to the heart, not to the mind, that feeling, not doctrine, made converts. But in his bizarre exaggeration of the importance of a single, yet-to-be-established seminary, he plainly did not realize how far church influence had declined. With so many families moving west, it simply seemed to him that America's future and perhaps the world's lay in the Ohio Valley.

Soon the entire Beecher clan was fired with enthusiasm for the move. Catharine, having lost interest in her school once it was established, prepared to leave Hartford. She tried to get her old associate Mary Dutton to take over the school, but Mary preferred to stay in New Haven. So Catharine turned to John Pierce Brace, the much admired headmaster—and Hattie's idol—of Miss Pierce's school in Litchfield. He accepted the call; as head of the Hartford Female Seminary he would become known as an outstanding educator. Catharine was free to dream of a bigger and better school on the banks of the Ohio.

And so, at the age of fifty-seven, the Reverend Lyman Beecher tore up all his roots—deep as seven generations and two centuries of New England life could make them—and launched the journey into the "western wilderness."

It was quite a caravan—a preview, in a way, of the greater, far more trying journey westward that tens of thousands of American families were to make sixteen years later. There was Beecher himself and his wife, Aunt Esther, Catharine, George, Hattie, and the three children of Beecher by his second wife—Isabella (called Sister Belle or Bella), ten years old, Thomas, eight, and James, four. The Reverend Dr. Wilson would have found his worst suspicions confirmed had he known that George, now twenty-three, was transferring to Lane from Yale Divinity School, where he had been thoroughly converted to Dr. Taylor's New School heresies.

Of the five children who did not go with the party, Edward was already in Illinois, Mary, happily married, was settled in Hartford, William was in Newport, Rhode Island, trying to cope with his first pastorate, Henry Ward was at Amherst, and Charles was at Bowdoin.

Although Esther, the maiden aunt, fated to go wherever her family went, was beset by many fears, it was Harriet Porter who was truly heartsick at being uprooted. Coming from a distinguished family, reared without pressures except from her own religious conscience, she had never adjusted to the teeming, highly charged Beecher household. The strain of caring for her alternately buoyant and depressed husband and his eight children and of bearing four of her own, all on Dr. Beecher's pathetic salary, had undermined her health and spirit, leaving her much of the time an invalid. Although she was as devout as any Beecher, no missionary fire burned in her veins. But in Boston she had managed to find a setting and a milieu that had made life tolerable. Boston had at least been hallowed soil, "pressed by the feet of the Pilgrims and watered by their tears."

Now all that had been abandoned and they were heading literally like gypsies into a strange land.

The first stop, New York, proved very exciting for the young ones because it was their first trip so far from home, and for Lyman because he found himself caught up in raising twenty thousand dollars for a professorship of Biblical literature at Lane. ("The incumbent," Harriet wrote, not dreaming what it would mean to her, "is to be C. Stowe"— then a professor of languages at Dartmouth.) Beecher rushed about from one rich church member to another, and with every donation his spirits rose. "He is all in his own element," Harriet observed, " . . . going around here, there, and everywhere—begging, borrowing, and spoiling the Egyptians—delighted with past success, and confident for the future."

Next came Philadelphia, where the weather was all dull drizzle but where a local editorial hailed Dr. Beecher and his clan as having bravely gone forth into the wilderness like Jacob and his sons.

On the stagecoach journey to Downingtown, Pennsylvania, and then to Harrisburg, they whiled away the time by singing hymns and psalms, led exuberantly by George. It was George, too, along with the younger ones, who began tossing religious tracts (he had brought a boxful) to all and sundry wayfarers, "peppering the land," as Harriet said, "with moral influence."

After Harrisburg they were in the mountains, surrounded by the splendor of the Alleghenies in October. When young Charles Fenno Hoffman described the same journey, made exactly a year later, he spent ten pages on the magnificent vistas—all glorious golden brown, russet and green—the wild ravines, and the pleasure of coming upon hidden hamlets, with meadows, orchards and barns, and, once, "a train of huge Pennsylvania wagons."

But Puritans had no eye for wild, untamed nature; it was the abode of devils and of no use. It would take a generation or more of Romantic poets to change all that. In any event, missionary ardor made the Reverend Beecher so impatient that he insisted on abandoning the stage and hiring a private coach. The horses turned out to be poor, and where the mail coach regularly made the trip to Wheeling, Virginia (now West Virginia), in two days, it took the Beechers eight.

Throughout the journey, Lyman—and sometimes George—missed no opportunity to preach, spreading "Taylor heresies" everywhere. So, for a few weeks on the hegira to the Promised Land, Lyman Beecher was an itinerant evangelist bringing the word of God to the people of the wilderness.

At Wheeling they were to take a boat down the Ohio to their destination, but they learned that Cincinnati was in the grip of that chronic scourge of early American cities, a cholera epidemic. Travelers coming up the river from the beleaguered city told of many hundreds of people stricken, coffins lined up in the doorways, and a pall of smoke from coal fires lit in the streets to combat the plague. It was two weeks before they heard that the epidemic had waned and they could move on. But the servants of the Lord were unafraid. They made the last stages of their trek by coach, jolting miserably over rough roads of corduroy—massive logs laid sidewise. Brimming with zeal and high expectations, the Reverend Lyman Beecher, spiritually a prophet leading an army with banners, entered Cincinnati on November 14, 1832.

5

ENTER, A NEW GENERATION

It was evident at a fairly early stage that each of Lyman Beecher's two oldest sons, William, born in 1802, and Edward, coming a year later, was of a very different mold. Edward became, like his older sister, Catharine, an excellent student; William, while by no means backward, was simply not one of the more gifted or brilliant members of the Beecher clan.

It was inevitable that Dr. Beecher should have expected his firstborn son to become a minister and a scholar, and it is ironic that William should have been the least successful minister of Lyman's seven sons. One of William's problems was that he soon realized that both his brother Edward and his sister Catharine were brighter than he was, at least where study was concerned. He was an imaginative boy and somewhat romantic, he later wrote, but with

a feeling that I never should be anything. . . . I did not know how to study and none showed me. Edward, on the contrary, learned easily. . . . the fact was I had trouble in my head—a gathering and discharge from my left ear . . . the whole outer ear was poisoned by the discharge . . . and my left breast bone being much smaller than the other they feared rickets.

We do not need to know anything about sibling rivalry or inferiority complexes to appreciate William's problems. When he reached twelve, a special effort was made to help him: he was sent to be tutored in such subjects as trigonometry by a Reverend Mr. Daggett in New Canaan, Connecticut. He made no progress at all and soon developed dyspepsia—the usual way for a Beecher to respond to frustration or defeat.

Because William did have an aptitude for things mechanical, he was next apprenticed to a cabinetmaker in Hartford, but he was so unhappy there that he had to be allowed to come home. In slow succession he served as a clerk in a general store in New Milford, Connecticut, in a dry goods store in Hartford and in another store in New York. He was the only one of the Beecher sons who did not go to college.

At twenty-one he was home again; all he later recalled of that interlude was that the great question around the house was "What shall we do with William?" Although Dr. Beecher had long since given up hope that his son could become a minister, he had never lessened his efforts to bring the youth to conversion. As early as William's seventeenth year, when the young man, in response to a prodding letter from his father, asked how a man could "feel sorrow for sins of which he does not feel guilty," Lyman wrote:

His ignorance of himself is voluntary and inexcusable, and his stupidity [that is, spiritual inertia] and insensibility are his crime. . . . Can not you read the law of God? . . . Can you not perceive you are constantly transgressing it . . . but have sinned constantly, ever since you have been capable by age of knowing and loving God?

The elder Beecher was completely unconscious of his impatience and harshness. As with Catharine, so now with William he simply could not understand why the youth should not recognize and acknowledge his own sinfulness.

As though he suddenly realized that it was one way in which he could easily fulfill his parents' expectations, William underwent conversion. He was spurred on to another step, surely anticipating how pleased his father would be: he decided to become a minister. To his surprise and disappointment, he got little encouragement from his father. Lyman evidently realized how unsuited William was for the ministry, especially as compared with Edward, who was already in divinity school. Nevertheless, William went off to Andover. But theological studies were no easier for him than trigonometry, and soon he was suffering from sleepless nights and dyspepsia. So it was decided that he should continue his studies at home. After a while, a committee of Boston ministers, which happened to include Lyman Beecher, granted William Beecher a license to preach. Following some itinerant preaching, he was again rescued by his father: Lyman secured him a place as a licentiate in a parish in what was, in 1830, the quiet seaside town of Newport, Rhode Island.

Momentarily encouraged, William decided to marry Katherine Edes, a girl he had been courting for a number of years. Perhaps it was his lack of self-confidence or the aura of defeat that clung to him, but even his wedding was disappointing. As he himself recalled it, "Harriet was bridesmaid, no company, no cake, no cards—nothing pleasant about it."

Before long the steeple on the Newport church became shaky and William himself, to everyone's admiration, managed to rope it and pull it down. But when it came to raising money for a new church, he failed. So he left Newport and found a pastorate in Middletown, Connecticut. But hard luck went with him: within a year the minister he had replaced decided to return.

Inspired by his father's vision of converting the West to God and Presbyterianism, William Beecher and his wife and baby joined the other Beechers in Cincinnati in 1832. As always, his father helped him get a post—this time in a church that was being organized in Putnam, Ohio. He got it, it was said, only because he was the first applicant on the scene.

Everyone knew from his boyhood on that Edward Beecher would, in his dedication to God and Church, realize his father's hopes for him. An excellent student, conscientious and methodical, he entered Yale at the age of fifteen and did outstandingly well there. Indeed, his interest in his secular studies made his father warn him against any intellectual activities that might cause him to neglect "the reading of the Scriptures and daily supplication to God." He was scarcely seventeen when his father, as with William the year before and Catharine before that, began pressing him toward conversion.

Perhaps Lyman was spurred by the death from scarlet fever—called the black canker—of baby Frederick, the first of his children by Harriet Porter. He urged Edward to beware "the mighty ruin which all your capacities and improvement will constitute in another world, should they continue under the dominion of a heart unsanctified and unreconciled to God." Any New England cemetery of that period, with its rows of stones memorializing dead children, may help to explain the elder Beecher's almost hysterical sense of urgency. The evening before little Frederick died, he wrote to Edward:

Most earnestly do I pray that I may never have the trial of weeping over you, on a dying bed, without hope. What shall it profit you though you should gain all knowledge and lose your own soul?

A few months later he burst out:

My heart overflows with grief and fear, and my eyes with tears while I write to you. *You must not continue stupid.* . . . Let nothing interfere now with the care of your soul.

By the spring of 1821, his appeal to Edward has become still more importunate:

how dreadful to my soul is the thought that you shall never serve God in the Gospel of his Son; and how still more dreadful that your powers should be forever perverted, and the perversion followed with suffering self-inflicted, and also divinely inflicted forever.

Oh, my dear son, *agonize* to enter in. You *must* go to heaven; you *must not* go to hell!

It would be another year before Edward achieved the shining goal. As morbidly despairing as father Beecher had been before, so joyful was he now: "It is also a feeling which no lapse of ages will obliterate from the heart. The reality of the fact will become unquestioned, but the wonder will increase forever."

Growing up in Litchfield, Edward had been surrounded by Congregational conservatism. But even before he reached Yale in 1818 he was aware that a new sect, the Unitarians, was challenging orthodox doctrines and displacing orthodox divines. Though he sympathized with his father's wrath at this "enemy" within the ranks, he himself belonged to another generation and could not simply brand them "pernicious infidels" and dismiss their views. Caught between the two forces, he would try desperately to reconcile the differences between them, to accommodate, for example, the Unitarian belief that God acts according to human standards of justice.

Meanwhile Edward was the ideal son. On some weekends while he was at Yale he would walk all Friday night the forty-odd miles from New Haven to Litchfield, work on the family farm on Saturday, sing in the choir of his father's church on Saturday evening and again on Sunday morning, and start back to New Haven Sunday evening. To save money he would carry a week's food back to school. (Yet his father denied him a watch, saying that until he earned it, wearing one would be foppery.) He met his college expenses by teaching, between college sessions, at the Hartford Academy.

His regimen as a teacher is a paradigm of the Protestant work ethic and the Puritan fear of idleness. He had twenty-six students, whom he met in classes of three, two or even one at a time. So, he reported to Catharine,

I always employ at least seven hours in the school, besides this I sleep seven hours, and in order to preserve my health I exercise one hour every day—this I do by cutting wood. . . . Of course to balance all this I must take something to eat but I make my meals as short as possible, but I will allow forty-five minutes for the three. Besides this I allow 1½ hours for reading the bible and prayer. These . . . leave me six hours and forty-five minutes. . . . I have in the first place the translations and Latin compositions of my scholars to correct . . . and a thousand little things that occur every day. . . . And I forgot to mention . . . washing and dressing which takes me about twenty minutes every day.

He then apologizes for his inability to do all the things he wants to do. And he does not even mention his study of music, his athletic activities or his interest in mathematical problems. His progress in "oratory" brought the ultimate compliment: hearing one of his exercises, his father said that "he poured it out Lyman Beecher like." Not surprisingly, he was valedictorian of his class.

Edward's sense of communion with God was already so deep that he began to see himself as mystically dedicated. " . . . whether I live or die," he wrote to Catharine, "am prosperous or unfortunate, am distinguished or unknown matters little to me. I feel willing to trust all to providence. I feel assured that I have something to do before I die and when that is done, I should rejoice to leave this for a better world."

It was evidently this assurance together with his maturity and Biblical learning that led Catharine, Harriet and Mary to turn to him with their spiritual and religious problems ("Oh how I wish you could sit by our fire, evenings, and help us out of our conjectures," Catharine wrote). He was not yet twenty years old when Professor Fisher—under whom he had studied mathematics at Yale—drowned, but his advice to Catharine shows a compassion that makes his father's attitude seem unyielding and harsh. Later, when young Harriet was tormented by her inability to accept her father's austere God, Edward comforted her with a vision of a God of mercy and pity, who "sympathizes with his guilty, afflicted creatures," a God whose nature is reflected in the image of Jesus as "the man of Sorrows."

After serving as headmaster at Hartford for two more years, Edward had had enough of the "cares of schoolkeeping" and trying to "beat knowledge into thick skulls." Ready at last to become a minister, he entered Andover Theological Seminary in 1824. But he was not happy with the emphasis on dogma and disputation, and when, a year later, Yale offered him a tutorship, he accepted.

At Yale, religion was once again at a low ebb. The students were disorderly, one wild group setting off a packet of gunpowder that blew out the windows of the school building. Edward organized prayer meetings and Bible classes—his brother Charles later made this sound like a revival—and helped to restore order. While he was still at Yale, and only a few months after his father went to the Hanover Street Church in Boston, Edward was repeatedly invited to preach at Boston's Park Street Church, one of the leading revivalist churches in America, so militantly orthodox that it was called "Brimstone Corner." Such was Lyman Beecher's influence that he soon persuaded the Park Street Church to make Edward its pastor, despite his youth, lack of experience, and inclination toward a more scholarly way of life. Lyman, glorying in a revival campaign of his own, urged his son to join him in the work of "resurrecting" Boston, New England, and eventually all America—and, incidentally, fighting the Unitarians. Thus inspired, Edward arrived in Boston late in 1826.

The Calvinist dogma that tormented Edward most of all was that of innate depravity. A child of the Age of Reason, he could not understand how man could be held responsible for a sinfulness that was inborn. Isn't a system, he asked, that dooms everyone at birth a malevolent one? Didn't it call into question the rectitude of God?

Such inner conflicts drove some into abysses of guilt and shame, others into camp meeting frenzies, and still others into the ranks of the Unitarians, Universalists, Swedenborgians, or any one of scores of utopian sects. It led learned, sensitive Edward Beecher into a theory of the origins of sinfulness that bordered on fantasy. Aided by what he believed was a divine illumination, he became convinced that souls came into this world not corrupt as a result of Adam's fall but as free spirits who fell from innocence in a previous existence. Since they had free choice in that existence, God could not be blamed for their fall.

As critics have noted, Edward's theory was much like that of Wordsworth's "Ode on Intimations of Immortality from Recollections of Early Childhood"—which Beecher had of course read—except that the soul came bearing sins from another sphere instead of "trailing clouds of glory."

Edward had solved the conflict to his own satisfaction, but neither his father nor Catharine showed any enthusiasm for the solution. As he himself admitted, even those who respected him wondered whether he had not lost his mental balance and "become unconsciously the slave of that visionary certainty which is caused by nervous excitement." Fearing his theory would be labeled mystical and arrogant, if not heretical, he waited twenty-five years before publishing it in his magnum opus, *The Conflict of Ages*.

Because he shared his father's dedication and faith, Edward's four years at the Park Street Church were so crowded with evangelical campaigns and surges of religious excitement that he twice had to take long vacations to relieve the "nervous strain." Once he went to Maine. Even there he preached revival sermons, but he had at least the special satisfaction of converting a young woman named Isabella Porter Jones, a distant relative of his stepmother's; he married her the following year and they set up housekeeping in Boston. Stimulated by such minglings of religion and love, he experienced at times a religious ecstasy that bordered on the erotic. Describing his love of God, he wrote:

I felt that the exciting cause of such love must be the knowledge of his love to me and of his infinite desire to communicate his Essence to me in full and overflowing communication of love such as should affect my whole frame until I could feel that the love of God is strong as death, that the coals thereof are coals of fire

. . . yea, so intensely did I desire the love of God that I felt willing that it should burn me up if it were but love, and I could rejoice to die by such a death.

He found relief from such intense experiences in physical exercise and especially in sculling in the harbor; characteristically, he used a most difficult technique, standing like a gondolier with one oar thrust out in a notch in the stern, and making the boat vibrate forward. It was, as Charles described it, "mathematics and boating combined."

But all Edward Beecher's piety, learning and mystical fervor did not prevent some of his leading parishioners—doubtless disappointed that he was no Lyman Beecher—from criticizing him for what they chose to call "defective preaching." Lyman insisted that it was all a matter of personal animosity. Whatever the reason, by the end of 1829 Lyman was trying to head off action by his son's critics. The end came when Ebenezer Parker, speaking for a dozen members of the congregation, notified Edward that they were deriving no benefit from his preaching and saw no prospect that he would improve. Edward himself, weary of the rigid orthodoxy of his church and the lack of freedom to explore his own views, was apparently not disturbed by the prospect of leaving.

It was only a little later that Dr. Beecher began talking enthusiastically about going to "the West." So when Edward was invited to become president of Illinois College, a tiny new school on the prairie, he welcomed the opportunity. The invitation came from a group of earnest citizens in the town of Jacksonville, Illinois, who had heard of Edward's abilities from several Yale theological students pledged to promote religion in the West. Late in 1830, inspired by his father's newfound missionary zeal, he accepted the post. Like his father, he was leaving the ministry for the sake of a college presidency that he thought would enable him to help create an ideal society in the West. He also hoped that it would allow him to return to the world of scholarship. .

But it was all quite different from what he expected. The college, established only two years earlier, was even poorer than Lane Seminary, and Edward would spend much of his time trying to keep it going. His salary, which eventually reached $1,100 a year, would have been adequate—if it had been paid in full or had not, at times, been omitted altogether.

Edward and his family had at first to make do with a log house and cope with so much malaria that a local jest was: "Everyone is shaking so hard with the durn ague, they can't find time to die." The daily routine of the school was austere, starting at five o'clock in the morning with prayers and closing with more prayers at five or six in the afternoon. The students worked betweentimes on farms or in shops in order to pay about one hundred dollars a year for tuition, room and board—and everyone, including the president, tended vegetable gardens.

Edward would remain at the college for thirteen years, faced with constant lack of funds—especially during the depression of 1837—distrustful politicians, and the slavery problem. In such respects his course would be remarkably like his father's, who arrived in the West only a few months later.

The fourth of Lyman's children by Roxana Foote, and the last to be born in East Hampton, was Mary. Among Lyman Beecher's children she stands out in reverse, for she never sought a career or fame and was the most "private" of the Reverend Beecher's children.

Perhaps she turned out as she did because she grew up in Litchfield, where the main goal for a young woman was a good marriage, and because, judging from her portraits, she was an attractive young woman. She was never troubled by crusading urges or by talents that clamored for expression.

But at least once—in 1826—even she protested against the absurdity of certain Calvinist concepts. If at the creation, she wrote Edward, God knew perfectly well what would take place to the end of time, including man's fall and the dooming of most of the human race to eternal misery, "How do you reconcile that with Infinite Benevolence?" And try as she might, she could not achieve that consuming commitment to God that her father had taught her was essential. Like Catharine and Harriet, she appealed to Edward as the one among her siblings who had reached the ideal with the least struggle. She wrote to him:

I lay plans and form resolutions ... but I accomplish nothing. ... You will say perhaps that I do it trusting in my own strength, but dear brother I feel myself to be "all weakness." ... If you were to see how little control I have over wrong feelings and desires, how little love to God or benevolence toward man, how unwilling to deny or exert myself for the cause I ought most to love, you would think I had sufficient reason for unhappiness and despondency. ... when I go to my closet for the sole purpose of spending an hour or a few minutes in prayer, I go too much as to a task ... and if I ever go with feelings of pleasure, I soon become wearied and cold.

"What shall I do?" she asked. But she did not wait for an answer. She had made her confession and, apparently reconciled to her shortcomings, went on her way.

Where Catharine would devote much of her life to education, Harriet to writing, and Isabella to women's rights, Mary, after teaching and acting as chief assistant in Catharine's Hartford Female Seminary, married Thomas Perkins, a Hartford lawyer, when she was still in her early twenties. Perhaps because he soon became a successful lawyer and business counselor, he was able to draw her off the Beecher path of reform and moral guidance.

So Mary Beecher Perkins became a proper and handsome matron, welcoming all her duties as wife and mother. She would have her share of problems, but it may say something about ambition and public achievement that the most conventional of Lyman Beecher's children seems to have been the most content.

6

HATTIE

"She went owling about"

Hardly four when her mother died, Hattie would recall only the aura of restfulness that surrounded Roxana. One of her earliest memories was that of hearing her mother gently say, as the children came running and dancing into the sitting room, "Remember the Sabbath day to keep it holy." For the rest, there were such mementoes of a nineteenth-century gentlewoman's accomplishments as miniatures on ivory, painted chairs, fine stitched doilies, handmade lace, and painted copies of birds which are still sold as postcards in Litchfield today.

To help Hattie escape the period of mourning in the house after Roxana's death, she was sent to her mother's family home in Nutplains to stay with her grandmother Foote and her aunt Harriet Foote. Aunt Harriet was an energetic woman whose ideas of education were those of an Englishwoman of the old school: belief in King and Church—High Church, of course, with only a bare tolerance of Congregationalism. As for little girls, Aunt Harriet thought they should move gently, speak softly, spend time sewing and knitting, go to church on Sundays and, on coming home after church, be catechized. Yet she managed somehow to combine these qualities with a keen sense of humor.

By contrast, Grandmother Foote was indulgent, sympathizing with Hattie when she annoyed her aunt, and generally overlooking the child's little faults. What Grandmother Foote and Aunt Harriet shared was a devotion to prayer. Grandma Foote was hardly ever without her huge prayer book. And Hattie never forgot how her aunt made her learn the mild Episcopal version of the catechism and then decided that since Hattie was a Congregationalist minister's daughter she should also learn the grim Presbyterian recitation. This was quite a concession, since Aunt Harriet, with her aristocratic, High Church sense of superiority, never considered her brother-in-law genuinely ordained. But after a few half-hearted attempts, Aunt Harriet concluded that it might be best to leave the Presbyterian version to Hattie's father. Long years later, Harriet

Beecher Stowe in her *Oldtown Folks* (1868) has Ellery Davenport, who is in violent revolt against his Puritan upbringing, say to Miss Debby, an Episcopalian:

"Your catechism is much better for children than the one I was brought up on. . . . tell a child that he is 'a member of Christ, a child of God, and an inheritor of the kingdom of heaven,' and he feels, to say the least, civilly disposed toward religion; tell him 'he is under God's wrath and curse, and so made liable to all the miseries of his life, to death itself, and the pains of hell forever,' because somebody ate an apple five thousand years ago, and his religious associations are not so agreeable—especially if he has the answers whipped into him, or has to go to bed without his supper for not learning them."

The influence on Hattie of Church of England attitudes in the household at Nutplains went even deeper than this: long afterward it contributed to her momentous shift into the Episcopal Church.

A spinster, Aunt Harriet treasured every family relic and memory— Aunt Catherine's embroidery, the objects Uncle Samuel Foote brought back from foreign shores, ranging from frankincense out of Spain to mats and baskets from Mogador. . . . "At Nutplains," Harriet wrote long afterward, "our mother, lost to us, seemed to live again. We saw her paintings, her needle-work . . . and though the place was lonely, yet . . . scarcely ever without agreeable visitors."

It was there that she first heard poetry—the romantic ballads of Walter Scott—read to her by Uncle George. As she remembered it,

the lonely little white farmhouse under the hill was such a Paradise to us, and the sight of its chimneys after a day's ride were like a vision of Eden. . . . To us, every juniper-bush, every wild sweetbrier, every barren, sandy hillside, every stony pasture, spoke of bright hours of love, when we were welcomed back to Nutplains as to our mother's heart.

Harriet's recall had plainly gathered a golden glow with time; thus when she visited Nutplains in later years she was surprised to find "the hills so bleak and the land so barren." Of course, compared to her own home, where she was subject to her father's constant assumption of her sinfulness, Catharine's domination and her stepmother's cold elegance, Nutplains was a paradise. And since her recollections were part of the family contribution to her father's *Autobiography,* how could she talk about the oppressive aspects of life in the Beecher household? As a famous novelist, she found it much easier to recapture the more agreeable family activities, even if she herself, as the seventh child and a girl to boot, had been more like a spectator on the fringes of the domestic pleasures. Referring to her brother Henry's childhood, but also obviously to herself, she wrote that a late-born child in such a household had "constantly impressed upon it a sense of personal insignificance" and the "absolute need for passive obedience." All that a child could expect was to be "statately washed and dressed and catechised, got to school at regular hours . . . and to bed inflexibly at the earliest possible hour at night."

It helped, of course, that the Litchfield into which Hattie was born in 1811 was by all accounts a very pleasant place to live. So she recalled such moments as the chestnut- and walnut-collecting expeditions in the autumn, how her father, full of pent-up energies, led in climbing trees to shake down the nuts. There was also the annual cutting of wood—most of it contributed by parishioners—needed in those cold New England hills to warm a drafty old house. After her father and brothers had cut and split the logs, Hattie was drawn into all the hustle and bustle in the yard by her father's outwardly flattering yet subtly belittling declaration that he "wished Harriet was a boy, she would do more than any of them." Putting aside needle and thread, and donning a little black coat which she thought looked more like that of the boys, she worked like a slave for as long as a day and a half until all the wood was neatly piled and the chips swept up. Then Lyman would announce a grand fishing party as a reward and they would all go off to Little Pond and float around among the lily pads till everyone could go triumphantly home with a string of fish. What a privilege it was to be treated, even for a day, like a son!

Each autumn, too, there was the task of making an entire barrel of "cider applesauce," which would then stand frozen in the milk room and be cut, when needed, in chunks like "red glaciers." With baskets of apples and quinces all around the kitchen and a huge brass kettle aboil in the deep fireplace, the entire family and the servants would set to work. To make the evening go off, Lyman, working the apple peeler, would propose that he and George—bright and hungry reader—take turns in seeing who could "tell the most out of Scott's novels," for those were the days when *Ivanhoe* and *Tales of My Landlord* had just appeared. And so they would go through novel after novel, from *The Black Dwarf* to *The Bride of Lammermoor,* reciting scenes and describing incidents. Occasionally Lyman would raise a point of theology on some passage, challenge one of his boys on it and argue it out with him, presumably preparing the youth for a lifetime of theological controversy and confrontation.

Scott had achieved this special dispensation by accident. Like most pious New Englanders, Lyman Beecher looked on novels as a self-indulgence fraught with dangers. Then in 1823 Catharine had returned from her winter-long stay with the Fisher family, bringing all the books and papers of her dead beloved. Happening to browse among the books in the attic, Lyman had come upon some of the Scott novels and had begun to read them. They had soon worked their magic on him. He had come downstairs and announced: "George, you may read Scott's novels. I have always disapproved of novels as trash, but in these is real genius and real culture." For all his Calvinism, there was an emotionalism in Lyman Beecher that left him susceptible to certain Romantic influences and gods. He was seduced not only by Scott but by Byron and Napoleon.

Thereafter, in one summer, Hattie and George went through *Ivanhoe* seven times and came away able to recite many scenes word for word.

Because there were very few children's books and no toys or ready-made games, the garrets in the house were at once secret refuges and excellent places for play and dreams. In one there were bins of quinces, shelled corn, oats and onions, and—like some fearful scene from *Pilgrim's Progress*—the yawning cavern of a smokehouse built into the chimney, where hams and dried beefs were cured. In another garret were rows of bonnets and old hats, spinning wheels, cabinets of mineral specimens collected by the boys, medicinal herbs—dried bundles of tansy, pennyroyal, catnip, boneset, elder blow. . . .

And in all the garrets stood barrels of sermons and tracts. Rummaging one day among these dusty relics, Hattie found an enchanting book called *The Arabian Nights*. Again and again she stole away to feed on its fantasy. Another time, working her way through her father's library in search of morsels of history, she came upon a commentary on "The Song of Solomon" and devoured its Oriental sensuality as though it, too, were something out of *The Arabian Nights*.

Cotton Mather's *Magnalia Christi Americana*, meant to be an edifying history, furnished a feast of horrors—Indian raids, witches, the punishment of sinners. Even such a solemn tract as *The State of the Clergy during the French Revolution* yielded fascinating accounts of bloodcurdling events. A fragment of *Don Quixote* was at once enthralling and tantalizing. And the discovery of a torn old copy of Shakespeare's *The Tempest* would become the source some forty years later of a similar discovery that sets little Mara, in Harriet's novel *The Pearl of Orr's Island,* to dreaming of an enchanter on a lonely island, a Caliban-like sea monster, and a handsome young prince.

A favorite retreat of Hattie's—and indeed of the whole family—was Aunt Esther's room in a house just up the street. Compared to the Beecher ménage it was a haven of quiet and unchanging order. After Esther had served the dainties for which she was famous, she would talk, loosing a surprising flow of wit, anecdote and miscellaneous information. She was well read in chemistry, philosophy and physiology and most of all in natural history. (The Reverend Beecher regularly sought her opinion of his sermons before he delivered them.) Hattie was spellbound no less by her narrative gifts than by her knowledge, and she soon learned from her aunt the effectiveness of a story well told.

It was at Esther's one afternoon that Hattie, searching as usual for

something to read, came upon a stray volume of Lord Byron's poetry—
The Corsair. It astonished and electrified the ten-year-old girl. As she
read she kept calling out to her aunt to hear wonderful passages in it and
to ask the meaning of some of them.

"Aunt Esther, what does it mean, 'One I never learned to hate'?"

"Oh, child, it's one of Byron's strong expressions," came the answer.

Thus, in one afternoon, at the most impressionable age, this child of
a New England Congregationalist parsonage of the 1820s was exposed to
the most insidiously seductive of Byronic heroes, the darkly handsome
rebel, disillusioned and reckless, brooding over some mysterious grief, all
the while hiding a deep capacity for tenderness and love behind a satur-
nine mask. What an escape it offered from the grim figures in the Puritan pantheon!

The very fact that Byron was deplored for mysterious reasons whetted curiosity. The influence of that experience is inestimable: it would
make itself felt again and again in Harriet Beecher Stowe's work—all
the way from an unfinished piece of juvenilia called *Cleon* to the figure of
Augustine St. Clare in *Uncle Tom's Cabin*. Like the other girls in Miss
Pierce's academy and the young men in Judge Reeve's law school—who
were already wearing Lord Byron collars and cravats—Hattie was
caught up in the Byron fever. She read all his work that she could find
and listened raptly to everything her mother and father said about him.
She heard about his separation from his wife—never dreaming that long
years later she would throw herself into a bizarre effort to defend Byron's
widow against the charges the poet had made against her.

She was only thirteen when one day she heard her father exclaim to
her mother, "My dear, Byron is dead—*gone*," and after a moment add,
"Oh, I'm sorry that Byron is dead. I did hope he would live to do something for Christ. What a harp he might have swept!" Hattie was too
young to see the incongruity of her father's vision of Byron as a Christian
evangelist. (Of course, Byron's death in the swamps of Missolonghi while
fighting for Greek independence struck a chord such as might inspire any
American in the 1820s.) That afternoon Hattie went out to pick straw-
berries, but too dispirited, she lay down among the daisies, "looked up
into the blue sky and thought of that great eternity into which Byron had
entered, and wondered how it might be with his soul." She would never
be able to allay that doubt: There was simply no way for either Hattie or
her father to reconcile the unrepentant, profligate poet with an acceptable
Christian image.

So the following Sunday the Reverend Beecher made up for his moment of sentimental sorrow by preaching a funeral sermon on the text:
"The name of the just is as brightness, but the memory of the wicked
shall rot." No degree of genius, he declared, could redeem vice from

doom. He did think that some things that Byron had written would prove as imperishable as brass, but the "impurities" in other works, he hastened to add, like those in Sterne and Swift, would doom them to oblivion. Untroubled by such arbitrary distinctions, Hattie noted only the admirable way her father had shown the sons and daughters of some of the leading families how to discriminate between genius and evil. A young law student, Edward Mansfield, who heard the sermon, recalled, fifty years later, that it was dull and "prosy" until Beecher suddenly raised his spectacles and began to talk first of Byron's genius and gifts and then of his lack of virtue and religion and "finally described a lost soul and the spirit of Byron going off, wandering in the blackness of darkness forever." It struck the young listener "as with an electric shock, and left an imperishable memory."

In later years Beecher would even assert that if he and the Reverend Taylor could have talked to Byron they "might have got him out of his troubles." It is hard to imagine a greater faith in the power of Gospel doctrine. Although he firmly believed in total depravity, Beecher was persuaded that unbelievers only needed someone—preferably Lyman Beecher—to show them the light.

Almost as much of a pleasure as reading Byron was the music the family began to make after Father came home one day with a "magical instrument," an old piano that he had picked up as a bargain. Catharine and Mary had already learned to play. With father accompanying them on the violin, Edward and William playing flutes, and a lovely young boarder named Louisa Wait singing, they often had impromptu concerts. The psalm tunes and Scottish ballads they preferred were hardly fine music, but Hattie would long remember how they filled the house with a cheerful sound.

One other figure played a special role in Hattie's education: Miss Pierce's nephew John Pierce Brace, head teacher at the academy and the kind of inspiring instructor that appears in the background of many writers. Not only was Brace well read in the classics but he wrote poems that were circulated among the young ladies of the school as well as the local literati. Reading these poems in manuscript introduced Hattie to the immensely exciting experience of writing creatively. Brace was no narrow teacher of rhetoric: a devoted student of the natural sciences, he was constantly corresponding and exchanging specimens with European geologists and botanists. But it was in teaching composition that he excelled. In his classroom even such subjects as "The Difference Between the Natural and the Moral Sublime" became exciting. Each week when Brace called for volunteers to write compositions, Hattie responded without fail. Although never an outstanding student like Catharine or Mary, Hattie soon began to win praise for her writing. And as early as her seventh year, her father wrote in a letter, "Hattie is a genius. I would give a hundred dollars if she was a boy. She is as odd as she is intelligent and studious." It would not be the last time he would mingle extravagant praise of his daughter with devastating regret that she was a girl.

Hattie displayed other familiar signs of an addiction to the world of words and fantasy: she read everything that came to hand and fell into reveries so deep it took a little shock to rouse her from them. Everyone but her father tolerated these moods; he crushed them with: "I knew a person who was wont to retire into this garden of reverie whenever he wished to break the force of unwelcome truth. I told him he must break up the habit or be damned."

But this rejection of her emotions only intensified them. Speaking in the person of a boy (who may have been her brother Henry) in a sketch called "Aunt Mary" in her earliest book, *The Mayflower* (1843), she wrote:

I was timid, and shrinking, and proud, and I was nothing . . . to my parents but one of half a dozen children, whose faces were to be washed and stockings mended on Saturday afternoon. . . . But the feelings of grown-up children exist in the mind of little ones oftener than is supposed; and I had, even at this early day . . . the same discontent with latent, matter of course affection, and the same craving for sympathy, which has been the unprofitable fashion of the world in all ages.

The high point of her school career came when at the age of twelve she was among those chosen to write a composition for the school's annual "exhibition" of student accomplishment. The subject that year—it had been discussed in Mr. Brace's class—was: "Can the Immortality of the Soul Be Proved by the Light of Nature?" As she later pointed out, it was at least not the kind of "trashy and sentimental" theme assigned in many academies for young women. Hattie took the negative. Born to the task, she rejected all answers not based upon the Bible. Avoiding the grim Calvinist notion that our fate is predestined, she managed to close on a note of consolation:

The sun of the Gospel has dispelled the darkness that has rested on objects beyond the tomb. In the Gospel man learned that when the dust returned to dust the spirit fled to the God who gave it. He there found that though man has lost the image of his divine Creator, he is still destined after this earthly house of his tabernacle is dissolved, to an inheritance incorruptible, undefiled, and that fadeth not away, to a house not made with hands, eternal in the heavens.

It was a brave ending, but as she herself wrote in *Oldtown Folks* in an essay on almost the same subject by Esther Avery, a character very much like Harriet, "It was condensed and logical, fearfully vigorous in conception and expression, and altogether a very melancholy piece of literature to have been conceived and written by a girl of her age." It was remark-

BELMONT COLLEGE LIBRARY

able enough to persuade some persons that her father had helped her with it. The compositions were read in a hall crowded with the leading citizens. As the reading of Hattie's piece came to a close, she saw her father, who was seated on the platform, lean over and ask who had written it. Someone promptly answered: "Your daughter, sir!" It was the proudest moment of Harriet's young life. "To have interested him," she recalled, "was past all juvenile triumphs."

Insulated though the parsonage was, a few incidents of life in the larger world left their mark on Hattie's spirit. One was the story of her beloved Aunt Mary's experience when she married a planter from the West Indies and found that he already had a family by one of his slave women. For Mary the shock was traumatic. Later Harriet wrote: "She has said that she has often sat by her window in the tropical night, when all was still, and wished that the island might sink in the ocean, with all its sin and misery, and that she might sink with it."

Since Hattie was little more than two years old when her aunt died, her vivid description of what Mary said was something she must have heard from others. But the story had burned itself so deep into her consciousness that she obviously thought she had heard it directly from her aunt. Its effect can hardly be exaggerated. The image of innocent young Mary trapped on a Caribbean island amidst a sea of fathomless evil would haunt her forever. Her earliest impression of slavery was thus personal and emotional. And it involved sin—unspeakable sin—as well as misery.

Since slavery was still legal in Connecticut when Hattie was a child, there were a few Negro slaves in Litchfield. But their condition as servants or coachmen seemed hardly distinguishable from that of such "bound girls" as Rachel and Zillah, who worked in the Beechers' kitchen. No one in democratic, Christian, civilized Litchfield found this surprising, not to say intolerable.

Hattie's first awareness of slavery as a national problem came in 1820 with the furious controversy over admitting Missouri as a slave state. Suddenly slavery was no longer a peculiar Southern institution but a matter for everyone's conscience. Years later, not long after she had published *Uncle Tom's Cabin*, she wrote to the black abolitionist leader Frederick Douglass:

I was a child in 1820 when the Missouri question was agitated, and one of the strongest and deepest impressions on my mind was that made by my father's sermons and prayers, and the anguish of his soul for the poor slave at that time. I remember his preaching drawing tears down the hardest faces of the old farmers of his congregation.

I well remember his prayers . . . in the family for "poor, oppressed, bleeding Africa," that the time of her deliverance might come; prayers offered with strong crying and tears, and which indelibly impressed my heart and made me what I am . . . the enemy of all slavery.

In the light of her father's clash only a few years later with William Lloyd Garrison in Boston and later with other abolitionists in Cincinnati, Harriet Beecher Stowe read a great deal more into her father's vague sympathy for slaves in "bleeding Africa" than was actually there. And here once again she saw slavery more as a sin against God than as an offense against humanity.

Where Aunt Mary's experience gave Hattie a chilling glimpse of what human beings could do to each other, the drowning of Alexander Metcalf Fisher and its effect on Catharine gave her an equally frightening glimpse of what God could do to man. Hattie was hardly eleven when Fisher died, but the tall young professor with the sensitive, aristocratic face had already become a fairly regular visitor at the Beechers'. More than once Harriet had heard Catharine playing the piano and both of them singing together. She had more or less witnessed their friendship grow into a deep attachment and sensed that her father approved. Even though she may not have realized the full meaning of such a relationship, she knew that Catharine, who was always so lighthearted and witty, was happier than ever.

Then the dreadful news and the nightmarish images: storm on a vast dark sea, a sailing ship staggering among wild waves and bitter winds, and Professor Fisher dragged down, down, down. After that, for endless months, the figure of Catharine, brooding and haunted—tormented not only by the loss of her beloved but by the fear that he had died unconverted and was doomed to wander eternally in an unimaginable underworld. Gone was the carefree Catharine. In her place a sorely beset young woman challenging the indifference of the Puritan God. And all the Beecher children who were old enough to understand were troubled and confused and prayed that God would be merciful.

It would remain an indelible memory, and years later Harriet would use it as an agonizing episode in *The Minister's Wooing,* when the heroine, Mary Scudder, learns that her beloved has been drowned at sea.

In time, Catharine found a way out of her despair by immersing herself in her school in Hartford. Soon Mary followed. The reports they sent back were increasingly hopeful and when they returned for a stay at home in the summer of 1824, Catharine was brimming with ambitious plans. All the school lacked was money and teachers. Catharine suggested that Hattie go back with them, first as a student and then, perhaps the following year, as a teacher.

So Hattie, small and quiet and hardly more than thirteen, was suddenly lofted from the snug domain of the Litchfield parsonage into the noisy world of twenty-five adolescent girls in what was to Harriet the busy city (its population was at least five thousand) of Hartford. Through its Main Street, impressively cobblestoned, rumbled stages from Boston and New York. It had a variety of shops—not just a general store, as in Litchfield—a fine statehouse befitting a capital city, and a daily newspaper.

Hattie boarded with the family of Isaac Bull, who owned a wholesale drugstore on Front Street. The Reverend Lyman Beecher could afford this arrangement only by giving lodging, in turn, to the Bulls' daughter when she attended Miss Pierce's seminary in Litchfield. Living among strangers might have been a trying experience for Hattie had there not been compensations: she had a room of her own at last. ("If my good, refined, neat, particular stepmother could have chosen," Hattie wrote, "she could not have found a family more exactly suited to her desires. The very soul of neatness pervaded the whole establishment.") Mrs. Bull, moreover, was a kindly woman. And the morning and evening prayers were often enlivened by the singing of hymns to the accompaniment of flutes played by the grown sons of the family. Finally, the daughter, Mary Anne, was a model of decorum: Hattie never forgot how sedately she entertained a suitor, one Samuel Collins, in the parlor.

Adjusting to the new school was also made much easier by the fact that sister Catharine had seen to it that two students, Catherine Cogswell and Georgiana May, befriended Hattie. The daughter of the leading physician in Hartford, Catherine was lovely, vivacious and very popular, the kind of figure younger girls adore from afar. But it was Georgiana, an older girl and plain, who became Hattie's intimate friend. In her, as they walked on the pleasant banks of the nearby Park River, Hattie at last found someone to whom she could talk of her hopes and fears. They came to love the grassy, tree-shaded riverside, which explains why long years later Harriet Beecher Stowe chose that site for a home. And Georgiana would remain one of the very few close friends Harriet Beecher Stowe ever had.

A thin, small girl—she would never be more than five feet tall—and inhibited in games and play by the competition of five older brothers and sisters, Harriet retreated to the world of dreams, especially the dream of becoming a poet. In Hartford she had become aware of a woman poet, Lydia Huntley Sigourney. Facile, sentimental, moralizing, Mrs. Sigourney was celebrated as "the sweet singer of Hartford." Despite the long hours devoted to Latin and being tutored in French and Italian, Harriet began to compose a tragedy in blank verse. Soon she was spending stolen hours filling notebook after notebook with an imitation of a classical epic.

Combining her studies and preoccupations—Roman history, classic poetry and Byronic heroes—she set her tragedy in Nero's court and portrayed its hero, Cleon, as a rich Athenian youth and an Olympic victor who has become a favorite of Nero's. A typical Byronic protagonist, Cleon is cynical and dissipated. But Hattie, as an author with a power her father never had, has Cleon converted to Christianity. Nero at first angrily condemns the youth to torture but, relenting, suggests that Cleon keep his faith—as follower of "a crazy Jew"—but hide it from the public eye. Cleon is outraged. . . .

At this crucial point in Hattie's creative orgy, Catharine happened into her young sister's room, saw the notebooks filled with poetry and put an end not only to Cleon's saga but to all such light-minded enterprises. If Hattie had so much spare time, Catharine pointed out, she had better use it to study such a worthy work as Joseph Butler's *The Analogy of Religion, Natural and Revealed, to the Constitution and Course of Nature.* Hattie dutifully obeyed.

The world will never know what became of Cleon. It is no great loss; nevertheless, as the product of a fourteen-year-old, the treatment is mature, the verse fluent and the vocabulary remarkable. The influence on her work of the Byronic hero would remain almost undiminished. And with it, like a form of penance, would go the pious urge to redeem such attractively wicked men for Christianity.

When Hattie returned to Hartford in the fall of 1824, Catharine set her the task of teaching Butler's *Analogy of Religion* to a class at the academy. It was a formidable responsibility for a conscientious adolescent, and Hattie had all she could do to keep even one lesson ahead of her class.

The drowning of Professor Fisher had been a shattering object lesson in the inscrutability of God's ways and, even more, in the dangers faced by the unconverted. Hattie had long been aware of the challenge of conversion—an event at once intimidating and full of glorious promise. After she had gone off to school in Hartford she came upon a deeply inspiring book, Richard Baxter's *The Saints' Everlasting Rest.* The raptures, sometimes almost mystical, of the saintly seventeenth-century English divine as he described the heavenly bliss awaiting true believers transported her. For a time everything on earth seemed like dross. "As I walked the pavements," she wrote, "I used to wish that they might sink beneath me if only I might find myself in heaven."

But it was her father who precipitated the crucial experience. Harriet Beecher Stowe told the story, in a letter to her son Charles, only when she was an old woman. First admitting—as she had never done in any public statement—that most of her father's sermons were "as unintelligible to me as if he had spoken in Choctaw," she told of a sermon that he preached spontaneously out of the deepest feeling:

Forgetting all his hair-splitting distinctions and dialectic subtleties, he spoke in direct, simple and tender language of the great love of Christ and his care for the soul. He pictured Him as patient with our errors, compassionate with our weaknesses, and . . . how He was ever near us . . . comforting our sorrows with a love . . . unchilled by ingratitude, till at last He should present us faultless before the throne of his glory with exceeding joy.

I sat intent and absorbed. Oh! how much I needed just such a friend, I thought to myself. Then the awful fact came over me that I had never had any conviction of my sins, and consequently could not come to Him. I longed to cry out "I will," when father made his passionate appeal, "Come, then, and trust your soul to this faithful friend." Like a flash it came over me that if I needed conviction of sin, He was able to give me even this also. I would trust Him for the whole. My whole soul was illumined with joy, and as I left the church to walk home, it seemed to me as if Nature herself were hushing her breath to hear the music of heaven.

As soon as father came home and was seated in his study, I went up to him and fell in his arms, saying, "Father, I have given myself to Jesus, and He has taken me." I never shall forget the expression on his face as he looked down into my earnest, childish eyes; it was so sweet, so gentle, and like sunlight breaking out upon a landscape. "Is it so?" he said, holding me silently to his heart, as I felt the hot tears fall on my head. "Then has a new flower blossomed in the kingdom this day."

We detect a novelist's hand here, but in *The Minister's Wooing* Harriet Beecher Stowe lets us see how a young girl could have been captured by the visions and the faith of the New England preachers of the time. Having served in a political revolution on earth, they were, she wrote, again ready to give their lives, but this time for an invisible sovereign—a King Eternal. They were servants willing to do anything to help bridge the chasm over which the redeemed should pass to the commonwealth of glory.

But it was not in the Calvinist code that a young girl should be allowed so easy an entrance into the kingdom of the saved. Remembering her own agonizing experience, Catharine received the news skeptically; she simply doubted that this particular lamb would enter the fold "without being first chased all over the lot by the shepherd." And so it was. While in Hartford, Hattie went to the Reverend Joel Hawes, pastor of the First Congregational Church and a good friend of her father's, to join his congregation. She told him, of course, how naturally and happily she had achieved conversion. It proved to be too simple, too lacking in struggle or in recognition of her own sinfulness, to satisfy Dr. Hawes. He must test her, and so, much as Lyman Beecher had tested both his wives before he married them, the Reverend Hawes asked, "Harriet, do you feel that if the universe should be destroyed, you could be happy with God alone?"

It was a possibility calculated to shake even the stoutest believer. Hattie managed to stammer that she thought she could. As though she might not be sufficiently humbled and crushed, the minister added, "You realize, I trust, in some measure at least, the deceitfulness of your heart and that in punishment for your sins God might justly leave you to make yourself as miserable as you have made yourself sinful."

She was fourteen years old and it would be a long, long time before she would recover from the deep shame and doubt into which the seemingly harmless preacher had plunged her. To her sympathetic brother Edward, who was studying divinity at Andover, she wrote despairingly: "My whole life is one continued struggle: I do nothing right. I yield to temptation almost as soon as it assails me. My deepest feelings are very evanescent. I am beset behind and before, and my sins take away all my happiness. . . ."

Hattie's appearance seemed to have reflected her moods. When she was lost in unhappy thoughts, and went, as her brother Henry put it, "owling about," she seemed dull and plain, her shoulders drooping and her small body shrinking into insignificance, her Beecher nose too prominent, her cheeks—indeed, her whole personality—colorless. When she was stimulated, her face and eyes became animated, one noticed her lustrous, dark-brown silky hair falling in long curls at the sides of her head and the full, curving, almost sensual lips, so much like those of both Henry and Catharine.

For the next four years she struggled not only with the problems of adolescence but with a crippling sense of her unworthiness and sinfulness. Not only had she no answer for Dr. Hawes's terrifying questions but, after the carefree years in the bosom of the Beecher family, she no longer seemed to fit in anywhere else. Suddenly discovering that she was sinful in the eyes of God and useless in the eyes of man, she found herself wandering all alone in a kind of limbo. Promising a glorious reward, the Calvinist code exacted a heavy toll: the *rites de passage* were merciless. Perhaps because she was so young, Hattie showed none of the rebelliousness that had marked Catharine's religious maturation.

In 1827, after her family had moved to Boston, she was still writing to Catharine in Hartford:

I don't know as I am fit for anything, and I have thought that I could wish to die young and let the remembrance of me and my faults perish in the grave rather than live, as I fear I do, a trouble to everyone. You don't know how perfectly wretched I often feel: so useless, so weak, so destitute of all energy. Mamma often tells me that I am a strange, inconsistent being. Sometimes I could not sleep, and have groaned and cried till midnight, while in the daytime I tried to appear cheerful and succeeded so well that Papa reproved me for laughing so much. I was so absent sometimes that I made strange mistakes, and then they all laughed at me, and I laughed, too, though I felt as though I should go distracted. . . .

Detecting in her sister an acute case of the family tendency to hypochondria, Catharine was much concerned. By now an experienced adviser to adolescent girls—her school had grown to one hundred students—Catharine was convinced that Hattie needed an occupation and cheerful young friends to talk to. So she urged her young sister to return to Hartford and prepare for teaching. When Hattie did return, in the fall of 1827, she was thrust into a busy routine of studying painting (a lifetime later she would still love to paint), drawing, French and Italian, teaching Latin and, later, rhetoric and composition. But writing and literature had already become her main interest. Innocent as these may seem, they nonetheless aroused in her an acute sense of guilt. In the spring of 1828 she wrote to Edward:

You speak of your predilections for literature having been a snare to you. I have found it so myself. I can scarcely think, without tears and indignation, that all that is beautiful and lovely and poetical has been laid on other altars. . . . I do not mean to live in vain. He has given me talents, and I will lay them at His feet, well satisfied if He will accept them.

There is hardly more subtle evidence of the grip of her religion than this regret that all the great poetry of the world had not been devoted to religious purposes. Nor was the vow of the last lines an empty one: twenty-five years later she would put all her talents into a book dedicated to freeing a race of God's children from bondage.

At eighteen still pathetically insecure, she tells Edward: "I believe there never was a person more dependent on the good and evil opinion of those around than I am. This desire to be loved forms, I fear, the great motive for all my actions." She then goes on to tell him of her religious doubts. Perhaps they were less agonizing than Catharine's had been, but they were nonetheless sufficient to leave her, in her own words, perplexed and bewildered:

The wonder to me is, how all ministers and all Christians can feel themselves so inexcusably sinful, when it seems to me we all come into the world in such a way that it would be miraculous if we did not sin.

Even as early as this she touches the crux of the Calvinist's dilemma:

The case seems to me exactly as if I had been brought into the world with such a thirst for ardent spirits that there was just a possibility, though no hope, that I should resist, and then my eternal happiness made dependent on my being temperate. Sometimes when I try to confess my sins, I feel that after all I am more to be pitied than blamed, for I have never known the time when I have not had a temptation within me so strong that it was certain I should not overcome it. This thought shocks me but it comes with such force, and so appealingly, to all my consciousness, that it stifles all sense of sin.

She was thus already tantalized by a vision of eternal bliss without ever being able to achieve it. In later years, no longer intimidated by Calvinism or its spokesmen, she occasionally brought to bear a hardheaded Yankee realism on such doctrines. In *Oldtown Folks* she has the shrewd, tough-minded Sam Lawson declare, after hearing a sermon:

"Parson Simpson's a smart man; but, I tell ye, it's kind o' discouragin'. Why, he said our state and condition by nature was just like this. We was clear down in a well fifty feet deep, and the sides all round nothin' but glare ice; but we was under immediate obligations to get out, 'cause we was free, voluntary agents. But nobody ever had got out, and nobody would, unless the Lord reached down and took 'em. And whether he would or not nobody could tell; it was all sovereignty. He said there wa'n't one in a hundred,—not one in a thousand,—not one in ten thousand,—that would be saved. Lordy massy, says I to myself, ef that's so they're any of 'em welcome to my chance. And so I kind o' ris up and come out, 'cause I'd got a pretty long walk home, and I wanted to go round by South Pond, and inquire about Sally Morse's toothache."

Because she was often sunk in one of her distracted, self-probing moods, it is hardly surprising that she did not attract young men. Nowhere is there any mention of beaux in all the years before she married Calvin Stowe. Lacking suitors, she spent her affections on her brothers and her friend Georgiana.

As the school grew and Harriet herself became a full-time teacher, she had to share a room with other teachers. Only one of these, Mary Dutton, seems to have made a lasting impression on her. Mary was a New Haven girl, bright, small and, like Hattie, the daughter of a Congregational minister. She excelled in mathematics and Hattie was convinced that she knew as much science as men who had gone to college—a rare achievement for a woman in the 1820s. In the year she lived with Mary, Hattie developed an immense respect for her abilities and something like a crush on her. Mary was also a good teacher, so that both Catharine and Hattie were disappointed when she decided in the fall of 1829 to teach in New Haven and not return to Hartford.

But it is to that separation between Hattie and Mary that we owe a letter from Hattie that shows another, far more flippant and gossipy, side of her personality, a side that she would draw on heavily when she came to write novels of domestic life.

Preparing for her composition class, Hattie writes, she has been reading Samuel Johnson's *Rasselas* and thinks some fairy has spellbound the Doctor into putting every word from his dictionary into his novel. She goes on to report on students whom Mary knew: "S. Willis . . . is a lovely girl, but a proud one. . . . J. Strong is . . . much-improved. . . . S. Ladd's character rises daily in my estimation. . . . " Then comes an account of a horseback ride with Catharine, slyly mocking Catharine's rejection of the use of prizes to inspire students to emulate the winners: "All the difficulty is that my horse has so much of the evil spirit of emulation in him. . . . The moment he hears the hoofs of 'Tinker' behind him, he goes like all possessed, and I am forcibly reminded of that line in Horace which begins, 'Jounce, jounce, jounce.' "

After a while she gets around, rather condescendingly, to men and marriage:

If you see A. Baldwin, tell him that I shall write him a series of "Sketches of Female Character" as soon as I get a letter from him to make it excusable for me to write to him. Miss Fisher [a protégée of Mary Dutton's] says, "Tell her I hope she'll enjoy herself and get a husband into the bargain." If such an acquisition would be to you the *summum bonum* of earthly felicity, I heartily join in the request. I think you spoke to tolerable purpose on the felicity of the wedded state, Mary; suppose you try. Miss Degan is launching out into the praise of the Eighth Wonder of the World, her brother Charles. . . . By her description it is *death* for a female eye to rest on one so fascinating.

Like the novelist she will become, she is capable of playing several roles as a letter writer: yesterday the intense young woman discussing God and theology with her brother Edward; today the schoolgirl indulging in chit-chat. Fully aware of this, she adds in a postscript: "This letter is for news and the lighter particles of thought. In the next you shall have wise saws and grave reflections, profound speculations, and all that might become the female *Savante*."

Perhaps it was simply the passing of the insecurities of adolescence, but as she approached her twentieth year Harriet began to achieve a measure of faith in herself and in her God. At the end of the following summer she writes to Edward: "I have never been so happy as this summer. I began it in more suffering than I ever before have felt, but there is One whom I daily thank for all that suffering, since I hope that it has brought me at last to rest entirely in Him."

Her son Charles later wrote of this development as of a ship that has come through storms to a quiet anchorage. But there is no evidence that her questions and challenges had been answered—only that she had given up trying to press such questions home. She had begun to find— more or less like Catharine—that the only way to cope with the wrathful

Calvinist God was through Christ, in his humanity and compassion, as an intermediary.

Doubtless the juices of youth were also at work, encouraging her to live with something like hope and confidence. But it was only years later that she would arrive at a faith as steady as her father's or Dr. Hawes's and yet without their masochistic severity and disparagement of man.

Meanwhile those years of self-doubt proved to be a deeply debilitating experience. Much like Catharine after Fisher's death, Harriet would never again enjoy complete physical well-being or freedom from worry about her health. Unlike her father, she was allowed no such release as sawing wood, swinging on high bars, shoveling sand in a cellar or plowing and planting. Only endless chores, from mending to kitchen work, or reading, brooding, dreaming.

Since Harriet later tells us that she became aware of the slavery problem as early as 1820, when the "Missouri question" focused attention on it, she must have been interested in the news that a radical young New England journalist named William Lloyd Garrison had started a periodical, the *Liberator,* dedicated to freeing Negro slaves. She had a special reason to take note of Garrison: an earnest Calvinist, believing in the power of evangelism, he had joined the Reverend Lyman Beecher's Boston congregation.

Garrison was in his early twenties when he moved to Boston in December 1826, but he was already what he would always be: a rigid idealist, courageous, impatient and utterly uncompromising. He had immediately seen in the famous Dr. Beecher, with his muscular, action-oriented evangelism, a leader to be emulated—and recruited. Although he was aware that Beecher favored some such answer to the slavery problem as sending Negroes back to Africa, and he himself had accepted this solution, Garrison was soon urging his pastor to help abolish slavery forthwith.

Isn't slavery, Garrison asked, a national sin? Beecher of course agreed. Then, Garrison argued, using Beecher's doctrine of immediate repentance, was it not the duty of the nation to repent at once and emancipate the slaves? Plainly disturbed by the fierce intensity of this angular young man with the thinning hair, steel-rimmed glasses, and punctilious manners, Beecher answered that such monstrous problems couldn't be solved so easily, and that one had to consider what was expedient as well as what was right. In any event, he added, he already had "too many irons in the fire." According to Oliver Johnson, one of Garrison's disciples, Beecher summed up his view with: "your zeal is commendable; but you are misguided. If you will give up your fanatical notions and be guided by us [the clergy], we will make you the Wilberforce of America."

Garrison's disappointment in Beecher was great. To him this was a counsel of defeat; it served only to exasperate him and increase his intransigence. The clergy in general, he discovered, were essentially conservative. Many of them pointed out that they found in the Bible as much acceptance of slavery as disapproval of it. And even those who, like Beecher, opposed slavery believed that the only genuine solution was for each slaveholder to be regenerated, to see the light and give up his slaves of his own free will.

As for the American Colonization Society, it had in ten years sent only a pathetic handful of freed slaves to Liberia and Haiti. For Garrison it was only a sham and a delusion: he attacked it ferociously—his capacity for vituperation and abuse was boundless—as simply a conspiracy to rid America of Negroes.

So Garrison's answer in the first issue of his newspaper was the electrifying declaration: "I am in earnest—and I will not equivocate—I will not excuse—I will not retreat a single inch—and I will be *heard.*" Of those who heard him only a few hearkened. And some of those who heard and understood him most clearly were Southerners: in Georgia a price was put on his head, and in other places in the South, the *Liberator* was strictly prohibited.

There were other omens of the struggle to come: in Virginia in the summer of 1831 a slave named Nat Turner, inspired by heavenly voices and portents, led an insurrection against the master race, slaying sixty-one white men, women and children. Turner and other leaders of the insurrection were captured and hanged. But the incident was full of signs for those who could read them, such as that slaves could be unbearably unhappy with their lot; that aroused slaves could be deadly; and that they could be aroused.

It was shortly after this that the Reverend Beecher and his eldest daughter took off on their reconnaissance of faraway Cincinnati and Catharine sent her glowing report back to Harriet. Soon the whole family was excitedly ready for the great hegira.

Having at twenty-one emerged from her years of anxiety and of wrestling with her father's gods, Hattie groped longingly for a way to throw off her habit of introversion and move out into the world. She had to rid herself, she knew, of the tendency to pass moral judgments on those she met. Almost pathetically ready to make the best of things, she picked up crumbs of guidance wherever she could. One morsel came from her uncle Samuel Foote while he was visiting Nutplains that summer. Out of his rich experiences he had distilled an attitude summed up in an inscription on a sundial in Venice: *Horas non numero nisi serenas.* "I take account of no hours except the unclouded ones." Seizing on it, she wrote, a bit wishfully, to Georgiana May: "I have come to a firm resolution to count no hours, but unclouded ones and to let all others slip out of my ·memory . . . as quickly as possible." It was a far cry from the world view of John Calvin. And it was far easier to declare it than to live it.

In the same letter she talked even more plainly of her efforts to escape from the dark maze of her soul-searching:

The amount of the matter has been, as this inner world of mine has become worn out and untenable, I have at last concluded to come out of it and live in the external one, and . . . to give up the pernicious habit of meditation to the first Methodist minister that would take it, and try to mix in society somewhat as another person would.

After proclaiming the adoption of Uncle Samuel's sundial philosophy, she goes on:

I am trying to cultivate a general spirit of kindliness towards everybody. Instead of shrinking into a corner to notice how other people behave, I am holding out my hand to the right and to the left, and forming casual or incidental acquaintances. . . . In this way I find society full of interest and pleasure—a pleasure which pleaseth me more because it is not old and worn out. From these friendships I expect little; therefore generally receive more than I expect. . . . The kind words and looks and smiles I call forth by looking and smiling are not much by themselves, but they form a very pretty flower border to the way of life. . . . This kind of pleasure in acquaintanceship is new to me. . . . When I used to meet persons, the first inquiry was, "Have they such and such a character, or have they anything that might possibly be of use or harm to me?"

Before she departed, she received from Georgiana a response so warm that in return she poured out her heart like a lover.

This evening I have spent in a little social party—a dozen or so,—and I have been zealously talking all the evening. When I came to my cold, lonely room, there was your letter lying on the dressing-table. It touched me with a sort of painful pleasure, for it seems to me uncertain, improbable, that I shall ever return and find you as I have found your letter. Oh, my dear G_____, it is scarcely well to love friends thus. The greater part that I see cannot move me deeply. They are present, and I enjoy them; they pass, and I forget them. But those that I love differently; those that I *love,* and oh, how much that word means! I feel sadly about them. They may change; they must die; they are separated from me, and I ask myself why should I wish to love with all the pains and penalties of such conditions? I check myself when expressing feelings like this, so much has been said of it by the sentimental, who talk what they could not have felt. But it is so deeply, sincerely so in me, that sometimes it will overflow. Well, there is a heaven,—a heaven,—a world of love, and love after all is the life-blood, the existence, the all in all of mind.

There is no echo here of the adolescent girl who worried herself sick over the fate of her soul. There is simply an upwelling of emotion—romantic, sentimental (notwithstanding her disclaimer) and verging on the sexual. In its celebration of heaven as love and as a kind of continuation of worldly love, it is a striking anticipation of what would be the overriding theme of her brother Henry Ward Beecher's preaching and practice.

We know about the journey to Cincinnati mainly from Hattie's letters to relatives in Boston and Portland. At the first stop, New York, the exhilaration of the trip itself, the wonders of the city, the glamour of her father's preaching in such a place as the Chatham Theatre, and his success at collecting large sums for Lane Seminary, all left her dizzy with excitement: "I believe it would kill me dead," she wrote, "to live long in the way I have been doing since I have been here. It is a sort of agreeable delirium. There's only one thing about it, it is all too scattering. I begin to be athirst for the waters of quietness."

Later, when her father was invited to preach from pulpits along the way and the family passed the time in singing hymns, life resumed a somewhat more familiar character. And when the young people backed up their father's efforts by passing out tracts, the trip became part pilgrimage, part crusade. On arriving at an inn in Downingtown, Pennsylvania, Hattie wrote: "Here we all are—Noah, and his wife, and his sons, and his daughters, with the cattle and creeping things, all dropped down in the front parlor of this tavern."

Then at last they were in Cincinnati, where Hattie Beecher was to find a husband, bear children, grope toward a career and pass eighteen burdensome and frustrating years.

7

HENRY

"My nature was enthusiastic and outgushing"

We have come to distrust the tracing of major aspects of character back to childhood experiences. But the fact is that the man who became the most eloquent preacher of his time, celebrated for his many-toned voice and consummate delivery, had throughout his early years such thick speech that almost everyone was sorry for him.

Little Henry's poor speech, it was said, was partly the result of enlarged tonsils and partly of bashfulness. "When Henry is sent to me with a message," one of his aunts reported, "I always have to make him say it three times. The first time I have no manner of an idea than if he spoke Choctaw; the second, I catch now and then a word; by the third time I begin to understand." Exaggerated as such descriptions may have been—and Charles, his closest brother, denied them vigorously—Henry, by Beecher standards, was a slow learner.

As the eighth child in the family, Henry's birth—in 1813—was hardly a special event; followed within two years by another son, Charles, Henry could not help knowing that he was but one of many. Only three when his mother died, he held on desperately and adoringly to whatever memories he had of her: almost the first thing his sister Catharine noted about him—she was seventeen—was how affectionate he was. In that respect he would never change.

Hattie, only two years older, was closest to him among the children. He clung to her and when she was sent away for a long stay in Nutplains after their mother's death, he waited impatiently for her return so that she could go with him when he started school. He was a chubby, round-faced child, not four years old, when he began attending the Widow Kilbourne's school in West Street, Litchfield. At first he still wore the long, girlish curls of infancy, but after a while his hair was cut short and, dressed in trousers, suspenders and a jacket and always barefoot, he entered boyhood.

The Widow's idea of education was rigid discipline and learning by endless rote. Juiceless and severe, she reinforced her instruction with a ferule and a hickory switch. It would not be unfair to say that like Calvinism, it was a method that had little faith in the nature of children. Poor at memorizing—as he would be all his life—Henry did not do well.

After a few years he moved on to the "district school," only a stone's throw from the parsonage. But that proved even more of a trial. Like the other children, Henry carried sewing and knitting with him to help keep himself usefully occupied. Harriet tells us how the "bashful, dazed-looking boy pattered barefoot to and from the little unpainted school house, with a brown towel or a blue-checked apron to hem during the intervals between his spelling and reading lessons."

Any nostalgic notion of what primary education was like in early-nineteenth-century America should consider the description of a district school by the Reverend Henry Ward Beecher in one of the essays in his popular *Star Papers:*

It was a little, square pine building, blazing in the sun, upon the highway, without a tree for shade or sight near it; without bush, yard, fence or circumstance to take off its bare, cold, hard, hateful look. . . . In winter we were squeezed into the recess of the farthest corner, among little boys, who seemed to be sent to school merely to fill up the chinks between the bigger boys. Certainly we were never sent for any such absurd purpose as an education. There were the great scholars—the school in winter was for *them*, not for us pickaninnies. We were read and spelt twice a day, unless something happened to prevent, which *did* happen about every other day. For the rest of the time we were busy in keeping still. . . . Our shoes always would be scraping on the floor. . . . All of our little legs together . . . would fill up the corner with such a noise that, every ten or fifteen minutes, the master would bring down his two-foot hickory ferule on the desk with a clap that sent shivers through our hearts . . . and then, with a look that swept us all into utter extremity of stillness, he would cry, "Silence in that corner!". . .

A woman kept the [summer] school, sharp, precise, unsympathetic, keen and untiring. Of all ingenious ways of fretting little boys doubtless her ways were the most expert. . . . The benches were slabs with legs in them. The desks were slabs at an angle, cut, hacked, scratched . . . until it then wore cuttings and carvings two or three inches deep. But if *we* cut a morsel . . . or pinched off splinters, the little sharp-eyed mistress was on hand, and one look of her eye was worse than a sliver in our foot, and one nip of her fingers was equal to a jab of a pin; for we had tried both.

Such a passage may seem like an exaggeration intended mainly to amuse—until we come to the summing up:

I have not a single pleasant recollection in connection with my school-boy days. The woods were full of temptations, the trees called me, the birds wanted me.

... It seemed cruel to be shut up. The brooks, birds, flowers, sunshine, and breezes were free; why not I?

All the Beecher children had chores. When the Reverend Beecher had the alders at the bottom of the east lot cut down so that he could plant corn and potatoes, Henry, then nine, and Charles, even younger, helped with the hoeing. They took care of the horse and the cow, carried in wood for the fire and in spring planted the garden. On winter mornings it was Henry's task from the time he was eight to go downstairs in the freezing cold to make a fire and draw water from a well that was often choked with ice.

Perhaps the Reverend Beecher was not so strict as some other fathers, yet occasionally the boys were given a taste of the switch, with Henry, as the older of the two youngest, bearing the brunt of the punishment. His father, Henry recalled long after, "found it a good deal easier to box our ears than ... stop and reason with us. As I take account ... I see that I was governed by fear." But what Henry remembered most vividly about his parents was that his father was so busy with church duties and his stepmother had so many children to take care of, especially after she had borne several of her own, that he was left pretty much to himself.

There were no children's books or special toys or festivals. Saturday night was a particularly dreary time, for then he faced the prospect of a whole day with nothing interesting to do. Sunday morning was a ritual of washing, donning go-to-meetin' clothes—round, stiff hat, new jacket with nothing in the pockets, hair brushed—and then standing inspection before being sent off to church. For a boy of nine or ten the church service was torture. If sometimes he was lucky enough to doze off, he was soon awakened by some emphatic passage in the sermon or by a prod from his stepmother.

The preaching meant little to Henry until he was at least fifteen, but he defends the sense of awe that the very rigor of the Sunday routine inspired. Sixty years later he would say that a day that stood out from others even in a "hard and gaunt way" left its mark:

It did its work upon the imagination.... It had power in it; and in estimating moral excellence power is an element of the utmost importance. Will our smooth, cosy feeble modern Sundays have such a grip on the moral nature? They are far pleasanter. Are they as efficacious? Will they educate the moral nature as much?

Playful as his father could sometimes be, the Reverend Lyman Beecher's religion admitted no beauty of ritual, ceremony or holiday. Henry Ward would know nothing of the joys of Christmas until he was thirty years old. As a child he passed the tiny Episcopal church in Litchfield while the choir was practicing Christmas carols. He stood outside the open door, enchanted by the lights and sounds. "That is about all I knew of Christmas in my younger days," he recalled. "I never heard anybody speak of it. It was not known in the house of my father, for a Puritan of the Puritans was he."

Then there was that other onerous Sunday duty, reciting the catechism, a routine that Harriet Porter supervised with religious rigor. This was a special ordeal for Henry: where the other children memorized readily and recited fluently, he stammered and blushed, got hopelessly hung up on strange words and was taken to task for idleness and inattention. With a small regiment of other children, mostly Roxana's, to cope with, Harriet Porter soon ran out of patience.

Whatever other qualities Henry's stepmother had, affection, he maintained, was not one of them. And if there was one thing the eighth child born to the Beechers craved, it was warmth and love.

It pleased God to give me a second mother [he wrote], a very eminent Christian woman. Now, my nature was enthusiastic and outgushing; I was like the convolvulus—I wanted to be running on somebody all the time. But my second mother was stately and not easy to approach. She was a beautiful person, serene and ladylike. She never lacked self-possession in speech, gesture, or posture. She was polished; but to my young thoughts she was cold. As I look back I do not recollect ever to have had from her one breath of summer. Although I was longing to love somebody, she did not call forth my affection; and my father was too busy to be loved. Therefore I had to expend my love on Aunt Chandler, a kind soul that was connected with our family, and the black woman that cooked, who were very kind to me.

He not only could not love her but was alienated and intimidated by her iron commitment to her God:

I revered her but I was not attracted to her. I felt that she was ready to die, and that I was not. I knew that at about twilight she prayed; and I had a great shrinking from going past her door at that time. I had not the slightest doubt that she had set her affection on things above, and not on things beneath. I had the strongest conviction of her saintliness. It stamped itself upon my youth.

This recollection, with its overtones of jealousy of his stepmother's affair with God, was written by the Reverend Henry Ward Beecher not many years after he had been tried for seducing the devout Elizabeth Tilton and had been accused of having sexual relations with other older women in his Brooklyn congregation. Whether the charges were true or not, he certainly achieved an intimacy with pious women that he had been denied in his childhood.

It is remarkable, too, that it was not from either of his devout parents that Henry got a sense of God as a living presence or of religion as a personal experience; that came rather from an old black servingman whose room he shared between his eighth and tenth years. Charles Smith worked on the little Beecher farm; he was, Henry recalled, "a godly and hymn-singing man" who would lie on his bed and read the New Testament as though there were no one in the room with him. Henry wrote:

he would laugh and talk about what he read, and chuckle over it with that peculiarly unctuous throat tone. . . . I never had heard the Bible really read before; but there, in my presence, he read it, and talked about it to himself and to God. He turned the New Testament into living forms right before me. It was a revelation and an impulse to me.

Nothing in the change that took place in the religion of the Beechers is more striking than this declaration by the celebrated preacher who came to know God intimately and warmly not through his celebrated father or his mother or through churchgoing or catechism or prayer but through an old black man's simple, direct apprehension of God and Christ. Like some quaint episode contrived by a novelist of the time, it summed up the shift of Protestantism from a God of wrath to God as a benign uncle, from religion as a path riddled with cruel pitfalls to religion as a friendly counseling service.

No less marked than Henry's disappointment in his second mother's detachment was his idealization of his original mother. Roxana had died when he was hardly three, but as soon as he was old enough for such thoughts he began to envision her as saintly and full of love. Although he asserts that all his life the memory of his mother exerted great moral power over him, he describes her in terms that seem more than filial:

After I came to be about fourteen or fifteen years of age I began to be distinctly conscious that there was a silent, secret, and, if you please to call it so, romantic influence which was affecting me. It grew and it grows, so that in some parts of my nature I think I have more communion with my mother . . . than with any living being.

So Henry Ward reached manhood with two frustrating images of women: one of a loving mother who had been carried off too soon and the other of a substitute mother who had proved unapproachable.

In the hope that special attention might help his son, the Reverend Beecher had Henry transferred to a school run by that outstanding teacher John Pierce Brace. But when the boy showed no improvement after a year, he was sent off to board in Bethlehem, seven miles away, and study with a Mr. Langdon. The latter's boast was that his method with beginners consisted of "extended, minute, and reiterated drilling." But Henry, lonely and homesick, spent most of his time in the nearby woods and very little in drill, minute or otherwise. In the woods he was free of school, of church, of his father's exhortations and proddings and his stepmother's glacial piety—free to imagine a deity represented not by dogma, catechism and hellfire but by quiet ponds, green fields and birdsong. Returning to a Latin lesson, he would have to cheat, reading the answers hidden in his hat.

So after another year the Beechers decided that Catharine should try to do something for her young brother at her school in Hartford. If Mr. Langdon's regimen had made Henry flee to field and stream, Catharine's female seminary and an audience of forty girls seem to have inspired him mainly to pranks and practical jokes. Shrewdly, Harriet later described this constant flippancy as really a yearning for attention. It was in part a way of coping with studies that did not interest him.

Meanwhile the pressures to convert, repent and submit—all a permanent part of the Beecher atmosphere—were adding to his woes. His stepmother had prayed with him and solemnly explained to him his religious obligations. But all this had meant little to him, partly because there was no communion between them or, for that matter, between him and anyone else within the Calvinist fold. There were times when he longed for someone who would listen to him, listen sympathetically to his fears and yearnings. That ruled out his stepmother: "It would have been easier for me to lay my hand on a block and have it struck off than to open my thoughts to her." He could not know, of course, that the gap between him and almost the entire older generation of believers was already unbridgeably large—and growing larger.

And when his next older brother, George, who had been a confidant and companion, was converted, Henry felt that he had been left alone in outer darkness. He did not dare go to his father, there was no mother to turn to, and now there was no one else.

Whatever hopes Henry Ward had of being one of the elect and escaping damnation were crushed at every turn. Once, on coming home, he heard a church bell tolling and learned to his astonishment that one of his companions, who had been ill, had died. The "ringing, swinging, booming" of that bell sent him into an "ecstasy of anguish." At intervals, for days and weeks, he cried and prayed:

There was scarcely a retired place in the garden, in the woodhouse, in the carriage house, or in the barn that was not a scene of my crying and praying. It was piteous that I should be in such a state of mind, and that there should be nobody to help me and lead me out into the light. I do not recollect that to that day one word had been said to me . . . that led me to think that there was any mercy in the heart of God for a sinner like me.

It would take fifteen or twenty years—almost to the middle of the century—before Henry Ward Beecher was able to throw off the sin-haunted, guilt-ridden atmosphere of those early years.

Henry was a sturdy, red-cheeked country boy of thirteen when the Beecher family moved to Boston in 1826. In one way the city was acutely disappointing to him: it had none of the woods, fields and streams he loved to wander in. But in other ways it was full of excitement and challenge.

Instead of the peacefulness and the deliberate pace of a Litchfield, there was noise and competition and a sense of strife—violent street games and furious gang fights between the Salem Streeters and the Prince Streeters and then between both of them, as North Enders, and their "natural enemies," the South Enders. The Reverend Henry Ward Beecher liked to tell how in a game of Follow the Leader he once led a dozen boys such a wild chase that he shook off all but two of them, and left those two behind when he climbed onto the deck of a ship in the wharf, scrambled out on the bowsprit and dived off, clothes and all, into deep water.

Sunday, of course, offered a moving contrast—a deep quiet broken gradually by hundreds of church bells filling the air with marvelous accidental harmonies. But most exciting of all were the tall ships that crowded the great harbor. In a time when planes and space flight have usurped the place in a youth's dreams of adventure and travel, it is not easy to appreciate what an array of great sailing ships meant, in 1826, to a country boy of thirteen or fourteen.

Meanwhile the ordeal of school continued. The place of trial was now the famous Boston Latin School. Although Greek and Latin bored him, he did begin to make some progress. But he was restless, churned by powerful, frustrated urges. In *Norwood,* the novel he wrote in later years, he describes what can happen in the heart of a fourteen-year-old:

The young nature, swelling to the new influences with a sense of immeasurable strength—sometimes turbulent with passions, but always throbbing with excited feelings, led on and fed by tantalizing fancies—seems transformed from its previous self. . . . A mild and docile boy springs up before his astonished parents defiant and unteachable. A conscientious . . . nature is seized with willful impulses, and seems by an insane attraction drawn to bewildering courses.

Even if this is not entirely autobiographical, it gives a striking glimpse of what sometimes lurked beneath Henry's lighthearted behavior. Harriet Beecher Stowe, made sympathetic by memories of her own troubled adolescence, described the Henry of these years as in a period of fermentation. "The melancholy that brooded over his childhood," she recalled, "waxed more turbulent and formidable." The city was a wilderness of meaningless forms and sounds. He grew moody and restless. School became intolerable and like so many adolescent boys, he was stirred by an urge to break the parental bond, to leave home and live independently. Encouraged by his father to read, he chose biographies of Captain Cook and Admiral Nelson and other great sailors and commanders. Soon he came to the classic decision of so many rebellious youths: he must go to sea. That way lay escape forever from classrooms, teachers and the relentless urging to "awaken" and "submit." More than once he bundled up some clothes and hurried down to the wharves. But he never could banish the awareness of how his running away would hurt and shock his father. He did not leave.

But neither could he stay. Finally he wrote a note to one of his brothers telling of his plan. He added that he wanted his father's permission but would go away even without it. He left the note where his father would be sure to come upon it. His father found it and said nothing, but a few days later he asked Henry to saw wood with him. It was a flattering invitation, for the woodpile was a place where men talked as equals and companions.

Casually the Reverend Beecher asked his son how old he was. When Henry answered that he was almost fourteen, his father exclaimed:

"Bless me! How boys do grow! Why, it's almost time to be thinking what you are going to do. Have you ever thought?"

"Yes—I want to go to sea."

"To sea! Of all things! Well, well! After all, why not? Of course you don't want to be a common sailor. You want to get into the Navy?"

"Yes, sir; that's what I want."

"But not merely as a common sailor, I suppose?"

"No, sir; I want to be a midshipman, and after that a commodore."

"I see," said the doctor cheerfully. "Well, Henry, in order for that, you know, you must begin a course of mathematics and study navigation and all that."

"Yes, sir; I'm ready."

"Well, then, I will send you up to Amherst next week, to Mt. Pleasant, and then you'll begin your preparatory studies, and if you are well prepared I presume I can make interest to get you an appointment."

It was a sly performance, worthy of the most manipulative of parents. Soon Henry was packed off to the Mount Pleasant Institution at Amherst, Massachusetts. Whereupon the Reverend Beecher remarked, "I shall have the boy in the ministry yet." Lyman Beecher prayed daily for all his sons to become ministers, but at the same time he spared no effort to help the Lord answer his prayers.

Mount Pleasant in 1827 was a brand-new, unproved school, but it had an impressive group of buildings and a lofty-sounding program for preparing poor but pious young men for the ministry. The tuition was

$250, not counting uniforms—it had a semi-military regimen—and books; but Lyman, having contributed a flattering tribute for use in the school's catalog (by the time Henry was graduated, Lyman was not so laudatory), was allowed to pay only one hundred dollars a year for his son.

As far as fourteen-year-old Henry was concerned, the school had an ideal setting: Amherst was a quiet village surrounded by fields and groves of oak and chestnut—much like the landscape he had learned to love around Litchfield. Here, too, when Latin declensions, military drill, and a code of discipline that included floggings and a dungeon cell became too much for him, he could go swimming or fishing in summer and skating or coasting in winter. Once he built a slat house in a tree; there "I used to sit wind-rocked and read, or muse and cry and laugh, just as the fancy took me." A gardener in the village even allowed him a plot of ground where he was able to raise flowers. Unbelievably, when the chaplain of the school came upon him admiring his asters and pansies, he reproved the youth for wasting time on things not connected with saving his immortal soul! As soon as he had gone, Henry returned stubbornly to his flowers.

The schedule at Mount Pleasant was rigorous: up at 5:30, drill, chapel, classes that began at 8 A.M. and, with a free hour at noon, ended at 4:30, evening service at 8 P.M. and call to rooms at 9 P.M.

Fortunately the school had some very able teachers, and two of them influenced Henry in crucial ways. One was W. P. Fitzgerald, a twenty-year-old West Pointer who not only made mathematics tolerable for Henry but, more important, taught him the satisfactions of intellectual discipline and achievement. He crushed Henry's excuses and evasions with scorn, demanding that each lesson be mastered completely. Once, when Henry was in the middle of a blackboard demonstration, Fitzgerald suddenly cried, "No!" Henry started over again but at the same point came another icy "No!" Henry sat down in confusion. The next boy was stopped at the same point with a similar "No," but he went right on and was commended.

"Why," whimpered Henry, "I recited it just as he did, and you said No!"

"Why didn't you say *Yes*, and stick to it? It is not enough to know your lesson. . . . You have learned nothing till you are *sure*. If all the world says *No*, your business is to say *Yes* and to *prove it!*"

But as a later associate pointed out, Henry Ward Beecher did not often stand up against the world. He found it much easier to anticipate when the world was going to say no, and then lead the chorus.

A far more important influence on Henry's personality as well as his career was John E. Lovell. Lovell was an outstanding teacher of elocution at a time when oratory was esteemed almost as much as states-manship, when the speeches of Webster, Hayne, Clay and Calhoun were admired and quoted everywhere. In his brief stay at Mount Pleasant, Lovell began the miracle that would transform a tongue-tied boy into the most eloquent speaker of his time.

Lovell's "secret" was endless drill applied to every detail of voice, gesture and posture—all of which was discussed and some of it illustrated in his book *The United States Speaker*. He would recite a piece and the student would then repeat it again and again, slavishly imitating every inflection, movement and even glance until Lovell was satisfied that it was as good as could be expected. What is significant is that Henry coop-erated completely, spending as much as an hour practicing the delivery of a single statement or even word. Although his progress in other studies was slow, in elocution it was soon notable. It was a classic example of compensation for a physical handicap. In Lovell's method Henry found not only a solution for his speech problems but release from embarrass-ment and clumsiness. Soon he was performing in school plays, finding in them an undreamed of opportunity to express emotions to the full. And instead of being chided for his efforts, he was applauded.

Having once tasted his power over an audience, he was inevitably drawn to the one pursuit in which a Beecher could reach people through the spoken word—the ministry. His performance in the role of the tyrant Gessler in a play about William Tell, staged in his second year at Mount Pleasant, was remembered by a classmate sixty years later. Indeed, there would be some who would say that the Reverend Henry Ward Beecher was all his life an actor who chose the pulpit as his stage, a minister who was always playing a role.

At the end of Henry's second year a religious revival took hold at Mount Pleasant. Caught up in the general excitement, Henry experi-enced such a hope of being converted that after a week or two he wrote his father about it. The Reverend Beecher took him at his word and promptly insisted that he come home and join the church on the next Communion Sabbath. Sad to say, Henry's excitement ebbed as quickly as it had come. In a few weeks he was, as he put it, already "beginning to feel quite jolly again"—which suggests that it had all been much more than he was ready for. But he went home as his father had urged, be-cause "pride and shamefacedness kept me from saying I did not think I was a Christian."

Once home, he was confronted by a church committee. Many years later he described how "cold and almost paralyzed" the fifteen-year-old felt when his elders questioned him about his "hope" and his "evi-dences." The committee finally decided that the son of such a father must surely be a good and pious boy. He adds:

On the morning of *the* day he went to church without seeing anything he looked at. He heard his name called from the pulpit among many others, and trembled; rose up with every emotion petrified . . . looked piteously up at the cornice, heard the fans creak in the pews near him; felt thankful to a fly that lit on his face, as if something familiar at last had come to break an awful trance; heard faintly a reading of the Articles of Faith; wondered whether he should be struck dead for not feeling more—whether he should go to hell for touching the bread and wine . . . and at last walked home crying, and wishing he knew what, now that he was a Christian, he should do, and how he was to do it.

It would not be the last time that Henry Ward Beecher would allow earnest church people to think he was something other than he actually was. Nor was it the last time he would admit without embarrassment to a lack of moral candor. In later years he would make that weakness an object lesson. When I did something wrong, he wrote,

I had not the courage to confess, and tell the truth. First, shame hindered me; second, fear. . . . And when I got to going wrong, I went on going wrong. . . . I was afraid of being found out; and then I prevaricated a little; and that made the matter worse . . . and for days, when my father came home, I would watch his face to see if he looked as though he knew it . . . and the anxiety and pain grew on me . . . and out of that depression and low state it was easier to be tempted again. . . . So one thing led to another and I was under a sense of condemnation. The very fear which I experienced bred suspicion and jealousy, and irritation, and unhappiness.

The very readiness with which he admitted all this was plainly meant to make it seem only a weakness of his immaturity.

But the episode did have its aftereffects. Almost without realizing it, Henry abandoned his dream of becoming a sailor and gradually began to give thought to entering the ministry. His letters to Harriet and Edward are sprinkled with pious sentiments and he even complained that his roommate's use of the "free hours" to practice on musical instruments left him little privacy for prayer. Probably to impress Edward, he later reported to his older brother that he had acquired a more devout room-mate who joined him in prayers every evening and allowed him an hour of private devotions. Although he was active in sports and games and was hail-fellow-well-met among his classmates—they called him "Hanck"—his letters to Harriet righteously deplored the fact that some students played cards on the sly and that boys of eight or nine swore shockingly. But once again he adds an ingenuous admission of his desire to play an approved role: "When I mix with the boys I . . . do talk and act unworthy of a disciple of Christ."

The number of students from abroad was remarkable. Before long, the New England parson's son came to know youths from such places as

Greece, Colombia, Cuba, Brazil and England, including quite a few of that much feared breed, Roman Catholics. In fact, the object of Henry's first deep emotional attachment was a Greek lad.

Constantine Fondolaik was the son of parents who had lived on the Aegean island of Scio and had been among the Greeks massacred by the Turks in 1822. Constantine, about eight years old at the time, had managed to escape and make his way to Boston. There he had been adopted by a Mrs. Newell of Amherst.

Dashing, handsome, popular—he commanded a student division in military drill—and with a romantically tragic history, he trailed a Byronic aura. Truly an exotic figure, he was temperamentally as remote as one could imagine from a son of New England Puritans. Which is plainly why he struck the pent-up, affection-craving Henry, with his frustrated hope of escaping to distant lands, as God-sent. Recalling his enthrallment, Henry later wrote: "He was the most beautiful thing I had ever seen. He was like a young Greek god. When we boys used to go swimming together I would climb out on the bank to watch Constantine swim, he was so powerful, so beautiful."

So close did their relationship become during their three years at Mount Pleasant and in the next two years that when Constantine left to go into business in Boston, they signed a covenant that was as close to a marital vow as it could be. It began with several pledges of undying brotherhood and love and with promises to defend each other and overlook each other's faults. It concluded:

And now we consider ourselves as *brothers,* and we are bound together by ties and obligations as strong as can be placed upon us. But we rather rejoice in the relationship, as now it has converted our friendship into brotherly love . . . now we are connected by a love which *cannot* be broken. . . . But we do not sorrow on this account—far from it, we greatly rejoice—for we have not done this thoughtlessly, but being convinced by *three years'* friendship that we mutually love one another. . . . And to all the foregoing we cheerfully and voluntarily subscribe our names. And now may God bless us in this our covenant. . . .

H. C. Beecher
Constantine F. Newell
Amherst, April 1832

Such was Henry's commitment to their oneness that here and elsewhere he used the middle initial "C," standing for Constantine. It was a time when fervent attachments between young men as well as between young women were accepted because they were automatically assumed to be innocent. Sometimes it was an emotion born of frustration: confronted by the untouchable purity of "good" girls and the sinfulness of any relationship with a prostitute, some men fixed their affections on other men.

Unfortunately, just as Constantine Fondolaik had begun life amidst tragedy in Greece, so he ended it: returning to his homeland in 1842, he died suddenly of cholera.

But for Henry Ward Beecher the memory of the beautiful Greek youth remained fresh and poignant. In 1848 he gave his third son the middle name "Constantine." And in 1849, when he visited Mount Pleasant seventeen years after leaving it, and wandered about his old haunts, the ghosts of boys he had known rose up around him, with the one he cherished most coming forward to greet him. But in a moment they vanished, and he fled, never to return.

For Henry's emotional life the relationship with Constantine was momentous; it taught him that an unreserved attachment was an endless source of joy and gratification. Such relationships with men as well as women were to be part of his religious life as well as his whole philosophy. In a way like his father, he was to be a man of feeling, guided as often by his heart as by his head. The word "love" would become a magic talisman for him and his circle.

Although his relationship with Constantine may have been latently homosexual, we do know that at the same time he was strongly attracted to the opposite sex. One girl who caught his fancy was the sister of a friend. Suddenly displaying great fondness for the friend, Henry began visiting him regularly but spent much of his visits watching sister Nancy with calflike longing. When she sewed he could not take his eyes from her hands, but as soon as she looked up, he was "covered with hot and awkward confusion." Slyly his mother observed that Mount Pleasant must be a remarkable school since it had led Henry to dress more carefully, shine his boots and brush his hair. As much as a year later, among the rather commonplace entries in a diary he kept at college, are occasional pen decorations in which the name Nancy figures repeatedly. But Nancy was older than Henry and she married someone else before very long. When he met her years later, the charm was gone. Shaking her hand, he felt "neither awkward nor hot."

At the Mount Pleasant graduation exercises in 1830, Henry Ward Beecher won no prizes or academic honors, but his burgeoning elocutionary talents were nicely recognized: he played a part in three numbers— one a comic scene, another a dramatic dialogue, and the third a reading from the somber warnings of the prophet Joel.

Even though Amherst College was only nine years old, had only six professors and was poorly endowed, Lyman Beecher sent Henry Ward there instead of to his own alma mater. He did so for two reasons: Amherst had been founded by intensely orthodox Congregationalists to counter the Unitarian "heresies" of rich old Harvard (then called Cambridge). He also thought that such a small school might give his son the kind of help in important subjects (elocution was definitely not one of them) that Henry had presumably failed to get at Mount Pleasant. Rather officiously., he wrote to the Reverend Heman Humphrey, president of the college:

After much deliberation and some hesitation I have concluded to send my son Henry to Amherst. One of the reasons of this decision is that in his preparation at Mount Pleasant he has been taught carelessly & has formed a habit of getting his lessons (I speak of the languages specially) superficially. . . . I understand that teaching by professors and having smaller classes and more particular attention . . . is paid to each student than might be practicable at Yale. . . .

Revealing a shrewd distrust of his son's capacity to resist temptation or self-indulgence, he adds:

Tho I have good hope of his piety yet his temperament & spirit is of a kind which would make him susceptible to Southern influence assailing him on the side of honour & spirit. As far as I know his conduct has been circumspect, but on the whole I shall regard his safety greater in Amherst than at New Haven.

At home in Boston that summer of 1830 Henry began to hear of the threat of a Roman Catholic occupation of "the West" and of his father's conviction that the religious fate of the nation would be settled in the Ohio Valley. With Edward leaving to take on the presidency of Illinois College, George at Yale, his three older sisters in Hartford, and his father's gaze turning westward, Henry Ward went back to school that fall realizing that he would again be left to his own inclinations. How far he had grown apart from the family became clear when he visited his sisters in Hartford before going on to college. Neither Mary (now Mrs. Perkins) nor Hattie (she who had been his closest companion in his years at home!) recognized him. With this amusing but hardly heartwarming proof of his transition to manhood, he went on to join the forty other members of the freshman class at Amherst.

At Amherst, as at Mount Pleasant, he showed no interest in mathematics or Greek and Latin, declaring he would study only what he wanted to know. Again he did well only in elocution and debating. His deficiencies did not disturb him. When he pointed out to a professor that mathematics was of no use to a minister, the professor tried to tell him that it would discipline his mind. "If that's all, I shan't go to class any more," Henry retorted. "My mind gets enough discipline inventing excuses for not being there." We wonder what kind of professor would have tolerated such a cheeky reply.

His love of flowers and wildlife remained as strong as ever and eventually he became president of the college's Society of Natural History. He also developed a taste for the classics of English literature. On the lighter side he marched, in full uniform, in the school band, and he was an entertaining companion, ever ready with a witty reply or a bit of clowning, already enjoying attention no matter how he got it.

He still had a weakness for practical jokes. His early biographers, all worshipful, cite elaborate pranks as evidence of his rich sense of humor, as when he made a very tall tutor, who came for a solemn conference, sit in a chair with legs sawed short so that the poor man had to look out from between his upthrust knees. But such stories seem somewhat less amusing when told of an eighteen-year-old at Amherst than of a fourteen-year-old at Mount Pleasant.

He was good at sports and games, and no other than Oliver Wendell Holmes declared that at Amherst he was "chiefest among their football kickers." Partly for the exercise, he would at vacation time walk the one hundred miles home to Boston. He also did it to save money; although his tuition was less than forty dollars a term and his board came only to a dollar and a half a week, his father, forever short of funds, was barely able to keep him in school.

Much as at Mount Pleasant, a revival was getting under way at about the time he arrived at college. And again, as at Mount Pleasant, he was "prodigiously waked up" by the event. But this time it was nearly traumatic:

I had begun to pass from boyhood to manhood, but I was yet in an unsettled state of mind. . . . I was beginning to slough hereditary influences without being able to take on more salutary influences, and I went through another phase of suffering which was far worse than any I had previously experienced. It seemed as though all the darknesses of my childhood were mere puffs to the blackness I was now passing through. . . . There was no humiliation that I would not have submitted to . . . if thereby I could have found relief from the doubt, perplexity, and fear which tormented me.

Even if he was, as usual, dramatizing his religious experiences, he was clearly unable to treat this episode as the qualms of a bewildered youngster. So he went to President Humphrey, moaning, "I am without hope and utterly wretched, and I want to be a Christian." The Reverend Humphrey declared that it was the spirit of God working within him and that he dared not interfere. Henry crept away "in blacker darkness" than ever. He continued to seek help from others, finally coming to an upperclassman, one Moody Harrington, a young man of the most intense religious conviction. Harrington gave him unstinting sympathy and encouragement, so that he came away at last with some sense of hope.

It was near the end of his freshman year that Henry first met Eunice Bullard, the sister of a classmate. Her brother Ebenezer had invited Henry and Constantine to spend their May holidays with the Bullards. To save the coach fare, the three youths walked the fifty miles to the Bullard home in West Sutton, Massachusetts.

The Bullards were of old Puritan stock on both sides of the family. The father, Dr. Artemas Bullard, was a dignified country physician with the strictest notions of proper behavior. (Once when Eunice and her sister came to table with low-cut dresses that they had made, he flung hot soup over them, remarking that they seemed to be cold.) Mrs. Bullard (she was Dr. Bullard's second wife) had made her contribution in the form of nine children.

Daughter Eunice was a tall, well-featured girl of nineteen, blue-eyed and with light-brown hair that came down the sides of her face in the customary ringlets. In a portrait—surprisingly bare-shouldered—made some years later, she is Junoesque. After graduating from an academy near Amherst, she had taught school for a year. Eunice was a competent young woman, and the teaching experience had added to her self-assurance. A bit patronizingly, she at first saw her brother's friend Henry as "exceedingly homely" and rather boyish (she was a year older than he), but like everyone else she was soon disarmed by his good humor and wit. In her recollections nearly sixty years later she pictured herself as a mature and accomplished person who took her chances with a youth who had little to offer except a ready tongue and charm.

Henry was, for his part, flattered by the rapid growth of Eunice's interest in him. At the same time, increasingly aware that his family would be moving to Cincinnati before long, he began to have romantic visions of himself as a frontier preacher—with of course a capable and loving woman at his side.

That fall, while Eunice was teaching at Clappville, Massachusetts, Henry learned that when the term closed she intended to spend the winter studying Latin at the home of an aunt in nearby Whitinsville. Before long, Henry turned up at the Bullard home with the news that he would be teaching school in the vicinity of Whitinsville and planned to board with Eunice's aunt. Considering Henry little more than a schoolboy, Dr. Bullard ingenuously suggested that Henry could help Eunice with her Latin when they were together. Even though Eunice doubted Henry's capacity to teach her Latin ("I didn't believe he could help me much—I who have been a schoolma'am for three terms!"), she later claimed that she did not suspect that he had any other motives.

Arriving at the home of Eunice's aunt early in January 1832, Henry wasted no time: the very first evening, while Eunice's aunt and uncle were out visiting, he gave Eunice a little Latin test—it coyly included conjugating the verb *amo*, "I love"—and then slipped a note onto her writing desk. It read: "Will you go with me as missionary to the West?"

Eunice raised a question or two about the seriousness of his intentions, but Henry swept such considerations aside, including the probability that it would be years before they could get married. As for Henry, how could he be anything but pleased to have captured an able and virtuous young lady of good family who would furnish him with admiration and eventually love.

The following Sunday he rode to West Sutton and declared his intentions to Dr. and Mrs. Bullard. Mrs. Bullard was hardly pleased by the news but it was Dr. Bullard who became genuinely angry. "Why, you are a couple of babies!" he cried, falling back on the classic response of parents caught napping by time. "You don't know your minds yet, and won't for years to come." He was above all mortified that he had been outgeneraled by a mere youth. But Henry was already a master in the art of charming foes as well as friends. The stiff-necked doctor was soon persuaded not only that Henry would remain true to Eunice even during a long engagement but that he would "make his mark in the world."

The talent with which Henry Ward would make his mark was manifest when he began giving talks on religion in the evening meetings of the Whitinsville church. He made an excellent impression, Eunice reported, never once hesitating for a word. The talent was again manifest when he gave his first lecture, near Amherst, and was rewarded with five dollars for his performance. He used the money to buy Eunice a piously proper if somewhat unlikely love token—a copy of Baxter's *The Saints' Everlasting Rest*.

His elation was boundless when late in the spring term he was invited to give a lecture on temperance—obviously on the basis of his father's reputation—on July 4 in Brattleboro, Vermont. He walked all the way to save the fare and received the munificent fee of ten dollars. Drunk with earned money and public success, he threw frugality to the winds and treated himself to the works of Edmund Burke, model of all would-be orators. Out of the little that remained of his fee he bought Eunice a plain gold engagement ring for something less than a dollar.

Like other hard-pressed students, he worked whenever he could, teaching for eight weeks during the long winter vacation. In one school, the boys—some of whom were larger and stronger than he was—became so belligerent that he had to beat them back with a stick. When the school committee did nothing about punishing the troublemakers, he resigned. Enterprisingly, he started private classes and soon had thirty pupils.

Henry's expectation that his future lay in the West was reinforced in the spring of 1832 by word from Harriet that the move to Cincinnati was not far off. He responded: "I fairly *danced* the first half hour after I read your letter. I sang, whistled, flew around like a mad man. Father's removal to the West is my 'heart's desire.'"

At about this time Henry and his classmate Orson Squire Fowler were also caught up in the phrenology craze. This pseudoscience, brought to Boston by its leading proponent, Dr. J. K. Spurzheim, had achieved popularity as a kind of respectable form of fortunetelling. With its claim of being able to determine the "faculties" of the brain from the contours of the skull, it was a glamorous addition to Henry's repertory as a performer. It had another attraction: unlike Calvinism's depressive view of man's nature, it allowed for such amiable characteristics as Amativeness, Philoprogenitiveness, Wit and Wonder. It also encouraged the un-Calvinist belief that each individual could develop his own faculties. Henry not only started a phrenology club at the college but, accompanied by Fowler, he went around delivering lectures while his classmate gave cranium readings. Henry Ward Beecher would continue to have faith in phrenology throughout his life. He conceded that it was not a science but asserted that it brought new "aid to the statesman, the lawyer, the physician and the minister of Christ in their benevolent efforts to benefit society and gives them a new power of the intellect and the will."

Orson Fowler made even more of it: he became the best-known phrenologist in America, opening an office in New York soon after he graduated, organizing a national society, publishing the *American Journal of Phrenology* and writing books on the subject. Phrenology proved, however, to be one of those fads that, like spirit rapping, reached its peak in the Victorian era and then—with advances in the biological sciences— faded away.

Although Henry Ward's achievements as a debater in college were exaggerated by his early biographers, his classmates clearly recalled his fluency as an extemporaneous speaker. Armed with the techniques Lovell had taught him, he soon joined a debating club, the Athenian Society. The subject of the debates and orations was often academic or highflown, but occasionally it engaged a vital issue. One such, in Henry's senior year, mooted the question whether the Anti-Slavery Society or the Colonization Society was more worthy of support. That Athenian Society debate has been used to show how early in his career Beecher espoused complete emancipation. In a sermon on the death of the great abolitionist Wendell Phillips in 1884, the Reverend Henry Ward Beecher solemnly declared:

during my college life, I was chosen by the Athenian Society to debate the question of African colonization, which then was new, fresh, and enthusiastic....

Fortunately I was assigned to the negative side of the question. . . . I contended against colonization as a condition of emancipation—enforced colonization was but little better than enforced slavery—and advocated immediate emancipation on the broad ground of human rights.

But we now know that Henry had been elected president of the society just before the debate and only presided at it. Had he in the course of fifty years of the slavery struggle come to believe his claim? Or was it only another example of being loose with the truth when it served his purpose? Significantly, the proponents of colonization—its foes called it "deportation"—won the debate. They were simply reflecting the view of the college authorities and of almost every leading New England clergyman, including the Reverend Lyman Beecher.

Outside of his activity in the Athenian Society and the Society of Natural History, Henry's college career was undistinguished. So when he thought about his family he still felt a sense of inferiority and, even more, of having been wronged. Once, in a rare moment of confession, he gave Harriet a glimpse of his secret resentment:

Dear sister, in sober truth I find no place with so little sympathy as home and I must say it—I almost always feel that my friends despise me. I know I don't deserve it . . . for I am not deceitful as mother has said. I *am careless* and I never found freedom in telling my plans. I shrink from my own kindred for it always seemed they looked coldly upon me. I ought not to have written this—but I could not help it, for it swelled as it often does till it seems as tho' my heart would burst. I never tell Eunice of it. . . . Don't you show this to *anybody*. I don't want father to know I feel bad, ever, for he is *always* kind to me—but I think he feels a *sorrowful* kindness and that is what *cuts* me more keenly.

We can already see in him most of the qualities that made up the man he became: eloquence, love of an audience, a craving for affection, a tendency to color the truth for the sake of approval, an antipathy to the grimness of Calvinism, and the first signs of personal magnetism.

At his graduation in 1834, Henry would have been a lonely young man had not Hattie—in tribute to their childhood companionship—made the long and costly trip back from Cincinnati to be with him. She found him much matured: a portrait shows him with a youthful leanness of face and figure, dark hair worn long in the back, the prominent nose, wide mouth, full lips and slightly protuberant eyes that would always characterize him. But of the thirty-nine graduates, he was one of the few who played no part in the commencement ceremonies.

Afterwards, Henry spent a few days with Eunice at West Sutton—they had been together only during his vacations in the two and a half years since their engagement. Then he set out for the West to rejoin his family and begin his theological education at Lane Seminary.

In her recollection of the parting, Eunice Beecher casually notes that they bade farewell with the prospect of not seeing each other again for four years.

II

❧

WINNING
THE WEST FOR
CALVINISM

1832–1850

8

CINCINNATI
Rebellion at Lane

The Cincinnati to which the Beechers came was a nineteenth-century American miracle. What had been a muddy riverside village of five hundred souls in the far southwestern corner of Ohio in the early years of the century—just about when young Reverend Lyman Beecher was settling in East Hampton—was now a thriving city of thirty thousand. It was, so to speak, in the right place at the right time—on a bend of a great river leading into the heart of the continent during a tidal surge of westward migration.

The town was still surrounded by an amphitheater of green hills rising as much as five hundred feet at the highest point, with a splendid view across the Ohio into Kentucky. As many as thirty vessels could dock at its landing at one time—not to mention long-oared flatboats and rafts—and the local boosters claimed that it built more steamboats than any other place in the world. A manufacturing center serving a vast hinterland, it slaughtered one hundred twenty thousand hogs a year, had no less than sixty foundries, and its factories and mills produced everything from flour and whiskey to barrels, glass and cotton gins.

Many travelers from the East or Europe visited Cincinnati and almost all were impressed by its lovely setting, its vitality and its cultural aspirations. At first those who lingered and settled there were mostly Americans of English descent, but increasingly immigrants, and especially Germans, added a cosmopolitan leavening to its society. The "Queen City of the West," and "another Genoa the Superb," as it was already being called, had two colleges, a score of churches—including, it was said, thirty-seven varieties of Presbyterians—ten bookstores, a dozen newspapers—most of them ephemeral—printing houses, several fine hotels and even a ladies' magazine. Its professions were served by sixty lawyers, eighty physicians and forty clergymen, and lecture courses on the arts, philosophy, economics and religion flourished. Each day, scores of stages swept down its paved, mile-long Main Street and at times the roadway was as crowded as any in New York. There well-groomed merchants, Southern planters and their ladies mingled with rough-hewn keelboatmen, drovers, stevedores and workingmen, called "mechanics." Travelers were impressed by the many well-built brick houses and even a few mansions surrounded by gardens. Charles Fenno Hoffman, New York magazine editor and novelist, made special note of the number of "pretty faces and stylish figures" he saw in the streets—"western beauties" he called them—and during his stay was treated to a literary soiree, a sporting club dinner and several lively parties.

Not everyone, however, found Cincinnati such an admirable place. An English Congregational clergyman, the Reverend Andrew Reed, was understandably astonished at the number of grogshops—two hundred was his estimate—and since he also saw barbershops everywhere, he concluded that many of the male inhabitants were not only too lazy to shave themselves but also intemperate.

But it was an articulate Englishwoman, Frances Trollope—wife of a lawyer, mother of a master novelist of English manners, and later a novelist herself—who weighed Cincinnati and found it wanting. Her famous, or as many Americans labeled it, infamous, account, *Domestic Manners of the Americans* (1832), had a solid basis—a three-year sojourn in America, including two spent in Cincinnati.

Mrs. Trollope, a dowdy little woman, was well read and widely traveled but she had too keen an eye and too sharp a tongue for her own good. Her opinions of America were colored, or as Americans claimed, discolored, by her foolish expectation that she and her family could make their fortune in America by establishing a "bazar" that would offer fine foreign merchandise, an ice cream bar, an oyster bar, a ballroom, an art gallery, a cyclorama exhibit and heaven knows what else. Hearing of Cincinnati's growing wealth and enterprise, she had chosen it as the site of her venture. The result, in 1828, was a Greco-Moorish-Egyptian building that was a monstrosity as architecture and, before long, a disaster as a business. It is said to have cost her thirty thousand dollars.

Accustomed as she was to time-mellowed European cities and the decorum of English cathedral towns, it was a pity that Mrs. Trollope entered America by way of New Orleans and came up the lower Mississippi on a primitive steamboat, and that she made a disastrous side trip to Fanny Wright's "Nashoba," a utopian communal experiment in a swampy forest in Tennessee. Making no allowances for the rigors of pioneer life, Mrs. Trollope was appalled by the coarse table manners, the constant spitting by men who chewed tobacco, the rawness of backwoods settlements. For her there was something incomplete about a community that lacked an old castle, a cathedral spire and a ruined abbey.

Cincinnati itself was a relief after her trip, but she complained that it was small, muddy in the low-lying areas, lacking in beauty in its homes and churches, and still allowed pigs to scavenge among refuse thrown into the streets—that it was, in short, a city only in its noise and bustle. What kind of a society was it that had, as far as she could see, almost no diversions, that banned (she claimed) cardplaying and even billiards and lacked concerts and dances. (Her critics retorted that she was simply not invited to the best homes and they cited other visitors who told of elegant parties and gambling in the more fashionable circles.) There was only one theater, she reported, and respectable women avoided it. As for cultural standards, they were warped by narrow religious and moral scruples. She quoted one leading member of the local literati as declaring that Byron was scandalous, Chaucer obsolete, Pope and Dryden outmoded, and Shakespeare—"Shakespeare, madam, is obscene, and thank God, *we* are sufficiently advanced to have found it out."

Relentlessly she asserted that Cincinnatians attended church so faithfully because they had so few diversions. She shrewdly noted that since democracy allowed for little social distinction between the rich and the poor, only the clergy were treated with deference. Women were the main supporters of the church, and clergymen rewarded them by giving them most of their attention. With a Dickensian sense of the grotesque, she described a revival service in a Presbyterian church—it was far more typical of a "camp meeting"—in which the preacher, one of a team of three, delivered a hellfire-and-damnation sermon: "The perspiration ran in streams down his face; his eyes rolled, his lips were covered with foam, and every feature had the deep expression of horror it would have borne had he, in truth, been gazing at the scene he described." It was so frightful that it reduced a number of listeners, most of them young women, to hysteria. The preachers then comforted their victims with "mystic caresses": "More than once I saw a young neck encircled by a reverend arm." She concluded:

It is thus the ladies of Cincinnati amuse themselves; to attend the theatre is forbidden; to play cards is unlawful; but they work hard in their families, and must have some relaxation. For myself I confess that I think the coarsest comedy ever written would be a less detestable exhibition for the eyes of youth and innocence than such a scene.

Even as Mrs. Trollope raps the contradiction between the ladies' moral standards and their sexual urges, she herself betrays a Victorian revulsion against all the emotions involved in the scene. It was a preview of a day when the standards of propriety would replace the standards of Puritanism.

Just as mixed was the city's response to Fanny Wright, disciple of Paine, Godwin and Mary Wollstonecraft, when she came to Cincinnati in 1828 during a lecture tour. Frances Wright was an ardently idealistic young Scotswoman who was trying—and failing miserably—to establish in backwoods Tennessee a communal utopia that would buy slaves, educate them and then free them. To many that seemed audacious enough, but when she also attacked the institution of marriage, organized religion and the subjugation of women, Victorian America was scandalized. Her critics labeled her "the Angel of Infidelity," "voluptuous preacher of licentiousness," and founder of a "free-love colony."

That was doubtless why proper Americans everywhere flocked to hear her, and listened with thrills of shock, guilt, excitement and even, in rare cases, admiration. In Cincinnati, Mrs. Trollope was struck by the stir Miss Wright's arrival caused. "But all expectations," she reported, "fell far short of the splendor, the brilliance, the overwhelming eloquence of this extraordinary orator. . . ."

Except perhaps for a few kindred spirits, Cincinnati in time forgot Fanny Wright. But she did not forget the city: years later, after a turbulent career, she retired to it. Once, in 1845, when Bennett's New York *Herald* made a slighting reference to her assaults on marriage, she emerged to lash out as vigorously as ever at a system that, she charged, deprived women of their independence and self-respect.

Other testimony to the tolerance, or perhaps the curiosity, of Cincinnati citizens was the debate between the Reverend Alexander Campbell, defender of Christianity, and Robert Dale Owen, famous Scottish socialist and enemy of all religions. Campbell, a Baptist who later founded the Disciples of Christ, had a nationwide reputation for marathon debates; on this occasion the pious—and more durable—citizens came in huge numbers twice a day for eight days. It was hardly surprising that the audience almost unanimously voted Campbell the winner. But it had at least listened politely to Owen declare in a dozen ways that Christianity, like all religions, was a fraud.

For more than six months after their arrival in Cincinnati the Beechers lived in a rented house in the city itself while a house was being built for them in Walnut Hills, two miles to the north. The rented house was, Hattie reported, "the most inconvenient, ill-arranged, good-for-nothing, and altogether to be execrated affair that was ever put together." When they finally moved into their new home, Hattie, writing to her friend Georgiana in her most romantic vein, declared that the road that climbed up to it was as picturesque as one could imagine, passing through every variety of hill and vale, with "beech of noble growth" and a "velvet richness of turf"—in short, nothing less than "Arcadian." Others described it as little more than rough track, alternately dusty and muddy.

The house itself was a comfortable, two-story brick building set in a pretty garden and backing up against a grove of beech, oak, elm and tulip trees. In the backyard a barn housed a cow as well as the horse that drew the family carryall. A flock of chickens rounded out the rustic setting. During the first year Mrs. Beecher helped Aunt Esther with the household duties, but as her health declined Esther took over more and more of her responsibilities. As in Litchfield and Boston, the household was large, with no less than thirteen in the family circle, including two servants, and a constant flow of visitors.

It was not only a full household but a very lively one. What with the troubled affairs of the infant seminary and its students, the Second Presbyterian Church and its congregation, and the coming and going between home and town—the old carryall constantly clattering down the road—life, especially for the Reverend Beecher, went on at full stretch. The members of the family who edited his autobiography speak lyrically of a household atmosphere "replete with moral oxygen—full charged with intellectual electricity . . . a kind of moral heaven, the purity, vivacity, inspiration and enthusiasm of which those only can appreciate who have lost it."

But how far can we trust this rhapsodic tribute when we learn from one young member of the family, Thomas, of "long, long discussions, lasting until past midnight and resumed at every meal, of 'free agency,' 'sovereignty,' 'natural and moral ability,' interpretations and such." What is apparently meant by "moral oxygen" and "intellectual electricity" is theological indoctrination and debate imposed unsparingly on young minds, including three children under eleven years of age. What effect this routine had on the nervous, not to speak of digestive, system is another matter. After a visit to the Beechers in February 1833, one member of the Foote family wrote to another: "Catharine has had a bilious fever. . . . George has the dyspepsia all the time dreadfully. Mrs. Beecher is always sick and Aunt Esther is suffering from a sore mouth." As a marginal note, she adds: "and they all have nerves."

Lane Seminary was only a short walk from the Beechers' house. The school itself, Catharine's glowing advance report notwithstanding, was only a few plain buildings on a stump-dotted slope. Since the seminary had been established to train indigent young men for the ministry, the trustees decided that it should also be, like several similar institutions, a "manual labor" school. This was supposed to guarantee that it would be healthful, instill habits of self-help and, even more reassuring to the Puritan temper, encourage hard work. As a onetime farm boy who continued to put much store in physical activity, the Reverend Beecher subscribed wholeheartedly to this program.

So the school promptly started a farm and an orchard, and soon after—too soon—tried to organize a printing shop and even a furniture and broom "manufactory." A few students managed to earn much of their expenses—a commons board of eighty-seven cents a week and an annual total of about seventy dollars—from these enterprises. But it also became evident that the students were eating about as much as they produced. Although most of them were pledged to austere living, a few betrayed a weakness for roasted oysters and entire pies evening after evening. Beyond that, the world, alas, showed no great interest in Lane's printing, furniture or brooms. So much of the program languished.

But soon the school—and its president—faced a far more disturbing problem: a band of students who had come from Oneida Institute, a theological seminary in upstate New York. Fanatically seeking a "new Jerusalem," these young men were engaged in a holy war against sin, infidelism, drink, self-indulgence and, even more, slavery. Their idol was an older student, Theodore Weld.

Descended from a long line of ministers, Weld, with a dedication characteristic of him, had studied so hard at Phillips Andover Academy that he had become almost blind. While recovering, he had for a few years tried to support himself by lecturing on what he described as the "science of mnemonics." It was during a tour through the South that he first saw slavery up close and began to develop a hatred of it that was to become the ruling passion of his life.

Just as crucial was his meeting with that fireball of revivalism, Charles Grandison Finney. On a visit to Utica, New York, Weld was outraged to hear how a close cousin of his had been left terror-stricken by Finney's preaching. ("Ye generation of vipers," was Finney's salutation, "how can ye escape the damnation of hell?") "My father," Weld wrote, "was a real minister of the Gospel, grave and courteous, an honor to the profession. This man is not a minister, and I will never acknowledge him as such." But his aunt tricked him into entering a church where Finney was preaching. As Weld later reported,

by and by Mr. Finney rose, with those great staring eyes of his (never was a man whose soul looked out through his face as his did), and took for his text, "One sinner destroyeth much good." I stooped down and took hold of my hat; but just as I rose, Aunt Clark . . . whispered, "Theodore, *you'll break my heart* if you go." I gave it up, and resigned myself to my fate; and then, for an hour, he just held me up on his toasting-fork before that audience.

The next day, while Weld was in a store in town, Finney, alerted by friends, entered the place. Weld, trapped, poured out a torrent of abuse. It was the kind of outburst that often precedes a reconciliation between quarreling lovers. Finney answered quietly and meekly. Weld suddenly turned away and went home. "I was so ashamed," he admits, "I could not live. Finally, I made up my mind I'd go and ask his pardon." When he appeared at Finney's lodgings, the minister cried: "Ah! Is it not enough? Have you followed a minister of the Lord Jesus to his own door to abuse him?"

"Mr. Finney, I have come for a very different purpose. I—"

Finney instantly understood. Throwing his arms around Weld's neck, he dragged him down till they were on their knees, both men "sobbing and praying and sobbing and praying." Weld left school and all that summer accompanied Finney and his "holy band" on their revival circuit. Later that year Weld enrolled at the Oneida Institute. At Oneida the aim was service to God and the routine was Spartan. As part of the manual labor program, Weld supervised the milking of thirty cows and the dispatching of the milk to Utica before dawn each morning.

Before long, the president of the school, recognizing Weld's talents, began sending him on fund-raising lecture tours. Now at the height of his powers, Weld was a strange mixture of qualities: dark, twisted features, boundless energy, austere habits, disheveled clothes and unkempt beard, iron integrity, deep gloom or periods of trancelike distraction, incandescent fervor when aroused—the aura of a man possessed. The product of almost two centuries of Puritan breeding, he was at once a high-minded idealist, a relentless reformer, a self-effacing Christian and an intractable individualist.

Weld's fund-raising work and his stand on slavery and temperance now brought him to the attention of Arthur Tappan and his brother Lewis, wealthy New York silk merchants and leading philanthropists. The Tappans were fanatically pious men. Accepting the Puritan doctrine of community responsibility for sin, they made their employees pray morning and evening, abstain from smoking, drinking, attending the theater and staying out after ten o'clock at night. But above all they were dedicated to improving mankind through reform societies and missions of every conceivable kind. Arthur, irritable and humorless, was the better known, but Lewis, though retiring, was even more tenacious in his reform efforts.

At their behest, Weld came to New York and delivered several temperance lectures. The Tappans offered him a pastorate but he insisted that he was not ready. Then, in July 1831, they asked him to become the "general agent" of their newly organized Society for Promoting Manual Labor in Literary Institutions. It was an opportunity Weld could not resist.

One of Weld's first tours in his new capacity took him to Cincinnati. Lecturing on temperance, he drew such a large crowd that he continued to speak on the subject for eight more nights. A typical reaction was that of James Fairchild, later president of Oberlin College: "I have seen crowds of bearded men held spellbound by his power for hours together, and for twenty evenings in succession." And Joseph Tuttle, also later a college president, declared: "His imagination was brilliant, his humor at times overpowering, and his invective in all respects the most terrible ever heard."

After the lectures, Weld visited Lane and began to think of it as the site of a great institution that would be devoted to God, manual labor and the struggle against slavery. He had now read William Lloyd Garrison's *Fiery Thoughts on Colonization* and become convinced that slavery was a sin, slaveholders were criminals, and the Colonization Society only a compromise with evil. Quickly he brought the Tappan brothers around to his position, and in December of 1833 they founded the American Anti-Slavery Society.

After a year with the Manual Labor Society, five thousand miles of travel and more than two hundred and fifty speeches, Weld, convinced, like Beecher, that the great battlefield for men's souls lay in the West, resigned his post and began looking westward. At the urging of Arthur Tappan, F. Y. Vail, who was Lane's financial agent, had begun to court Weld as early as November 1831:

We only need to have your plan and efforts identified with our own in order to secure the influence of New York, and make it strictly a national, model institution. . . . We want now, my dear brother, just such a man as you are (I do not flatter you) to be the mainspring in the whole concern. We want the funds promised you . . . for buildings for 500 or 600 students, for more land . . . workshops, tools. . . .

The following August, Vail offered Weld the chair of Sacred Rhetoric and Oratory, apparently ignoring the fact that this was the Reverend Beecher's special field. Almost perversely resisting formal recognition of his influence, Weld declined. Curiously, despite such acts of humility, Arthur Tappan, Lyman Beecher and others thought that Weld often behaved as though his views and his way of doing things were divinely inspired. And in a moment of extraordinary self-analysis he himself wrote to his wife: "I am too proud to be *ambitious,* too proud to seek applause. . . . There is no end to my pride." At last, early in 1834, Weld and three of his Oneida friends took deck passage on a steamboat and worked their way to Cincinnati by helping to load wood.

There was nothing callow or unfledged about the first group at Lane. Of the forty students in the theological class, the majority were over twenty-six years old, and ten, including Weld, were over thirty. All were college graduates, six were married and a dozen had served as agents of benevolent societies. The fifty-six students in the "literary department" were only a little younger and a little less experienced.

The faculty of the seminary was undistinguished except perhaps for John Morgan, a huge, virile young Irishman who excelled in explicating Scripture and in reading hymns and was as reform-minded as the students, and Calvin Stowe, professor of Biblical Literature, a learned, quaint and rather quirky man in his early thirties.

The members of that first class were, as Charles Beecher, who was in the next class, put it, "uncommonly strong, a little uncivilized, entirely radical, and terribly in earnest." Something of their mettle, and especially Weld's zeal, was demonstrated when a cholera epidemic struck the school soon after they arrived. Scores of students were stricken—some mildly, but others so acutely that they died within twenty-four hours. Weld and others who remained well were concerned to care for the ill but just as intent on seeing that the dying embraced salvation before they died. Weld himself tended the sick for ten days and nights almost without rest. With an exaltation amounting to ecstasy, he tells, in a letter to a friend, of those who, despite their final agonies, died with a prayer on their lips or describing visions of bliss. He devoted most attention to George, a sensitive, brilliant eighteen-year-old who had been exposed to several revivals but "still resisted the Spirit." He had, Weld adds, "hardened his heart . . . to an appalling extent." The youth fell ill in the afternoon; by midnight he was declared to be beyond recovery. Weld writes:

we looked in each other's faces in speechless agony—he was an infidel! . . . it was agreed I should tell him that it was certain *he must die soon,* and urge on his soul *the great salvation* provided for the chief of sinners. . . .

Weld did so and adds:

He was in a rage—thrust me from him with violence: "Let me die in peace," said he.

I endeavored, with the utmost . . . tenderness, to press the subject at intervals for an hour and a half, but, the more affectionate the approach, the fiercer did he repel it, till at last he screamed to drown my voice.

Weld went upstairs. But in a moment he heard George calling his name with "frightful energy." When he returned the dying youth grasped him convulsively and cried:

"Dear—dear Mr. Weld, *now I'll hear you! now I'll hear you!* Oh, tell me, *is there* an eternal hell? Convince me by sure arguments. Oh, to be damned! to be damned! Oh, for a light! for a light! Bring me a light—the light of my salvation! No, never, never, never!"

This word he repeated as many as twelve or fifteen times, all the while tossing his body from side to side. . . . He stopped, and, with a phrensied look of horror, died! . . .

Having described this agonizing scene in such detail, Weld closes his letter with some casual remarks on how satisfied he is with his teaching situation. Like Lyman Beecher after the drowning of Alexander Metcalf Fisher, he is less moved by the agonizing death of the youth—increased by the torment he himself has contributed—than by the fate of a young man's soul.

The first Lane group, forming a state within a state, did not easily accept the rule of the school. Weld led them as readily in rebellion as in cooperation. Even before his arrival they had looked on the school not as an academic enclave but as a base of operations. They went out into what they called the "waste places" of the city to preach or, as they said, to "prophesy."

When they found the daily lectures of Thomas J. Biggs, professor of church history, insufferable, they simply refused to attend his classes. Dr. Beecher finally persuaded them to accept the professor once a week, with the understanding that Beecher himself or Professor Stowe would take the class on the other days. Beecher managed to cope with such minor mutinies, but he was utterly unprepared for the full-scale revolt that broke out over the antislavery issue.

In New England, slavery had been a remote problem, an issue that even Garrison had not yet managed to make immediate or urgent. But in Cincinnati, just across the river from Kentucky, it was on one's doorstep. The city itself was an outpost of the South, combining much of Southern culture and speechways with Northern drive and enterprise. Family servants were often slaves hired from masters across the river, and 2,500 free blacks clustered in a large district known as Green Town. Vessels whose decks were loaded with chain gangs of slaves were constantly passing down the river, on the way to the sale of their wretched human cargo in the South.

Since local merchants depended heavily on the Kentucky trade, there was a profound reluctance in the city to make an issue of slavery. But all that was changing. Wealthy Kentuckians had not in other days hesitated to cross the river into Cincinnati accompanied by their slaves, but after 1830 they increasingly ran the risk of having the slaves escape into the "Underground Railroad."

The students at Lane were another, even clearer manifestation of the change. When Weld arrived at Lane he found an active Colonization Society there, with abolitionism regarded as both absurd and fanatical. Shrewdly starting with one of the considerable number of Southerners at the school, he began systematically converting his classmates to outright abolitionism and emancipation.

Beecher was at first indifferent to the ferment among the students.

Even if he had heard, just before he came West, of the slave insurrections led by Nat Turner in Virginia and by Samuel Sharp in Jamaica, he paid no attention to them. Nor did he show any concern over South Carolina's effort to nullify the federal government's power to tax the states—or President Jackson's gloomy prediction that the next cause of Southern defiance would be the slavery issue. Like many other well-intentioned Northerners, Beecher favored the colonization solution, essentially because it did not arouse the fears or wrath of slaveholders. It was a solution that appealed to those who hoped to banish the issue, to get the victims out of sight and thus out of mind. Beecher even denied that there was any ground of controversy between the colonizationists and the abolitionists. "I am myself both," he insisted, "without perceiving in myself any inconsistency." (Had he turned to almost any freed slave, he would have had a stunning explanation of the inconsistency.)

Wasn't it, Beecher felt, sufficient evidence of his tolerance that a former slave, James Bradley—a Negro who had bought his own freedom—had been admitted to the school and was one of the first of his race to be accepted in such an institution? Had Beecher not also preached most successfully to an audience of two thousand blacks? Of course, in both instances he had been in a privileged position, one that involved no personal relationship. The fact was, according to Calvin Stowe, who would later marry Harriet Beecher, that Beecher retained, "without being conscious of it, not a little of the old Connecticut prejudice about blacks."

To the Reverend Beecher slavery was indeed an evil, but the millennium, which with God's help would come first in America, would usher in a righteousness that would sweep away all evil.

Meanwhile Weld, having committed himself heart and soul to abolitionism, identified himself—and far more personally than Garrison—with black people. In a letter in March 1836 he wrote:

If I ate in the City, it was at their Tables. If I slept in the City it was in their homes. If I attended parties, it was *theirs—weddings—theirs—Funerals—theirs—Religious meetings—theirs—Sabbath schools—Bible classes—theirs.* During the 18 months that I spent at Lane Seminary *I did not attend Dr. Beecher's Church once.* Nor did I ever attend any other of the Presbyterian Churches in the City except brother Mahan's and did not attend there more than half a dozen times. . . .

At this point Weld proposed a student debate on abolitionism versus colonization. So buoyantly sure of himself was Beecher that at first he consented and even offered to take part—defending colonization. But soon, cautioned by conservative faculty members, he tried to postpone the confrontation. It would be divisive, he announced, and likely to arouse antagonism: down in the city there were not only proslavery businessmen but rough dockworkers and drifters who might easily be aroused against students with radical views. It was a counsel of caution such as he had given young Garrison only a few years before—and it was rejected just as impatiently.

Weld was not to be thwarted. Although as devoted to his religious calling as Beecher, he and his classmates saw the older man as out of touch with the realities of the age. If they were ahead of their time on the issue of slavery, Beecher was barely abreast of it.

The first part of the "debates" turned out to be evenings of "annihilative discussion" of slavery. At one point Weld held the floor for eighteen hours, delivering a complete history of slavery through the ages. The student vote was almost unanimously for immediate emancipation. It was followed by nine evenings devoted to the colonization program. Weld and others made much of how utterly ineffectual it had proved—fifteen hundred Negroes freed in fifteen years. The vote on that program was overwhelmingly for rejection.

The "Lane debates" were an extraordinary anticipation of things to come. Although they received much attention in the antislavery press of the time, histories have not given them their due as a thorough and radical exploration of the slavery question long before it became a national issue. And they served to put Weld in the forefront of the antislavery movement.

The results of the debates were all that Weld and his followers needed: tremendously emboldened, they immediately undertook to "elevate the colored population in Cincinnati," establishing a lyceum with lectures in grammar, geography, arithmetic and natural philosophy, and classes in reading and the Bible. After a series of visits to thirty black families, Weld reported that some members of more than half of these families were still in bondage. The more he saw, the more fierce became his indignation.

Growing vaguely apprehensive, Beecher now warned Weld of the danger of arousing pro-slavery fanaticism: "If you want to teach colored schools, I can fill your pockets with money; but if you will visit in colored families, and walk with them in the streets, you will be overwhelmed." As late as June 1834 he was still saying: *"if we and our friends do not amplify the evil by too much alarm, impatience and attempt at regulation, the evil will subside and pass away."*

In one respect Beecher proved right: a Cincinnati magazine declared that the "sophomore declamations" of the Lane students were arousing malignant passions and rancorous party spirit. In an impassioned reply, Weld scoffed at the journal's references to the rebels as schoolboys and minors, and in tones reminiscent of Garrison's *Liberator,* announced:

"Sir, you have mistaken alike the cause, the age, and the men, if you think to intimidate by threats, or to silence by clamors, or shame by sneers, or put down by authority . . . those who have put their hands to this work."

Beecher now saw how self-willed these young men were, but he still did not realize how deeply they were stirred by the issue. He charged them with a "headlong, reckless purpose . . . and an affected childish pity." They were, he chose to think, hotheaded boys who would soon get over their fever. So in May, with the approach of the summer vacation, Beecher calmly went off to raise funds for the school.

Weld and more than fifty of his followers remained at the seminary for the summer. Released from their school duties, they moved forward with their activities among the blacks, even inviting several young black women to picnic on the school grounds. The only professor on the scene, the unpopular Biggs, harsh foe of the rebels, now asserted that the seminary had become "a reproach and a loathing in the land." Goaded by his mutterings and by rumored threats of mob violence, a committee of trustees, most of them business or professional men who dealt with Southerners, took action. At a meeting on August 20 it declared that slavery was not a subject for immature minds and especially not for theological students. Disdaining to wait for Beecher's return, the trustees went on to prohibit any societies, public statements or even discussions not related to theological studies. They went so far as to have the bans published in the Cincinnati *Daily Gazette.* In justifying their acts, the trustees echoed Biggs, declaring that "many of our best citizens" looked upon the seminary as a nuisance more to be dreaded than the cholera. They saw in the students' "insubordination, resistance to law and civil commotion" a prelude to the kind of scenes they associated with the revolutions in France and Haiti.

The edict revealed an abysmal ignorance of the identity of the students. The antislavery press immediately denounced the resolutions as an intolerable attack on freedom of speech. The New York *Evangelist* asked:

In what age do we live? and in what country? and who are the persons thus restrained? and with whose endowments was the seminary founded? . . . Nor do we see how such men as Dr. Beecher, and Professor Stowe, and Professor Morgan could consistently remain, nor how those subscribers to the funds of the seminary . . . could make any farther payments to trustees so incompetent to appreciate the wants of the age. . . .

The question of whether it was proper for theological students to occupy themselves with slavery was more important than the trustees realized. And Theodore Weld's approach to it, like his approach to the question of slavery itself, was unhesitating. Shall those soon-to-be "ambassadors of Christ," he asked, avoid speaking of that "accursed thing that . . . shakes its blood-red hands at heaven? . . . Is it not the business of the theological seminaries to educate the *heart* as well as the head?"

Suddenly, and for an unenviable reason, Lane Seminary began to attract nationwide attention. Even more unfortunate, Arthur Tappan, now as ardent an abolitionist as any, learned that the school he had helped to found and foster had summarily prohibited even the discussion of slavery.

Weld advised his fellows to ignore the injunctions of the trustees. He also took it upon himself to write to Beecher urging him to return at once. Beecher started west but then wrote Weld that it was more important for him to continue his fund-raising work. With an incongruous jauntiness, he declared that the students were still "a set of glorious fellows" whom he would not exchange for any others. But all he could offer by way of advice was that they should be patient until his return. His conclusion could not have been more exasperating: "Pray much, say little, be humble and wait." He simply could not believe, much less take seriously, so fundamental a threat to everything he was trying to do. And he obviously resented being directed by Weld. Whatever the explanation, his failure to return was a tragic error.

The students, having trusted and admired Beecher, were doubly disappointed and shocked. So was the Reverend Asa Mahan, revivalist pastor of the Sixth Presbyterian Church of Cincinnati and the only trustee sympathetic to the rebels. He, too, wrote to Beecher of "the peril of the Seminary" and pleaded with the wandering president to hasten home to "prevent the dismantling of the institution."

On October 4, just before the opening of the fall term, the trustees indulged in another high-handed act: they dismissed Professor Morgan, a strong supporter of the rebels, and threatened Weld with expulsion. Meant to smother the fire, these decisions served only as a bellows. One of the rebels, Huntington Lyman, wrote to another: "Truly madness rules the hour," and, "Who that has an opinion and a soul will enter L. Sem. now?"

Beecher returned at last. And he even persuaded the trustees to modify their resolutions. But it was much too late. The students had seen that he was not only unsympathetic but ineffectual. A student meeting marked by solemn appeals to God, country and conscience resulted in the overwhelming repudiation of the school's actions. When the term opened, the rebels requested permission to discuss the new rules: the request was curtly denied. Weld immediately drew up a statement of the student position. Fifty-one students signed it, and then, like the delegates of an offended nation, they seceded from the school. Forty-one of them bravely moved out and took refuge in a deserted tavern in nearby Cummingsville. Others transferred to other schools.

Beecher met with the rebels in a last desperate attempt to get them to return. He argued that a professor—obviously meaning Biggs—had frightened the trustees into their decisions and that the rebels had "ignorantly" done just what the professor wanted them to do—leave Lane.

"Well," the rebels asked, "what can be done?"

Beecher's answer was partly conciliatory but it was also a warning: "That is for you to determine. . . . You are excellent men, but I am afraid it will wreck you. . . ."

The students stood fast. The news of their action, spread by the antislavery press, reached Arthur Tappan. He promptly sent money to the refugees. And the *Liberator,* with its flair for the inflammatory phrase, announced that Lane Seminary was now to be regarded as "strictly a Bastile of oppression—a spiritual Inquisition."

The rebels, encouraged by Tappan's generous support, decided to start a school of their own. As Asa Mahan said, Cincinnati would now have two Lane seminaries, one at Cummingsville, with students but nothing else, and one at Walnut Hills, with everything but students.

It was then that the Reverend John Jay Shipherd, agent for a small Ohio school called Oberlin Collegiate Institute, moved in. Hardly a year old, impoverished, without a president and with barely one hundred students, Oberlin was fighting to survive. Shipherd saw in the Lane rebels not only a sizable group of students but, more important, Tappan's support. He invited the refugees to come to Oberlin.

It was an ideal solution for the rebels, but they refused to come unless certain conditions were met, to wit: the Reverend Asa Mahan must be made president, John Morgan and Charles Grandison Finney must join the faculty, freedom of speech must be guaranteed and students be admitted "irrespective of color"—meaning Negroes. Several of the conditions disturbed the Oberlin trustees, but it was the last demand that seems to have frightened both officers and students most of all. Although they themselves had been admitted as a result of an enlightened admissions policy, several women students threatened to "wade Lake Erie" to escape if colored men entered the school. But Oberlin capitulated, the rebels relented and the women students stayed on.

Time would show that Lane's loss was Oberlin's gain. The Reverend Asa Mahan became president of Oberlin, John Morgan came to teach and remained for almost half a century, the Reverend Charles Finney, lured from his post at the Broadway Tabernacle in New York City, was made head of a newly formed Theology Department and later President of the College. Almost overnight Oberlin became a haven of freedom and religious idealism, while Lane shrank abruptly, its reputation tarnished and its prize patron alienated.

As for Theodore Weld, he continued his passionate crusade, training scores of agents for the American Anti-Slavery Society and speaking tirelessly on behalf of the cause. Although repeatedly beaten and stoned by pro-slavery mobs, he continued to give himself with such feverish intensity that by 1836 his health was impaired and his great voice reduced to a whisper. A few years later he married that equally unusual and equally passionate reformer, Angelina Grimké. She and her sister Sarah, daughters of a wealthy South Carolina planter and slaveholder, had astonished and dismayed their entire Southern world by going north and becoming Quakers, ardent abolitionists and women's rights advocates.

For a time Weld maintained his influence with his writings: his *Slavery As It Is* (1839), based on thousands of accounts of slaveholders' cruelties routinely recorded in Southern publications, sold one hundred thousand copies in a single year, and Harriet Beecher Stowe said she kept a copy of it in her sewing basket while she was writing *Uncle Tom's Cabin*. But Weld disdained public life: "I am a *backwoodsman* untamed. My bearish proportions have never been licked into *city shape....* A stump is my throne, my parish, my home; my element the *everydayisms* of plain common life." In the end his scorn for honors or publicity deprived him of his due as an inspired leader in the abolitionist cause and as one of the most remarkable men of his time. Whatever his psychological motives, he was that absolute rarity, a man who served in a great cause but sought neither power nor credit. He spent much of the remainder of his life as a teacher in small experimental schools and died in 1895 in a community near Boston, honored locally but forgotten by the nation at large.

In the calm of later years, Beecher, at once magnanimous and rueful, would say, "Weld was a genius. First-rate natural capacity, but uneducated. Would have made a first-rate man in the Church of God if his education had been thorough. In the estimation of the class, he was president. He took the lead of the whole institution. The young men had, many of them, been under his care, and they thought he was a god." But at the time, in the heat of charges and countercharges, Beecher understandably blamed all Lane's troubles on Weld. It was Weld's design, he declared, to make the seminary serve the cause of abolition even if it meant undermining the school itself. "We regard it," he said, "as an eminent instance of monomania."

He was right, but his role had been a misguided and feckless one. Brought to the West by a dream, Beecher had proved unwilling to cope with the reality and had suffered a grievous defeat. Within a few months the shining hope of creating a citadel of Calvinism in the West, of leading America and the world onward and upward to salvation, had dissolved—replaced by the sad task of getting enough students and funds to keep a small, shattered backwoods college going.

Later, Beecher's friend Oliver Johnson claimed that the example of a strong clergyman like Beecher could have rallied the churches around the antislavery cause. But there were at least two reasons why Beecher could not have been that man: in spiritual matters his eyes were fixed on the millennium, and in worldly affairs he looked backward for his models.

If any man had a right to think that he had been deserted by his God in the very midst of an effort to serve that God, it was Lyman Beecher in October 1834. Nothing could have seemed more perverse than that a band of theological students should suddenly have staged such a devastating revolt against an obscure little school.

Yet, with his still abounding vitality and homely ways of speech, Beecher would by July 1835, in a letter to his son William, be characterizing the rebels as "he-goat men, who think they do God service by butting every thing in the line of their march which does not fall in or get out of the way. They are . . . made up of vinegar, aqua fortis, and oil of vitriol, with brimstone, salpetre, and charcoal, to explode and scatter the corrosive matter."

Just as interesting and even more revealing is the practical advice he gave William:

As to abolition, I am still of opinion that you ought not, and need not, and will not commit yourself as a partisan on either side. The cause is moving on in Providence, and by the American Union, and by colonization, and by Lundy in Texas, which is a grand thing, and will succeed, as I believe.

The Lane debates and rebellion clearly had no effect on his basic attitudes toward slavery and the slavery controversy. It was simply not a clergyman's province.

So he went forward once again, trying to patch up the great rent in the fabric of his life.

9

LYMAN BEECHER
Trials and Tribulation

When the Reverend Lyman Beecher went east that summer of 1834, he planned to collect funds for Lane but he also made a point of telling everyone about the importance of the West—not only in its boundless promise but in its hidden dangers.

In sonorous phrases he described the West as a young empire "rushing up to a giant manhood," a vast region where the destiny of America would be decided. That was why schools, superior schools, inspiring schools, must be provided for the great role that the people there would play.

That was the promise. He would then spend the rest of his sermon or talk on the perils. No, the danger came not from pioneering or Indians or wild beasts but from the flood of poor and uneducated immigrants. Playing on familiar fears, he declared that many of the newcomers were paupers "emptied on our shores" to crowd the prisons and the poorhouses and to quadruple taxes. Such poor souls were susceptible to every demagogue. Most dangerous of all were the Catholics, for their priests were subject to a "foreign potentate," the Pope, whom they considered infallible. Catholics, Beecher said, were taught that their church was the only church, they were forbidden to read the Bible without permission, and their priests, who were anti-republican, even told them how to vote.

Then, one day in August, Beecher delivered such a sermon in Boston, and on the following night a mob burned down a Catholic convent in Charlestown, just across the Charles River. For several days after that, gangs of rowdies roamed riotously through the streets. If the militia had not been called out and a Catholic bishop had not pleaded with his people for restraint, Irish laborers in railroad camps on the outskirts of Boston would have attacked the city.

Catholics promptly charged that the Reverend Beecher's sermon had incited the mob. Beecher vehemently denied this; he pointed out that the mob could not even have known that he was in the city. Since anti-

Catholic feeling had been mounting for some time before the nunnery was burned, it is unlikely that Beecher's sermon had any connection with this incident. But obviously shaken by the violence of the episode, Beecher repeatedly insisted, in *A Plea for the West,* a book that grew out of his sermons and talks, that he had no quarrel with Catholicism as a religion and deplored any violation of either the civil or the religious rights of Catholics. They should not, he wrote—with what he doubtless thought was great magnanimity—be held responsible for what had happened in the Middle Ages, and any virulent or taunting denunciations of them were, to use his rather mild terms, "as unchristian as it is in bad taste and indiscreet."

But then, he went on, it is treason and folly not to recognize that Catholics are like a state within a state, Greeks in the midst of Troy, and bringers of Jesuit intrigue. He charged that they ignored the separation of church and state—he himself conveniently forgetting how long the Congregationalists had ignored it in New England. "Did Catholics not try to undermine the religion of our children?" he asked. He had been told that they had reformed, but that was not to be trusted. Lamenting a lost purity, he spoke nostalgically of a time when Americans were a "homogeneous people." It was a plea for the West—but a West without ardent Catholics or poor foreigners.

In private he was much more bitter. In a letter written after he returned to Lane, he said of the crisis in Boston:

For what was the city of Boston for five nights under arms—her military upon the alert—her citizens enrolled, and a body of five hundred men constantly patrolling the streets? . . . Has it come to this, that the capital of New England has been thrown into consternation by the threats of a Catholic mob, and that her temples and mansions stand only through the forbearance of a Catholic bishop? . . . Will our great cities consent to receive protection from the Catholic priesthood, dependent on the Catholic powers of Europe, and favored by his Holiness?

Thus even as he was prompted by expediency to avoid the slavery issue, he was prodded by prejudice to seek a confrontation on the Catholic question. At least one prominent Cincinnatian, Judge James Hall, writing in the *Western Monthly Magazine* in December 1834, attacked Beecher's anti-Catholic outpourings as bigoted and a foisting of eastern problems on the West. Hall was a formidable opponent. He had studied law and had served as a circuit judge in Illinois. A confident, vigorous man, he had valiantly sought to clean up a frontier area swarming with horse thieves, murderers and "regulators." All the while he had written and published colorful stories, poems and sketches of the western scene and had established the first literary periodical west of the Ohio, the *Illinois Monthly Magazine.* Moving to Cincinnati, he had launched the

Western Monthly Magazine in 1833. Hall had a ready eloquence that made him popular as a speaker, and he was an able editor—the first, indeed, to recognize the talents of one shy young contributor, Harriet Beecher.

Several Cincinnatians and various western magazines came to Beecher's defense and denounced Judge Hall. Hall's magazine lost so many of its subscribers that he soon abandoned it. Nevertheless, the Catholic imbroglio, following hard on the antislavery affair, marked Beecher as a source of contention and ill-feeling. There was resentment, too, at this Easterner who assumed that he was coming as a kind of savior to helpless Westerners.

Even Harriet Martineau, the British author whose account of a stay in America from 1834 to 1836 is one of the ablest of its kind, reported that the coming of Dr. Beecher to Cincinnati had "much quickened the spirit of alarm in that region," and she echoed the tale that Beecher had "preached in Boston three sermons vituperative of the Catholics the Sunday before the burning of the Charlestown convent by a Boston mob."

Hardly had Beecher sustained the shock of the Lane rebellion when he was confronted by an equally galling assault from a fellow clergyman. Giving Beecher little chance to recover from his ordeal at the seminary, the Reverend Joshua Lacy Wilson had him brought before the local presbytery on charges of heresy, hypocrisy and slander.

The epitome of an Old School Calvinist, Wilson was tall, pale, stern-faced and severe. He had been brought up on the Kentucky frontier in the 1780s and 1790s, and had as a youth indulged in free living and wild company. But after a lively party, a "conviction of sin" had turned him to religion with all the fervor of a convert. He was ordained in 1804, but his contentiousness gained him such bitter enemies that in one town they burned down his place of worship and in another he had to carry a gun.

He came to his pastorate in the hamlet of Cincinnati in 1808 and in time became the archdefender of Presbyterian orthodoxy and the watchdog of local morals and manners. Imperious and overbearing, he did not hesitate to make such statements as that eloquence, poetry and music were not as rejoicing "to the heart of a sincere enquirer after truth as downright controversy." His belligerence was all-embracing: when volunteers were going off to war in 1812, he took his text from Jeremiah: "Cursed be he that dealeth deceitfully, and cursed be he that keepeth back his sword from blood." Apparently convinced that God was made in his image, he once declared that the Lord "approves *slavery* as he does *war* as one mode of punishing sin in the world." His attacks on what he considered sinful conduct caused him to be satirized in local plays, but he thrived on such disapproval.

Wilson had at first hailed the appointment of Dr. Beecher to the presidency of Lane, but alerted by Old School conservatives in the East, he soon began to challenge the "big gun" of eastern Congregationalism and his New School theology. Doubtless he was further nettled by Dr. Beecher's selection as pastor of the Second Presbyterian Church, since that congregation had broken away from his own First Presbyterian Church and was attracting some of the most influential Presbyterians in the city.

But Wilson did not need such motives as envy, malice or personal pique. He found justification enough in the conviction that he was preserving the purity of the faith against those who would distort it even in the slightest degree. Righteousness sanctioned every measure he took, no matter how divisive or spiritually sterile.

The Reverend Wilson assailed the Reverend Beecher on a variety of counts. Presbyterians and Congregationalists had in 1801 signed the Plan of Union, which allowed pastors to move more or less freely from one of these church bodies to the other, and F. Y. Vail, the trustee who had persuaded Beecher to come to Lane, declared that there would be "no difficulty in having the Doctor Presbyterianized." But he had reckoned without Wilson; that worthy now asserted that Beecher was not in fact a proper Presbyterian.

Turning to theology, Wilson charged that Beecher pretended to subscribe to the basic Presbyterian creed as set forth in the Westminister Confession of Faith (adopted in England in the 1640s) but all the while was undermining it with New School interpretations. All his darkest suspicions were substantiated when an Old School colleague of his, the Reverend James Weatherby of Mississippi, charged that Beecher on being asked whether he could "sincerely receive and adopt the Confession . . . as containing the system of doctrine taught in the Holy Scriptures," had answered, "Yes, but I will not say how much more it contains." Only when Weatherby had retorted—or so he claimed—that "no such Yankee answer would do," had Beecher replied with a clear "yes." Stirring up old fires, Wilson asserted that Beecher had long proclaimed man's accountability for his actions, thereby denying original sin. Which also meant, Wilson insisted, that Beecher was denying God's complete sovereignty.

We would need to know much more about Wilson, son of the frontier, accustomed in his youth to maximum independence and self-reliance, before we would venture to explain his efforts to enforce utter submission to such an intractable deity. The controversy was an exercise in futility—the last gasp of a two-hundred-year-old tradition of Puritan heresy-hunting. The Old School position, proclaiming man's innate depravity, reduced men—so the New School argued—to resignation and even despair. The New School, granting man free agency, canceled—so the Old School claimed—dependence on God's grace, on Christ's intervention and the services of the church.

It had all become only a debate in which the opponents were trying to score points rather than arrive at any better understanding of their own beliefs. The differences between the Beechers and the Wilsons were simply doctrinal—in a world moving inexorably away from doctrinal contests. All the average churchgoer knew was that one pastor was conservative or strict while another was more liberal or flexible. And in Cincinnati by 1835, people were more concerned with other matters than theology—with trade, property, politics, to name only a few. Beyond that, the temper of the people and the place—ambitious men on a frontier rich in worldly promise—favored any system that allowed one a chance, however slight, to escape the darker labyrinths of Puritanism. It was ironical, of course, that a man who had given his life to his religion—climaxed by volunteering at the age of sixty to go as a missionary into a far-off land—should be brought to trial for betraying his faith and for spiritual dishonesty. The members of Beecher's family were all convinced that the true motive was church politics: a shameful effort by Old School clergymen to destroy a leader of the New School invasion of the West. Later, a letter by one of the children characterized the entire attack as base, malignant and demoralizing.

But Beecher, far from being shocked by the charges or the possibility that if convicted he would be ousted from his office and even barred from heaven, was almost gleeful. Never, as far as we know, did he question the injustice of it or the waste of spirit. Pressed hard on all sides, his wife sick unto death, his school tottering, he nevertheless responded with sublime confidence. He saw it simply as a play in which he would have a splendid chance to confound an opponent. A trial would translate an abstract dispute into a duel of personalities. It would convert metaphysics into emotions, dogma into drama. When the charges were broached before the local presbytery in November 1834, his reaction was:

I laughed in my sleeve, and said to myself, "You think you know more of Presbyterian management than I do; but I have as much common sense as you have, and have attended several ecclesiastical trials in my day, and all those councils and consociations in Connecticut were not for nothing."

For help in marshaling learned citations he turned to Calvin Stowe, the immensely erudite professor of Biblical Literature at Lane, who would soon become his son-in-law. Stowe dragged stacks of arcane tomes to Beecher's study and began to ply his victim with quotations. Soon Beecher, as Stowe reported, grew "cloudy, bewildered and perplexed; and at length exclaimed, with an impatience that was laughably pettish,

'Pish! Pshaw! Take your books away, Stowe; they plague me!' " So Beecher went his own way, content to rely on his wits rather than his learning. On the eve of the trial he took all his books and sat down on the stairs of the pulpit in his church:

I looked so quiet and meek, my students were almost afraid I shouldn't come up to the mark. I had everything just then to weigh me down. My wife was lying at home on her dying bed. She did not live a fortnight after that. Then there was all the wear and tear of the seminary and of my congregation. But when I had all my references, and had nothing to do but extemporize, I felt easy. I had as much lawyer about me as Wilson, and more. I never got into a corner, and he never got out.

The trial lasted eight days. Lyman met the charges with countercharges, denials, tears, rhetoric, floods of learned quotations and a variety of ingenious defenses. Far from admitting any form of error, he grew ever more confident and assertive. It is I, he boasted, who preach true Calvinism. He was provocative: "Calvin was as bad as I am. The doctrine for which I am to be turned out . . . is not new divinity but old Calvinism."

The presbytery acquitted him by a vote of twenty-three to twelve, and he crowed in triumph. When Wilson stubbornly decided to appeal to a higher Presbyterian body, the synod, Beecher welcomed the new challenge. Instead of having only the clergy of the local presbytery as his audience, he would have the brethren of all Cincinnati. "My trial," he wrote in a letter in July 1835, "was the greatest blessing I have had happen to me in many a day, and the prospect is fine of two more opportunies of . . . defending and propagating all I believe and teach."

Henry Ward Beecher, now twenty-two and not especially absorbed by his divinity studies at Lane, accompanied his father to the meeting of the synod. The trial, held in Dayton, had its amusing as well as depressing aspects. The setting out was hectic:

As I emerged from my room, the doctor was standing in his study doorway, a book under each arm, with a third in his hands, in which he was searching for quotations. In an hour and a half all his papers were to be collected (and from whence!), books assorted, breakfast eaten, clothes packed, and horse harnessed.

After a hasty meal, he goes up stairs, opens every drawer, and paws over all the papers, leaving them in confusion, and down stairs again to the drawers in his study, which are treated in like manner. He fills his arms with books, and papers, and sermons, and straightway seems to forget what he wanted them for, for he falls to assorting them vigorously *de novo*.

Eight o'clock, and not half ready. Boat starts at nine.

"Where's my Burton?"

"Father, I have found the *Spirit of the Pilgrims*."

"Don't want it. Where did I put that paper of extracts? Can't you make out another? Where did I lay my opening notes? Here, Henry, put this book in the carriage. Stop! give it to me. Let's see—run up stairs for my Register. No. No! I've brought it down."

Half past eight, not ready. Three miles to go. Horse not up.

At length the doctor completes his assortment of books and papers, packs, or rather stuffs his clothes into a carpet bag—no key to lock it—ties the handles, and leaves it gaping.

At length we are ready to start. A trunk tumbles out of one side as Thomas [his eleven-year-old son] tumbles in the other. I reverse the order—tumble Tom out, the trunk in. At length all are aboard, and father drives out of the yard, holding the reins in one hand, shaking hands with a student with the other, giving Charles directions with his mouth—at least that part not occupied with an apple; for, since apples were plenty, he has made it a practice to drive with one rein in the right hand and the other in the left, with an apple in each, biting them alternately, thus raising and lowering the reins like threads on a loom. Away we go . . . the carriage bouncing and bounding over the stones, father alternately telling Tom how to get the harness mended, and showing me the true doctrine of original sin. Hurra! We thunder alongside the boat just in time.

That was the amusing part.

At the meeting itself, the preparations on the morning of the trial were, as Henry Ward described them, like those for a battle: "overhauling knapsacks, fixing flints, picking locks, fixing ammunition, cleaning muskets . . . then aids-de-camp riding to captain and corporal, from tent to tent, from man to man. It's all fever, all expectation—a bracing up the mind to meet all things. . . ."

Then, quite suddenly, young Henry puts flippancy aside; for one revealing moment, like the child who saw through the emperor's "new clothes," he perceives the men of the synod with a pitiless clarity bordering on contempt:

I never saw so many faces of clergymen and so few of them intellectual faces. The predominant expression is that of firmness (in many cases deepening into obstinacy), kind-heartedness, and honesty. As for deep thought seen in the eye or lineaments—for lofty expression—for the enthusiasm of genius—for that expression which comes from communion with great thoughts, with the higher feelings of poetry and religion, and even of speculation, there is an utter want of it. There is very little dignity of expression: It is homespun, sensible integrity which characterizes them; and the elders are just what forty or fifty common farmers would be supposed to be, except that for *eldership the soberest men are chosen, and as stupidity is usually graced with more gravity than great good sense,* the body of elders are not quite so acute in look as the higher class of working men.

The observation is all the more striking because it comes from a youth about to enter the church. Henry would never quite get over the disenchantment with presbyteries and other such bodies that he experienced in the time of his father's trials.

Once again Wilson thrust and Beecher parried, and once again, in the end, their peers voted to clear Beecher. They agreed that the charges of hypocrisy and unsound faith had not been proved, but they also declared that Beecher had "philosophized instead of exhibiting in simplicity and plainness" the doctrines of the Scriptures and that he had conveyed ideas inconsistent with the word of God. They therefore ordered him to be more guarded in the future and to publish his views just as he had presented them to the synod.

Again Beecher rejoiced, but again Wilson, fueled by endless reserves of zeal and sanctimony, served notice that he was appealing the decision, this time to the highest Presbyterian tribunal, the General Assembly. It was not until the assembly met, in Pittsburgh in May 1836, and Wilson saw that he would again not win that he consented to withdraw his charges.

But the orthodox were not appeased. Beecher's case dramatizing the difference between the Old School and the New School, now at the breaking point, had become a *cause célèbre*. The machinery of ecclesiastical politics ground on. Soon hostile articles, harsh reviews of his *Views in Theology*—the book written to satisfy the synod's order—and embarrassing extracts from his private correspondence began to appear in church periodicals. Their refrain was that he had equivocated, shifted his position from early to late, said one thing in public and another in private. Even some of his former supporters were drawn into questioning his integrity. Dr. Samuel Miller of Princeton, who had once urged him in a very flattering letter to accept a prominent pastorate in Philadelphia, now wrote to the Reverend Asahel Nettleton: "Is it possible to reconcile that man's whole course with a sound, honest, straightforward purpose? It would give me more pleasure than I can express to see him come out *bright*, and *entirely consistent*."

Bitter at last, Beecher cried out that all this was a trial without a trial, half truths, character assassinations, fanaticism, outright falsehoods. "They took burning arrows dipped in gall," he wrote, drawing on his rich store of military metaphor, "and shot them over into the Presbyterian camp. They rifled the graves of my dead friends, out of their ashes to evoke spectral accusations against me." For once he did not bounce back with a blithe quip. Years later he would still speak of those attacks with pain and indignation.

The fact was, in church disputes Beecher was often—whether out of honest doubt, or expediency, or a bit of both—betwixt and between. He was neither an unquestioning follower of Dr. Taylor, who wanted an open break with the Old School, nor a subscriber to the iron dogma of the Wilsons. It wasn't surprising that diehard conservatives believed that he did not preach "genuine, old-fashioned New England divinity." In their camp, zeal was tolerated but conformity was demanded.

If Lyman Beecher thought that the dismissal of Wilson's charges by the General Assembly was a triumph, he was soon to learn that it was the kind of victory that leads to ever more determined attacks.

As though a rebellion in the seminary and a trial for heresy—not to mention blame for the burning of a Catholic convent—were not enough tribulation for one year, private woe was added to Lyman Beecher's public ordeals: his second wife died in July 1835. Outwardly she died of consumption, but although she was only forty-four, she had long before died of morbid melancholy.

The obituaries and other references to her death fell back on platitudes, stressing her piety, refinement and intellect. Her children and husband spoke of her with respect but without love or the anguish of true loss. Indeed, one blunt obituary, signed "C"—was it by Catharine, who had never really accepted her?—declared that it was only after she had contritely acknowledged "her failings in her duty to others . . . that her spirit found peace." Some of the older children observed that they had not really known her. The younger ones remembered her as, at first, cool, neat and smiling, but as depression and illness took over, unsmiling and, so Hattie said, "hard, correct, exact and exacting."

The truth is that Harriet Porter Beecher had led a shadow life, the remote, passionless, resigned existence characteristic of many of the daughters of upper-class New England families of the nineteenth century. Her upbringing had unfitted her for any life except as a daughter in just the kind of family she had come from. She was not prepared for sexual love, children, a household not amply staffed, or any of the world's work that a woman might do.

Harriet Porter had all the makings of a spinster, and forlorn as spinsterhood might be, she probably would have been less unhappy in that role. But when Lyman Beecher arrived on the scene, she had reached the age of twenty-seven, she was commendably devout, and she had the elegance and beauty of a Sèvres figurine. And the eminent Dr. Beecher had carried her away with Scriptural quotations and little sermons combined with metaphors of love reminiscent of Donne. Your affection, he wrote, is like "gold shut up in a box," but your heart has made it "a box of perfumes," and he rejoiced that for him she had "broken the box & poured it out."

So Harriet Porter had committed herself to a poor man's parsonage. Although she had stayed on for eighteen years and borne Beecher four children (typically, the one that haunted her thoughts most was Frederick, who had died in infancy) and taken care of his other children, she had remained a visitor—a troubled, pensive transient. Increasingly, she had been unable or unwilling to cope with that swarm of individualistic children and their father—all of them, whether outgoing or inturned, making emotional demands she could not meet. Nor did it help matters that most of the children were not her own and were ever ready to compare her with the increasingly idealized image of their first mother.

The more that worldly problems faced her, the further Harriet Porter retreated into the darkling depths of her spirit. And the greater the vitality of those around her, the more she looked forward to the quiet of the grave and the peace beyond. After the shock of being torn from the old and settled world of Boston, hallowed home of the Pilgrims, she was relieved to find a secluded little graveyard "set about with weeping willows and shrubs" on the grounds of the seminary at Walnut Hills. Later it was reported that she had often spoken of the cemetery with delight, obviously as one who looked forward to resting there before long. When Calvin Stowe's lovely young wife, Eliza, with whom Harriet Porter had formed a close and tender friendship, died at the age of twenty-five, her grave became a haven where the ailing and despondent Harriet would go to rest and to commune with the spirit of her departed friend. Although illness and suffering darkened her last years, reaching a pitch of agony, Lyman's *Autobiography* makes much of the fact that in her final moments "the veil was lifted" and she died hearing the sounds of celestial music.

The assumption that the American family up to the twentieth century was a stable unit, remaining for generations in one home or at least one locality, is hardly borne out by the record of Lyman Beecher and his children. By 1832 he had moved from Guilford, Connecticut, to East Hampton, Long Island, to Litchfield, Connecticut, to Boston, to Cincinnati—and would later go back to Boston and finally to Brooklyn. His older children were already scattered over half a dozen states, and the "circular" letters to which each member of the family added a message sometimes went to as many as eight different addresses.

The more widely his offspring were scattered, the more the Reverend Dr. Beecher—especially as he grew older—tried to bring them together in a reunion. Now, ironically, while the earth was still fresh on Harriet Porter's grave, he succeeded.

Edward, returning to his Illinois college post after his annual trip east, persuaded his sister Mary in Hartford to go with him on a visit to Walnut Hills. William, who now had a church in Putnam, Ohio, and George, who was in Batavia, New York, settling into his first pastorate, decided to join them. Since Catharine had returned from one of her trips, and Hattie, Henry and Charles were home, as were Harriet Porter's three young children, Isabella, Thomas and James, suddenly all eleven of

Lyman Beecher's surviving children were together for the first time. So great were the gaps between them—Catharine was thirty-five years old, while James was seven—that Mary had seen Thomas only once and James not at all.

The "old doctor" was transported with joy: when all his children first gathered around him he attempted to say a prayer but could only weep. Finally they all joined hands and sang "Old Hundred." Edward preached in his father's pulpit in the morning, William in the afternoon and George in the evening. The event was fulsomely reported in the Cincinnati *Journal*. It was the first sign that the Beechers were becoming a famous family.

The harmony that reigned for those few days was a momentary flame lit by an aging father's spirit. It was a tribute, mostly by the older sons and daughters, to memories made precious by time. For three days all the differences in temperament and principle that would eventually dissolve family ties were swept away. For three days there were prayers and dinners, and reminiscences and hymn singing and finally a kiss from each to each and a prayer from Lyman as though it were the last time he would ever see them.

But life was hardly over for Lyman Beecher. Even though he no longer had an ever increasing brood to take care of, he soon set about getting a third wife. (After all, his father had had five.) This time it was Mrs. Lydia Jackson, a widow whom he had known as a member of his Bowdoin Street congregation in Boston. The owner of a boardinghouse frequented mostly by ministers, active in various benevolent societies, and the mother of six children, two of them married, she was a mature and very competent woman.

As usual, Beecher moved impetuously. Surprised by his blunt proposal, Mrs. Jackson pleaded for time: "Doctor, this is wholly unexpected. . . . It is a very serious question. I will think of it and make it a subject of prayer, and—" That was all Lyman Beecher needed. "Yes, yes . . ." he exclaimed, "let us pray over it now," and sinking to his knees, he began praying with all his natural fervor. His prayer was answered.

Far more practical minded and energetic than her two predecessors, Mrs. Jackson put the Beecher household—it included two of her own children—in order. To the amusement of his older children, she also soon had Beecher, for the first time in his life, looking spruce. "Our only fear is that father may yet turn out a dandy . . ." Catharine wrote in 1837. "And she is such a fine-looking woman herself that both together make folks turn around to see if that *can be* Dr. Beecher."

Lydia Jackson even helped the Doctor with his church duties, especially when these began to try his patience. It was fortunate for Lyman Beecher that he found Lydia Jackson when he did; it was a pity for her that she was not with him in his best years but only in the troubled aftermath of the Lane rebellion and the trials and in the long years of his decline.

Contributing to the split between the New School and the Old was the growing quarrel over slavery. Although the Presbyterian Church as a whole was unsympathetic to the radical antislavery movement, such rabid abolitionists as William Lloyd Garrison, Theodore Weld and Elijah Lovejoy were Northerners, Presbyterian, and puritanical to boot. Moved by the same spirit as the revivalist preachers, they constantly branded slaveholders sinners. By the late 1830s, Southern Presbyterians were already taking a violent stand against such radicals.

The slavery question was argued in the Presbyterian General Assembly of 1836, the same meeting that acquitted Beecher. When a report of this discussion reached the Reverend Witherspoon, a South Carolina clergyman, he poured out his passions in a letter to Beecher. He deplored the whole idea of a split in the Presbyterian Church, he wrote, but if a division was inevitable, it would take place at the Mason and Dixon line; then Southern ministers would surely be excluded from Northern churches, and Northern ministers would be "driven from the South" or hung from the nearest lamppost. "Yet *so it will be* if the Abolitionists rule," he continued. ". . . I have been a slaveholder from my youth, and yet I detest it as the *political and domestic curse* of our Southern country; *and yet I would contend to the death* against Northern interference with Southern rights. . . ." Well before it became standard Southern doctrine, he put the blame for all unrest and trouble on Northern agitators:

Abolitionism leads to *murder, rapine,* and every vile crime that an enthusiastic ignorant slave could commit, and therefore I *abhor* Abolitionism and *detest the Abolitionist.* It was well that I was not on the floor of the last Assembly; but if God spare me, I shall be on the floor of the next; and let Lovejoy, or Patterson, or Dickey [New School clergymen], or any like them, *dare* to advance the opinions I have expressed, and—the consequences be *theirs.*

As early as 1832 the *Princeton Review,* an Old School journal, had recommended a plan of reorganization by which the churches in the slaveholding states would be separated from those in the Northern states. Years later, looking back, Beecher himself saw abolitionism rather than slavery itself as the underlying cause of the split in the church.

The South [he said] had generally stood neutral. . . . But they got scared about abolition. Rice [a Virginia clergyman] got his head full of that thing, and others. John C. Calhoun was at the bottom of it. I know of his doing things—writing to ministers, and telling them to do this and do that. The South finally took the Old School side. It was a cruel thing—it was a cursed thing, and 'twas slavery that did it.

Beecher refers to the great South Carolinian—senator, secretary of war, twice vice-president, secretary of state—as though Calhoun's part in the struggle between North and South were only an aspect of the Presbyterian controversy. Calhoun was a staunch Presbyterian, but his concern was not with New School or Old but with church support for the Southern slave power.

The fuse finally reached the powder keg in the General Assembly of 1837. The Old School, holding a majority, summarily renounced the 1801 Plan of Union that had linked the Presbyterians and the Congregationalists. They thereby cut away four synods, representing six hundred churches in New York and Ohio. Outraged, the New School faction waited till the next annual General Assembly and then went to the meeting place, a church in Philadelphia, determined to regain at any cost a place for the ousted synods.

But the Old School party was ready for them. When a New School spokesman—urged on by cries from Beecher and Taylor—demanded an explanation of the ouster, he was told, "We do not know you, sir," and "It is out of order, sir." Amid a bedlam of shouting from both camps, with ministers standing on the seats of their pews, a New School leader announced that the four synods had been unlawfully expelled and would withdraw at once and form a new general assembly. Then the rebels, with Lyman and Edward Beecher (who had become a leading defender of the militant abolitionist Reverend Elijah Lovejoy) among them, marched down the aisle and out of the church.

Beecher triumphantly asserted that the assembly, taken by surprise, was left in a state of "utter paralysis." But one church historian declares that the assembly considered itself well rid of a source of discord and resumed its business without a qualm. And the following year it elected Joshua Lacy Wilson its moderator.

The episode would have been the sensation of the season in Philadelphia had not the Anti-Slavery Society at the same time held a convention in its new, forty-thousand-dollar building, called Abolition Hall, on Sixth Street and promptly brought an attack by a mob. A Lane Seminary student who witnessed the episode reported how Angelina Grimké—married only a few days earlier to Theodore Weld—had addressed the convention, giving a firsthand account of the horrors of slavery and urging immediate emancipation. The mob responded by breaking the windows of the hall. Miss Grimké talked on, delivering a memorable address. The following afternoon the rioters again gathered outside the hall and watched in tense silence until, seeing "a huge Negro darken the door arm-in-arm with a fair Quaker girl, they screamed and swore vengeance." They set fire to the hall while the mayor, the sheriff and firemen looked on and did nothing. An investigation later revealed that the "huge Negro" and the "fair Quaker girl" were a black couple, Robert Purvis and his light-skinned wife.

The next day crowds raged through the streets once again and, encouraged by their success of the day before, set fire to the Shelter for Colored Orphans, called African Hall, on Thirteenth Street. This time the authorities managed to save the building. "That the Convention had been imprudent there is no doubt," the young seminarian concluded, "but that the rabble in the midst of an enlightened and powerful community should be permitted to trample on all laws is shameful."

So, amid the mutual rage of Old School and New, and the wrath of a rabble against both black and white abolitionists, the Presbyterian Church of the United States broke in two. It would not come together again in the lifetime of Lyman Beecher.

Meanwhile Lane languished. The result of the Weld rebellion was the loss not only of more than fifty students but of prospective students and supporters alienated by Lane's position on both the antislavery issue and freedom of speech. Ironically, even as the antislavery press stigmatized Lane as unfriendly to their cause, groups in Cincinnati continued to refer to the school as a center of antislavery activity—and would do so for many years.

Once, in 1841, after days of riots between Irish and Negroes had rocked the city, a gang of roughs, believing rumors that Negroes had taken refuge at Lane, threatened to attack the seminary. The road to Lane was long and very muddy, but the students began to prepare themselves. As Beecher gleefully recounted it, "I told the boys that . . . they could arm themselves and if the mob came they could shoot." His voice dropping to a stage whisper, he would add, "but I told them not to kill 'em," just to "hit 'em in the legs! hit 'em in the legs!"

Neither view—that Lane was actively for or against the antislavery cause—was justified. But both views hurt the school.

The financial panic of 1837 was another blow. Lewis Tappan's business suffered and he curtailed his philanthropies sharply. A terse note in Beecher's daybook in July 1837 records one painful result: "I have this morning received a letter from New York informing me that my draft on Mr. Tappan has been dishonored on account of his suspension of payments."

The impact on Lane of all these events was disastrous: the entering classes from 1836 to 1840 averaged only five students. Salaries ceased and friends fell away. Everyone connected with the school was discouraged—except Lyman Beecher. Whenever Professor Stowe grew particularly gloomy, Beecher would say: "Come, let us get by this pinch, and then we'll have plain sailing." When Stowe's bleaker predictions came true, Beecher merely shifted to saying, "Come, Stowe, let us get by this pinch, and then we'll get ready for the next." It was useful to be able to view everyday events in the light of eternity.

But a day finally came, in 1845, when there were no students at all for the next class. (It was also a year of drought so acute that people could wade across the Ohio River.) Stowe despaired. Several other professors left. But Beecher, a high-pressure salesman in the name of the Lord, simply went out and scoured the countryside: he got five students from Marietta College, lured a young businessman from Louisville, and begged half a dozen other young men from Illinois College, where his son Edward was president. When he returned to the seminary he found Stowe in bed, sick with despair. According to Beecher, Stowe thought it was "all over—of no use—might just as well leave, and go back East. . . .' 'Stowe,' said I, 'I've brought you twelve students. You've got no faith, and I've got nothing but faith. Get up and wash, and eat bread, and prepare to have a good class.' The consequence was a class of thirteen next year, and the following year thirty-five."

Meanwhile Beecher was forced to borrow and scrounge to keep himself and his family, small though it now was, clothed and fed. At one point he had to beg his son George for two hundred dollars even while admitting that he could not be expected to pay it back. "Poverty and debt," he said, "added to all that is on me, will break me down and end my life." Repeatedly he raised money from affluent friends of the seminary for his personal support as professor and president. Later he declared that he felt no embarrassment in making such an appeal because he had secured the primary endowments for the school as well as the means to erect its buildings and furnish its library—not to mention the thousands of dollars the seminary owed him in back salary. Whatever weaknesses he may have had, hunger for money or property was not one of them. As soon as the crises had receded and he had resumed a stable way of life, he was content to scrape along.

Preaching as often as ever, hurrying around the countryside to help with revivals and prayer meetings, he could assume that he had weathered the worst and that quieter days lay ahead. He could even acknowledge how painful the period of crises had been. In the privacy of a letter to Lydia, written while he was at a revival in Oxford, Ohio, in 1839, he says: "The Lord has permitted the accumulation upon me, for the last two years, in domestic and public cares, and anxieties, and labors, a greater pressure of responsibility and suspense, and baffled plans and hopes, than ever before in my life." Only to his wife did he admit that his heart had been "sickened by hope deferred" and his nervous system taxed to the breaking point.

But one thing Beecher would never admit was that he had made a mistake in leaving Boston and going West. Beecher was a spiritual and emotional force, not a logician or a church diplomat: in going West he had lost his way. As the Reverend James White, one of his "converts" in Boston and then one of his older students at Lane, declared, "Like a mighty locomotive engine he had leaped his track in coming West." He was never at home with his Cincinnati congregation, White said, and his power as a preacher was never the same again.

Nor did Beecher ever acknowledge that his dream of winning the West for Calvinism and leading in the grand procession toward universal redemption had been shattered. Despite Calvinism's lack of faith in man's capacity to choose good over evil, Beecher, with typical pioneer optimism, had gone West confident that men would achieve the millennium there. His hopes had been frustrated not because men preferred evil but because they had other dreams—dreams in which the church played no part.

Born in 1775 into a world where the great Puritan divines were still revered figures dominating New England society, Beecher simply did not see that the Revolution, democracy and the pioneer condition were all reducing clergymen to the status of mere functionaries in a secondary social institution. Nor did he realize that the very drive westward was motivated in part by an urge to be free of the constraints of a Puritan theocracy.

Even as Lane limped along with only forty or fifty students, Beecher's relationship to his congregation deteriorated. Although he had brought hundreds of communicants into the fold in his eleven years at the Second Presbyterian Church, in time the gulf between him and the social elite in his congregation widened. Just as he had impressed polite society in Boston as something of a curiosity, with his country humor, temperance campaigns and evangelical ardor, so in Cincinnati he antagonized the wealthier families in his church with criticism of what he considered their extravagances. As late as 1840 he took to task Nathaniel Wright, prominent lawyer, Lane trustee, and elder of the church, for lavish entertainment and balls. He even asserted that these hampered his efforts to bring young people to conversion. "My heart is sick" he wrote, ". . . in the prospect of my unsustained and obstructed ministry."

The charge was presumptuous and tactless, and Wright rejected it as such. He gave Beecher to understand that it was really none of his business and that such a view would be held only by someone unacquainted with the ways of polite society. It was a confrontation between rural New England, puritanical, frugal, and provincial, and urban America, affluent, successful, and relatively sophisticated, between religion as all-pervasive and religion as confined to the church. In the end a policy disagreement with Beecher led the congregation to ask for his resignation. So in 1843 he left his post at the church.

For the first time in forty years the Reverend Lyman Beecher had no pulpit or congregation of his own. Although he continued periodically to help with revivals around the countryside, the big gun of eastern Calvinism was more and more an aged clergyman whose great days were past. Not that he accepted his fate readily: when a speaker at a Missions Board conference in New York in 1845 was introduced in his stead and explained that "owing to the infirmities of age or the fatigue of travel, the celebrated Dr. Beecher" would not be able to deliver an address, Beecher leaped to his feet, crying, "Infirmity! Why, sir, I was never better in my life," and gave a missionary speech "full of fire, impulse and Beecherism."

At another time, when a speaker at an antislavery temperance meeting described Massachusetts as having retreated from its former temperance position and "let go" some fundamental principles, Beecher literally vaulted onto the platform in the midst of a crowd of distillers and saloon-keepers and shouted, "Old Massachusetts 'let go'! Old Massachusetts 'let go'! *I tell* you she has only let go to spit on her hands!" And then he launched into a scorching attack on the enemy. There were also the residual honors accorded an elder statesman of the church. When General William Henry Harrison came to Cincinnati in 1840, campaigning for the Presidency with his tale of being born in a log cabin, Dr. Beecher was seated on the speaker's platform as evidence of Harrison's support among the most respectable citizens, especially those who had the ear of God. And a few years later, when Lyman and Lydia visited Washington, they were received by President Polk at the White House. But these were only polite gestures, agreeable but of no consequence. Obsessively Beecher continued to issue warnings of the dangers of Catholicism and Unitarianism, but few paid any attention: the Queen City on the Ohio was becoming more mixed and cosmopolitan with every passing year. Its population of almost fifty thousand now included fifteen thousand Germans, most of them Catholic, and an increasing number of Irish, almost all of them Catholic, a sprinkling of Jews, and other "alien" elements. Gone was any possibility of achieving the homogeneity, the pristine "purity," of New England.

Long after it should have mattered to anyone, the Old School adherents returned to the assault on Lyman Beecher. Having allowed him to complete one last act of public service, a trip to London in 1846, to attend a World Temperance Convention, David Kemper, an Old School man and a member of the family that had founded Lane, sued to have Dr. Beecher ousted as professor and president at the seminary. The writ with which Beecher was served demanded *quo warranto,* by what right, he held his posts at Lane Seminary. The claim was that Lane was a Presbyterian institution and that only Old School ministers were true and legal Presbyterians. Beecher was fortunate enough to get Salmon P. Chase, later a senator, the secretary of the treasury in Lincoln's cabinet, and finally chief justice of the Supreme Court, to defend him.

Chase argued that it was foolish to claim, fifteen years after the fact, that Beecher had not been a Presbyterian when he was appointed or that he should be held responsible for the split in the Presbyterian Church that had given rise to the charge. Beecher was upheld, but it tried him sorely to be called an impostor and usurper in a cause for which he had worked with immense hope, energy and devotion. "It was a vexatious suit," he said, "and vexatious enough they found it . . . but we outwinded them."

But he was approaching, as he said, three score and ten, and his days at Lane were numbered. To Henry Ward, who had been called from an Indiana parish to a prominent church in Brooklyn, he wrote ruefully: "For the first time in my public life I have now no pastoral responsibilities and stated preaching on the Sabbath. . . . What shall I do—a soul without a body? But . . . preach I must, so long as flesh and heart fail not."

Still deeply attuned to her father, Catharine was saddened to see him being thrust aside. Remembering his days of glory in Boston, she wrote to Henry's wife, Eunice: "There are *small minds* at helm now in these parts and the sooner father is put where he can have full scope and fair appreciation the better for him. . . . It will add years to his life to put him in the right place, and that *now* is not *at the West.*"

There were other evidences of Lyman's age: all his children had grown up and gone from home, and when those who were married wrote to him they spoke more and more often of their own children. Several members of the family who had gone west were now returning to the East. Not only was Henry Ward in New York but Edward had resigned as president of Illinois College in 1844 and gone to Salem Church in Boston. Thomas, having graduated from Illinois College, was at Yale Divinity School, and Harriet had moved to Brunswick, Maine, where her husband, Calvin Stowe, was teaching at Bowdoin.

So when he retired from his professorship at Lane in 1851, Beecher found his gaze turning back to the place where he had begun, had spent his best years, and brought up his brood of extraordinary children. Perhaps it was another sign of growing old that while most Americans were dreaming of going west, he should, like sap retreating to roots in late autumn, be readying to withdraw to the country of his fathers.

Even after working for eighteen years in triple harness—as pastor, professor and president—he was once again penniless. "When we closed up at Lane," Lydia reported, "we sold all our goods and chattels for $300"; and even this pittance, which they were supposed to receive in monthly installments, was never paid in full. Beecher had always been not so much improvident as vaguely, almost blithely, reliant on Providence and the good will of God. Because Lydia was so expert at making ends meet, it had been easy for him to say, "The Lord has always taken care of me, and I am sure he always will." Lydia, not at all so sanguine, worried herself sleepless.

Significantly, there is no description of how Lyman Beecher and his wife left Cincinnati and returned to Boston. It must have been a quiet, perhaps even poignant departure, not an actively unhappy moment but with no band of high-spirited children to accompany them—no army with banners flying—no sense of embarking on a great mission or a noble adventure, no grand hopes and shining visions. Only an old man and his wife closing out a career.

Beecher's main plan was to write his autobiography and publish his sermons and other papers—in short, to spend much of his time looking backward.

Lyman Beecher in the 1840s during his presidency of Lane Seminary.

Alexander Metcalf Fisher, a brilliant young professor of mathematics at Yale as painted by inventor-painter Samuel F. B. Morse about 1820, shortly before Fisher's betrothal to Catharine Beecher.

Catharine Beecher in a
photograph by Mathew Brady,
probably made when she was in
her early fifties and at the peak of
her career as an educator
of young women.

Mary Beecher Perkins, wife of a
Hartford lawyer, was the only
Beecher who had no professional
career. She lived to the age of
ninety-five.

Edward Beecher in 1855, before
leaving Boston's Salem Street
Church to become pastor of a
church in Galesburg, Ohio.

Harriet Beecher Stowe, from a
daguerreotype by Southworth and
Hawes, probably made in
the early 1850s.

Henry Ward Beecher and Thomas K. Beecher in the early 1840s, when Henry was about thirty years old and Thomas about nineteen.

Charles Beecher in about 1859, not long before he was charged with heresy by his fellow ministers in Massachusetts.

10

CATHARINE

A Dream for Women and the West

Except for Lyman himself, none of the Beechers came to Cincinnati with higher hopes than Catharine. The city had everything she could desire: a pleasant setting, an intelligent, sociable and prosperous upper class, and above all a group eager to have a good school for young women.

Since many of the leading citizens came from Litchfield, Hartford and other familiar New England places, Catharine had immediate access to the city's social elite. Her uncle Samuel Foote, retired sea captain, was now a successful investor in western public works. And because he was related to Harriet Porter, she considered Edward King, who had married Sarah Worthington, daughter of the governor of Ohio, a cousin. Long before, King had attended Litchfield Law School and had even squired Catharine here and there.

Perhaps the most conspicuous way this elite carried on New England cultural traditions was in its literary and intellectual cliques. Pretentious though they might seem by Boston standards, they were impressive evidence of how far and fast the city had come from its pioneer origins. The best known of these groups was the Semi-Colon Club. Its weekly "soirees" were usually held in Samuel Foote's spacious Georgian home and its members included such local luminaries as Judge James Hall, editor of the new *Western Monthly Magazine,* Caroline Lee Hentz, the leading "literary lady," and young Salmon P. Chase. The meetings were given over to polite conversation, music, poetry and the reading of an essay or literary contribution by one of the members. Afterwards, refreshments were served and the group danced a reel or two.

Both Catharine and Harriet soon joined the club, Catharine delighting almost as much in the elegance of the gatherings as in the intellectual stimulation, and Harriet timidly trying out her first literary efforts there. It was also one of the few groups in which women were on the same intellectual footing as men. (Even such a professional association as the Western Literary Institute and College of Professional Teachers ex-

cluded women except as observers.) One of Catharine's contributions was
a description of "Castle Ward, the residence of my ancestors on my
mother's side." Giving the impression that the home in Nutplains was a
mansion on an estate, the piece was evidently intended to establish her
social credentials—as much for the sake of her school as for her personal
luster.

Catharine was also a regular guest at literary evenings in the home
of the Beechers' family physician, Dr. Daniel Drake. A controversial,
many-sided figure, Drake had earned the title "the Franklin of Cincinnati" with his remarkable scientific, cultural and philanthropic activities.
He had helped found a college, a hospital, two medical schools and a
library, and as early as 1815 had published a celebration of his adopted
city, *Picture of Cincinnati*. At his place as well as the homes of other
leading families, Catharine was at first welcomed as an informed, able
and very bright if rather opinionated young woman.

Before long she was riding to church in the carriage of Mrs. Jacob
Burnet, wife of a judge of the Supreme Court of Ohio, and spending time
with Charles Hammond, editor of the influential *Gazette*. In summer,
along with the wealthier families of the city, she went north to Yellow
Springs to escape the cholera that still scourged Cincinnati from time to
time.

Her ascent of the social ladder had been very rapid and her hopes
ran high.

Catharine had lost no time in getting a new school under way.
Within two months of her arrival at Walnut Hills she was writing to
Mary Dutton, her favorite assistant in Hartford, urging her to come to
Cincinnati to start "a school of the first-rate order, which shall be a
model to the West." But she also made clear that she herself would not
teach. She was not only subject to periods of poor health—chiefly nervous
exhaustion—but tired of classroom routine. Just as important, she now
saw herself as an originator of new types of schools, an educator who
should be free of any duties except the recruiting and training of young
women to teach in the deprived regions of the West. "I should love to
come and *preach* and sometimes to *teach* and Harriet would like the
same," she wrote to Mary Dutton, "and if we assumed no obligation or
responsibility, we could do it without feeling burdened." Miss Dutton
succumbed to Catharine's blandishments, and a week after she arrived, in
April 1833, Catharine announced the opening of the Western Female
Institute.

For a time Catharine lived in the city itself in order to be close to the
school. But for the next two years, conveniently supported by the school,
she divided her time between social activities and writing, lecturing or

otherwise spreading the gospel of education according to Catharine Beecher. Finally, in the spring of 1835, in a lecture sponsored by the American Lyceum in New York, she presented a plan for employing women as teachers and, at the same time, educating the "ignorant masses." It was so well received that the sponsors published it as *An Essay on the Education of Female Teachers.*

Here again is the characteristic mixture that made Catharine Beecher at once a pioneer and a conservative—original and innovative in some respects, cautious and even reactionary in others. The traditional image of a woman, she asserts, must be discarded: " . . . instead of the fainting, weeping, vapid, pretty play-thing, once the model of female loveliness, those qualities of the head and heart that qualify a woman for her duties are demanded and admired." This seems to promise a new ideal—until Catharine defines the word "duties," to wit: acting as "guardian of the nursery," "presiding genius . . . of domestic business," accommodating to the "peculiarities and frailties of a husband," and controlling the "indolence" and "waywardness" of servants. Husbands, be it noted, are problems and servants are untrustworthy. In other words, instead of being playthings, women are to be homebodies—always mothers and wives but never independent human beings. Even as she liberates women—that is, of the upper class—from idleness, she announces that their place, their power base, the headquarters of their operations, is in the home.

Catharine's recommendations for courses of instruction are also a mixture of the new and the traditional. Committing facts to memory is not enough; just as important is cultivating accuracy, as in the study of mathematics, or stimulating the imagination, as in the study of poetry. But even more important is moral and religious education, with the Bible as the arbiter of right and wrong. Such instruction is the chief safeguard against vice, indolence and irreligion. Still clinging to a Calvinist dictum, Catharine asserts that such education has been neglected because intellectual superiority has been valued too highly. And it is women as wives and mothers, she concludes, who are best fitted and in the best position to set standards of virtue and piety as well as intelligence. In her eagerness to win for women both teaching opportunities and control of the domestic scene, Catharine reinforces the Victorian view that women are and should be more virtuous and pious than men.

The increase in the number of teachers, she continues, will also serve to bring education to the vast number of native children who get no schooling at all and to the hordes of "degraded foreigners . . . pouring into this nation at every avenue." Much as her father had argued in *A Plea for the West* for training ministers who would save the souls of benighted immigrants, Catharine pleaded for teachers who would lead the same immigrants away from otherwise inevitable barbarism and anarchy.

Marching side by side under the banners of education and religion, Catharine and her father would save the West from darkness and damnation.

But just as Lyman Beecher's vision of himself as the spiritual savior from the East irked independent-minded Westerners, so did Catharine's assumption that she had the magic educational formula for protecting the West from degenerate foreigners. When, moreover, word came that her father's diatribes against Catholics in Boston had been followed by the burning of a convent, many Cincinnatians saw both father and daughter as agitators bringing eastern discord to the West.

The East-West antagonism was underscored when, as we have seen, a magazine article by James Hall, judge and editor, ridiculed the Reverend Beecher's fear of Catholics. Such antipathies help to explain why Catharine's campaign to gain moral and financial support for her school failed. Even though a meeting intended to raise the thirty thousand dollars she needed was chaired by influential Nathaniel Wright—it would have been most unladylike for Catharine to conduct it herself—it came to naught. There was no active hostility, but simply a lack of enthusiasm, especially of the kind that leads people to open their purses.

As damaging as her sharing of her father's prejudices was the shadow cast over her by his troubles at Lane. To the older families the abolitionist uproar at the seminary was disturbing because it threatened the friendly relations between Northerners and Southerners in the town, sowed unrest in the black community, and was in general a source of dissension. No matter that Beecher had not encouraged the rebels; neither had he suppressed them, and he had even participated in their incendiary debates.

Ignoring such signs, Catharine continued to assert herself. Accustomed to domineer, she now tried to stir up opposition to Hall and Drake. She even urged that they be excluded from the homes as well as the clubs of the socially elect. This was a double mistake: it converted a matter of principles into one of personalities and it provoked the gentry into closing ranks against her as a presumptuous outsider. Considering her youth, lack of social standing and late arrival on the Cincinnati scene, it is surprising how much hostility she managed to arouse.

A basic blunder was her special effort to enlist Edward King and his wife, Sarah, in her campaign against Hall and Drake. Mrs. King, daughter of the governor, and King himself, the son of austere Rufus King, ambassador to Great Britain and senator from New York, would have been a powerful pair of allies. Although she thought of Ned King as an "old Litchfield beau," he was actually a snobbish aristocrat. This may explain his harsh warnings against "cousin" Catharine. Tell Catharine, he wrote his wife in December 1834, that she is "a guest and not a director in our home," and tell all the Beechers that "if they choose to visit and partake when invited, it is well, but . . . not as our advisors as to when and how and with whom they are to mingle at our fireside."

Only an inflated notion of her importance could have persuaded Catharine Beecher to oppose such prominent\men as Hall and Drake. Her error was in supposing that her intellectual accomplishments would offset the fact that she was a poor and very distant relation. With the condescension of the chosen, King found Catharine too enthusiastic, too aggressive and much too ambitious.

In a remarkably candid letter, King gave his wife a withering account of Catharine's endless inquisitiveness during a visit to Chillicothe in the summer of 1835. As they toured the countryside, he writes, she asked "more questions than anyone could answer in a day. Why the fields were so square! Why there were not better houses! . . . Whose property was this and that!" Later she asked "whether mother managed her farm, whether she gave orders to the men . . . what was the price of *help*. . . ." Seizing on that ultimate test of good breeding, table manners, he wrote: "She devoured all before her and *licked her fingers*." Catharine went further: in her association with King's niece Lizzy she assumed that she was a model even in the matter of clothes. "She asked Lizzy how she liked her riding dress," King wrote, "if she had ever seen one like it, that she had made it and set the fashion in Cincinnati. . . ."

Just before she left, Catharine climaxed her breaches of propriety by asking King to join in her feud with Hall. King, his patience exhausted, told her that the difficulty had begun with the Beechers' attempt to lord it over the intellectual society of the city, and that he himself would "promote the Western Society until the emigrants thought proper to yield to the customs and habits of the people amidst whom they might come and not endeavor to establish their own rules for the regulation of society." He warned Catharine that her hope of replacing Hall as editor of his journal with someone more favorable to her views would not succeed. King even drew satisfaction from the way Mrs. King's mother had spoken out against "the abolitionists and peace destroyers in the church."

"I think," he concluded, "*cousin* had on the whole a hard time."

But Catharine was either insensitive to snubs or too engrossed in her schemes to take note of personal rejection. When a project was thwarted or defeated, she simply lost interest in it and moved on.

Aware by 1836 that her school was foundering, she began to pursue her goals elsewhere. But first she attempted, in a book entitled *Letters on the Difficulties of Religion*, to set forth her own position on the controversies vexing the church. Obviously to disarm the orthodox, she pleaded for tolerance of other people's views and the avoidance of "personalities." But her bias in favor of her father's position, especially on the outworn issues of free agency versus "fatalism," is clear. With even more confidence than her father, she asserted she was sure "God does not require anything of us but what we have *full ability* to perform." According to one legend, it was such a passage that led Catharine's new brother-in-law, Professor Stowe, to tell a famous German theologian that his sister-in-law had written the ablest refutation of Jonathan Edwards's celebrated discourse on the will.

"What a woman!" the theologian is said to have exclaimed, "refute Edwards on the Will! God forgive Christopher Columbus for discovering such a country!"

Even more challenging was Catharine's blithe declaration that "any man who sincerely and habitually loves his Maker, so as to make it the chief object and effort to discover his will and obey it, will secure eternal happiness." According to this theory, a shocked critic wrote, "it is our own inherent righteousness or moral goodness by which we are rendered acceptable to God, and not by the merit or righteousness of Christ, which is never once mentioned. . . . This is surely . . . completely subversive of the gospel of Christ."

Nor did her promise to avoid personal attacks prevent her from holding up Robert Owen's utopian colony, New Harmony, as an example of the folly of "practical atheism" and the "wild vagaries of lunacy." But it was her assault on Fanny Wright that revealed her willingness to damn even a pioneer in the women's rights movement to serve her own ends: " . . . who can look without disgust and abhorrence upon such an one as Fanny Wright, with her great masculine person, her loud voice, her untasteful attire . . . her mingling with men in stormy debate, and standing up with bare-faced impudence to lecture to a public assembly. . . . " Recalling that Mrs. Trollope, who could be as cruel a critic as any, thought Fanny Wright a quite wonderful woman, we may well see Catharine's description as a spiteful appeal to absurd prejudices. Just so had her father declared that no woman could address a public meeting without loss of that female delicacy which is above all price.

Having found an excuse to get away from the problems of the school, Catharine spent from April to October 1836 visiting cities in half a dozen states. At each stop she announced that she hoped to form an organization that would help women find, and reach, suitable teaching posts. She collected the names of over one hundred women willing to serve as "missionary teachers" as well as of various women and men who would help finance the project. It was all intensely gratifying to Catharine, combining a position of importance, a chance to travel, wide social acceptance and the promise of a new career.

The opportunity came not a day too soon. When Catharine set out on her grand tour as educational apostle, she had told Mary Dutton not to trouble her with the school's problems. But the problems, and especially the falling away of students, were too much for Miss Dutton. Repeatedly she sent discouraged reports to Catharine; the latter either ignored them or, what was more exasperating, sent back such lofty exhortations as ". . . we teachers are to work not for money, nor for influence, nor for honor, nor for ease, but with the simple single purpose of doing good."

Finally in the spring of 1837, it became evident that the school was doomed. Catharine's response was to fire off a long letter, signed "Charitus," to the Cincinnati *Gazette,* blaming the city for its lack of interest in educating its young women. But several other female academies in the area were doing well enough. The fact is that Catharine—and Lyman as well—had antagonized many of the middle-class and socially ambitious families to whom the school was meant to appeal. In a petulant letter to Mary Dutton, she typically glossed over her responsibility for the school's failure with exaggerated claims of altruistic motives and sacrifices:

I began this school as a matter of self-denial, giving up ease and literary pursuits and the ability to make more money by my pen for the responsibilities, care, and vexation of a school that has been more plague to me than all I suffered in Hartford for ten years. I did it because father wished it, because Harriet needed some means of immediate support . . . and from the hope of doing good.

So after only four years, the Western Female Institute closed its doors. Since she had raised the money for the school, Catharine did not hesitate to pocket all tuition fees still due and whatever was realized from the sale of furnishings. When Mary Dutton protested rather pathetically that she had lost five hundred dollars in the school, an unseemly exchange followed, with Catharine tartly rebuking both Mary and Harriet. She argued over sums as little as fifteen dollars until Harriet, normally no match for Catharine in such matters, finally exclaimed, "What is that between thee and me?" And Mary Dutton was deeply offended.

Insult was added to failure when the institute was reopened by the Catholic church as a school for nuns.

As a leader in educating women and in helping them secure independence as teachers, Catharine Beecher had achieved a reputation second only to that of Emma Willard and Mary Lyon. But her experiences, together with the influence of the Bible and perhaps the example of her mother, had convinced her that women must accept or, rather, make the most of a dependent and submissive role. Women could accomplish more, she firmly believed, through persuasion and guidance than through the militant assertion of their rights or through challenges to male supremacy.

Now, quite suddenly, several women, and one in particular, Angelina Grimké, stood up and declared that there was no reason whatever for women to accept an inferior position. Because she felt the same way about blacks, Miss Grimké was also an uncompromising abolitionist. It was hard to explain her away as a malcontent or misfit; she came from a leading South Carolina family; she was a religious woman who had changed from Presbyterian to Quaker out of the profoundest principles; she had seen slavery firsthand and, except in defense of her social views, she was a decorous young lady. There is, in short, no simple explanation of why she and her much older sister Sarah should have, almost alone among Southern women of the time, questioned the entire institution of slavery, the inferior position of women, and even the dominant Protestant churches of Southern culture.

On religious, moral and humanitarian grounds, the sisters had been appalled by the treatment of slaves. Sarah had seen a friend's handsome mulatto girl, who had repeatedly tried to run away, subjected to whippings, to an iron collar with iron prongs jutting from it, and to having a sound front tooth knocked out so she could be easily identified if she ever tried to escape again. Angelina had witnessed similar punishment in a Southern workhouse.

Both women were also unsatisfied with the empty and vain lives led by many Southern belles. So when Sarah visited Philadelphia, she found in the Quaker persuasion something closer to her dream of what one's spiritual and daily life should be. It set her once and for all on unorthodox paths. Angelina, a much more self-confident young woman, followed these paths even more readily.

Both women were thus ripe for rebellion when anti-abolitionist riots broke out in New York and Philadelphia and soon included Negroes and such moderate antislavery figures as the poet John Greenleaf Whittier and the Quaker teacher Prudence Crandall. Along with these outbursts came William Lloyd Garrison's *Liberator,* challenging white hypocrisy and inhumanity with an intensity that troubled Angelina Grimké beyond all bearing. Indeed, Angelina's first act in support of abolition was a passionate letter to Garrision. "The ground upon which you stand is holy ground," she wrote; "—never surrender it." It was meant as a personal tribute, but Garrison, recognizing its extraordinary significance, printed it.

Overnight Angelina Grimké became a model of the sensitive Southerner who abominated slavery and wanted it abolished immediately. Deeply stirred by the strong reaction to her letter, she was drawn heart and soul into the abolitionist movement. The result, in the fall of 1836, was her *Appeal to the Christian Women of the Southern States.*

She called upon women to persuade all the men they knew that *"slavery is a crime against God and man."* She urged immediate action: women who owned slaves should set them free and begin to pay them for their work. They must also educate their slaves whether or not it was against the law. Finally, women must petition their legislators even though they might be met with jeers. The arguments were not new but the appeal was bold, unequivocal, and immeasurably ahead of its time.

The Grimké sisters had met Theodore Weld and were deeply impressed by him, Angelina referring to him as "the lion of the tribe of Abolitionists." Along with forty men, they now submitted to intensive instruction by him in antislavery theory and practice. They emerged from the training as the first female abolitionist agents and plunged at once into a crowded schedule of lectures and debates, many in churches. So effective were such lecturers that Connecticut Congregationalist ministers, led by Leonard Bacon and his friend Lyman Beecher, soon voted to ban all "itinerant agents" from speaking in churches without special consent. The Quakers took similar steps. To the growing disappointment of the Grimkés, the Friends also disapproved of their activities. Indeed, the sisters found that they were being attacked more as militant women than as abolitionists. Perhaps piqued by the increasing fame of the Grimkés as champions of women as well as of slaves, Catharine now joined the assault on them.

Cincinnati's situation in a North-South border state had made abolition a dangerously divisive issue there. After an outburst of racial violence in 1829, the city introduced restrictive codes that drove out a majority of the large population of blacks. In mid-decade the Lane debates aroused bitter anti-abolitionist sentiment, and in the summer of 1836, in a landmark in antislavery history, the press where abolitionist James Birney published the *Philanthropist* was demolished and shacks in the Negro slums were burned by white mobs. Henry and Harriet had deplored the lawlessness of the mobs and the destruction of Birney's press, but only Edward in 1838 in his *Narrative of Riots at Alton* would break through the Beechers' cautious opposition to slavery.

Such caution marked Catharine's *An Essay on Slavery and Abolitionism with reference to the Duty of American Females* (1837), an open attack on Angelina Grimké and abolitionism. Catharine, echoing her father, asserted that all Christian women were abolitionists but that they believed in gradual rather than immediate emancipation. Captive to gentility, she argued that the attacks on sincere and respectable foes by advocates of "immediation" were so harsh that they aroused only anger and increased oppression. The evil was great but the question of removing it, she asserted, was a matter of expediency. At once Romantic and Victorian is her warning that a woman who succumbs to "the promptings of ambition or thirst for power" loses all claim to the protection of religion, chivalry and "romantic gallantry." Incongruously she pleads for tact and meekness in reproving slaveholders.

But what is likely to give a modern reader most pause is Catharine's insistence that woman's relationship to man is one of dependence and subservience. If education leads women to ignore the value of "dignified retirement and submission," it is dangerous. Surely speaking as a child of Calvinism, she declares: "Heaven has appointed to one sex the superior, and to the other the subordinate station." Woman's duties and influence are no less important than man's, but her sphere and her appeal are entirely different. Reacting to a decade of Jacksonian democracy, she announced, with rhetorical flourishes, that the "storms of democratic liberty" threaten us with "disunion and civil wars." Our best hope, she concludes, is women working at the nation's moral center, the home, and as teachers building character in children. To achieve such goals women must be so cultivated in intellect, so benevolent in feeling, so unassuming and gentle that every father, husband and son will yield to them. The description is of a woman so different from Catharine Beecher herself that we must view it as the romantic ideal she had used to inspire adolescent girls. Since she had no husband and does not mention brothers, it is possible that she is describing an idealized version of her mother's relationship to her father.

Angelina Grimké's answer came in twelve letters published in the *Emancipator* and the *Liberator* and then in book form as *Letters to Catharine E. Beecher in Reply to an Essay on Slavery and Abolitionism* (1838). In the militant tradition of Weld and Garrison, she brands every slaveholder a "master-stealer" because he robs a slave of himself. Northerners are just as guilty because they do nothing to end slavery. The colonization scheme is a cloak to hide the monster Prejudice, which can love the colored man only after he has been sent to Africa. "Surely," she wrote, "you never want to *'get rid'* of people whom you *love*." True emancipation means freeing slaves, paying them for their labor, allowing them to marry and keep their children, educating them and letting them read the Bible. Catharine's notion that woman must win everything by peace and love she scornfully dismisses as a rule suitable for a "fashionable belle whose idol is herself." This nation, she cries, is *"rotten at the heart,* and nothing but the most tremendous blows with the sledge-hammer of abolition truth" will break the acquiescence into which it has sunk.

But Miss Grimké saved her most savage indictment for two letters answering Catharine Beecher on the rights of women. She rejects completely the idea that Heaven has appointed woman to an inferior station and she denies that there is any evidence of this in the words of the Bible or Christ. Catharine's prediction that women would sacrifice all the impulses of chivalry unless they asked for no rights except those that come as "the gifts of honor, rectitude and love," evoked Miss Grimké's boundless contempt: Any self-respecting woman "turns with disgust from all such silly insipidities." Women's rights are not the "gifts" of man or even of God. She concludes that a slave's rights may be wrested from him but they "cannot be alienated. . . . it is stamped on his moral being, and is, like it, imperishable." A dozen years before the manifesto of the first Woman's Rights Convention, she declares, with all the ardor of a Mary Wollstonecraft or a Fanny Wright:

Now, I believe it is woman's right to have a voice in all the laws and regulations by which she is to be governed, whether in Church or State; and that the present arrangements of society, on these points, are *a violation of human rights, a rank usurpation of power,* a violent seizure and confiscation of what is sacredly and inalienably hers.

Catharine Beecher and Angelina Grimké represented two extremes in the struggle to achieve greater influence and more opportunities for women. Catharine believed that these ends could be reached by the calculated use of methods women had always used because they were readily available. Her approach accepted subservience to men, especially in such areas as politics, where the game seemed hardly worth the candle, but it did have the virtue of being available, practicable and nonviolent.

Angelina Grimké's approach was bold, noble and committed to the full self-realization of each woman as both a woman and a human being. But it was rash, and it dealt in absolutes that ignored the time, the place and human nature. A small band of women chose the Grimké approach and helped lead the way through civil war and its aftermath, but in other directions made little progress for almost a hundred years. The great majority of women adopted or, rather, slipped into the roles recommended by Catharine Beecher.

This attack, along with the failure of her Cincinnati school, left Catharine once again deeply depressed. She was approaching forty years of age and it had become evident—especially to associates such as Mary Dutton and her sister Harriet—that she was far more interested in starting schools than in working in them.

Catharine now turned to writing to support herself and keep her reputation alive. Like Harriet, but without Harriet's gifts, she tried doing stories for the very popular sentimental ladies' magazines and gift annuals, but she had little success. She had already published half a dozen books, including two textbooks on arithmetic; now, inspired by the popularity of William McGuffey's "Readers," she put together a textbook, *The Moral Instructor for Schools and Families: Containing Lessons on the Duties of Life.* Shamelessly exerting pressure on friends and acquaintances, she tried to have it adopted in the common school—that is, public school—system. But Horace Mann, her friend from Litchfield days and now an influential educator, and others had begun a movement to keep sectarian religious education out of the schools. Despite her claim that it was nonsectarian and even nonreligious, Catharine's book, with all its lessons based on texts from the Bible, which would certainly offend Unitarians and Universalists, was disqualified.

It did not help her personal situation that she now had to return to her second-floor bedroom at Walnut Hills. Seven of her brothers and sisters were married and all but two of the others were grown, so that there was no excuse for her to resume her position as the dominant oldest child in the family. Nor could she function as substitute mother, for Lydia Jackson had taken over the household and needed no help. Indeed, not surprisingly, Catharine had soon fallen out with Mrs. Jackson and quarreled bitterly with her. (Years later, Harriet Beecher Stowe, referring to her second stepmother, wrote to Catharine, "She has never loved or trusted us.") She also irritated her female in-laws with unsolicited advice on domestic matters and argued with her brothers on theological questions.

Catharine's arguments with her brothers were not accidental. She had made a gesture toward returning theologically as well as physically to her father's house when in 1839 she published in *The American Biblical Repository* an essay "On Fatalism and Free Agency." As though to give further proof that she was doctrinal heir to the Reverend Dr. Beecher, she disputed points of theology constantly with Edward and Charles. She dueled so aggressively with Charles, a sensitive young divinity student, that he was driven to pouring out his exasperation in a letter to his father:

I have simply to say in respect to these controversies, that (1) with Edward I consider them as barren of wholesome fruit as the scholastic jargon of the middle ages, (2) as to Catharine's mind, it is the last that should flatter itself with the hope of disentangling the subject, (3) that as to Edward, she neither does nor can comprehend him, by reason that his region of truth and thought is too far above her.

Lyman was aware of the disturbing form taken by Catharine's tendency to domineer. Since her challenges were not directed at him, it was easy for him to sympathize with her frustrations and the awkwardness of her situation in the family. ". . . with her nervous incapacities," he wrote to

Henry, "she feels deeply any appearances of light estimation on the part of her family friends who she so sincerely loves." Perhaps he was also subconsciously aware that it was part of his legacy to her. So he urged his sons to spare her their resentment.

It may seem surprising that Catharine Beecher's greatest fame and success should have come from her books on home economics and the household arts. But her schools had always tried to train young women in such fields. And her overriding view, as we have seen, was that home was woman's empire, arena, pulpit and stage and that women should make themselves masters of every aspect of it.

Temporarily frustrated in her effort to prepare women for teaching, Catharine now undertook to prepare them for home management. Just as she had sought to establish teaching as a profession, and a noble one, she now presented homemaking as a high calling and as worthy of study as history or mathematics.

So in 1841 she published *A Treatise on Domestic Economy for the Use of Young Ladies at Home and at School.* It was clear, practical, and remarkably broad in scope, covering not only every household activity, room by room and day by day, from carving a roast to packing a trunk, but also the physiology (illustrated) and ills of the human body, the care of infants, building a house (complete with expert floor plans), and even gardening. Again and again the reader today comes upon advice as informed and enlightened as any in a comparable recent book: get more air and exercise; eat moderately; take less meat and more vegetables—or even try a vegetarian diet; drink less coffee and tea; amusement is necessary and laughter is good. Occasionally a primitive theory crops up: decaying vegetables in a cellar create "miasmas" that cause fevers. Or there is Victorian prudery: children's "impure thoughts" lead to frightful consequences such as can be seen in any asylum; and dancing, licentious fiction—especially the novels of Edward Bulwer—cards and theaters are dangerous.

The book constantly goes beyond the purely practical to matters of character and behavior: domestics should not be blamed for seeking higher wages or changing jobs to improve their condition; children should be guided more by rewards than by penalties, and neither children nor domestics should be corrected continually or disagreeably.

But Catharine Beecher could not be content with a merely practical handbook; she had to set forth her views on woman's place in American society. So in a lofty prefatory chapter—with extensive quotations from Alexis de Tocqueville's *Democracy in America* (1835)—she points out that in American society men and women have equal rights and equally important roles. But then both she and Tocqueville weaken this assertion with several qualifications. First she declares that in the family, as in every department of life, there can be only one head—as though, indeed, the family were an army, a business or a political body. Man, she observes, has always been the head of the family and must remain so. The American system, in its wisdom, also excludes women from any part in political life, commerce or rough labor. Catharine of course was aware that these exclusions restricted women to a very few roles, most of them considered unimportant or even menial, but she was firmly convinced that such roles would enable women to bring unity and harmony to American life. American society, moreover, unlike Europe with its privileged classes, allowed a woman more freedom of choice in a mate, an employer, and political leaders—the last claim remains unexplained—and far more hope of improving her social position.

As further proof of the superiority of American standards, Catharine cites Tocqueville's view that American women have stricter morals and are more chaste than their English counterparts. Most travelers agreed with Tocqueville; but Harriet Martineau came away with the impression that there was as much "vice" and intemperance among women in America as in England; for which opinion Catharine, with all the conviction of a Puritan daughter and a Victorian spinster, branded her a pitiable dupe and spreader of falsehoods. More convincing is Catharine's use of Tocqueville's observation that in Europe men flatter women and pretend to be their slaves yet think of them only as "seductive but imperfect beings." By contrast, in America, he wrote, women are subordinate in station but always treated as superior, especially in the education of children, in the selection of clergymen, in benevolent works, and in morals and manners. They are, moreover, accorded all the courtesies of life. Within a few years the leaders of the women's rights movement would be labeling such courtesies a sop. And the code of chivalry, which was reaching its most glorified form in the South, would in time be criticized as putting woman on a cloud or a pedestal, and thus removing her from any active role in society.

At the same time, with the rapid growth of cities, more and more men were going off each morning to work in mill, plant, shop or office, leaving women to run the household as they saw fit. One result was what Charles Dudley Warmer, a writer who was later a next-door neighbor of Harriet, Mary and Isabella Beecher, termed the "feminization of the age." This was another aspect of the shift from Puritan standards set by the church and the Bible to Victorian standards set by the middle class. Carried away by her own missionary enthusiasm, Catharine, like her father in similar moments, grew exultant at the prospect. American women are engaged, she wrote, in the building of a glorious temple . . . whose summit shall pierce the skies, whose splendor shall beam on all lands; and those who hew the lowliest stone, as much as those who carve the highest capital, will be equally honored, when its top-stone shall be laid, with new rejoicings of the morning stars, and shoutings of the sons of God.

To achieve such goals young women must be properly trained. Catharine said that this included all women because in America, where "everything is moving and changing," where the poor can rise to riches, and the rich can sink to poverty, every woman must be ready to meet every kind of household problem.

Domestic Economy was an immediate success and was reprinted almost annually for many years. Catharine followed it a year later with *Miss Beecher's Domestic Receipt-Book,* offering, she said, simple, healthful and not too expensive dishes tested by "the best practical housekeepers." These were especially useful to housewives who saw more and more servants going off to mills and plants. But most welcome of all, the book provided a vision of a healthy, happy and well-fed family living harmoniously in a well-built, well-furnished and well-kept house.

So Catharine Beecher, who had never had her own home and family, and was not even on friendly terms with most of her closest kin, became the chief promoter of family life and patroness of the cult of domesticity.

After three or four years of casting around for a means of resuming her career as an educator, Catharine found her way again during a trip east in the summer of 1843.

After several months she came to rest in New York City in the home of Courtlandt Van Rensselaer, a prominent raiser of funds for religious schools. The Rensselaers' support revived Catharine's dreams and schemes, and she set off around the country, organizing committees, especially of churchwomen, to raise money and help find teachers for the West. Her well-publicized visits, combined with the increasing sale of her *Treatise on Domestic Economy,* made her one of the best-known women in America. Evangelist, organizer, distinguished visitor—these were roles she relished.

Soon she became convinced that a man should head the organization: Professor Calvin Stowe, now Harriet's husband, had made a study of European schools for the state of Ohio—and was not, incidentally, the kind of man to contest her leadership—so Catharine dragooned him into serving as leader of what she called the Central Committee for Promoting National Education.

In all her talks—summed up in *The Evils Suffered by American*

Women: The Causes and the Remedy (1846)—she had a few major themes. First she dwelt in graphic detail on the two million children who were getting no education at all or doing so under the most primitive conditions. She quoted a report from New York, a state with one of the best educational systems, telling of indescribably dilapidated schools where many of the "self-styled teachers, who lash and dogmatize in these miserable tenements of humanity, are shown to be low, vulgar, obscene, intemperate, and utterly incompetent to teach anything good." While women who enjoy all the pleasures of life sit idly by, prevented by social custom from doing useful work, Catharine charged, many young children are turned over to "coarse, hard, unfeeling men, too lazy or stupid" to perform their duties.

Catharine then calls attention to the young women who leave jobs as seamstresses, nurses and domestics to work in shops and mills. In eastern cities, she points out, manufacturers are growing rich on the labor of ten thousand women, most of them American born, who work for a pittance and live in squalor. Nor are the vaunted mills of Lowell, Massachusetts—which she had visited—the answer. There, young women work from 5 A.M. to 7 P.M., for an average of $1.75 a week. And too many of them, Catharine primly adds, spend their few free hours in extravagant indulgence, dancing and idle flirtations. Young women trained as teachers will not only save neglected children but stay out of the factories and mills. Proper education will also prepare such women for their duties and difficulties as wives and mothers. Catharine's celebration of domestic economy was hardly unselfish: she promptly added that complete information on the subject was available in her *Treatise on Domestic Economy* and in *Miss Beecher's Domestic Receipt-Book*. She also declared that profits from the sale of the books would be devoted to teacher recruitment and placement. There is no evidence that this was done; and it is clear that she tended to consider support for Catharine Beecher as support for the cause.

Later, she added what was spiritually the most challenging argument for her scheme. The Catholic Church, she pointed out, welcomed women willing to devote their lives—as nuns—to the service of the church. Why not a Protestant equivalent made up of women who would be sent out to teach and set a moral and religious example—a missionary corps supported by other women? Like nuns, the teachers would be practicing sacrifice and self-denial, but unlike nuns, they would be doing so not for their own salvation but for society. Resigned to having no husband or children of her own, Catharine obviously saw herself, and thought others saw her, as a model of such self-denial and sacrifice.

It was perhaps the first shift by a Beecher from the gospel of salvation to the creed of social service, from a preoccupation with conversion, sin, hell and heaven to educating neglected children and protesting the exploitation of working women. The creed still made obeisance to the Bible and God, but it was far more concerned with women's lives than with their souls.

By the summer of 1846, Catharine had collected enough money to replace Calvin Stowe with a paid agent. Not really as pliant as he seemed, Calvin had come to resent intensely the way she manipulated everyone who joined her. She persuaded William Slade, governor of Vermont, whose term of office was coming to an end, to accept the post. She then assembled a group of thirty-five prospective teachers in Albany in the spring of 1847 and another group in Hartford in the fall and gave each a month's training. The program was mainly practical but it managed to imbue the young women with a remarkable sense of religious and moral mission. They were then sent to posts Slade had found for them, mostly in rural settlements. The missionary training may account for the fortitude and spirit with which many of these women, mainly from well-established areas of New England, confronted poverty, prejudice, ignorance, illness and the most primitive living conditions. The letters they wrote to Catharine are filled with graphic glimpses of their trials and achievements. One wrote of never finding the promised school, another of being supplanted by a teacher of a different sect, still another of having her school almost broken up by a struggle over the admission of colored children.

One of the most vivid came from a young woman who had opened a school in a log house in January with forty-five pupils, including some grown boys. The settlers, she wrote, were mainly farmers from North Carolina and Tennessee and from Germany. When the teacher arrived they warned her that she would not be paid for more than three months a year. At first they distrusted her but she finally gained their good will and they built her "a good frame school-house, with writing desks, blackboard, and promise to support her all the year round." Much distressed because they spent their Sundays in hunting, fishing and visiting, she started a Sunday school and succeeded in getting as many as fifty to attend. But her greatest trials were

the want of religious privileges . . . the entire want of social sympathy, and the manner in which I am obliged to live. I board where there are eight children and the parents, and only two rooms in the house. I must do as the family do about washing, as there is but one basin and no place to go to wash but out the door. I have not enjoyed the luxury of either lamp or candle, their only light being a cup of grease with a rag for a wick. Evening is my only time to write, but this kind of light makes such a disagreeable smoke and smell I cannot bear it, and do without light except the fire. I occupy a room with three of the children and a niece who boards here. The other room serves as a kitchen, parlor, and bedroom for the rest of the family.

She had also begun reading Catharine's *Domestic Economy* to members of the family—a detail that surely pleased Catharine—and they were already heeding some of its suggestions, such as drinking one cup of coffee a day rather than three, and using yeast to lighten their heavy, half-baked bread. "I intended to stay only one term," she concluded, "but the people urged me so much to remain . . . that I concluded to stay longer. I did not leave my home to seek pleasure, wealth, or fame, and I do believe my Heavenly Father will bless my labors here. . . . " Catharine could hardly have wished for a more edifying combination of a success story with pious genuflections and moral overtones. And its flattery of Catharine made it a perfect testimonial.

As might have been expected, Slade, unlike Stowe, had no intention of remaining Catharine's shadow. He soon took over the leadership of the organization, moved it from Cincinnati to Cleveland, and changed its name to the National Board of Popular Education. For a number of years it was fairly successful, placing about 450 teachers in the West. This may seem like a vindication of Catharine's faith in the superiority of women teachers. But the main reason for the rapid increase everywhere was the fact that women could be paid much less than men. A master of expedients, Catharine did not hesitate to make open use of this circumstance. Woman, she declared, is "the best, as well as the cheapest guardian and teacher of childhood." In the long run her goal was achieved, with women teachers, a minority in the 1830s, becoming an overwhelming majority by the 1880s. It would be unjust to conclude that Catharine's campaign was simply fortunate enough to come at a time when women began to be accepted in a variety of occupations. A dedicated, practical-minded publicist, she spread far and wide the message that women should be trained for work.

Slade's assumption of leadership in the association (later she bitterly described how he ignored and finally ousted her) left Catharine at loose ends once more. Faced by another interruption of her career, she again suffered a nervous collapse, including a "weakness" or partial paralysis in a foot. All kinds of "cures" and treatments—some of them quack and many of them outlandish—had become available for such ailments, and Catharine tried a remarkable number of them—mesmerism (she was hypnotized eight times in ten days), galvanism, electromagnetic machines, weird diets, and even clairvoyants.

But her favored treatment, one to which she resorted for as much as six months every year from 1843 on, was hydropathy, popularly known as the "water cure." Shorn of most of her duties by Slade, she retreated in 1845 to a rest home in Brattleboro, Vermont, known for a water cure practiced by a German political émigré, Dr. Robert Wesselhoeft. Sister Harriet, exhausted by childbearing and family cares, joined her. After a month of study, the doctor diagnosed Catharine's case as "bad humors," which, he said, should be brought to the surface. The treatment was apparently based on the theory that any genuine remedy must be painful. Patients were awakened at 4 A.M., packed in a wet sheet for two or three hours and then "in a reeking perspiration immersed in the coldest plunge-bath." After that they walked as far as strength allowed and drank five or six tumblers of ice-cold water. Breakfast consisted of mush, brown bread and milk. At 11 A.M. they were stood under "a douche of the coldest water falling *eighteen feet, for ten minutes,*" which felt like a torrent of rocks but, so patients said, left one exhilarated. Then more walking and three or four more tumblers of cold water; at 3 P.M. a session in a sitz bath of cold water; more walking and water drinking; and at 9 P.M. half an hour of soaking the feet in cold water and massaging them. Finally, with part of the body swathed in wet bandages, the patient was put to bed. The same wet bandage was worn all day.

Although this drastic regimen did not cure Catharine, her stay at such places was always deeply gratifying. The constant attention of doctors, nurses and attendants (in 1846 the Brattleboro water cure had more than thirty attendants) could be very comforting, especially for a woman who had no family of her own. It was also a relief to live for a while among women of breeding and wealth—it was the most expensive water cure in the country—and discuss intimate female ailments freely. Indeed, the self-indulgence of these long retreats suggests that much of Catharine's arguments for self-denial and sacrifice were efforts to convince herself, and the world, that her aims were purely altruistic and high-minded.

Her breakdowns, as she herself acknowledged, were "nervous" or psychological in origin. They always came just when she needed an excuse to escape from an uncompleted or failing enterprise, and they never, even in her old age, prevented her from resuming her activities.

It was at Brattleboro in the fall of 1846 that Catharine's life became bizarrely entangled with that of Delia Bacon. Miss Bacon, sister of Dr. Leonard Bacon, well-known Congregationalist clergyman and professor of theology at Yale, had been one of Catharine's outstanding students at Hartford. She was now a woman of thirty-five who had won attention as a writer of fiction and as a lecturer on history and literature, and especially on Shakespeare's plays.

In the spring of 1845 Miss Bacon had become interested in—some said infatuated with—Alexander MacWhorter, a young minister who had studied under Dr. Nathaniel Taylor, Lyman Beecher's old friend at Yale. Because MacWhorter was very wealthy and more than ten years younger than Miss Bacon, unkind gossip about the pair began to circulate in New Haven and Hartford church circles. By September 1846 Miss Bacon, disturbed by MacWhorter's failure to declare his intentions (he loved her deeply, he said, but like a brother), fled to Brattleboro for rest and treatment.

Catharine and Harriet, who had been at Brattleboro all summer, welcomed Delia into Dr. Wesselhoeft's watery Eden. Catharine soon developed a proprietary interest in this student of hers who had blossomed into a writer and teacher so stimulating that she was being compared to the intellectual heroine of Madame de Staël's *Corinne*. But when Mr. MacWhorter suddenly arrived in Brattleboro, and Catharine happened upon Delia and MacWhorter in intimate conversation in the boarding-house garden, all her instincts as an oldest sister and head of female seminaries were aroused. Without telling Delia, she asked the Reverend Mr. Clapp, a classmate of MacWhorter's, what his friend's intentions were. To her dismay, Clapp ridiculed the idea that MacWhorter would marry a woman so much older than himself.

As though dealing with an adolescent student, Catharine demanded of Delia how the relationship should be explained to their friends in Hartford. Delia answered, "Say what you please." The result was two shocking items of news when Delia returned to Hartford in November: first, Catharine had declared that Delia and MacWhorter were engaged, and far more shattering, MacWhorter had authorized his friends to deny the story.

Delia's brother Leonard immediately forbade her to see Mac-Whorter again, calling the man a villain and a fool. Dr. Taylor descended on Delia and demanded that the episode be closed and the story suppressed. Frantically, Delia appealed to Catharine and Harriet to intercede with Taylor. Harriet backed away. Catharine went straight to Taylor. "It was," she later reported to Dr. Bacon, "one of the most painful interviews of her whole life. It seemed as if the *whole being* of a . . . surpassing intellect . . . and of almost unbounded power of influence over other minds, was now . . . in a struggle to overthrow those principles of truth and justice that are the pillars of human society. . . . "

Acrimonious charges, no credit to Yale, the local clergy or their gossipy wives, were now flung back and forth. Finally Dr. Bacon, charging MacWhorter with "slander, falsehood, and conduct dishonorable to the Christian ministry," forced the New Haven West Ministers' Association to bring the young man to ecclesiastical trial.

On August 4, 1847, Catharine Beecher escorted Delia Bacon into the "courtroom"—the home of the ex-president of Yale, Dr. Jeremiah Day—feeling as though she were leading a martyr to "torture and fiery wheels." Catharine testified frequently, but not always as wisely as she thought. Hearsay as well as betrayals of confidences abounded. The trial dragged on for two weeks; the verdict was that MacWhorter had been guilty of nothing more than "imprudence."

For Delia Bacon the trial was agony followed by unbearable humiliation. For Catharine it was like living over again the horror of the days after Fisher had been snatched from her. After a period of seclusion, Delia Bacon gradually returned to her work. (But her brother believed that the episode began the derangement that ended in her madness ten years later.) For Catharine, however, it remained a wrong that had to be righted. She began to put together an exposé of the injustices and cruelties to which Delia Bacon had been subjected by MacWhorter, Taylor, Yale University and the entire local Congregational establishment. Late in 1849, quite insensitive to the effect it might have, she showed Delia the half-finished manuscript.

Delia, all her suffering revived in an instant, begged Catharine to destroy it. In a highly emotional letter, she wrote: "I am tired of being a 'victim.' I do not wish to be a 'heroine.' " But Catharine, headmistress and avenging angel, was not listening. "I have planned to save your feelings," she wrote, "if you will but return to the fealty of your childhood, and obey me as you did then." It was an aging mother longing for the domination she had once enjoyed. Warming to the role of Defender of Slandered Maidenhood, Catharine declared, "The blame and the outcry of those who would still 'hush up' this monstrous outrage will be turned on me. Let it come. I cannot suffer in a better cause."

The Reverend Leonard Bacon forbade her to publish the book. Her father and brothers, aghast at her presumption, joined the effort to stop her. The public would have found it a strange sight, she acknowledged, if it could have witnessed "my recent *hegira,* with my various brothers in full pursuit, some of them fancying an insane hospital my only proper residence." All opposition swept aside, she published *Truth Stranger Than Fiction: A Narrative of Recent Transactions involving Inquiries in regard to the Principles of Honor, Truth and Justice which obtain in a distinguished American University* (1850). She printed it at her own expense and then unblushingly wrote to all the women on her educational committees urging them not only to buy it but to publicize it in every way. If the trial was an absurd exaggeration of a matter of local gossip, writing a book about it two years later compounded the absurdity. A reviewer in a New York periodical, *The Literary World,* derided it as an attempt "to interest all mankind and command the sympathy of the whole country in a squabble in a country town" and a critic in the New

York *Herald* dubbed Catharine "busybody general."

Truth Stranger Than Fiction is of interest only for what it tells us about Catharine Beecher. Throughout, she pictures herself as the champion of abused womanhood, ready to sacrifice herself for the cause. Like a novelist, she dwells on Delia's sufferings and dramatizes crucial scenes. To justify having spread the story that precipitated the crisis, she overstates Delia's innocence as well as the charges against MacWhorter and his "patrons." Most significant is her resentment at the self-serving behavior of churchmen in high places and her frustration at the helplessness of women in their relationships with men.

Strange as had been the MacWhorter affair, it was as nothing to the surreal events of the last ten years of Miss Bacon's life. In her study of Shakespeare's works, the meager details of his biography led her to conclude that only a writer with the intellectual powers and worldly wisdom of a Francis Bacon could have written the plays. This farfetched theory soon possessed her uncontrollably. As early as 1852, her brother Leonard, convinced that her obsession was undermining her sanity, urged her to give up this "delirious fancy." Far from giving it up, she went off to England and for five years, often nearly penniless, sought "lost manuscripts" of the plays which would confirm her thesis.

Delia Bacon's remarkable knowledge of both Shakespeare's plays and Bacon's works coupled with her demonic intensity made her seem a romantic figure to Nathaniel Hawthorne, then the American consul in Liverpool; he helped her find a publisher for her book *The Philosophy of the Plays of Shakespeare Unfolded* (1857). Tragically for Miss Bacon, the reviewers either were baffled by the book or ridiculed it mercilessly. Her mind already unhinged, she went completely mad and died in a Hartford asylum in 1859.

Once the Bacon-MacWhorter trial was behind her, Catharine resumed her travels, at first to gather support for her missionary teachers or to rescue those in distress, but later to find a site for a model seminary. She had meanwhile persuaded a young teacher, Nancy Johnson, to try the water cure for her crippled foot, and now Nancy joined her as secretary, protégée and companion. Despite her handicap, Nancy was a lively and mettlesome young woman and for two years the pair toured the country in fine style. They drew liberally on the funds collected for their work, and everywhere they were entertained in the best homes, with Catharine received as the fairy godmother of female education in the West. To Catharine this easeful life—a far cry from the self-denial she advocated—was simply compensation for her efforts and for illnesses contracted in the service of the cause. At the same time, Nancy Johnson was a hedge against loneliness, obviously acting not only as a daughter or younger sister but as a substitute for a husband.

In the spring of 1848 the couple came upon a promising site in Burlington, Iowa, and Catharine organized a small school there. But the community failed to carry through the program she set up, and again she was drawn into serving as principal, majordomo and financial manager. Again she collapsed and fled to her water haven in the East. Nancy struggled along until winter and then gave up. The school had lasted barely seven months.

After a rest, Catharine returned to the struggle. She was fifty years old and more than ever she wanted a permanent home in a college setting. She also now knew that the kind of school she envisioned needed a continuing endowment. So when she found some influential citizens in the rapidly growing city of Milwaukee who wanted a good local school for their daughters, she established the Milwaukee Female College and then organized the American Woman's Educational Association to support it.

She had at last found a working formula for her vision, and the school would become her one enduring monument in the field of education.

11

A FATHER AND FOUR SONS

By the time Lyman Beecher arrived in Cincinnati in 1832, only Edward of his eight surviving children by Roxana Foote had begun to fulfill his ambitions for his offspring. William was, for the moment, working as an agent for the Sunday-School Union of New England. Catharine, with the help of Harriet, was about to start a small seminary for women in Cincinnati. As Mrs. Thomas C. Perkins, Mary was contentedly being a wife and mother in Hartford. George had left Yale Divinity School to go west with his family. Henry Ward was a junior at Amherst, and Charles, at seventeen, was a sophomore at Bowdoin; within two years both of them would go to Walnut Hills and enter Lane Seminary.

William Beecher was still the victim of hard luck, stingy congregations and petty intrigues. Hardly had the Beecher clan settled in Cincinnati than he followed them with his wife and baby. He followed partly to join in the family effort to win the West for God and Protestantism but also to break the succession of mischance and personality differences that had sent him from job to job ever since he had been an adolescent.

Although he was thirty-one when he came to Cincinnati, the refrain in the family circle was once again: "What is to be done with William?" As usual, his father was equal to the occasion, helping him get a post as pastor of a newly established church in Putnam, Ohio. Although Lyman himself had had misgivings about William's qualifications for the ministry, it never occurred to him that he had made the ministry the only goal that William could respect.

William organized the Putnam church and a small school along with it, and for a number of years managed to scrape along on a salary of five hundred dollars a year. In desperate need of money for an ever-increasing family, he finally asked for a raise. But some of his parishioners had been antagonized by his strong antislavery views—he and his wife, along with George, were among the first Beechers to favor abolition—and others had been displeased by his sermons on intemperance.

The response to his request was so niggardly that, badly as he needed the post, he felt that he must resign.

Luckily for William, his brilliant brother George was leaving a desirable pastorate in Batavia, New York, and was able to arrange to have William succeed him. The congregation, a large one, paid him one thousand dollars a year. So William seemed at last to have found a very respectable place for himself. It was too good to last. Eventually a group of women in the congregation took a dislike to him and made his situation so uncomfortable that once again he had to resign. The impression that these misfortunes give of a socially inept and bumbling man is hardly borne out by his half sister Isabella's view of him after a visit. She thought he showed a loving heart and she found him most like her father in quick thinking and fluency. His trials, she wrote, had improved his religious character and she was convinced that he would have ranked high among preachers if he had had more of an education.

"What to do with William" was once more a family concern, and more pressing than ever because he now had six children. He tried earnestly to find work, but having learned to expect difficulties and defeats, he was soon discouraged. He had also become accustomed to relying on his father. With good reason: Lyman brought his forty-two-year-old son with him to a convention of ministers in 1844 and found a place for him in a church being planned in Toledo. Toledo had only 1,800 inhabitants but the congregation managed to offer him eight hundred dollars a year. He soon set about raising money for a new church building and was approaching his goal when he discovered that his leading deacon, who was also one of his more generous subscribers, owned a hotel that had a particularly busy bar. As a champion of temperance, William challenged the deacon; instead of resigning his post or closing the bar, the deacon angrily organized a campaign to starve him out. William held on until his congregation owed him a thousand dollars in back pay. With Christian humility he offered to accept eight hundred dollars; the congregation offered him one hundred. All patience exhausted, William sued. He won, collected all that was owed him, and resigned. No one praised him for his courage or his principles in challenging the deacon, and no one, he sadly noted, expressed regret at his leaving.

After another painful interval of unemployment, he heard that the little town of Euclid, outside Cleveland, had been left a farm to be used as the site for a church and a school. The salary was pathetic—only four hundred dollars a year—but he had no choice, and he still had some pioneering spirit left. So he begged for a little more money and was promised another hundred dollars. This time he succeeded in getting a church and school built. It was a noteworthy achievement. His reward, after three years of work, was a salary fallen three hundred dollars in arrears. Once again a congregation had made him work for a pittance and in the end had cheated him even of that.

That he maintained any faith in congregations of professing Christians is a wonder. Almost fifty years old and disillusioned with pioneer communities, he turned against the tide and in the early 1850s, like his fellow Beechers, moved eastward.

Fired like his father by the challenge and promise of the West, Edward Beecher had accepted the presidency of a small new college, but, like his father, found himself heading a school that was struggling to survive. And Jacksonville, Illinois, was no Cincinnati. After a visit there in 1832, William Cullen Bryant described it as "a horridly ugly village, composed of little shops and dwellings stuck close together around a dingy square, in the middle of which stands the ugliest of possible brick courthouses."

Edward and Isabella had their own problems. At first they had to make do with a small cottage, cope with malarial surroundings and a cholera epidemic that carried off their second child, and take care of another child who was mentally deficient. Although Isabella went on to bear six more children in this period, she suffered an attack of cholera that left her almost an invalid. For three years a hostile state legislature refused to give the college a charter, one of its members boasting: "I was born in a brier thicket, rocked in a hog trough, and have never had my genius cramped by the pestilential air of a college." But the cultural level of the community continued to rise, and Edward, along with visiting members of his family, managed to create a quite interesting social circle. His colleagues in the college looked on him with affection and admiration, one old friend later describing him as a "great-brained and great-hearted man . . . with the guilelessness of a child."

From the very first he had to make arduous trips, usually to New England—just getting back to Illinois in the early years took almost a month—to plead for money for education in the present and to build a better society in the future. The latter goal helps to explain why he became so deeply involved in the antislavery movement. How far, he asked, could Christianity go in a society half of which rested on human slavery?

When he left Boston late in 1830, Beecher still believed in colonization in Africa as the solution for slavery. He rejected Garrison's extremist position (which Garrison had adopted only the year before) and described himself as merely a "thoughtful spectator" of the antislavery struggle. By the close of 1835, however, a few shocking events had convinced him that "the doctrine of gradual emancipation was fallacious, and that of immediate emancipation was philosophical and safe." The events included attacks on abolitionists by rioting mobs, especially the dragging of Garrison through the streets of Boston by respectable citizens, and the suppression of antislavery discussion in Congress. Other factors played a part: the failure of the colonization scheme, experiments in emancipation in the British West Indies, and right at home, the Lane debates.

Beecher had also become friendly with the Reverend Elijah P. Lovejoy. Lovejoy was a minister's son who had gone west in 1827. He had returned east to become a minister himself and finally settled in St. Louis as editor of a Presbyterian weekly paper, the *Observer*. Caught up in the shift from strictly theological concerns to "benevolent causes," he had begun to campaign against slavery and intemperance. When he visited Edward during the commencement at Illinois College in 1835, he, like Beecher, was still strongly opposed to Garrison's intransigent abolitionism. (In a letter to his mother he went so far as to call Garrison an "incendiary fanatic.") But he, too, was shaken by the events of that fall and in October he came out in support of the radical position of the Anti-Slavery Society.

At this point a group that included leaders in the Presbyterian Church urged him to "pass over in silence every thing connected with the subject of Slavery" lest it offend the slaveholding states, lead in time to a "disseverment of these United States" and reduce our nation to "what Europe was in the dark ages." After the most intense soul-searching, Lovejoy answered: "I cannot surrender my principles, though the whole world besides should vote them down—I can make no compromise between truth and error, even though my life be the alternative." Thus began his march to martyrdom.

When he was asked to resign from his paper, he turned to Edward Beecher for advice. Beecher promised full support, declaring, " . . . the time for silence has gone by. . . . I say go on." Lovejoy stayed on and was even chosen moderator of the Presbyterian churches in the St. Louis area.

But by the fall of 1836 the threats against him had grown so fierce and the vandalism directed at his shop so frequent that he decided to move across the Mississippi to Alton, a busy town in Illinois—a free state. Hardly had his press been landed on the Alton wharf than a mob threw it into the river. Antislavery groups helped Lovejoy replace the press and he carried on.

When Lovejoy and Beecher attended the Presbyterian General Assembly in Philadelphia in July 1837, they watched in anger as the Old School forces ousted four synods ostensibly because of their New School views but mainly because they opposed slavery too actively. Charles Beecher in his unpublished biography of his brother Edward would later come up with a chilling interpretation of this event:

It may not be clear at first to the ordinary mind why slavery and theology should go hand in hand in national affairs. But if we reflect that theology is but another name for the politics of the universe, or the Kingdom of God, the problem becomes simple. . . . Old School theology enthrones a great slave-holder over the universe; New School enthrones a great Emancipator.

It was a remarkable insight into the way religious orthodoxy had aligned itself with political conservatism, while religious liberalism turned to social reform.

As Lovejoy's editorials became more and more outspoken, the hostility of businessmen who had Southern connections grew sharper. The collapse of a land boom in Alton and the financial crash of 1837 frayed men's nerves and made them resentful of anyone who stirred dissension. In October 1837 Lovejoy was attacked by armed intruders while he was visiting a clergyman friend and was saved from harm only by the intervention of his wife. Thereafter he slept with a loaded musket at his bedside.

The following August a mob dessended on the *Observer* office and again threw its press into the river—and again Lovejoy's supporters replaced it. In a desperate effort to head off even more violent confrontations, Edward Beecher invited all "friends of free inquiry" to attend a meeting in Alton. He was dismayed when Colonization Society members, led by a visiting New Orleans apologist for slavery, the Reverend Joel Parker, packed the meeting. After two days of fruitless contention, the frustrated abolitionists withdrew and reassembled in private to pray and ask counsel of God.

When the antislavery forces called another convention, Beecher declined to attend unless his views were adopted by the group. Acknowledging his influence, the others let him draw up a "Declaration of Sentiments." It asserted that slavery was in all cases sinful, but Beecher, still avoiding Garrisonian extremism, added that a slaveholder who wanted to free his slaves but was unable to do so was not to be blamed: the community, Beecher insisted, was guilty and the sin was "organic," that is, a part of the system. Beecher's view may seem like sophistry, but it is really not very different from what we now call collective guilt.

Excitement in the town mounted rapidly. To cope with it, leading citizens met to hear both sides. Beecher tried in vain to convince the group that the true issues were freedom of the press and Lovejoy's rights. But at a meeting the following night, with Lovejoy present, a committee recommended that the editor abandon his paper and leave town. Lovejoy rose, and speaking softly, with serene conviction, said:

You have been exhorted to be lenient and compassionate; and in driving me away to affix no unnecessary disgrace upon me. Sir, I reject all such compassion.

You cannot disgrace me. Scandal and falsehood and calumny have already done their worst. My shoulders have borne the burthen till it sits easy upon them. You may hang me up, as the mob hung up the individuals at Vicksburg! You may burn me at the stake, as they did McIntosh at St. Louis; or you may tar and feather me, or throw me into the Mississippi . . . but you cannot disgrace me. I and I alone, can disgrace myself; and the deepest of all disgrace would be . . . to deny my Master by forsaking his cause.

At one point, speaking of his family, he wept, and his friends wept with him. But his critics muttered that he was a fanatic and mad.

A new press, the fourth, was on its way, but to avoid violence, it was delivered at three in the morning. Lovejoy, Beecher and a crew of volunteers were at the dock and had the crate placed for safekeeping in a large stone storehouse at the riverside. A guard was set up. In the cold November dawn Lovejoy and Beecher went back to Lovejoy's home and joined his wife and family in prayer. Although all business in the city was suspended that morning, Beecher, believing the crisis was past, left for Jacksonville.

He could not have been more mistaken. After dark, a mob of armed men, some of them grotesquely got up in high hats and tail coats, and many of them inflamed by drink, marched to the warehouse and tried to break into it. Shots rang out and one of the rioters was struck down. Raging, the crowd started to set fire to the building. A figure stepped out of the dark of the warehouse. It was met with a volley of rifle shots, and Elijah Lovejoy fell with five bullets in his body. The guards in the building fled and the press was destroyed.

On January 20, 1838, a jury in Alton exonerated the leaders of the mob. A week later, young Abraham Lincoln, speaking at the Lyceum in nearby Springfield, denounced mob lawlessness. In Hudson, Ohio, another young man, John Brown, hearing of the murder, is said to have consecrated himself to wiping out slavery at any cost. Owen Lovejoy, carrying out a vow made over his brother's dead body, became a leader of the radical abolitionists.

When news of the killing reached the East, anger in some quarters rose to a fever. Old John Quincy Adams wrote that Lovejoy's death shocked the American conscience like an earthquake. At a mass meeting held in Boston's Faneuil Hall to memorialize Lovejoy's heroism, a proslavery faction took over—until a young man named Wendell Phillips leaped onto the platform and with a stirring plea for liberty of the press began his career as the voice of abolitionism.

For all these men the shots fired at Alton on November 7, 1837, would be, in one sense, the beginning of the Civil War.

Meanwhile Edward Beecher, working feverishly, completed his *Narrative of Riots at Alton*. Even more than an indictment of slavery, it was a defense of freedom of inquiry and the rights of the individual. Its closely reasoned arguments are suffused with anger against lawlessness and it strikes again and again at "that bloody, thousand-headed, murderous tyrant, the mob." Almost as often, Beecher reproaches the decent citizens who allowed the mob to have its way. Occasionally he is carried away by rhetoric, but at its best the *Narrative* is an eloquent and moving document.

The fearful drama of Lovejoy's death was a high point in Beecher's life. It contrasted sharply with the routine at Illinois College to which he returned and which he endured for six more years: the genteel beggary of his perennial fund-raising activities, the day-to-day problems of a struggling college, especially during the depression of 1837, and the hostility of politicians and others who resented the antislavery position of Beecher and his faculty.

Beecher continued to insist, even more than had his father, that the future of America would be decided in the West. But after fourteen years in Jacksonville he was exhausted, and particularly weary of the obligations that kept him from his theological studies and literary work.

He was more convinced than ever that the theological system, based on the preexistence of souls, that he had been gestating over the years would revolutionize Christianity and bring him everlasting fame. It possessed him to such an extent that his outspoken young half brother Thomas, after studying at Illinois College for several years, said that on some points Edward seemed insane. And, Thomas added, "if religion were to make me another Edward—I say God deliver me from being pious."

So when an opportunity came in 1844 for Edward to return to the pulpit in Boston's Salem Street Church, he embraced it. As the other Beechers had followed him west, so in the next six or seven years they would follow him east, tacitly acknowledging that the West would not after all be the stage of a crucial spiritual struggle. Indeed, in 1848 it would become only a station on the road to gold and free land.

Although no one in the family ever admitted it, George Beecher may well have been Lyman Beecher's most tragic failure as a father. Lyman had contributed to a deep wound in Catharine's psyche and he had repeatedly led William beyond his depth, but Catharine had grown a scar over her wound and William had simply endured. George was not so strong as Catharine or as resigned as William.

George, the fifth of Lyman's children by Roxana and only a few years older than Harriet and Henry, grew up in Litchfield, going first to Miss Collins' School and then joining Catharine and Mary at Miss Pierce's academy. He was a bright student and such a remarkable reader that one of the family recreations on a winter's night was, as we have seen, a contest between father Beecher and George to see who could recall the most scenes out of Scott's novels.

At fourteen he went off to the Hartford Grammar School partly because his brother Edward had become its headmaster and George could attend it without paying tuition. He was also able to live in the Beechers' "Hartford Annex" with Catharine, Mary and Edward.

Two years later he moved on to Yale. There, under the tutelage of Edward, who was in the divinity school, his interest in religion was awakened and with it his long struggle with self-doubt. In his freshman year he was already answering his father's prodding with the admission that he still had no hope of conversion. When he came home in November he was caught up, like the rest of the family, in the excitement of one of his father's revivals and went through a period of emotional turmoil. "We have been this three weeks in a state of deep sympathy for George," Lyman wrote, "whose distress precluded sleep, almost, for many nights, and his voice of supplication could be heard night and day." The sympathy here is clearly professional and with no thought that such a prolonged ordeal might be damaging to a sensitive seventeen-year-old. True, George soon came out of his depression and swung to the other extreme, engaging in lively conversation with the girls and singing, his father reported, louder than he had prayed: "All his quickness and characteristic ardor seems now to be heightened by the contrast of joy with recent distress." The manic mood did not last. Under continuing pressure, both open and implicit, he broke down in his sophomore year and again in his junior year, suffering a "nervous dread of all feeling and action for months." In his senior year one of his eyes failed him and he had to give up his studies for two years.

When he was finally able to return to school, his father sent him to Yale Divinity School to study under Dr. Taylor. Extremely receptive to new ideas, he was much excited by Taylor's New School doctrines. But besides the burden of his sense of guilt, he was worn out by the need to teach part time to help support himself.

When Lyman decided to move to Cincinnati, George welcomed the change. On the journey west he was, as we have seen, one of the merriest of the family cortege, leading in the singing of psalms and hymns and exuberantly tossing tracts on Taylor's heresies to everyone along the way.

Not long after the family was settled in Walnut Hills, George went before the Cincinnati presbytery for his license to preach. The Reverend Joshua Lacy Wilson and his followers, having declared war on the Reverend Beecher, saw in George's examination an excellent opportunity to prove that this youth was, like his father, a New School heretic. A description of the trial comes from Harriet and it is a brilliant example of how well developed, at twenty-two, was her gift for narrative and characterization, her wit and her contempt for the mumbo-jumbo of her father's Old School enemies.

Dr. Wilson, chief inquisitor, she reported, led off with a cross-examination in "Philosophy":

"Mr. Beecher, what is matter and what is mind, and what is the difference 'twixt and 'tween . . . and what is right and wrong, and what is truth, and what is virtue . . . and what is intellect, susceptibilities, and will, and conscience—and every thing else, world without end, amen!"

Later came what Harriet called the "fiery trial"—questions at random from any of the brethren at the meeting:

"Mr. Beecher, do you believe in the doctrine of election?" . . . "Mr. Beecher, do you believe infants are sinners as soon as they are born?" "Do you believe that infants have unholy natures?" . . . "Mr. Beecher, do you think that men are punished for the guilt of Adam's first sin?" . . .

There was George—eyes flashing and hands going, turning first to right and then to left—"If I understand your question sir"—"Do you mean by nature thus and so? or so? . . ." "Yes, sir" (to right). "No, sir" (to left). "I should think so, sir" (in front).

Harriet confessed that her "Beecher blood boiled" when she learned that a few of these men "had actually been preaching such broad nonsense for many years." At the end, the Reverend Beecher spoke, defending his son's views, and the Reverend Wilson answered, declaring that the candidate was clearly not a Christian and knew nothing about Christianity and that he and his like "would never see the gates of eternal bliss." His speech, Harriet noted, was said to be the mildest he had ever made.

The Beechers prevailed: George was ordained and soon was assigned to a well-established church in the upstate New York town of Batavia. Overly conscientious, he was depressed and even reduced to tears by what he considered the low state of religion and the prevalence of vice everywhere. He began, he writes, to look forward to heaven as an escape from "this world of sin and sorrow." Among the sins that he most deplored was slavery. Passionate in his commitments, he joined the Anti-Slavery Society in 1836, the first Beecher to take so radical a stand. And as a minister in Ohio he was a leader in the movement to get the synods of the West to insist that their members speak out against slavery.

George was almost thirty years old when he married Sarah Buckingham, daughter of a prosperous Batavia family. When their first child died seven weeks after it was born, George characteristically tried to see the death, as had Harriet and Henry in a similar situation, as "a severe yet healthful discipline."

His health continued to deteriorate and after four years at his post, his father and friends all urged him to leave his work and rest. He agreed and for a time attended lectures at Lane and pursued his hobbies. Wearying of this, he accepted a call to the Brick Church in Rochester, New York. His shyness made some of his duties as pastor a trial, but he served zealously. One of his parishioners remembered him as "a guileless and affectionate minister" but with a tendency to respond too impulsively to new theories and movements.

One of these theories was Perfectionism, which set up as its goal nothing less than perfect holiness. In an amusing circular letter, the other members of the family commented on George's new preoccupation, each responding to it in a characteristic way: Henry warned him against committing himself too hastily, Charles analyzed it with witty skepticism, and Harriet, declaring that it was too metaphysical for her, asked instead for his advice on planting dahlias.

But such concerns haunted George and left him "unstrung by disease and exhausted by excitement." He sought refuge in gardening and music and he collected shells until he had five hundred of them, including a few valuable specimens. Finally, the poor health of both his wife and himself led him to accept a post in Chillicothe, Ohio. Except for an interval of illness that sent him to rest at a spring in Virginia, he carried on dutifully for the next few years. Near the end of that time he was heard to say that he hoped his Saviour would come for him that very year.

Then, one hot day in July 1843, he took his double-barreled muzzle-loading shotgun and went out presumably to drive away the robins that were stripping the fruit from his beloved cherry trees. A little later a servant girl found him dead in the garden, with a bullet through his mouth.

The coroner's verdict was accidental death, and Henry contributed the information that George had the bad habit of blowing smoke out of the barrel of his gun. No one publicly pointed out how curious it was that George had overlooked the fact that the gun was loaded and that he happened to pull the trigger just as he put the muzzle to his face. And a few days later Harriet, in a letter to Henry and Charles, disclosed that on the evening before his death, George had told his congregation that he thought he would soon die.

The tragedy tested Dr. Beecher's convictions to the limit. Someone blurted out the news to him on a Cincinnati street; for an endless moment he was unable to breathe, and then he burst into tears. Lest anyone think that he wept only because a dear son had died, he said, " . . . they were not the tears of the father which flowed first, but the tears of disappointed hope for so much and so needed usefulness in the cause of Christ cut off." Later he wept simply the tears of a father.

Harriet, after a broken-hearted description of the funeral, admitted that unless in such a moment one could fall back on faith in Christ, all would be confusion, agony, dismay and waste. And two years later, in a letter to her younger half brother, Thomas, she admitted: "The sudden death of George shook my whole soul like an earthquake; and as in an earthquake, we know not where the ground may open next. . . . Such unexpected, stunning agonies show us heart secrets before undreamed of."

Catharine had by some terrible coincidence come to visit George and Sarah on the day before the accident. Perhaps to exorcise that harrowing memory, she prepared George's journals and papers for publication. She made much of his struggle with his failings, but her tone is sometimes that of a headmistress talking of a flawed child. Thus she tells of his efforts to modify "habits formed while destitute of religious principles, in regulating strong passions and quick impulses, and especially in controlling the impatience and nervous irritability occasioned by disease." It was an apologia for a failed life. But it may well be that she realized that George's breakdowns came from the same sources as her own periodic nervous prostration: the lifelong pressure from her father and his religion. Whatever the reason, she never again returned to the Beecher fold.

Henry was on the road returning to Indianapolis with Eunice when a friend stopped him and told him that George had "killed himself." George had been his dearest brother. Eunice never forgot the look on Henry's face as they rode on home. But he was stricken as much by the sin of George's self-destruction as by the death itself. When he learned the official verdict his relief eased the agony of the loss. It was a month before he could get himself to write to George's widow. He tried words of solace but the cry that came from his heart was: "Oh, what can Christ mean—how can he *afford* to take only his Servants from the battle. . . ."

The question remained forever unanswered, leaving behind more pain among the Beechers than the death of any of their infants or their beloved mother or Alexander Metcalf Fisher. Perhaps it was the dreadful fact that one of their own had destroyed himself. So George, himself tormented, left a legacy of torment to those who were closest to him.

Charles Beecher's first love was music and his first youthful response to basic Calvinist doctrine was a deep skepticism. Yet, like Lyman Beecher's six other sons, he became a minister—never quite orthodox but a minister nonetheless. He later said that his father was alone responsible for his entering the church. But he never resented this because his father had acted, he believed, with noble intentions and with love.

Long afterward he described his father's influence on him in his childhood as all-pervasive: "I grew up into life one intellect, one heart, one will with him." He recalled grave homilies addressed to him and Henry when he himself was seven years old: "Henry, do you know that every breath you breathe *is sin?* Well, it is,—every breath," and he remembered sitting, at the age of nine, below the pulpit in Litchfield and beginning to tremble and weep as he listened to his father's appeal to sinners to save themselves.

In Litchfield, Charles, along with Henry, roamed the countryside and did the usual chores in garden, yard and barn. He was hardly eleven when Lyman proudly reported that Charles and Henry had been "awakened" and were "seriously disposed." Lyman was aware that the effect was "like the wind in the willow, which rises as soon as it is passed over," but he thought it was beneficial because it would strengthen conscience, moral principles and conduct.

In the streets of Boston, it was fourteen-year-old Charles and sixteen-year-old Henry, again always together. Tom, their small brother, recalled them as his heroes, renowned for their daring—riding sleds down Copp's Hill, skating, "whirling round the horizontal bar," running to fires. Charles attended the Boston Latin School but he was already drawn to music; soon he was playing the violin and studying church music under Lowell Mason, who directed all the music in his father's church and was becoming famous as a composer of hymns.

After preparing at Lawrence Academy in Groton, Charles went on to Bowdoin. Despite his feeling that he was too young for college ("Father was in a hurry to get us all through and into the ministry"), he excelled: he was as scholarly as Edward, had a gift for languages and stood near the top of his class. Six feet tall and athletic, he was, like his father and Edward, a gymnast. And by the time he graduated he was an accomplished violinist and a dedicated student of music theory.

With youthful idealism he set for himself the impossible goal of perfection in his religious life. But on being exposed to that awesome classic of American Calvinism, Jonathan Edwards's *Freedom of the Will*, he soon concluded that since all things were decreed by God, man really had no freedom of will. Much like his brother Henry at Amherst, he turned to phrenology for help, but where Henry had drawn encouraging conclusions from that source, Charles found that it only confirmed the view that man's fate was predetermined. He was plunged into a state in which, he said, he sounded "all the depths of fatalism, pantheism, atheism." He even boasted to his father how he had shocked Bowdoin orthodoxy with a poem in which the hero was an unbeliever, a murderer of his father, and finally a suicide. Not surprisingly, his family tended to treat these postures as the emotional self-indulgence of a high-strung young man, a sowing of intellectual wild oats.

Charles was still at Bowdoin when his family left for Cincinnati, but when Henry, having graduated from Amherst, decided to go west, Charles became homesick and followed him. The two of them entered Lane together, doubly welcomed by Lyman because the departure of Weld's "rebels" had nearly emptied the seminary classrooms. For the young men life in Walnut Hills was pleasant enough. Going to class was, at least as their much younger brother Tom saw it, a lark:

A foot-path led through the woods, over which came three times a day the heroes, shouting, exploding the vowel sounds, and imitating frogs, cows and crows—a laughing menagerie.

The Academy of Music, two miles off downtown—Henry primo basso, Charles violin and tenor; and the little boy, at last an alto, permitted to run between the heroes and sing, while eyes feasted on Charles's violin bow-hand, and ears were filled with Henry's basso.

Just as Henry had become engaged to Eunice before going west, so Charles, although hardly sixteen at the time, pledged himself with boyish impetuosity—as he later said—to a young cousin, Sarah Coffin. Thus there were letters going off from Charles and Henry to "two far-away beings, and the little boy [Tom] sometimes took them to the post office . . . wondering what they could find to write such long letters about." On Saturday mornings as many as nine members of the family gathered for prayers and hymn singing, and in the evenings "long discussions lasting past midnight and resumed at every meal" made theological questions as familiar to every Beecher as events and issues in America's history.

But where Henry managed to set aside his doubts and dutifully prepare for the ministry, Charles continued to resist all efforts to bring him into line. He even let his relationship with Sarah Coffin founder on the grounds that so religious a woman should not have to marry an infidel. This seems most considerate of him until we learn that he had fallen passionately in love with a Mary Wright. Unfortunately, Miss Wright was only in her early teens, she was not well and she was the daughter of a prominent member of Lyman Beecher's congregation who viewed Charles's suit with chilling disapproval.

Desperate to escape from the domination of his family, Charles now fled to a rented room in Cincinnati proper, hoping to support himself by giving music lessons. But he was so miserable that after a while he let Lyman fetch him home. It was a humiliating episode and it seems only to have increased his yearning for freedom.

He had meanwhile begun to contribute a weekly letter on music to the Cincinnati *Journal*, edited by Henry while its regular editor, the Reverend Brainerd, was away. Later in the year, when Henry's custodianship ended, Charles was able to continue the series in the *Chronicle*. This recognition strengthened his urge to become a musician. His father's reaction was characteristic: "Charles has founded his determination on *feeling,* his plans on *hopes,* and his arguments on *obstinacy.*" He was probably right, but no one noted that what he said applied just as well to his own view.

By this time Charles's infatuation with Mary Wright had become an open secret, especially after he allowed some thinly disguised love poems to be published in a local newspaper and had engaged in such moonstruck antics as peeping into the window of Mary's room. Whether prodded by the exasperation of her parents, the embarrassment of his own family or Mary's failure to return his love, Charles wrote Mr. Wright a long, desperate letter of confession and apology. Whatever he expected to come of it, he must have been disappointed: Wright was totally unsympathetic.

So Charles once again fled, but this time much more convincingly: he went off to New Orleans. In his father's autobiography, which Charles edited many years later, he pictures himself as a kind of prodigal son who stonily rejects all his father's arguments and pleas. His father's farewell is made into a Victorian drama: " 'My son,' he [Dr. Beecher] said with quivering lip, 'eternity is long!' and, with a glance of anguish . . . he turned away."

In New Orleans Charles took a job as a countinghouse agent, part of whose task was to ride the countryside collecting debts. That incongruous outcome of his rebellion may well have shocked the family as much as his abandonment of the ministry: the entire clan joined in a "weekly concert of prayer" for the wanderer. Clinging desperately to his musical ambitions, he also served as a church organist.

What Charles saw of opulence in New Orleans, poverty in the bayou country, and slavery on the plantations (Harriet would use his stories when she wrote *Uncle Tom's Cabin*) repelled and depressed him. A series of letters he wrote in the late 1830s to his seventeen-year-old half sister, Isabella, is an outpouring of tortured emotions. It is sprinkled with effusive expressions of love for Isabella and apologies for his neglect of Sarah Coffin: I am, he says, the enthusiast and idealist; she is "practical—real—common sense." Pathetically, he still yearns for Mary Wright. Surrounded, he wails, by "the hateful world of business," where everyone is pursuing "cursed Money! Money! Money!" he is kin to Werther in his hypersensitivity, his adoration of an unattainable woman, and his suicidal impulses.

Writing to a sympathetic younger sister, he may have exaggerated his malaise. But as a moody, high-strung young man caught between religious pressures from his family and a bill collector's work, his turmoil is understandable. As a worshiper of Rousseau—who had also been a wanderer for many years, rejecting institutions, cultivating emotions and adoring music—Charles's life in New Orleans was as much a betrayal of his ideals as it had been in his father's house in Walnut Hills.

Languishing in what he called the "midnight of fatalism," and plainly under the influence of Byron's "Childe Harold," another Romantic model of the alienated spirit, Charles published a poem that began:

> Oh, must I live a lonely one
> Unloved upon the thronged earth,
> Without a home beneath the sun
> Far from the land that gave me birth.
>
> Alone—alone I wander on,
> An exile in a dreary land. . . .

Beset by frustrations, much of it obviously sexual, he abandoned all pride and in an almost hysterical letter pleaded with his father to intercede for him with Nathaniel Wright, promising that if he won Mary he would return to religion and conventional paths. Defending his passion, he added: "You may call this idolatry—But I tell you—it is *Nature*." The alternative, he declared, was a descent into vagabondism. To Isabella he gave a Poe-like description of what he faced if his plea failed:

You have never stood by the dark cave of Insanity—and looked with horror in at the dark door—and down the frightful chasms—nor heard beneath—the hurrying waters—the hideous noises—the shrieks and the laughter—feeling meanwhile your own brain boil—and every nerve thrill with a dreadful joy mingled with horror.

Having been subjected to other of Charles's macabre visions, Isabella was evidently not alarmed. At this point Lyman, perhaps inwardly resenting Wright's rejection of Charles, attacked his parishioner for corrupting his children by encouraging the sin of social dancing. Wright answered angrily, scorning Beecher's criticism as officious, bigoted and guilty of mistaking gravity for piety. Mary was so agitated by the whole affair that she needed medical treatment to calm her heart.

Defeated at last, Charles abandoned his bizarre courtship and faced what he now called "the realities of the world." Although still unsure of himself ("I believe it would be safe for me to marry Sarah," he wrote to his father and Isabella), he turned back to patient Sarah Coffin, married her, and settled down in New Orleans. Thus tamely, at the age of twenty-five, did Charles Beecher's act of rebellion against Church, father, family, Mammon and American society come to a close.

As remote as a divinity school graduate in the Ohio Valley in the 1830s may seem from the sophistication of European Romanticism, Charles Beecher had been for almost ten years mastered by that movement. He was listening not to the sermons of his father or the advice of his sisters and brothers but to the siren songs of Byron, Rousseau and Goethe's Werther. But like so many followers of great rebel spirits, he had much of their torments and none of their triumphs.

The end of his youthful dreams is reflected in a brief narrative that he contributed to *Godey's Lady's Book* in 1840. "Eoline" is a cross between a Rhine legend, Poe's tales and *Faust*. Full of echoes of his own career, it tells of the son of a Rhineland blacksmith, Karl, who longs to become a great violinist but when he cannot achieve perfection destroys his violin. Then, with an Aeolian harp he summons up Eoline, a wind spirit, and possesses her. In a Faustian pact she grants his wish to be a master musician, but when he deserts her for a simple earthly maid, Bertha—obviously Charles's wife, Sarah—Eoline calls down spirits who strike him dead in the middle of a concert. So even Charles's farewell to his romantic dreams is pure fantasy.

In real life, Charles, forced to earn a living for his wife and, soon, a son, began teaching music in a school run by Eunice Beecher's brother Talbut Bullard. He also began to move, as had Henry and Harriet, toward a religion of the heart, one in which creeds and strict doctrines were replaced by love of Christ and a reliance on the Bible. In a family circular letter in 1840 he even indulged in a bit of joking about his progress: "Times is not quite so hard with me as they used to was. . . . Have just cleared $100 by a Singing School. . . . With a fair prospect of an income next year [of] say $150 a month." Unfortunately, the school failed and the fair prospects faded. (It was just as well for Talbut: he turned to the study of medicine and eventually set up a practice in Indianapolis.) So in 1841, after three years of exile, Charles came back north with his wife and child.

He turned now to Henry, companion of all his days from Litchfield to Walnut Hills. Realizing how desperately Charles was struggling to find a faith, Henry proved completely sympathetic and helpful. So Charles took a house near Henry's and soon became a kind of general assistant in his brother's church. Compared to Henry, Charles was a striking-looking young man with a background of artistic aspiration and spiritual anguish that evoked the tender sympathies of young women. They had heard how he had gone off to New Orleans to devote himself to music and escape the clutches of Calvinism. It was in church that Jane Merrill Ketcham first saw him: "He was sitting on one of the seats near the platform . . ." she wrote. "He was singing alone—'Do not I love thee, Oh, my Lord.' Never can I forget how his countenance shone with that love."

Julia Merrill and Betty Bates, already mooning over Henry, now extended their affections to his younger brother. At first it was only an adolescent infatuation, but by 1845 they were mature young women and their intimate messages to the two young men, both of them married, take on poignant overtones.

Charles not only became the church organist and directed the choir but took charge of the Sunday school. Unlike his father and Henry, who saw church music essentially as an emotional stimulus to worship and prayer, Charles loved it for itself. "The whole soul of our organist was in his music," Mrs. Ketcham wrote. Under Charles the choir became known throughout the state and gave public concerts—with solos on violin and organ—that included the religious works of Haydn and Mozart.

But the church could not afford to pay Charles and although he earned some money by tutoring and giving music lessons, he was frequently, like his father and Henry, in debt. And his wife, Sarah, like her sisters-in-law Harriet and Eunice, had problems with health, household work and lack of money. Nevertheless, amid the glow of Henry's optimism, Charles began to accept, as Henry and Harriet had, a relatively Christ-centered faith. Finally, during a revival in 1843, he achieved conversion. With the pride of a successful conspirator, Henry reported to his father:

Charles has been very deeply affected—has most heartily dedicated himself to Christ and tho' as yet he experiences no such *fullness* of intense personal love to Christ . . . I thought it would be balm to your feelings to hear me say . . . that on the whole, *I feel that Charles is safe.*

It was balm indeed to Lyman—a consummation he had sought stubbornly for ten years.

Charles's decision seems to have tapped wells of feeling and imagination in him. Encouraged by Henry, he preached repeatedly, bringing to bear a touch of mysticism and imagination. He drew sizable audiences and held his listeners interested for hours. In her reminiscences long afterward, Jane Merrill Ketcham recalled the "pathos and beauty" of his sermons on the Virgin and the young Jesus. He incorporated this material in a book, *The Incarnation,* a rather flowery and "picturesque" retelling of the New Testament story of the Virgin and the birth and youth of Jesus.

Compared to what George and Henry had faced, Charles had no difficulty in passing the presbytery examination for his license to preach. He did so despite the fact that, as Tom declared and Henry knew, not all his doubts about Calvinist doctrine had been laid to rest. It was not so easy to find a church. But just as Lyman had come to the aid of his four oldest sons, so Henry helped Charles now. He learned from Samuel Merrill that a few members of an Old School congregation, the First Presbyterian Church of Fort Wayne, a prosperous trading center in northeastern Indiana, might be persuaded to transfer their allegiance to a

New School pastor. Seeing an opportunity to win a church for the New School cause as well as create a post for Charles, Henry went to Fort Wayne openly intent on splitting up the Presbyterian congregation there. Despite his insistence that he abhorred dissension in church ranks, he mounted a campaign to capture enough parishioners for a second Presbyterian church. He won only six converts but scraped together a few others and in June 1844 organized the Second Presbyterian Church of Fort Wayne, with brother Charles as its pastor.

No sooner had Henry returned home, however, than he learned that Charles was having trouble keeping his pathetic little congregation—all of sixteen women and three men—together. In a bitter report to the secretary of the Home Missionary Society, Charles charged that new settlers were being misled by "ultra high Calvinistic and Old School influences." ". . . as I have," he added, "the misfortune to be . . . rather original, I am represented as anything but sound in faith." He declared that the Old School clique,

rich, aristocratic, and formerly idle, are now . . . kept vigilant and active. Every new arrival is visited, courted, told that they are New School in sentiment, and we Unitarian etc. . . . and thus is fully organized a most excellent system of opposition. . . . it is their fixed resolve to cut off our supplies . . . and starve us out. They do nothing openly. . . . All is civil, polished.

Henry immediately wrote to his father urging him to come to Charles's rescue, pointing out that Lyman Beecher's known antipathy to Unitarianism would carry great weight. There was, he added, an even more important task: "*Besides* (and sub rosa) I am anxious that you should *commune with Charles*. I do not believe that he is *tainted*." They must, he wrote, get Charles "to repress . . . any new views, and to urge . . . *practical preaching*. If you can stand in the gap *once more,* I think you may dismiss all *care* of [Charles] from your mind and regard him as safely launched. . . ." It was at this point, as we saw, that Henry also wrote to Charles, urging him to preach only "mouldy orthodoxy" as long as captious critics were lurking about.

Henry's fears were not unfounded: Charles warned his father how troubled he would be if his forthcoming ordination ended his right to differ with the church whenever he felt that it did not agree with Scripture. Lyman answered in a long letter exhorting Charles not to do or say anything rash and then set out for Fort Wayne. A newspaper later carried the story of how the seventy-year-old minister left St. Mary's on the Ohio on horseback, covered over sixty-five miles of wilderness roads and arrived at the home of his Fort Wayne host, Judge McCulloch, twenty hours later, "besplashed and bespattered, with smoking steed and saddlebags crusted with mud . . . weary and stiff, but still hale and hearty."

After a good meal, a bath in cold water and a whiskey rubdown, he went to bed and came down the next morning as "sound as a nut." Lyman Beecher's reward came a few days later when members of the presbytery, Charles's congregation and his family gathered to witness the ordination of the last of Lyman's five sons by Roxana Foote. Lyman shed tears of joy.

But ordination did not work a miraculous transformation in Charles Beecher. Still trailing shreds of idealism, he was sorely disappointed when his congregation proved more intent on scoring points against their Old School rivals than achieving grace. Contemptuously he reported their coarse proddings on a Sunday morning:

"Beecher you must *put in your best licks today!*" "You must *knock the socks* off those Old School folks!" And so they stood by to see me fight. Fight? for what? for Christ? They never dreamed of that, they wanted to hear what I had to say for *New School.* Now I had nothing particular to say for New School. . . . I *didn't,* and told them so. "Well," said they, "What did you come up here for?"

Considering the near poverty in which he lived, such a question must surely have depressed him. Once when Aunt Esther came to visit and to help Sarah, she found that because Charles's quarterly check from the American Home Missionary Society had not arrived, there was almost no food in the house.

All seemed to go fairly well for almost a year, but then rumors of discontent in his congregation drifted back to his family. For all her romantic notions about Charles and Henry, Julia Merrill had to admit, after a visit to friends in Fort Wayne, that Charles was not so popular as she thought he would be. She reported a variety of carping criticisms— that he was conceited, made too much of his relation to Dr. Beecher, lacked tact. "He seems to be common property," she wrote, "and every [one] that pleases picks at him."

But such critics were only mildly annoyed; it was his fellow clergy whom he genuinely shocked. The provocation was two sermons he delivered in 1846 at the dedication of a church building. As part of a reaffirmation of the authority of the Bible, he made as militant an attack on suppression of free thought in the church as anyone there had ever heard:

. . . liberty of opinion in our theological seminaries is a mere form. To say nothing of the thumbscrew of criticism by which every original mind is tortured into negative propriety, the whole boasted liberty of the student consists in a choice of chains . . . whether he will wear the Presbyterian handcuffs or the Methodist, Baptist, Episcopal or other Evangelical handcuffs. Hence it has secretly come to pass that the ministers themselves dare not study their Bibles. . . . There is something criminal in saying anything new. It is shocking to utter words that have not the mould of age upon them. . . .

With amazing boldness he concluded that any church that imposed its own creed on that of the Bible was taking a step toward apostasy. His father and his brother Henry were in the audience and Henry, if not Dr. Beecher, must have realized that Charles was not only rejecting their advice but making it seem devious and shameful.

The presbytery promptly sent a committee to examine him. They found him friendly and so they contented themselves with declaring that his opinions were "subversive in the house of God" and "a total misapprehension of the views and practices of the Presbyterian Church." Perhaps because he was Lyman Beecher's son and Henry Ward Beecher's brother, the presbytery took no further action. Thirty years earlier, clergymen had been suspended for far less of a challenge to the church code. Indeed, encouraged by a few equally brave souls in his congregation, he published the sermons in a tiny book, *The Bible, a Sufficient Creed.* It was quoted widely but in the long run it marked Charles as unreliable and hurt his career.

A few years later when he decided to follow other Beechers in returning to the East, he had to settle for a decaying church in Newark, New Jersey. In location it was not far from Henry's church in Brooklyn, but in prestige it was nowhere.

HARRIET AND CALVIN STOWE

"As domestic as any pair of tame fowl"

An advertisement in Cincinnati newspapers on March 8, 1833, read:

A NEW GEOGRAPHY FOR CHILDREN
Corey and Fairbank have in the
press, and will publish in a few days a

GEOGRAPHY FOR CHILDREN
with numerous maps and engravings
upon an improved plan
By Catharine E. Beecher

The ad was curiously misleading: the book had been suggested by Catharine but it had been written entirely by Harriet. It was only a textbook for children, but, produced by a woman of twenty-two and written as a readable narrative rather than as a compendium of data and dates, it was a significant performance. And it was all hers.

When Catharine, with an eye to income as well as usefulness, had suggested the book, Harriet had promptly put aside her lofty literary ambitions and set to work. Her teaching duties were a burden but they took little of her creative energies, and like any young writer, she yearned for publication. She was surely a bit unhappy to see the book credited entirely to Catharine—obviously because of Catharine's reputation as an educator; but she was on the title page and her share of the profits— Catharine had sold the manuscript outright to the publisher—was $187. Best of all, the book sold very well, going through five editions in six months. There were even collateral benefits: when Bishop Purcell of the Cincinnati diocese visited the school, she wrote: "He spoke of my poor little geography and thanked me for the unprejudiced manner in which I had treated the Catholic question." In view of her father's attitude, the bishop's comment was both generous and well deserved.

But her endless school duties soon left her exhausted. By the time she finished her long letter to Georgiana several days later, she had lapsed into one of her gloomy, introverted states; and it was no longer an adolescent mood but a frustrated woman's analysis of what she saw as a condition of her sex in American society.

Contributing to her malaise was her reading of Madame de Staël's novel *Corinne* (1806) and an account of the life of that remarkable author herself. Madame de Staël had become famous in Paris for her glamorous salon, her independence, and her celebration of the free emotional life. When Napoleon exiled her for criticizing and even mocking him, she profited from her life abroad by writing *Corinne,* a novel set in Italy. It told of Corinne, a young Italian of mysterious background—she spoke English perfectly—who captures society in Rome with her wit, learning, beauty, talents and zest for life. She falls deeply in love with a handsome and intelligent but melancholy English lord and when a series of fateful misunderstandings separates them, Corinne dies, a sacrifice to love.

Romantically overdrawn in every respect, it was nonetheless profoundly influential in its portrayal of an emotionally liberated woman. In Hartford, a copy secretly passed around among the students in Catharine's school had caused a minor sensation.

We cannot fully understand how the inhibited daughter of New England Puritans could have written *Uncle Tom's Cabin* if we do not realize that she was also a product of the Romantic age, deeply affected by the lives and works of Byron, Scott, Madame de Staël and their like. For some young Americans no sermon could quite counteract a taste of that wine. Speaking of *Corinne,* Harriet wrote to her friend Georgiana:

I have felt an intense sympathy with many parts of that book, with many parts of her character. But in America feelings vehement and absorbing like hers become still more deep, morbid, and impassioned by the constant habits of self-government which the rigid forms of our society demand. They are repressed, and burn inward till they burn the very soul, leaving only dust and ashes. It seems to me the intensity with which my mind has thought and felt on every subject presented to it has had this effect. It has withered and exhausted it. . . .

. . . All that is enthusiastic, all that is impassioned in admiration of nature, of writing, of character, in devotional thought and emotion, or in the emotions of affection, I have felt with vehement and absorbing intensity,—felt till my mind is exhausted, and seems to be sinking into deadness. Half of my time I am glad to remain in a listless vacancy, to busy myself with trifles, since thought is pain, and emotion is pain.

Coming from a twenty-two-year-old in 1833, the perception that emotions forbidden by society are simply repressed and "burn inward" is of course remarkable. More than that, it suggests that her effort, and power, in *Uncle Tom's Cabin* to bring suppressed emotion to the surface was no accident.

Both *Corinne* and Madame de Staël herself must also have increased

Harriet's awareness that at twenty-two she had never had a beau. But that was soon to be remedied in a most unexpected way.

In late August of 1833, Calvin Stowe arrived at Lane Seminary to take up his duties as professor of Biblical Literature. Stowe, a protégé of her father's in Boston in 1828, had been a professor at Bowdoin and then Dartmouth and was already known as an outstanding scholar. At first Harriet found herself more interested in Stowe's young bride, Eliza Tyler, daughter of Dr. Tyler, president of Dartmouth and a leader among Old School Calvinists. Harriet, lonely for such a friend as she had had in Georgiana, "fell in love with her directly," and Eliza responded. (She responded in the same way to Harriet's equally lonely stepmother, Harriet Porter.) Harriet described her to Georgiana as a delicate, pretty little woman with a fair complexion and "a most interesting simplicity and timidity of manner." In the fall, when Harriet and Catharine moved into town to be close to the school, Calvin and Eliza remained in Walnut Hills, but there was constant visiting back and forth. It was thus, more or less inadvertently, that Harriet came to know her future husband.

Although Harriet Beecher Stowe spent eighteen years in Cincinnati, the city would play no part in any of her thirty-odd books. But had she not lived there and learned through it about slavery, it is unlikely that she could have written *Uncle Tom's Cabin*. As a gateway to the South, with many Southerners moving constantly through it, the city gave her opportunities to get glimpses of slave society and yet not be identified with it. She came close enough to slaveholders to feel that by and large they were not inhuman and to hear their arguments firsthand. At the same time she learned the inhumanity and agony of the system in personal terms. She was exposed to the shock of newspaper advertisements for runaway slaves; below a crude woodcut of a skulking black man the announcement might read: "100 DOLLARS REWARD! . . . *will be paid for the apprehension and delivery of Humphrey, a slave, who is about 17 years of age, and who made his escape from the undersigned in Boone County, Ky., on the 22nd ult.* (signed) A. W. Gaines."

Occasionally, too, an editor would see something that was more than he could stomach and would dare to speak his mind. Such a one was young Reverend Thomas Brainerd, editor of the Cincinnati *Journal*. Like many other Northerners, he thought slavery was evil, but he could see no way of ending it: taking slaves away from their masters was confiscation of private property and would be resisted with violence; buying the freedom of slaves with government money was beyond the nation's capacity; and slavery had after all served to convert African blacks into American Christians. . . .

But one March day in 1833 down at the wharf he saw a steamboat crowded with 150 slaves, including males and females of all ages. He discovered that they had been bought in Virginia and Kentucky and were being taken south to be sold in Mississippi. So he wrote an editorial called, with deceptive mildness, "Unrighteous Traffic":

... They were under the care of two beings in human shape, named Dorsey and Miller, who it seems make the purchase, transporting, and sale of slaves a gainful business. ... The traders pass through the northern slave-holding States, and whenever they find (which is a rare case) a master willing to sell his slaves to he knows not whom, to be carried he knows not where, a bargain is struck. Husbands and wives are torn asunder—parents and children are forcibly separated. ... While the process of buying is going on, the victims are collected at certain points and lodged for safe-keeping in jails, etc. When enough have been purchased for a *drove,* all are brought together, chained two and two, and ... are driven to the place of embarkation. They are crowded into the upper deck of a steam boat, confined in irons if necessary ... and are landed, sold and distributed in the lower countries. The trader often gains a hundred percent on the entire lot. ...

Of those fellow citizens in adjoining States who have inherited slaves from their ancestors ... we have never been disposed to complain. Many masters and mistresses in these circumstances, by giving their slaves proper instruction and uniform kind treatment, make the best of an evil which they have inherited ... and which they have a disposition, but not the power, to remedy.

But no apology can be offered for the master who raises *human beings to sell,* and no character on earth is more intrinsically hateful or more universally despised, than that of a slave jockey. We could wish such persons no heavier punishment than ... to have them see in one deep, broad stream the blood which their merciless thongs have drawn from human flesh—and to have their consciences tell in accents of dreadful truth the guilt which those incur who make their wealth by adding mountain weights to the already grievous load of human misery.

Since the Reverend Brainerd would before long become Dr. Beecher's assistant in the Second Presbyterian Church and since his weekly was the foremost Presbyterian newspaper in the West, Harriet surely read this editorial. And just as certainly its emotional concern with individual lives, with human suffering rather than abstract issues or arguments, sank into her consciousness. She would in time use precisely that personal approach.

She also had at least one intimate glimpse of slavery; it came when she accompanied Mary Dutton that first summer on a visit to a student's family in Washington, Kentucky, about sixty miles from Cincinnati. According to Mary, they also went to a large plantation nearby. Harriet seemed to pay little attention to what they heard and saw there. But Mary was astonished twenty years later when scenes from that visit turned up in the most vivid detail in the pages of *Uncle Tom's Cabin.*

One scene was of the master laughing, as though at a monkey, at the way one of his black boys entertained a party after a dinner. Another, in the local church, was of a beautiful young woman who seemed to be white, but who was, Harriet was told, an octaroon. Harriet was left forever with the tormenting thought that someone with skin hardly darker than her own was doomed by men to all the barbarities of slavery, including submission—as the octaroon's mother had submitted—to the sexual advances of a white master.

Soon, too, there were increasing signs close to home of the rise of an aggressive opposition to every aspect of slavery. The most arresting representative of that was, as we have seen, Theodore Weld. He arrived like an itinerant evangelist, filled to overflowing with his message, a knight with no armor but his fiery conviction, no sword but his voice. He came to Lane as a thirty-year-old freshman who was treated as a professor and would exercise more power than the president of the school.

Weld would, like Garrison, Birney, Lovejoy, the Grimkés, and a few others, demand that all Americans join in wiping out slavery or accept their share of the blame for it. He would bring this message painfully home to all the Beechers. In the battering attack of the Lane antislavery debates Weld supplied not only the wrath but the reasons. What had been considered a paternalistic, family institution, sanctioned by time and tradition, began to appear, under his assault, as a national sin, a darkly spreading stain, a wound which Livingstone, fighting slavery in Africa twenty-five years later, would call "the open sore of the world."

Amid the wearisome routine of teaching there was one special solace for Harriet in Cincinnati—the literary groups, and especially the Semi-Colon Club. While Catharine delighted in the select company, the conversation and the opportunity to promote her school, Harriet found in them her first audience. The geography had after all been only a textbook for children; ever since her triumphant school composition and her exciting, if abortive, experience with *Cleon*, she had dreamed of being a genuine writer—author of stories, sketches, plays, perhaps even novels. Catharine was justified in claiming that teaching was the only professional work open to the average young woman, but there were already many well-known women writers—so many that Hawthorne would some years later refer to them as "the d——d mob of scribbling women." Some women, such as the Brontës, George Eliot, George Sand and, later, on a few occasions, Harriet herself, still thought it wise to use a male *nom de plume*, but others—Fanny Burney, Jane Austen, Maria Edgeworth, Madame de Staël, and in America, Lydia Sigourney, and in Cincinnati itself, Caroline Lee Hentz—had achieved fame without such a disguise.

One custom of the Semi-Colon Club was particularly comforting to a shy novice: contributions could be presented anonymously. After trying out a few humorous trifles on the group, Harriet undertook a character sketch of her father's uncle Lot Benton, with whom Lyman had lived as a youth. She had been listening to her father's wry and vivid stories of his uncle ever since her childhood and it was no task at all for her to present him in sharp detail.

The piece (first published as "A New England Sketch" but later known simply as "Uncle Lot") was read to the club one night in November 1833—a memorable date, for it marked the debut of a major American writer. The members had heard nothing like it, and judging from the reaction of James Hall, editor of the *Western Monthly Magazine,* they were delighted and impressed by it. Hall, who encouraged local color, humor and high moral standards, invited her to submit the story in a fiction contest being conducted by the magazine. We can imagine the excitement that gripped her as she did so. Soon Hall announced that it had won the prize—the handsome sum of fifty dollars. Although a case has been made for her authorship of a pseudonymous sketch in an issue two months earlier, the publication of her first signed story in Hall's highly regarded magazine was triumph enough, and winning the prize was sweet beyond all dreams.

The story, the wooing of Lot Griswold's daughter, serves only as a framework for portraits of Lot, his wife, Sally, his daughter, Grace, and her suitor, James. The characterizations are shrewd, supported by homely details and by dialogue that reveals an ear for New England speech. But most surprising is Harriet's dry humor and satiric thrusts. Having often seen her in despondent or even morbid moods, we are unprepared for the breezy style and the sunny atmosphere: Grace is pretty, pleasant, chatty—a "universal favorite"—James is irrepressibly buoyant and flirtatious, and Aunt Sally is as "cheerful and domestic as the teakettle that sung by her fire." Only the character of Lot has any shading: "a chestnut burr, abounding with briers without and with substantial goodness within . . . a kindly heart; but all the strata of his character were crossed by a vein of surly petulance, that, halfway between joke and earnest, colored everything that he said and did." If Lot seems like a stock figure, he seems so partly because Harriet Beecher drew him so expertly that dozens of later writers imitated her. In Lot we get the first signs of her mastery of that combination of Puritan earnestness and Yankee humor called "New England doubleness."

Mainly because of the way it captured a regional type, "Uncle Lot" is sometimes said to represent the beginning of literary realism in America. But sentiment romanticizes all: even the death of the Griswolds' beloved son George, a young minister who literally wastes away through the intensity of his devotion, somehow becomes a blessed event. Harriet repeatedly sentimentalizes the death of the young, plainly a device for making bearable what was then a common tragedy. True, she was only twenty-two years old; thirty years later she would, in *Poganuc People* and *Oldtown Folks,* produce a much richer and more enduring treatment of the same kind of material.

Almost immediately she undertook another character sketch, this time of a woman, "Aunt Mary." Based upon her mother, it is a memorial to the self-sacrificing women found in so many New England families; the result is a figure without color or substance—a saint, not a human being. Nevertheless Hall printed it and paid for it, confirming Harriet's—and her family's—belief in her great literary gifts.

These sketches, together with other of her earliest efforts, were later collected in her first book, *The Mayflower.* It also contained an essay called "Feeling," which proclaimed the need for emotional expression and the free exercise of sensibility. It is a slight piece, but taken along with her letter to Georgiana on her adoption of her uncle Samuel's "sundial philosophy" of counting only unclouded hours, and her receptivity to Madame de Staël's faith in self-expression, it is significant. It was all part of an intense effort to escape from the sense of guilt and inadequacy—and perhaps even the lack of a mother's love—that had haunted her from her childhood on.

In June, when Henry Ward was to graduate from Amherst, it was agreed that Harriet, his companion of old, should attend his graduation. Accompanied by Mary Dutton, she made the journey by stagecoach to Toledo, by steamer across Lake Erie to Buffalo, and then by stage to Amherst. The trip was exciting enough in itself, but finding Henry grown from a thick-tongued boy into a witty, popular youth of twenty-one was a delight. After the graduation, and while they were busy visiting old friends, painful news came from Cincinnati. The conflict with Weld's rebels was persisting ominously, but far more shocking, as far as Harriet was concerned, was word that a cholera epidemic—sweeping Cincinnati for the third year in succession—had struck down Eliza Stowe. No matter how accustomed Harriet may have become to the terrible ways of the disease, its sudden destruction of that gentle soul—hardly twenty-five years old—shook her.

Perhaps it reduced Harriet's sorrow to learn, when she returned to Cincinnati, that Eliza, like Roxana Foote, had died blissfully. In her last hours, seeing Calvin weeping, Eliza had gently said, "Weep not for me," and at the end she had exclaimed, "Oh, joy—joy unspeakable and full of glory—full of glory!" In this her religion served her well. But Calvin was left prostrate with grief.

Harriet was accompanied back to Cincinnati by Henry and by

Charles, who had become homesick at Bowdoin. Both young men were to enter the pathetically diminished classes at Lane.

Harriet's deep sympathy with Calvin and her willingness to talk lovingly and long about "dear departed Eliza" drew the pair very close. Later, they had a portrait of Eliza painted by an artist who had known her, and each anniversary of her death they would sit before it and talk about her. It was as though their love of Eliza were transferred to each other in the act of mourning, and death sanctioned an unaccustomed unlocking of the gates of feeling. So, truly phoenix-like, a new love rose out of the embers of the old.

They were not alone in mourning Eliza; often in the tiny cemetery in Walnut Hills, Lyman's wife Harriet sat beside Eliza's flower-strewn grave, envying the peace the younger woman had achieved.

For a young woman who had been tantalized if not enchanted by the men in the works of Byron, Scott, Richardson, and Madame de Staël, Harriet could not have chosen for herself a more unlikely lover than Calvin Stowe. At thirty-two, he was a professor of Biblical literature and probably the leading Hebrew scholar of his time. When he traveled he usually carried two books—the Bible in Greek and Dante's *Divine Comedy* in Italian. Physically he was hardly a figure of romance: short, stocky—later fat—almost bald, with a squarish face, wide mouth and generally rumpled clothes. He was a voracious eater, helpless in matters of money or manual skill, rather indolent, and subject to fits of hypochondria verging on the morbid. Most curious of all, he had weird visions.

Yet even at worst he seems to have been merely exasperating. Harriet—and everyone else—found him amiable and sympathetic. He was an able teacher and lecturer, with a keenly logical mind, and he had a droll sense of humor and an endless fund of stories of his native Massachusetts village. Most of all, his religion rested on a warm personal view of God, quite without her father's intensity and sense of mission.

Born into a desperately poor family, Calvin Stowe was brought up by a widowed mother. At a most impressionable age and with what he himself described as a highly excitable nervous system, he was fascinated by the more unearthly episodes in Job, Revelation, Daniel and Ezekiel. He was haunted by stories of witchcraft and demonic Indians. But it was John Bunyan's *Pilgrim's Progress*, with its fiends and giants, as well as the voices and terrors abounding in Bunyan's own boyhood, that made the deepest impression on him. At the least they prepared him to accept his own visions and delusions without fear or surprise.

At the age of fourteen he became an apprentice in a paper mill: one of his more unsettling duties there, and one that surely contributed to his visions of hell, was to rise at 3 A.M. and fire the boilers to make steam before the workers arrived at six. How he managed at eighteen to afford to go to college is something of a mystery. At Bowdoin he was by far the most pious student—although skepticism was the fashion—and the most studious, and yet quite popular. Not surprisingly, he was valedictorian at graduation. It tells us something about his personality that while teaching at Dartmouth he wooed and won the daughter of the president of the college.

Professor Stowe first revealed his rich psychic life in a paper read before the Semi-Colon Club early in 1835. Because he had been familiar with his astral visitors since he was four years old, he recounted his experiences like a physician reporting a case history. The facts, he observed, were curious enough to warrant the attention of a psychologist. He disarmed skeptics by adding that he had no "taste or talent for fiction or poetry" and barely imagination enough to enjoy such works by others. (The vividness of his account soon proved that this was a decided exaggeration.) He continued:

As early as I can remember anything, I can remember observing a multitude of animated and active objects, which I could see with perfect distinctness . . . passing through the floors, and the ceilings, and the walls of the house. . . . These appearances occasioned neither surprise nor alarm, except when they assumed some hideous and frightful form . . . for I became acquainted with them as soon as with any of the objects of sense.

Lest his spellbound audience suppose he was describing only dreams or nightmares, he disclosed that they also occurred in the daytime and when other people were present. He did not reveal that he still had such visions; that might have given his audience pause.

He told how at the age of four he slept in a bedroom that had a staircase leading into a garret. After he had gone to bed and the candle had been removed, a figure with a very pleasant face would thrust itself part way through an opening in the staircase and then withdraw. "He was a great favorite of mine," Calvin added, "for, though we neither of us spoke, we perfectly understood, and were entirely devoted to, each other." He called this favorite phantom "Harvey" because it resembled an older boy by that name whom Calvin knew.

Sometimes, especially when he was sick or depressed, "there were visitations of another sort, odious and frightful." Thus one night he was deeply alarmed by the appearance of agitated black clouds. Harvey appeared, but "with an expression of pain and terror," and soon left. Next Calvin saw far below a vision of hell swarming with inhabitants, just as it was pictured in sermons. Suddenly, near his bed, he saw four or five "sturdy devils" trying to carry off a "dissipated" local character named Brown. (Since Brown had repeatedly terrified little Calvin, he was obviously now about to be suitably punished.) Strangely, the devils had no horns, hoofs, tails or red faces, but were all "well-dressed gentlemen." Brown resisted the devils fiercely. Finally a thick cloud whirled up to him and when he struck at it, it turned his hand and arm black. But Brown sprang into the cloud and tore it apart, exclaiming hoarsely, "There, I've got out! dam'me if I haven't!" Undiscouraged, the devils brought in an iron frame with a pair of enormous rollers of the kind used in iron mills, seized Brown and began to crank him into the rollers. Calvin continued:

Not a word was spoken, not a sound was heard; but the fearful struggles and terrified, agonizing looks of Brown were more than I could endure. I sprang from my bed and ran through the kitchen into the room where my parents slept, and entreated that they would permit me to spend the remainder of the night with them. . . .

"Poh! poh! you foolish boy," replied my father sternly. "You've only been dreaming,"

and he ordered the boy to go back to bed or be whipped. Calvin returned to his room, found all quiet, and soon fell asleep.

An even more macabre experience was his awakening one bright, moonlit night to find an ashy-blue human skeleton in bed with him! He screamed but when the family came running, he refused to tell them what had frightened him. He was, however, allowed to go to another bed; there the mood of his vision changed completely: he saw on the window benches tiny fairies "in white robes, gamboling and dancing with incessant merriment." They soothed and cheered him.

Almost naively candid, Calvin revealed that he had always been subject to extreme moods, wandering about on dark nights in a deep melancholy. At other times he burned with a "morbid love" of his friends and yet at the slightest provocation would "fly into an uncontrollable passion and foam like a little fury."

If such visions had ended with his childhood, they might be dismissed as the hallucinations of a sensitive boy overstimulated by alternately terrifying and heaven-promising sermons and a spiritual climate in which reports of occult occurrences were not considered especially eccentric. Protestant religious history from John Calvin himself and John Bunyan to Joseph Smith and his Book of Mormon was strewn with stories of men and women who heard voices, were guided by angels or beset by devils. Stowe knew of the German mystic Boehme's familiarity with the spirit world and he had read the speculations of Kierkegaard. Besides this there was the tradition of the supernatural that saturated

Romantic literature, from the Gothic novel and Goethe's *Faust* (which Stowe admired greatly) to Poe's horror tales and Irving's specter-haunted legends of Sleepy Hollow. Calvin Stowe's account must have seemed simply like testimony close to home.

It is customary to think of early New England as peopled by a hardheaded, sober-sided race, but the region produced—perhaps as a reaction to the rigors of New England life and Calvinist rule—more than its share of utopian dreamers, religious visionaries and "spiritualists." Catharine Beecher repeatedly resorted to clairvoyants, and William, Harriet, Charles and their half sister, Isabella, all became actively interested in spiritualism.

So it was not difficult for Harriet to find in Calvin Stowe's recital evidence of mysterious depths and far more imagination than he himself realized. And it is clear that he was never truly possessed or disordered by his visions. Since Harriet also found his learning most remarkable, his humor and stories beguiling and his company congenial, it is not altogether surprising that after communing so intimately with him about Eliza, she should have seen herself as Eliza's successor.

But the year that followed was full of disturbing experiences in other directions.

Late in 1834 Harriet accompanied her father and Calvin Stowe to a meeting of the Presbyterian synod in Ripley, a town on the Ohio side of the river near Maysville, Kentucky. There they were guests of the Reverend John Rankin. Rankin's tiny house was situated on a bluff that overlooked the river. There would have been nothing memorable about their stay with Rankin had they not noted the lantern he put in his window every night. Then, perhaps because he found them sympathetic, he made a startling revelation: his house was a "station" on what was to become known as the Underground Railroad. The lantern was a beacon: escaped slaves in Kentucky learned that if they could cross the river and reach the house in which that light shone, they were on their way to Canada and freedom. The evidence of that modest man's willingness to risk everything to free even one slave must have shown Harriet how timid was her opposition to slavery.

As though that were not enough, Rankin told his guests of a slave escape that they would never forget. The runaway was a young black woman who had been treated so cruelly that even though she had a baby in arms and had to leave without her husband, she had bundled up her child and fled. She reached the Kentucky shore of the Ohio on a March evening only to find that the great river was still frozen and, far more ominous, that a spring thaw had begun to melt the ice.

A riverman, it is said, took pity on the wretched woman and told her that if she could reach the light visible in the house across the river, she and her baby would be safe. Frantic in the dark and the cold, she started across the ice, the baby clutched in her arms. How she made her way across, climbed the bluff and reached the cottage no one knows. Magically the door opened and merciful white folks—the Reverend Rankin— gave her food and dry clothes. Afterwards, Rankin drove her to a house in nearby Greenfield, another refuge a little farther along the road to liberty.

The story is told that the runaway's husband soon fled his master, reached Rankin's cottage and was passed along till he was reunited with his wife and child. Later, when *Uncle Tom's Cabin* made the story of a slave woman's escape across a frozen river famous, various escaped slaves each claimed that she was the original of Harriet Beecher Stowe's character.

Rankin's story must have touched Lyman Beecher and Calvin Stowe, but we know beyond all doubt that the images it evoked burned themselves into Harriet's brain and heart.

Perhaps because she was not happy as a teacher in her sister's school and was, after all, twenty-four years old, Harriet became engaged to Calvin Stowe. The engagement was kept secret, probably because it was fairly soon after Eliza Stowe's death, but it explains why Harriet decided in November to quit teaching.

The marriage itself, in January 1836, was as private as it could be, with Mary Dutton the only outsider at the ceremony. Hardly an hour before the ceremony, when she should have been too excited, too nervous, and too full of mixed emotions for everyday tasks, she sat down and calmly wrote a letter to Georgiana May:

Well, my dear G., about half an hour more and your old friend, companion, schoolmate, sister, etc., will cease to be Hatty Beecher and change to nobody knows who. My dear, you are engaged, and pledged in a year or two to encounter a similar fate, and do you wish to know how you shall feel? Well, my dear, I have been dreading and dreading the time, and lying awake all last week wondering how I should live through this overwhelming crisis, and lo! it has come, and I feel *nothing at all*.

The wedding is to be altogether domestic; nobody present but my own brothers and sisters, and my old colleague, Mary Dutton; and as there is a sufficiency of the ministry in our family we have not even to call in the foreign aid of a minister. Sister Katy is not here, so she will not witness my departure from her care and guidance to that of another. None of my numerous friends and acquaintances who have taken such a deep interest in making the connection for me, even know the day, and it will be all done and over before they know anything about it.

Well, it is really a mercy to have this entire stupidity come over one at such a time. I should be crazy to feel as I did yesterday, or indeed to feel anything at all. But I inwardly vowed that my last feelings and reflections on this subject should be yours, and as I have not got any, it is just as well to tell you *that*. Well, here comes Mr. S., so farewell, and for the last time I subscribe

Your own
H.E.B.

The letter is so detached and matter-of-fact that it may seem that Harriet went through with the marriage at least partly because the "connection," as she phrased it, had been made for her. But it is more likely that she was emotionally exhausted after months of anticipation. Although Calvin Stowe was the last person to inspire fear, Harriet after twenty-five years of Puritan sermons and little or no intimate contact with other suitors could not but dread the moment in which she would engage in the most passionate and yet unmentionable of all acts. She had been bred in the Calvinist tradition of the pitfalls of sexuality but she had also grown up in the age of Byron and she had come to know strange yearnings and unbidden impulses. As she would say in *The Minister's Wooing,* when Mary Scudder, also a daughter of Puritans, finds herself in love: "... what did it avail her that she could say the Assembly's Catechism from end to end without tripping ... ? The wildest Italian singer or dancer, nursed on nothing but excitement from her cradle, was never more thoroughly possessed by the awful and solemn mystery of woman's life than this Puritan girl."

Then, too, after reading Madame de Staël's *Corinne,* she had complained that in America the repression of such desires made them "burn inward" till they left only dust and ashes. It was a penetrating insight, but in the days and nights that followed she apparently discovered that she had been unduly fearful.

She did not send off the letter to Georgiana immediately, partly because mail, particularly to distant places, was expensive; it was not uncommon for a writer to add installments over a period of time. Three weeks later, after a wedding excursion to Columbus, where Calvin lectured on the much admired methods of education in Prussia, she added a second installment: it described Calvin and herself seated by their fireside "as domestic as any pair of tame fowl you ever saw." "And now, my dear," she adds, "perhaps the wonder to you, as to me, is how this momentous crisis in the life of such a wisp of nerve as myself has been transacted so quietly. My dear, it is a wonder to myself. I am tranquil, quiet, and happy, I look *only* on the present and leave the future with Him who has hitherto been so kind to me."

A month later she added an exciting conclusion to the letter: in April she and Calvin were leaving for the east and on May 1 Calvin was sailing to Europe.

Lyman and Calvin had long discussed the need for someone to go to Europe to buy books for the seminary library. The school had funds for the books but not for an extended European trip by a buyer. Now, as a result of Calvin's efforts to further the development of "common" or public schools and raise teaching standards, the Ohio legislature, trying, like many other states, to establish such schools, voted to have Professor Stowe report on public education in Europe. So Calvin had a doubly distinguished mission. Then, in March, just as they were about to leave, Harriet discovered that she was pregnant. In later years she would not hesitate to travel at such a time, but it seemed too risky while she was carrying her first child.

She was sorely disappointed. She did not dream of resenting her duty as a mother, but it seemed unfair to be deprived of the trip and in addition to face eight or nine months and the birth of their first baby alone. Still, she was proud of Calvin and happy for his sake. Addressing him—as she often would—as though he were a child, she warned him against his tendency to depression, what she called "the cultivation of indigo." "You are going to a new scene now," she wrote, "and . . . I want you to take the good of it." But she could not help closing with a rueful exclamation: "My dear, I wish I were a man in your place; if I wouldn't have a grand time!"

13

HARRIET

"I have six children and cares endless"

After Calvin had left for Europe, Harriet moved into her father's house in Walnut Hills. It was hardly an ideal arrangement. Having been little more than a visitor in the Beecher home since she had gone off to school in Hartford at the age of twelve, she returned to the crowded household with mixed feelings. It was, after all, still dominated by her father and managed by Aunt Esther and was soon to be occupied by her father's newest wife, Lydia Jackson. Henry Ward and Charles continued to attend the seminary (although Charles was far more interested in music), and Harriet Porter's children were still home.

It was not entirely a happy time in the Beecher world: Harriet Porter's death was not long past, Lyman faced another heresy trial, and Lane was staggering from the defection of Weld and his rebels. Even the Western Female Institute, with both Catharine and Harriet gone, and all responsibility resting on Mary Dutton, was in trouble.

It was, however, a far more uneasy time in the city around them. There had been an antislavery movement in the South well before it took hold in the North. But as the cotton gin and other developments made cotton king, and as cotton required more and more slaves to serve it, this movement aroused increasing opposition. This hostility remained unfocused until the rise in the 1830s of abolitionism in the North. Then a Southerner like the Reverend Dr. Witherspoon of South Carolina would tell Lyman Beecher that he detested slavery but would "contend to the death against Northern interference with Southern rights." And the Cincinnati *Journal* would reprint an offer of ten thousand dollars by the city of Savannah for the capture of a prominent abolitionist, A. A. Phelps. As an important border city, Cincinnati became the scene of ugly incidents. In April 1836, a street fight between a white boy and a black boy triggered a race riot. Blacks were killed and a few of their houses were burned. The state militia had to be called out to end the clash.

It was at this point that James G. Birney, forced out of the town of

New Richmond, near Cincinnati, brought his antislavery weekly, the *Philanthropist* (signifying "friend of man"), to Cincinnati. It was a particularly inopportune moment, because plans had been completed for a railroad—it was the beginning of the railroad building boom—that would run from Cincinnati through Kentucky and the Carolinas to the Atlantic coast. Cincinnatians in general and businessmen in particular, looking forward to a great increase in trade with the South, were excited by the prospect.

Birney, Kentucky-born but educated at Princeton, had been a district attorney, cotton planter and Presbyterian elder in Huntsville, Alabama. He was already active in the Colonization Society when Theodore Weld came to Huntsville on one of his tours and gave his talks against slavery and the colonization plan. Birney, deeply impressed, decided to devote his life to abolition. He freed his slaves and began his efforts to establish his paper. But if Birney thought that Cincinnati would welcome his high-minded enterprise, he was grievously mistaken. Early on, several editors and politicians called a meeting to exert "every lawful effort" to prevent him from publishing. But Birney went to the meeting himself and disarmed it by his reasonable demeanor. Soon he also acquired an able assistant editor, Gamaliel Bailey, a young surgeon from the Cincinnati Hospital. A devout Methodist, Dr. Bailey had become an abolitionist and was one of the few Cincinnatians who had befriended the Lane secessionists.

In May Dr. Beecher went off to the Presbyterian General Assembly meeting in Pittsburgh, prepared, as we have seen, to face Dr. Wilson's charges once again. With him went the Reverend Brainerd, editor of the Cincinnati *Journal* and Beecher's assistant at the Second Presbyterian Church, which may explain why he left seminary senior Henry Ward as acting editor of the paper. Looking over Henry's shoulder as he wrote his editorials during the next few months, Harriet, despite her pregnancy, was constantly close to the Birney affair.

Rumblings of disapproval of what was called Birney's "Abolitionist rag" continued through the spring. Jacob Burnet, Ohio Supreme Court judge and a deacon in Beecher's church, led a committee to warn Birney that unless he stopped publishing the *Philanthropist,* his office would be sacked by a mob that would include two thirds of Cincinnati's property owners.

In July, Southern buyers and planters made their semiannual business visit to Cincinnati, and the merchants who welcomed them became more and more hostile to Birney. On the evening of July 12, a mob composed mainly of "young men of the better class" broke into the shop of Achilles Pugh, a Quaker who had bravely undertaken to print the *Philanthropist,* and damaged his press and type. As in most early attacks on abolitionists, respectable citizens looked on and did nothing; Harriet wrote to Calvin that many of them were "disposed to wink at the outrage" because it lined up with their prejudices. Birney and his printer promptly patched up their equipment and put out the next edition. Mayor Davies denounced the rioters and even offered a reward of one hundred dollars for the arrest and conviction of any one of them, but he undercut his action by also issuing a warning to the abolitionists.

At Henry's urging, Harriet wrote a letter (over the pen name "Franklin") to the *Journal,* defending Birney on the grounds of freedom of speech and press and a citizen's right to hold an unpopular opinion; but she avoided the slavery question itself and disclaimed any abolitionist sympathies. Henry took much the same position in his editorials.

Outraged by the action of the mob, several prominent Cincinnatians, including E. D. Mansfield, Hammond of the *Gazette* and Salmon P. Chase, called a protest meeting. The anti-abolitionists came in force and proceeded to shout down Chase and other speakers. Then they held a meeting of their own and chose a committee to warn Birney to leave town. "I wish father were at home to preach a sermon to his church," Harriet wrote in her diary, "for many of its members do not frown on these things as they ought." Appalled by the mob's behavior but, as a pregnant woman, doubly conscious of her helplessness, she poured her feelings into a journal which she sent to Calvin regularly:

For my part, I can easily see how such proceedings may make converts to abolitionism, for already my sympathies are strongly enlisted for Mr. Birney, and I hope he will stand his ground and assert his rights. The office is fire-proof, and inclosed by high walls. I wish he would man it with armed men. . . . If I were a man, I would go . . . and take good care of at least one window.

That Sunday, July 31, a mob gathered in the evening heat and moved toward Pugh's printing office. Blacks fled before it and locked themselves in their houses. The mob smashed Pugh's type and press and threw the wreckage into the river. Mayor Davies, who was standing by, was all paternal approval. "Well, lads," he said, "you have done well so far. Now go home before you disgrace yourselves."

But the "lads" had tasted violence and wanted more. Armed, drunken, shouting, they started toward Franklin House, where Birney lodged. Salmon Chase ran on ahead to forestall them. It was an act of pure conscience; he came of a socially distinguished family and he was legal counsel for a Cincinnati bank with pro-slavery officers. He had never even met Birney.

When the rioters reached Franklin House, Chase was there, barring the way. There were shouts and threats from the crowd. At that moment Mayor Davies appeared in the doorway and announced that Birney was not home. He pleaded with the mob to disperse. Sullenly the crowd turned away, roamed aimlessly about, and finally burned down some shacks in the Negro slum.

When the rioting started up again the next day, the mayor hurriedly swore in a volunteer patrol and authorized it to shoot to kill. Harriet later heard that Henry had loaded a pistol and rushed out to join the patrol.

For a day or two [she wrote in her journal] we did not know but there would actually be war to the knife, as was threatened by the mob, and we really saw Henry depart with his pistols with daily alarm, only we were all too full of patriotism not to have sent every brother we had rather than not have had the principles of freedom and order defended.

At last the community was frightened by the violence it had tolerated. The rioters, shorn of support, Harriet reported, "slunk into their dens and were still." Hammond of the *Gazette* now printed a grim account of what the mob had done; and he placed the blame squarely on the committee. Harriet agreed, declaring that the members of the committee were "justly punished . . . for what was very irresolute and foolish conduct, to say the least."

More in disgust than out of fear, Birney later quit the editorship of the *Philanthropist*. Anti-Birney sentiment in Cincinnati lingered: the following summer a professional slave-hunter discovered that a fugitive slave—light enough to pass for white—was working in the Birney household. The young woman was dragged into court, Birney was indicted, and it took a great effort by Birney, with the help of Salmon P. Chase, to free them. Instead of retreating, Birney dedicated himself to making the antislavery movement a political force. Openly opposing Garrison's rejection of political action, he helped found the Liberty party and was its Presidential candidate in 1840 and 1844.

The Birney incident was not the most violent slavery riot in Cincinnati history but it may well have been the most fateful: it turned Birney into an even more ardent abolitionist and it moved Salmon P. Chase, Henry Ward Beecher and Harriet Beecher Stowe another painful step away from a merely passive opposition to slavery.

As a scholar, a devout Protestant, a thrifty New Englander and a sentimental "family man," Calvin was delighted with Germany and the Germans. His letters were published regularly in the Cincinnati *Journal*. Having caught glimpses of Frederick William III, the aging king of Prussia, and heard gossip about the royal family, Professor Stowe even wrote an admiring account of the Kaiser's private life. It was intended to be read to the Semi-Colon Club. But before she received it, Harriet was occupied with a far more pressing matter: on September 29, 1836, she gave birth to twin daughters, Eliza Tyler Stowe and Isabella Beecher Stowe.

Calvin completed his tour in grand style, visiting universities and buying books in England and Scotland. He arrived back in New York in January 1837, and learned to his surprise and delight—since Harriet's later letters had apparently not caught up with him—that he was a father twice over. When he reached home he gallantly insisted that little Isabella Beecher Stowe be renamed Harriet Beecher Stowe.

In July, Lane Seminary held an exhibition of the books Professor Stowe had brought back from Europe. It consisted of five thousand volumes—the works of church fathers, Protestant martyrs, Catholic historians, and Greek and Roman classics. The world of literature was allowed one hundred and twenty-six volumes of poetry, seventy by British authors and fifty-six by German and French poets.

But Lane's pride—and doubtless awe—at Calvin's accomplishment was cut short by the deepening panic of 1837. Without warning, the draft covering Dr. Beecher's salary was returned from New York unhonored: the firm of Arthur Tappan had gone down in the crash. The Reverend Beecher was forced to borrow from his friends and his son George in order to survive. Uncle Samuel Foote went bankrupt, lost his mansion and had to move into quarters over a row of offices in town. Deprived of its elegant meeting place, the Semi-Colon Club collapsed and never recovered.

Once again, the cruelties of slavery intruded on the Stowes, and this time more intimately than ever. Not long after Calvin and Harriet reoccupied their house in Walnut Hills, they hired a young mulatto who said she was legally free. Then one day the woman came hurrying back from town in an agony of terror, declaring that her former master was in Cincinnati looking for her. Although he had no legal right to her, she—and Harriet—knew that some trick might be used to retake her. She begged the Stowes for help. Nervously they agreed.

Calvin set about spiriting the woman away, trying desperately to recall how the Reverend Rankin had carried off such exploits. It is hard to imagine Calvin Stowe managing such a risky business alone. One version has it that Charles Beecher (another declares it was Henry Ward) joined him and while Harriet stood by, shaken by pity and fear, the pair put the woman in the family carriage one stormy night and drove her over back roads to the farm of John Van Zandt. Van Zandt was a Kentucky farmer who had freed his own slaves and come to Ohio to help free all other slaves. Like Rankin, he received the fugitive without question.

The episode—a terrified young black woman hunted like an animal in Harriet's own home and fleeing into the night—would be memorably recreated in *Uncle Tom's Cabin* in the fugitives' escape from Tom Loker and Marks and in the figure of the compassionate farmer John Van Trompe.

Then Harriet found that she was pregnant again. Feeling ill, and desperate for a change, she fled with the twins, taking advantage of an invitation to visit her brother William in Putnam, Ohio. But there the slavery issue seemed to be even more challenging, with William and his wife leaning strongly toward abolitionism. Even while Harriet was there, a leader in local society brought an account of the radical proceedings of a Female Antislavery Convention. Ever fearful of what she called "ultra" positions, Harriet pleaded for an "intermediate" solution:

If not . . . all the excesses of the abolition party will not prevent humane and conscientious men from joining it.

Pray, what is there in Cincinnati to satisfy one whose mind is awakened on the subject? No one can have the system of slavery brought before him without an irrepressible desire to do something, and what is there to be done?

Even as she acknowledges the need to act, she reveals that she is temperamentally unable, like her father and her brother Henry, to commit herself to any position while it is still unpopular or imprudent.

On returning to Cincinnati, she found the old problems unsolved and new ones developing. That fall only fifteen students registered in the beginners' class at Lane. Then news came of the murder of the abolitionist editor Reverend Elijah P. Lovejoy in Alton, Illinois, and with it a paralyzing rumor that his close friend and supporter, the Reverend Edward Beecher, had been killed at his side. The murder sent shock waves all across America and created more abolitionists than had all Lovejoy's editorials combined. And for one heart-chilling moment—before word came that Edward had left Alton just before the attack—the monster that was slavery seemed to have struck the Beechers themselves. It had certainly come close. And it was the kind of incident that, more than any argument, would light a flame of anger in Harriet Beecher Stowe's heart.

In January 1838 Harriet gave birth to a son, Henry Ellis. Incredible metamorphosis: within two years to have acquired a husband and three children. . . . To help her cope, a nurse was brought in and Calvin's mother came from Massachusetts.

Now Harriet's letters to Georgiana are dominated by a new theme—babies. "Only think how long it is since I have written to you," she writes, "and how changed I am since then—the mother of three children!" To explain the lapse in her correspondence she describes her day:

I waked about half-after-four and thought, "Bless me, how light it is! I must . . . wake up Mina, for breakfast must be had at six o'clock this morning." So out of bed I jump and seize the tongs and pound, pound, pound over poor Mina's sleepy head, charitably allowing her about half an hour to get waked up in— that being the quantum of time it takes me,—or used to. Well, then, baby wakes—quâ, quâ, quâ—so I give him his breakfast, dozing meanwhile and so-liloquizing as follows: "Now I must not forget to tell Mr. Stowe about the starch and dried apples"—doze—"ah, um, dear me! why doesn't Mina get up? I don't hear her"—doze—"ah, um—I wonder if Mina has soap enough! I think there were two bars left on Saturday"—doze again—I wake again. "Dear me, broad daylight! I must get up and go down and see if Mina is getting breakfast." Up I jump and up wakes baby. "Now, little boy, be good and let mother dress, be-cause she is in a hurry." I get my frock half on and baby by that time has kicked himself down off his pillow, and is crying and fisting the bed-clothes in great order. I stop with one sleeve off and one on to settle matters with him. Having planted him bolt upright and gone all up and down the chamber barefoot to get pillows and blankets to prop him up, I finish putting my frock on and hurry down to satisfy myself . . . that the breakfast is in progress. Then back I come into the nursery, where, remembering that it is washing-day . . . I apply myself vigorously to sweeping, dusting and the setting-to-rights so necessary when there are three little mischiefs always pulling down as fast as one can put up.

While the twins are "chattering, hallooing, or singing at the tops of their voices," the nurse readies their breakfast. When this is finally cleared away, the husband, as was common in such households, is dis-patched to market. Harriet continues:

. . . baby being washed and dressed, I . . . start to cut out some little dresses . . . when Master Henry makes a doleful lip and falls to crying with might and main. I catch him up and turning round see one of his sisters flourishing the things out of my workbox in fine style. Moving it away and looking the other side, I see the second little mischief seated by the hearth chewing coals and scraping up ashes with great apparent relish. Grandmother lays hold upon her and charitably offers to endeavor to quiet baby while I go on with my work. I set at it again . . . when I see the twins on the point of quarreling with each other. Number one pushes number two over. Number two screams: that frightens the baby, and he joins in. I call number one a naughty girl, take the persecuted one in my arms, and endeavor to comfort her. . . . Meanwhile number one makes her way to the slop jar and forthwith proceeds to wash her apron in it. Grandmoth-er . . . drags her away, and sets the jar up out of her reach. By and by the nurse comes up from her sweeping. I commit the children to her, and finish cutting out the frocks.

But let this suffice, for of such details as these are all my days made up. Indeed, my dear, I am but a mere drudge with few ideas beyond babies and housekeeping. As for thoughts, reflections, and sentiments, good lack! good lack! . . .

Well, Georgy, this marriage is—yes, I will speak well of it, after all; for when I can stop and think . . . I must say that I think myself a fortunate woman both in husband and children. My children I would not change for all the ease, leisure, and pleasure that I could have without them.

Despite our suspicion that the future novelist in Harriet is making all this seem more amusing than it was, she is still in the first flush of marriage and motherhood and she can still brush aside problems. Foremost among these was the approaching fall term at Lane with not a single new student in sight and only ten old ones remaining. Professor Stowe was ready to give up. He took to his bed, wallowing in melancholy. Here he was, thirty-six years old, an international authority on education, famous Biblical scholar, sought-after lecturer, languishing in a destitute backwater seminary and suddenly burdened with a full-fledged family.

As we have seen, it was the Reverend Beecher, as manic as Stowe was depressive, who flushed a handful of students from the Ohio and Kentucky countryside, and saved the day. It was he who hauled Calvin out of the swamps of dejection and back to work. Calvin kept insisting, in the privacy of his home, that he would resign, but inertia, his ties to the Beechers, and especially his admiration of Lyman, would keep him at Lane for another dozen years.

Harriet did not seem to be disturbed by Calvin's helplessness in the face of such crises; even more than the need for money, it gave her a reason to make more time for writing—and spend less time doing housework. A few dollars she had saved from sundry pieces sold to magazines enabled her to hire a "stout German girl" to do the housework, leaving Anna, the English nursemaid, to devote all her time to the children. This was not such an extravagance as it may seem, for immigrant servants could be had for little more than their board and lodging.

The arrangement gave Harriet about three hours a day for writing. Suddenly very businesslike, she wrote to Mary Dutton, "And if you see my name coming out everywhere, you may be sure of one thing—that I do it for the pay. I have determined not to be a mere domestic slave." So she studied the formulas of the "annuals." Daintily decorated and with such names as *Affection's Gift, Token, Lily, Keepsake,* and *Souvenir*—the latter published in Cincinnati itself—these periodicals were filled with romantic, highly moral stories and sentimental trifles. Occasionally she tried the religious papers, which were, as far as a Beecher was concerned, practically a family tradition. She never published these pieces in a book, but she sold enough of them to allow her to consider herself a professional writer.

A friend who sometimes helped her in her literary work thought it a great pity that Harriet's talents should lie idle because of her family obligations. Years later, in an amusing sketch, she pictured Harriet as bravely managing to write amidst a hundred household distractions. Alternating snatches of Harriet's dictation with her instructions to a new servant in the kitchen, the sketch contrasts the romantic world of popular fiction with the humdrum realities of housework. The friend starts by insisting that Harriet finish the story she has promised the editor of *Souvenir*. Harriet answers that she has housecleaning and mending to do. The friend points out, rather flatteringly, that in three hours she can write enough to cover her sewing expenses for a year.

Seated next to the stove, and surrounded by rolling pins, flour, ginger, lard, the baby and dark-skinned Mina, they set to work.

"Now, this is the place where you left off," the friend says, ". . . the last sentence was, 'Borne down by the tide of agony, she leaned her head on her hands, the tears streamed through her fingers, and her whole frame shook with convulsive sobs.' What shall I write next?"

"Mina, pour a little milk into this pearlash," said Harriet.

"Come," the friend says, ". . . What next?"

Harriet paused and looked musingly out of the window, as she turned her mind to her story . . . and she dictated as follows:

"Her lover wept with her, nor dared he again to touch the point so sacredly guarded"—"Mina, roll that crust a little thinner." "He spoke in soothing tones."—"Mina poke the coals in the oven."

Now for a time Harriet writes while the friend guides Mina. Then Harriet dictates again:

"I know my duty to my children. I see the hour must come. You must take them, Henry; they are my last earthly comfort."

"Ma'am, what shall I do with these egg-shells and all this truck here?" interrupted Mina.

"Put them in the pail by you," answered Harriet.

She continued to dictate—"You *must* take them away. It may be—perhaps it must be—that I shall soon follow, but the breaking heart of a wife still pleads, 'a little longer, a little longer.' "

"How much longer must the gingerbread stay in?" inquired Mina.

"Five minutes," said Harriet.

"A little longer, a little longer," the friend repeated in a dolorous tone and we burst into laugh.

It is a rather cheery picture of talent and determination "conquering all." Like the letter to Georgiana, it makes light of problems and gives the impression that the self-deprecating, introverted adolescent Harriet has given way to a happy, outgoing and resourceful mother and wife.

But much as she loved her babies, when she found herself pregnant with a third child after only fifteen months of marriage, she evidently decided to put off another pregnancy as long as she could. Catharine, dismissing Biblical injunctions about multiplying abundantly, wrote to sister Mary:

Harriet has one baby put out for the winter, the other at home, and *number three* will be here the middle of January. Poor thing, she bears up wonderfully well, and I hope lives through this first tug of matrimonial warfare, and then she says she shall not have any more *children, she knows for certain* for one while. Though how she found this out I cannot say, but she seems quite confident about it.

Harriet's method was probably simply abstinence, which was most easily achieved by feigning illness or fatigue or through the extended trips and visits that she or Calvin made in this period. Catharine continued to take the position that in such matters wives had to protect themselves from their husbands if they were not to become slaves to their families. After a visit to Walnut Hills Catharine reported to Mary Dutton: "Harriet is not so well as to nerves, but no discouraging prospects as yet in the maternal line. I hope she is to have an interval of rest from further service in that line."

The "interval of rest" would be very brief. After she accompanied Calvin on a trip to Dartmouth College, where he had been invited to give the Phi Beta Kappa address, and then to a summer resort in the White Mountains, they returned to Walnut Hills. Even though they moved into a new house, it was depressing to be plunged again into all the cares and chores. Soon, too, Harriet was in "the maternal line" again. And this time the pregnancy was an ordeal. A "severe neuralgic" condition that settled in her eyes confined her to a darkened room for two months. The birth itself was hard and left her bedridden for another two months.

In Cincinnati, the periodic street riots were like knives ripping the fabric of life. Border city, river port, and still a gateway to the West, Cincinnati was in a constant state of growth and flux. Perhaps it was this ferment, the constant mixing of not always compatible peoples (almost fifty thousand by 1840), and the alternation of boom and panic, that brought mob outbursts so often.

Racial clashes throughout the summer of 1841 culminated in riots in September. Mobs attacked the black quarter and the casualties on both sides were frightening. The turbulence continued for a full week and the governor had to call out the militia to restore peace. Then Van Zandt was caught helping nine slaves escape. Sued by the owner of the slaves, a Kentuckian, he fought the case, with the help of Salmon P. Chase, all the way to the Supreme Court. But he lost and was ruined. That, too, contributed to Harriet's portrait of old John Van Trompe in *Uncle Tom's Cabin*.

Despite family duties and servant problems, pregnancies and illnesses, Harriet had accumulated by 1842 enough published tales and sketches of New England life to make a book. But it remained for Catharine, self-appointed negotiator, to approach publishers in New York. When she reported a favorable reception from Harper's, Harriet's spirits soared and she promptly decided that she must talk to New York editors herself. Using Mary Beecher Perkins's home in Hartford as a base—half sister Isabella, now twenty years old, was also staying there while she went to school in Hartford—Harriet descended on New York.

Negotiating a contract with Harper's—although they allowed her only a meager royalty—and talking to editors of well-known magazines and annuals were immensely stimulating. Now truly she was no longer just another harried housewife or overworked teacher, but a full-fledged Author. In the offing were fame, money, influence. Harriet Beecher, formerly just another of the Reverend Beecher's many children, was now Harriet E. Beecher Stowe, a woman with a special gift, with boundless potentialities.

When she wrote to Calvin of her ambitions and plans, to his everlasting credit he encouraged her wholeheartedly and even offered what he considered practical suggestions:

My dear, you must be a literary woman. It is so written in the book of fate. Make all your calculations accordingly. Get a good stock of health and brush up your mind. Drop the E. out of your name. It only incumbers it and interferes with the flow and euphony. Write yourself fully and always Harriet Beecher Stowe, which is a name euphonious, flowing, and full of meaning. Then . . . your husband will lift up his head in the gate, and your children will rise up and call you blessed.

His compliments became even more lavish. Even if they were meant only to fetch her back without delay, they are meltingly generous:

And now my dear I want you to come home as quick as you can. The fact is I cannot live without you, and if we were not so prodigious poor I would come for you at once. There is no woman like you in this wide world. Who else has so much talent with so little self-conceit; so much reputation with so little affectation . . . so much enterprise with so little extravagance; so much tongue with so little scold; so much sweetness with so little softness; so much of so many things and so little of so many other things?

Soon she is writing him with all the confidence of an experienced author, peppering her letter with professional references and even a bit of boasting:

I have seen Johnson of the *Evangelist*. He is very liberally disposed, and I may safely reckon on being paid for all I do there. Who is that Hale, Jr., that sent me the *Boston Miscellany,* and will he keep his word with me? His offers are very liberal—twenty dollars for three pages, not very close print. . . . I shall get something from Harpers some time this winter or spring. Robertson, the publisher here [Hartford], says the book [*The Mayflower*] will sell, and though the terms they offer me are very low, that I shall make something on it. . . . On the whole, my dear, if I choose to be a literary lady, I have, I think, as good a chance of making profit by it as anyone.

Perhaps remembering that Calvin was at home with two of their children, she makes a gesture toward her family obligations. "Can I," she asks, "lawfully divide my attention by literary efforts." She evidently thinks she can, because she goes on to say that she must have a room to herself, a room where she will not be disturbed by the children, the setting and clearing of tables, coal, dust. . . . All she would need in it would be a few pieces of furniture, a stove and her beloved plants.

With supreme faith in her talents, he answers:

You have it in your power by means of this little magazine [*Souvenir*] to form the mind of the West for the coming generation. . . . God has written it in his book that you must be a literary woman, and who are we that we should contend against God?

Stirred by his admiration, she sought to reciprocate: "I was telling Belle [her half sister Isabella] yesterday that I did not know till I came away how much I was dependent upon you for information. . . . If you were not already my husband I should certainly fall in love with you." In the warm glow of his flattery, she grows humble and reverts for a moment to her old posture of self-deprecation:

One thing more in regard to myself. The absence and wandering of mind . . . that so often vexes you is a physical infirmity with me. It is the failing of a mind not calculated to endure a great pressure of care, and so much do I feel the pressure I am under, so much is my mind often darkened and troubled by care, that life seriously holds out few allurements—only my children. . . . It appears to me that I am not probably destined for long life; at all events the feeling is strongly impressed upon my mind that a work is put into my hands which I must be earnest to finish shortly.

Although her next few years were troubled and occasionally anguished, her expectation that she had not long to live was simply a throwback to one of her morbid moods. (She would live for another fifty-four years!) As for the premonition of a great work to be done, that was ten years too soon.

Despite how "prodigious poor" they were, Calvin came east to meet

Harriet and accompany her home. They lightened the long journey by staying with members of the family along the way. First they went to visit George in his new and prosperous parish in Rochester and then to the church in Batavia, New York, that William had taken over from George. They could not have known that both William and George had begun the Beechers' retreat from the West, reversing the movement started with such joyous anticipation eleven years before.

Once home, Harriet tried to carry out her writing program. She had hardly started on it when she found herself pregnant again, and again she felt miserable. "That winter," she wrote, "was a season of sickness and gloom." Typhoid fever struck the seminary and President Beecher's house became a hospital, with his family nursing the sick and the dying. Now, too, the seminary failed to pay Professor Stowe his full salary, leaving him more hard-pressed than ever.

There was a brief interlude of pleasure and pride when Harriet received copies of her book. How exciting the look of her name on the binding and how impressive the title she had chosen: *The Mayflower; or, Sketches of Scenes and Characters among the Descendants of the Pilgrims*. It was an uneven collection, ranging from the confident characterizations of "Uncle Lot" to the cloying sentiment of "The Tea Rose," in which an old maid, a woman of means, expresses her sympathy for a poor family by giving them a rose. There are signs of the mature novelist of later years and anticipations of her principal themes, but much of it is simply genteel trivia.

But all Harriet's plans for following up *The Mayflower* with a stream of literary works that would bring her money and fame soon crumbled, buried under the daily round. Much of what she suffered was the cumulative effect of petty problems and annoyances. But one blow was not petty at all—George's death. That it should have resulted from an improbable accident, and just when he had taken a major step in his career, was a cruelty not to be explained or even understood. . . . George, the brilliant one, the life of the family on the road to Cincinnati—dead, destroyed, annihilated. After the funeral, the only consolation Harriet could muster was that the power of faith was, in such a moment, the strongest argument for the religion of Christ: "Take from us Christ and what he taught, and what have we here? What confusion, what agony, what dismay, what wreck and waste! But give Him to us, even the most stricken heart can rest under the blow; yea, even triumph!" Just so had Harriet in "Uncle Lot" converted the pitiable death of Lot's beloved son George, the pious young minister, into a blessing.

Summer brought another slavery riot. The provocation this time was local abolitionists who aided in the escape of a slave girl belonging to a traveler from New Orleans. The mobs attacked, among other targets, the home of an abolitionist named Burnett. Burnett collected the stones thrown through his windows and for years kept a barrel of them on his front porch with a sign on it reading "Pro-Slavery Arguments."

Harriet's fifth child, called Georgiana May, born in August 1843, was a cranky baby and left the mother an invalid for several months. Even Anna, the once ideal nurse, became difficult. And the professor's income sagged to a new low that year, Calvin receiving only half of the $1,200 due him.

For Harriet the winter of 1843–1844 was nightmarish. Recalling it in a letter to her half brother Thomas a year or so later, she was, she wrote, "haunted and pursued by care that seemed to drink my life-blood. A feeble, sickly child—a passionate, irritable nurse, with whom I feared to leave it, from whom I feared to withdraw it—slowly withering in my arms . . . harassed, anxious, I often wondered why God should press my soul . . . with a weight of cares."

When we learn that the baby not only survived but became the liveliest of the Stowe children, Harriet's description seems somewhat melodramatic.

In the same letter to Thomas, which runs to eight printed pages, she sets forth passionately the faith she has finally achieved. In the past her failure had been, she says, to have more thoughts of herself than of Christ:

. . . if you see that entire union and identity of your will with Christ is the thing, why don't you have it? . . . Why not? ah! why not? Words of deep meaning to any one who tries that vain experiment! . . . We reason, reflect, resolve, and pray—weep, strive, love—love to despair, and all in vain. In vain I adjured my soul, Do you not *love* Christ? Why not, then, cut wholly loose from all these loves and take his will alone? . . .

But the pressure of outward cares prevented her. She began to see, she says, that her love of Christ had been transient, not permanent. So she "prayed with prayer unceasing" and finally was able to resolve to "go for the whole."

Then *came* the long-expected and wished help. *All* changed. Whereas once my heart ran with a strong current to the world, now it runs with a current the other way. . . . The will of Christ seems to me the steady pulse of my being, and I go because I cannot help it. Skeptical doubt cannot exist. . . . I am calm, but full—everywhere and in all things instructed. . . . Now if this is, as you say, a dream, so is certainly every form of *worldly* good; but this, if it be a dream, answers the purpose entirely, and I shall never wake till I awake "in His likeness."

It was an eloquent, if rather self-conscious, statement, calculated to reassure a younger brother. Probably it was such letters that led Charles a few years earlier to write to his young half sister Isabella from his exile in New Orleans:

Nobody writes such letters as you write. All else are in comparison cold and awaken only an emotion of disappointment. Harriet tis true wrote some beautiful letters. But she is a little too wise withal—and . . . is irresistibly inclined to assist others in their passage thro' the same path (as she thinks) by telling them how she felt, and how she came to stop feeling so. . . . this is not Harriet's characteristic but her occasional failing. Probably she considers it as the exclusive prerogative of Cate [Catharine] . . . . Nevertheless—she does not as you do satisfy herself with the artless expression of spontaneous emotions. She is not in her letter pouring forth feeling merely because she feels it but planning by the combination of such and such feelings . . . to produce a given effect.

It is a revealing glimpse of three sisters, with an objectivity made possible by distance.

The letters Harriet and Calvin wrote to each other during this period reflect the strain their problems put on their relationship. Neither of them could have been easy to live with at this time, he with his hypochondria and she with her illnesses, real and imagined. Of all the qualities they might have criticized in each other, it is astonishing that they repeatedly charged one another with too little devotion to God. Or was this the safest criticism because no one, as Harriet had observed, could ever achieve all the devotion that Calvinism demanded. "If you had studied Christ," she wrote to Calvin, "with half the energy that you have studied Luther—if you were as eager for daily intercourse with him as to devour the daily newspaper—if you . . . loved him as much as you loved your study and your books, then would he be formed in you, the hope of glory."

She even warns him that when he becomes "nervous, anxious, fretful and apprehensive of poverty" he has wrongly taken matters out of Christ's hands and is "doing what he is very sorry to see you do." She here seems curiously close to recommending passivity—a kind of advice that Calvin Stowe hardly needed. Far from resenting such criticism, Calvin chides her when she fails to insist on ever more piety and prayer, and he indulges in one of his favorite postures—self-abasement: "It was my chief hope in the darkness and despondency of my own mind that you were continuously approaching nearer . . . to Christ . . . that you could be . . . a guide and support to my feeble and tottering steps in the way of life."

All Calvin Stowe's Biblical scholarship and contacts with the spirit world did not save him from sensuality. He ate gluttonously, liked liquor and was stirred by libidinous urges. In a curiously ambivalent letter to

Harriet in June 1844, he tells her how difficult it is even for a minister to resist sexual temptation. After assuring her that when he is with her, "every desire I have, mental and physical, is completely satisfied and filled up," he gives her a detailed account of the "melancholy licentiousness, recently detected, of several clergymen of high reputation in the east." A Philadelphia bishop, long addicted to drink, "while half boozled has caught young ladies who were so unfortunate as to meet him alone, and pawed them over in the most disgusting manner . . . and now it all comes out against him." In what seems to be a kind of rationalization of his own inclinations, he adds, "Bless the Lord that with all my strong relish for brandy and wine, and all my indescribable admiration and most overflowing delight in handsome young ladies, no offenses of this kind have yet been written down against me." Next in what he calls "this dreadful catalogue" of ministerial lechery is a well-known pastor and editor in New Jersey who has long been in the habit of "visiting brothels and bawdy houses where he would get beastly drunk and revel and swelter with the vilest harlots." Last is fifty-five-year-old J. H. Fairchild, formerly pastor of the Orthodox church in South Boston, who "seduced one of his own kitchen girls, committed adultery with a member of his own church and lately . . . has cut his throat . . . in the agony of his shame."

Although he concludes, "Is there anyone we can trust? . . . Are all ministers brutes?" there is a relish in the graphic detail that belies his posture of disillusion. The more shocking the example, the more admirable will his own self-control appear.

Like a sinner hoping that confession will bring him absolution and sympathy, he says in a letter to Lyman:

I try to be spiritually minded, and find in myself a most exquisite relish and deadly longing for all kinds of sensual gratification. I think of the revival ministers who have long lived in licentiousness with good reputation, and then been detected, and ask myself, who knows whether there be any real piety on earth? O wretched man that I am!

Calvin knew, of course, of the camp meeting revivalists who took advantage of the tempestuous passions they aroused in young women. And behold, Harriet is not only aware of the power of sexuality—had she not read Richardson and Byron and Shakespeare?—but she thinks she has a prescription for men who are tempted. Hearing her brother Henry also speak of "falls" among highly placed churchmen, she had a presentiment of how horrible it would be if she found that her husband or one of her brothers had had such a fall. The thought pursued her like a nightmare and seemed to ask, "Is your husband any better-seeming than so-and-so!" It left her full of pity for those "wives worse than widows, who are called to lament that the grave has *not* covered their husband." (There is an uncanny augury here not only of her brother Henry's "fall" but of her sensational attack on Byron for his unfaithfulness to Lady Byron and his other sins.) The thought then evokes a confused sequence: Victorian shame, Puritanic revulsion, and naive, not to say absurd, advice:

I can conceive now of misery which in one night would change the hair to gray and shrivel the whole frame to premature decrepitude. . . . What terrible temptations lie in the way of your sex—till now I never realized it. . . . I have no jealousy—the most beautiful woman in the world would not make me jealous so long as she only *dazzled the senses,* but still, my dear, you must not wonder if I want to warn you not to look or *think* too freely on womankind. If your sex would guard the outworks of *thought,* you would *never* fall, and . . . so astounding are the advantages which Satan takes, it scarce is implying a doubt to say "be cautious."

If such warnings seem exaggerated, we soon get another clue to her uneasiness. Although she has learned from hard experience a degree of self-control, there are times, she admits, "when the old fountain rises again, warm, fresh, and full." Speaking of her visit to Henry's that summer, she wrote:

I love him so much . . . it really makes me cry to think of it. Oh this love. If we only could have enough of it. I could be any thing and do any thing for and by love, but without it how desolate and waste and cheerless. You will love me very much at first when you come home, and then will it be as before, all forced into months of cold indifference. . . . It is thoughts like these that often sadden my anticipation of your return which though I desire I sometimes dread.

As easily as Calvin confessed to weaknesses—knowing full well that he would continue to indulge them—so easily could he be critical of Harriet. In one letter, which must have irked her greatly, he gave an inventory of her deficiencies: (1) he anxiously takes thought beforehand, whereas she has a hopeful temperament that makes her quite heedless of the future; (2) he is very methodical and anything out of place, whether it be a morning paper or a newspaper—which he always folds up but she and Anna leave "sprawling on the floor"—gives him "inexpressible torment"; (3) he takes offense easily and expresses his vexation at once but then forgets it, whereas she takes offense less readily but remains silent and retains the wound. (Ironically, using a similar figure of speech, she later claimed that he said unjust things in haste and never retracted them, leaving the "poisoned arrow in the wound.") A few days later he added another charge: like her father and her sister Catharine, but not quite so carelessly as either of them, she makes promises whether she can keep them or not.

There were others who thought she had faults. Her mother-in-law, who had lived with her, let her know, as a mother-in-law will, that she was extravagant, needed much waiting on, and kept too much help. Even if we concede that mother Stowe took a jaundiced view, her criticisms make Harriet's complaints about her burdens seem a little overdone.

Harriet recovered her health only very slowly after Georgiana's birth. Her illness, one feels, was as much of the spirit as the body, a mixture of headaches, unpaid debts, trouble with her eyes, more and more mouths to feed—by 1845 there were already nine in the Stowe ménage—and ever less prospect of escape. She continued to sell occasional pieces to the *New Evangelist,* but that brought almost nothing.

Calvin managed in June of 1845 to get away for a trip to Detroit as a delegate to a church convention. Afterwards, preparing to go east on a mission for Lane, he suggested that Harriet come with him. The invitation found her in one of her most despondent moods. Her answer was the immemorial litany of unhappy housewives. My dear husband, she wrote,

It is a dark, sloppy, rainy, muddy, disagreeable day, and I have been working hard (for me) all day in the kitchen, washing dishes, looking into closets, and seeing . . . that dark side of domestic life which a housekeeper may who will investigate too curiously into minutiae. . . . I am sick of the smell of sour milk, and sour meat, and sour everything, and then the clothes *will* not dry . . . and everything smells mouldy; and altogether I feel as if I never wanted to eat again.

His letter, she said, formed "a very agreeable contrast to all these things," but it can hardly have cheered him when she complained that her health was daily growing worse. "I feel no life, no energy, no appetite. . . ." Little Georgiana, she added, is "weak, nervous, cross, and fretful, night and day," and all the children were "like other little sons and daughters of Adam, full of all kinds of absurdity and folly." As though to match him in hypochondria, she wrote, "All common fatigue, sickness and exhaustion is nothing to this distress." As to accompanying Calvin: "If God wills, I go. He can easily find means. Money, I suppose, is as plenty with Him now as it always has been."

Whether or not it was God who helped her, Harriet was able to make the trip. Once again she went where her heart lay: Hartford, Boston, Natick, visiting Mary, Edward and Calvin's family. Too soon she was back in Walnut Hills, but this time she brought back word of a remarkable new cure for just such complaints as hers—a hydropathy sanitarium in Vermont. She began to dream of going there.

Again she left it to Providence to help her get away. Perhaps she encouraged Providence by telling friends of her hopes, because, miraculously, "donations" came from this one and that one, and Harriet, not too proud to accept charity from God, began to plan for a long vacation in a waterborne Paradise. She easily persuaded herself that Calvin could get along without her. "My husband has developed wonderfully as a house-father and nurse. You would laugh to see him in his spectacles, gravely marching the little troop in their nightgowns up to bed."

This time the trip east, in March 1846, took only six days. What with visits to family and friends, she stayed away thirteen months. Patient as he might be, Calvin complained of the disorder in the house. Overcome with guilt, Harriet wrote: "I really pity you in having such a wife. I feel as if I had been only a hindrance to you instead of a help."

Like Catharine, she went through the bone-chilling ice-water regimen, the bread-and-milk diet, the long walks. But for her, as for Catharine and Mary, and later Isabella, the water-cure was far more than just a health program; it was in general a pleasant social experience, and beyond that, an escape from all daily responsibilities, a magical transfer from serving everyone else to being served by everyone else. To Harriet in particular, it was a release not only from a housewife's duties and cares but from life in the shadow of a church seminary, a preacher father, and a Biblical scholar husband. It was a lotus land that lulled her into ignoring the cost of her stay and the welfare of her family. Like a drunkard who craves company in her indulgence, she became a champion of recreation, an expert on diversions. When Calvin kept complaining about his ailments, she urged him to get out of his airless study and take a long walk before breakfast. ". . . above all," she wrote, "do amuse yourself. . . ." With what must have seemed like shameless hedonism, she wrote:

I should really rejoice to hear that you and father and mother . . . and a few others of the same calibre, would agree to meet together for dancing cotillions . . . and if you took Mr. K's wife and poor Miss Much-Afraid, her daughter, into the alliance, it would do them good. Bless me! what a profane set everybody would think you were.

As if it were not incongruous enough to recommend cotillions to pudgy, middle-aged Calvin, she goes even further: "I wish you could be with me in Brattleboro, and coast down hill on a sled, go sliding and snowballing by moonlight! I would snowball every bit of the *hypo* out of you! Now, my dear, if you are going to get sick, I am going to come home." Her very gaiety and the carefree life it reflected must have plunged Calvin into an abyss of self-pity. So lugubrious were his letters that Harriet could not help making fun of him: "My dear soul,—I received your most melancholy effusion, and I'm sorry to find it's just so. I entirely agree and sympathize. Why didn't you engage the two tombstones—one for you and one for me?" But she soon swung back to acid charges that his "vindictive" fault-finding resulted from a "morbid" state of mind and his mother's influence.

It was late spring before she was back in Walnut Hills. Within a month or so she was pregnant again, feeling wretched and again reduced by her "neuralgic" eye condition to groping her way around the house. No writing, not even thinking—only enduring. Had the fear of this been the main reason she had stayed away for thirteen months? Her sixth child, Samuel Charles, was born in January 1848.

Neither Harriet's blithe advice nor her sharp criticism had apparently done Calvin any good. Indeed, hearing her description of the sanitarium, he was soon convinced that it was just the place for him. He had weathered fifteen years at Lane and now he needed a long rest. Providentially, vineyards in the Walnut Hills area had for several years been producing an excellent Catawba wine, making the Lane acres increasingly valuable. So the trustees, breathing more easily, granted Professor Stowe a sabbatical year. He left for Vermont in June of 1848. Attached to him as she may have been, Harriet was surely relieved: it meant one less in the family to take care of and no new pregnancy in the offing.

Once the baby was born, Harriet revived. She was also cheered by the news that after several years in Indiana, brother Henry had accepted a call from a rich new congregation in New York—the Plymouth Church in Brooklyn. Since Edward Beecher had long since left Illinois College to return to a pulpit in Boston, and Catharine was traveling almost constantly, only Harriet and Charles of the younger generation were left in the West.

Thus even as the discovery of gold in California was setting off the greatest westward movement in American history (posters on the Cincinnati waterfront were soon advertising the fares to Sacramento, heart of the Gold Rush country), the Beechers were drifting back to the East. Their deepest roots were in New England, and when their efforts to capture the West for Calvinism failed, they retreated, almost instinctively, to the scene of ancestral triumphs.

Harriet was hardly idle while Calvin was away: "I have six children and cares endless," she wrote to Georgiana May. "They are my work, over which I fear and tremble." To cope with the expense of Calvin's stay in Vermont, she took in boarders and even opened a small school next door. But when she began to tell Calvin of her interest in some of Catharine's enterprises, he exploded:

[it is] as much your duty to renounce Cate Beecher and all her schoolmarms as it is to renounce the Devil and all his works. . . . Cate has neither conscience nor

sense—if you consent to take half a pound, she will throw a ton on your shoulders, and run off and leave you, saying—*it isn't heavy, it isn't heavy at all, you can carry it with perfect ease.* I will have nothing to do with her in the way of business, any more than I would with the Devil . . . and you ought not to have. She would kill off a whole regiment like you or me in three days.

To the big river port, now a city of 100,000, with slum areas, and slaughterhouses on the road to Walnut Hills, cholera came again. The Beechers had become inured to outbreaks of the disease almost every year; but this siege grew more and more frightening. By early July as many as 120 deaths were reported in one day. Fires of soft coal, whose smoke was supposed to neutralize the plague, burned on every corner and covered everything with soot. Business came almost to a halt, and carts as well as hearses filled with the dead, as during a plague in the Middle Ages, constantly rolled by on the way to the cemetery near Lane.

Then baby Charley developed disturbing symptoms; they receded but ten days later he went into convulsions. The doctor simply shook his head in despair. Bravely, Harriet warned Calvin not to come home. Helpless and frantic, she watched the child writhe in agony, and finally she prayed that he would die. He died, and grief would have consumed her had it not been for her faith. "He is now among the blessed," she wrote to Calvin. "My Charley—my beautiful, loving, gladsome baby, so loving, so sweet, so full of life and hope and strength—now lies shrouded, pale and cold, in the room below." Later, in the figure of Senator Bird's wife in *Uncle Tom's Cabin*, she revealed what it was like to go through a drawer containing a dead baby's clothes and toys.

Finally Calvin came home. He was truly rested, and, even more important, he brought almost unbelievably good news: he had been offered the professorship of Natural and Revealed Religion by his old college, Bowdoin, in Maine.

A deep relief and joy filled Harriet. For eighteen burdensome years she had made the best of Cincinnati while her heart lay elsewhere. She could not know that what she had seen of slavery throughout all those years lay in her like a banked fire ready to flare up when she needed it. But now she was going home. Calvin would have to give the seminary a year to replace him, but with the East awaiting them in the end, that seemed no great hardship. Harriet was not even disturbed at finding herself pregnant again.

But she could not wait until the end of the school year: taking three of the children—the oldest, Hattie, was already fourteen—and disregarding her condition, she boarded a riverboat and started for Maine.

She would in later years tell the story of how, when they had to change trains at a Pennsylvania depot at two o'clock in the morning, a churlish station agent, seeing the tired little woman—she was six months pregnant—wearing a shawl and surrounded by three children in hand-me-downs, thought they were immigrants and made them wait outside. Occurring less than two years before she wrote *Uncle Tom's Cabin,* it was like some Victorian melodrama wherein the humble, careworn but brave heroine reaches bottom just before she rises victorious.

On the way to Maine, Harriet stayed with Henry in Brooklyn, Mary in Hartford and finally Edward in Boston. It was April 1850 and in each house her ears were filled with troubled and sometimes angry discussion of what had now become the Great Debate—Slavery versus Abolition. In Congress since December, three old men—Calhoun for the South, Webster for the North, and Clay for the border states—had devoted all their remaining energies and extraordinary eloquence to differences that threatened the Union as no other issue ever had or ever would.

The crisis had been brought on when California, swarming with gold-hungry immigrants, applied to join the Union as a free state. Calhoun, seeing this as a wedge for admitting all the vast western lands as free states, cried "No" in a last outburst before his death. Clay offered a "compromise" that accepted California as a free state but allowed slavery to enter the new territories, and supported the forcible return of fugitive slaves. But it was Webster, in his fateful address of March 7, 1850, who made the concessions that would lead to more and more bitterness and finally civil war: he opposed a ban on slavery in the new territories and he accepted a fugitive slave code—it became a law in September—that harshly penalized all who obstructed its enforcement, barred an accused Negro from offering a defense, and rewarded officials who favored a slaveholder's claim.

In Brooklyn, Harriet heard Henry Ward denounce it, and in Boston she heard Edward—he had been an abolitionist for fifteen years—and his wife revile it. She seemed too preoccupied with her own problems to take part in the discussions. In any event, it was never arguments based on principles or theories or reason that moved Harriet Beecher. It was when she heard of black men seized in the streets of Boston and dragged away that she knew that this law would be like a deadly poison in its effect not only on all black men but on all white men.

She arrived in Brunswick, Maine, full of hope for herself and her family but haunted by the fear, anger and frustration that had been loosed in the land.

14

HENRY

Frontier Interlude

At Amherst College and later at Lane, Henry Ward encouraged a view of himself as a fun-loving, lighthearted fellow. That role, he had learned, served his deeper self in several ways: it made him popular and it won the affection he craved. The earnest demeanor expected of a divinity student was more than he could manage, and a carefree air simply made life more bearable.

In a journal entry at Lane in October 1835, he gives a flippant but revealing opinion of three classes of ministers, "the ascetic, the neuter and the sunshiny." The first, he wrote, "conceive the chief end of man to consist in a long face, upturned eyes, a profound sanctimonious look. . . . And though I think many such are truly pious men, yet such endowments are the deformity and misfortune, not the ornament, of their piety." The second class, the neuter, adapt to every change of company in which they find themselves and though it is proper not "to jest at a funeral, laugh at church, or dance in a hospital," nothing, he insists, will ever make him "disown mirth." It is the third class, the "glorious, sunshiny ones, those who think there is a time for relaxation and elegant enjoyment" that he will emulate. "To be mirthful," he declares, "is part of our constitution, and I believe God never gave us that which it is a sin to exercise."

His diary remains a fragment, for, as he admits, "I am not enough contemplative to make a record of reflections and feelings very definite," and—an even more curious admission—"I never could be *sincere*," meaning that he dared not entrust his innermost thoughts to a journal that someone might see. He dwells on this possibility at length, his main concern being, as always, that he should be seen as he wants to be seen, not as he is. With a flourish, he concludes: " . . . in mental dishabille I will stroll thro' my mind and do as I choose."

Free of responsibilities, he carries his blithe philosophy into practice. Mornings he and Charles cross the lovely old woods separating the Beecher house from the Lane campus, singing and imitating musical instruments. He finds time to do a dozen things more enjoyable than studying theology: he sings in the choir in his father's church and sometimes leads it, gives a Bible class for young ladies, and lectures on temperance and phrenology, the latter encouraging an un-Calvinist interest in self-improvement. Echoing his father's prejudices, he writes a series of anonymous articles on the Catholic question for the *Daily Evening Post.* He reads Wordsworth, Burns, Byron and Coleridge and tries his hand, rather amateurishly, at literary criticism. But what he really learns from these writers, and especially Wordsworth and Burns, is the power of an appeal to the emotions and the inspiration to be found in nature. Like Harriet and Charles, he was a child of European Romanticism as well as American Calvinism.

Eunice, as well as other young women, often occupies his thoughts. His diary references to her are tinged with gush emphasized with underlinings and exclamation points: "What a noble creature E——— is!" "How dearly do I love her!" "Found a packet of letters from my dearest E———. Oh, how dear!" He takes her portrait to bed, puts it on his pillow, and then, "It soon underwent another migration—*where,* one may imagine if he will recall all such doings as depicted in novels."

He addresses at least one other young woman in equally effusive terms. When Catherine Dickinson tells him she is getting married and moving to New York, he burbles: "You know how deeply I love *all* when I love at all." I will cherish your memory, he declares, with deep and single-hearted affection. "Oh, Catherine, it will be long ere I find another for whom I shall feel all that I did and do for you." "I do love you," he concludes, "and shall ever."

Another distraction was writing and editing. When the Reverend Thomas Brainerd, editor of the Cincinnati *Journal & Western Luminary,* a Presbyterian weekly with a circulation of 3,600, accompanied the Reverend Lyman Beecher to the Presbyterian Assembly in May 1836, he left Henry in charge of the paper, at a salary of forty dollars a month. After all, had not young Beecher established his competence, both in style and judgment, with his anti-Catholic articles?

Borrowing some of his father's standard themes, Henry devoted editorials to the evils of intemperance and the theater. But soon the slavery controversy demanded attention. First he denounced slavery as an unmitigated evil, but he hastily followed that with an editorial rejecting the radicalism of the abolitionists. When mobs attacked the printing office of James Birney's *Philanthropist,* Henry wrote a long defense of freedom of speech and press. He said little about Birney's abolitionism and made much of the sanctity of private property. When the mob violence continued, he volunteered for street patrol. The story is often told how Harriet, seeing him pour lead into molds in the kitchen at Walnut Hills, asked him what he was doing. "I'm making bullets," he answered, "to kill men with." He didn't, of course, fire a shot.

He was genuinely disappointed when Brainerd returned in October and he had to go back to the classrooms at Lane.

But one experience at Lane was truly rewarding—his friendship with Calvin Stowe. Henry not only studied under the quirky, marvelously learned professor but roomed with him. And just as an earlier roommate, the old black man who had worked on the Beechers' tiny "farm" in Litchfield, had introduced him to God as a living presence, so Stowe taught him—as he would later teach Harriet—to see the Bible not as a record of "guilt, wrath and penalty" or a machine, "formal and dead, but as a body of truth instinct with God, warm with all divine and human sympathies." It was the intimate and personalized kind of approach that would make the Reverend Henry Ward Beecher the most influential preacher of his time.

Henry's experience with church officialdom was by no means so agreeable: as the oldest son at home, he was at his father's side in almost all the heresy trials and was thoroughly disenchanted by the Old School stalwarts who sat in judgment on his father. He was disillusioned not only by the personal prejudices and the intrigue at the meetings but by the mean-spirited character of the men who made up the hierarchy. But he did learn from his father how to outwit such adversaries at their own game. Those experiences also explain his lifelong lack of enthusiasm for ecclesiastical organizations.

Despite his commitment to the ministry, he was easily unsettled by the attractions of Cincinnati. Yearning to enjoy life without feeling guilty and at the same time troubled by what he saw of the workings of the church, he was confused and repelled by his "experience of religion." As usual, he dramatizes his situation: "My mind," he declared, "took one tremendous spring over into skepticism." He remained in that "malignant" state for two years. Then, in his last year at the seminary, he suddenly began to see Christ—or so he said long afterward—in a new light. With some of the embellishments of the style of his later years, he writes:

It came to me like the bursting forth of spring. It was as if yesterday there was not a bird to be seen or heard, and as if today the woods were full of singing birds. There rose up before me a view of Jesus as the Saviour of sinners . . . because they were so bad and needed so much. . . . but from that hour I felt that God had a father's heart; that Christ loved me in my sin . . . [and] cared for me with unutterable tenderness. . . . When that vision was vouchsafed to me I felt that there was no more for me to do but to love, trust, and adore.

Actually this benign and undemanding creed was one that he

achieved many years later. Calling it a "vision" was an effort to give a lofty significance to his desire to be comforted, loved and absolved of any guilt. In later life he himself would point out that his temperament was poetic and emotional and that when in his youth he had tried a reasoned or logical approach it had led only to skepticism and anguish. "... an abstract philosophical statement of the truth never met my wants," he said.

Another experience in his last months at Lane opened his eyes to sectarian prejudices: a nine days' debate between the Reverend Alexander Campbell, a founder of the Christian Church (later the Disciples of Christ), famous for his exhaustive debates with Robert Owen and others, and John B. Purcell, Catholic bishop of Cincinnati. The exchange, which drew large audiences, exposed the bigotry behind charges of papist plots and perfidy. Considering what his father and he himself had written, Henry must have been chagrined when Bishop Purcell remarked that anti-Catholic literature had become as much of an industry in America as making clocks or nutmegs. It taught him a lesson, Henry said, about religious intolerance and the animosities that Calvinism bred in the bone.

From time to time he cried out against the demands that he saw would be made upon him by the orthodoxy. Putting on a brave show, he wrote to Eunice: "There are some points which I must not, *will* not subscribe to. . . ." If the council would not license and ordain him, he asserted that he would preach, "licensed or not," and then, with a romantic flourish, "If I can do no better, I will go far out into the West, build a log cabin among the lumbermen and trappers . . . and devote myself to . . . trying to interest them in religious services. . . . Will you go with me into the wilderness?"

Faced by such a challenge, poor Eunice stoutly declared that it was her duty to follow her betrothed wherever he went. Or did she suspect that it was only a flourish?

The Reverend Henry Ward Beecher's first post as a pastor was hardly a glorious one: Lawrenceburg, in southeast Indiana, was a low-lying, malaria-ridden frontier town with a population of about fifteen hundred, not counting emigrants on their way west, boatmen, gamblers and itinerant evangelists. Although it was a busy and relatively prosperous center for Indiana wheat and corn growers and hog breeders, most of its houses were little more than log cabins along unpaved and treeless streets. ". . . a destitute place indeed," was Henry's own first reaction to it. It achieved townhood by virtue of a brick courthouse, two brick churches, two newspapers, nine stores, three taverns and its main industry, several large distilleries, from which a steamboatload of liquor was carried to market every day.

Henry's appointment came thus: Just before graduating from Lane in the spring of 1837, he preached a few sermons in a hall across the Ohio, in Covington, Kentucky. Martha Sawyer, a remarkable young woman from Lawrenceburg, heard him, and liked what she heard. Since she was treasurer, manager, trustee and, as Beecher described her, almost everything else in the small Presbyterian Church of Lawrenceburg, she invited him to preach a trial sermon for the minister's post there.

Henry's family and friends thought it a dreary prospect but Henry, easily flattered, accepted the invitation. His trial sermon was a dismal failure but he tried again on a few other Sundays, carefully keeping to orthodox themes, and was rewarded with a call to the church. He was offered only four hundred dollars a year, most of it guaranteed by the American Home Mission Society and part of it to be paid in provisions. Since he was constantly running into debt, he accepted promptly.

Henry entered on his first pastorate with a careful plan for winning favor. He must, he told himself, build up a large congregation, "visit widely and produce a personal attachment; also wife do the same," "get the young to love me," and, rather obviously, "preach well uniformly." In his place, his father's first objective would have been to save souls.

Unfortunately, only a few souls were waiting to be saved. ". . . the flock which I found gathered in the wilderness," he wrote, "consisted of twenty persons. Nineteen of them were women and the other was nothing." He also found that, unlike ministers in Boston or Cincinnati, he had a number of menial duties. He had to be his own sexton, opening the church, making the fire, sweeping and dusting, and locking up. He had to raise money to buy badly needed oil lamps as well as install, fill and trim the wicks, and then raise more money to buy hymn books. Long afterward, when it had become an amusing memory, he said: "I did all but come to hear myself preach—that they had to do."

Alone in Lawrenceburg, he suddenly felt the need for a home, a confidante and love. Having bided his time, like Jacob, for seven years, he wrote to Eunice urging marriage straightaway, and then impatiently started east, arriving almost as soon as his letter. Sweeping aside all objections, he arranged the ceremony so hastily that Eunice had to stay up all night to sew her India tulle wedding dress and, after breakfast, bake her own wedding cake—with Henry stoning the raisins and beating the eggs.

When they returned to Lawrenceburg, the best the couple could find—or afford—was two rooms over a livery stable near a wharf on the Miami River. The rent was forty dollars a year and the rooms were so filthy that it took days and days of scrubbing to make them bearable. The backyard was littered with debris and bordered by tenement houses: it was hardly the wide-open spaces of the "golden West."

At one point a count showed that Henry had a total of sixty-eight cents and Eunice not a penny, so Eunice sold a new cloak and added thirty dollars to their fortune. They then set up house, using a three-quarter bed out of Henry's seminary room, a table salvaged from a back-yard rubbish heap, and knives, forks, a cook stove, calico curtains and a husk-filled mattress and pillows contributed by friends. They were particularly moved when Mrs. William Henry Harrison, wife of the famous old general—soon to become President—gave them a bureau, brass and-irons, and a shovel and tongs, with all of which, she said, she had begun housekeeping over forty years before. The boxes in which Henry's books had been packed were converted into bookcases, and his saddle, bridle and buffalo robe were hung on a hook behind a curtain. When he needed a horse he had to borrow one. Later, lacking money for a new suit, he accepted a hand-me-down from one of his parishioners, a judge, regret-ting only that the man was so meager in the shanks. Eunice cut his hair; Henry, with his phrenological interest in the shape of the cranium, had her cut off her ringlets, part her hair and brush it tightly back. Few as their needs were, Eunice had to do seamstress work and, after a while, take in boarders.

Despite his resolutions, Henry did not visit widely and neither did his wife. Where he succeeded was in his preaching. Compared to the almost illiterate pastors who had gone before him, he shone. At first he approached every sermon with misgivings, but gradually he began to dis-play some of the characteristics—fluency, glowing rhetoric, humor and homely illustrations—of his later style.

Still facing him was his examination for ordination by the presby-tery—a mere formality had not the board been made up of such rigid Old School Scotch-Irish Presbyterians as were hounding his father. But Hen-ry had mastered the passwords of orthodoxy at his father's knee. "I had been stuffed with these things. I had eaten and drank them. I had chopped and hewed them. . . . I had had them *ad nauseam*," he wrote long afterward. So he faced the test confidently, ready, like his father, to outwit his judges—most of them country parsons.

In a letter to his brother George he describes the presbytery session with boyish boastfulness and not so boyish mockery:

Father Craigh was appointed to *squeak* the questions. . . . I was a model to be-hold, and so were they! Elders . . . gave their noses a fresh blowing, fixed their spectacles, and hitched forward in their seats. . . . There he sat, the young candi-date begotten of a heretic, nursed at Lane; but with such a name and parentage and education, what remarkable modesty, extraordinary meekness, and how def-erential. . . . Then questions on all the knotty points. "Still the wonder grew" for the more the lad was examined the more incorrigibly orthodox did he grow.

There is no embarrassment at his deviousness. Even thirty years later he would proudly assert: "I knew all their proofs, all their dodging cuts, their ins and outs. . . . the questions came like hail. . . . Some of them I answered directly, some ingeniously . . . and others somewhat obscurely . . . and the Presbytery, without a dissenting voice, voted that I was orthodox—to their amazement and mine!"

But the next day the enemy stiffened: they asked him to declare plainly that he was of the Old School. He refused, whereupon they turned him down. When Beecher reported this to his congregation, they voted unanimously to withdraw from the Oxford Presbytery and declare themselves independent. (A few months later, the Cincinnati Presbytery, a New School group, conveniently guided by Lyman Beecher and Calvin Stowe, confirmed Henry Ward Beecher's ordination.)

Henry's willingness to feign any degree of orthodoxy was hardly an impulsive act. A few years later, when Charles, his next younger brother, had just become a minister in Fort Wayne, Indiana, Henry wrote to him: "Preach little doctrine, except what is of mouldy orthodoxy. . . . Take hold of the most practical subjects; popularize your sermons. I do not ask you to change yourself; but, for a time, while captious critics are lurking, adapt your mode." Perhaps he spoke as he did because he suspected that Charles had not completely discarded his deep skepticism. Even so, its cynicism is surprisingly blatant. Charles disregarded it. Henry's apologists argue that he considered the privilege of preaching the gospel of Christ worth any concessions or compromises in theological doctrine. And did he not, they add, flatly refuse to join the Old School faction? Beecher himself later observed that the main effect on him of the Old School and New School quarrel and of the enmity between Protestants and Catholics was to make him vow never to attack another Christian sect.

The fact that they had a home of their own, created with loving labor together, was for a time sufficient source of happiness for the young couple. It reconciled Henry to the limitations of life in Lawrenceburg. But for Eunice adjustment became more and more difficult. It was not altogether surprising: the daughter of a well-to-do physician in a genteel old Massachusetts community, she suddenly found herself in a raw western farming center, the wife of a poor minister, doing all the housework—and pregnant. Water had to be fetched upstairs from a backyard well, and not only had wood to be carried in but ashes had to be carried out. Some of her neighbors thought she was not a good housekeeper and they were piqued because she insisted on serving every meal on a tablecloth. Her sister-in-law Harriet, who had learned that she could earn money by writing and then pay others to do her housework, advised: "If you can make money by sewing and it hurts you to wash and iron . . . why not hire the latter with the avails of the former?" So Eunice sewed for several hours a day and earned, at most, two dollars a week.

The baby, Harriet Eliza, was born in May 1838. Henry spread the news joyfully. Eunice was not so happy about it. Indeed, she afterward wrote to George Beecher and his wife, Sarah, that at times during her pregnancy she felt that "it would be no great trial to me—and release me from a load of responsibility, which I felt unfit to sustain, should the baby be stillborn." Even if she was recalling what she felt in a period of illness or deep depression, the statement is chilling. She eventually became fond of little Hattie but still tended to be jealous of Henry's affection for the child.

Eunice was also jealous of the hours her husband spent relaxing with the men of the town. In fine weather they could be found on or near the river, hunting, fishing, catching driftwood for use as fuel, or just lounging on the banks. In bad weather they paused to exchange banter and news in one of the local stores. In her autobiographical fiction *From Dawn to Daylight,* Eunice later described the young minister's wife as pleading with her husband to spend some of his free time with her, but to no avail. It was a way of life quite suited to Henry's temperament; he was, he later said, never happier in his life.

Eunice was even more annoyed by the failure of the townspeople to give her husband the respect she thought a minister and the son of Lyman Beecher deserved. Coming from Amherst, where everyone automatically deferred to a clergyman, she was provoked by the familiarity with which the cruder members of the congregation—the more genteel citizens attended the Methodist church—treated their pastor. In a region where many were still struggling to tame the wilderness, a clergyman—who after all was supported by his neighbors—was not considered a particularly valuable member of the community. Henry's growing popularity did bring promises of more money from his congregation; meanwhile the Beechers had to rent a larger house, mainly to accommodate boarders. To a son of Lyman Beecher—but not to Eunice Bullard—it was a familiar answer to financial problems.

As he had planned, the Reverend Beecher took an active part in community affairs. When the Lawrenceburg *Political Beacon* proposed a Fourth of July program to collect funds for the colonization cause, Beecher promptly made his church available for the occasion. On the Fourth, after opening prayers, a resolution was offered favoring the colonization of free blacks on the coast of Africa or elsewhere. But, the speaker added, he had no intention of interfering in the relations between masters and slaves. Henry seconded the resolution. He declared, magisterially, that colonization would free America from "the pest of slavery" and that it was impossible for whites and blacks to live together without one ruling the other. Colonization, he assured his audience, not only was totally different from abolition but was the one way to get rid of the pernicious doctrine of abolitionism. Once again he was telling people what they presumably wanted to hear. Forgotten were his pistol-toting role in quelling the anti-Birney riots in Cincinnati, brother Edward's support of martyred Elijah Lovejoy and Theodore Weld's stirring pleas. Henry would be the last of Lyman Beecher's sons to move away from his father's ever-prudent position on slavery.

It worked. Respectable citizens across the state read young Beecher's words and nodded approvingly. Among other things, they were still in the grip of the panic of 1837 and wanted no one to rock an already unsteady boat.

But before long the increasing hostility between the two camps gave Henry second thoughts. Untroubled, as always, by any inconsistencies in his views, he decided that it was impractical to try to move all blacks to Africa. He had also noted how often whites and blacks interbred not only in the South—the many mulattoes were ample evidence of that—but in other civilizations, such as ancient Egypt. So he decided that it might after all be God's will that the two peoples should live together and eventually merge. He confided such thoughts only to his journal, certain that they would not be welcomed.

But on such a subject as intemperance he was fiercely outspoken, even though Lawrenceburg was, as he said, "the very metropolis of whiskey." Like his father, he attacked drunkenness constantly; and he was pleased to be a delegate to the State Temperance Convention in Indianapolis in 1839.

At first, while he was still, as he himself put it, fresh out of the seminary, he introduced theology into his sermons, especially when he had little else to say: "As a man chops straw and mixes it with Indian meal in order to distend the stomach of the ox that eats it, so I chopped a little of the orthodox theology, that I might sprinkle it with the meal of the Lord Jesus Christ." In time he reduced the theology till all he preached, he said, was "the unsearchable riches of His grace.

In his efforts to arouse his congregation he also tried fiery warnings and threats, but they proved ineffective and he began to realize that the day of the hellfire-and-brimstone sermon was past. Of Edwards's famous "Sinners in the Hands of an Angry God," he said: "I think a person of moral sensibility alone at midnight, reading that awful discourse, would wellnigh go crazy." By 1839 Indiana was a far cry, both in space and time, from the Puritan theocracy of old New England.

Whatever the tradition had been, he knew that he was by nature unable to subscribe to the idea of an angry or vengeful God. Increasingly, he offered a vision of a compassionate, loving Christ—a wishful reflection of his own needs and desires. In this he was stimulated by the example of the Reverend John Newland Maffit, a Methodist evangelist who came through the Ohio Valley converting as many as one hundred sinners in an evening. A pulpit actor, Maffit used appeals to the imagination and a perfervid, almost amatory tone. It was exactly the approach toward which the Reverend Henry Ward Beecher was groping.

Like his father in East Hampton days, Henry Ward found that he could not get along on a country parson's salary, especially when part of it was late or never paid. He and Eunice were finally forced to ask her brother-in-law Ira M. Barton for a loan of two hundred dollars. But Barton could not help them. Henry interpreted this as a rebuke by God and, momentarily humbled, resolved to reduce his debts, devote more time to his church duties, and control his desire for "fine living." But Henry Ward Beecher was not made for frugality, and he had already been subjected to as much of it as he and his wife could stand.

The record of the Reverend Beecher's conversions and additions to church membership was poor; he himself later acknowledged his disappointment at his failure to start any kind of revival. Despite this, his reputation as a preacher, if not as a pastor, and his genial way with people of all classes, spread rapidly. Martha Sawyer helped in this, singing his praises among the socially elect, especially on her visits to the family of Samuel Merrill, a civic leader in Indianapolis. Merrill was influential in a small group that had broken away from the local Old School Presbyterian Church and formed a New School congregation. As president of the State Bank, Merrill visited Lawrenceburg regularly; there he heard young Beecher preach, and he arranged for him to deliver a trial sermon in Indianapolis. Beecher did so, made an excellent impression, and in May 1839 received a call to serve as minister in the new Second Presbyterian Church of Indianapolis.

It was a distinct step upward. The couple had no regrets about leaving Lawrenceburg—except perhaps for being a hundred miles away from Walnut Hills. The town had served well enough as a training ground and for the first years of marriage, but it had also left them burdened with debts. More important, its horizons were far too narrow for so gifted a son of Lyman Beecher.

Indianapolis, hardly twenty-five years old and with less than four thousand inhabitants, was not much more of a city than Lawrenceburg. The stumps had not yet been cleared from all the streets, the wagon tracks and corduroy roads in the surrounding countryside were often impassable sloughs, refuse trickled through open ditches in the streets, and "the ague"—malaria—was everywhere from early summer to late fall. The town's main contact with the world was still by stagecoach. The poor lived in rented cabins on "Smoky Row," with as many as a dozen persons occupying a small unventilated shack. The mainstays of diet in many households were fried cornmeal, pork, game and saleratus biscuit. A vast quantity of corn whiskey was consumed and few men would refuse a drink. Women wore gingham, calico, or woolen dresses that reached from the neck to below the ankles, and many families made their clothes at home.

When the Beechers arrived, the city was still in the throes of the panic of 1837, and it would be until the early 1840s. A boom in land, based on the expectation that a canal as well as a railroad would soon reach the capital, had collapsed and many laborers were unemployed. A goodly number of Indiana settlers had come from the South, and as North-South antagonism grew, the state was increasingly unfriendly to blacks. They were not allowed to vote, serve in the militia or on juries, or send their children to public schools.

But Indianapolis was the state capital: it had been carefully laid out, with a few wide streets radiating from a hub called the Circle, and here and there it had fine houses surrounded by gardens. It also had all the machinery of culture: two literary societies, a library, a lyceum, a music society—and, surprisingly, a piano factory—an anthenaeum, a female collegiate institute, an academy, two newspapers. . . .

Unfortunately Eunice's first experience there was bitterly disappointing. When the Beechers arrived, in July, the Merrills generously invited them to stay in their home, one of the finest in the city, until the newcomers found a place of their own. One of the main reasons Eunice had been glad to leave Lawrenceburg was to get away from the malaria there. But on entering the Merrill house, she found Mrs. Merrill almost an invalid from chronic malaria—not to mention consumption and too much childbearing—and three of her children in bed and showing all the telltale symptoms. Eunice burst into tears and cried, "Oh, Henry, they are all sick with 'chills,' and you were told no one ever had them here!" Mrs. Merrill was astonished: all visitors to the city soon knew, she said, that everyone there had the "chills and fever" regularly. Henry denied this. Even friendly biographers assume he knew about the malaria but did not tell Eunice for fear she would refuse to move. Theodore Parker reported that he saw not a single rosy cheek among hundreds of Indianapolis schoolchildren and that the women were all thin, bony and flabby-cheeked.

Fulfilling Eunice's fears, both she and Henry fell ill. And they had to move several times before they found an acceptable house. It was only ten feet wide and the bedroom was so small, Eunice said, that she was "obliged to make the bed on one side first, then go out on the veranda, raise a window, reach in and make the bed on the other side." Now, too, she was pregnant again. Whether it was due to poor health or overwork, she gave birth to a dead baby. She did not go to the burial and she and Henry seemed hardly to mourn. Perhaps it was that death in infancy was so common, or that Eunice was physically and mentally too weary to care. Harriet, only a year or so older but combining four years of marriage and childbearing with a streak of Puritan iron, assured her that it was plainly part of God's plan and, considering Eunice's poor health, probably just as well.

During Henry's first year in Indianapolis, the new congregation met on the second floor of a seminary building. The community was still so rural that stray sheep gathered under the open stairway leading to the upstairs meeting place. Often in the course of his missionary duties Beecher preached at a distance from the city. These trips, on horseback, could be exhausting, and if he had to ford rivers, dangerous: twice he was nearly drowned. The food and the beds in taverns, moreover, were usually so bad that if he was not invited to stay in someone's home, he preferred spending the night in a barn or even in the open.

The congregation built its own church the following year. Beecher saw to it that the building had a dais at the front rather than the conventional pulpit stuck, as he put it, like a swallow's nest, high up on the church wall. He had begun to rely on that intimacy with his audience that would become one of the secrets of his power.

He had learned to preach, but he had still to discover how to get results from his efforts. "I can preach so as to make the people come to hear me," he said, "but somehow I can't preach them clear into the Kingdom." That he learned, he says, by studying the Apostles. He read their sermons until he realized that they sought out a common ground "on which the people and they stood together . . . then they heaped up a large number of the particulars of knowledge that belonged to everybody . . . [and] brought it to bear upon them with all their excited heart and feeling." He discovered, in short, how to dramatize his message and make use of accepted attitudes, which he presented in vivid figures and with an uninhibited show of feeling. A sermon was good, he declared, only if it had "power on the heart."

But Henry Ward Beecher did not achieve success as a preacher by reading the Acts of the Apostles. He did so by a gift of nature—his overflowing health and energy (some called it "animal spirits")—his hopeful temper, his fertile imagination, and his friendliness and informality. Whatever the source of his power, his sermons began to draw visitors from other churches and even from other cities. Members of the state legislature, when it met in Indianapolis, came to hear him. He was consulted by high-placed Presbyterian churchmen in the Indiana synod. His favorite teacher at Lane, Calvin Stowe, who had refused to preach in his church in Lawrenceburg because he thought Henry should stand on his own feet, now came to Indianapolis and preached twice in his church. His family talked proudly of his progress. "Brother Henry . . . feels much encouraged," his half sister Isabella reported in December 1839. ". . . I think he is going somewhat in father's track and will perhaps one day come somewhere near him in eminence." Considering that Henry was only three years out of seminary, it was a remarkable vote of confidence even from a sister.

Eunice, almost as rapidly as nature would allow, had become pregnant again. Such was her dread of bearing a child in the malaria-ridden Indianapolis summer that in November 1840 Henry took her and little Hattie back to the Bullards' home in Massachusetts. She had not seen her parents in three and a half years and she knew that she looked careworn and old beyond her years, but she was shocked when she walked alone into the Bullard home and first her mother and then her father thought she was one of Dr. Bullard's new patients—and an ailing one at that.

Many members of Beecher's congregation in Indianapolis were aware that their minister's wife had fled not only because of the climate but because she was unhappy about the treatment she and her husband had received in the West. They had noted that she was often absent from church services and rarely made the calls expected of a minister's wife. They also found her changeable. "I had never yet seen such a woman; she could be as beautiful as a princess and as plain and homely as possible," wrote Jane Merrill Ketcham. "So she could be sparklingly bright and bitterly sarcastic."

Eunice in turn could not bear the way the congregation kept the family of their religious and spiritual guide only a step away from want and seemed to consider his salary a form of charity, payable when they pleased. Once when Henry listed his debts he found that he owed money to seventeen creditors, including $175 to one of them. In *From Dawn to Daylight* Eunice declared that the minister's family could have lived for a year on what prosperous members of the congregation "wasted" on a single "blowout." Then there were her constant complaints about servants; whether Hoosier, German or black, they were, she said, lazy, dirty or ignorant. After a visit in 1840, John Parsons, a Virginian, said of the difference between Henry and Eunice:

His greeting was hearty and sincere. I knew he meant his welcome and the invitation he extended to me to his church and his home. The latter, a neat, one-story cottage in Market Street . . . I soon visited, meeting his wife, a rather discontented woman, complaining constantly of chills and the unhealthy nature of the town.

Difficulties gave Henry Ward Beecher only momentary pause; his naturally buoyant and hopeful temper soon asserted itself. After the tension and the challenge of preaching, he, like his father, sought physical release. Although he was now over thirty, a minister and a father, he thought nothing of rolling downhill with children in a round of copenhagen at a church picnic or of playing parlor games with young people; he would join the youths in a street near his church and compete with them in vaulting over a board fence; he chopped down trees on William Bradshaw's farm "just to hear them fall"; and he joined a volunteer fire company and more than once fought a fire until he was streaked with soot. Once he astonished the carpenters working on his new house by "skinning the cat" on an exposed joint. Finally, the presbytery rebuked him for the disorderly way he ran his church. It is doubtful that he cared.

There was a certain boyish swagger about the way he disregarded the forms of dress and grooming. He had lost the lean face of his college days and his hair was long and stringy. He was the first clergyman in the region to wear a soft felt hat, he usually stuffed his trouser legs into his boot tops, and he sometimes turned up in church in pants stained from gardening or, after a horseback trip, in muddy leggings. But for what he lacked in dignity he made up in vitality. Samuel Bowles, later the well-known editor of the *Springfield* (Massachusetts) *Republican,* would say: "He has no reverence and inspires none, only wonder and admiration for his mental gymnastics and his physical freshness and vigor." Even in a minister it was an image that suited "western" America in the 1840s. Thus he drew his color from his environment: in the West he was a Westerner; in the East he would be an Easterner—with perhaps a dash of western flamboyance.

As in most controversial matters, in politics Henry was a middle-of-the-roader—a moderate Whig. He had known General William Henry Harrison in Cincinnati when the old Indian fighter, onetime senator and active Presbyterian, lived in nearby North Bend. Later, as we have seen, Mrs. Harrison had given Eunice and Henry some precious wedding presents. So Beecher followed Harrison's Presidential campaign against Van Buren in 1840 with intense interest. As pleased as he was when the luxury-loving Harrison with his "log cabin and hard cider" pose—and his pro-slavery views—won overwhelmingly, so stunned was he when the President died a month after his inauguration. It was quite a tribute to Beecher—or to his claims of friendship with Harrison—that at the memorial services in the state capitol, Governor Samuel Bigger and the Reverend Henry Ward Beecher delivered the main addresses.

Henry's enthusiasm for gardening continued undiminished. It satisfied both his love of flowers and his need for outdoor work. (When practical-minded farm folk asked him what good flowers were, he would exclaim, "What good! Why, make you happier and better everytime you look at them.... Try it a year and you will never ask that question again.") As soon as he was settled in Indianapolis he began planting fruit, vegetables and flowers in his cottage garden. That was evidently not enough, so he rented two lots and then, although he really could not afford it, bought the lots. Soon, too, he helped organize the Indiana Horticultural Society and was a judge at its exhibitions. So successful was his vegetable gardening that by the second spring he was pushing wheelbarrow loads of produce to the city market. Rhubarb, or pie-plant as it was called, was one of his specialties and he sold as much as he could grow, enjoying not only the fellowship of the market but the income.

Although he was an eager student of books on horticulture, it was probably his way with words as much as his knowledge of gardening that led to his being asked in 1844 to edit a new journal, the semimonthly *Indiana Farmer and Gardener.* Serving without pay but reveling in the opportunity to publish, he wrote lively and engaging articles not only on farming and gardening but on temperance, prostitution among farm-born girls in England, and the rowdyism of some urchins during college commencement exercises in Bloomington. He encouraged useful articles, scorning "fine writing" and "senseless gabble about dew and zephyrs."

After a few years his interest in the journal waned and when he left Indianapolis in 1847 it ceased publication. But his passion for flowers and gardening, begun in the Litchfield hills of his boyhood, would never leave him. Indeed, the natural world, from the cycle of the seasons to the magic of a single flower, became for him as convincing proof of God as he needed.

Fluent, agreeable, witty, his essays attracted attention and a following. To the end of his career he would continue to pour out such pieces effortlessly and for an ever larger audience.

When Eunice gave birth to a son at her parents' home in Massachusetts in July 1841, Beecher prepared to go east. He agreed to take along Julia, the lovely fourteen-year-old-daughter of his friends the Merrills, who planned to visit relatives in New England. With them went Julia's best friend, Betty Bates. Beecher had taught both girls, and Julia had come to idolize the ingratiating young minister. Although his wife had been away for nine months, no one—and apparently Beecher least of all—saw any impropriety in his escorting two attractive and admiring girls across the country and back.

Ironically, as soon as Beecher went away, a revival started in his church. For three years he had tried his utmost to arouse his parishioners, but in vain. Vexed at his absence, the congregation was inspired to ask the help of their minister's famous father, Lyman Beecher. At odds with his own congregation, Dr. Beecher was happy to be called on to practice his favorite art, especially in his son's church. Although sixty-six, he labored with all his old-time energy for ten days and brought a dozen souls into the fold before he went home.

Like a scattering of brush fires, revivals started up elsewhere in Indiana, and a few months after Henry returned to Indianapolis with his wife and newborn son, he was invited to assist in a revival in what was then the village of Terre Haute. It went so well that he started back home in a state of exultation. Many years later he wrote that his return to the ordinary round of church life

. . . from this glowing centre seemed so intolerable that my whole nature and all my soul rose up in uncontrollable prayer. Through the beech woods, sometimes crying, sometimes singing, and always praying, I rode in one long controversy with God. "Slay me if Thou wilt, but do not send me home to barrenness. Thou *shalt* go with me. I will not be refused. . . . I will prevail or die!"—these and even wilder strains went through the soul.

At length the clouds rolled away. . . . An unspeakable peace and confidence filled my soul. The assurance of victory was perfect.

He was sure that the fire in him would kindle a flame in his congregation. But there was no response. Only after weeks of intensive preaching, prayer meetings and personal appeals ("I can see him still," a friend recalled, "in his rough brown overcoat, his trousers tucked in his heavy boots, flying around full of zeal and inspiration") did the revival take hold. It filled the lives of church members through the long winter weeks from February to April and added about ninety persons to the church rolls. The climax came when, at the urging of a few initiates, Beecher joined the pastors of the Baptist and Methodist churches in arranging a riverside baptism. The ceremony took place on the banks of the White River and is said to have drawn two to three thousand spectators.

Word of Beecher's success as a speaker spread and he was soon asked to help with revivals in Indiana from Madison to Logansport. At the latter he spoke first in the tiny Presbyterian church, but was then called on to preach to a large camp meeting on the edge of town. Such meetings had erupted in the Cumberlands early in the century and had periodically swept the western land like waves of fever or some ancient nature rite. They were perhaps a reaction to centuries of Puritanical discipline as well as the loneliness and emotional starvation of frontier life. Frontier settlers, seeking a religion that did not depend on an inscrutable Providence or God's pleasure, welcomed revivals because they were a formula for instant salvation.

Thousands gathered in a primeval woods and listened as in a trance, all swaying and moaning and crying out as one. Often, buried impulses surged to the surface, expressing themselves not only in religious hysteria but in drunkenness, violence and sexual license. "Religious passion includes all other passions," a Methodist minister with twenty-five years of experience told an English editor in Indiana; "you cannot excite one without stirring up the others." Babies born to unmarried as well as married women were common enough to warrant the name "camp meeting child."

Many Presbyterian clergymen, especially in older communities, considered the meetings barbaric and mistrusted them because they bypassed churches. Much as Beecher believed that religion should rule through the heart rather than the head, he too was troubled by the unruly character of the crowds. But he saw in them the power of a speaker to release pent-up feelings and arouse an audience. And occasionally the experience could be enchanting:

The night, beautiful in its radiance overhead . . . the songs of Zion sung by three thousand people, the strange mingling of light and dark; and after the great meeting is over and the people have retired to their tents . . . I have lain in my little bunk and heard, in the night, six, eight, or ten little meetings going on all around me. One dies out, another dies out, and another . . . and finally, as the last bell strikes, I hear but one. After that, low murmurings, and then . . . all is still.

At the Logansport meeting, seeing that no one had been appointed to police the huge crowd—he estimated it at five thousand—Henry pleaded with it to maintain order. The meeting went off without incident. But he could hardly have been entirely satisfied to pour himself out to people he did not know and would never meet again.

Beecher led another revival in his own church in 1843 and a third in 1845. It was not simply a coincidence that all three began in February and petered out in April. They brought excitement and drama into the dull round of village life in winter. Orator, poet, showman, Henry gave what amounted to a series of theatrical performances and lit up the bleak days with the hope of salvation. But it was one of the shortcomings of revivals that their manufactured intensity was always followed by a relapse into indifference and a return to the duties of daily life.

Despite all the revivals and preachments, sinfulness rocked the congregation from time to time. Whether it was lingering Puritanism, Victorian prudery or provincial narrowness, Beecher and the elders of the church repeatedly censured members for immoral conduct. One of the very first members that Henry had enrolled, Mary Harman, was publicly excommunicated for breaking the Seventh Commandment. Later Owen Tuller was similarly humiliated after he admitted being guilty of adultery. A young woman of a prominent family and her husband were suspended when she bore a child only a few months after they were married. Others were rebuked and punished for drunkenness, gambling, profanity, breaking the Sabbath or visiting a house of ill fame.

Even the coming of a dancing master brought mutterings of disapproval—led by the Reverend Beecher. True, the teacher wore a frilled shirt, silk stockings, and pumps with silver buckles, and the hornpipes he played were enough to quicken the bones of the dead. Henry could hardly be blamed if his disapproval was an effort to please his older and more important parishioners.

Social visiting was the most popular recreation, and as the Reverend Beecher's reputation grew, family and friends often crowded his little house. To avoid travel at night, the friends would come late in the morning, have dinner—usually lavish—early in the afternoon and leave before dark. Henry, born actor, always took a main part in the talk and games, and once or twice even Eunice joined in, surprising everyone with her performance. When Thomas Worthington Whittredge, a young artist and daguerreotypist, later a famous landscape and portrait painter, fell ill, Beecher took him in and he stayed as their boarder for a year. One of Eunice's brothers, Dr. Talbut Bullard, who lived nearby, and other of her relatives came and lingered.

Harriet, escaping from her household burdens, made a longish visit to Henry's home in 1843. It was a delight to indulge once again in "soul to soul" confidences with her brother. Clearly resenting Eunice because she had taken Henry away, Harriet made a point of reclaiming him when she visited him. (She did not realize how very condescending she was when she later wrote to Eunice: "I thought . . . that tho' you were such a good for nothing saucy baggage, yet I could not help loving you, sins, sinner, and all, as I always did and do.") So she and Henry stayed up late, talking, drinking spruce beer and renewing their old communion.

One of the diversions she described was Henry's repeated success in mesmerizing her:

The first session he succeeded in almost throwing me into convulsions—spasms and shocks of heat and prickly sensation ran all over me. My lungs were violently constricted and my heart in dreadful commotion and I was so frightened that I called out for quarter. This strange tempestuous effect was occasioned simply by our sitting opposite to each other with our eyes fixed and our thumbs in contact for about thirty minutes, and it was dissipated by making reverse passes which relieved first my head, then my lungs, then my lower limbs and lastly my arms. . . . after being thus violently possessed with the demon of mesmerism I began to have rather reverend ideas of the same.

She was convinced, she reported to Calvin, that she had been brought to "the verge of the spirit land." Eunice was upset by the experiment and fled from the room—or so Harriet said—as though she thought she had "some hobgoblin magician for a husband."

Soon afterward Harriet consulted a pair of mesmerists and invited one of them, a Mrs. Bonneville, a "pretty little graceful creature," to visit with her at Walnut Hills. Mrs. Bonneville persuaded her, she told Henry, that the "mesmeric fluid" was a "powerful remedial agent in the cure of nervous diseases." Harriet urged Henry to continue to work with it because, she wrote, "I think you have an immense power in this way and the time may come when you can relieve pain by trying it."

In considering mesmerism as a medical technique, Harriet's interest in it is not remarkable, but she seems to have been just as much attracted to it as a way of communicating with the spirit world. Henry did not share this urge. Despite his belief in personal magnetism, he almost alone of the Beechers rejected spiritualism and the use of mediums as tending to weaken the reliance on religion and the Bible. He seems to have sensed that in its way it was a rival in the field of the supernatural.

Henry's young half brothers, Tom and James, stimulated by his vitality and optimism, stayed with him for long periods. That same buoyancy of spirit also drew brother Charles to his side: In the summer of 1841 Charles, trailing a romantic aura as musician and skeptic, came north with his wife and child. He settled in Indianapolis and became Henry's all-around assistant. Working with Henry, he gradually shed enough of his doubts to allow him to win a license to preach. And it was Henry, as we have seen, who then found him a pastorate in Fort Wayne, Indiana.

With Charles, James and Tom turning to him, Henry, although only in his early thirties, was already beginning to do for Lyman's younger sons what Lyman had once done for his older sons. They plainly sensed that Lyman's day was past and the future was Henry's.

Thirty years earlier, Lyman Beecher had achieved nationwide recognition with a series of six lectures on a single sin—intemperance. Now his son, in the winter of 1843–1844, gave seven lectures for young men; but he took an entire range of temptation and immorality for his theme: idleness, dishonesty, lust for wealth, "dangerous" men (cynics, libertines and demagogues), gambling, prostitution and popular amusements such as horse racing and the theater. Set forth in a highly colored style with vividly drawn, or overdrawn, portraits to illustrate every vice, and lurid scenes of the seduction of youth, they simultaneously fascinated, horrified and edified his listeners.

In outlook they represent a transition from religious to ethical values, from Puritan to Victorian standards. The sins that once led to damnation and hell have here become vices leading to sickness, disgrace, failure and the gallows. The penalties are almost all paid in this world rather than the next. And society, not the church, passes judgment.

Aside from their theatricality, the lectures abound in moral absolutes and sounding generalizations: "The poor man with industry is happier than the rich man in idleness"; "Riches bought with guile God will pay for with vengeance"; "If in every community three things should be put together . . . the front would be a *grog-shop*, the middle a *jail*, the rear a *gallows* . . . and the recruits for this three-headed monster are largely drafted from the lazy children of worthless parents." Industry, thrift and honesty are the most reliable qualities; so Beecher opens his lecture on dishonesty with a description of the panic of 1837 as an object lesson in the dangers of financial speculation. But beneath this statement of faith in the Protestant work ethic, Beecher reveals a curious distrust of wealth. His is not the code of a Franklin who said, "Time is money," nor does it anticipate the Horatio Alger who sold young people on the goals of "success" and "getting ahead." Later, as the famous pastor of an affluent Brooklyn congregation, Beecher would change his tune—although occasionally echoing his earlier warnings—but in small-town Indiana in 1844 he was still reflecting the rural distrust of wealth that is not earned by sweat or strenuous service. And he repeatedly declared that unless the rich man helped the needy, he would never derive true happiness from his wealth. Addressed to the new middle class, the appeal was not for Christian charity but for social benevolence. The goal was ethical, not spiritual—suitable, whether he realized it or not, for an increasingly business-oriented society.

Similarly, the lecture on gambling combines a New Englander's misgivings about risking hard-earned money in a game of chance with a stereotype of the country boy succumbing to big-city corruption. With an almost Dickensian vividness, he describes the stages in the life of a youth who becomes a gambler:

Scene the third. Years have passed on. . . . Go with me into that dilapidated house, not far from the landing at New Orleans. Look into that dirty room. Around a broken table, sitting upon boxes, kegs, or rickety chairs, see a filthy crew dealing cards smouched with tobacco, grease, and liquor. One has a pirate-face burnished and burnt with brandy; a shock of grizzly, matted hair, half covering his villain eyes, which glare out like a wild beast's from a thicket. Close by him wheezes a white-faced, dropsical wretch, vermin-covered, and stenchful. A scoundrel Spaniard and a burly negro (the jolliest of the four) complete the group. They have spectators—drunken sailors, and ogling, thieving, drinking women, who should have died long ago, when all that was womanly died. Here hour draws on hour, sometimes with brutal laughter, sometimes with threat and oath and uproar. The last few stolen dollars lost, and temper too, each charges each with cheating, and high words ensue, and blows; and the whole gang burst out the door, beating, biting, scratching, and rolling over and over in the dirt and dust. The worst, the fiercest, the drunkest of the four is our friend who began by making up the game.

How much of this view of country innocence and city evil represented Beecher's true convictions and how much was designed to fit the prejudices of his audience is a question. Much the same question is posed by the prudery and bigotry of his moral standards. But here the answer must be that no one who did not believe in such a code of conduct could have presented it in such detail and with such conviction. Thus he fires not only at large targets such as dishonesty, prostitution and drunkenness but even at "mere pleasure sought outside of usefulness," at French novels and their English imitators ("the sewers of society, into which drain the concentrated filth of the worst passions"), dancing, boxing, racing and the theater. In Beecher's judgment on writers, Bulwer is the "implacable corrupter," Chaucer is gross, Moore offers a "perfumed" license, Swift (a clergyman, he moans) is Belial and guilty of "abominable vulgarities," Sterne (another clergyman!) deals in "scoundrel indirections," and the Elizabethan playwrights, the early Shakespeare, Fielding and Byron—not to mention those depraved sensualists the French—"give currency to filth by coining it in the mint of beauty."

For the theater he has only boundless contempt. It is a "vagabond prostitute" whose day is long past. Despite such exceptions as Mrs. Siddons, Ellen Tree, Fanny Kemble and Garrick, actors are "licentious wretches": "Half the victims of the gallows and the penitentiary will tell you that these schools for morals were to them the gate of debauchery, the porch of pollution, the vestibule of the very house of death."

But it is for the harlot, the "strange woman" of the Bible, that he saves his most glittering descriptions and most terrifying warnings. It tells us something about his own fantasies when he assumes throughout that this woman is irresistible: "simple man, trust not thyself near the *artful* woman, armed in her beauty, her cunning raiment, her dimpled smiles ... her look of love, her voice of flattery; for if thou hadst the strength of ten Ulysses, unless God help thee, Calypso shall make thee fast, and hold thee in her island."

In his complete distrust of youth's capacity to resist temptation, he is still echoing the old Puritan belief in innate depravity. In scenes that make Hogarth's *Rake's Progress* seem tame, he traces the stages of the victim's downward path—Pleasure, Satiety, Disease, Death—making as much of the loathsome as he does of the seductive. After the banalities of the average sermon, his Biblical curses against the "corrupters of youth" must have been almost as satisfying to his audience as his fantasies of sensual indulgence.

Even as he gives his own overheated imaginings free rein, he warns youth that the only safe way is to shun such thoughts altogether. Apparently no resolutions, principles or ideals are in themselves sufficient. Such an exaggeration of the harlot's charms can only be explained as a result of Puritan and Victorian prohibitions against any sexual contact between young men and women. Prostitution was simply the other side of the coin of Victorian prudery.

Although every adult knew there was prostitution in Indianapolis, several members of Henry's church violently opposed any public mention of the subject and a few women and children stayed away from the lectures. More than one critic later remarked that Beecher knew suspiciously much about all the vices, so Beecher let it be known that his information came from interviews with gamblers and their kind. But no one could doubt that he had read all the "filthy" literature he deplored.

Despite this, or perhaps because of it, a local printer offered to publish the lectures in book form. At first Beecher hesitated, aware of their shortcomings, but he was soon persuaded. The book won testimonials from various prominent citizens, and the Indiana Synod recommended that it be given to every young man and placed in every Sunday school, hotel and steamboat in the state. (A dozen publishers in the United States and Europe would keep the book in print for half a century.) It gave Beecher his first taste of nationwide recognition and surely whetted his appetite for a larger audience than the Second Presbyterian Church of Indianapolis.

Freely as the young Reverend Beecher spoke out on all such matters—who was not against sin?—he remained conspicuously cautious in his utterances on slavery. When he arrived in Indianapolis, the local presbytery was urging its members to give at least one antislavery sermon a year. The Indiana Synod had also called on the church for "decisive measures to purify itself from this . . . enormous evil" and had dismissed the colonization scheme as inadequate. Beecher nevertheless continued to avoid the subject. Long afterward, when he had at last joined fully in the struggle against slavery, he declared that he recalled a time in Indiana when "no prayer meeting or church gathering allowed men to speak on the subject of liberty . . . when in Presbytery and Synod it was considered heresy to advocate freedom." This was a distinct exaggeration. Several leading members of his congregation had made their opposition to slavery clear. Samuel Merrill had had Frederick Douglass as a guest in his home; Dr. Luke Munsell, an elder, had once worked with abolitionist

James G. Birney; and John L. Ketcham, later the clerk of the church, had gone to great lengths to help the husband of Henry's black maid win his freedom.

Years later, Beecher rationalized his failure to act by asserting: "I knew that just as sure as I preached an Abolition sermon, they would blow me up sky high, and my usefulness . . . would be gone." Apparently he meant only his usefulness in preaching against prostitutes and gamblers.

Of course there were risks in taking a radical position. He knew what had happened to such extremists as Birney and Van Zandt in Cincinnati and Lovejoy in Alton, Illinois. Closer to home, there were frequently violent outbursts by supporters of slavery in Indianapolis. One of the more shameful incidents involved a family that had emigrated to Missouri. The father had died there and the mother, her three daughters and a light-skinned black who had worked with the family started back to Massachusetts. They paused in Indianapolis and there one of the daughters, reportedly a genteel young woman, married the black man. A mob had descended on the family, the black man had fled, and the mob had paraded the girl through the streets. When a Dr. Stipp tried to intervene he was knocked down.

At another time Henry was in Pendleton, northeast of Indianapolis, when the townspeople learned that abolitionists, including a white woman and a former slave (said to have been Frederick Douglass) were holding meetings nearby. Assuming the worst, a mob attacked the abolitionists and drove them away. When the leader of the mob was arrested and jailed, three hundred armed men rode into Indianapolis and demanded his release. Governor Whitcomb capitulated. As in the editorials Beecher wrote for the *Philanthropist* in the Birney affair, he protested violently against mob rule but said nothing about slavery:

What can the community expect but growing dishonesty . . . when honest men and officers fly before a mob . . . when the Executive, consulting the spirit of the community, receives the demands of the mob and humbly complies, throwing down the fences of the law, that base rioters may walk unimpeded to their work of vengeance, or unjust mercy?

When he finally did preach an antislavery sermon, it drew a number of distinguished visitors. As one of those visitors recalled many years later, the church was already crowded when a "young man from the country . . . of a stout, clumsy figure" entered. He was carelessly dressed, his face was "full, heavy and flushed," and he uttered the prayer with a "gush of fervor." But as soon as he plunged into his sermon he became "inspired, radiant, glorified, transfigured face aflame, eyes flashing, voice reverberating. . . ." The visitor listened with rapt attention for two hours. Even allowing for an exaggeration of both Beecher's boorish appearance and his later transformation, the visitor's reaction was typical of Henry's effect on audiences throughout his career.

To make the sermon safe, Henry buttressed it with Biblical evidence, and he contented himself with calling slavery a moral evil that must be ended gradually and by law. The degradation of blacks, he asserted, degrades all men, but he also trotted out the old argument that slavery was not prohibited by the Bible. "True wisdom," as his father had said, consisted in "advocating a cause *only so far as the community will sustain the reformer.*" As might have been expected, the sermon caused no stir whatever.

Even a dreadful incident within earshot of Beecher's church seems to have added more to his fear of the slavery forces than to his anger against them. During a Fourth of July celebration in 1845, boisterous behavior led to rowdyism, and when a black man, John Tucker, tried to pass a drunken white youth, Nicholas Wood, the youth began to badger him. Tucker stood his ground and soon the two men came to blows. Other white men, enraged by the sight of a black man daring to strike back at a white man, joined the attack. Terrified, Tucker tried to run away, whereupon William Ballenger, owner of a "grocery"—another name for a saloon—struck him down with a club and beat him to death.

Less than a hundred yards away, the respectable folk in Beecher's church, hearing screams, curses and the sound of men fighting, were horrified. Beecher and a few others rushed down the street to where the murdered black man lay. By that time, one version declares, the mob, looking for other prey, had come upon Henry DePuy, a mild little man who was editor of the local abolitionist paper, the *Indiana Freeman*. The rioters were beating him when Beecher caught up with them. Turning to DePuy, he cried, "Get out! Run! You have no friends here!" Reluctantly DePuy retreated to his office. When the story of Beecher's behavior got around, more than a few found it shameful. Wood was tried, convicted and sent to prison, but Ballenger left town and escaped prosecution.

No one ever accused Henry of lack of physical courage. There were some rough fellows in Indianapolis and Henry repeatedly outfaced men who threatened to whip him. Once when DePuy told Beecher that a certain bartender had mocked and abused him, Beecher made little of the bartender and his threats. DePuy promptly printed Beecher's comments in the next issue of his paper. When Beecher passed the bartender's place that day, the man called him into the bar and roared, "If it were not for your cloth, sir, I'd give you the damnedest thrashing." Beecher calmly took off his coat and declared, "Never mind the cloth," and offered to accommodate him. His bluff called, the astonished bartender backed down and did nothing.

But at least once, Henry was arraigned for pussyfooting on the slavery issue. It came about when he made the mistake of attacking an Indianapolis merchant and prominent temperance advocate, Cornelius G. W. Comegys, for building a distillery—Henry called it a "fiendhouse"—in Lawrenceburg, with a capacity of 150 barrels of whiskey a day. When Comegys soon afterward sued the *Greenburg Repository* for libel, Beecher mockingly observed in his *Indiana Farmer and Gardener* that he knew no one who could so ill afford to lose his character as a distiller but that the loss would not of course matter so much to a Christian distiller as to an "ungodly, impenitent distiller." The criticism was not only unprovoked but malicious; and Comegys, barely containing his anger, published an open letter to the citizens of Indianapolis declaring his pain at seeing "how very frequently the Rev. (?) H. W. Beecher attempts to hold me up to public derision and contempt. . . . His pulpit and his press have both been used to gratify his petty malice, his unmanly and ungentlemanly attacks." Caught off guard, Henry resorted to righteousness and ridicule. Apparently referring to a threat by Comegys to beat him, he wrote:

While, then, my unfeigned regard for his courage in thrashing a minister will make me very prudent in my language, I must inform him that if worst comes to worst, I shall engage a Quaker and a woman to stand by, and fight for me in that disastrous hour; and if he vanquishes the three—a Quaker, a preacher, and a woman, the scene shall be engraved . . . upon the head of each whiskey barrel, reminding every beholder, both of what the manufacturer has done, and what the contents of the barrel will enable others to do.

Comegys retorted in kind, charging that Beecher had deserted his church in Lawrenceburg in its moment of need and spent his time there in reading corrupt works of fiction. After another lengthy reply by Beecher, Comegys fired a devastating last shot:

Slavery—that is a rather delicate subject with the gentleman. . . . But slavery is an *evil,* and by its laws men without the exercise of their will or inalienable rights . . . are held by *iron law* fast in its chains. Does alcohol do that? Or does the distiller do that? . . . You cannot justify slavery, then, by talking about the making of whiskey. . . .

Why is thy tongue still and thy pen idle when the sentiments of thy brother [Edward Beecher] and thy church on slavery are promulgated? Thou idle boaster—where is thy vaunted boldness? . . . When a moiety of true, philanthropic, Christian courage is needed . . . thy tongue is still, thy hand forgetteth its cunning.

You are greatly to be pitied—even by a distiller!

It was an unseemly exchange, and many believed that Henry had the worst of it.

The slavery charge rankled. Although he still feared that he might lose his post ("It seemed to me that my church would be shut, and that I should be deprived of the means on which I depended for the support of my family"), he ro longer dared to remain silent. So, early in 1846, he gave two sermons. In the first, as cautious as ever, he assailed the tyranny of the Egyptians in enslaving Moses and the Hebrews. Getting no protests, he finally ventured in the second to denounce the evils of slavery in America.

At least one newspaper in the East reprinted the sermons, but there was no earthshaking reaction to them. Young Julia Merrill, still adoring Henry, wrote to a friend that they had caused much excitement in Indianapolis, but her father, somewhat more objective, reported that Beecher had preached two sermons because the synod had directed him to do so and that they had suited neither "the abolitionists nor the other extreme."

Fate seemed determined to keep Eunice Beecher unhappy in the West. Quite suddenly, fifteen-month-old Georgie fell ill, was seized by convulsions and died. Six years earlier, when their second baby was still-born, they had grieved only briefly, but Georgie was a favorite of theirs, and his death left them badly shaken. Helplessly, Henry fell back on the traditional view that bitter medicine was good and that one must yield "dumb, unreasoning submission to the will of God." But Eunice was once more borne down by their troubles. She was somewhat cheered when they started work on a new house, but a letter to Harriet at the end of 1846 is a catalog of Henry's and her duties and burdens. "My heart," she cries, "is almost broken by this year's trials." Nearly ten months after Georgie's death, she wrote, "I miss his small step by my chair. I miss him at the morning prayer. I miss him *all day everywhere!* and I have the wildest longings to *look into his grave and see* if he is indeed there—or if this be not a horrible dream." She ends the letter with a wail of self-pity: If you were to step in, she writes, "I think you would have some trouble to recognize your sister in the thin-faced, grey-headed, toothless old woman you would find here."

Later Beecher would claim that it was Eunice's health that first made him consider returning to the East. But he certainly had other reasons: he had served almost ten years in the West, his salary was still only eight hundred dollars a year and usually in arrears, and perhaps most important, a vision of fame and a great audience had suddenly been opened up to him by overtures from a Congregational church being organized in Brooklyn. A New York businessman, William T. Cutler, who had long known and admired Lyman Beecher, heard Henry preach in Indianapolis and talked to him about returning to the East. Cutler was impressed not only by young Beecher as preacher and writer but by his many other achievements: the increase in his congregation from 33 to 275, the building of a new church, his work in establishing the Indianapolis Benevolent Society to aid the poor, a Deaf and Dumb Institute, a school for the blind, temperance societies, the Indiana Horticultural Society—of which he was president—and publicly supported education. Not least was his feeling that Beecher had qualities that middle-class Americans were coming to prize more and more: a comforting interpretation of Christian doctrine, a faith in America's future, a moderate position on public issues, a reliance on persuasion rather than threat in moral matters, and a natural optimism. Cutler carried his enthusiasm back to his associates in Brooklyn and especially to Henry C. Bowen.

Bowen, a prosperous Broadway merchant whose young wife, Lucy Tappan, was a niece of Arthur Tappan, Lyman Beecher's patron at Lane, was an energetic organizer. He quickly spread word of Henry Ward Beecher as an eloquent young frontier preacher who would be just right to launch a new church. Responding to several invitations, Henry came east—at Bowen's expense—in May 1847, addressed the Home Missionary Society in New York and then the newly formed, as yet unnamed, Congregational church in Brooklyn. Both efforts, bold in tone but reassuring in point of view, were widely praised, the second being reprinted on the front page of the New York *Daily Tribune*.

Quickly, excitingly, word circulated of the young clergyman who held audiences spellbound with the warmth and poetry of his preaching and the magnetism of his personality. Henry was promptly invited to Boston and delivered almost a dozen lectures and sermons there, including one at the very influential Park Street Church, where his father, his brother Edward and he himself during his wedding trip east, had preached. Afterwards, leaders of the congregation offered him the post of assistant pastor, reminding him that he would thus be returning to "the heart of New England."

Spurred by the competition, Bowen, with the emotionalism that would mark all their relations over the years, told Henry that he was "the man of our choice—'our first love,' the desire of our hearts."

A last obstacle was Lyman Beecher's opposition; he himself having failed to win the West for Calvinism, the old man clung to the hope that this one of his sons might still carry the day. But Henry had spent thirteen years in the West and he knew that opportunity for him, if not for the church, lay in the East.

Returning to Indianapolis, he held off until he received an offer from Plymouth Church—as it was finally named—of twelve hundred dollars a year along with one thousand dollars to pay off his debts, and promises of increases to come. Finally, in August of 1847, after both churches had begun to show impatience, he accepted the Brooklyn offer. He had heard the song of the Sirens and it came from New York, not Boston.

Eunice Beecher and Indianapolis parted company without any regrets on either side. Even her friends seemed to have felt little affection for her. "Mrs. B. has not, I really believe, a real friend in the church," John L. Ketcham, husband of Jane Merrill, and a charter member of the church, wrote to the Reverend David Merrill. "Full of large tales, and enormous exaggerations, no one believes a word she says. And I believe the opinion is general that her recent sickness [he called it "palpitation of the heart"] was *for the occasion.*"

Eunice waited twenty-two years before presenting her side of the picture in *From Dawn to Daylight; or, The Simple Story of a Western Home,* a thinly fictionalized account of the couple's life in Indiana. (When Henry, by then a famous preacher, heard that a publisher had accepted the book, he said: "Tell Derby, if he wants to be fool enough to publish a book written by my wife, to go ahead.") Its recurrent theme is the trials and indignities the couple suffers at the hands of thoughtless and unkind townspeople. Here and there a barb is directed at the minister for letting his wife bear the brunt of their hardships. All in all, it is one of the few unsympathetic pictures of small-town life in the early Midwest, and for many years the book was banned in Indianapolis.

The attitude toward Henry himself was one of admiration mixed with a feeling that he was not reliable or disciplined. "We have liked him as a preacher but many of the Church as I now learn," wrote Samuel Merrill, "complain much of him as a pastor"—which had of course been the criticism of Henry in Lawrenceburg.

John Ketcham had a similar reaction. He thought Beecher was

a great man in the pulpit—but woefully deficient in every other respect. Often he has failed to attend prayer meeting without any excuse. Never has been in Sabbath School more than thrice in his residence here of seven years. Visits almost none among his people. Makes appointments for meetings of Session, and half the time forgets them. Always funny and often frivolous.

Ketcham's view was obviously a very sober-sided one, but it would be echoed again and again by critics in the years to come. Ketcham also noted that Beecher had constantly gone off on "preaching and other excursions" and that the congregation had tolerated this because "he always made a noise wherever he went and we were flattered by it and held on."

He concluded that "as a *town*," Indianapolis was losing a valuable citizen, but that he had not been "a pastor at all—only a brilliant preacher."

But there was one person whose regrets at Henry's departure were genuine and overwhelming—Julia Merrill. At the age of twelve she had helped the Beechers in their transfer from Lawrenceburg to Indianapolis and was immediately smitten by the young minister. At fourteen she and her friend Betty Bates had accompanied him to New England and back. He had become her spiritual guide and gradually her relationship to him had ripened from adolescent hero worship to a romantic and possibly passionate attachment. Once when Henry went to Madison for a revival Julia turned up there; when Eunice heard of it she wrote to Henry that she envied the girl. Henry dismissed her envy but he closed his answer to Eunice with a gushing, "Give my love to Elizabeth [Bates] and a good warm kiss, as the kiss for Julia is at hand." Since Julia was a vibrant nineteen and Eunice a careworn thirty-four, perhaps the openness of the reference to Julia was meant to allay any suspicions.

Again, when Beecher was invited in 1847 to deliver sermons in New York, Julia and Betty sent him money; his letter of thanks concluded "And now dear Julia, you may well imagine how much more I think and feel than I can write. So you must call upon your *imagination* to interpret an ampler meaning than these hasty lines can give."

When Julia learned that Henry was moving east, she was disconsolate. Desperate to spend as much time with him as possible, she no longer concealed the depth of her attachment to him. When she had to accompany her dying mother to Cincinnati, she wrote to her sister Catharine: "Oh Kate, what am I to do? You know how badly I want to get home to see Mr. Beecher before he goes—I must," and she went so far as to say that she would even leave her mother's bedside to be with Beecher. But she was able to return to Indianapolis before Beecher left. By that time Eunice had already gone east with the children.

By coincidence, Henry was scheduled to depart aboard the first railroad train that had reached Indianapolis. Only Julia Merrill came to see him off. We do not know what passed between them as they waited for the train that was to take him away from her, but the very next morning he wrote to her from Madison a letter full of veiled allusions to what seemed a deep communion in the past and the possibility of a reunion in the future. While Beecher was still in Indianapolis, Julia Merrill curtly rejected a marriage proposal from Dr. Talbut Bullard, Eunice's younger brother. She did not marry until 1854, when it had long been evident that Henry Ward Beecher was gone forever.

15

CHILDREN OF A LATER TIME

At the Beechers' grand family reunion in Cincinnati's Walnut Hills in 1835, the gap between Lyman Beecher's older children by Roxana Foote and his three children by Harriet Porter was startling: Catharine, the oldest, was thirty-five, while James, the youngest, was seven. Not only would Harriet Porter's children, Isabella, Thomas and James, come of age a generation later but they had first known their father when he was already middle-aged or older, past the days of his triumphs and beset by troubles. To some extent, too, they were overshadowed by a father and several older brothers and sisters who were already making a name for themselves when the younger children were still in school or college.

Despite Lyman's unifying influence, their birth by another mother set the three later children apart as what has been called "the second Beecher brood." This gave them an acute sense of responsibility for each other, which became a solemn obligation when their mother charged seven-year-old Isabella with taking care of little James when Harriet herself died. With an ambivalence that often goes with such a relationship, the three later Beechers criticized each other freely and sometimes cruelly.

Despite this background, or perhaps because of it, Isabella and Thomas would distinguish themselves in their fields and all three would turn out to be as unusual, not to say eccentric, as any of the older children. James himself thought that there was a touch of madness in them, inherited from their mother, who in her last years sank into melancholia. But the histories of several of the older children, not to mention Lyman's own deep depressions, suggest that the father contributed in both genes and training to the psychic unrest of his family.

But it was probably the increasingly humanitarian climate of the age as much as the personalities of the "other Beechers" that put them beyond the reach of the darkling God of their fathers. It also freed Isabella and Thomas to reflect new influences and move in new directions.

By the time she was in her teens, Isabella Beecher was aware that she was pretty and had a way with people. She was not only the baby sister of five brothers but the most attractive of four daughters. Eleven years old when the family moved from Boston to Cincinnati, she attended Catharine's Western Female Institute and was thus exposed at an impressionable age to her sister's conviction that women should prepare themselves for independence. But when her mother died two years later, she was sent back east to live with her half sister Mary Perkins in Hartford. Mary was a well-settled matron in her early thirties, her husband was a successful lawyer and they moved in a social circle marked by affluence, respectability and refinement. There Isabella seems to have acquired that respect for decorum and good breeding that would mark her even in the most militant days of her suffragist period.

At fifteen she was back in Cincinnati and once again in Catharine and Harriet's school. Even more important was the time she spent in a home constantly stirred by lively discussions.

I date my interest in public affairs [she later claimed] from those years between eleven and sixteen, when our family circle was ever in discussion on the vital problems of human existence, [where] the United States Constitution, fugitive slave laws, Henry Clay and the Missouri Compromise alternated with free will, regeneration, heaven, hell, and "The Destiny of Man."

One of these issues was brought ominously home to her when Cincinnati mobs sacked James G. Birney's abolitionist newspaper office and her brother Henry went out, pistol in belt, to patrol the streets. But it is doubtful that she was as much concerned with such issues as she later professed. Similarly, when many years later she complained that after her mother died, her "dear good father (instigated, of course, by his new wife) . . . suggested that I should begin to teach school and support myself," she was conveniently forgetting how many less serious interests she had when she was fifteen years old. Intelligent, accomplished, a trifle indulged because of her delicate health, she was admired by Henry and adored by Charles. She has taken up, Harriet reported to her father, with "companions with whom dress and amusement are the absorbing topics and who will lead her farther and farther from all serious and profitable habits."

This development was so disturbing that at sixteen Isabella was once more packed off to sister Mary's home in Hartford—an environment that would presumably return her to more serious and profitable pursuits. She was again sent to the Hartford Female Seminary, the school Catharine had established fourteen years earlier, but remained there for only a year. Her father, she would later say, managed to send six of his sons to school until they were twenty-two years old, but "never a daughter cost him a hundred dollars a year after she was sixteen."

Isabella was, however, almost alone among Lyman Beecher's children in escaping the Beecher *rites de passage*—that traumatic period of guilt and self-doubt that almost all the young Beechers underwent before they were admitted to the sanctum of the Elect. Where her father would have put nerve-racking pressures on her, Mary and her aunt Esther merely prodded her gently. It says something about the male sense of authority that Mary felt not quite competent to guide Belle, whereas her fifteen-year-old brother, Tom, urged her to turn to the Bible and prayer lest her heart grow callous. Perhaps because a "terrible accident," as she mysteriously called it, and poor treatment had undermined her health, she was spared any further prodding. Soon word went out to Lyman in Cincinnati that his youngest daughter had been saved. This evidence of the goodness of God, her father announced with his usual ebullience, was "like the bursting out from darkness of an effulgent sun, and made me weep for my past distrust."

He must also have seen that his influence had made some of his children too aggressive in their effort to save mankind; he did not mean, he added, that she "should every day slam-bang at somebody as a matter of duty without rule or reason." How much effect she did have is evident in the highly emotional letters her half brother Charles, although seven years her senior, sent her from his exile in New Orleans. Again and again he told her, with lover-like expressions of affection, how much more beautiful and sympathetic than her sisters she was.

In the Perkins home Isabella now met John Hooker, a tall student clerk in Thomas Perkins's law office. A descendent of Thomas Hooker, the great colonial clergyman and founder of Hartford, John was a mild-tempered, modest young man some six years older than Isabella. While at Yale he had—like George Beecher and Theodore Weld—permanently weakened his eyes with too much study. To regain his health, he had left school and spent two years before the mast, making trips to the Mediterranean and China. Unlikely as this may seem for someone with weak eyes and a sheltered background, it was not uncommon for young men of good families—the most familiar are Herman Melville and Richard Henry Dana—to go to sea before they settled down.

Isabella and John Hooker were soon engaged, but considering that both were ardent, they made a remarkable pact: "If either of us found we had made a mistake we were at liberty to choose elsewhere." Isabella went further. On reading the marriage vows, she protested that they said everything about a bride obeying her husband but nothing the other way around. This reduced women, she declared, to a gallingly submissive state, robbed them of a will of their own or simply spoiled them. She said all this even though she surely knew that John Hooker was the last man to tyrannize over a woman he loved.

But once Isabella returned to Walnut Hills and that high-tension assemblage of God-oriented brothers and sisters, she began a campaign, charged with pious exhortations, to get her betrothed into the ministry. Inspired by her "old, almost idolized father" and her brothers, she decided that serving God was the only worthwhile work. Ministers, she asserted, were the only men who could "accomplish any considerable amount of good without turning aside from their usual business—*all* that a minister does is designed some way to save the souls of his fellow beings. . . Now it seems to me that it is not thus with a *lawyer.*" Forgetting her constant complaints of ill health, she declared that she would be happy to be a home missionary's wife. Neither Lyman nor Catharine could resist joining in the campaign. Barred from making his daughter into a minister, Lyman did not hesitate to recruit his future son-in-law. Catharine, the family's self-appointed career guide, got off several urgent letters to young Hooker, culminating in a massive document that ranged from warning to flattery. In her usual blunt way she declared that neither he nor Isabella was fitted for life as a missionary, especially in the West. The choice lay, so she claimed, between being a lawyer in the village of Farmington and a popular and distinguished minister in a New England city. Your character, she observed, is unsuited to the legal profession because it is a cold and calculating activity dedicated to the clashing interests of selfish men, whereas the ministry is a noble, useful and enriching pursuit. Nor need he give up social enjoyments and "the pleasures of taste," for with his refinement, reasoning powers, unction and eloquence, he could become as successful as the celebrated Dr. Bushnell.

She added a remarkably prophetic insight into Isabella's character: "Belle is formed by nature *to take the lead*. She will every year learn more and more of her power *to influence others.*" Since she has been home, Catharine wrote, she has been more effective than her father in leading young people away from fashionable amusements. "She is growing fast in piety, in power of intellect, in . . . controlling other minds. What will you find for her to do . . . ? I do not want to see a woman of her talents and powers put out of her place as a *leader.*" Despite Catharine's analysis, Isabella's own letters to Hooker dwell on her poor health and disordered nervous system and how unworthy she is of him. That this was in part a strategy, perhaps unconscious, to win love and attention, a technique for manipulating people, seems to be borne out by Catharine's statement that Isabella's "complaint" was not serious and could easily be cured. But it worked with John Hooker: he responded with a passionate declaration that he wanted her even if she remained an invalid for the next ten years.

Hooker's parents as well as the Perkinses and other friends—a Hartford circle in which lawyers were as influential as clergymen and generally much more prosperous—opposed his leaving the law and strongly resented the Beechers' interference. But the Beechers proved too much for the young suitor. He capitulated and in a mood of lofty dedication went off to Yale Divinity College. But one season of theology was all he could endure: he returned to Farmington and promptly opened a law office.

Isabella and John Hooker were married the following year and went to live with his parents in Farmington, a pleasant community only a few miles from the center of Hartford, overlooking broad green meadows of cultivated land. Soon Isabella began going to her husband's office with her knitting and listening to him read from his lawbooks while he waited for clients to call. Because he could not read by artificial light, she in turn read literary works to him in the evening. They did this for four years—a supplement to Isabella's education that explains why women's rights leaders later found her so expert in legal arguments and constitutional law. The first book they read was that eighteenth-century classic of English law, Blackstone's *Commentaries*. Everything in it seemed quite wise and just until they came to the duties and rights of husbands and wives in a chapter called "Domestic Relations." The resentment she had felt at the wording of the marriage vows was as nothing to her consternation—the word is hers—on learning that the legal identity of a woman who married was thereafter incorporated in the person of her husband. For some "misdemeanors" a husband even had the right to whip his wife. Isabella stopped the reading, looked up into her "young lover's face," and exclaimed, "And this is your code that is to bring peace on earth, good will to men and harmonize the universe." Although they discussed both conditions—the domination by man and the subjection of woman—again and again and John was increasingly sympathetic, the injustices in the marriage contract continued to nag at her.

But it was Hooker who first took a strong stand on that equally troubling subject, slavery. Even before they were married he challenged Isabella sharply for refusing to listen to anything on that "immense and sublime question." Perhaps her closeness to her father, Catharine and Harriet in Cincinnati and to Mary in Hartford led her to adopt their cautious approach rather than the vigorous position of her older brothers Edward, George and William. Or perhaps she was intimidated by the violence of the anti-Birney mobs in Cincinnati and the assassination of Edward's friend Lovejoy.

Once they were married, however, she came quickly around to her husband's view. By 1842 she was saying of the Perkinses' indifference to the cause, "I suppose they talk here very much as I used to—but it does not strike me either pleasantly or as becoming intelligent, reading, Christian people." And she could only have been dismayed when Mary's husband, Thomas, declared that Northerners had no more to do with slavery than they have with "hindoo idolatry." Still, Hooker felt it necessary to defend himself to Isabella after he addressed an antislavery meeting from the same platform as an abolitionist whom she considered rabid and "prejudice-inciting." He pointed out that her father's famous sermon against the dueling code, aimed especially at Southerners, was as violent and abusive as any abolitionist attack on slaveholders.

Although he disliked the "ultraism—the garrisonianism, Abby Kellyism . . . and above all the anti-clerical spirit" of the more radical abolitionists, Hooker's sympathy with the slaves ran deep and strong. He was shocked to discover that a black man—"a fine, noble fellow"—working for his parents was a slave who had fled from a Virginia master because he was about to be sold apart from his wife and four children. A "justice-loving God," Hooker wrote, "could not much longer withhold his avenging thunders." At another time he had a black man share his church pew, and when he found that the Reverend James W. C. Pennington, a well-known black minister in Hartford, was in fact James Pembroke, a slave who still feared that his former master might reclaim him, Hooker purchased him and freed him.

When at last Isabella joined him in his commitment, he wrote: "I love this Anti-Slavery cause more and more every day . . . and it makes me sad, very sad to see so many good men and women so bitterly opposed to it," and then added: "How I thank God that you are a whole-souled abolitionist." In time he even brought her around to the support of the antislavery Liberty party. Respected and well liked, Hooker was elected—by forty antislavery people who held the balance of power in Farmington—to a term in the Connecticut House of Representatives. But he had no hankering for a political career and soon returned full time to his law practice.

Despite Isabella's anxieties about remaining only a housewife, the birth of children and the increase in household duties left her too busy or tired to concentrate on social problems. Her first child, a boy, died soon after birth, but within a few years she bore two daughters and, later, another son. Evidently hoping to reconcile her activities as mother and wife with establishing an independent identity, she tried to run her family by principle and method.

But her daughters proved quite normal in their revolt against such rule. Once when four-year-old Mary reacted with an hour-long tantrum to a seemingly reasonable request, Isabella whipped her until her own hand hurt. Although the journal she kept of their childhood development shows how dearly she loved her daughters, she beat both of them, thinking that they needed the kind of disciplining she herself had never had.

As the 1840s slipped away, Isabella, despite her pleasant social life, was not content. Although she enjoyed the parties—at which she charmed the company with both her singing and her conversation—"picnics," visits to well-to-do friends in New York and Boston, and vacations in the mountains or at the seashore, she continued to complain of inadequacies and ailments. In an especially revealing letter to her husband in 1849 she laments how "tame and insipid" her life has become. She assumes he will not be jealous when she tells of meeting an old friend of theirs, a man whom she has always liked, and of the "spontaneous flow of more than common regard towards me." It made her happier than she had been since she was a "young dreamer, save in the ecstatic hours of our own peculiar wedded bliss." The friend's advances, she hastens to add, "were both unexpected and unsought," but she also adds that he admitted being irresistibly drawn to her. The letter is a curious mingling of innocence and yearning, of pleasure in her continued desirability and a signal that someone else can stimulate her. In later years there would be evidence that their own sexual "bliss" was rather limited.

Whether it was a result of the Hookers' growing concern with social reforms or the increasing sophistication of their circle, the old Puritan sense of sinfulness and guilt began to seem dated and dour. As late as 1844, John Hooker would still apologize for writing a letter on the Sabbath and he rose an hour before dawn to spend the morning reading the Bible and preparing to teach his Sabbath school class. A strict temperance advocate, he was shocked, when he visited the region around Albany during the Anti-Rent Rebellion, at the number of men, including lawyers, who swore, drank and used foul language.

So, too, Isabella at first declared—perhaps to impress her fiancé—that she tended, like her father, toward Old School doctrine and New School practice. Her faith in Christ remained intense, but by the end of the decade the pious injunctions were gone from her letters and the urge to be a missionary's wife had disappeared. Harriet even felt it necessary to point out, with older-sister authority, that Isabella was abandoning the traditional beliefs too rapidly.

There were other signs that Victorian aspirations were replacing Calvinist standards. Early in the 1850s John and Isabella would build a spacious home on the outskirts of Hartford. They would soon be followed by a small but distinguished group of writers and professional men, and in the Nook Farm Literary Colony, as it was later known, Isabella Beecher Hooker would emerge from the cocoon of domestic life and begin her long struggle to achieve a new identity.

Free of vanity, forthright, with a grim humor and a not too hopeful view of human nature, but stubbornly devoted to helping his fellow man, Thomas Beecher was at once the most unorthodox of the seven sons of Lyman Beecher and perhaps the most truly Christian.

Although he was the tenth of Lyman's children and only eight years old when the Beechers arrived in Cincinnati, he did not escape the family debates and his father's importunities. Like his brothers and sisters, he was troubled by his inability to feel a profound religious conviction. That, along with the somber atmosphere surrounding his mother in her later years—he was only eleven when she died—left him with an almost morbid view of man's fate.

Like Charles, he found a confidante in Isabella and poured out his troubles to her, but where his older brother was moody and impetuous, Thomas was analytical and earnest. He was no more than fifteen years old when he wrote to her, "I am not one of those who are to be happy in this world, for if anything . . . can give me a conception of the *lower* regions it is to sit down and think of my lot." This was not simply an adolescent pose; a few years later he writes: "constituted as I am, I have but little happiness to look for in this world, and tormenting doubts and fears sometimes whisper that I have less to look for in the next." Such melancholy moods would haunt him throughout his life.

The first of the Beecher children to grow up in Walnut Hills, he had such vivid memories of the Ohio woods as "the whistle of the quail . . . the heavy busky flight of the wild turkey . . . and the breezy rush of wild pigeon." In later years those who did not know of his western background would be surprised by his love of wilderness vacations, physical work, and plain clothes, and his easy mingling with workingmen.

After his school years in Cincinnati, Thomas went off to Illinois College, where his brother Edward was president. By the end of his sophomore year, finding himself much more interested in mechanics and the sciences than in theology, he decided that he was unsuited for the ministry. In a similar situation a few years earlier, Charles, musician and Romantic, had rebelled and fled; Thomas, much more strong-minded, tried to persuade his father to let him follow his own bent. Looking for a more active life, he talked of going to West Point and even dreamed of becoming a Rocky Mountain trapper. At one point his unrest led to his suspension for "repeated disorders tending to disturb the worship of God in chapel." Another account of the suspension is more revealing. Tom sometimes indulged in the old sophomore prank of yelling "Heads out!" from his top-story window and then dousing whoever responded. But once he went up on the roof and was about to throw down scraps of mortar when Edward appeared beside him. Mockingly Tom asked, "Have I the pleasure of addressing my beloved brother or the honor of reporting to our revered president?" Whereupon Edward, to the glee of a crowd of students in the yard below, suspended Thomas on the spot.

Part of Thomas's lack of enthusiasm for the ministry grew out of an increasing disillusion with Edward. It was awkward enough to be the twenty-years-younger brother of the president of the college, but it was even more disturbing to a scientifically minded youth to see his brother preoccupied with theological dogma and farfetched theories of the universe.

The more Thomas drew away from Edward, the closer he moved toward Henry. Between college terms he made visits to Henry's place in Indianapolis and shared not only his brother's churchwork but many of his other activities. Henry was, he told Isabella, most like their father. As a speaker and writer he surpassed any divine that Thomas knew and he was unmatched in the "versatility of his talents." For Thomas, as for others, Henry's virtues were enriched by his warmth.

Thus inspired, Thomas returned to college. But his doubts were soon as strong as ever. In a long letter to Isabella he declared that, seeing no proofs of the existence of God or the authenticity of the Bible, he had come very close to skepticism. Even his personal experiences with churchmen, including those in his family, were discouraging. They left him with disrespect for religion and for a system "whose lights and glory appear to me so dim and faulty." Now completely alienated from Edward, he adds that on some points his brother is either insane or is not the same kind of Christian as their father or their brother Henry. If this is what religion does, he continues, God deliver me from being pious. A younger brother ostentatiously asserting his independenence, he concludes that he loves Edward as a brother but feels more pity for him than respect.

Henry returned Tom's affection: he traveled three hundred miles to attend his brother's graduation. But graduation did not solve Thomas's dilemma. Back in Walnut Hills, he spent a year filled with "cavil and controversy," arguing that church doctrines were based on "shadowy nothings." He finally suggested that he should stay at Henry's for a few months. Lyman agreed and wrote "long letters to Henry as one physician to another when he transfers a patient." At Henry's, Tom recalled years later, he and his brother

sawed and split wood together; sat on rail fences and told stories; raised sweet potatoes weighing five pounds each; wrote articles for the *Farmer and Gardener;* banked up celery till it was nearly three feet tall, white and crisp; picked blackberries as big as my thumb; and hunted squirrels, rabits and smaller game. Tom went down to meeting every night for sixteen weeks, to laugh and sing and hear Henry talk about Jesus Christ.

I did not know it at the time. There were no arguments. Nothing was proved. Can you tell how the bones of the unborn babe grow in the womb? So Christ was formed in Consciousness.

Like some white bird high-flying, that drops down through the smoke into a walled city fortified against all comers, carrying under its wing a message from afar, so came to me the vision of Christ, as with matchless words brother Henry told the story, without theology or dialectic.

Thomas's feeling of independence was heightened by his mechanical aptitude. All his life he would be immensely proud of his capacity to earn a day's pay as a house painter, a carpenter, a machinist, or in building construction. Still unreconciled to a career in the church, he worked for about a year making astronomical instruments—earning, he boasted, as much as five dollars a week—and then for another year as assistant to a Dr. Lock, professor of chemistry and pharmacy at Ohio Medical College. He proved so competent in both capacities that even Lyman seemed to realize that his unrelenting effort to make a minister out of every one of his sons was neither kind nor wise. Lyman disclosed his ambivalence in a letter to Henry, his family understudy:

His bent of mind is so strong for the natural sciences, and his originality and power of mind, and mechanical execution, and his attained qualifications are so distinguished for a professor of chemistry . . . that my heart had let go of its favorite purpose that he should preach; and yet I feel reproved almost in giving it up . . . though, as in the case of Charles, I do not give it up, still hoping and desiring yet he may be a minister.

He then boasted to Henry of Lock's praise of Tom's great skill in making and repairing "beautiful and efficient instruments" and in performing experiments. Few teachers, Lock had said, knew more about chemistry. Yet, Beecher concludes, whether Thomas becomes a preacher or not, "I cannot think without pain and fear of his character being formed as a man of talents and celebrity without religion, every year adding to the chances that he may spend his life and die without holiness." It was just how he had written to William and Edward almost twenty-five years before.

There was one difference in his attitude toward Thomas: more and more as he himself grew older he clung to this next to the last of his seven sons. Tom would not forget the morning when the old man came to him with a letter in his hand. His income gone, Lyman was living mainly on "donations." He had just received such a contribution and he offered it to Tom, telling him to buy himself the boots and vest that he had long needed. Almost tearfully he added: "and now you'll stay with me."

Even after Tom had graduated from college, his father, fearing that he was still "unsettled in religion," urged him to stay home so that he could be led to safety. But Thomas, irritated by people who reproached him for "living on his father," was impatient to be gone. More and more often, Thomas later wrote, he and his father fell into passionate discussions of the matter:

I never gave up entirely until one morning, as I stood impatient on the south step of the study in the sun. He came out suddenly, not knowing I was there. He sniffed the air, looked up into the maples, down upon me, put both hands upon my shoulders, looked me full in the face, and said, with broken utterance, "Tom I love you; you musn't go 'way and leave me. They're all gone—Jim's at college, I want one chicken under my wing."

Of course I staid by until I left with a blessing.

Harriet, hearing of Thomas's indecision, added her voice to her father's: in a long letter she mixed descriptions of her own spiritual struggles with a sermon on the bliss of submission and faith. Whether it was all this prodding or his desire to judge for himself, Thomas decided to try a year of theological study at Yale. So, late in the summer of 1845, Dr. Beecher wrote to Dr. Taylor that he was putting the latest of his sons in the hands of his old friend. "He possesses . . ." he added, "a mind not inferior to any of my sons, and quickness, depth, and comprehension . . . surpassing any mind I have come in contact with."

After a year at Yale, Thomas found himself still drawn as much to teaching as to preaching. Teaching, after all, was in the Beecher blood; every one of Thomas's nine older brothers and sisters, except William, had taught in some kind of school. But first he let Catharine inveigle him into escorting her around the country on one of her speaking tours and delivering the public lectures that were considered an unfeminine activity for a respectable woman. Although it was a useful experience in both public speaking and educational problems, Thomas soon began to resent serving as a kind of live marionette.

So when an opening was found for him to take charge of a school in Philadelphia, he looked forward to the challenge. The Northeast Grammar School, once the best in the city, was now the worst. Given a free hand to revive it, Thomas reveled in his independence. But it was a mixed experience, and within a few months he was lamenting what a "dirty, ragged, lousy, and obscene" lot his boys were. They glory in cheating, he wrote, and take pleasure in watching him whip one of their classmates. He tried desperately to accept Edward's contention that the public schools were designed to help just such pupils, but it took, he said, "a heart full of love and faith to persevere, and a body of iron, and nerves of steel to bear the labor."

Just as in his preaching he would think of himself as a teacher, so in his classes he tried to set a Christian example, teaching as he thought Christ would have taught. In his first months at the school he asked one of the rougher boys, by the name of Brown, to shut the door. When the youth muttered, "See you in hell first!" Beecher answered quietly, "In that case I will shut it myself." In a time of strict discipline, Thomas's reaction was unheard of, and for several days the disorder in his class-room increased horridly. Finally one day Thomas broke down, put his head on his arms on the desk and wept. Later he prayed for help.

During a spelling lesson a few days afterward, a boy leaped up and declared excitedly that he had seen in a flash how to spell; the class was "awakened" and joined in his enthusiasm, and soon other classes fell into line. In another, somewhat less inspiring version of the story, Thomas was said to have given Brown a beating before he would behave. But all versions agree that the youth then became Beecher's greatest admirer. In time Thomas abandoned whipping and reported that he was getting more and more of his pupils to love him. But, like Catharine, he deplored teaching by rote and stuffing pupils with words rather than ideas simply so they could pass examinations.

His social life in Philadelphia was meager, and despite his lack of money, he began to think of getting married. A few years earlier he had met Catherine Mussey, the daughter of a Cincinnati physician. Now, he confessed to Isabella, he was desperately in love with her. Thinking that he lacked polish and accomplishments, he asked Isabella for advice. We do not know what she told him, but while he was still making plans for capturing "Catie" he learned that she was about to marry a well-to-do Cincinnati lawyer. His castles in air having toppled, he decided that he couldn't after all afford a wife.

He had begun to spend his summers at home studying theology with his father. But in Philadelphia he attended Episcopal services because he loved the music and singing and scorned the "slab-sided Presbyterians" who thought such practices were "unclean."

Frustrated by menial duties and a feeling of intellectual stagnation, Thomas left Philadelphia in 1848 and turned to an old Beecher gathering ground, Hartford. Probably through the influence of the Perkinses and Hookers, he was offered the post of principal of the public high school established a few years before. He stayed there only two years, but it was a crucial period because it brought him under the influence of Horace Bushnell, the gifted Hartford preacher, and his belief that religion was an individual experience. Thomas had been uniquely prepared for Bushnell by Henry's warm personal approach to faith, but hearing someone outside the family reject institutional religion and appeal to an instinctive spirituality excited and inspired him. Bushnell's involvement in community affairs such as the cleaning up of blighted factory, tenement and railroad areas also made a deep impression on him.

Thomas now began to see a way in which he could be both a preacher and a teacher. So he turned back to Walnut Hills and spent another year at home working with his father. Like Charles he had protested, groped and floundered until he had found a way of serving in the church that would satisfy his innermost nature. But unlike Charles, he would turn further and further away from doctrine and toward religion as a private experience. In this he had learned much from Henry. His relation to his older brother now bordered on adoration. As late as 1848–1850 he wrote:

Henry, I never can show to you my whole heart for words will not suffice and actions are forbidden ... I am so filled and led captive by an association with you that it passeth my love to woman ... it is not because of *yourself* that I so love. But the common love we bear to Christ.

The resistance of Lyman Beecher's children to his unremitting pressure surfaces first in Catharine (after Fisher's death), appears at an early stage in George in the form of breakdown after breakdown, and then, skipping Harriet and Henry, reappears in Charles, the fatalist who dreamed of being a great musician, increases progressively in Harriet Porter's three children—Isabella, who wanted to function as more than a wife and mother; Thomas, who could have been an excellent teacher or scientist; and at last, almost violently, in James, who was a man of action, not doctrine.

James, the last child of an old man, was overshadowed by an array of brothers and sisters forever occupied with their own souls and everyone else's. By the time he was old enough to be aware of such matters, his older brothers and sisters were already well-known teachers and preachers. His response as soon as he had reached Dartmouth College and found himself free of family dominion was a defiance of authority. He studied what he pleased and as he pleased; he joined wild young men and rode about doing the wicked things that wild young men did at Dartmouth in 1845. The president of the college was soon reporting to Lyman that James was "rude, ungoverned [and] impatient of discipline." But he did have hope that the youth would settle down.

James himself may have known that, like George and Charles and Thomas, he would end up, willy nilly, in the church, so like an unbroken colt he ran free as long as he could. Finally, in his junior year, he was suspended for neglecting his studies, being absent for two weeks, and because of unpaid bills for board, shoes and laundry. Far from being contrite, he was quite unconcerned, telling a relative that he had left simply to give his class a chance to catch up with him. He was soon readmitted and managed to graduate in 1848.

But he had had his fill of classrooms; there were many far more exciting things for a young man to do than study theology. Hadn't Charles at the same age gone off to be a musician and Thomas to make beautiful instruments and remarkable experiments? And weren't other men rushing off to gather gold in California? So James announced to his father that he was shipping out to the Orient and even asked for money to do so. The old man not only withheld consent but resorted, as with Thomas, to emotional blackmail, adding that it would cause him enough grief to shorten his life. Unlike Thomas, James departed.

He would spend five years on clipper ships in the East India trade, first as an ordinary seaman and later as an officer. On his return, he would, as Thomas had predicted, reenter the fold, but there would always be something restless in his nature.

The landing place on the Ohio River in Cincinnati in 1841, a few years after the Beecher family arrived there.

The home in Walnut Hills, then on the outskirts of Cincinnati, that the Beechers occupied from 1832 to 1851.

The faculty of Lane Seminary in the 1840s, when Lyman Beecher was president and Calvin E. Stowe (left), Harriet's husband, and D. H. Allen (right) were professors there.

16

LYMAN BEECHER

Death of a Patriarch

Toward the end of his years in Cincinnati, Lyman Beecher would occasionally try to put his papers—a lifetime of sermons, lectures and records, many of them yellow with age—in order, but they would soon be scattered around his study again. Then, in the summer of 1851, after he and Lydia had moved in temporarily with the Stowes in their big house in Maine, he began, with the help of one of Lydia's daughters, to prepare his writings for publication: selected sermons, lectures on atheism, temperance, dueling and such, together with his *Views in Theology.* Despite the fact that Harriet was already working on installments of *Uncle Tom's Cabin* for the *National Era,* her father and his assistant took over the kitchen table while Harriet sat on the back steps with her writing portfolio on her lap.

Theology had never been Dr. Beecher's strong point, and now many of his writings seemed only echoes of bygone issues and controversies. In print, without his vital presence and verve, they were lusterless and lacking in urgency. They would have received little attention had they not begun to appear not long after the sensational publication of *Uncle Tom's Cabin* and shortly before Edward Beecher's *The Conflict of Ages* stirred the church world. How strange it must have seemed to Lyman Beecher to be increasingly identified as the father of Harriet Beecher Stowe and Edward Beecher—not to speak of Henry Ward Beecher. Lyman hardly knew what to make of the astonishing success of Harriet's novel, but his opinion of Edward's book he packed into one pungent sentence: "Edward, you've destroyed the Calvinist barns, but I hope you don't delude yourself that the animals are going into your little theological hencoop!"

For a few years, Lyman and Lydia lived in a rented house near Edward's home in Boston, Lyman preaching now and then, sometimes with surprising vigor. From time to time he tried to work on his autobiography, but it was too much for him. Finally he turned over a mass of papers, letters and records to Charles, who had been chosen to act as editor for the family. At the same time he began relating his recollections to his children, and particularly to Harriet and Catharine.

Although his memory for names and places had become unreliable, he still recalled men and events shrewdly and colorfully. Much more vivid were scenes from the distant past—plowing the steep acres on Uncle Lot's farm, courting the lovely Roxana at Nutplains, his great sermons on dueling and intemperance, the wheeling of the gulls over the beach in the Hamptons, nut picking with the children in the Litchfield hills. . . .

Harriet and Catharine in turn added their own reminiscences, and these, together with hundreds of letters, form a unique composite, a large, many-faceted, if somewhat haphazard, family chronicle.

To celebrate Lyman's eightieth birthday, the family held a reunion at the Stowes' "Stone Cabin" in Andover. It was meant to be like the one in Cincinnati on his sixtieth birthday, but there was little of the carefree rejoicing that had marked the earlier party. They were all much older and too aware that this might be the last such gathering of the clan. The family was, moreover, no longer a small, close-knit unit; indeed, there were and would remain, unresolved discords and antipathies.

But another gathering did take place a few years later at Henry's home in Brooklyn—and that one yielded the memorable group portrait (see the frontispiece) taken at Mathew Brady's famous studio. Present were five of Lyman's sons and all four of his daughters (only George, long gone, and James, managing a seamen's mission in Hong Kong, were missing), with Catharine and Mary, the oldest daughters, sitting next to Lyman and holding his hands to keep them still . . . all the women with the wide Beecher mouth and dark hair parted in the middle, and all of them in rich decorous black—a phalanx of dignity and pride.

If Lyman's mind was failing, his physical vitality, the legacy of his blacksmith forebears, was still remarkable. While visiting the Stowes he decided to attend one of Calvin's lectures. Calvin had already left the house, and Lyman, hurrying after him, took a shortcut; coming to a five-barred fence, he promptly vaulted over it and arrived in the classroom before Calvin.

To be near Henry, now his most famous son, Lyman moved to Brooklyn in 1856. Using money that had long been due him from Lane Seminary, he and Lydia bought a house on Willow Street. His pleasure was to attend services and prayer meetings at Plymouth Church. There he would sit, a short, square-set, white-haired old man gazing with deep satisfaction at that astonishingly eloquent son of his. Once he said, "Thought I could preach till I heard Henry."

At first he was sufficiently aware to question Henry's way of making salvation easy for his parishioners. Occasionally, too, he betrayed a restlessness at the lack of purpose in his life. But after a while he seemed to be living behind a veil. At times his speech became unintelligible and he did not recognize old friends. At rare intervals he did surprise those around him with flashes of his old wit. Once, as he rested on a sofa, Harriet, sitting by his side and stroking his hair, said, "Do you know that you are a very handsome old man?" His eyes lit up and he quickly answered, "Tell me something new."

Unlike Roxana Foote and Harriet Porter, he did not resign himself to death or look forward to the possibility of heaven. He had had too purposeful a life, enjoyed fame and influence too long to want to give it up. In one of the last times he spoke in the lecture room at Plymouth Church he said, haltingly at first but vibrantly at the end: "If God should tell me that I *might* choose—that is, if God said that it was *his* will that I *should* choose whether to die and go to heaven, or to begin my life over again and work once more, *I would enlist again in a minute.*"

Such was the effect of Calvinism that even this passionately committed man had doubts and fears about what lay before him: it left him at times, as the autobiography puts it, with "little appetite for heaven." He was confident that he had devoted all his powers to God, yet such was his sense of his imperfections that even for him there was no end to the ordeal of the Puritan conscience.

As a preacher—far more than if he were a blacksmith like his father or a farmer like his uncle Lot—Lyman Beecher challenges us to consider his influence not only on his family but on his congregations and the entire religious life of his time. Personally, his commitment as a Congregational divine served him well, bringing him respect and eminence, persuading him that he was saving souls from endless torment, and above all, giving him an all-embracing purpose that kept him living with bright intensity—if we except those desolating periods when even he went through agonies of self-doubt. It granted him a vision of a millennium that nothing could mar. Whether his hopefulness came from this source or from his native temperament or from the spirit of the times, it endowed him with an exuberance and a zest that, for many of his parishioners, offset the gloom of his theological message. It enabled him in his finest hours to bring to his more devoted listeners a sense of excitement, the joy of utter submission, and the dazzling possibility of ultimate bliss.

But this same creed touched him with fanaticism. It made him ruthlessly confident that his way, and no other, was the right one. So he waged a holy war against not only infidels and skeptics but Catholics, Unitarians, Episcopalians and Old School Presbyterians, and he preached tirelessly against a score of man's little pleasures, from drinking and gambling to circuses, the theater and Sunday excursions. It made him at once humble and intolerant—supine before God but imperious before man. It led him into the Puritan labyrinth of obsessive concern with the self and the next world as against society and this world. It caused him to hedge or advise expedience on social issues and look to a millennium in which evils such as slavery would be magically swept away.

Although Lyman Beecher had tried to soften some of the harsher doctrines of his faith and even seemed a heretic to the orthodox, he never abandoned certain of the most oppressive Puritan dogmas. As late as 1836 he wrote, with a kind of perverse fervor:

Total depravity includes the absence of all holiness. . . . It is universal—there being not a mere man of all the millions of Adam's posterity that hath lived and not sinned. It is entire—every imagination of the thoughts of the heart being evil only—there being none that do good, no not one.

What could have been the effect of such beliefs? How many did they leave guilt-ridden as compared with those who were comforted? To how many did Beecher bring a message of hope as against those whom he left helpless in the hands of a vengeful God? In its closing pages, his autobiography contains glowing testimonials from friends and associates, all of them fellow clergymen. But understandably, it contains nothing from critics either of the man himself or the religion he represented.

It was hardly surprising that Colonel Robert G. Ingersoll, lawyer, orator and America's most famous—some would have said infamous— agnostic, should view him with abhorrence. In a tribute to Henry Ward Beecher in 1887, Ingersoll wrote:

Henry Ward Beecher was born in a Puritan penitentiary, of which his father was one of the wardens—a prison with very narrow and closely-grated windows. Under its walls were the rayless, hopeless and measureless dungeons of the damned, and on its roof fell the shadow of God's eternal frown. In this prison the creed and catechism were primers for children, and from a pure sense of duty their loving hearts were stained and scarred with the religion of John Calvin.

Although Ingersoll went on to acclaim Henry's escape from this prison, some may perhaps discount this attack as the overstatement of an avowed enemy of all religions. But what is to be thought of the revulsion that, as we have seen, young Theodore Parker, later a notable spiritual leader himself, felt after attending Beecher's church in Boston in the late 1820s? And what of the verdict of Horace Mann, an outstanding educator of his time and an acquaintance of the Beechers as far back as the early 1820s:

I feel constantly and more and more deeply, what an unspeakable calamity a Calvinist education is. What a dreadful thing it was for me! If it did not succeed in making me that horrible thing, a Calvinist, it did succeed in depriving me of that filial love of God, that tenderness, that sweetness, that intimacy, that desiring, nestling love, which I say is natural that a child should feel toward a Father who combines all excellence.

We come finally to Lyman Beecher's effect on those dearest to him, his children. They revered and loved him and all of them followed in his footsteps—the sons by profession and the daughters by avocation—in their concern with religion and their zeal as reformers. Yet they all abandoned or even repudiated his church and its pitiless tenets. A year after her father died, Catharine said that in his later days he admitted—but apparently without remorse—that the system he had used with his children was "not the best." Although she affirms that his method was carried out with love as well as firmness, she adds:

What a record of vain attempts for *twenty years,* not in a single case rewarded with success! What anxiety, perplexity, disappointment, and agonizing fear are there recorded [in the *Autobiography*] on the part of the father, and what suffering and vain efforts on the part of the children! And has not this experience been thus preserved to aid in the rescue of other such sufferers?

In *The Religious Training of Children* Catharine points out with characteristic bluntness that five of Lyman Beecher's children, including herself, had publicly rejected his system. We suspect, too, that the pressure he put on two others, George and James, may have contributed to the fearful way they ended their lives. As for his three youngest children, the times soon put them beyond the reach of his more oppressive beliefs.

Because they loved him, his children tried to separate Lyman Beecher's religion from his theology, to distinguish between the man and his profession, between his heart and his mind. But it is difficult, if not impossible, to judge him apart from his calling: he alone was responsible for setting himself up as a spiritual guide and for spending his life telling everyone else how to live. It was the kind of vanity and pride—sinful pride, as the religious would say—that crusaders of every sort are often guilty of.

In the lucid moments of his last years Lyman Beecher was sure that he had served his God well; it did not matter how he had served his fellow men as long as he had brought them to the feet of God. He died peacefully on January 10, 1863, at the age of eighty-eight. He was eulogized as an eminent religious leader of another time; and within a generation after his death his basic beliefs were thrust aside by Protestant churches as though they were savage superstitions.

III

RETURNING EAST

1850-1870

CATHARINE

The End of Many Beginnings

Milwaukee was a small, rapidly growing frontier city when in 1850 Catharine Beecher chose it for her last attempt to establish a college on her own principles. She chose it because its leading citizens seemed ambitious, culturally, to live up to its growth. In particular, the social elite, annoyed at having to send their daughters east to be educated, were eager to have a superior school for girls.

The rapid growth of cities everywhere in the West also led Catharine to modify her goals: she decided to put less emphasis on training women to act as missionary teachers in frontier settlements and more on preparing them, as professionally as possible, for a role as homemaker, mother and spiritual guide. Indeed, she soon left the teacher-training program to her latest protégée-companion, Mary Mortimer, and concentrated on "domestic science." Mary Mortimer, like Nancy Johnson, had a lame foot, and Catharine took her, as she had taken Nancy, under her wing. She invited Mary to share a rest at a water cure in Northampton, Massachusetts, in the fall of 1849 and showered her with guidance, care and affection. The rest cure cleared up Mary's lameness and left her deeply grateful to Catharine. For a while she became, like Nancy and like Delia Bacon, the daughter Catharine had never had.

Lyman Beecher and Lydia had now established themselves in Boston and since Catharine spent much time collecting donations in the East, she made a last, rather desperate attempt to rejoin her father's household and create a permanent home for herself. "I wish it could be so arranged that I could keep house, and you and he [Lyman] board with me," she wrote to Lydia. "I could do twice as much *head* work if I could have the gentle exercise and the *amusement* of housekeeping." With unusual humility, she added that if this was not possible, she would be content simply to board with them. But Lydia clearly had no desire to share the "amusement" of housekeeping with her fifty-year-old stepdaughter. So the famous expert on homemaking went back to her curiously homeless existence, alternating fund collecting with sojourns at some comfortable health resort or with relatives or at the college in Milwaukee.

To raise funds for a building to house the college, Catharine wrote *The True Remedy for the Wrongs of Women* (1851). Repeating what she had already said about the education of women and making much of her illnesses and sacrifices, it is not one of Catharine Beecher's more notable performances. Evidently piqued by the attention given the first national convention of the woman's rights movement, held at Seneca Falls, New York, in 1848, and its sensational demand for woman suffrage, an equal voice for women in domestic affairs and the right of women to hold property, bring suit and obtain a divorce for just cause, Catharine overstated the merits of her own "remedy."

Deploring the call for equality of man and wife in marriage, she fell back on the authority of the Bible. Astonishingly for a woman of such force of character and independent spirit, she explained—and seemed thus to justify—man's dominant position in the family as a result of "the power of physical strength and the power of the purse." With the assurance of someone who has never been married, she cites the Biblical dictum that if a woman chooses to put herself in the power of a man by becoming his wife, she should submit to that power and obey her husband. He in turn should honor his wife—as "the weaker vessel." Catharine dared to challenge time-honored traditions in the education of women and in basic church doctrine, but submission to man as father, minister, husband or God was too deeply ingrained in her to be rejected. Since she had never had a husband and would mourn forever the one she had almost had, the idea of domination by a husband came easily to her.

From the days in the 1820s of her first post as headmistress of a school, Catharine in and out of the classroom had stressed good health and physical activity. Her father had always thought vigorous exercise and gymnastics were healing activities and several of her brothers were athletic. She had repeatedly reported in her books that she had met an extraordinary number of women who suffered from chronic ailments. Now, as was her habit, she put her observations and advice in a book, *Letters to the People on Health and Happiness* (1854). It admittedly borrowed some of its information and attitudes from *The Laws of Life with special reference to the Physical Education of Girls* (1852) by Elizabeth Blackwell, the first woman physician in the United States, but it is a useful work in its own right.

Catharine opened her book with the startling declaration that the parents of America were systematically bringing up a generation to be "feeble, deformed, homely, sick and miserable." In her youth, she recalled, one saw healthy, rosy-cheeked children everywhere. Now, in both city and country, most youngsters were pale and "delicate-looking." And every family was beset by ailments. To support her observations, she asked one woman in each of two hundred communities to report on the health of ten married women among her friends. The answers seemed to show that the great majority were either "habitual invalids," "delicate" or "diseased," with only a small number well and strong. A typical response, from a woman in Whitestone, New York, read: "Mrs. A. consumptive. Mrs. P. well but delicate. Mrs. M. well but delicate. Mrs. P. pelvic disorders. Mrs. R. dropsy. Mrs. B. pelvic disorders. Mrs. H. sick headaches. Mrs. K. organic disorder. Mrs. B. well but delicate. Mrs. T. bronchitis."

Many of these disorders, Catharine believed, resulted from ignorance. Her most frequent target, besides the lack of fresh air and exercise, was the tight-waisted garments worn by women. To these she attributed the displacement of almost all the internal organs. From this in turn came the disorders of bladder, uterus and stomach that left women invalids.

Some of the conditions Catharine lamented were probably the result of poor diet. But there was also the attitude of a growing middle class that strenuous physical activity was unbecoming to a well-bred woman and that frailty, a listless air and a tendency to faint were signs of gentility. Some of these conditions may well have been aggravated by the suppression of sexuality in women and the glossing over of ailments resulting from too much childbearing. It has also been said that "pelvic" (a euphemism for "genital") disorders were mentioned so often because some wives used such a complaint to avoid coitus or, rather, pregnancy.

As evidence of the effect of an unwise regimen, Catharine unabashedly offers her own life. Although she alone of her mother's eight children, she writes, was born with a "delicate constitution," a simple diet—more the result of poverty than of choice—and outdoor play in all weathers kept her from having a single sick day until she was in her twenties. Then, intensive study and teaching, a great sorrow and religious responsibilities brought "cutaneous difficulties." They also brought a nervous sensitivity in which any slight wound to a limb resulted in months of partial paralysis. Repeatedly she had suffered nervous prostration. Had she known better, she says, this condition could have been cured by fresh air, exercise, frequent bathing, and no "carbonaceous foods." Instead she subjected herself for many years to all kinds of medicines, a surgical severing of injured nerves, electromagnetic machines, psychology (mainly staring at a silver sixpence for fifteen minutes at a time), Russian, Turkish, sulfur, vapor and sun baths, and rest cures at thirteen health resorts in a dozen years.

The way in which Catharine established relationships with such young women as Delia Bacon, Nancy Johnson and Mary Mortimer at water sanitariums suggests that her motives were largely psychological—a search for a substitute for a husband and family. In the end she found in the health resorts not so much a medical cure as companionship, care, sensual indulgence and freedom from responsibilities. The retreats were, above all, compensation for her inability to fulfill herself as a wife and mother and for what she considered her sacrifices in a noble cause.

Far less enlightened than her attitudes toward physical health are her views on intimate relationships between the sexes. There morality supersedes physiology, and the preacher displaces the teacher. There all her comments reveal a distrust of men. It is as though she realized that she had been blind to the power of sexuality and was trying to make up for her failure to alert innocent women to the danger. Perhaps, too, the militancy of some of the women's rights advocates spurred her to sharpen her criticism of men. Thus even as she bemoans women's ignorance of the body functions, she circulates one of the sorriest of Victorian pruderies: she warns parents that their children at boarding schools are learning an unmentionable vice—obviously masturbation—that leads to horrible diseases and eventually the madhouse. She urges the sternest suppression of such practices even though this approach may sometimes leave the victims paralyzed by fear.

It is perhaps the virgin and spinster in her speaking when she violently rejects the idea that all body functions must be exercised for full health—that would simply punish the chaste. Elsewhere she lifts the curtain on another danger of sexuality—teachers, physicians and clergymen who arouse what she calls "morbid" affections in the young, especially of the opposite sex. Having lifted the veil, she quickly drops it. Similarly she describes her shock at meeting people who hold that the only true marriage is the one between a man and a woman who are in love, even though they are not united by legal or religious rites. The true adulterers, these same people claim, are a married couple who remain together after they no longer love each other. What is surprising is not that she was shocked by such attitudes but that she acknowledges them and even admits that they are held by people of "cultivation and refinement." Her awareness of such views is striking evidence of how early were the signs of the pluralism that would eventually mark America's sexual morality. Meanwhile she dismissed such people with what was still her most damning indictment: they simply have no reverence for the authority of the Bible in such matters.

In 1831, in her privately printed *The Elements of Mental and Moral Philosophy,* Catharine had first revealed, rather guardedly, her loss of faith in Calvinist doctrine. Now, believing that the nation was ready for revolt, she published *Common Sense Applied to Religion; or, the Bible and the People,* a frontal assault on church dogma. She began by offering her own history as a lesson in the effect of such teachings: her acceptance, as an adolescent, of the fact that she, like everyone else, was born with a "wicked heart" and did not know whether God would favor her with a new one; the horrifying thought, after Fisher's death, that he was damned forever; and then, after endless torment, her resignation to that most forlorn conclusion: *"There must be a dreadful mistake somewhere, but I will trust and obey and wait quietly for the light."*

But as soon as she began to teach she was confronted, and shaken, by young women troubled by the very questions that troubled her: How could God be wise, just and good when he did things that in anyone else would seem utterly cruel—the work of an abominable being.

Almost ruefully Catharine observes that she has seen another, better way of training children—one in which they are taught that Christ is the friend and father of all, ever ready to help them when they fail and forgive them when they do wrong. It was of course like the creed Henry and Harriet were evolving in the same period. But where Catharine arrived at her position by intellectual steps, Henry and Harriet were spurred by temperament and emotional needs. If Henry's is the poet's way, and Harriet is the soul searcher, Catharine is, or tries to be, the disciple of reason.

Lashing out at the more oppressive doctrines—not only in *Common Sense Applied to Religion* but also in its sequel, tortuously entitled *An Appeal to the People on Behalf of Their Rights as Authorized Interpreters of the Bible*—she blames Saint Augustine for the degrading view of man as conceived in sin, prone to evil, and doomed to punishment in this life and misery in the next. Common sense, she claims, has always waged "a feeble but ceaseless warfare" against this system, but the churches use all their resources to defend it and their clergy dare not criticize them. As an educator, she herself has had to mask her views and avoid revealing them even to her family. But at last, she says, mothers and teachers are rejecting these "soul-withering" doctrines.

Common Sense Applied to Religion is remarkable evidence of Catharine Beecher's independence of mind. Combining an insider's knowledge of churches and church history and a lay person's freedom to criticize the establishment, she exposes the cruelties and contradictions in Augustine, Calvin and Edwards with astonishment that they were ever accepted.

As for her brother Edward's attempt to exonerate God by theorizing that man was created perfect but that in a preexistent state he chose to sin, she tartly observes that preexistence is supported by neither reason nor revelation. In a letter to him she voices an even harsher objection. If you claim this is a revelation from God, she writes,

> I say before I can confide in his teachings I must have *proof* that all this horrible misery and wrong resulting from the wrong . . . nature of mind is not attributable to the Creator of All Things. His mere word is nothing from the Author of a system which is all ruined and worse than good for nothing. He must clear his character before he can offer me a Revelation.

Had those who were already attacking the Beechers as disturbers of the (religious) peace seen this letter, they would have been convinced that all their suspicions and fears were justified.

Having abandoned much of her father's system, Catharine had tried to find a substitute for it. She had broached a new code of ethics as early as 1831 in her book on moral philosophy, and she now summed it up in the concept of self-sacrifice. In both *Common Sense Applied to Religion* and *An Appeal to the People* she proclaimed it in oracular tones as "the *grand law of the system.*" It was justified, she claimed, by reason and the experience of the ages.

Sacrifice was not simple or easy—in fact, if it came too easily it was plainly not a sacrifice. It required constant struggle against indulgence and temptation. Clinging to the Puritan faith in suffering, she insisted that self-denial must be carried to the point of pain. Such suffering led to the greatest happiness. Enjoyment was acceptable and right only if it served the general good. The code was, in effect, a Victorian alternative to Calvinism, making the individual responsible not so much to God as to other people.

Seeing, moreover, what she considered the demoralizing effect of the spread of wealth and luxury, she urged self-denial as a way of counteracting that evil too. In her distrust of both enjoyment for its own sake and increasing luxury, she is still a daughter of the Puritans. She would later see even in the Civil War a supreme demonstration of her code—great masses of men sacrificing themselves for the common good.

Catharine may be forgiven if this code seems to glorify her own career and the fact that she had supposedly denied herself a husband and family in order to devote herself to improving the lot of women. It gave a meaning to her life not possessed by that of any of her brothers or sisters.

Periodically, Catharine renewed her effort to set up a permanent home for herself. Soon after she published *Letters to the People on Health and Happiness* and a textbook, *Physiology and Calisthenics for Schools and Families,* which was based on the therapeutic exercises developed by a Swedish philosopher, Per Henrik Ling, she made a triumphant sales tour around the country. In Cincinnati, five hundred teachers, given half a day off, gathered to hear her lecture. Stimulated by her success, she decided to have a house built for herself in connection with a science building that she was planning for the college in Milwaukee. She would thus be able to bring her work and her homemaking together in a way she had always dreamed of. "There I hope to complete the plan so many years aimed at and so little understood," she wrote to her father in the fall of 1855.

She presented her plan to the most influential trustee at the college, Increase Lapham, a geologist and a prominent figure in local society. She also sent him her design for the building and offered to invest three thousand dollars in it, that is, about half the cost. She wanted, she told him, a place where two teachers could enjoy "the quiet and comforts of an independent home," and not be "crowded into a great family of boarding scholars." With her customary aplomb, she asked that construction be started without delay so that she could organize the Domestic Department of the college the following spring.

She was obviously unprepared for Lapham's reply: he was, he said, surprised by her letter and he implied that he and other trustees thought it not quite proper for them to finance such a plan. Humiliated, she ended her official connection with the college and resigned from the supporting group, the American Woman's Educational Association. The association soon collapsed and plans for the new building were shelved. When the college in 1861 did erect a building for the domestic science department, Increase Lapham invited Catharine to take charge of it. She refused, observing that the building, mainly a dormitory, did not suit her.

In an official history of Milwaukee College published in 1891, William W. Wight gives a blunt but not unkind assessment of Catharine's behavior and role:

That Miss Beecher's plan was inflexible, unyielding, not pliant to the circumstances of local environment, that in some of its details it was impractical, even visionary, must be conceded; that she herself was often arbitrary, dictatorial, inconsiderate, under the pressure of her resistless activity, cannot be doubted; but, barring these blemishes, one cannot repress an utterance of admiration for the nobility of her nature, the loftiness of her aims, the unselfishness of her disposition, her untiring devotion to a great cause, the persistent energy with which she met and thwarted obstacles. A character so majestic may well be the model, at this institution of her own creation, for those pupils who, still unborn when she planned and toiled, were yet the objects of her vigilant and fostering care.

So she returned once again to her itinerant existence. She stayed more often with Harriet and with other Beechers, but she still took every opportunity to maneuver herself into visits with wealthy patrons. Planning a trip to Cincinnati in 1859, she wrote to the Beechers' influential friend Nathaniel Wright that she was in such a condition of nervous excitability that rather than tax him with repeated calls, she asked "the privilege of the hospitalities of your house for two or three days." He overlooked her presumption and welcomed her, for the truth was that she could be a lively and very interesting guest.

The older she grew, the more confidently she played whatever role she assumed. Once when she was nearly seventy she came to the office of Dr. Andrew D. White, president of Cornell, and announced that she had found that the college was giving a course she had long sought. Apologetically he explained that courses at the school were not open to women. "Oh, that is quite all right," she replied. "I prefer to take it with men."

Disarmed by her assurance, he asked whether he could find lodging for her in town. She declined, calmly adding that she would room in the dormitory. "But that is a dormitory for young men," White exclaimed. "I have inspected the accommodations and find them entirely satisfactory," Miss Beecher responded, "and as for those young men, they will not trouble me in the least." She not only took the course but became one of the most popular residents in the dormitory. Under the guise of innocence, she had completely breached a hallowed male barrier.

She assumed authority almost automatically. During a visit to a niece, Mrs. Edward Everett Hale, she decided to try out some recipes for one of her books on housekeeping. Her niece's maids obeyed her but with increasing resentment, and finally refused to go on. Catharine promptly discharged them. When Dr. Hale came home, he found his wife and daughter preparing supper and Aunt Catharine writing in her room. Furious, Hale rushed upstairs and shouted, "Aunt Catharine, your visit is over! Pack up your things. A hack will call for you first thing in the morning." She left in the morning.

Two years later Hale happened upon Catharine in Boston Common. Acutely embarrassed, he tried to pass unnoticed, but she saw him and called out, "Edward, do come and see the wonderful books I have just bought at that second-hand store on Tremont Street." They talked, and he was so touched at finding that she bore him no ill will that he said, "Aunt Catharine, couldn't you arrange to visit us right now?" She was delighted. She accompanied him to his home and stayed two weeks without the least discord.

She was equally authoritative with children. Mrs. Porter, a neighbor of the Stowes in Hartford, told how Catharine during an evening visit noted that the Porters' nine-year-old son was still up, and abruptly declared: "Isn't it time Robert went to bed? All children should go to bed at eight!" Poor Robert was promptly banished.

But it was Isabella who, losing all patience, finally wrote Catharine a letter that was as overbearing and righteous as Catharine had ever been—a Beecher quality turned by one Beecher against another. You show, Isabella wrote, no concern for your host's convenience or wishes, you give away your money so openhandedly in your causes because you assume that relatives and friends will support you in your approaching old age, and you disclose, sometimes with unpleasant consequences, what you have seen or heard in the privacy of homes in which you were a guest. Catharine could not afford to be offended but neither did she mend her ways.

Not even for the sake of praising God would Catharine deny her own worth and dignity. When the company at a friend's house started singing a hymn in which the chorus was: "I am nothing, Lord, Oh nothing—thou art all, all, all!" she refused to join in, crying, "I am *not* nothing!" And that settled that.

As Catharine grew older, the agonizing effect of the religious training that Calvinist children received continued to prey on her mind. Privately she expressed an increasing bitterness over such teaching. Paradoxically, her own heritage had given her the strength to cope with an oppressive code, but what it did to weaker or gentler natures left her furious. Her sister Harriet's daughter Hattie had such a nature and, as usual, Catharine did not hesitate to speak her mind about the girl's plight. For once she is genuinely touching in her compassion. I plead with you, Catharine writes to her brother Henry, to preach one sermon for me as advocate of a large class of suffering souls who can find no teachings that give them any hope of heaven. I am, she says, self-reliant enough to pick out what suits me, but the Hatties are helpless. Hattie, Catharine continues, is a young woman of clear intellect, a little culture, strong will, an appreciation of all that is noble and self-sacrificing, an abhorrence of all that is cruel to helpless creatures, fastidiously averse to demonstrating feelings of love and tenderness, nervous, sensitive, and worst of all, lacking in hope and self-appreciation. The girl, Catharine goes on, is torn to death by Andover Calvinism, with all its hideousness shown up by her uncles Edward and Charles, her mother and her aunt. Nor does "the emotive experience toward Christ which her mother exhibits . . . suit her taste or nature any more than it did Uncle Samuel's or mine. . . ."

I have tried to tell her, Catharine writes, that she need only do the best she can and if she fails she must confess and try again, and that Christ, like a tender mother with a child who has tried to please but failed, will forgive her. Hattie's answer is that her uncle Henry says she must believe that Christ is willing to save her, but she does not know why Christ doesn't do so. She has decided that "it is all a dreadful mess" and once even said that "all the ministers deserve a good whipping for not knowing better what they are about." So, Catharine concludes, whenever I read your account of faith in Christ . . . and love to Christ . . . I say, such feelings and views I never had for years and years (I have them now) and yet I was as truly a Christian as I am now. And some of the best people . . . are to be shut out of Heaven if what you describe faith in Christ to be is a *sine qua non*.

Now please make me a sermon that will meet the wants of such minds as little Hattie . . . and thousands more.

Finally, in 1864, she published these views in *The Religious Training of Children in the School, the Family and the Church*. One explanation of her open revolt was her discovery in the Episcopal Church, which she joined even as she was writing the book, of a more tolerant and humane attitude. She had become an Episcopalian—as would Harriet a year later—because, she said, any virtuous person could enjoy its privileges without being "interfered with" or questioned by anyone. Even more important, it considered children "lambs of the fold" and not corrupt creatures who must face the fearful ordeal of conversion. The Episcopal was, moreover, her mother's church and, like Harriet, she had become eager to establish a spiritual relationship with her mother. Another liberating factor was the death of her father: she was at last free not only to leave his church but to reveal how his system had made his children suffer and how in fact it had failed. What a relief, she pointed out, for a mother not to find—as Catharine had found when Alexander Fisher died—that an accident could plunge a beloved one into the eternal misery of hell. *The Religious Training of Children* was a 410-page exorcism, not of demonic spirits but of a demonic conception of God.

The view she had adopted, that children began in simple ignorance and had only to be taught self-denial and the great law of sacrifice for the good of others, was clearly Victorian in its humanitarian direction. What you did for your fellow beings mattered as much as what you did for God. It was another step toward the religion of social service.

After the years in Hartford and Cincinnati in which Harriet taught in Catharine's schools, Harriet's marriage and Catharine's travels had separated the sisters. Then in the late 1840s, especially after their long sojourn together at the Brattleboro water cure, they drew together again; and in 1851 Catharine joined the Stowes in Maine and for a year shared the household burdens while Harriet worked on *Uncle Tom's Cabin*. Deeply grateful, Harriet, after reading Catharine's *True Remedy for the Wrongs of Women*, wrote to both her father and Henry that the family had completely failed to appreciate the magnitude of Catharine's vision and the nobility of her dedication: "I considered her strange, nervous, visionary and to a certain extent unstable. I see now that she has been

busy for eight years about *one thing* . . . educating our country by means
of its women and this she has steadily pursued in weariness and painful-
ness . . . in peril of life and health. . . ." If it has failed in certain respects,
Harriet declares, it has done so because it was so great a plan.

Catharine continued to visit the Stowes after they moved to Andover
and until Harriet was caught up in the turmoil of the Civil War. But
their affinities brought them together again even more intimately in the
late 1860s, when the Stowes went to Hartford. There the sisters worked
together on *The American Woman's Home or the Principles of Domestic
Science,* the first of several books on housekeeping and family care that
Catharine published between 1869 and 1873. The books combined the
same kind of material that had earned *A Treatise on Domestic Economy*
a dozen printings since its publication in 1841. Typical was the last volume, *Miss Beecher's Housekeeper and Healthkeeper.* Much like its modern counterparts, it contained hundreds of recipes, chapters on designing,
furnishing and managing a home, on clothing and health, on gardening,
animals, amusements, manners and religious training. Efficient and commonsensical as it is, the personal note intrudes only in the section on
religious training; there, one autobiographical passage is about as revealing as anything she ever wrote. In it she declares that her father's "over-
mastering passion" was to save as many as possible, and especially his
own children, from "eternal ruin," and that it was this dreadful threat
that

changed a frolicsome, hopeful, light-hearted girl to a serious, hard-working
woman as nothing else could have done. It was this that stimulated a mind
whose natural tendency was to works of taste, light literature and fun to anxious
investigation in theology, metaphysics, and Biblical science.

It was surely compensation for a life she had never had that as this
spinster neared the end of her long career, her most successful books were
devoted to homemaking and an almost religious sense of a woman as
wife, mother and household deity.

The years Catharine spent with the Stowes at Nook Farm on the
outskirts of Hartford, not far from where she had started her first school
almost half a century before, were among her most contented. She was
seventy years old, but freed of any sense of guilt, with her frustrations
and her tragic loss growing dim, she was as full of zest as ever. "I have
been for many years a wanderer without a home, in delicate health, and
often baffled in favorite plans of usefulness," she wrote. "And yet my life
has been a very happy one, with more enjoyments and fewer trials than
most of my friends experience who are surrounded by the largest share of
earthly gratifications." The circle at Nook Farm, cultured, affluent, ac-

complished, including Harriet, Mary, Isabella and their families as well as distinguished literary and political figures, could not have been more congenial.

Nearby, Catharine's school, the Hartford Female Seminary, was still functioning, but the competition of the burgeoning public high school system had reduced it to a fraction of its former size. Now the trustees decided that if Catharine would take charge again, and if Harriet, now the world-famous Mrs. Stowe, would lend a hand as of old, the school could be revived. As always, Catharine responded enthusiastically. Soon she was telling one of her publishers of this splendid new opportunity: "I have secured fine teachers to do the work, and my first move will be to introduce *our book.* . . . I never saw fairer prospects of success!"

So she moved into a boardinghouse with the teachers and twenty students and did her quaint best to create a homelike atmosphere, spending the very considerable sum of one thousand dollars in the process.

Long afterward one of her pupils recalled with the clarity of a fine old daguerreotype the daily routine during the few months that Catharine reigned in her resurrected seminary:

Every morning the girls, wearing small white aprons, and with laurel wreaths of paper on their hair, would march into the assembly hall to piano music. Miss Beecher, standing alone on the platform, in her self-made black lace dress over pink paper cambric and her self-made shoes with soft soles and velvet uppers, and with her cork-screw curls bobbing up and down, would sing the following song, in which we girls joined in the chorus. She would sing in a faint quavering wreck of a voice:

> "Let us cherish
> While yet the taper glows
> And the fresh floweret
> Pluck ere it close.
>
> *Chorus*
> "Why are we fond of toil and care
> Why choose the laurel wreath to wear
> And heedless by the lily pass
> That blossoms in our way."

Now a small, thin old woman with scraggly gray hair, she was a relic and a bit absurd, but she had been a pioneer for an ideal and even as the girls made fun of her they admired her.

Her attempt to revive the school was foredoomed. She held out for five months and then, as so often before, went off, leaving the school in the hands of a young woman, her cousin Katy Foote. Catharine tried for years to recover the thousand dollars she had invested in the school but in vain. As for the school, it lapsed into apathy again, remaining only feebly alive until 1888.

In the early 1850s, almost as soon as the women's rights movement emerged as a national organization, Catharine Beecher had opposed it. In her *True Remedy for the Wrongs of Women* she had condescendingly declared that it was unwise to ridicule such "ultraism" even though it was a disastrous and fatal approach. Now, twenty years later, she was still opposing women's suffrage, no longer condescendingly but with sweeping disapproval. The women's movement, she claimed in *Woman Suffrage and Women's Profession* (1871), is uniting all the forces that are destroying the American family: free love, free divorce, spiritualism, vice, and the avoidance of maternity, often by sinful means. With an ingrained elitism, she declared that the latter practice would eventually let the control of society fall into the hands of the "ignorant masses."

She conceded that women had too long been denied equality, but she saw grave dangers in upsetting ancient balances. Giving all women the vote would, she feared, enfranchise women who acted on impulse or would simply vote as their menfolk did, or were controlled by a "foreign or domestic priesthood," or were "degraded." But more important was her conviction that it would take much too long to achieve such a goal and that political rights could be gained, as they had in New York State, by direct appeal to men.

She was right about the length of time the suffrage campaign would take and in her feeling that voting in itself was not of primary importance. But in other ways her opposition was riddled with inconsistencies. In describing women who were impulsive or easily swayed, she accepted Victorian stereotypes of feminine characteristics. Yet she herself had always insisted that women were capable of as much education as men. And elsewhere in this very book she asserts that although her mother and her aunt Mary never went to college, they were her father's superiors in various intellectual and creative respects, and that although she and her sisters also lacked a higher education, they were the intellectual equals of their five well-educated brothers.

Just as baffling was her willingness to deny the vote to women because some of them were ignorant or superficial or degraded, and yet overlook men who had the same defects.

It is almost impossible to reconcile such contradictions. And yet we cannot treat Catharine Beecher like any other opponent of the women's rights movement. As a leader in educating women for independence, she was convinced that she had the true remedy for their dependent state. Of course, behind the show of reason in her opposition lurked such personal factors as the influence of her father's image on her acceptance of male domination in the family. Perhaps she was also a little too old in the 1850s, when women's rights became a national movement, to accept the leadership of Elizabeth Cady Stanton and Susan B. Anthony, who were much younger—and militant to boot. There was also her urge to be headmistress in every situation, and finally, her dislike for publicly aggressive women. When Isabella became an outspoken champion of women's rights, Catharine wrote to the Beechers' old friend the Reverend Leonard Bacon of Yale:

My soul is cast down at the ignorance and mistaken zeal of my poor sister Bell and her co-agitators. Can you not lend a pen to show what a mercy it is to woman *to have a head* to take the thousand responsibilities of family life, and how much *moral* power is gained by taking a subordinate place?

The feeble yielding of responsibility and the vague talk of "moral power" in this letter lead us to suspect that Catharine was really provoked because a sister twenty-two years her junior had invaded her professional territory. Even when in her last book, *Educational Reminiscences and Suggestions,* she concedes that women might be allowed to vote, she wants to restrict the right to those who are well educated and pay taxes— who are, that is, more or less like Catharine Beecher.

Most of the glimpses we get of Catharine at this time are mellow and engaging—playing croquet on Nook Farm lawns, giving a "doorstep concert" on her guitar, organizing dances for the students at the school. . . . But there were rueful moments too, as when she recalled how a famous medium, Kate Fox, told her she had seen Dr. Beecher kneeling before Catharine and offering her a rose as an emblem of her purity: "Such nonsense! When my father never in his life praised me, although he used to say I was the best boy he had." How ironic that because she was a woman and therefore not allowed to become a preacher she was doubly wasted in her father's eyes!

But one glimpse of her is poignant beyond words: she visited the farmhouse where Alexander Fisher had lived—it was occupied by a nephew—and sat by the fire in the guest room reading old letters for hours at a time and then dropping them slowly into the fire. . . .

Was she destroying the evidence of the one time when she was ready to give all of herself to a man . . . or was it the one memory she felt should be hers alone?

For a few years Catharine lived with her brother Edward in Brooklyn. Nearby was Henry's home and the Plymouth Church that he had made famous. She had long since become accustomed to the astonishing fact that the thick-tongued child she had known had become the most popular preacher in America. Even his harrowing trial on the charge of seducing Elizabeth Tilton, a parishioner's wife, had not shaken her faith in him.

In her last year she retreated to the home of the kindest of her brothers, Tom, and his equally compassionate wife, Julia. They lived in Elmira, New York, close to Gleason's, her favorite water cure. When she wrote to Harriet complaining of restlessness, her sister, now elderly herself, answered: "I am relieved and glad to think of you at home at last with Brother Tom. Too many years have passed over your head for you to be wandering like a trunk without a label." It was hardly kind of Harriet to add: "The government of the world will not be going on a whit worse that you are not doing it."

Late in April 1878, only a few days before her death, Catharine was still full of schemes and dreams: "My plan is to consult the heads of women's institutions and superintendents of common schools this summer. . . . [I] am going to Philadelphia and New Jersey to see others and am forming women's committees to cooperate. . . . I am stronger than for years but take no new responsibilities. . . ."

Describing her last days, her brother Tom wrote:

Like a mirror fractured . . . so sister Catharine "went to pieces." Incessantly, yet incoherently active, now with her hands fixing her well-worn conveniences of dress, shoes and writing apparatus; now writing a page or two of educational . . . correspondence with bishops, statesmen, and capitalists, running ten times a day to play snatches of tunes from her antique repertoire, always ending with a quavering hymn refrain, "It's better farther on." Then back to her room, ready for metaphysics until would come the explanation, "My head is tired, Tom."

With all her faults, Catharine Beecher was a remarkable woman. If she was autocratic, it was often for the sake of others; if she did not finish the formidable projects she started, they were nonetheless brave and admirable efforts; if she was neurotic about her own health, she was helpful and sound in her advice to her many readers. Even though she never had a husband, children or a place of her own, she poured out wise and practical counsel that made many an American home a little more comfortable and attractive. Although bound in part to a Biblical view of women and too genteel to approve of militant women reformers, she helped point many a young woman toward independence. She was the first of the Beechers to rebel against Calvinism and although she received no recognition as a critic of religion, her influence on her brothers and sisters was great. Through them she freed a host of the faithful from the threat of a wrathful God.

If some of her twenty-five books are overly didactic or metaphysical, they are often rich in learning, in high purpose and in common sense. As a writer and educator she broke new ground for women and as an individual she exploded the belief that an unmarried woman was doomed to become an old maid and live only vicariously.

Despite the trauma of her beloved's death when she was twenty-two, she lived a full and productive life. She has received increasing attention but she has not yet been given her due.

18

HARRIET
Days of Glory

As soon as Harriet reached the East in the spring of 1850 on her way to her new home in Brunswick, Maine, she became aware of the bitterness aroused by the Fugitive Slave Law. Episode after episode for twenty-five years—race riots, the attacks on Lovejoy, Garrison, Birney, Weld, Phillips, Lewis Tappan, the Grimkés and others, the insurrections led by Nat Turner and Denmark Vesey, the mounting threats by Northern abolitionists and Southern secessionists—had marked the increasing tension on both sides. At first the South had been partly defensive and partly scornful, the reaction of a people charged with a shameful practice of long standing; then came nettled pride, the resentment of natives at outsiders—themselves not altogether innocent—who censure righteously. But those had generally been the responses of extremists or mobs. Now the Fugitive Slave Act was a law of the land.

Senator Clay of Kentucky, in his seventies, had framed it as a compromise in which California would enter the Union as a free state if Congress would strengthen the laws requiring the return of fugitive slaves and the punishment of those who aided in their escape. Another great Southerner, Calhoun, raged against it. But Webster of Massachusetts, now also old, pleading that he wanted only to preserve the Union, had accepted it. Harriet would later describe him as the "lost archangel of New England," the leader who spoke with a serpent's voice.

If it was a victory for the South, it was a fatal victory. Before it, many Northerners had made little of the controversy or blamed it on hotheads. Now suddenly they saw Southerners licensed to penetrate the North to reclaim escaped blacks—with the help, if needed, of federal judges and even troops. Northerners felt betrayed, made accessories to acts that were morally wrong, personally repugnant and certainly undemocratic—a dark stain on the record of the new republic.

Before going on to Maine, Harriet paused for a visit with Henry in Brooklyn, Mary in Hartford and Edward in Boston, and found each in his own way disturbed by the new law. Henry, basking in the sun of success, admiration and a handsome salary at Plymouth Church, had dramatized his protest by raising money in his church to buy the freedom of two quadroon slave girls. Edward and his wife, Isabella, true to the memory of their martyred friend Elijah Lovejoy, denounced the proposed law as immoral and lamented Boston's failure to rise up in rebellion, and even Mary Beecher Perkins and her husband, secure in their fine Hartford home, sounded an alarm at the prospect. In each place, Harriet said little and seemed to listen only in a distracted way. But she heard.

She reached Brunswick late in May and was immediately caught up in furnishing the big house they had rented on Federal Street, revarnishing furniture, making bedspreads, and coping with scrubwomen, plumbers, coopers and three children. She was, moreover, in the last months of pregnancy and not only was Calvin still in Cincinnati but he had—as she reported with a great show of patience—written a typically doleful letter complaining that he was sick abed, all but dead, didn't expect to see his family again, knew they would never get out of debt, and thought Harriet should be prudent in case she was left a widow. . . . It would have been deeply depressing if it hadn't been ludicrous.

Harriet may as usual have exaggerated her problems, for the house was a fine old structure, Calvin would have been more of a hindrance than a help, and several of the Bowdoin faculty wives were immensely helpful. And far from being a rustic community, Brunswick, a busy little port with fine old houses, prosperous shipbuilders and world-traveling sea captains, was as civilized as Boston.

Calvin, bringing the other two children, arrived a week before Harriet gave birth to her seventh—and last—child. He had already extracted from the Bowdoin trustees a five-hundred-dollar bonus above his pathetic thousand-dollar-a-year salary, but the new baby and the expense of moving forced him to ask for another bonus. The trustees granted him a hundred dollars. At the same time he revealed that Lane Seminary had failed to replace him and was insisting that he return for at least the winter term. The patient trustees agreed. Then, as so often happens when recognition comes, another institution sought his services: the prestigious Andover Theological Seminary offered him a post as professor of Sacred Literature, a generous salary and a house to live in.

Jubilant, Calvin accepted without hesitation and even allowed Andover to announce his appointment. Learning of his three teaching commitments, the New York *Independent* dryly observed that Dr. Stowe had apparently acquired the faculty of omnipresence. Harriet piously warned him that he was betraying his friends at both Bowdoin and Lane. The Bowdoin trustees were exasperated, but they finally agreed to release him if he would give them a full year after his term at Lane. So at fifty years of age Calvin Stowe was at last to receive his due in pecuniary rewards as well as honors.

But the Stowes still faced a year of living on a meager salary, with six children, a new governess and, as a summer guest, father Beecher. So Harriet turned again to writing "sermonettes" and light-handed sketches for sundry periodicals. But one theme kept resisting her—the plight of slaves. A reading of the autobiography of the Reverend Josiah Henson, and perhaps a meeting with him, added to her growing indignation. Henson was a former slave whose arms had been crippled in a beating by a neighbor's white overseer. An able and ambitious man, he had become the trusted overseer on a Maryland plantation. He had finally arranged to buy his freedom but his master, a drunkard and a brawler, had deceived him and then decided to sell him. Outraged, Henson had escaped to Canada with his wife and children and after educating himself, established a black cooperative settlement there. "Father Henson"—he had learned to preach during his slave days—had become a well-known lecturer and "exhorter," so pious that he had forgiven his former masters and prayed for their souls. Although he may have been a model for both the saintly Uncle Tom and the escaped slave George Harris, he was, as one critic points out, quite unlike Uncle Tom in that he occasionally did his master's bidding, even though it went against the grain. But perhaps that difference is what makes Henson human and Uncle Tom too good to be true.

As soon as the Fugitive Slave Act became a law in September 1850, a new type of horror story began to appear in the press, especially in abolitionist papers. It told of "slave-snatchers" and "man-stealers" who tore escaped slaves from their families and jobs in Northern communities. Pouring out her anger in a letter to Harriet, Edward's wife, Isabella, concluded: "Hattie, if I could use a pen as you *can,* I would write something that will make this whole nation feel what an accursed thing slavery is." With its flattery, its accent on Harriet's power to make readers feel, and in the religious force of "accursed," the letter struck home. Her children never forgot how Harriet, obviously deeply stirred, read the letter to them and then rose, letter in hand, and said: "I *will* write something. I will if I live"—the last words her usual reflex obeisance to God's will.

She not only lived but even defied household duties and the long Maine winter by going sleigh riding and "snowballing" with her children. But delivering a blow against slavery was not so easy. Then one stormy January night in 1851, Henry, after a lecture in Boston's Tremont Temple, rode up on the railway to visit Harriet, arriving at midnight amidst a blizzard. They spent the rest of the night talking, he at the height of his powers, flushed with success, she gathering her resources and all the experiences of eighteen long years on the Southern border. Aroused to a pitch of excitement by Henry's bold schemes for awakening the nation to the evils of the Fugitive Slave Act, she finally disclosed her own plan for contributing to the cause. With his ever-ready enthusiasm, he cried, "That's right, Harriet, finish it and I will scatter it thick as the leaves of Vallombrosa." He spoke as if he would be essential in gaining attention for what she wrote.

At last, so one story goes, the inspiration came. In church on a Communion Sunday in February, as she sat in the dreamlike state that often stole over her, she had a vision of unusual intensity: urged on by a brutish white master, two slaves, equally brutish, are flogging a white-haired old slave. The slave will not betray his fellows or his faith in Christ, and he prays for his murderers as he dies.

She could hardly wait until she had recorded what she had seen in her vision. When she read the result to her children, thirteen-year-old Henry cried, "Oh, mamma! slavery is the most cruel thing in the world!" But it was only a single incident, no more than the sketches she had been doing all along. So she put it aside. A month later Calvin, back from his stint at Lane, came upon the manuscript, read it, and with tears streaming down his cheeks, turned to Harriet to learn what it was. When she explained, he said, "Hattie, you must go on with it. You must make up a story with this for the climax. The Lord intends it so." Thus encouraged, she set down a few more episodes. Excited by the result, she wrote to Dr. Gamaliel Bailey, editor of the *National Era,* an eight-page antislavery paper to which she had become a contributor. She was working, she said, on three or four sketches of slave life that would show

the best side of the thing, and *something faintly approaching the worst. . . .* The Carthaginian women in the last peril of their state cut off their hair for bowstrings to give to the defenders of their country; and such peril and shame as now hangs over this country is worse than Roman slavery.

My vocation is simply that of painter, and my object will be to hold up in the most lifelike and graphic manner possible, Slavery, its reverses, changes, and the negro character. . . . There is no arguing with *pictures,* and everybody is impressed by them, whether they mean to be or not.

Bailey, a veteran abolitionist who in his Cincinnati days had succeeded Birney as editor of the *Philanthropist,* was most sympathetic. He offered her three hundred dollars—a generous sum for what he assumed would be a modest number of installments. Tremendously stimulated, Harriet drove on. Characters, scenes—*pictures*—welled up inexhaustibly, as astonishing to her as they would be to everyone else. Soon she saw that she would need five, six or even more installments and might even have enough—the thought made her heart leap—for a novel. Soon, too, she had a title for it: *Uncle Tom's Cabin; or, The Man that Was a Thing.* The subtitle must have seemed too bitter, for when the first installment appeared on the front page of the *National Era* on June 5, 1851, it was *Life Among the Lowly.*

From the very first installment, in which the ordinarily kind slaveholder Shelby is driven by debts to sell "Uncle Tom," his most trusted slave, along with the appealing little son of Eliza, another slave, readers were enthralled. Pathetically small though the readership of the *National Era* was, word of the new serial spread amazingly. One reader later recalled how in his remote New England village people who had never before taken fiction seriously were so deeply affected by the novel that they "read it to their children; and how the papers which contained it, after being nearly worn out in going through so many hands . . . were as carefully folded up and laid away as if the tear stains on them were sacred." Once, when Harriet, exhausted, missed a deadline, the paper was deluged by letters of protest.

In August, Catharine came and took charge. Having read the installments, she resumed her managerial role and tried to get her latest publishers to take the book. They rejected it, fearing it would hurt their Southern trade. But in September, Mrs. Jewett, wife of a small Boston publisher, talked her husband into reading the serial and he decided to risk publishing it. When, however, the installments continued on and on, threatening to become a two-volume work, he tried to get Mrs. Stowe to cut it short. She was, she intimated, in the hands of a higher agency and could not stop. Jewett then proposed that she bear half the costs and take half the profits. But the Stowes had neither the money nor the desire to take a risk the publisher himself was trying to avoid. They accepted a more or less standard royalty, ten percent of the sale price—thereby losing the fortune they might have earned. But Harriet was delighted. "I hope," she said, "it will make enough so I may have a silk dress."

Even after it had appeared in book form, she still did not realize the extent of her reputation: when Sarah J. Hale, editor of the tremendously popular *Godey's Lady's Book,* asked her for biographical information for use in a book on the most distinguished women writers, she replied that her life had been "so thoroughly uneventful" that she could not see how it warranted any attention. She suggested that Mrs. Hale consider Catharine instead.

Calvin, in Boston for the negotiations with Jewett, visited his father-in-law's new home on Hayward Place. They agreed that it was a triumphant time for the Beechers as far as publications were concerned, with the second volume of Dr. Beecher's sermons just out, both Catharine's *True Remedy for the Wrongs of Women* and Charles's *The Duty of Disobedience to Wicked Laws* (an attack on the Fugitive Slave Act) still causing ripples, Edward's *The Conflict of Ages* being readied for publication, Henry doing featured contributions to the *Independent*—and now Harriet's book.

Uncle Tom's Cabin was published on March 20, 1852, in an edition of five thousand sets of two volumes each, bound in cloth at one dollar fifty per set, in paper at one dollar, and in "cloth full gilt" at two dollars. The first printing was sold out in two days and fifty thousand sets followed in the next eight weeks. At that point, the *Boston Traveler* reported, three power presses running twenty-four hours a day and one hundred binders were unable to keep up with the demand. By the end of the year, 300,000 copies had been sold in the United States and a million and a half copies in Great Britain and its colonies.

A number of modern critics of *Uncle Tom's Cabin,* including Van Wyck Brooks and Edmund Wilson, have expressed astonishment at its range, insights and emotional force. The explanation is simple: for almost a century, hundreds of unauthorized but immensely popular stage versions made the story into a melodramatic, tear-wringing folk play with minstrel or even circus trappings. Such characters as Topsy, Simon Legree, little Eva and eventually Uncle Tom himself became comic bywords. The reputation of the book also later suffered from an increasing distaste for Victorian sentimentality and piety. All this makes it difficult for anyone who has not read the book to understand its popularity in its own time or the impression it makes on most critics today.

There is no way to explain why no other novelist had written about slaves intimately and as individuals even though at least a hundred narratives by slaves themselves were published after 1831. It took a sensitive foreign traveler, the Swedish novelist Fredrika Bremer, to note this curious lack. With an uncanny anticipation of Harriet's book, she wrote to her sister late in 1850:

I have heard histories of the flight of slaves which are full of the most intense interest, and I cannot conceive why these incidents do not become the subject of romances and novels. . . . I know no subject which could furnish opportunities for more heart-rending or more picturesque descriptions or scenes. . . . I cannot understand why, in particular, noble-minded . . . American mothers who have hearts and genius do not take up the subject and treat it with a power which should pierce through bone and marrow, should reduce all the prudential maxims of statesmen to dust and ashes. . . . It is the privilege of the woman and the mother which suffers most severely through slavery. And if the heart of the woman . . . would heave warmly and strongly with maternal life's blood, I am convinced that the earth, the spiritual earth of the United States, must quake thereby and overthrow slavery!

When *Uncle Tom's Cabin* appeared, Miss Bremer greeted it as the book she had hoped for.

In range, Harriet's book went well beyond Miss Bremer's prescription, portraying not only slaves in flight but many who could not or would not flee. Because she made her principal fugitives attractive as well as light-skinned—Eliza is beautiful, her child, Harry, is a darling and her husband, George, is a gifted mechanic—Mrs. Stowe's two most hostile modern critics see this treatment as evidence of Harriet's deep-rooted prejudices concerning what makes a black admirable, while Harriet and her champions say that it simply served to point up the absurdity and cruelty of slaveholders' standards.

So it goes with almost all Harriet's characters. To her early readers Uncle Tom's Christ-like qualities underscored the wickedness of his destroyers, while to many black critics today he represents the utter futility of Christian submission and faith; for Harriet (as she tells us in *The Key to Uncle Tom's Cabin*) Topsy is an incorrigible delinquent because she knows intuitively that there is no place for her anywhere in the white world, while to Harriet's detractors she is simply a monkey; Cassy, the quadroon mistress of Legree, seems admirable in her fierce resentment of her condition but Harriet's treatment of her has been faulted for the Gothic claptrap with which she outwits her master; it is understandable that Sambo and Quimbo have been brutalized by their brutal master Legree, but not that they become instant Christians when Uncle Tom forgives them as they kill him.

The few hostile critics notwithstanding, such characterizations exploded the legend of happy, thoughtless, insensitive darkies—a legend long circulated by slaveholders and accepted by most Northerners.

Perhaps because she knew them better, her white characters have aroused fewer objections. Shelby is the kind master whose good intentions quickly fade when he falls into debt; his wife is shocked by his betrayal but she herself proves utterly ineffectual; Augustine St. Clare, the kind of Byronic figure who appears in many of Harriet's novels, is the brilliant, moody individualist, too disillusioned to cope with the realities he describes so well; his wife, Marie, spoiled, jealous, hypochondriacal, prefigures women in latter-day Southern novels; their child Eva is, everyone agrees, an insufferable combination of sugar and piety; their nephew Henrique is the "hot-blooded" young Southerner who shows his mettle by beating a black boy for not obeying him quickly enough; and Ophelia, St. Clare's New England cousin, is a prim, devout and efficient spinster who hates slavery but cannot stand the slaves themselves.

In a strategic if rather strained effort to spread the guilt around, Harriet makes the villain of the book, Simon Legree, a renegade Northerner. A crude precursor of Faulkner's grotesques, Legree makes it a practice to work blacks till they drop, and then replace them. When a respectable planter tells a Northerner that Legree is not typical, the Northerner—anticipating our theories of community guilt for atrocities—declares that respectable slaveholders must be held responsible for the Legrees.

Harriet establishes many of her characters in almost Dickensian detail, but Dickens would never have been guilty of the moralizing passages, the contrived debates on social issues, the occasional affectations in style, the vague connections between the various plots, or characters overdrawn to the point of caricature.

Some of this can be blamed on Harriet's writing at white heat to meet a weekly deadline—which is the way she would write most of her novels—as well as her belief that there were more important things in creating a novel of this kind than aesthetic niceties or psychological refinements. She had "no more thought of style or literary excellence," her son said in his biography of her, "than the mother who rushes into the street and cries for help to save her children from a burning house."

Nothing was clearer support for this view than the praise she won from those masters of the well-fashioned novel Henry James and George Sand. James called *Uncle Tom's Cabin* a "triumphant work," as wonderful as a fish that flies; it had, he writes, "the extraordinary fortune of finding itself, for an immense number of people, much less a book than a state of vision, of feeling and of consciousness, in which they didn't see and read and appraise . . . but walked and talked and laughed and cried." In short, it successfully defied James's most cherished literary principles.

Even more generously, George Sand—Harriet thought her a great artist but a scandalous person who spent her talents on deplorable themes—said that the book had faults only in terms of the conventional rules of art: "If its judges, possessed with the love of what they call 'artistic work,' find unskilled treatment in the book, look well to see if their eyes are dry when they are reading this or that chapter. . . . She has . . . the genius of goodness, not that of a man of letters, but of a saint."

Not that *Uncle Tom's Cabin* was in any sense the work of an untaught or unsophisticated writer. Harriet was after all part of an intellectual elite and her comments on literary figures from Scott, Byron and Milton to Madame de Staël and Voltaire, when not blinded by a puritanical morality, reveal a wide and careful reader. Her mixing of tragic and comic characters is a crude but calculated strategy; and her treatment of the sexual license of slaveholders and the selling of black girls into prostitution is far from naive. Her enemies even charged her with prurience and exploiting stories of lust. It was a fact of Southern life; but talking about it was taboo.

But the extent of Harriet's social awareness is most strikingly illustrated by some of St. Clare's remarks. In one conversation he tells his conservative and elitist brother Alfred that the inhuman treatment of the lower classes everywhere will one day drive them to rise up in revolt. Alfred declares that they will never be allowed to rise up. "That's right, said St. Clare; 'put on the steam, fasten down the escape-valve, and sit on it, and see where you'll land.' " Alfred's answer is that he is not afraid to sit on the valve as long as the boilers are strong, to which St. Clare responds that the nobles before the French Revolution thought so too, and that all such men may meet each other in the air when the boilers burst.

"I tell you," said Augustine, "if there is anything that is revealed with the strength of divine law in our times, it is that the masses are to rise, and the under class become the upper one."

"That's one of your red republican humbugs, Augustine! Why didn't you ever take to the stump;—you'd make a famous stump orator! Well, I hope I shall be dead before this millennium of your greasy masses comes on."

Even though St. Clare's views are hardly Harriet's own and were borrowed from the writings of the most socially radical of New England clergymen, Orestes Brownson, she does attribute them to a character with whom she often seems to identify.

Two other aspects of *Uncle Tom's Cabin* are at once a source of its wide appeal and, at least for modern readers, its weakness—the almost mystical worship of motherhood and its view of the powers of Christian faith. As the devoted mother of seven children, and as a daughter who idealized and continued to miss a mother she had scarcely known, Harriet saw slave mothers as the most tragic victims of slavery (unlike men, they were after all used for pleasure as well as profit) and mothers in general as a primal force for social good. But this adulation—which she shared with most of the women in her audience—is carried to absurdity when Simon Legree is portrayed as haunted by the mother he ran away from in his youth or when St. Clare dies with his mother's name on his lips.

So, too, Harriet's faith in religion gives the book its spiritual conviction but opens it to the charge that religion served the slaves only as an opiate. The hope of heaven may have helped slaves like Uncle Tom carry on in the face of every torment and indignity; but it also reconciled them to their fate and allowed their masters to rest easy.

That no doubt is why Uncle Tom has become a symbol of abject servility among many blacks. The harshest of such attacks came in 1949, when James Baldwin, then a very young novelist, charged that the emotions in *Uncle Tom's Cabin* were spurious and that of the three most admirable slaves, Eliza and George were simply disguised whites and

Tom was esteemed only because he was robed in the white garment of salvation. In its use of "theological terror," Baldwin asserted, the book breathed the spirit of witch-burners and lynch mobs. It was, he concluded, only another dishonest white way of approaching blacks. Understandable as Baldwin's bitterness may be, his attack was guilty of as many excesses as the book he criticized.

Clergymen fare badly in *Uncle Tom's Cabin*. Only a Beecher would have had the self-confidence to picture them as hypocritical apologists for slavery. Harriet was even rash enough to add a footnote identifying one of them as the Reverend Joel Parker. That brought from Parker a demand for a retraction and spilled over into a long, unpleasant and inconclusive exchange in the press. Perhaps she could be so critical because she clung to the belief that regardless of the clergy, a spiritual awakening would lead each slaveholder to free his slaves. And yet, as though she knew this was only a dream, she had such a rebel as George Harris turn to the old scheme of colonization in Africa.

Abandoning the role of the storyteller, she concludes with an apocalyptic warning to the churches to stop protecting injustice, cruelty and sin lest the nations bring down on themselves the "wrath of an angry God." No preacher could have closed on a more Calvinistic note.

Ironically, she would have been devastated had she known that her prediction would come true barely ten years later, with violence, ruin and death on a scale beyond her imagining. All that the little housewife hoped was that people would see the error of their ways and repent.

Before *Uncle Tom's Cabin*, American fiction had had only the fantasies of Poe, Irving and Charles Brockden Brown and the romances of Cooper, the early works of Hawthorne and Melville and a host of "women scribblers." Such powerfully original works as *The Scarlet Letter* and *Huckleberry Finn* were still to come and *Moby Dick* had just been published but was fated to be neglected. And none of these would reach readers everywhere with anything like the force of *Uncle Tom's Cabin*. At her best, Harriet Beecher Stowe was the first American realist of any consequence and the first to use fiction for a profound criticism of American society, especially its failure to live up to the promises of democracy.

Hardly less satisfying than the sale of *Uncle Tom's Cabin* were the reviews and congratulations. In the influential *Independent,* a well-known clergyman called the book a mighty and moving sermon and concluded: "Let ALL MEN read it." Longfellow congratulated Mrs. Stowe on a great moral as well as literary triumph. Almost ruefully he wrote in his diary: "At one step she has reached the top of the staircase up which the rest of us climb on our knees year after year." Heine, ill in Paris, said it led him back to the Bible and faith, and Tolstoy ranked it with *Les*

Misérables and *A Tale of Two Cities* as high moral art. Jewett now began to advertise it as "The Greatest Book of Its Kind Ever Issued from the American Press." When Dickens declared the book "noble but defective," it was something of an anticlimax.

With large royalties in the offing, Harriet decided to treat herself to a leisurely trip to New York. She had a good excuse: the editors of the *Independent* wanted her to consider becoming a weekly contributor. Along the way she stopped to see relatives and old friends—Edward and her father in Boston (Lyman thought he was jesting when he said she might become more famous than he), Mary Beecher Perkins and her husband, Thomas, in Hartford, and finally Henry and his wife in Brooklyn. It was a triumphal progress, with everyone at gatherings crowding around to talk to the little woman who had written not only a worldwide best-seller but a great humanitarian work.

Harriet began to enjoy other fruits of success. John T. Howard and his wife, two of Henry's wealthy supporters at Plymouth Church, became her social guides. They decided that she must hear Jenny Lind, who had captured America with her singing. But the singer's last concert had long since been sold out. Then the "Swedish nightingale" heard of Harriet's interest and sent her not only two tickets but a note telling her how beautiful she had found her book. Harriet thought the performance, the first of its kind she had ever attended, "a bewildering dream of sweetness and beauty," adding to the illusion that she herself was living in a dream.

Now, too, she was able to play the benefactress. Three years earlier, Henry in a sensational gesture had raised $2,250 in a New York church to buy the freedom of two quadroon girls, daughters of a slave, Milly Edmonson, and her free husband, as the girls were waiting to be sold in a Virginia slaveholders' warehouse. Now Mrs. Edmonson came to Henry with a plea to save her other two children. Henry promptly turned her over to his famous sister. Harriet had Milly address women in various churches and collected enough money to free not only the children but Milly herself.

Although Harriet was now assuming control of her family's financial affairs—she had made her brother-in-law Thomas Perkins, a conservative lawyer, her adviser—it was typical of her relationship to Calvin that despite all the attention she was receiving, she should write to him: "It is not fame nor praise that contents me. I seem never to have needed love so much as now. I long to hear you say how much you love me." Impractical and inept though Calvin might be, he was still her beloved, the man with whom she had lain and begotten her children. Her marital attachment would remain inviolable.

On Harriet's journey home, Mrs. Howard accompanied her as far

as the Perkinses' home in Hartford. There the two women shared a guest
room overnight. Mrs. Howard was already in bed when Harriet began to
undress. Dropping her petticoats and undoing her stays, she sat down
cross-legged on the floor and in a reverie began brushing her hair. Mrs.
Howard never forgot how astonishing it seemed that this little, girlish
woman, so pensive and detached, should have caused such a stir. At last
Harriet spoke, telling of a letter from her brother Edward in which he
cautioned her against letting fame "induce pride and vanity." Then, as
Mrs. Howard reported it,

She dropped her brush from her hand and exclaimed with earnestness, "Dear
soul, he need not be troubled. He doesn't know that I didn't write that book."
    "*What!*" said I. "*You* did not write *Uncle Tom?*"
    "No," she said. "I only put down what I saw."
    "But you have never been at the South, have you?" I asked.
    "No," she said, "but it all came before me in visions, one after another, and
I put them down in words."

To the end of her days Harriet would continue to give such explanations of the authorship of *Uncle Tom's Cabin*, sometimes adding that
God had guided her pen and even that in transmitting the harsher details
she was a reluctant instrument. Perhaps that was why adulation never
made her self-important and criticism never weakened her conviction.
She was, after all, the Lord's amanuensis. Some critics have considered
this a delusion or an affectation in a woman whose sudden fame had gone
to her head. But it is hardly uncommon for a writer, especially when
passionately involved, to write like someone possessed, drawing mysteriously on subconscious sources. In what other way can we explain how a
forty-year-old housewife could create so powerful a work on so original a
theme? She herself simply never believed that she could have written the
book without God's help.

Then a secondary reaction set in. Southern and other pro-slavery
reviewers, at first truly surprised by Harriet's view of blacks and of the
slave–master relationship, treated her as misguided and refused to take
her seriously. The *Alabama Planter* declared that the woman who wrote
it must be "either a very bad or a very fanatical person." Planter interests
in the South and cotton and banking interests in the North, more concerned about money than morality, and shocked by the popularity of the
book, suddenly saw its dangerous potential. The New York *Journal of
Commerce* opened this attack by questioning its veracity. The New York
Observer, a rigidly conservative, pro-slavery and anti-women's rights
journal, announced: "We have read the book and regard it as anti-Christian." Amidst the paeans in the British press, the London *Times*, after

conceding that the book showed a mastery of human feeling as well as great skill, dismissed the sudden conversions of Sambo, Quimbo, Cassy and others as "audacious trash" and concluded: "Let us have no more *Uncle Tom's Cabins* engendering ill will" and preventing "the spread of the glad tidings from Heaven." No one has ever explained what rosy Victorian expectation the last words were based on.

Where the book had at first been tolerated in the South, it now became anathema. Henry Pellew, son of the Earl of Exmouth, having read and been moved by the book, spoke of it to a young woman in Charleston, South Carolina. When she showed interest in it, he managed to get a secondhand copy for her. He was soon visited by several young men who told him that he had insulted the young lady and should expect to be challenged to a duel. A wise youth, he left town immediately.

Now, too, there were hate-filled and obscene letters from the South, including one from which, as Calvin opened it, fell a blackish ear, obviously of a slave. . . . All Harriet could do was block these out—simply deny that there could be such malignity in the world.

Somewhat easier to ignore or cope with was the "anti-Tom" literature, mainly novels that sought to offset the effect of Harriet's book. Most of these were feeble performances. One of the best of them, *Aunt Phillis's Cabin; or, Southern Life As It Is,* by Mary H. Eastman, was dismissed by the reviewer for the *Independent* with the comment that "the pictures of the intense happiness of the slaves are so very charming one wonders why the inventors do not make haste to sell their children to the slave-traders."

After her return to Brunswick, Harriet took steps to make more time for her writing: besides a governess for the six children, she hired a cook and a housekeeper. When the time came for Calvin to take over his duties at Andover Theological Seminary, she also decided, after rejecting the free house offered by the seminary, that she must at last have a home done to her own taste and needs. Fortified by a royalty check for more than ten thousand dollars, she offered to remodel an old stone building that had been used as a carpenter shop—if the trustees would promise to reimburse her. They agreed, bowing not so much to the professor as to his famous wife. Harriet left Calvin and the children and went happily to Andover to supervise the rebuilding and furnishing of what was to be their home for the next eleven years.

It was a very pleasant summer for her: alone . . . building a home for herself . . . composing poems and hymns . . . luxuriating in the bright morning of her fame. . . . It was a relatively tranquil time even on the national scene: the Democratic Presidential candidate, Franklin Pierce, Calvin's onetime schoolmate at Bowdoin, was an amiable and undistinguished figure, considered safe even by the South; he managed to defeat an aging general, Winfield Scott, popularly known as "Old Fuss and Feathers."

The record of *Uncle Tom's Cabin* abroad grew ever more amazing. When British publishers realized that there was no European copyright on the book, a score of them issued editions of it. So great was the sale that it gave rise to a business based mainly on pirated American books—turning the tables on American publishers, who paid almost no royalties to British authors. The book soon appeared in a score of other languages, including Wallachian, Illyrian and Welsh, and in no less than six translations in France—greatly stimulating, it is said, the sale of the Bible. In Italy it was serialized separately in Genoa and Turin—but the Vatican, apparently seeing it as a product of militant Protestantism, banned it—and a Portuguese edition in Rio de Janeiro challenged slavery in Brazil. And readers everywhere took the book to their hearts.

By the fall of 1852, "Tom-mania" (called *l'oncletomerie* in Paris and *Onkeltomerei* in Germany) began, with Americans singing or playing eight different Uncle Tom songs. Soon, too, the stage versions, opening in New York, Boston and London, became the rage. By the 1890s four hundred to five hundred troupes were performing the play. For seventy-five years no day passed, it is said, without a performance in America. Since authors did not have drama rights, Mrs. Stowe received not a penny from these performances. One story has it that when a troupe put on the play in Hartford, Harriet went to see it with her neighbor Charles Dudley Warner, editor and critic. She laughed and cried along with everyone else but was confused by the bizarre additions and changes—such as the bloodhounds used to pursue Eliza and the wires that literally wafted Eva from her deathbed to heaven—and Warner later claimed that he had to explain parts of it to her. The pity of it was that the distortions would live on, overshadowing the original. It was doubly ironic because like her father, she continued to consider the theater sinful and corrupting.

Mrs. Stowe would have been mortified to learn that the plays would increasingly become extravaganzas whose interpretation of Negro types made a mockery of the book and its intentions. The only explanation for the freedom with which all troupes converted the work into pure entertainment—made respectable by a gloss of pious moralizing—was a feeling that it was a folk drama to be played not for meaning but simply for laughter and tears—or in some versions, for a morbid pleasure in cruelty and violence.

Because critics both in the South and in the North questioned the veracity of *Uncle Tom's Cabin,* Harriet decided to publish a collection of firsthand evidence in support of her work. This took her an entire winter and cost her, she said, incalculable anguish. The result, *The Key to Uncle Tom's Cabin; the Original Facts and Documents upon which the Story is Founded, together with Corroborative Statements Verifying the Truth of the Work,* is a scrapbook of advertisements for runaways, slave laws, notes on the origin of the characters, and sundry borrowings from Theodore Weld's *Slavery As It Is.* It bore out many of the horror stories in the novel—even though some of the examples had turned up after the serial was published and although a few of the explanations differed from those she gave elsewhere.

But much more relevant then the factual accuracy of *Uncle Tom's Cabin* is its spiritual authenticity—and that needed no documentation. Far more significant, too, were its psychological sources: her frustrations as a girl in a family and a world dominated by men, then her years serving Calvin and her children in Cincinnati, and finally rebellion, long suppressed, against the relentless pressure to submit to a God who did whatever he pleased with his helpless human slaves. She had expressed such rebellion in George and Eliza and Cassy and in gestures by other slaves. As for Uncle Tom, he represented the other side of the coin, her hope of making love prevail, of conquering by forgiveness and by accepting death not as punishment but as a gateway to eternal peace. If Tom is pathetic in this respect, so, one might say, was Christ.

The publisher had no trouble selling 150,000 copies of *A Key;* Harriet Beecher Stowe's name had become magical. Despite this, she clung, almost coyly, to the image of herself as an obscure housewife. When Eliza Follen, author of popular children's books, asked for information as a sister foe of slavery, she was surely surprised by the answer: "So you want to know something about what sort of woman I am! To begin, then, I am a little bit of a woman—somewhat more than forty, about as thin and dry as a pinch of snuff; never very much to look at in my best days, and looking like a used-up article now." Such self-disparagement was surely meant to evoke a flattering denial. It also served to heighten the contrast between her obscurity and her accomplishment. As observers described her and as pictures more or less confirm, she was plain but her face had a spiritual quality and was lit by large dark lustrous eyes.

Her letter to Mrs. Follen also contained a characterization of Calvin Stowe that is often quoted: "I was married when I was twenty-five years old to a man rich in Greek and Hebrew and Latin and Arabic, and, alas! rich in nothing else." It was of course funny but also a bit rueful if not unkind.

In this letter, too, Harriet described how much she had learned about slave women from her cook Eliza Buck, and especially how she had discovered that Eliza's pretty quadroon daughters were fathered by Eliza's last master. Humbly Eliza had said: "You know, Mrs. Stowe, slave women can't help themselves."

If she had doubts about the extent of her fame, they must have been swept away when she and Calvin received a letter from a prominent Scottish clergyman inviting them to visit the British Isles as a guest of antislavery societies. It was a rare honor and they accepted with pride and delight.

It was agreed that Charles, now a minister in Newark, tall and looking like an artist, should accompany them as secretary. Then Sarah, George Beecher's widow, a woman of means, asked to join them with her son and brother. So it was a family group of six that sailed from Boston and arrived in Liverpool on April 10, 1853.

A crowd was waiting on the wharf but the Americans paid no attention to it until, to their astonishment, the people surged around Harriet, everyone bowing and greeting her as she walked toward a hack. They then crowded so densely around the vehicle that it could hardly move. And all along the way there were knots of people waving as she passed. She realized then what Charles Kingsley, the British novelist and clergyman, meant when he warned her of "the foolish yet honest and heartfelt lionizing which you must go through." It was all like a dream and it would go on for months, in Glasgow, London, Paris, Geneva, Cologne. . . .

They stayed in an old English mansion that night, and the following morning were guests at a formal breakfast—the ladies wore their bonnets throughout—attended by forty leading citizens. A clergyman gave a welcoming address and since it was not proper for a lady to speak to an audience, Calvin replied—as he would do again and again in the months to come. Afterwards, out on a broad lawn, a group of children from a local charity or "ragged" school, all shined up for the occasion, sang a hymn proclaiming how happy they were to be English children and not slaves in America. It was the Stowes' first glimpse of a certain smug superiority in the British attitude. This was even more conspicuous in a letter addressed to the women of the United States by a score of notable English women and signed by no less than 500,000 other British women. In the name of Christ it exhorted the Americans to abolish slavery. When it was presented to Harriet—in twenty-six huge volumes—she was evidently too flattered to see how self-righteous the letter was. But Calvin fumed over it.

At Glasgow, Harriet was met by cheering crowds and was taken to the cathedral in the luxurious carriage of the lord provost of the city. Such throngs lined the streets that with her usual self-deprecation she wrote: "I could not help saying, 'What went ye out for to see? A reed shaken with the wind?'" The next day she was so ill that she spent the day in bed. But in the evening she managed to go to a "tea party" at the city hall attended by two thousand guests; in her bemused way all she could think of was how large the teapot must be. . . .

One weekend the group sailed down the Clyde to the Duke of Argyll's estate. When Harriet was introduced to his farmers, one of them, a huge man, said he had read her book and would any day walk six miles to see her. She added: "when I put my hand into his great prairie of a palm, I was a grasshopper in my own eyes." They rode through several villages and she later wrote of the welcome:

What pleased me was that it was not mainly from the literary, nor the rich, nor the great but the plain common people. The butcher came out of his stall and the baker from his shop, the miller dusty with flour, the blooming comely young mother, with that hearty, intelligent, friendly look as if they knew we should be glad to see them.

After another overwhelming reception in Edinburgh she resigned herself, she said, "as a very tame lion, into the hands of my keepers." The climax of her visit was a presentation to her of one thousand gold sovereigns collected penny by penny from the people of Scotland.

It was much the same in London. After a dinner given in her honor by the lord mayor, he invited her to go to the House of Commons with him. "With all my heart," she replied, "if I only had another body to go into tomorrow." She had hoped to get some rest by staying in the parsonage of a dissenting minister in the rather unfashionable suburb of Walworth. But the carriages of the great and the wealthy swept up to the door night and day—past and future prime ministers, royalty in droves, clergymen from the archbishop down, judges, literati, reformers—all of which was reported in the press until it became a matter of jest to some and of annoyance to others. Calvin was sure that his modest little wife would never be the same again. She did complain, understandably, that artists' portraits of her in London shopwindows looked either like the Gorgon or the Sphinx. "They will be useful," she wrote to Mrs. Howard, "like the Irishman's guideboard, which showed where the road did not go."

But it soon became evident that her hosts were so worshipful partly because her book arraigned the American social system; it gave the British, who had abolished slavery a score of years earlier, a grand opportunity to denounce the inhumanity and wickedness of their former colony, now grown high and mighty. All this irked Calvin far more than it did Harriet. Finally, before a huge audience at an anniversary meeting of the British and Foreign Anti-Slavery Society, he stopped playing the homespun humorist and pointed out that it had been easy for Britain to free her slaves because she had so few of them; in America slavery was a three-billion-dollar business whose sudden abolition might well prove ruinous. Britain itself, he charged, was responsible for slavery because it consumed four-fifths of American slave-grown cotton. "But are you willing," he asked, "to sacrifice one penny of your own profits for the sake of doing away with this cursed business?" His conclusion was harsh: "The receiver is as guilty as the thief." Most papers reacted with veiled disapproval and several thought he would have been sharply rebuked if he had not been the husband of "Mrs. Beecher-Stowe." But no one would say that his charge was not justified, and it made clear that there was something of the tough-minded Yankee in this Biblical scholar.

Before leaving England, Harriet had a fateful meeting—she visited Lady Byron. That the widow of the great poet should still be alive and that Harriet should visit her seemed as uncanny to her as if she were meeting a figure out of mythology. But finding that Lady Byron was not the coldhearted and priggish wife who had made Byron bitter, but a spiritually sensitive woman, was even more astonishing. Only a brief encounter, it was nonetheless enough for them to discover a deep affinity for each other. Lady Byron's Calvinist piety, which others found objectionable, only ennobled her in Harriet's eyes.

Eager to get back to his own work and weary of acting as his wife's aide-de-camp, Calvin returned to America when Harriet left for the Continent. In France, and later in Switzerland and Germany, she had more time for herself. Thereafter her letters home, published, with extracts from a journal kept by Charles, under the title *Sunny Memories of Foreign Lands*, dwell, like those of any new tourist, on the pleasures and disappointments of museums, cathedrals, mountains, lakes, sightseeing excursions, and unfamiliar customs. In Paris one night, she visited the Jardin Mabille, where couples danced and made assignations under gas lamps hung in the trees, and although she could not approve of the waltz—which, after all, brought bodies into shocking contact—she was beguiled by the carefree atmosphere and the typically Parisian gaiety of the place.

The trip was truly a liberating experience and she tried to respond to it with a worldliness befitting her new stature. Although she was still conservative in her moral judgments, an innate romanticism persuaded her to let down her guard. Most striking were her reactions to art. At first shocked by Rubens's flauntingly fleshly women, she was soon writing rapturously of "great, joyous, full-souled, all-powerful Rubens!" and hailing his revolt against the "cadaverous outlines of womankind painted by his predecessors, the Van Eycks, whose women resemble potato sprouts grown in a cellar." On seeing Rubens's *Descent from the Cross,* she added, "I was lifted off my feet. . . . Art has satisfied me at last." Brave indeed was the daughter of Lyman Beecher when she declared that great artists seem to have "a beauty and worth independent of their moral character. That ethereal power which shows itself in Greek sculpture and Gothic architecture, in Rubens, Shakespeare, and Mozart has a quality to me inexpressibly admirable and lovely. We may say . . . that there is no moral excellence in it, but none the less, we admire it." But the most poignant statement of all, wrenched from her innermost being, is that in New England there is a "long withering of the soul's more ethereal part—a crushing out of the beautiful—which is horrible. Children are born there with a sense of beauty equally delicate with any in the world . . . [but] it dies a lingering death of smothered desire and . . . starvation. I know because I have felt it."

Just as she was seduced by Europe's art, so she was intoxicated by the sensuous rituals—the incense, organ music, stained glass—of the great Catholic cathedrals. Surely, she wrote from Cologne, "there is some part in man that calls for such a service, for such visible images of grandeur and beauty." Rationalizing her heresy, she adds that the wealth spent on such churches was "a sublime . . . protest against materialism." But she was appalled to see poor people in a corner of a cathedral praying to the Virgin in the form of a tinsel-covered doll hung, by those who hoped to be healed, with wax effigies of arms and legs.

Growing homesick at last, she hurried through the cities of Germany and sailed for America early in September.

No writer had ever won such instant fame everywhere. One modern critic explains this by describing *Uncle Tom's Cabin* as like a chemical that brings out the images latent in photographic film. But far from being merely a passive agent, Harriet was a woman with an acute New England conscience, a Puritan capacity to face evil, and the power to give dramatic form to a welter of emotions. She did far more than focus feelings; she aroused them.

But because it is motivated by social and moral convictions, *Uncle Tom's Cabin,* despite all the testimonials of recent critics, has not won the continuing attention given such novels as *The Scarlet Letter, Moby Dick* and *Huckleberry Finn.* Unlike them, it was a plea for a cause, a book with a mission, and once the mission—abolition—was achieved, it became a historical landmark. Too often the moral subverts the art. Social and religious motives fueled her fervor but also overheated her imagination. (Even in her own time, that shrewd critic James Russell Lowell warned Harriet against letting doctrine dominate.) But that is partly why the book appealed to many people who had never read novels; they were not only moved but edified. It was as absorbing as any popular romance and uplifting as well. The remarkable thing is that with all its faults, certain episodes still move us and the message still has meaning.

19

HARRIET

"The little lady who made this big war"

Harriet Beecher Stowe had gone to Europe a famous novelist; she returned to America the leader of a cause. But where Garrison was the fiery militant, Mrs. Stowe was the moderate who still cherished the hope that slaveholders would see the light. She was a leader but not an activist or an organizer: she brought back twenty thousand dollars—a very large sum in 1853—from collections made in Europe, but she had no practical program and used very little of the money in any systematic way.

She did entertain a good deal more than ever before, stirring up and even disturbing staid, seminary-oriented Andover with parties and little concerts and, on one occasion, a "levee" given by her sixteen-year-old twin daughters, Hattie and Eliza, for their school friends. The community seems to have been of two minds about her, partly proud of her presence but a bit jealous of the attention she was getting. She herself was healthier than ever before, probably because of her carefree life abroad but also because fame and fortune had relieved her of the sense of frustration as well as the periods of exhaustion and morbid fears.

She even found an excuse for drinking wine daily. Once when she felt faint in her publisher's office, he revived her with a glass of champagne and then sent her several bottles of Catawba wine. Shortly afterward, she asked him to order a dozen more bottles for her. Later, in a letter to her daughter Hattie, she writes: "The wine I have usually taken at 11 o'clock to be placed *in the dining room closet where I can get at it at 6 o'clock in the morning.*" In a second letter she asks to have the drink after breakfast instead of at 11 o'clock, and another "portion" before her afternoon walk. "The *stimulus,*" she writes, "will be used up in active out-of-door exercise which will strengthen my general health."

Now, as suddenly as a bomb explodes, the South, confident of a majority in Congress, announced that it intended to repeal the Missouri Compromise of 1820. That compromise, which everyone had come to think of as immutable, had fixed the northern limits of slavery in the West at roughly the northern border of Arkansas and on a line westward through northern Oklahoma. In return for this "concession" by the South, Missouri, which was north of the compromise line, had been admitted as a slave state. Now settlers were pouring into the vast territory west of the Missouri River. With the spread of the antislavery mood, induced in part by *Uncle Tom's Cabin,* it was generally thought that any state carved out of the new territory would be free. And not a few Southerners, engaged in the breeding and sale of slaves, saw the territory as a huge new market for their human livestock.

The Southern plan, incorporated in the Kansas-Nebraska Bill, proposed that the territory just west of Missouri and Iowa be divided into two states, Kansas to the south and Nebraska to the north. To make the plan seem democratic, the two states were to be allowed self-determination. But everyone knew that Kansas was being settled mainly by a lawless breed of slaveholders from Missouri. Coming not too long after the Fugitive Slave Bill, the new proposal seemed to Northern antislavery forces an even more barefaced aggression. In a rage, William Lloyd Garrison warned that the South, holding a majority in Congress, had the power to legalize slavery everywhere in the Union. Harriet's first response was an impassioned appeal to the women of America to unite in opposing the bill. Unaccountably putting faith in the power of the church, she had several clergymen draw up a petition against the bill and, with the help of Calvin, her father and her brother Edward, and encouragement from Senator Charles Sumner, who had repeatedly cited *Uncle Tom's Cabin* in his antislavery speeches, she collected the signatures of 3,050 New England clergymen. The petition, two hundred feet long, looked most impressive. But the South had its own loyal clergymen and late in May 1854 the Kansas-Nebraska Bill became a law.

Harriet was busy that summer with visits from her father, Catharine and Charles as part of the family effort to help Lyman, now almost eighty, finish his "autobiography." Avoiding the slavery issue in her writings, she filled her weekly column with pious parables and her contributions to the ladies' magazines with innocuous trifles.

In the November election in the Kansas Territory, lawlessness prevailed: armed men, soon dubbed the Border Ruffians, crossed from Missouri into Kansas and, while President Pierce looked the other way, seized the polls and sent a pro-slavery delegation to Congress.

The year-end holiday season gave Harriet a further excuse for escaping from the ever-increasing tensions of the slavery issue. Another sign, small but clear, of the relaxing of Puritan taboos came when she again had a Christmas tree and decorated her house with holly. But pressures continued to build in the West: In May 1855 the Border Ruffians captured the election of the legislature in Kansas, whereupon the "free-soil" men promptly elected their own legislature. So the territory now had two governments, both armed and ready to fight. It was a prophetic development, a full seven years before the Civil War. Just as ominously, Northern newspapers and churches now urged young men to migrate to Kansas and stand ready to keep it free. Among those who went west were the five sons of a poor, fanatically religious farmer and abolitionist named John Brown.

Meanwhile, with his matchless flair for the dramatic, Henry Ward Beecher was having his Plymouth Church followers dispatch barrels of rifles to Kansas Free-Soilers. At the same time he sent a collection of hymns to the press. Harriet, who had composed one of the hymns, approved of the book; what she thought of the guns we do not know. The vengeful God of the Old Testament was in the ascendant.

Prodded by her publishers to do another novel on slavery and spurred by her ever-increasing sense of mission, Harriet began to write, calling the work *Dred: A Tale of the Great Dismal Swamp*. This time she planned to show the slave system's fearful effect not on the slaves but on the master race. Where she had undertaken *Uncle Tom's Cabin* with the modest intention of "painting pictures," her commitment to a cause now led her into concentrating on the lesson she would teach. In a column in the *Independent* reviewing several antislavery books in 1856, she declared that the use of novels in the great questions of moral life was coming to be one of the features of the age, and added, "A novel is now understood to be a parable—a story told in illustration of a truth or fact." Prohibited from becoming a preacher like all the men in her family, she was trying to convince herself that she could use novels as her pulpit.

Fortunately, once she began work on *Dred,* the painter of pictures took over and she became absorbed once again in the godlike act of creating characters and incidents. To demonstrate the demoralizing effect of slavery on the master class she used the grown daughter and son of a slaveholder. The daughter, Nina, is a charming but heartless flirt. The spoiled darling of the Gordon family, she is faced, after her parents' death, with acting as the mistress of the plantation. Her brother, Tom, is as debauched and insolent a youth as Harriet could conceive. Luckily, Nina has one suitor, Edward Clayton, a young lawyer, who is well-born, high-minded, cultivated and compassionate—in short, everything Harriet admired. When he is ostracized for defending slaves, his nobility points up the debasement of Southern society. Harry, a quadroon, the secret son of Nina's and Tom's father by a mulatto slave, is the all-capable overseer of the plantation—and a replica of George in *Uncle Tom's Cabin.* The lesson is obvious: part-black Harry is all energy and resourcefulness, while pure-white Tom is all corruption and destruction.

Like Uncle Tom, the blacks who claim our attention in the first part of *Dred* are natural Christians. Despite having seen all fourteen of her children sold off, Milly, a majestic serving-woman, teaches Nina to find hope in Christ. Milly was clearly modeled on regal, African-born Sojourner Truth, a famous "preacher" and reformer who visited Harriet in the mid-1850s. Her mystical fervor and personal magnetism had made a profound impression on Harriet. Even more of a true Christian is Old Tiff. Completely faithful to a poor-white family despite their degraded condition, he shines out amidst the decay around him. Again like Uncle Tom, both Milly and Tiff are often too good, wise and forgiving to be believed.

Much as in *Pilgrim's Progress,* each character in *Dred* tends to represent certain virtues or vices: the message is unmistakable but human nature is naively oversimplified. This was the age of Thackeray and George Eliot, and *Dred,* though it has its vivid characters and powerful scenes, is, by comparison, too programmatic, too intent on its moral lessons. Sometimes Harriet abandons the narrative completely, as when she devotes two chapters to a pitilessly satirical picture of several Old School clergymen discussing slavery. Her portrait of the Reverend Dr. Shubael Packthread, described as a leading Northern preacher—and easily identified as the Reverend Joel Parker, whom she had already impaled in a footnote in *Uncle Tom's Cabin*—is worthy of Dickens. Packthread's face, she wrote, was part of his stock-in-trade,

and he understood the management of it remarkably well. He knew precisely all the gradations of smile . . . for accomplishing different purposes. The solemn smile, the smile of inquiry, the smile affirmative, the smile suggestive, the smile of incredulity, and the smile of innocent credulity, which encouraged the simple-hearted narrator to go on unfolding himself to the brother, who sat quietly behind his face, as a spider does behind his web, waiting till his unsuspecting friend had tangled himself in incautious, impulsive, and of course contradictory meshes of statement, which were, in some future hour, in the most gentle and Christian spirit, to be tightened around the incautious captive, while as much blood was sucked as the good of the cause demanded.

It was revenge in full measure for all the trials and harryings of her father and Henry, George and Charles by their Old School foes.

Harriet was halfway through the novel when an act of violence rocked the nation. Her friend Senator Sumner had made a speech, "The Crime Against Kansas," in which he attacked the pro-slavery faction, and particularly an absent senator, Butler of South Carolina, with merciless invective. Considering the speech an intolerable insult to his family and his state, a young relative of Butler's, Congressman Preston Brooks, also of South Carolina, worked himself into an ungovernable rage over it.

On a dark day in American history, while Sumner was writing at his Senate desk just after the close of a session, Brooks came up to him and beat him on the head with a gutta-percha cane until he fell bleeding and unconscious to the floor. "I wore out my cane completely," Brooks remarked later, "but saved the head which is gold." This act, so insolent in its brutality, would send shock waves down the years until it was expiated in the blood of war.

The wrath of the North was boundless. Indignation meetings were held everywhere. Brooks was forced to resign, but his constituents immediately reelected him and presented him with a score of souvenir canes. In Kansas, John Brown, hearkening to the voice of his God, and aided by his sons, butchered five pro-slavery settlers at Pottawatomie Creek. In Brooklyn, Henry Ward Beecher auctioned off attractive slave girls from the pulpit of Plymouth Church. And Harriet changed the entire direction and tone of her novel.

Dred, a black fugitive from the law who speaks in the exalted language of an Old Testament prophet, predicts death and destruction for the white world. Described as a son of Denmark Vesey, who had led a slave insurrection in Charleston in 1822, Dred is literally a voice crying in the wilderness—awe-inspiring and God-obsessed, but little more.

In the second half of the novel, reason and legal argument give way to death and violence. Nina is matured by Clayton's love and Milly's example but dies, rather pointlessly, of cholera. Clayton, like Senator Sumner, is beaten almost to death, Dred is murdered, Harry flees. Tom goes on his atrocious way unpunished; he is obviously a more corrupt version of Preston Brooks, while Dred is Harriet calling on God to punish the wicked and save the innocent. But God is not listening. If the atmosphere in the second half of Dred is that of Elizabethan tragedy, the ending is virtue triumphant: Harry, Milly and Old Tiff escape safely to the North. But the South, ominously, is abandoned to its evil ways.

Even before she had finished the novel Harriet was off to Europe again, this time with Calvin, Henry, the twins and her sister Mary. Who could blame her? Europe had been the scene of her greatest glory as well as the freedom to live without worries about money, a household, or the hounds of a New England conscience.

Dred was published soon after the Stowes reached England. Some of the reviewers there, Harriet herself reported, came down on the book with "waspish spite." But again the demand for copies was great. And again Harriet attributed her success to divine favor: "God, to whom I prayed night and day while I was writing the book, has heard me and given us of worldly goods *more* than I asked." When other reviewers charged her with ridiculing religion, she wrote to Calvin: "One hundred thousand copies ... sold in four weeks! After that who cares what critics say?"

Among the paradoxes in Harriet's personality was a modesty that amounted to pride. It allowed her to play the country mouse, yet spend so much time visiting with British nobility and writing about their castles and clothes as to suggest that her own plain living was hardly a matter of choice. She was apparently disappointed at Queen Victoria's failure to see her (it was later said that a meeting would have implied official recognition of abolitionism), and when she was not invited to a royal reception attended by all her noble friends, she said, rather huffily, "Merely to see public people in public places ... was never interesting to me." Nevertheless, when she and Calvin reached England on their second trip, they let the Queen's emissaries arrange what Calvin termed "just an accidental, done-on-purpose meeting at a railway station, while on our way to Scotland." He reported that they exchanged bows with the Queen and Prince Albert and that the royal children stared wide-eyed at the "little authoress of Uncle Tom's Cabin." A copy of *Dred* was presented to the Queen, but Calvin later protested that neither he nor Harriet had sanctioned that gesture.

Far more significant were Harriet's visits to Lady Byron. The poet's widow, now in her early sixties, was in poor health but the two women at once resumed their intimate relationship. They met repeatedly. Then one day, after they had lunched with Mary and friends, Lady Byron led Harriet into the privacy of another room. Speaking hesitantly, she said that she was going to tell Harriet something about Byron that would shock her beyond measure. She was doing so to clear her own name but also because, she added flatteringly, "I think *you* could have understood him."

She then spoke of a dreadful knowledge that she had lived with all the years since Byron's death—his incestuous relationship with his half sister Augusta Leigh. Harriet had heard the story as a piece of ancient and horrid gossip. But now, hearing it from Lady Byron herself, she was dumbstruck. As Lady Byron talked, lurid images flashed through Harriet's mind and the figure of the poet glowed with a hellish light. For Harriet it was not simply disillusionment—Byron's reputation as a free spirit had after all been part of his glamour—but a shattering blow to a Romantic impulse that had defied all the Puritan warnings. Like her, Byron had been brought up in a Calvinist home: Was this where rebellion led?

Meanwhile Lady Byron was explaining that she had told Harriet the story because the publisher of a new edition of the poet's works would surely revive the old charge that Byron had been driven into exile and death by his wife's cold and selfish nature. She was now faced with agonizing questions and Harriet must help her answer them: Was it not time to expose what she claimed was a monstrous falsehood? Then, piously picturing herself as Byron's redeemer, she asked how the poet's soul could rest in peace till the truth was made known.

Swept by indignation and pity, Harriet immediately saw Lady Byron as a martyr, sacrificed to save the reputation of a lecherous, God-abandoned man. The truth, she declared, must be revealed at once. But when she told Mary the story that night, her sister was appalled by the thought of the scandal that would surely follow. So Harriet asked Lady Byron for more time. Six weeks later she wrote from Paris as solemnly as though it were a state secret: "I would say, then, Leave all with some discreet friends, who, after *both* have passed from earth shall say what was due to justice." It seemed like prudent advice but it would in time return to entangle her disastrously.

Although she went on to spend the winter in France and the spring in Italy ("Rome is an astonishment! Papal Rome is an enchantress!"), she could not put Lady Byron's story out of her mind. On her return to London, she saw the older woman once more and then, just before leaving for America, she wrote her a letter that mingled the spiritual and the romantic just as she had, long before, in letters to Georgiana May and Mary Dutton. "I left you," she began, "with a strange sort of yearning, throbbing feeling—you make me feel quite as I did years ago—a sort of girlishness quite odd for me." She vowed that they would meet after death and love each other eternally. Deceived by the same man, it was as though they were now transferring to each other the adoration they had felt for him.

When Harriet returned to Andover in June 1856, she had been away a year and she was delighted to see the three children who had remained home. She was disappointed that Henry, who had returned from Europe much earlier in order to enter Dartmouth College, was too busy with examinations to meet her.

But everything had gone too well too long. On the evening of July 9, 1857, while Harriet was visiting her friend Susan Howard in Brooklyn, a telegram came from Dartmouth. It brought unbearable news: Henry had drowned while swimming in the Connecticut River in New Hampshire.

The cruelty seemed diabolically calculated: her eldest son and most beloved child, strong, tall and in the full flush of youth—annihilated. She went about in a daze and Calvin took to his bed. When the coffin was lowered into the grave in the cemetery that the seminary provided—as a constant reminder of life's brevity—she longed, she said, to lie down by her son's side.

Uncannily like Catharine's experience thirty-five years earlier, Harriet could at first find no solace in religion or God. It was as if the devil, she wrote to Catharine, was trying to "separate me from the love of Christ." Then, too, the old Calvinist fears, never completely exorcised, surged up from the depths of her being:

The most agonizing doubts of Henry's state were thrown into my mind—as if it had been said to me: You trusted in God, did you? You believed that He loved you! You had perfect confidence that He would never take your child till the work of grace was mature! And now He has turned him out without warning, without a moment's preparation, and where is he?

But Harriet, like Mary Scudder in Harriet's *The Minister's Wooing*, was among those who "never reason abstractly, whose intellections all begin in the heart." Her emotional needs proved stronger than religious doctrines. There were, besides, five other children to care about. So, much sooner than Catharine in 1822, she was able to put aside her doubts and turn to Christ. But there were still periods of depression. As much as a year and a half later, she wrote to her daughter Georgie:

I am cold, weary, dead; everything is a burden to me.

I let my plants die by inches before my eyes, and do not water them, and I dread everything I do . . . so when I get a letter from my little girl I smile and say, "Dear little puss, I will answer it"; and I sit hour after hour . . . looking at the inkstand and dreading to begin. The fact is, pussy, mamma is tired. . . . Henry's fair, sweet face looks down upon me . . . from out a cloud, and I feel again all the bitterness of the eternal "No" which says I must never, never, in this life, see that face, lean on that arm, hear that voice.

Sympathize with Harriet as we may, the letter was, up to that point, a frightening one to send to a sixteen-year-old. Apparently realizing this, Harriet adds:

Not that my faith in God in the least fails, and that I do not believe that all this is for good. I do, and though not happy, I am blessed. Weak, weary as I am, I rest on Jesus in the innermost depth of my soul, and am quite sure that there is coming an inconceivable hour of beauty and glory when I shall regain Jesus, and he will give me back my beloved one.

Still not free of the fear that Henry was damned, Harriet turned to spiritualism in an effort to make contact with him. Close to sisters and brothers who visited mediums, and to Calvin with his visions (he now often saw Eliza, his dead wife) and coming from a home in which an afterlife was an unquestioned reality, she was peculiarly receptive to any promise of communication with the spirit world. Her first article in the

Independent after Henry's death was "Who Shall Roll Away the Stone?" connecting spiritualism with Biblical miracles. But she knew enough about such mediums as the Fox sisters, who in 1848 in upstate New York had popularized "spirit rapping" and table tipping, to be wary of pretenders. She wanted an "unquestionable angel" who could truly roll back the stone at the door of the tomb, and she added that if communion came only in raps on tables and other such "mountebank tricks," she wanted none of it. "If the future life is so weary, stale, flat and unprofitable," she wrote, "as we might infer from these readings," immortality would be intolerable. Skeptical as this seems, she continued to attend séances, looking pathetically for a genuine angel. And spiritualism would be a main subject of her correspondence with another famous author—George Eliot.

The remarkable upsurge of interest in spiritualism that began in the 1830s resulted in part from the increasing rejection of the Calvinist conception of hell. Freed from the straitjacket of fear, a credulous minority began to entertain the notion that the departed were hovering about in some nearby realm, waiting to communicate with those they had left behind. As pictured in Elizabeth Stuart Phelps Ward's tremendously popular postwar novel *The Gates Ajar* (Mrs. Ward was the daughter of a professor at Andover Theological Seminary in the 1850s, when Harriet was there), that realm was simply a mirror of Victorian America but with all the comforts, none of the cares, and as Mark Twain parodies it in *Captain Stormalong Goes to Heaven*, an insufferable bore. To families like the Beechers, in which almost every couple had lost at least one child, it offered irresistible promise of happy reunions. In this respect spiritualism was a characteristically optimistic Victorian answer to Calvinism.

Meanwhile Harriet visited Henry's grave daily—a Puritan would have frowned on such attention to the physical state of the dead—and Calvin often went to it twice a day and wandered around it until he was exhausted.

It was clearly the death of Henry and, long before, of Alexander Metcalf Fisher, both by drowning and both raising the same harrowing questions about the state of the dead person's soul, that led Harriet to undertake *The Minister's Wooing*. That and her need to distinguish the dross from the gold in the Puritan way of life.

The time of the novel is the 1790s but the Puritanism of Jonathan Edwards still dominates. Harriet based her narrative on a story she had heard of an eminent New England divine, Dr. Samuel Hopkins. A pastor in the seaside town of Newport, Rhode Island, long before it became a resort of the wealthy, Hopkins had won the hand of a young woman but had released her when her former suitor turned up and claimed her. Fleshing out this outline, Harriet created a heroine, Mary Scudder, who is a paragon of Puritan devotion and innocence. Even more than that, she is Harriet's effort to show how Calvinism could inspire a truly mystic exaltation. Had she been born in Italy, Harriet declares, she would have lain "entranced in mysterious raptures at the foot of altars"; instead she reads scholarly treatises on the will.

The hero, Jim Marvyn, is an impulsive youth who has decided to go to sea. His irreverence and his thoughtless joy in life fill Mary, his childhood companion, with fears for his soul. The third corner of the triangle is Dr. Hopkins, a boundlessly high-minded minister, a bachelor who looks on romantic love as somewhat foolish and profane. He boards with Mary and her widowed mother, and they revere him. His sermons, learned and metaphysical, enthrall a Mary Scudder but leave a Jim Marvyn unmoved. In what has become a classic description of Calvinism's "rungless ladder" to heaven, Harriet tells us that he conjures up a ladder

whose base God has placed in human affections, tender instincts . . . sacraments of love, through which the soul rises higher and higher, refining as she goes, till she outgrows the human, and changes, as she rises, into the image of the divine. At the very top of this ladder, at the threshold of paradise, blazes dazzling and crystalline that celestial grade where the soul knows self no more. . . . This highest step, this saintly elevation, which but few selectest spirits ever on earth attain . . . for which this world is one long discipline . . . this Ultima Thule of virtue has been seized upon by our sage as the *all* of religion. He knocked out every round of the ladder but the highest, and then, pointing to its hopeless splendor, said to the world, "Go up thither and be saved!"

When word comes that Jim has drowned at sea, Mary is stricken, but submissive to the will of God, she carries on. It is Jim's mother who rebels. Her intellectual inclinations, Harriet says, surely thinking of Catharine, have unfitted her for "regions where spiritual intuitions are as necessary as wings to birds." In a frenzy of grief, Mrs. Marvyn cries:

"I must speak or die! Mary, I can not, will not, be resigned!—it is all hard, unjust, cruel!—to all eternity I will say so! To me there is no goodness, no justice, no mercy in anything! Life seems to me the most tremendous doom that can be inflicted on a helpless being! . . . Brides should wear mourning—the bell should toll for every wedding. . . ."

She is Harriet as well as Catharine, raging against the unbearable annihilation of their loved ones. Harriet prepares us for the bitterness of this outburst by a chapter on New England Calvinism. It may not be good fiction but it is an extraordinarily sensitive account of the Puritan code. Of the earliest New Englanders Harriet declares that there never was a community where the roots of common life were "so intensely grappled around things sublime and eternal." In the intervals of planting and harvesting, she writes, "They were busy . . . adjusting the laws of the universe. Solemnly simple, they made long journeys in their old one-horse chaises to settle with each other some nice point of celestial jurisprudence, and to compare their maps of the Infinite." But a system in which every human being was presumed to be born under God's wrath and curse affected certain minds like "a slow poison." While "some strong spirits walked, palm-crowned . . . along sublime paths, feebler or more sensitive ones lay . . . bleeding away in lifelong despair."

Although Mrs. Marvyn repeats Catharine Beecher's anguished "there must be dreadful mistakes somewhere," she is at last reconciled through a vision of Jesus brought to her by Candace, the Marvyns' cook. With a rich, native wisdom, Candace, like several other blacks in Harriet's stories, softens and humanizes Calvinism with large doses of simple feeling. The Platonic love between Mary and the minister, directed by Mrs. Scudder, moves them to marriage. But on the eve of the wedding, with no regard for credibility, Harriet brings Jim Marvyn back not only well but rich and full of Christian faith.

Mary's joy is of course great; that is why her decision that she is nevertheless bound to marry the minister is so stunning a statement of Puritan values: "Self-denial and self-sacrifice had been the daily bread of her life. Every prayer, hymn and sermon . . . had warned her to distrust her inclinations and regard her feelings as traitors." Neither Mary nor her mother sees any spiritual deception in Mary's marrying one man while she loves another. It takes the simplehearted, gossipy dressmaker, Miss Prissy, to tell the truth to the minister. Virtually a disembodied spirit, he, matching Mary sacrifice for sacrifice, relinquishes her.

Only one person in the book, aside from Candace, perceives how excessive is Mary's submissiveness: Virginie de Frontignac, the young wife of a French aristocrat who is visiting a Newport planter. Joyful, impulsive, passionate—and Catholic—she is unimaginably exotic against the New England background. The two young women also anticipate a favorite theme of Henry James, the contrast between American innocence and European worldly wisdom. Virginie sees the error in Mary's course—but she herself goes to the other extreme, throwing herself at the feet of a famous political figure, Aaron Burr.

Clearly using what she has learned about Byron from Lady Byron, Harriet paints Burr as a hypnotically fascinating mixture—brilliant, charming and gifted, yet heartless and unscrupulous, especially in love. Having abandoned the religion of his grandfather Jonathan Edwards, he seems to illustrate the dangers of both religious overindoctrination and complete rejection. Where St. Clare, Harriet's Byronic figure in *Uncle*

Tom's Cabin, has many redeeming features and dies reconciled to Christ, Burr remains a child of Satan. (As we have since learned, Aaron Burr was indeed sexually a satyr.) Although Virginie's advice to Mary—that true love should not be denied—makes her appear wiser than Mary, the superiority of the New England code is, we suppose, demonstrated when Mary saves Virginie from her enslavement to Burr.

Both Virginie and Burr appear curiously out of place in *The Minister's Wooing* until we realize that each character in the book represents a different relationship to the Calvinist creed. Thrusting through the rarefied air near the summit of faith are Mary and the minister. Not far off is Candace, moving securely along with her gospel of love; elsewhere, clinging by her fingertips to the cliff face, is Mrs. Marvyn; then there is Jim, groping manfully for the true path; Mrs. Scudder, a proper Pilgrim, looking neither right nor left; and finally Burr, headed toward the abyss.

As a picture of New England religious types, *The Minister's Wooing* is impressive. It is the plot that disappoints. Jim's failure to communicate with family or friends during his long absence, his opportune return, converted to Christ as well as rich, and the minister's acceptance of his eleventh-hour displacement (the historical Dr. Hopkins was a young man and soon married someone else) are equally unconvincing. In the end, true love conquers all—including Calvinism. In her treatment of New England types and customs, Mrs. Stowe could be a realist; as a storyteller she was too often seduced by the traditions of Victorian romantic fiction.

But just as the narrative of *Uncle Tom's Cabin*, with all its melodrama, rallied the opposition to slavery, so the love story in *The Minister's Wooing* proved an attractive medium for the message: the book went through forty printings. The sense of the message was that the old religion was an invaluable discipline, a tempering by fire, but only for a few "strong spirits" such as Mary Scudder and the minister. The strength bred in Mary by her creed is captured in a memorable image: "Aerial in her delicacy, as the blue-eyed flax-flower with which they sowed their fields, she had yet its strong fiber, which no stroke of the flail could break; bruising and hackling only made it fitter for uses of homely utility." As for weaker spirits, they languished "in lifelong despair," among "shadows that lay over the cradle and the grave."

The Minister's Wooing gave such vivid expression to a spreading discontent with the more austere aspects of Calvinism that it was criticized by clergymen. But anyone outside the church establishment must have realized that it was at the same time a tribute to the pure spirituality of the old religion and its courage in confronting pain and death.

The clearest evidence that Calvinism was in full retreat was that it could be freely satirized. It was Harriet's new friend Dr. Oliver Wendell

Holmes who brought to bear his wit and common sense to riddle the extremes of dogma. Holmes's father was, like Harriet's, a Calvinist minister, but Holmes's training as a physician and in the sciences had made him utterly impatient with such doctrines as original sin. So in 1858, in his "The Deacon's Masterpiece," he had described Edwards's Calvinism in terms of a certain parson's "one-hoss shay." It was, he wrote, "built in such a logical way/It ran a hundred years to a day" and then, because it had no weak spot,

> ... went to pieces all at once,—
> All at once, and nothing first,—
> Just as bubbles do when they burst.

Humorous verse, apparently meant only to amuse, it dissolved dogma with laughter.

Harriet was now a prominent literary figure. When a young Bostonian, Francis Underwood, decided to establish an antislavery magazine featuring literary contributors, he quickly gained the cooperation of Holmes, Lowell, Whittier and Longfellow. But the publisher hesitated to proceed unless he could get a serial by Mrs. Stowe. Lowell and Underwood visited the Stowes and easily persuaded Harriet to join them. The magazine, soon named the *Atlantic Monthly*, picked up circulation sharply as soon as *The Minister's Wooing* began to appear in it.

While at the Stowes', Lowell remarked to Calvin how very lively and ready of speech his children were. Calvin proudly responded, "Yes. Beechers every one of them!" Lowell found something touching in his self-effacement, his resignation to being known as "Mrs. Stowe's husband." But that gives us a much too pathetic view of Calvin Stowe. Very different was the impression of crusty Samuel Bowles, who knew him some years later: "Big, burly, sledge-hammery, with a loud voice and a good deal of intellectual power.... He looks like one class of German professor,—poor clothes, red nose, opinionated, and wise; or an old-fashioned country New England tavern-keeper, the oracle of the village."

It is easy now to see how inexorable was the march of events toward war. In Kansas, the border bands avenged John Brown's slaughter of proslavery settlers by murdering a few of his followers, including one of his sons. In 1857 the Supreme Court, with Justice Taney, a Southern slaveholder, presiding, delivered the Dred Scott decision, another blow to the antislavery cause. It declared that a Negro had no legal rights and remained only a piece of property no matter where in the United States his owner took him. The Northern states responded by declaring the Fugitive Slave Bill unconstitutional and forbidding anyone to help enforce it.

In Illinois in 1858, a lanky prairie lawyer, Abraham Lincoln, was nominated for the Senate by the new Republican party. In debates with the Democratic candidate, dynamic little Stephen Douglas, Lincoln stated his position unforgettably: "A house divided against itself cannot stand. I believe this government cannot endure permanently half *slave* and half *free*. . . ." Later he moderated his position, but Southerners had already marked him down as a threat. Douglas straddled the issue and won the election.

But no one reckoned with the fanatics. Seeing himself as a burning brand in the hand of the Lord, John Brown was moved to lead.a slave revolt, convinced that great numbers of blacks would rally behind him. On October 16, 1859, he fell upon and captured the United States arsenal at Harpers Ferry, Virginia. Not a single slave joined him. At first the reaction in the North was one of condemnation. But the response of the South soon changed that. An officer named Robert E. Lee laid siege to the arsenal and recaptured it quickly, killing most of Brown's men and seriously wounding Brown himself. Virginia tried, convicted and hanged Brown within two months. That was meant to teach the North and all slaves a lesson, but it served only to make a martyr out of Brown. Before a large audience in Boston's Tremont Temple, Ralph Waldo Emerson hailed Brown as a new saint.

Traveling in Europe and hearing only of Brown's mad courage and calm death, Harriet wrote that the entire country under martial law could not "subdue the tremor caused by his great quiet spirit." She was right. John Brown's body would go marching on, doing more than any political act to fill the North—and the South too—with the will and the anger to engage in civil war. He was a fanatic who served a great purpose.

When a radical abolitionist, Joshua R. Giddings, defended Brown's raid, an ad in the Richmond *Whig* offered ten thousand dollars for Giddings, dead or alive.

After finishing *The Minister's Wooing*, Harriet again fled to Europe and, as in a lotus land, again stayed for almost a year. In Florence, an acquaintance with Elizabeth Barrett Browning ripened into friendship when they found that they were both interested in spiritualism. In Florence too, while she was visiting a "very powerful medium" and had a feeling that her Henry was close by, a guitar on the wall was plucked loudly and later strummed, whereupon the medium declared that she had asked the spirits for such a sign. Attempting to justify her interest in such a demonstration, she wrote to Calvin that spiritualism was "a reaction from the intense materialism of the present age" and that the "real Scriptural spiritualism" should be revived through persons especially sensitive to "impressions of the surrounding spiritual world." She avoided making such opinions public, knowing that some of her admirers would reject them, perhaps with scorn.

In Rome Harriet was entranced by the papal pageantry during Holy Week, but it was the exotic and history-encrusted countryside as well as the people farther south, especially around Sorrento and Amalfi, that stirred her imagination most powerfully. Inspired by a beautiful girl selling oranges in Sorrento, Harriet suggested that her entire party collaborate in making up a story about a saintly peasant girl. The others gave up when Harriet with amazing fluency poured out several episodes. Carried away by the praise of her companions, she promised to complete *Agnes of Sorrento,* as she named it, when she returned home.

On her trip to Europe three years earlier, Harriet had met John Ruskin, the English art critic, and they had quickly formed an intimate friendship. They had corresponded cordially in the interval and now they appeared to have carried the relationship to a point that has piqued the curiosity of biographers. Months later, when Harriet embarked from London while Ruskin was in Geneva, he wrote her a letter referring to how "cruelly pleasant" she had been to him and expressing acute regret at having missed seeing her again. The fact that she gave this letter to her son Charles only when he was writing her biography near the end of her life has suggested that the relationship aroused stronger feelings than she cared to acknowledge. But she was forty-eight at the time (eight years older than Ruskin) and with her scruples and his sexual problems, the relationship could hardly have been more than a titillating friendship.

Harriet returned in June 1860 to an America in which regional hatred had taken over. The issue in the South was no longer simply opposition to abolitionism or a desire to see slavery extended, but freedom from Northern criticism and denunciation as well as the increasing threat of Northern economic domination. When Abraham Lincoln, homespun "Honest Abe" to the North but an "ape" to the South, was elected President in November 1860, the states of the lower South were filled with a perverse satisfaction: the North, they said, had given them no alternative but secession. In February 1861 the delegates of seven Deep South states voted to secede and set up the Confederate States of America. Colt revolver and Sharps rifle factories were already working overtime. As markets were cut off, the price of slaves dropped by half or more. Before Lincoln took office, the secretary of war, a Southerner, surreptitiously shipped 65,000 rifles from Northern arsenals to Southern depots. President Buchanan cast impotently about for a compromise solution, and in preparation for the inauguration turned Washington into an armed camp.

Harriet was busy with matters far removed from sectional discord and the threat of war. In Europe she had become friendly with a sympathetic publisher, James T. Fields, and his gifted, beautiful young wife,

Annie. Annie Fields, who would remain Harriet's lifelong friend, later wrote that she and her husband first saw Harriet as "wrapped about . . . with a kind of sacred awe." Now Fields was succeeding Lowell as editor of the *Atlantic,* and Harriet arranged with him to publish *Agnes of Sorrento,* first as a serial and then as a book.

Out of Harriet's visits to lovely old homes in Europe came another undertaking—a series of articles on ways to beautify American homes. She sold this project to the bright young managing editor of the *Independent,* Theodore Tilton, a protégé of Henry Ward's. But Tilton also wanted fiction from Mrs. Stowe. Recalling a story of Maine coast people that she had started in 1853, she promised him a serial called *The Pearl of Orr's Island.*

Then, too, there were her children. The twins, Hattie and Eliza, were twenty-seven now. Having devoted themselves as housekeepers and secretaries to their mother, they seemed resigned, though they were elegant and pretty, to becoming old maids. Despite their devotion to her, they were of another, more self-indulgent generation, and Harriet repeatedly chided them for not taking on enough of her burdens or working as hard as she did. When the two young women went to Paris in 1859 or to rest cures, she harried them with endlessly preachy letters not unlike those her father had fired off to all his children in their formative years. Even though she herself had joined in mimicking some of the uncouth missionaries they had met, she scolded them when they ridiculed any servant of religion for any reason.

We also know now that Fred Stowe, undersized and not robust, had problems, especially with liquor, well before the war. He was not even seventeen when the Stowes, worried by his drinking, put him in the care of Harriet's brother Thomas, who was boarding at Gleason's water cure in Elmira while he served in the local Congregational church. Early in 1857 Thomas reported that Fred had made too many undesirable acquaintances in Elmira and had been taken to Glen Haven, a completely isolated retreat, and would remain there until he was abstinent.

Apparently Fred recovered, at least temporarily. When he finally agreed to study medicine, Harriet, zealous mother, called on Oliver Wendell Holmes to help him get started at Harvard Medical School, where Dr. Holmes taught anatomy.

The twins, together with Georgiana, a vivacious seventeen-year-old, and Charley, ten, as well as their friends, filled the Stowe house with life.

Although Lincoln's inaugural address was firm, putting the Union above everything else, it did not threaten slavery in the slave states. Yet when he sent ships to supply Fort Sumter, off the Charleston coast, Southern guns on the mainland fired on the fort. Suddenly—too suddenly for its full significance to be appreciated—the civil war had begun.

Even before the call for volunteers, Fred Stowe, obviously oversensitive to being the son of Harriet Beecher Stowe, wanted to leave his medical studies and enlist. But Harriet decided that he was not strong enough spiritually or physically to be "a mere soldier." Trying to explain her muddled views, she wrote to her daughter Hattie: "It is not that I would not give my son's life, but [it is] the temptations and dangers of the camp and the fears that . . . obtrude of his being prisoner of barbarians or wounded and helpless." So Fred tried to go as a surgeon, that is, as a medical officer. He was turned down and immediately left Harvard and joined the first company of the Massachusetts Volunteer Infantry.

Soon four or five other Beechers, including Harriet's half brother James, were in uniform. Without a qualm, she wrote in the *Independent*: "this is a cause to die for and—thanks be to God!—our young men embrace it as a bride and are ready to die." Because it was a war for a cause she had espoused—with God's convenient cooperation—this otherwise mild little woman did not hesitate to send the youth of the nation into battle. She had no idea, she later admitted, of the price they would pay. So she watched with pride as Andover students began to drill on the campus in front of the Stone Cabin, and she was thrilled when she heard their impromptu marching song—it would soon inspire Julia Ward Howe to give it its classic form—which began "John Brown's body lies a-mould'ring in the grave" and ended: "Glory, glory, hallelujah! His soul's marching on."

Everyone on both sides was sure the war would be short.

Then came the reality. When a blockade of Southern ports virtually closed down British cotton mills, the British, including Harriet's erstwhile antislavery admirers, blamed the North and predicted the success of the "rebellion." Aghast at such treachery, Harriet wrote: "O England, England! What, could ye not watch with us one hour?" and thereafter strove, along with Henry, to turn British opinion around.

The debacle at the battle of Bull Run, only fifteen miles from Washington, awoke the North from its dream.

Imperiously, Harriet declared that only a general emancipation would save the day. Without any responsibility for what she recommended, she ignored the fears of Lincoln and others that emancipation would alienate the border states and lead to a black reign of terror in the South. When General John Charles Frémont, glamorous "Pathfinder" of western exploration and the Republican Presidential candidate in 1856, a headstrong man, began to free slaves in the territories he conquered, Harriet and the abolitionists exulted; but when Lincoln relieved him of his command because he had acted outside the law, their anger burned high. Calvin Stowe wrote a virulent letter to his friend Salmon P. Chase, now a member of Lincoln's cabinet, accusing the administration of rewarding imbecility and treachery and punishing success. Lincoln listened and endured.

Harriet was meanwhile trying to work on two novels at once. The *Independent* began publishing *The Pearl of Orr's Island* early in 1861, and shortly afterward the first installments of *Agnes of Sorrento* appeared in the *Atlantic*. Convinced that *Agnes* was a masterpiece and *The Pearl* only run-of-the-mill, she was annoyed when Fields showed no enthusiasm for *Agnes* while Tilton was proud to have snared *The Pearl*. Again the judgment of her editors was far more reliable than hers. Dismissing these reactions, Harriet read parts of *Agnes* to her family and when they applauded, she determined to finish it. It was her "little darling," she wrote to Fields. "I have a pleasure in writing *Agnes of Sorrento* that gilds this icy winter weather. I write my Maine story with a shiver, and come back to this as to a flowery home where I love to rest."

It was more than climate that led her to write a novel on Italy in the time of Savonarola. Italy had become a favorite of British and American expatriates, and Italian themes had become fashionable, attracting such writers as Browning, George Eliot, Ruskin, Cooper and Hawthorne. Unfortunately, Harriet knew little about the Italian people. *Agnes of Sorrento* is thus a New England woman's fantasy of Renaissance life, a tedious tale in which lowly Agnes, an ideal embodiment of religious faith, with all the makings of a saint, incurs the wrath of the corrupt churchmen of Rome. She is saved by a mountain bandit who turns out, as in a fairy tale, to be a nobleman ruined by his papal enemies; Agnes in turn brings him back to Christ. Virtually without plot, the novel is pieced out with descriptions of the Amalfi countryside, Agnes's naiveté, and papal depravity. Seeing Savonarola as a Puritan reformer, it was easy for Harriet to relate to him. She responded equally to the rich texture of the Catholic tradition, from old Latin hymns to frescoed monasteries. She even found a virtue in the confessional, with its relief for the troubled, and in monasteries and convents as a physical as well as spiritual refuge. She had come a long way from her father's bitter broadsides against the Catholic power. Published in June of 1862, *Agnes of Sorrento* offered a completely romantic escape from the realities of war. Although it was recognized as something less than a masterpiece, it sold an astonishing 400,000 copies in the United States alone.

By contrast, *The Pearl of Orr's Island* has at least a basic authenticity. Set on an island off the Maine coast at Brunswick, it is, particularly in the first half, a sympathetic narrative of life in an old-time, sea-oriented, Bible-saturated New England community. In its picture of the order and serenity of such a place it is a nostalgic view of the stability that

Harriet obviously thought the old religion fostered. If the people seem too familiar, they do so because they are the originals of a long line of fictional characters. (Sarah Orne Jewett, later distinguished for her own faithful novels of Maine life, acknowledged *The Pearl* as a rich source of inspiration.) Here are old sea captains, mostly retired and rather mellow—the kind that Mrs. Stowe would be most likely to know; their wives, pious, sensible, and in all things thrifty; the old maid, Roxy, all angles, sharp-tongued and domineering, but strong in that all-round competence called "faculty," and her contrasting sister, the plump, ever agreeable Ruey; and flirtatious Sally Kittridge, who plays cat and mouse with all the young men but will, we are sure, mend her ways before very long.

As different as *The Minister's Wooing, Agnes of Sorrento* and *The Pearl of Orr's Island* are in many respects, the romantic relationship of the young lovers in all three is so similar that we detect in it the fantasizing of a woman who has herself never had such a relationship. We cannot help thinking that Harriet, married to a pudgy, aging Biblical scholar, repeatedly made her heroes bold young men spoiling for action because that is what the romantic tradition had taught her they should be. In his energy and ambition and his impatience with religion, the hero of *The Pearl*, Moses Pennel, is like Jim of *The Minister's Wooing* and, to a lesser degree, Agostino, the bandit-nobleman of *Agnes of Sorrento*. The heroine, Mara, "the pearl," is a self-sacrificing, God-adoring spirit, not of this world. She had grown up worshiping Moses and hoping—as Mary Scudder with Jim, and Agnes with Agostino—to save him for Christ. But Moses, like Jim, goes off to sea unconverted.

When *The Pearl of Orr's Island* was announced by Tilton in the *Independent*, Harriet rebuked him roundly for advertising it as "Mrs. Stowe's great story," and she herself described it—surely as compared with *Agnes of Sorrento*, which she had finished at the same time—as "pale and colorless as real life and sad as truth." Nevertheless she had been building up to it in sketch after sketch and in sundry characters in her other novels. So we are fully prepared for *The Pearl*'s mixture of realism, sentimentality and homely humor, its command of local speechways and even its morbid intimacy with death. But we also note an almost obsessive emphasis on the spiritual life, on faith in Christ and the promise of life after death. And yet there is at the same time very little of the rigorous religion formulated by Edwards: even the local minister is portrayed as a diffident and tolerant soul, very skillful at skirting the rocks of dogma.

The spiritual quality is most evident in Mara, who stands somewhere between the vacuous innocence of little Eva and the learned saintliness of Mary Scudder. She suffers silently as Moses toys with Sally

Kittridge and then sails away. By the time he returns, he has come to realize what a pearl Mara is, but it is too late—she has begun to die of consumption.

Harriet acknowledges that the reader, expecting a happy ending, will be disappointed. Such endings, she says, are unrealistic. But just as we are beginning to admire this courageous stand, she leads us into a long-drawn-out account of the bliss of Mara's final days. In Mara, as in little Eva and Uncle Tom, faith in Christ has magically transformed the early Puritan fear of hell into a welcoming of death as a paradisal sanctuary. Harriet might have pointed out that in their last moments her mother, Roxana, her stepmother, Harriet, and Calvin's first wife, Eliza, had all been similarly convinced that they were going on to eternal bliss. But as the ending of a novel in which separated lovers have just been reunited, it makes us frustrated victims of Harriet's evangelistic messages.

After a winter lull in the fighting, a Northern general named Grant, an unkempt, taciturn, fiercely tenacious commander, emerged in the West, capturing Fort Henry, Fort Donelson and Nashville, and driving back General Beauregard at Shiloh. But when the North's Army of the Potomac suffered a setback at Chickahominy in July 1862, Lincoln's critics once again clawed at him mercilessly. Harriet, a preacher hurling Biblical threats, exclaimed: "How many plagues must come on us before we will hear the evident voice, 'Let this people go, that they may serve me!'" God's spokeswoman, she ordered Lincoln to "obey the voice of the Lord." Challenged by two great objectives but never hesitating in his choice, Lincoln answered such attacks with inexhaustible patience: "My paramount object . . . *is* to save the Union and *is not* either to save or destroy slavery. What I do about Slavery . . . I do because I believe it helps to save this Union, and what I forbear I forbear because I do not believe it would help to save the Union. . . ."

Harriet responded—in the *Independent*—as though there were but one solution to America's problems. Almost contemptuously she turned Lincoln's statement inside out: "My paramount object . . . is to set at liberty them that are *bruised* and *not* either to save or destroy the Union. What I do in favor of the Union, I do because it helps to free the oppressed."

She who had so often complained of poor health and deep fatigue hammered away tirelessly at the administration. The modest little housewife had become not only the savior of the oppressed but the instructor of Presidents, eloquent and imperious: "Alas, our sons will be slain not because our God was cruel, but because He was good; not because He was angry with them, but because our Commander-in-Chief would hold them in the very way of God's thunderbolts, in the whistling path of His glittering spear." No wonder that when she received a sympathetic letter from the Duchess of Argyll, Harriet wrote a tormented answer, denouncing as "pious humbugs" the British antislavery group that had abandoned the Northern cause. But still harboring a snobbish admiration for British nobility, she described Prince Albert as having been "the ideal knight, the Prince Arthur of our times, the good, wise, steady head and heart *we*—that is, our world, we Anglo-Saxons, need so much."

In the *Independent,* which he now edited, her brother Henry, who had at first supported Lincoln, soon joined Harriet in clamoring for emancipation and, outdoing her, for the drafting of another million men. The moment finally came, in September 1862, after the strong Union stand at Antietam, when Lincoln decided he could safely issue the Emancipation Proclamation. It was to take effect on January 1 if the South did not surrender. All but the most fanatical abolitionists were satisfied. And at last Harriet felt she could answer those shameless English turncoats without quibble or apology, and perhaps with a touch of malice for their faithlessness.

But some doubters were asserting that if the South came back into the Union, Lincoln would not sign the proclamation. So Harriet concluded that she must see for herself what Lincoln's intentions were. "I mean," she wrote to Fields, "to have a talk with 'Father Abraham' himself."

She took one of her twins, Hattie, as well as twelve-year-old Charley with her and used her influence to get a special pass for Fred so that he could meet her in Washington. He had won a battlefield commission and she was pleased to see how he had matured: a year and a half before, in his first uniform, several sizes too large for him, he had seemed pathetic.

Isabella had also come to Washington and she joined Harriet and her children in the visit to the President. The meeting with Lincoln lasted, it is said, a "brief hour." As they shook hands, the contrast between that sparrow-small woman and that crane-tall man must have seemed bizarre. "So this," Lincoln is supposed to have said, "is the little lady who made this big war." There is no record of what they talked about, but Harriet apparently left the meeting persuaded that the President was a good and great man. And she was humbled at last by the realization of the weight of his cares as compared with hers. All that young Charley recalled was that the President, rubbing his hands before an open fire, had said, "I do love a fire in a room. I suppose it's because I always had one to home." Afterwards, Charley asked why the President had said "to home" instead of "at home." Quoting Saint Paul, Harriet answered: " 'Though I be rude in speech yet not in knowledge; but we have been thoroughly made manifest among you in all things.' "

But if we are to trust a neglected letter by daughter Hattie to her twin sister, Eliza, it was all so funny that they nearly "exploded" with laughter. " . . . we succeeded in getting through with it without disgracing ourselves," she writes. "But . . . we gave free vent to our feelings when we were safe in our rooms. There we perfectly screamed . . . [with] pent-up laughter." It was an unretouched view of a historic meeting.

Hesitating no longer, Harriet finished her "Reply to the Affectionate and Christian Address of British Woman." It was an eloquent document, reproachful but restrained, and if anyone had been listening to reason, it would have been compelling. But few were listening. Harriet never went back to England. (Henry Ward would be, as we shall see, far more successful abroad.)

On January 1, 1863, an Emancipation Jubilee—actually a prayer service—was held in Boston Music Hall to welcome word of the signing of the Proclamation. Harriet was there, modestly seated in the balcony. Emerson read his poem "Boston Hymn," and then news of the signing came. Amidst a great outburst of cheering, weeping and kissing, someone began calling, "Mrs. Stowe! Mrs. Stowe!" The crowd immediately took up the cry, suddenly recalling that this woman, long years before, had put together words that had touched the heart of the world and led to this moment. Hands pushed her toward the balcony rail, a small, middle-aged woman with a shawl across her shoulders and her hat askew. She looked down at the cheering throng with tears filling her eyes. After that, all would be anticlimax.

Many things came to an end in those midwar years. Early in 1863 Lyman Beecher died. Because he was very old, had lost touch with the world and had presumably gone to a better life, there was little mourning. Lady Byron and Elizabeth Barrett Browning were also gone. In the late spring Calvin taught his last class and retired, presumably to concentrate on his great work on the origins of the Bible. Harriet would have been sorry to leave the Stone Cabin, so closely associated with her years of glory, had it not meant that she could move back to Hartford, where Mary and Isabella lived. It also meant that she could realize a dream she had when, as schoolgirls, she and Georgiana May had strolled in a lovely grove on the bank of the Park River—a dream of someday living there in a beautiful home. Even though the city and its factories were already encroaching on the area, Harriet impulsively bought four and a half acres of woodland and began to plan a mansion built to her heart's desire.

But the war was not so easily put aside. There were dreadful losses at Fredericksburg and Chancellorsville, and horrifying tales of atrocities on both sides. And when the first general conscription bill was passed in

March, there were riots in New York, starting among the poor, whose young men could not afford to pay three hundred dollars for a substitute conscript.

Finally cheering news did come—of great victories at Gettysburg in the East and Vicksburg in the West. But any rejoicing in the home of the Stowes was short-lived: a heart-chilling newspaper list of casualties and then a letter from an army chaplain notifying them that Captain Stowe had been wounded at Gettysburg—struck in the right ear by a shell fragment. Although the chaplain added that Fred was resting quietly and a telegraph from a nephew, Robert Beecher, said Fred would soon be sent home, Calvin, frantic, took the first train to Gettysburg. But he was robbed—of $130, he said—by a gang of a pickpockets in the Springfield railroad station, fell ill, and crept sheepishly home.

Fred's wound never healed completely, and after he had spent months in army hospitals, Harriet helped him get a discharge. But something had happened to him besides the physical wound. We know from a letter he had written to Calvin in March 1863 that he had been drinking too much. But whether, as the family claimed, the open wound had left him more vulnerable to the effects of alcohol or he had also suffered a traumatic shock, he became a drunkard. Time after time he came home reeling and stupefied, shocking the sober seminary community and driving Harriet to every kind of effort to cure him. Years later, in a novel, *My Wife and I,* she would describe the agony of those who watch helplessly as the spirit of a dear one is broken by drink. Harriet could accept the wound as God's will, but no one ever knew how she, daughter of a leader in the temperance movement, coped with the shame of having a son who was a drunkard.

The Beecher family would come to know the horrors of war full well that summer of 1863: Lieutenant Frederick Beecher, Charles's eldest son, was also wounded at Gettysburg—and almost fatally.

Fortunately Harriet had learned to live on several levels. While the war dragged on and death haunted every home that had someone in the service, she busied herself with the building of her villa and, as a by-product, with contributions to the *Atlantic* on homemaking and decorating. Indulging her whims, she provided her new house with an abundance of gables, verandas, piazzas and bay windows, with oak paneling, statuary, ornate mantelpieces and, as a climax, a study looking out into a two-story conservatory containing plants and a fountain. "Tell Mrs. Fields," she wrote to James Fields, "that my house with *eight* gables is growing wonderfully, and that I go over every day to see to it. I am busy with drains, sewers, sinks, digging, trenching, and above all, with manure! You should see the joy with which I gaze on manure-heaps in which the eye of faith sees Delaware grapes and d'Angouleme pears and all sorts of roses and posies." The twins, their judgment fortified by their European experience, were an excellent sounding board, but Calvin, now without any income of his own, was appalled by the cost. Even after they moved into the house, in May 1864, unexpected expenses continued for years, with the plumbing a constant source of trouble. One winter night, the water pipes over Calvin's bed burst and the professor surged out of his room roaring, "Oh yes, all the modern conveniences! Shower baths while you sleep!"

In March, Grant, now general in chief, came east and began his hammering, bloody (eighteen thousand men lost in the Wilderness and twelve thousand at Spottsylvania five days later) and finally irresistible drive against Lee.

But Harriet found many ways to keep her mind off the devastation: twenty-one-year-old Georgie was being courted by a most eligible suitor, the Reverend Henry Allen, handsome, learned and well-to-do rector of the Episcopal Church of Stockbridge, Massachusetts; visitors came to the house with all kinds of appeals and offers; a new juvenile magazine, *Our Young Folks* (which eventually became the famous *St. Nicholas Magazine*), lured Harriet into contributing a leading piece every month. Out of the latter she accumulated material for four very successful children's books.

Now, too, she moved over into the Episcopal Church. Her twins and her sister Catharine had already done so and her ties with the Presbyterians had been broken by her father's death and Calvin's retirement from Andover Theological Seminary. But the shift had a deeper significance: her discontent with Calvinist austerity, heightened by her exposure to the Catholicism of Europe, and even more important, her freedom after her father's death to acknowledge her mother's spiritual influence by returning to Roxana's church. The move was made without fanfare but we must not underestimate it. The dominant religious figure in her life had been Lyman Beecher, a late Puritan but still a Puritan. By entering the Episcopal Church she and Catharine took a great step in the retreat from Calvinism to what skeptical Ellery Davenport in Harriet's *Oldtown Folks* would describe as "a nice old motherly Church, that sings to us, and talks to us, and prays with us, and takes us in her lap, and cuddles us when we are sick and says—'Hush, my dear, lie still and slumber.' "

At last Southern power and the Southern spirit began to crumble. (If might was on the side of right, it had taken an eternity to make itself felt.) Sherman savaged his way through Atlanta to the sea, and Grant battered Lee into submission. The curtain came down on the tragedy in a stark tableau at Appomattox Court House on April 9, 1865. To the endless—and justified—pride of the Beechers, Lincoln selected Henry Ward

Beecher to make the address when the American flag was raised again over Fort Sumter.

But the god of Violence had one more trick to play, changing a time of thanksgiving into one of horror: Abraham Lincoln was assassinated six days after the peace.

A month later Harriet published a tribute to the dead President that belatedly made some amends for her earlier misjudgment:

The kind, hard hand that held the helm so steadily . . . the fatherly heart that bore all our sorrows . . . and God, looking down . . . was so well pleased with his humble faithfulness, his patient continuance in well-doing, that . . . He reached down and took him to immortal glories. . . . He has been . . . a new kind of ruler in the earth. There has been something even unearthly about his extreme unselfishness, his utter want of personal ambition, personal self-valuation, personal feeling.

But the poignancy of these lines is almost destroyed when we learn that Harriet suggested to the publisher that if he combined it with a piece she had written on Andrew Johnson and issued them in "a little book with mourning decorations," it might sell thousands of copies. . . .

Perhaps, it was her changed attitude toward Lincoln along with her acceptance of atrocity stories such as those of the torture and starvation of Union prisoners in Southern jails that made her fiercely vindictive. Hardly had peace come when she wrote a bitter article for the *Atlantic* describing the "martyrdom of a Christian boy" from Andover in a Southern prison. In the accompanying letter to Fields, she heaped scorn on the "false, mawkish pseudo-talk of humanity and magnanimity to these cruel assassins, Davis and others." Even for a woman tormented by what had happened to her son, it was a singularly ferocious outburst.

Only Henry among the Beechers advocated leniency—and thereby antagonized any number of Radical Republicans. Soon Harriet, swayed by her brilliant brother ("I cannot but think it is the Spirit of Christ that influences him"), also relented. She began to advise conciliation and even opposed granting immediate suffrage to freedmen lest that precipitate a "war of the races." Not that the nation's leaders—first Andrew Johnson and then Ulysses Grant—were any wiser, or, if wiser, strong enough to make reason prevail.

And, as after every great war, there were many who were eager to make up for the years of sacrifice and suffering, happy to indulge themselves without pangs of guilt. Using the tools of the industrial revolution, merchants and financiers and contractors took over the world. The nation's industries and wealth increased apace but so did political corruption, extravagance and the relaxing of moral and religious standards. The result was what Harriet's neighbors Charles Dudley Warner and Mark

Twain called the "Gilded Age." In this sense, Harriet's "Oakholm," as she named her new home, which strained her resources and forced her to write a variety of potboilers, was, like Henry Ward's estates and Mark Twain's nearby mansion, a sign of the times.

When Calvin, that master of procrastination, failed, after three years of retirement, to organize his magnum opus, Harriet conspired to have Fields make him a publication offer. Calvin, immensely flattered, took the bait, and set to work at last. In a short time, he was ready to submit the first half of the manuscript. But Harriet, having seen Calvin leave unfinished too many projects he had started with equal zest, advised Fields to accept the fragment, pretend that he was setting it in type and then announce a crisis. Otherwise, Harriet wrote, "what with lectures and the original sin of laziness, it will be indefinitely postponed."

The ruse worked; Calvin finished the manuscript over the winter, and *The Origin and History of the Books of the Bible* was published early in 1867. It was surprisingly successful and would earn Calvin the very considerable sum of ten thousand dollars.

Postwar Hartford had become the center of a flourishing subscription book business, and an enterprising publisher decided that a volume of the Reverend Professor Stowe's sermons and lectures would be just right for his crew of door-to-door salesmen. Calvin, happy to be an author with such little effort, agreed. Now, letting his white beard spread and wearing a black skullcap, he settled into the role of Biblical patriarch, conversing impressively with a wide variety of visitors. Harriet referred to him as "my Rabbi," or, less flatteringly, "my poor Rabbi."

Needing money to maintain Oakholm, Harriet soon allowed the same publisher to inveigle her into making a book, *Men of Our Times; or, Leading Patriots of the Day,* out of a series of biographies she had been doing for a Baptist paper called *The Watchman and Reflector.* Even though it was undistinguished, mixing eulogy, worn anecdotes and dutiful credit to mothers and to abstinence from alcohol, it ranged from Lincoln to Henry Ward Beecher, and so was easy to sell.

At the same time, long flattered by the women who read the poems and hymns she turned out with such ease, Harriet proposed to Fields that he publish a volume of her religious poetry. Feeling that she was essentially a facile versifier whose work appealed mainly by its piety and sentimentality, Fields was reluctant. But envisioning herself as a famous poet as well as novelist, she insisted, and Fields gave in. Once again, time would show that her publisher's judgment was sounder than hers.

After four years of such by-products, Harriet started at last on a new novel, *Oldtown Folks.* It would be a masterly picture of the New England way of life, based on the stories Calvin had told her of Natick, his native Massachusetts village. But because she became increasingly aware of its rich possibilities, she was unable to hurry it along; it would take her almost three years to complete.

Then, in a totally unexpected way, her son Fred opened a new direction in Harriet's life. One day he came home from a tavern with two young war veterans, formerly Connecticut farmers, who had an unusual enterprise under way. Hearing of cheap land and cheap labor in Florida, they had rented a one-thousand-acre plantation on the St. Johns River not far from Jacksonville and were preparing to grow cotton on it. But running out of money, they had come north to get more capital and help.

With Fred himself obviously interested, Harriet immediately saw exciting possibilities in the proposal: above all, it would get Fred out of the city and into healthful, outdoor work and a position of responsibility. It would even have a humanitarian aspect, providing work for freed blacks. In the end she put enough money into the venture to justify her sending Fred down to Laurel Grove plantation as its superintendent.

By winter, Harriet was getting reports from Fred of progress on the plantation and, even more, the wonders of the Florida climate. She who had made much of the pleasures of sleigh riding in Vermont and snow-balling in Maine suddenly decided that cold weather "torpified" her brain and left her living half of each year like a "froze-and-thawed apple." Florida could be even more of a release than Europe. By March she was sailing south and was soon writing ecstatic letters from Charleston ("flowers everywhere, windows open, birds singing") and then from Florida itself.

Fred, looking tanned and healthy, met her on the boat landing. Although the plantation buildings seemed neglected and the fields were not yet planted, Harriet remained full of hope for the venture. The plantation was located in a scrub pine area cut by streams lost in tangles of evergreen shrubs. Across the river, which was extremely wide at this point and fringed with wharves, she found the town of Mandarin and was soon riding down sandy roads under giant live oaks festooned with Spanish moss. There she came on a cottage with a splendid view down the St. Johns River. Behind the house was a wide green grove alive with golden oranges. She was enchanted, and when she learned that the orange grove yielded two thousand dollars a year, she knew that she would buy the place.

Reluctantly she returned to the North, but by February 1868, she was on her way south again, taking eighteen-year-old Charley with her. Traveling by land this time, she became conscious that nowhere was there any hostility toward her—a woman who had been so cordially hated throughout the South that little children had chanted:

> "Go, go, go,
> "Ol' Harriet Beecher Stowe—
> We don't want you in Virginny."

Now when she and Charley reached Charleston they were invited to stay in a fine old house owned by a white-haired gentlewoman. Their hostess explained that during the war a band of drunken Yankee privates had invaded a home in Columbia, South Carolina, where she and her daughters were staying. Her screams had brought a Union colonel running, and he had driven out the looters at pistol point. That colonel had been Robert Beecher, one of Harriet's nephews. Harriet also learned that the woman's son had been a Presbyterian divinity student and that his last letter to his mother after he had been mortally wounded declared that he was dying gladly, having fought for God and against injustice and oppression. Harriet read the letter and wept, chastened and perhaps bewildered by the evidence that God and "justice" had been on the other side too.

She was again touched when on the steamer that took her and Charley from Charleston to Mandarin, the captain, who treated her with "almost pathetic solicitude," proved to have been a militant rebel and blockade runner. She had seen the barbarous enemy—the face of evil—and found that his sins had left no mark on him. . . .

This time the scene at the plantation made her heart sink: Fred had become a wretched creature with trembling hands and glazed eyes, and the plantation was a shambles. The Connecticut farmers had known nothing about raising cotton and the half-drunken blacks who lazed about were demoralized by the lack of direction. The ten thousand dollars Harriet had sunk in the venture was gone and the small quantity of cotton that had been harvested had been poorly stored and was ruined by mildew.

After three months in which Harriet tried to put the plantation in order, she gave up and in June 1868 returned to the North with her two sons.

Unable to concede that she could not cure her son of drink, she persuaded Calvin to abandon his easy chair and take Fred on a long voyage where he would have no liquor available. "My Rabbi and Fred," she wrote to Annie Fields, "have gone to the Mediterranean—in a sailing vessel, for the benefit of being at sea." The pair came back five months later. Fred was sober—but only until he could go off by himself and find liquor.

Harriet had now nearly finished writing *Oldtown Folks*, but she exasperated her publisher (he had paid her ten thousand in advance royalties) by constantly allowing herself to be distracted by other projects. Although Henry, on assuming the editorship of the *Independent,* had rather ungraciously taken over her front-page column, she was now conducting a weekly department in a farm journal—exploiting an old interest in flowers and fruits—and even planning an article on the newest craze in communicating with the spirit world, "planchette boards." But finally, early in 1869, she gave Fields the manuscript of *Oldtown Folks*.

Over six hundred pages long, *Oldtown Folks* is Harriet Beecher Stowe's richest book. Set in the 1790s and drawing largely on Calvin Stowe's recollections (the narrator, Horace Holyoke, is a youth who resembles Calvin), it abounds in crotchety, flavorous characters and in the country ways of what she describes as a fresher and more innocent time.

Once again there is an enchanting young woman, an array of strong-minded spinsters, a Byron-Burr figure, a do-nothing but know-all town handyman and his wife, "a gnarly, compact, efficient little pepperbox of a woman, with a mouth always at half-cock, ready to go off with some crack . . . at the shoreless, bottomless, and tideless inefficiency of her husband," a stiff-necked Tory family that despises democracy and Calvinism and reveres King, Queen and the "true Church," and long-suffering mothers who die in pious bliss. Unfailingly there is the gamut of preachers, from Dr. Stern, who saw an enemy of God in every human heart, to Parson Avery—plainly Lyman Beecher—"a cheerful, busy, manly man" who found some hope for almost everyone. There is, finally, Avery's daughter, one of several women who illustrate, almost better than the men, New Englanders in whom "thinking grew to be a disease." Only in a cruel farmer, "Old Crab" Smith, and his flint-hearted sister— the wicked witch of the folk tale—do we get a glimpse of the shriveling effects of the New England way. But all the characters are shrewdly and amusingly drawn, and if some of them seem like stereotypes, it is in part because they were, as we have said, so often copied by later writers.

More than ever, religion permeates life. Again and again Harriet struggles with the haunting question of Edwards's influence. But where in *The Minister's Wooing* at least two characters, Mary Scudder and the minister, are transfigured by his vision, in *Oldtown Folks* he is mainly a source of perplexity and debate. Although Edwards's denial of any hope for a world of sinners is described as slow poison to the sensitive, Calvinism is seen as the seedbed of New England discipline, integrity and intellectual mettle.

The contradictory effects of Edwards's code are illustrated by two characters, Ellery Davenport, a grandson of Edwards, and Emily Rossiter, Parson Rossiter's brilliant daughter. Both fall under the spell of Voltaire and Rousseau and both escape to Paris—the new Sodom. There Ellery gets Emily with child and then abandons her. Ellery returns home and, as wickedly fascinating as ever, bewitches Oldtown's fairy-tale heroine, Tina. Ellery continues on his shameless course until he is killed off in a duel. It is as though Harriet, captured of old by the satanic attractiveness and sexuality of the Byron-Burr types, is driven to exorcise them again and again. She must punish Tina—just as she punished Burr's lovely inamorata, Madame de Frontignac, in *The Minister's Wooing*—by making her the humiliated victim of a godless and licentious man. It requires no psychoanalyst to see that in Mrs. Stowe's repeated portrayal of sexually unscrupulous men she was titillating her readers and then assuaging their sense of guilt—and her own—by punishing both the sinful man and the too compliant woman.

Born to the tradition, Harriet everywhere scatters insights into the Puritan mystique: in New England, Nature itself with its stony soil and harsh climate is, she says, high Calvinist; as the subjects of English monarchs, the American colonists found it natural to bow to a remote, tyrannical God and to ministers who behaved like noblemen by divine right; Calvinism, shaped by the Old Testament as well as the New, united the extremes of the material and the spiritual, giving America Franklin as well as Edwards; and it was to Saint Augustine, who knew nothing of cultivated women, that Calvinism owed its view of woman as a snare and temptation.

In spite of such acute perceptions and a stream of vivid portraits, *Oldtown Folks* fails to take hold of the reader. It entertains, amuses and instructs, but its characters are psychologically slack, too rarely engaged by their situation in the novel. Forgetting Holmes's wise advice, Harriet allows morality to govern imagination. In her vision of New England society, genteel standards prevail. Eccentricity is tolerated but not genuine rebellion: an individual may be mean, cruel, bigoted or ne'er-do-well, but not an active critic of church, God, wealth, masculine domination or prudery.

Despite such shortcomings and although it lacks the purpose and passion of *Uncle Tom's Cabin* and the emotional drama of *The Minister's Wooing, Oldtown Folks* is a masterly evocation of old New England.

Harriet was, in her late fifties, still at the peak of her powers. Physically she had come far enough from the days of her complaints of deadly fatigue and year-long rest cures to be able to write to Fields: "I have worked so hard that I am almost tired." Except for Fred's condition, her personal life was relatively untroubled.

She did not dream that because of her loyalty to the memory of Lady Byron, her own reputation would soon be tarnished and that an unbearable scandal in her brother Henry's life would cast a deep shadow over the Beecher name.

20

HENRY

The Great Spellbinder

When Henry, Eunice and their three children arrived in Brooklyn in 1847, they were so short of money that Henry C. Bowen, the dry goods merchant who had helped found Plymouth Church, had to pay off eight hundred dollars in Beecher's old debts. Then Bowen and his wife, Lucy, daughter of the Lewis Tappan who had financed Lyman Beecher's post at Lane, outfitted the entire family in presentable clothes.

Calling a young minister out of the western hinterland to a church in Brooklyn was a remarkable tribute to Henry Ward Beecher. Encouraging his native optimism, it sent him forward with a confidence that would last, with only a few intermissions and one great setback, for the rest of his life. Henry's new position may not have changed his nature or personality, but it did produce a distinct shift in his frames of reference and his style of life. Overnight he moved from a provincial community (in leaving Indianapolis he had to sit on planks in a wooden boxcar in the first train to reach that city) into a metropolitan center with a mixture of cultures, a flourishing economy and a contagious vitality. Only a few years earlier he had peppered his *Lectures to Young Men* with references to cities as sinks of sin and vice.

Not that Brooklyn was such a place. Far from it. In 1847 it was a highly respectable suburb of New York, a refuge for a middle class intent on escaping from Manhattan's increasing congestion, rising costs and waves of immigrants. ("Cool, fragrantly airy, and no mobs!" proclaimed one of its contented residents.) It had begun an expansion that would take it from a population of 60,000 to 300,000 in twenty years and make it the third largest city in America. Substantial homes, pretty gardens and some forty churches framed its tree-lined streets, especially on Columbia Heights, overlooking the East River and New York Bay. And Manhattan—a metropolis crowding the southern half of a narrow island—was only a penny ferry-ride away. It was already "a caravanserai for the

whole world," as Fredrika Bremer called it, the horse-drawn traffic—
including four hundred buses—on its avenues was a torrent and the hotels on Broadway and the mansions reaching up to Gramercy Park were
the admiration of visitors from everywhere.

Life continued to be unkind to Eunice. She had lost a child before
leaving Indianapolis and seemed so aged—although scarcely thirty-six—
that on the journey east an elderly woman on the train, noting Henry's
effort to make her comfortable, observed that she was lucky to have so
attentive a son. Members of Eunice's as well as Henry's family and a few
friends were already settled in Brooklyn and Henry's income soon enabled Eunice to have several servants, but she had little time or inclination for the pleasures of the city. Although some of them pretended
otherwise, most of the Beechers did not like Eunice and she resented
Henry's attachment to them. Soon, too, she lost another baby and before
long she was carrying her sixth child. Even Henry's success left her fretful: more than ever she saw herself as the neglected wife. "When I got
here to Brooklyn," she wrote long afterward, "the public began to take
my husband away from me. His study was no longer in the house but in
the church. And when he went out I used to gasp for breath and my eyes
would fill with tears, for it seemed to me as if we had quarreled."

Henry's congregation, very small at the start but soon growing rapidly, was made up mainly of middle-class and a few well-to-do families,
many of New England stock. With the loss of Puritan guidelines and
with ever-increasing material temptations and the pressure to "succeed,"
they craved reassurance that they were not sinful, selfish or headed for
damnation.

Henry Ward gave them just that, trying as best he could to distinguish between wealth earned through honest toil or talent and profits
gained by hook or crook. Freed from the reins of Calvinism, the shadow
of a famous father and the near penury of his Indiana days, he blossomed. He also brought a self-confidence born of ten years on a frontier
where men and women were conquering a continent and preachers were
pioneers as well as apostles.

He declared his own independence on the first Sunday after his
arrival:

I want you to understand distinctly that I will wear no fetters; that I will be
bound by no precedent; that I will preach the gospel as I apprehend it, whether
men will hear or whether they will forbear, and that I will apply it without
stint, and sharply and strongly, to the overthrow of every evil and to the up-
building of all that is good.

It was a resounding statement and somewhat bolder than his performance. But, believing the first five years of a new church were crucial, he plunged into his work with immense energy, starting revivals, establishing a Sunday school, renting pews at ever higher prices, and preaching day and night. Declaring that it was a minister's right and duty to introduce *"every subject"* in which his people were concerned, his sermons dealt almost as much with social behavior as with religious doctrine. But his great contribution was what the age called personal magnetism.

His figure was not imposing. Compared with the form-fitting frock coat, tight pantaloons and towering stovepipe hat of fashionable men, his loose dark trousers and plain felt hat were unpretentious. "Out upon this idea," he exclaimed, "that a minister must *dress* minister, *walk* minister, *talk* minister, *eat* minister and wear his ministerial badge as a convict wears his stripes." His voice was not in itself remarkable but he had a hypnotic fluency and an almost kinetic intimacy with his audience. He was fully aware of this. Just as in Indianapolis, he had the pulpit in the church opened up so that he could move about freely, and when the building burned down two years later, the new one was constructed with a platform thrust out into the congregation. "It is perfect," he declared, "because it is built on . . . the principle of personal and social magnetism, which emanates reciprocally from the speaker and from a close throng of hearers. . . . I want them to surround me, so that they will come up on every side, and behind me . . . and have the people surge about me."

And they did, coming in crowds to hear him. The new church was built to seat two thousand, which seemed more than enough, but after a while it was rearranged to accommodate three thousand, with hundreds of others standing and sometimes many turned away. In time, New Yorkers would say to visitors who wanted to hear Henry Ward Beecher preach, "Take the ferry to Brooklyn and follow the crowd." Only a few months after he began preaching at Plymouth Church, Susan Howard, wife of a church trustee, wrote to a brother that one subject engrossed the neighborhood:

Beecher, *Beecher,* BEECHER! . . . Don't ask me what *I* think of him. I . . . only know that I am intensely interested. There is a sort of fascination about the man. . . . He carries one along with him by the power of his own flow. . . . The Unitarians like him because he preaches good works and calls no doctrine by its name.

Harriet Beecher Stowe once said that her aim in writing was to paint pictures because they would reach everyone; Henry Ward had much the same goal. "In writing or speaking when fairly roused up," he wrote to a friend, "I do not seem to think, I *see*."

"As a preacher he is a landscape painter of Christianity," observed Indiana's Senator Oliver H. Smith. Smith also noted that Beecher spoke as if "conscious that he is telling the truth, and the audience believes he thinks so." If this implies that Henry was something of an actor, it was meant as a compliment. Henry was indeed an actor. He often mimicked the voice and gestures of someone he was describing. If he spoke of a fisherman, he handled the rod and reeled in a catch so realistically that everyone saw the fish dangling from the hook. Once, speaking of an old sailor, he imitated the way the man took a quid of tobacco from his mouth and tossed it behind him; then, with a seemingly unconscious—but actually calculated—gesture, Henry wiped his fingers on the back of his coat. He composed sermons—much as his father had—shortly before delivering them so that they would sound extemporaneous. "Some men like their bread cold," he would explain. "I like mine hot." It was one of the secrets of his emotional effect.

Another was the way he introduced his own feelings and experiences into his lectures and writings, intuitively aware that an audience likes nothing more than a glimpse of a public figure's inner life. In his letters there are no such intimate passages; compared to Harriet's, they are curiously impersonal. He needed an audience to stir and release him.

Finally, there was the range of his styles. Scorning the "holy tone" of most preachers, he could by turns be ringingly eloquent, breezy, lyrical, salty, somber. He liked the statement that ended surprisingly, like the flick of a whip, and one of his favorite modes was a jaunty irreverence. He wept easily and he laughed easily. He could work up to a crescendo and then suddenly drop to a whisper. He was master of the soaring, rapturous climax that left listeners transfixed. Gently, then, he would call for a hymn.

Often his figures of speech, again like his father's, were surprisingly homely, drawn from everyday life—gardening, fishing, farming, sailing, the weather—and were singularly apt. Describing how easily he controlled the mood of a congregation, he said, in one of his lectures on preaching: "If I can make them laugh I do not thank anybody for the next move; I will make them cry. Did you ever see a woman carrying a pan of milk quite full and it slops over on one side, that it did not immediately slop over on the other side also?"

Above all there was his inexhaustible buoyancy and zest. "He is eternally young, and positively wears me out with his redundant, superabundant, ever-recovering and ever-renewing energy," admitted Theodore Parker, himself a preacher of no mean power. The sound of his own voice inspired him; the words stirred emotions, and the emotions flowed into words, until everyone within range was caught up in a swelling exaltation of sound and feeling. He could draw his listeners into the deepest intimacy and then carry them wherever he chose, making them not only cheer or sob but do so unashamedly. He played on them and on himself as on instruments so that a service in Plymouth Church was an overwhelming emotional experience.

As he pulled farther and farther away from his Calvinist roots, Henry's religious message became increasingly one of hope. He still accepted the idea of the sinfulness of man, but he had discarded not only the doctrine of original sin but even the need for a distinct conversion. He had, moreover, shifted the entire basis of faith from fear of a wrathful father figure, God, to the love of a pitying, almost motherly Jesus. In the process almost all the elaborate machinery of theology had been rendered superfluous—replaced by vague, easily accessible moods. He was only half jesting when he told a seminary student that theology was all right as long as he didn't take it seriously.

Henry was not the first prominent Congregationalist to substitute love for fear in bringing people to faith. By the late 1840s Horace Bushnell, the brilliant young Hartford minister, had, in his sermons and his *Views of Christian Nurture* (1846), clearly rejected the crueler aspects of Calvinism. When Thomas Beecher came to teach in the Hartford high school in 1848, he wrote admiringly of what Henry had called Bushnell's "scheme of love" and a "Christian philosophy that springs from the Bible as based upon the heart." But Bushnell was an intellectual and a theologian; his appeal lay more in his ideas than in his emotional impact. Henry admired him but said that his force was in thought, not feeling, and Bushnell in turn said of one of Henry's revival sermons that it greatly moved him despite the fact that it was "unspeakably crude and naturalistic." Bushnell, moreover, had little faith in reform, whereas Henry was a firm believer in social action. Our age, Henry declared, is a period of change: "The questions of our day are questions of . . . progress of reforms. The spirit of our people and, I think, God may say *the public spirit* of the world, is for amelioration and expansion and growth toward individual and social excellence." Such optimism was not Henry's alone but that of his age.

Suddenly America had become the land of boundless opportunity and abundance. After the gray Puritan dawn and the long hard morning of the pioneers, noon had come, astonishing in its rich warmth. All around him the poor pastor's son saw the glow of opulence and luxury. Overnight he himself was lapped in success, and the sensuous, self-indulgent part of his nature emerged and flourished almost rankly. With rhapsodic fervor he hailed the future, the prospects of the common people, and human brotherhood. Success fed his native buoyancy and his susceptibility to impulse and emotion. Adulation surrounded him, swept over him and drew from him gushers of love.

Henry enjoyed his journalistic writing in Indiana almost as much as preaching, so when Bowen proposed to establish a weekly paper edited by clergymen but free to speak out on social and political issues, Henry responded enthusiastically. An association with religion was still an advantage for a newspaper, and the *Independent* did moderately well. Henry's contribution sometimes struck a conspicuously lighthearted note among the earnest reports on mission work, intemperance, slavery and vice. His *Star Papers*, so called because he signed them with an asterisk, are traditional "familiar" essays in their humor and informality, but their verve and lyrical flights are Henry's own. Again and again he celebrates the delights of nature and the countryside—an indulgence that the old religion had discouraged—finding in flowers and sunsets "revelations of God's sense of beauty." A faculty for enjoyment is a gift of God, he announces in "Nature a Minister of Happiness"; with it we can "discern in everything some ray of brightness." "On such a glorious morning of such a perfect day as this . . ." he chants, "I wander forth, wondering how there should be sorrow in the world. . . . Each hour is a perfect hour, clear, full and unsated. It is the joy of being alive. . . . Such days are let down from heaven." No wonder Thoreau, despite his distrust of self-indulgence, came away from a Beecher sermon convinced that this preacher had more than a little of the pagan in him. Like Harriet, but much more naturally, Henry Ward had adopted his uncle Samuel's Venetian sundial motto—observe only the unclouded hours. Avoiding doctrine and dogma, he conjured up "a perpetual tropical luxuriance of blessed love" and he called for submission, not to God's will but to "the heart's instincts." Intoxicated by his own fervor and having thrown off the straitjacket of predestination and innate depravity, he cried out to his congregation, "Ye are gods!" and "You are crystalline to me, your faces are radiant; and I look through your eyes as through windows into heaven. I behold in each of you an imprisoned angel that is yet to burst forth." When they recovered from their surprise, the good citizens of Brooklyn, ranged row on row in front of him, glowed with pleasure and gratitude.

They responded by raising his salary and presenting him with a handsome horse and carriage. And when Fredrika Bremer arrived in America late in 1849, one of the first things she felt obliged to do was hear Henry Ward Beecher. She reported:

I am just returned from a Presbyterian church where I have heard a young preacher from the West preach on "the Positive in Christianity," one of the best extempore Christian discourses which I have ever heard. . . . The preacher is full of life and energy, and preaches from that experience of Christian life which gives a riveting effect to his words. . . . He has also considerable wit and does not

Harriet Beecher Stowe
in the 1850s.

Henry Ward Beecher, who held
America spellbound for forty years
as preacher, author and lecturer.

Henry Ward Beecher and Harriet Beecher Stowe in 1858 at or near the peak of their careers.

Henry Ward Beecher's Plymouth Church in Brooklyn, in its heyday the most famous church in America.

THE BROOKLYN RESIDENCE OF HENRY WARD BEECHER.

Henry Ward Beecher's Brooklyn home.

Eunice, wife of Henry Ward Beecher, with her twin sons about 1853.

William H. Beecher, called "The Unlucky" by his family. His trials and defeats as a pastor in many churches left him critical of his congregations but still dedicated to his calling.

object to enliven his discourse with humorous sallies, so that more than once the whole audience of the crowded church burst into a general laugh, which, however, did not prevent them from soon shedding joyful tears of devotion . . . and tears also streamed down his own cheeks as he bowed in silent, rapt contemplation of the splendid mystery of the sacrament.

As unique as Walt Whitman may appear, the more one considers the moods and messages of Henry Ward Beecher in the 1850s and '60s, the more these two men resemble each other as children of their time and place. In the selfsame city and period as the poet, dressing in loose pants and a wide-brimmed hat, Henry often, like Whitman, liked to wander Manhattan streets and talk to the workers on the docks and in the shipyards and foundries, to the pilots on the ferryboats and the men working in the silver-plating atelier at Tiffany's. And like Whitman, he celebrated himself endlessly, embracing all men and women, offering and inviting love, affirming the future of the race and especially of the free, self-reliant American. He, too, saw divinity in a flower, and sang of the steam plow as well as the dandelion. And he, too, was undisturbed by his inconsistencies. There were of course vital differences: in certain ways Whitman challenged his time and defied its conventions while Henry often, but not always, swam with them, and Henry loved everyone indiscriminately. Yet the parallels are remarkable and illuminating.

Expansive as he himself might be, the aggressiveness of the young republic was on a few occasions too much for him. Thus he attacked America's role in the Mexican War, describing the doctrine of "manifest destiny" as an excuse to despoil and murder, and he mocked the claim that the aim of the war was to Christianize the Mexicans. "To . . . pour armies upon a rude and undisciplined mob of half-starved slaves, to ravage provinces . . . has been common to all ages; but to do it for the sake of *civilization and religion* is an achievement of the Anglo-Saxon race." It was a pretense, he charged, that added hypocrisy to injustice.

For a time he avoided the slavery issue. But the force of events was irresistible. Invited to a meeting at the Broadway Tabernacle to raise funds to buy the freedom of two quadroon girls, the daughters of the slave Milly Edmonson (whose two other children his sister Harriet would ransom three years later), he saw at once the potential drama of their situation. When he rose to speak, he drove home not the inhumanity of their fate but the sexual depravity of it. "Shall this girl—almost as white as you are—be sold to the first comer to do as he likes with?" This is, he cried, a sale of Christian girls—Methodists—by a dealer in human flesh. In a moment he was transformed into a slave auctioneer: "And more than that, gentlemen, they say she is one of those praying Methodist niggers; who bids? a thousand—fifteen hundred—two thousand—twenty-five hundred! Going! going! last call! Gone!" By the time he was through he had the audience sobbing and frenziedly throwing money onto the platform to save Innocence from Lust. "Of all the meetings I have attended . . ." he later said, "for a panic of sympathy I never saw one that surpassed that."

Over twenty-two hundred dollars was raised and the girls were triumphantly freed. The attention Henry gained was dazzling. He had found a formula for dealing with the slavery question without becoming enmeshed in tortuous argument or bitter charges. When someone called it sensationalism, Henry retorted: "He is the best fisherman who catches the most fish."

But when the Gold Rush began pouring a great stream of settlers into the West and the issue of permitting slavery in the new territories became critical, a far more realistic response than a mock auction was required. When Clay, old master of compromises, proposed in 1850 that in return for allowing California to enter the Union as a free state a stricter fugitive slave law must be passed, it was a moral challenge that Henry could not ignore. He was outraged not only that any American should be required to help recapture a slave but that slavery should be considered an acceptable alternative for newly formed states. All at once the "peculiar institution" of the South was threatening the West and entangling the North.

Henry was still reluctant to abandon "moral suasion" or alienate the South. But slavery was not only a crime against slaves; it undermined all the virtues Victorians held dear. So in 1850, in a piece called "Shall We Compromise?" he denounced slavery because it destroyed the family, degraded honest labor, deprived the black man of his humanity and was motivated by greed and lust. The conflict was, he declared, a struggle between two "incompatible and mutually destructive principles . . . slavery and liberty." "One or the other," he concluded, "must die." As for helping to recover slaves, he refused to do so even though the Constitution sanctioned it: "I disown the act. I repudiate the obligation. Never while I have breath will I help any official miscreant in his base errand of recapturing a fellow-man for bondage."

"Shall We Compromise?" stirred much discussion, some of it favorable, some of it harshly critical. Although he was saying only what Garrison and Phillips and even Horace Greeley in his *Tribune* had been saying for years, he was still loath to align himself with the extremists. They sowed the whirlwind and no man knew what they would reap. Henry would always insist that, noble and brave and benevolent as Garrison might be, he inspired such bitterness and violence by his ferocity as almost to destroy his cause.

Soon he returned to the attack on slavery not as inherently unjust but as a source of depravity:

There is no sensual vice . . . which Slavery does not monstrously engender. . . . This vast abomination which seethes and smokes in our midst; which is . . . demoralizing the white by the oppression of the black; in which adultery, fornication and concubinage exist, that in comparison with it, a Turkish harem is a cradle of virgin purity . . . . in this huge, infernal system is the destruction of men, soul and body.

It was a strong blast and, like his *Lectures to Young Men*, lurid, but within a preacher's province.

Much as he tried to steer clear of the more rabid abolitionists, he was repeatedly thrown together with them. When Bowery hoodlums prevented Wendell Phillips from speaking in the Broadway Tabernacle, Henry arranged to have Phillips use Plymouth Church, and he even introduced him. But he made clear he was acting in the interests of free speech, not abolitionism. Later, in a letter to an associate, he revealed something close to envy of Phillips's performance: "I was amazed at the unagitated Agitator—so calm, so fearless, so incisive. . . . He had the dignity of Pitt, the vigor of Fox, the wit of Sheridan, the satire of Junius— and a grace and music all his own."

After he had suffered several periods of illness from overwork, Henry's church granted him a leave of absence in the summer of 1850. His trip, taken without wife or children, was curiously like his father's visit to Niagara and the extended rest cures almost all his sisters and brothers took when pressures became too great. Leaving his brother Charles to serve as preacher while he was gone, he spent three months in Europe.

He had come a long way from his father's parsonage but he was only three years away from Indianapolis and quite unprepared for the sensory richness of Europe, for places layered and encrusted with paintings and tapestries, mosaics and stained glass. Bedazzled, he responded rapturously. At his first sight of the ruins of Kenilworth Castle he wept, and when on that same day he visited Warwick Castle and Shakespeare's birthplace he could "neither eat nor sleep for excitement." Attending a service in the little church where Shakespeare is buried, he trembled so much he had to sit down, and every "Amen" brought tears to his eyes. The welter of religious and erotic paintings in the great museums sent him into transports. "I am here," he cried out to the pictures; "I am yours; do what you will with me; I am here to be intoxicated." (Three years later Harriet would respond in almost exactly the same way.) In the Louvre he found too much "French nakedness," which he excused only when the sentiment was "noble." Where Harriet would simply be overwhelmed by Rubens's genius, Henry noted only that the painter's women were too fat and that he thrust his wife into every painting, even making her, in *Abduction of the Sabine Women*, the prize captured by a Roman soldier.

As it would be for Harriet, Europe was a liberating experience for Henry. It encouraged his interest in the arts and nurtured an awareness that their beauty need serve no other purpose. It helped turn him into an ardent collector of art objects and apparently quieted any qualms about the extravagance of such an addiction.

Soon Henry returned to the assault on the Fugitive Slave Law, arguing that it commanded men to sin and thus break the laws of God. We should, he advised, let slavery alone because the "natural laws of God are warring" against it. Shut it up, he cried, and let it go to seed: "Time is her enemy." The statement stirred rage but counseled passivity. Frederick Douglass is said to have commented: "With a good cowhide, I could take all that out of Mr. Beecher in five minutes."

Now Harriet, also aroused, spurred him on. When Henry, as we have seen, came to Brunswick after a lecture in Boston, they planned how he in sermon, lecture and newspaper column and she in story and novel would awaken the nation to the monstrous tragedy of slavery.

Divided, trying to be both spiritual firebrand and social moderate, Henry swung from one position to another—sometimes in the same lecture or article. But there is little question about his courage when in May 1851 he took up the cause of the free blacks of the North. Everywhere, he protested, they were downtrodden and discriminated against, kept out of schools, barred from the trades, segregated in theaters, churches, trains and buses. But he undercut his radicalism with a conservative solution. With brisk paternalism he advised: "Educate them, Christianize them, and *then* colonize them," or in other words, treat them with benevolence and then send them away.

Henry spoke before the American Anti-Slavery Society in May 1853 along with Garrison and other radical abolitionists, but he still took pains in a letter to the *Tribune* to distinguish his position from theirs:

my earnest desire is that slavery be destroyed by the manifest power of Christianity. If it were given me to choose whether it should be destroyed in fifty years by selfish commercial influences, or, standing for seventy-five years, be then the spirit and trophy of Christ, I had rather let it linger twenty-five years more, that God may be honored, and not mammon, in the destruction of it.

It was doubly dismaying that he should be willing to prolong the sin of slavery for the sake of Christ's glory and at the same time believe that God would be honored by such a "trophy." When sharp criticism pointed to the cruel implications of his position, he simply replied: "This sentiment does not spring from any indifference to the slave, but from a yet greater sympathy with Jesus Christ—the slave's only hope . . . the Saviour of the world!"

Henry now began to reach the public through lectures as well as through sermons—his congregation hired a stenographer to record them—and his articles in the *Independent*. As a medium of education, inspiration and entertainment, lectures had come of age in the 1840s mainly because of a lack of adequate schools and colleges and a growing middle class that had some leisure and a desire for self-improvement. For at least seventy years lyceum lectures would remain a major source of instruction and edification for a host of Americans. As a man of God who spoke the language of the average citizen of both western towns and eastern cities, who was friendly, rich in humor and hope, and a natural actor, Henry Ward Beecher was ideal for the lyceum circuit. Where Webster and Sumner kept to political issues, Garrison and Phillips to abolitionism, and Emerson to the higher mysteries, Henry took almost all of life for his theme. With an approach that was far more personal and heartwarming than that of such specialists, he was after a while as famous as any of them.

In Paxton Hibben's muckraking biography of Beecher, the preacher of the Indiana period is seen as an opportunist who fed anti-city prejudices and a narrow morality to small-town folks, and later, in Brooklyn, equally an opportunist in his justification of the self-indulgence of prosperous parishioners. There is some truth in this view, but it makes no allowance for the fact that in the 1840s Henry was a poor young preacher coping with settlers on a raw frontier, while in Brooklyn in the 1850s he was a leading minister, riding the tide of liberal Protestantism and serving a congregation affluent enough for benevolence, culture and a measure of gracious living.

Nor was Henry's shift in values ever complete or consistent. Like many Americans in the mid-Victorian period, he was in passage between a rural society with its isolation and hidebound traditional values and burgeoning cities much more exposed to the winds of change. Henry's lack of a full commitment to either of these worlds is not difficult to understand. On the one hand, the small town offered roots and stability, a chance to breathe, neighbors who knew each other, country pleasures, simpler needs and a sense of identity. But it was also a narrow world, in thrall to hard work, troubled by fears of God and sexuality, and distrustful of leisure, intellect and the arts. Henry loved the country and spent as much time as he could in the gardens, farms and orchards of a succession of summer homes, but nothing could have made him go back to live in Indiana or even Litchfield.

Yet he was almost equally ambivalent about cities. By the end of the

1850s he saw the city as a restless, feverishly competitive arena, full of lonely individuals, alien neighbors and snares for the innocent. Cities, he wrote, are "whirlpools of excitement where men strive for honor and know not what is honorable; for wealth and do not know true riches; for pleasure and are ignorant of the first elements of pleasure." He dreaded hearing young men say, "I am going to the city," and notwithstanding his own triumphant experience there, he described it in chilling terms:

If they ask me what chances there are for lawyers in the city, I say, "Just the chance that the fly has on a spider's web; go down and be eaten up!" If they ask me what chances there are for a mechanic in the city, I say, "Good! good! there Death carries on a wholesale and retail business. . . ." If a man's bones are made of flint, if his muscles are made of leather; if he can work sixteen or eighteen hours a day and not wink . . . if in other words he is built for mere toughness, then he can . . . go through the ordeal which business men and professional men are obliged to go through . . . but there is connected with the business of the city so much competition, so much rivalry, so much necessity for industry that . . . it is a perpetual, chronic, wholesale violation of natural law.

It was easy for Henry to take such a view: where business was concerned (except for the annual renting of pews, at which he was so effective that fellow ministers thought the Plymouth rents scandalous), he was obviously above the battle. For him the city had every advantage: the opportunity for fame and influence, an electric energy, the challenge of other strong personalities, and tolerance for a variety of views.

There was also the miracle of the machine. Although Beecher acknowledged that railroads, which spread amazingly in the 1850s, defaced the countryside and shattered tranquillity, he admired them along with most other mechanical marvels. Side by side with charming essays on dandelions, trout streams and summer rain in his *Star Papers* are amusingly appreciative pieces on sewing machines and steam plows.

Paralleling his mixed view of city and country was his treatment of the scramble for money as ugly but of wealth itself as a civilizing influence. Just as in his *Lectures to Young Men* he had used the panic of 1837 to denounce the sin of speculation, so after the financial collapse of 1857—again following a time of rash speculation—he condemned the criminal practices of the managers of great corporations and the immorality of stock-market gambling. "A man who deliberately purposes to gain wealth without earning it by some substantial equivalent rendered to the community," he declared, "is a thief." Reverting to Calvinist attitudes, he at first treated the depression as God's punishment of man's greed. But when the anxieties and even hysteria aroused by the crisis set off a revival all across the land—the last great spontaneous revival before the professionals took over—he began to see it as a tempering by fire. That it was sparked by fear and not by principles did not matter. Any movement that revived faith was welcome. The depression was, paradoxically, a financial boon for Plymouth Church, bringing in 335 new members in the spring of 1858 and increasing the returns from pew rents by sixty percent.

Not that Henry was unaware that some people used the church as spiritual first aid in a time of crisis. At least once he lashed out bitterly at those who were devout only on Sundays. I look at the life of businessmen, he wrote,

who cry for the lullaby of love in the family, in the shop, in all the departments of life, and I find that they abhor love except on Sundays. . . . But if I were to go to them at their places of business, and say, "I understand that you take advantage . . . of your workmen, and employ them at one quarter of what they ought to have, so that they can scarcely subsist on what you pay them; and as you wanted me to preach about love, I thought I would come and tell you what the doctrine of love is as applied to matters of this kind"; they would say, "Religion is religion and business is business. Go home, and when I want you to come to my shop and preach to me I will let you know." In other words, they want sermon love, poetic love, theoretic love, love that makes them feel good during the insurance day—for Sunday is the insurance day of the week! And they want me to talk of love because it subdues their fears, soothes their hearts, and makes them feel pleasant.

It was an extraordinary statement, scorning the lip service that religion was becoming in an age of business and profit. And it reveals how aware Henry was that his preaching was a kind of spiritual massage, assuaging anxiety and lulling guilt.

Despite this challenge to the hypocrisy of businessmen, Henry found more and more ways to justify the prodigality of the rich. Such expenditures were, he suggested, a contribution to the welfare of the community. Self-serving as this may seem, it aroused no cries of protest. Opportunity seemed unlimited, hope was at the zenith, and Americans were assuming the right to spend their earnings as they chose.

In his praise of the embellished life Beecher was preaching what he practiced. On his return from his trip to Europe he began to accumulate all manner of art objects and decorative pieces. As much as he had disdained or been forced to forgo such luxuries in Indiana, so freely did he now indulge in them. He bought not only the usual paintings and engravings, but bronzes, enamels, porcelains and Venetian and Bohemian glass. He loved fine editions, spending no less than five hundred dollars a year on books, including, despite his attacks on licentious novels, the works of Rabelais, Boccaccio and Fielding. Soon his home was hung with velvet drapes and scattered with embroidered cushions, silken scarves and stuffed hummingbirds. The Puritan ideal of the modest dwelling rather plainly furnished, such as Lyman Beecher's Litchfield home, had given way by the 1860s to the high-Victorian town house awash in bric-a-brac and *objets d'art.*

But the most striking evidence of Henry's sensuous nature was his passion for unset gems, which he liked to carry loose in his pockets. He called them his opiates and when overstimulated he would take them out and with a mingling of the sensual and the possessive, handle them and gaze at them until he was able to relax. New York jewelers knew of his addiction and they called him whenever they thought they had gems he might like.

In addition to the house in town, there was a summer home in the country. The first one, acquired in 1854, was in Lenox in the Berkshire hills of western Massachusetts, not far from Litchfield. When that proved to be too far away for short visits, Beecher found a place on the Hudson River near Peekskill, about fifty miles north of Manhattan. Boscobel, as he named it, had thirty-six acres of rolling country overlooking a lovely sweep of the river.

Henry's success did little for his wife. The pride and pleasure Eunice experienced when twin boys were born to her in December 1852 was shattered by grief when they died less than six months later. Within two years she was pregnant again and gave birth to her last child, a son, in 1854. Having borne nine children and lost five of them, she was spiritually as well as physically exhausted. Her hair was gray and her expression was dour. She complained that the more popular her husband became, the less she saw of him. She was critical of his extravagance (in one essay he described the ruses needed to get expensive books past the sharp eyes of a disapproving wife), his disorderly habits, his boyish enthusiasms and some of his more liberated opinions. The more flamboyant he grew, the more she clung to the conservatism of her New England upbringing and her stern father. Henry in turn seems to have regarded her much as an impetuous youth looks on an overly strict mother.

Congressional action in 1854 should have persuaded Henry that it would take more than "moral suasion" or the spirit of benevolence to end slavery. In that year Stephen Douglas of Illinois led in the repeal of the Missouri Compromise of 1820 and introduced, in the Kansas-Nebraska Bill, the principle of popular sovereignty. It was immediately clear to Northerners that democratic though it might seem, "squatters' sovereignty," as they dubbed it, would open a dangerous breach in the wall around slavery. The clashes that soon broke out in Kansas between Free-Soilers and the pro-slavery Border Ruffians confirmed their fears.

Henry was aroused and in his "Defence of Kansas" he indulged his flair for the incendiary phrase. Blasting those who had promised peace, he cried: "We have been betrayed by kisses . . . compromises have bred cockatrices. We are spun over with webs . . . tangled with sophistries." The war can be stopped now, he declared:

But fear will not do it. A truculent peace will not do it. When tyrants are in arms they who cry peace become their confederates. . . . Let them that have sons in Kansas send them arms, and pray . . . if they must be used, that the son may so wield them that the mother be not ashamed of the son whom she bore.

If some were scandalized by such ferocious sentiments from a clergyman, what could they think when in 1855, in his *Conflict of Northern and Southern Theories of Men and Society,* he warned, "We will war it to the knife, and the knife to the hilt."

The gods must have been amused when amidst all this militancy Henry decided that America also needed a collection of hymns. Deploring the lack of a book that combined words with tunes, he assembled, with much expert help from his brother Charles and from John Zundel, organist of Plymouth Church, the *Plymouth Collection of Hymns and Tunes.* It was criticized for setting some of the hymns to popular tunes—Henry scoffed at such hidebound attitudes—but the book sold very well and was soon imitated in other collections.

Master of gestures, Henry now asked his congregation to send Sharps rifles to New Englanders on their way to join the Free-Soil settlers in Kansas. Rifles, he cried, are "a greater moral agency than the Bible." The weapons were shipped in boxes marked "Bibles" and soon all rifles sent to Free-Soilers were called "Beecher's Bibles." Not surprisingly, Henry began to be classed with the rabid abolitionists. Ironically, Garrison, opposing violence as un-Christian, was sharply critical of Henry's action. He never forgave the evangelist for having failed to support the abolitionists in earlier days and then encouraging bloodshed later on.

And yet Henry was not an abolitionist; he could still say concerning the slaves: "as they cannot be, will not be, [free] for ages, is it best that bitter discontent should be inspired in them, or Christian quietness and patient waiting?" Here he was the son of Lyman Beecher counseling caution and prudence; tomorrow he would be Beecher the incorrigible showman staging another slave "auction"—this time a girl who, it was said, had been offered for sale by her white father. The trader who had bought her had allowed her, with Henry's word as bond, to go north to raise money for her redemption. Without warning, after a Sunday service, Henry asked: "Is it lawful on the Sabbath day to do good, or to do evil? To save life, or to destroy it?" Then, turning to the platform stairs, he said: "Come up here, Sarah, and let us all see you." The young woman who came shyly up the stairs was nearly white.

"And this," Henry said, "is a marketable commodity. Such as she are put into one balance and silver into the other. . . . I reverence woman. For the sake of the love I bore my mother I hold her sacred. What will you do now? May she read her liberty in your eyes? Shall she go out free?" Once again an audience, this time his own congregation, responded uncontrollably. "Tears of pity and indignation," Eunice recalled, "streamed from eyes unused to weeping. . . . Women took off their jewelry and put it into the baskets. . . . Men unfastened their watches and handed them to the ushers. . . ." It was a stunning drama: a mid-Victorian audience confronted by an almost white girl who had been offered to any white man who would pay for her.

There is no record of Henry's ransoming a black male slave or an unattractive black woman.

Whether Henry decided that political action was necessary to halt the spread of slavery or he simply saw that politics was another arena in which his talents would shine, he joined in the Presidential campaign of 1856. The newly formed Republican party was made up of discontented members of the old Whig party, Free-Soilers, the violently anti-foreign Know-Nothing party and sundry reformers, all held together by their opposition to slavery. Casting about for a heroic figure with no political past to haunt him, they hit upon John Charles Frémont. At forty-three, Frémont was already known as the "Pathfinder" because of his exploration of trails across the western wilderness and his "conquest" of California. He was brave, handsome, ambitious, and opposed to slavery, and he was married to Jessie Benton, the strong-willed daughter of Senator Thomas Hart Benton of Missouri; but he was also headstrong, rash, and completely inexperienced in government.

Joining such New York bigwigs as Senator William Seward and *Tribune* editor Horace Greeley, Henry moved enthusiastically into the campaign. Taking a leave of absence from his church, he toured New York State, making two- and three-hour speeches several times a week to huge audiences. The Democrats nominated James Buchanan, an elderly bachelor, conservative, respectable and, as it turned out, willing to appease the South. Despite support from a rising western political figure, Abraham Lincoln, poetry by Whittier, praise by Emerson, and a rousing slogan, "Free Soil, Free Speech and Frémont," the candidate—doomed always to be the hero who failed—was defeated. Henry was left exhausted, subject to dizzy spells and in debt, but now known as a man to be heeded in other matters besides religion and ethics. The attacks of critics attested to his growing reputation. An abusive letter in the Hartford *Times* was headlined:

A Sermon by Henry Ward Beecher
Politics in the Pulpit
The Church of St. John C. Fremont
Blasphemy of a Rev. Political Buffoon

But slanderous journalism was common and public figures learned to take such insults in stride.

As the decade wore on, a kind of numbness alternated with periods of tension. Henry spoke out only intermittently on slavery. But at least once, amid all the rhetoric, he revealed that he knew there was more behind the Southern position than lust or an unawakened Christian conscience. With a sense of economic determinism worthy of a Marxist, he declared in one of his columns in the *Independent:* "It is a policy the necessity of which springs from the very organization of their society, from the irresistible nature of their industrial system. They cannot help themselves." He could be just as acute on the effect of the Northern industrial system:

The corrupt passions which lead in the Southern States to all the gigantic evils of slavery, in Northern cities break out in other forms. . . . The grinding of the poor, the advantages which capital takes of labor, the oppression of the farm . . . of the road [the railroad] . . . of the shop . . . of the ship, are all . . . as guilty before God as the more systematic and overt oppressions of the plantation.

And again:

If we have said: "To agitate the question imperils manufacturing . . . shipping . . . real estate" . . . and if we have bought the right to make money here by letting slavery spread and grow there—we have been doing just the same thing that they have.

Then in 1859, John Brown came to Virginia from years of bloody forays against the Border Ruffians in Kansas and was captured after he and his tiny band occupied the arsenal at Harpers Ferry. In an address two weeks later, Henry declared that he sympathizes with Brown and thinks the "poor, child-bereft old man is the manliest of them all," but he disapproves deeply of his "mad and feeble schemes." Taunting Northerners, Henry added: "What must be the measure of manhood in a scene where a crazed old man stood head and shoulders above those who had their whole reason? What is average citizenship when a lunatic is a hero?"

But the "crazed old man" had wrought better than he—or Henry Ward Beecher—knew. And in the hanging of Brown there was a drama Henry could not resist. He brought into Plymouth Church the chains that were said to have bound the old man, threw them down and, trampling on them, sent his audience into a paroxysm of grief at Brown's fate—and cries of admiration at Henry's nobility.

Swinging between benevolence and denunciation, Henry turned up on several sides of the conflict in those last years before the final breaking of ties. His favorite position, as we have seen, was that if slavery was prevented from spreading, it would die of its own weaknesses. But he never could say how long that might take. Another of his positions was that the slave must be educated and uplifted until he became so good a Christian that his master would be inspired, or shamed, into freeing him. The slave must be taught to be "an obedient servant and an honest, true, Christian man. . . . Truth, honor, fidelity, manhood—these things in the slave will prepare him for freedom. It is the low animal condition of the African that enslaves him." The point was not only sanctimonious but it suggested that Henry had missed, or dismissed, the message of Uncle Tom's fate.

Northerners should also, Henry insisted, work on the conscience of the slaveholder. "We love you and hate your slavery," Yankees should declare. Southerners must be persuaded through Christian love and prayer to give slaves the right to become Christians, to marry and keep their children, to read, and to testify in a court of law. It was, as one critic has said, "the veriest pipe dream."

Then there was the argument that has always been used against enslaved or downtrodden people everywhere: "Does any man believe that this vast horde of undisciplined Africans, if set free, would have cohesive power enough to organize themselves into a government and maintain their independence? If there be men who believe this, I am not among them."

In opposing a slave rebellion because it might prove a disaster, Henry was reflecting a middle-class fear of disorder and anarchy. This fear led him into ethical swamps. "The right of a race or nation to seize their freedom," he declares, "is not to be disputed. It belongs to all men . . . without regard to complexion." "But," he adds, "according to God's Word, so long as a man remains a servant, he must obey his master." Thus, while he denounced slavery in the most violent terms, he discouraged any active resistance to it. In response to a proposed boycott of slave-made products, he delivered a sermon called "Our Unworthiness," crying *mea culpa* and denouncing the "growing rottenness of politics" and the "luxury, extravagance . . . corruption of morals" resulting from prosperity. He went on to describe Northern wealth as partly the product of slave labor: "We clothe ourselves with the cotton which the slave tills. . . . Our looms and our factories are largely built on the slave's bones. . . ." But instead of supporting a boycott or even stronger measures, his conclusion was that they would do no good. Once again, he left his listeners filled with guilt but dissuaded from making even a gesture.

As his critics have said, compared to the active abolitionists and the faithful workers in the Underground Railroad, little that Henry did for the antislavery movement required a sacrifice, and almost all of it brought him publicity and acclaim. And yet, as a master of the emotional appeal, the phrase that stirred the blood, the gesture that dramatized the cold fact, he made his contribution.

With money coming in not only from Plymouth Church but from lectures and books and his contributions to the *Independent,* Henry was able to move his family into a spacious graystone town house not far from the church. It was a long, long way from the pathetically tiny cottage of the early Indianapolis days. But for Eunice it brought new problems: members of their families—Lyman and his wife, Catharine and Eunice's mother—came and some of them stayed until they or Eunice could not stand another day together.

Henry's days at home were filled with visitors, many of them seeking help or advice. It was an exhausting routine and whenever he could he rushed off to his Peekskill farm and his beloved flowers and fruits. He had had every foot of soil turned over twenty inches deep and planted, under the supervision of an able English gardener, with vegetables, flowers and what was said to be the greatest variety of trees and shrubs in any private collection in America.

When Henry first came to know Theodore Tilton, in 1854, Tilton was a twenty-year-old reporter on the New York *Observer.* He was tall and handsome, with auburn hair which he wore long; other reporters referred to him as "Apollo" and a "perfect Adonis." At first he was intensely religious and burned with the kind of passionate idealism that often consumes itself, leaving a desperate disenchantment. He had a style, somewhat Byronic, certainly Romantic, mingling a dedication to crusades and a touch of brooding for the world's ills. He was also talented and ambitious.

Henry, charmed by Tilton's enthusiasm, his promise and, not least, his admiration for Henry, persuaded Bowen to make him a general assistant on the *Independent.* Soon, too, Henry officiated at the marriage of Tilton to one of his other parishioners, Elizabeth Richards, eventually far better known as Lib Tilton.

When Tilton joined the *Independent,* in the late 1850s, it was a small sectarian weekly with a circulation of seventeen thousand. A resourceful editor, he began after a while to secure contributions, often controversial, on lively issues from such people as Garrison, Phillips, Greeley and the Hungarian patriot Kossuth. His vigorous editorials trou-

bled the quiet pages of the *Independent* with advanced views on abolition, women's rights and religion. He had imagination and temperament,
publishing Elizabeth Barrett Browning regularly and turning out half a
dozen volumes of poetry, mostly facile ballads on highly Romantic
themes. Within a few years the *Independent* reached a circulation of
sixty thousand and Tilton was earning many times as much as when he
started. He also developed a showy platform manner and in later years
often went on highly successful lecture tours.

Tilton had long idolized Henry from afar. Now he made no secret of
his worship. As he said some years later, the minister's influence on him
had been greater than that of all his books and teachers. Deeply flattered,
Henry responded warmly. Despite the gap of twenty-two years between
them, they became so intimate that Tilton later wrote:

The debt I owe you I can never pay. My religious life; my intellectual development; my open door of opportunity for labor; my public reputation; all these, my
dear friend, I owe in so great a degree to your own kindness that my gratitude
cannot be written in words, but must be expressed only in love.

That the relationship was not one-sided but a deeply shared experience is
made clear in another passage in the same letter:

Then, what hours we had together! . . . What mutual revelations and communings! What interchanges of mirth, of tears, of prayers! The more I think back
upon this friendship, the more am I convinced that, not your . . . fame, not your
genius, but just your affection has been the secret of the bond between us; for
whether you had been high or low, great or common, I believe that my heart,
knowing its mate, would have loved you exactly the same.

Were not the effusiveness, the rank emotionalism of such an outpouring
characteristic of their circle, we might suspect that the relationship was
something more than a friendship.

Henry's marriage had obviously become an emotional desert. Once
again he reveals his frustration not in letters but in his published writing.
In a column in the *Independent* in 1859 he wrote:

Domestic unhappiness comes from the fact that people do not . . . recognize the
peculiarities of each other's natures. They expect impossible things of each other.
If a flaming demonstrative nature and a cool, undemonstrative nature come together, neither of whom understands or makes allowances for the peculiarities of
the other, there can hardly fail of being unhappiness.

To someone with a "flaming demonstrative nature"—the phrase
characterizes Henry unmistakably—an affection such as Tilton's could
hardly have been completely satisfying. Later, in his novel, *Norwood*, he
observed that when love goes out of a marriage, some "distribute their
affection in many channels" while others "bury their Love and keep

watch as over a sepulchre." He also wrote of the effort it takes to divert worldly passions into holy channels and he marvels at the ascetics who sacrificed their affections for the sake of celibacy or virginity. When the "secret tide" of "mighty longings and yearnings" set in upon them, he writes, they "poured forth in mingled sobs and words those affections which were meant to be eased in the relations of life, but which, hindered and choked, found tumultuous vent in mighty prayer to God." Phrases such as "hindered and choked" tell us quite clearly what Henry thought of such suppression. Elsewhere he refers to the two lives that all men lead, lives that are "not always, or often, either parallel, or morally alike." It takes no special knowledge of Freud to recognize that Henry is talking here of repressed sexuality and the ways it expresses itself. Critics who believe that Henry was guilty of the secret sexual liaisons with which he was later charged see in such passages signs that he had already given way to his desires or realized how close he was to doing so.

Henry's routine on the day he did his weekly piece for the *Independent* was to rise at six and take the ferry to the newspaper office in lower Manhattan. After he had finished his work, he and Tilton would often go off to browse in bookshops and picture galleries. They also shared a dedication to their church, Tilton serving for a time as the superintendent of the large and active Sunday school and joining Henry and Bowen in what some called "the Trinity of Plymouth Church."

It was probably Tilton, too, who persuaded Henry to back the women's rights movement openly. Despite his wife's lifelong scorn of the "New Woman" and his sister Catharine's clashes with Angelina Grimké, Henry was fundamentally sympathetic to the movement. He had encouraged women to speak in church and they were his most adoring parishioners. Even the *Independent* had endorsed their cause.

When Henry finally lent his support to the movement he did so with a flourish, appearing on the platform of Cooper Institute with Lucy Stone, who had refused to change her name when she married, and Robert Dale Owen, the social reformer, who had gone so far as to describe methods of birth control. "The most natural and proper method of introducing information into public affairs," Henry declared, "is to give women a coordinate influence there. What man that is gross, what man that is corrupt, would not be blighted before woman's vote?" Proceeding cautiously, he was arguing not so much that women have a right to the vote as that they will bring to bear a superior refinement and a loftier morality. But during the Civil War he did help Susan B. Anthony raise funds for her Women's National Loyal League, and finally, when he was called on to make a major address at the Woman's Rights Convention in 1866, he was unequivocal in his support of suffrage for women.

When the women's rights movement split in two at the end of the 1860s, with the more radical New York reformers led by Elizabeth Cady Stanton on one side and a group of New England moderates led by Julia Ward Howe and Thomas Wentworth Higginson on the other, Henry tended to support the latter. The New England segment eventually formed the American Woman Suffrage Association and, to look as respectable as possible, asked Henry to serve as its president. He agreed, but although he was actually president in name only, the New York organization—the National Woman Suffrage Association—was angered by this move. This resentment was fateful, for it would later contribute to the decision of a radical feminist, Victoria Woodhull, to expose what she believed were Beecher's extramarital sexual activities.

One of the issues on which Henry and Tilton did not see eye to eye was slavery. Tilton simply could not believe that the leader who had long before attacked slavery so fiercely was not by now out of all patience with slaveholders. But Henry still clung desperately to the dream that conscience, Christ and uplifted slaves would lead slaveholders to modify their views. When as late as 1860 he recommended that Plymouth Church continue its contributions to the Home Mission Society even though it supported churches among the Cherokee Indians, who were slaveholders, Tilton was acutely disturbed. The younger man rose at a meeting in the Plymouth Church lecture room and reported in anguished terms that everywhere people were asking him, "Is the pastor of Plymouth Church changing his views? Is Mr. Beecher becoming more conservative?" And in a gesture reminiscent of Henry himself, he concluded by holding up a Sharps rifle.

Apparently upset at finding himself on the side of what he himself called a "holdback," Henry again resorted to a slave auction to reestablish his antislavery credentials. This time it was a nineteen-year-old girl named Pinky, "too fair and beautiful for her own good," and once again he stirred his audience to tears and prodigal contributions.

In 1927, on the eightieth anniversary of Henry's first sermon in Plymouth Church, Pinky, then seventy-six years old and the wife of a Washington, D.C., lawyer, told what she remembered of the day she was ransomed by Henry Ward Beecher.

Although he had his ear to the ground, Henry Ward Beecher failed to hear the sound of Abraham Lincoln approaching. He did not go to Cooper Institute during the Presidential campaign of 1860 to hear Lincoln's first speech in the East, whereas Lincoln, seeing in Henry an anointed spokesman for middle-class America, went to Brooklyn to hear him preach. Later Henry would describe Lincoln as a "considerate, prudent, honest politician," a characterization that damned with faint praise and had a sting in its tail. Although Henry never worked up anything like the admiration he had had for Frémont—next to the dashing "Pathfinder," Honest Abe obviously seemed countrified, cautious and utterly unheroic—he did campaign for Lincoln.

He was more surprised than jubilant at Lincoln's victory. But when the President in his inaugural address said that his supreme purpose was to preserve the Union, and the South ignored the message, Henry moved to his defense. Everyone, he said, was asking, "Will the South secede?" Henry's answer was: "I don't think they will and I don't care if they do."

He was wrong, and when the guns of the South opened up on the garrison in Fort Sumter, it was as if he personally, along with all his pleas for love and Christian conscience, had been spurned. If peace, he wrote, means that the North must give up its religious convictions and suppress every sympathy for the oppressed, "Give me war redder than blood and fiercer than fire."

He immediately threw himself into the war effort. When his eldest son, Henry, not yet twenty-one, asked him for permission to enlist, he replied, "If you don't I'll disown you." He led in equipping a local regiment, the "Fourteenth Brooklyn," and he opened his home to the storing of military goods. He addressed recruiting meetings, blessed flags, preached patriotic sermons, and dared such unpopular advice as: "Every honest man in America ought to send to Washington one message in two words, *fight*, tax." All his zeal ignited, he celebrated George Washington and the flag as symbols of national honor. Anticipating the jingoism of a later era, he flung harsh epithets at the less zealous: "God hates lukewarm patriotism as much as lukewarm religion; and we hate it too. We do not believe in hermaphrodite patriots." He even found a variety of moral uses for war. It would teach self-denial to a people "grown luxurious by prosperity" and turn men's thoughts from stocks and bargains to patriotism and the national heritage.

Henry's threefold position as preacher, writer and editor (in 1861, needing money, he had become editor of the *Independent*—with Tilton as his assistant) gave him tremendous influence. His fame was registered in many ways, ranging from articles about him in popular magazines and in books on notable men to having well-known painters come to do portraits of him. Having achieved authority without official responsibility, and impatient with Lincoln's efforts to conciliate the border states—"border state eunuchs" Henry called them—the apostle of love and good will now became a merciless critic of the administration.

Henry meanwhile had his own problems. One story is that his son Henry, caught in a breach of discipline, lost his commission. It took Tilton to repair the damage. He went to Washington and literally charmed the secretary of war, Cameron, into granting young Henry another commission in the regular army. Eunice never forgave Tilton for this favor; unlike Harriet, she was not at all willing to have her son risk his life for the cause.

Henry was further upset when Frémont, who had been serving as general in command of the Western Department, was charged with incompetence and was removed by Lincoln. Convinced that Lincoln was jealous of Frémont, Henry asserted that the general had been mistreated and he arranged a dinner for the fallen hero when Frémont returned to New York. Along with the violent letter of protest that, as we have seen, Calvin Stowe fired off to his old friend Salmon Chase, it formed a barrage calculated to annoy any harried official.

But most disturbing of all for Henry, as for most Northerners, were the defeats suffered by General McClellan in the spring of 1862. Henry's reaction was a series of almost weekly assaults on the administration. In one of the earliest of these, on July 10, 1862, he wrote:

What has Mr. Lincoln's education done for him—more than ours for us—to fit him to judge of military affairs? . . . We are sick and weary of this conduct. We have a sacred cause, a noble army, good officers, and a heroic common people. But we are like to be ruined by an administration that will not tell the truth . . . that is cutting and shuffling the cards for the next great political campaign.

A week later he asserted, with supreme cruelty, "The President seems to be a man without any sense of the value of time," and the following week, as though addressing some slow-witted underling, "It is war that we are making. . . . It is not Politics. . . . It is not the decision of legal niceties. . . . It is war, absolute, terrible, and immeasurable War!"

At the outset Henry had opposed emancipation by edict, believing, along with middle-class conservatives, that it would be arbitrary and unconstitutional for the federal government to take such action against private property. But when disaster followed disaster he at last decided that, in the declaration of men's "inalienable rights," "liberty" was now more important than "property." So he called for universal emancipation. Once again he seemed to be joining the radical abolitionists.

With this demand added to his exhortations, his scorn for Lincoln became limitless: "Never was a time when men's prayers so fervently asked God for a Leader! He has refused our petition! . . . Not a spark of genius has he; not an element for leadership. Not one particle of heroic enthusiasm."

All this was apparently too much for his brother Thomas. Writing from his parish in Elmira, New York, Thomas declared that he was doing great harm by "a most noble overestimate of men and public sentiment.... The more emancipation you talk, the less recruits you can enlist."

But Henry was not listening. Intoxicated by his influence and fortified in his bitterness by every announcement of a setback and by such private grievances as that his son, after fifteen months in the army, had never seen action, he stooped to open insult:

At present, the North is beaten.... His [Lincoln's] advisers clash. His generals quarrel.... What shall he do? So he does nothing.... It is a supreme and extraordinary want of executive administrative talent at the head of the government that is bringing us to humiliation. Be it known that the Nation wasted away by the incurable consumption of Central Imbecility.

To all of which Lincoln said only, "Is thy servant a dog?"

Even Harriet protested Henry's bitterness: "The general tone of your articles is deeply discouraging to that very class whose demoralization and division would be most hopeless defeat for us."

The Emancipation Proclamation seemed to be a vindication of Henry's position and it added measurably to his reputation. It even gave rise to the story, probably apocryphal, that one rainy night late in 1862, a tall, gaunt stranger muffled in a great cloak came to the house in Columbia Heights and spent several hours alone with Beecher in talk and prayer, and that only after the President's assassination did Henry tell his wife that the visitor had been Abraham Lincoln.

But the failure of the Proclamation to have any such effect on the South as Henry had expected took some of the fire out of his campaign. Spiritually as well as physically exhausted, he gladly accepted an offer from his congregation to send him to Europe for a long rest. But those who credit Henry Bowen's later statements about his wife's relationship with Henry believe that there was another reason for Henry's near prostration and his flight to Europe: Lucy Bowen's untimely death—she was only thirty-eight—in the spring of 1863. It was this warmhearted woman who had befriended the Beechers when they first came to Brooklyn and had been Henry's intimate associate in the fevers of the revival of 1858.

What Bowen revealed many years later when Henry was charged with the seduction of Elizabeth Tilton, was a shattering deathbed confession by his wife: She had had, she said, a sexual relationship with Henry Ward Beecher.

Once again leaving his wife and children, Henry sailed for Europe in June 1863. It was still a dark time for the Union forces, and in England Henry encountered in the upper class a belief, amounting sometimes to a hope, that the North would never defeat the South. He was persuaded, he wrote to Harriet, that with a few notable exceptions, the political leaders, the rich, and the professional classes were motivated by fear: "I do not mean fear of a narrow kind. But the shadow that the future of our nation already casts is so vast that they foresee that they are falling into the second rank." So he refused invitations to speak, believing it would be futile.

But in July, as he traveled on the Continent, news came of the great victories of General Meade at Gettysburg and of Grant at Vicksburg, and Henry's mood changed. By the time he returned to London he was ready to speak his mind. Meetings were quickly arranged and during October he delivered addresses in the key industrial cities of Manchester, Glasgow, Edinburgh, Liverpool and London.

In describing this tour, his worshipful early biographers picture Beecher as taking his life in his hands in facing huge and hostile audiences and as converting them by sheer courage, eloquence, common sense and personal magnetism. But historians point out that the first Union victories had already convinced the British that the North could win; that the Emancipation Proclamation made it morally difficult to defend the South, and that the common people with the exception of workers in mills that needed cotton, had long favored the North. According to this view, the scurrilous, blood-red posters that greeted Henry in Manchester and elsewhere ("Men of Manchester, Englishmen! What reception can you give this wretch save unmitigated disgust and contempt? His impudence in coming here is only equaled by his cruelty and impiety") were simply retaliation for Henry's declaration after the Trent Affair (in which the English had been found dealing with Confederate agents) that "the best blood of England must flow."

But no one could gainsay Henry's personal triumph, evidence once again of his power over an audience. Famous only for the brief flight of a sermon, a lecture or a newspaper column, he demonstrated in the five English speeches an ability to sustain a line of arguments and to orchestrate a variety of appeals.

He began with every disadvantage: he was almost unknown in Britain (Harriet was so much better known that he was once introduced as the Reverend Henry Ward Beecher Stowe), *Punch* greeted him with caricatures, and worst of all, English cotton mills were closed for lack of Southern cotton. His first audience, in a huge hall in Manchester, was made up one-fourth of toughs sent to break up the meeting. For an hour wild stamping and shouting kept him from being heard. He later said he felt like "a shipmaster giving orders to a mutinous crew in a tropical thunderstorm." Then his good-humored, cool defiance won him a hearing and he went on to capture his listeners with flattery, wit and hardheaded reasoning. In the end he was cheered tumultuously.

In Glasgow, where the shipyards were still building blockade runners for the South, he aimed at workingmen, arguing that slave labor anywhere was a threat to free labor everywhere. In the South, he pointed out, labor was a "badge of dishonor." In Edinburgh the crowd was so dense that he had to be handed over the heads of the people in the hall. At Liverpool, headquarters of Southern sympathizers, he received frightening warnings not to speak, but after overcoming his fears—partly by handling his precious stones—he went to the meeting. It took over an hour for him to make himself heard, but then his sharp sallies and extraordinary aplomb won again. Once more he used economics, observing that a South made up of slaves and poor whites would not be a good customer. After three hours his voice failed him—but he had had his say.

At the climax of his tour, in immense Exeter Hall in London, Henry asserted that the North was fighting not only for its life but for free labor and free institutions everywhere. He left London with colors flying and was greeted in New York as a conquering hero. In an *Atlantic Monthly* article, "The Minister Plenipotentiary," Oliver Wendell Holmes hailed Henry's journey as the most remarkable embassy since Franklin's to Versailles. Henry himself was quite modest about his role:

I believe I did some good service wherever I spoke [he said at a huge reception in his honor in Brooklyn]. But it should be remembered that a single man . . . would be eaten up by vanity if he said, or supposed, that he had done all the good that had been accomplished. . . . When, in October, you go to the tree and give it a jar, and the fruit comes down . . . it is not you that ripens it. A whole summer has been doing that.

But he also remarked that a committee in London had said: "If you can lecture for us, you will head off this whole movement," leaving the impression that he had indeed tamed the British lion single-handed.

Henry spoke now with soaring confidence, sending out even in the somber days of 1864 his old clarion call for love, liberty and benevolence. His harsh criticisms of the administration were forgotten. Indeed, as Congress was about to adopt the Thirteenth Amendment, abolishing slavery, he arrived at the White House and appeared at a window to share with Lincoln the cheers of the crowd. Later, when he heard that Lincoln was sending a delegation to confer with Stephens, the vice-president of the Confederacy, he hurried to Washington to caution the President against offering concessions; he reported that he had been reassured.

One unfortunate incident marred Henry's triumphs: in May 1863, brokers apparently seeking to panic the stock market bribed young Joseph Howard to forge an Associated Press dispatch so that it would appear to be a Presidential call for 400,000 additional troops and for a day of fasting and prayer. Howard was apprehended, tried and imprisoned. Because his father was the Beechers' closest friend and a founder trustee of Plymouth Church, Beecher persuaded Lincoln to arrange for young Howard's release. Isolated as the episode may seem, the young man's behavior was an omen of the corruption that would riddle business and politics in the postwar years. And as the press noted, it came rather close to Plymouth Church.

The high point of Henry's official recognition and perhaps of his career came in the closing days of the war. Fort Sumter had been recaptured, and Lincoln chose Henry Ward Beecher to deliver the address at the ceremony of the return of the American flag to the fort. It was a perfect opportunity for Henry and he delivered a speech both solemn and joyous. Standing amidst the ruins of the fort—in effect the desolation of the South—he dwelt on reconciliation and struck a note of magnanimity, blaming only the Southern leaders for all crimes and disasters. "But for the people misled . . . let not a trace of animosity remain," he declared. "The moment . . . they return to their allegiance, then stretch out your honest right hand to greet them. Recall to them the old days of kindness. Our hearts wait for their redemption." It was in the best sense a Christian speech, and a moment of true greatness.

Henry Ward Beecher would never have such recognition again and he should have been allowed time to savor it. But in the evening of that very day, in a box in the Ford Theatre in Washington, Abraham Lincoln was assassinated.

"Did ever so many hearts," Henry said in the sermon he later preached at Plymouth Church, "in so brief a time, touch two such boundless feelings? It was the uttermost of joy: it was the uttermost of sorrow—noon and midnight without a space between."

In his feelings for Lincoln, Henry had at last caught up with the common people.

During the war it was easy for antislavery forces to demand complete equality for blacks. But once the war was over and federal troops had been sent south to "restore order," and carpetbaggers were hurrying after them to gather the spoils, the problem of achieving such aims was baffling, especially to political moderates like Henry Ward Beecher. Trying as always to reconcile both extremes, he advocated suffrage for freedmen. But he added that the South must be permitted to regulate such matters itself and that there should be property and educational qualifications for voters. Once again he spoke for the majority, echoing a widespread Northern reluctance to give all blacks the right to vote. He was also reflecting a middle-class faith in education and, finally, a Protestant conviction that advancement must be achieved through hard work and self-discipline.

It was soon evident that his views were very close to those of the new President, Andrew Johnson. Although Johnson was a Republican, his Tennessee "poor white" origins made him peculiarly sympathetic to the problems of the South. Pleased to find a President whom he could support, Henry wrote to Johnson, stressing the need to secure for freed slaves "the kindness and good will of the Southern white man." Somehow, conciliating the South had come to seem more important than suffrage and full citizenship for freedmen. And quite forgotten was the rage he had expressed against the rebels after Lincoln's assassination: "no such man . . . should stand otherwise than as a branded and disgraced traitor. Pardoned he might be, and suffered to live; but he should live as Cain lived."

But both Henry and Johnson were reckoning without the Radical Republicans. As harsh as Henry was sentimental, they sent a message to Johnson demanding that the South should be policed until it was chastened and ready to cooperate.

In September 1866, Henry was invited to Cleveland to serve as chaplain at a convention of soldiers and sailors who were Johnson supporters. His annual hay fever attack prevented him from attending, but he sent a public letter in which he endorsed the convention's recommendations and criticized the Radicals for impeding reconciliation and for interfering in Southern local government. He then added a comment on the freedmen. They must, he said, "take their march. . . . If they have the stamina to undergo the hardships which every uncivilized people has undergone in its upward progress, they will in due time take their place among us. That place cannot be bought, nor bequeathed. . . . It will come to sobriety, virtue, industry, and frugality."

An essay could be written on the prejudices embedded in that statement: that blacks lack stamina and have not faced hardship, that they are uncivilized, that "progress" is always upward, that freedmen should be patient until whites decide they are worthy of a place in society; and that sobriety and frugality will make them worthy of such a place.

The letter drew down on Henry a storm of criticism not only from Radical Republicans but from his friends, other clergymen and even members of his church and family. He was lumped with Johnson, the "Copperheads," and those who raised the specter of black domination of the South. Even Tilton, who had taken over the editorship of the *Independent* in 1863, when Henry went abroad, turned on him. Where a short time earlier *Harper's Weekly* had referred to him as the most brilliant preacher who had ever appeared in America, Tilton now wrote that

Beecher had "done more injury to the American Republic than has . . . any other citizen except Andrew Johnson," and Horace Greeley of the *Tribune* declared:

It was ungenerous . . . to render his apostasy so base, so black, so hateful, so hideous. In pity, if not in decency, they [those who invited him] should have put something into their letter implying . . . that he might serve his new masters without . . . shaming the honorable record of his past years.

Bewildered, Henry wrote another letter, trying to dissociate himself from Johnson and yet stand his ground. "I am not a 'Johnson man,'" he declared, and, "I still think a middle course between the President's and that of Congress would be wiser than either." Although he would later point out that his approach to the South was finally adopted, he had blundered badly and his new effort evoked only further criticism. Even Harriet challenged him, posing some hard questions: Were the Southern states to be readmitted without any safeguards for the Negro? Would they repeal the "Black Codes"? Would they also raise up the poor whites?

His brother Edward went even further, sending a letter to the Chicago *Tribune* sharply criticizing Henry's position. When Henry wrote to him in protest, Edward answered with the formality of an older brother defending the honor of the family.

Despite Henry's avoidance of unpopular positions, he was inextricably linked to Johnson and to Johnson's ignominious defeat. He had advocated a Christian attitude of reconciliation, but it was reconciliation with the masters at the expense of the slaves. For twenty years he had hedged and paltered, attacked and retreated, swung this way and that; it was ironical that when at last he took a firm stand on emancipation he should nonetheless have been identified with Andrew Johnson.

Henry continued to turn out his ebullient sketches, and these as well as his sermons still appeared in the *Independent*. But so did Tilton's attacks on his political position. So in 1867, after almost eighteen years as its star contributor and for a short time its editor, Henry resigned from the paper. Although he objected to some of the advertising accepted by Bowen, he himself continued to give testimonials to commercial products ranging from Waltham watches to a truss, including such inanities as—of Pears soap—"Soap must be considered as a means of grace and a clergyman who recommends moral things should be willing to recommend soap."

There was little change in his home life. While driving their carriage Mrs. Beecher was thrown and suffered a blow on the head from which she never fully recovered. She was always so strict with the children and opposed the marriage of their daughter Harriet to young Reverend Samuel Scoville so firmly that Henry could hardly bear it. Cold, straitlaced, severe, she came to be known in some quarters as "the Griffin."

Perhaps that is why Henry bought fast horses and one country place after another, why he surrounded himself in church with masses of fresh flowers and acquired so many fine Persian rugs he had to use them three deep in his drawing room; why he visited Tiffany's regularly to see the latest in precious stones. When he was asked how he reconciled such indulgence with the way of the humble Jesus, he asserted that the belief in a relationship between poverty and sanctity was a product of the medieval church. In a lecture called "The Moral Uses of Luxury and Beauty," he said: "I don't know why [a man] should not indulge himself and his family with the elements of the beautiful . . . [or] should dress plainly when he is able to dress richly provided he cheats nobody." Even more provocative, especially since it came in the dark depths of the war, was his assertion that no one had a license to point to another and say: "He is a Christian, and yet he dresses in those jewels and feathers and trappings." A man has a right, Henry declared, "to do what he pleases in this regard, subject to God, and not to you, little godling." Henry himself was by then the highest-paid clergyman in America—with a salary of twenty thousand dollars a year and almost another twenty thousand dollars from lecturing and writing—and for fifteen years he had had one of the largest and most prosperous congregations in the United States.

With the release from austerity after the war, Beecher found other rationalizations for self-indulgence. In his novel, *Norwood,* his central character sees the elegance of the well-to-do as setting an example for their neighbors. Without going so far as to justify what Thorstein Veblen would call "conspicuous waste," Henry encouraged those who could afford to spend money freely to believe that they were benefactors of the community. Apparently he never felt a need to reconcile such views with his occasional outbursts against luxury and ostentation. It is not easy to serve impulse and hard reason at the same time.

During the war Henry had not appeared in the *Ledger.* In the interval, an astute publisher, Robert Bonner, had built the weekly into the most popular magazine in America. (Once a poor printer but now a millionaire and man of fashion, Bonner went out daily to race his trotters against the best that rivals could put on the road in Central Park.) Thus, when in 1865 Bonner offered Henry a contract for a novel that would run as a serial in the *Ledger,* Henry accepted it. Although he knew he was not a novelist, he had an inordinate respect for Bonner. That, along with the *Ledger's* circulation of 275,000 a week, envy of sister Harriet's success and, most of all, as high an advance as Bonner had ever paid,

$24,000, persuaded him. Because it did not come easily ("Oh, if I could make a story as easily as I can make a sermon!" he wrote to Bonner) and had to be fifty installments long, it took him almost four years to complete.

Norwood; or, Village Life in New England is the work of a fireside philosopher and essayist, not a storyteller. The narrative, such as it is, revolves around the relationship between the daughter of a New England physician and her suitors: a farmer's son who goes to Amherst, a Boston art student and a rich young Virginian. Ruth is pure, serious minded and bodiless, and her suitors are all manly, noble-hearted fellows. What there is of plot depends on coincidence or accident and is interrupted by metaphysical debates between Wentworth—a cosmopolite educated in Vienna and Paris as well as at Harvard—and an old-fashioned parson and a skeptical judge. Except for a few "quaint" characters, who appear only on the fringes of the narrative, there is little of the village life that the subtitle promises. Victorian gentility and a preference for what William Dean Howells—who had just become an editor of the *Atlantic Monthly*—called "the smiling aspects of life" barred Henry from anything like realism.

But *Norwood* does throw much light on Henry's beliefs. The most revealing of these, one that he had broached in essays and sermons, is the agreeable conviction that God manifests himself not in churches but in nature. "Your God is historic," the doctor says to the parson, "mine is living." Although it does not go as far as pantheism, for his God is still God, it is a long way from Calvinism. And tame as it may seem to us, it surely convinced Henry's readers that he had a touch of the pagan.

As befits such a lofty-minded New Englander, the doctor does retain a certain respect for the exalted tone of the old religion, defending it as a powerful agent against materialism. He argues, much as Harriet does in *The Minister's Wooing*, that a community brought up on "themes remote, difficult, and infinite, will be far nobler than if . . . fed upon easy thought." But Henry also gives us a more cynical view when he has a "pragmatical" Yankee say, "The church thinks that it will not do to make religion too easy; folks might take it up of themselves."

One of Henry's talents—if also sometimes a weakness—was his capacity to see several sides of a question; thus in *Norwood* he has the Virginian mock the intellectual pride of New Englanders:

"The fact is, there is too much brain here in New England. Everybody is racing and chasing after causes. I believe your people think they have the responsibility of the universe on their shoulders. When the Bible said, 'Canst thou find out the Almighty to perfection?' there were no Yankees about. Since then, five hundred ministers in this very New England think they have done it! They have found

God out—all that He has done, why He did it, what He has not done, and why He could not do it!"

Using a fictional character, Henry made light of two centuries of New England theology and religious speculation. And as he surely realized, the description applied perfectly to almost all the Beechers.

The doctor, not unlike Henry himself, is liberated in other ways. He admires "Beauty" and the arts. He attributes the lack of arts in New England not so much to Puritan prohibitions as to the fact that Puritanism forced the imagination of men into speculative channels and led to systems of thought rather than music or painting. "The poems of Dante," he asserts, "are not more complete pictures than are the sermons of Edwards." But even beauty, as one critic has pointed out, is subjected to genteel standards. The art student mocks an artist from New York who goes about painting pigweed, piles of stones and a board fence, knots and all, and who declares that an artist "must paint what he sees. Nothing in nature is to be despised." The artist's function, unlike that of the scientist, the student answers, is to "select only such things as are beautiful." The New York painter was not alone; Walt Whitman was taking much the same view.

As refined as is the portrait of the doctor, so crude is the portrait of Pete Sawmill, the one black in the book. He is a giant physically but mentally a child. Like Harriet's Dred, he is in tune with nature and the animal world because he is himself not far above the animal level. He is of course touchingly faithful, incapable of any moral or intellectual development, and unreliable because he drinks. Surely meaning to be kind, Henry created in him a stereotype of stereotypes, a figure that must have made Harriet cringe.

Although in his introduction Henry talks of a lower class of hangers-on who are "ignorant and imbecile, and . . . for want of moral health, have sunk, like sediment, to the bottom," and concedes that "perhaps nowhere in the world can be found more unlovely wickedness . . . than in New England," Norwood ignores the sordid and the cruel, moving in an intellectual and moral stratosphere. Thirty years in Indiana and Brooklyn had apparently left Henry with memories of a New England village as a kind of philosopher's republic. Where Calvinists made too much of innate depravity and the power of the devil, Henry, like so many Victorians, sees, hears and speaks no evil. Like the "mob of scribbling women," he accepts all the standards of the genteel tradition in fiction.

The reviews did not take Norwood too seriously, and Henry himself tried to pass it off as an amusing experiment. "People used to accuse me," he jested, "of being the author of Uncle Tom's Cabin—until I wrote

Norwood." But it was a success, and it paid off all Henry's debts. Because he was criticized for allowing it to be made into a stage play, he was glad to counterbalance it with a contract for two volumes of his sermons, a *Life of Christ*—on which he got an advance of ten thousand dollars—and a volume of *Prayers from Plymouth Pulpit*. Such an avalanche of churchly works was enough to smother any criticism of his dubious dabbling in politics and novel writing.

After Henry's resignation from the *Independent* in 1867, Tilton as editor increasingly filled the paper with radical views on a variety of subjects. The *Independent*, Tilton trumpeted, was now a journal of "practical Christianity" in which all "good men of all churches—yea, and good men of no churches—can Christianly unite." Although Henry cautioned Tilton against delivering religious opinions until he was completely sure of his ground, he also declared that the new truths of science could and should be reconciled with the old ones of religion. Tilton found this contradictory but he was much more disturbed when Edward Beecher led a group of midwestern ministers in a frontal attack on him and the *Independent*. Edward had already complained to Henry that Tilton had dared to recommend Emerson, a pantheist, and Spencer, who had reduced God to an unknowable force. Now he asked sharply where Henry stood. Just as sharply, Henry replied that his opposition to Tilton's views was well known, that he was no longer on friendly terms with Bowen, and that any quarrel Edward had with the *Independent* was his own affair.

This was the beginning of the bitterness between Henry and both Tilton and Bowen that would contribute to the greatest scandal of the age.

It was at this time, too, that Henry took the first step on the path to the scandal. Troubled by his difficulties in writing *Norwood*, he took to working on it with a very sympathetic and amiable Sunday school teacher who happened to be Theodore Tilton's wife.

21

SONS IN A TIME OF TRANSITION

Outwardly Edward Beecher was an unassuming Congregational clergyman; inwardly he believed he had a divine mission to change the Christian view of God and the origin of sinfulness. He wanted nothing less than to be a "moral Copernicus," to reorganize the religious universe as radically as the great Polish astronomer had reorganized the physical universe.

That was why he left the presidency of Illinois College and returned to Boston to become pastor of the Salem Street Church. For thirteen years he had periodically been called on to travel around the country begging for money for his school. To do any of the scholarly work he loved, he had to journey thousands of miles to the libraries of Boston, Cambridge and New York, endure long interruptions in his research, as well as "pecuniary cares and anxieties," and write on canal boats, in taverns and wherever else he found himself.

Except for his younger brother Charles, no one who knew his secret encouraged him: his father and his sister Catharine urged him to keep his more extreme theories to himself and his much younger half brother Tom, who studied at Illinois College, thought him obsessed. Paradoxically, as a clergyman he was acutely aware of the sin of pride, and for over twenty years he went through ordeals of self-discipline, sometimes stretching out face down on the floor of his study in an agony of prayer. Despite the temptation to correct what he considered a distorted and hateful conception of God, he managed to keep his revelation to himself for almost a quarter of a century.

Although the implications of his thesis were revolutionary, Edward was in practice as conventional as his father. Like Lyman, he believed in man's inherent sinfulness and the need for revivals. So as soon as he settled into his new post in Boston—not far from where he had started his career eighteen years before—he led revivals, preached loftily and poured out a stream of articles and lectures on religion, temperance, slavery, education and the Roman Catholic threat. In almost everything he did he carried the Beecher zeal to the point of obsession. " . . . his play," his sister Isabella declared, "is harder study than the labor of most men. Chess for instance is his diversion now, and he sits like a marble statue by the hour together, studying games from one of the five great volumes which adorn his library. I wouldn't be the wife of such a man for a great deal, but I like to observe such minds." But she found his preaching more "sprightly" than she had expected. And he mingled amiably with his fellow Bostonians, leading one of them to write: "You will see him in the streets, and at the exchange in the reading-rooms, and at the police court, at the public meetings in Faneuil Hall and Tremont Temple. He is a sociable, accessible, generous man and capital company when he is sufficiently acquainted to 'unbend the monkish brow.' " An Englishman who edited a Boston magazine, John Ross Dix, in his book on eminent American divines, describes Beecher's "fine Wordsworthian head," free and easy dress, and "nonchalantic air." His manner, Dix added, "is neither gaudy nor noisy, but he can sometimes abandon the sublime for the sledge-hammer style."

By 1849 his reputation was such that when a group of Bostonians established the *Congregationalist,* a weekly representing "the broad grounds of New England theology," they asked Edward to serve as editor. Little as the editor's work paid, he added it to all his other duties in an effort to meet the expense of half a dozen children, including twelve dollars a week for the care of his retarded son, Eddie.

The Beechers were now near the zenith of their influence, with Henry Ward and Harriet filling the columns of their New York *Independent,* Lyman preparing his collected sermons and other works, Catharine turning out book after book, and Charles publishing his attack on the Fugitive Slave Law.

Nor had Edward forgotten the struggle against slavery. Had he not been at Elijah Lovejoy's side only hours before that supremely brave man had been murdered in Alton, and had he not written a memorable account of that horrid event? And yet, as though the violence at Alton had confirmed his distrust of extremism, he still would not go as far as the radical abolitionists. Believing the guilt for slavery was shared by society as a whole, including the North, he refused to denounce all slaveholders. To the followers of Garrison this was an evasion and they felt sure of this when Edward, along with Calvin Stowe, supported the American Board for Foreign Missions in their policy of noninterference with slavery. As his brother Charles later said, Edward did not come easily to his decision:

How was it possible to be a true antislavery editor without being a disunionist and denouncing the Constitution [as Garrison had done] as a league with death and a covenant with Hell; and the churches as "a brotherhood of thieves"? How treat slaveholders politely without being called . . . "a mansteader," "a pirate"?

So Beecher, despite his support of Lovejoy, remained a "conservative Abolitionist." Harriet may well have been influenced by this attitude in her sympathetic treatment of slaveholders such as St. Clare in *Uncle Tom's Cabin.* Certainly she absorbed some of Edward and his wife Isabella's anger and dismay at the Fugitive Slave Bill when she stayed with them during her move from Cincinnati to Maine in 1850. And it was Isabella's letter urging her to write something heart-shaking about the sins of slavery that started her on the path to *Uncle Tom's Cabin.*

Edward had grown increasingly impatient with the church because of its inflexibility on matters of doctrine, especially when it came to coping with contemporary problems. Beyond that, brought up on the strictest notions of honor and right, he could not believe that God was not guided by such values. But the orthodox scoffed; imagine, they said, judging the deity by human standards. And a sentence of heresy, not to speak of damnation, still threatened any dissenter.

Whether he was fearless or naive or could no longer control his ambition to shake the world like a Copernicus, Edward, in a book called *The Conflict of Ages,* at last presented his ideas. Anticipating hostility, especially among the orthodox, he marshaled chapter after chapter of Biblical evidence and church history—and ended up completely obscuring his claim that he was writing from agonizing personal experience. The Bible, he maintained, contains no evidence that God doomed mankind because of Adam's sin. Far from being so callous and unjust, God was, Edward asserted, loving and forgiving. But unlike the Unitarians, he refused to reject the idea of man's inherited depravity; that, he said, ignored the endless history of mankind's wickedness, cruelty and corruption.

Thus did Beecher come to his divinely inspired theory—at once radical and bizarre—of the preexistence of souls. God had given the human race a previous cycle of life—a concept that was, he pointed out, an essential part of several world religions, especially in the East. In that earlier existence men had sinned. To God's sorrow, they had therefore come into this world in a fallen state, as into a kind of "moral hospital." Where Henry and Harriet, unable to accept a remote and unfeeling deity, had turned to Jesus, Edward simply humanized God.

Unfortunately Edward's two major theories had inherent weaknesses. In attacking the doctrine that man must bear the sin of Adam he was flogging a dying horse. For almost twenty-five years he had been so absorbed in perfecting his arguments that he was unaware how many of the faithful had already abandoned that belief. Its defenders seemed to be mainly clergymen who clung to it, perhaps as a way of disciplining their parishioners.

His other theory, the preexistence of souls, not only seemed farfetched and as fanciful as a fairy tale—an agnostic like Ingersoll or a Unitarian like Theodore Parker would have said that it was no different in this respect from the story of Adam and Eve—but was unheard of except among certain church philosophers.

As the work of a prominent churchman of a famous family, Edward's book commanded attention. It went into several printings, albeit small ones. More than that, it started a major debate, provoking five books and a shower of pamphlets, articles and reviews, and involving Emerson, Henry James, Sr., and Oliver Wendell Holmes among others. Most of the responses were unsympathetic and some were scornful. What astonished the critics was that a clergyman who had been considered orthodox, reasonable and free of what a Unitarian leader, Thomas Starr King, described as "the rhetorical and emotional friskiness of the Beechers," should have been torn by such doubts and arrived at such outlandish theories.

The sharpness of the reaction suggests that Beecher, if nothing else, had touched a sore spot. Conservatives said he had undermined orthodoxy and offered only an absurd alternative and that it was outrageous for men to judge God. They labeled preexistence a "fanatical delusion" and a "freak of the imagination." The more liberal critics, and especially the Unitarians, welcomed his attack on the significance of Adam's fall but decried his effort to revitalize the doctrine of inherent sinfulness. One of the more interesting responses was *The Nature of Evil* by the elder Henry James, a philosopher and the father of William, Henry and Alice. Because James had been scarred by a Calvinist childhood he viewed Edward's book as the last gasp of the old religion before it was "interred . . . on the shelves of disused libraries." He noted that the theory of preexistence still left God responsible for evil, although at some earlier period.

Despite the stir it created, *The Conflict of Ages* was a failure. It convinced most critics that Edward Beecher was extremely learned but had decidedly eccentric views. Only his good reputation saved him from being charged with heresy. Concerned lest the criticism of his book injure the *Congregationalist,* he resigned from his editorial post.

He continued to write as industriously as ever, but his next book, *The Papal Conspiracy Exposed,* published only two years later, was as narrow and bitter as *The Conflict* had been broad and benign. And it was even more paranoid than his father's anti-Catholic broadsides. Aroused by the missionary activities of what he called the "Romish" clergy, Beecher described the Papacy as a greedy and tyrannical "corporation" served by an arrogant priesthood. Its aim, he said, was to introduce Popish idolatry by infiltrating schools and accumulating land and property. Even allowing for his belief that Protestant and especially Congregational churches had achieved an ideal independence and an open organization after centuries of struggle, his book remains an assemblage of virulent charges. Most disturbing is its intolerant spirit: even as it defends freedom of worship it reminds us that it was New England Protestants who conducted the Salem witch hunts.

His dream of greatness fading rapidly and the East now associated with a humiliating defeat, Edward looked westward once more. His congregation liked him and wanted him to stay; like most churchgoers, they were far less interested in their pastor's theology than in his character and religion. But Edward was again convinced that he could exercise a much wider influence in the virgin West. And once more he found a post in Illinois, this time in a Congregational church being organized in the twenty-year-old town of Galesburg, about one hundred miles north of his earlier home in Jacksonville. Galesburg had other attractions: it was the seat of Knox College and a center of abolitionist activity. Beecher had also been invited to lecture at a new theological seminary in Chicago. Increasingly enthusiastic about the prospect, he finally wrote: "All the ties are now cut that hold me to New England and I begin to realize that I am a Western man once more."

In Galesburg, Edward and his family occupied a small cottage for two years. He then bought several acres a few miles from the center of town and built a comfortable home on a pleasant site. He would remain there for sixteen years. Friendly and unpretentious, he was soon as well liked as he had been in his Boston churches and at Illinois College. But with ailing children and school tuitions to be paid for several sons, he had to take finanical aid from the Stowes; and when a tornado in the summer of 1858 sent the steeple of his church crashing through the roof, Henry Ward came out and raised three thousand dollars to have the building repaired. For a brief period Charles, long a kind of disciple of Edward's, served as professor of rhetoric at Knox College. In time, too, four of his sons attended the college.

To deliver his lectures at the Chicago Theological Seminary he made a weekly three-hundred-mile round trip to Chicago even though he was paid only for his expenses. Less tolerable surely was the seminary's strict injunction against his preaching the theory of preexistence. His reward, he told Henry, was the knowledge that he was doing God's work of redeeming the West. "As I looked over the prairie," he said, "I saw the glory of God." Charles, judging the lectures—they dealt with the history of church institutions—from notes taken by Edward's son Frederick, thought they were "a work of genius."

Edward Beecher's years in Galesburg were, he later said, among the most pleasant in his life. But he was still a Beecher, that is to say, aggressive in a controversy, sometimes even when he was not directly involved.

So when a quarrel broke out between the Presbyterians, led by the Reverend George W. Gale, the aging founder of the town, and the Congregationalists, led by Jonathan Blanchard, president of Knox College, over control of the college, Edward, although he had no official connection with the school, sided with Blanchard. Aggravated, like many church disputes of the period, by differences over the slavery question—Blanchard was a firm abolitionist—the struggle grew witheringly bitter. Edward even went to other towns to spread word of the "moral assassination of Blanchard." Speaking in his own church, he accused the Gale forces of "atrocious acts of dishonesty and injustice." A trustee of the college, a Gale ally, described the speech as "distinguished by blasphemy and fiendlike malignity" and Beecher as a "sanctimonious hypocrite" guilty of "venomous scurrility." Even allowing for prejudice, it is rather hard to reconcile this description with Charles's later assertion that Edward "never uttered an impatient or unkind word concerning opponents" and never used ridicule or irony. Whichever characterization was true, Blanchard was forced out; he later founded Wheaton College. But only the war put an end to the dispute.

Perhaps because the criticisms of *The Conflict of Ages* were so diverse and in some instances so personal, Edward had not answered them. Now, having brooded over them long enough, he decided that most of them resulted from a misconception of God's nature. So in 1860 he published a sequel, *The Concord of Ages*, in which he restated his position with even greater force. The heart of the book, however, is its description of God as full of sympathy for fallen humanity but unable to prevent man's compulsion to sin. In the titanic struggle between God and Satan, God had finally won by assuming the form of Jesus, enduring the ultimate sacrifice, and thus demonstrating "the divine glory of suffering love." (Why God made man susceptible to sin in the first place and only later sent Jesus to redeem him is among the mysteries that Edward never satisfactorily resolved.) Edward went so far as to assert that it was orthodox Protestantism with its conception of God as unjust and heartless that had fostered in Americans an "insane love of money and tendencies to luxury and self-indulgence." He still talked of the millennium, but he added that it would not come until mankind adopted a new image of the deity. *The Concord of Ages* was virtually ignored; with war threatening, there was something unreal and irrelevant about a grandiose theory of the universe.

But Edward's brothers and sisters continued to involve him in their problems. In other days it had been Catharine and Harriet who called on him; later it would be Henry; now it was Charles. When his younger brother was brought before a Congregational council in Massachusetts in 1863 on a charge of heresy—partly because of beliefs he had borrowed from Edward—his brother acted as his advocate. But neither Edward's reputation nor his arguments saved Charles from being found guilty. It was a parting shot from orthodoxy's rear guard, doubly pathetic in that it was delivered in the midst of war.

Some of Edward's own foibles seem to have annoyed his parishioners in Galesburg. The church records for 1870 show that he was accused of moods of such abstraction that he failed to recognize church members when he met them on the street. He replied that he regretted the habit but that it was a family trait—only intense mental concentration had enabled him to achieve as much as he had. But there was apparently even stronger opposition, for the following year a small faction brought pressure on him to resign. Although most of his parishioners supported him, he withdrew rather than split the congregation. Despite their dedication, high ideals and willingness to accept low pay, Lyman and all his sons except Henry were harassed by such factionalism in church after church. Taught by their father, they were individualists and sooner or later bound to annoy a beleaguered orthodoxy.

Having twice given everything he had for Protestantism in the West, Edward now returned to the East. He was still full of zeal but the age had passed him by. It was not that he was sixty-eight years old but that he had had his great "revelation" forty years before and it was further than ever from being accepted.

The world and time are unkind to Romantic young rebels. Charles Beecher was such. In his youth, enamored of Rousseau and Goethe's Werther and Byron, he left home, dreamed of being a great musician, railed against the world of business and money-making, loved an unattainable young woman, wrote self-pitying poetry and talked of madness and suicide. Then reality, in the form of Lyman, Henry and other Beechers, a wife and child and the need to earn a living, did its work, and Charles came gradually around to serving his church and God. Still a passionate idealist, he held up the Bible and Jesus, not church creeds or theologians, as the sole source of spiritual truth. So it was a pity that his first parish had been in the raw Indiana town of Fort Wayne and that his tiny congregation had looked to him mainly to outwit and confound the local Presbyterian church from which it had split off.

By 1851, Edward, whom he revered, had long since gone back east, Henry had taken New York by storm, and Lyman and the Stowes were preparing to follow them. His wife plagued by malaria and his pay small, Charles found little to hold him in Fort Wayne. So he went off to Brooklyn and, while waiting for an opening, preached in Plymouth Church when Henry was on tour. At last he was called to the Free Presbyterian Church of Newark; and the first thing he did there was reorganize it into a Congregational church—the church of his fathers and relatively independent. Aroused, like Edward and Henry, by the Fugitive Slave Law, he was soon preaching fiercely against it. One of his sermons, "The Duty of Disobedience to Wicked Laws," published at the behest of his congregation, attracted much attention because it was by a Beecher but even more because it was so militant: "it is an unexampled climax of sin. It is the monster iniquity of the present age, and . . . the vilest monument of infamy of the nineteenth century." Some of the reactions to his outburst were almost as strong: opposition to slavery was acceptable but advocating civil disobedience and calling a law of the land infamous was not to be tolerated. Cravenly, the ministers of Newark expelled him from their association. Charles Beecher had, after all, a reputation for being "unsound."

Illness now forced him to take "vacations," and need compelled him to accept cast-off clothes as well as money from Harriet, Henry Ward, Isabella and other members of the family. Free of pretensions, he accepted such gifts without embarrassment. Isabella, his longtime confidante, found a lovely quality in him. While on a visit to Harriet in Brunswick, she wrote: "every look and laugh speak a childlike simplicity." He was, she said, so sure that man's original position was among the angels and he was so hopeful of regaining it that he suffered from none of the perplexities that disturbed her. But, she added,

he has troubles poor fellow . . . his health is miserable and so is his wife's. Newark is no place for either of them, and he has nearly concluded to go to California for a year or two, leaving his family here. I am so sorry for Sarah. She can't bear to be separated from him, yet she must come up here this summer to keep herself and her children alive. . . . They have five little children and no money.

She hardly needed to add: "just think of it and compare our lot."

Like many frustrated idealists, Charles was sometimes swept by an apocalyptic view of the world: What hope was there for sinners who would not put all their faith in Jesus? From a lovelorn youth who had bombarded his young half sister, Isabella, with letters of yearning and self-doubt he had become a Biblical prophet uttering cries of doom. His imagery was haunting and nightmarish. "Tell Father," he wrote to Harriet:

that the great Tribulation is begun. This guilty land will not escape. The church instead of premature paeans, had better weep in sackcloth and ashes. . . . The name of blasphemy is written no more henceforth on the imperial Head . . . but all over the *democratic body politic*. The Woman will first ride the Democratic beast and become drunk with blood. Then she herself will be destroyed. Democracy became Anarchy and universal confederacy against God. Antichrist will rise to the surface, and ride on the foam-wave, and then will come the End. Whom the *Lord* will destroy with the brightness of his coming. Father may not live to see it. But I for one expect either to die by violence or to live in the fastnesses . . . of the forest. The plot is laid. The explosion will come soon.

He is as alienated and overwrought in this, the religion of his maturity, as he was in the Romantic moods of his youth. Then his dream had been the utopia of an artist; now it was a vision of doomsday.

Charles had been fascinated at an early age by his older brother Edward's theory of preexistence, as much because it fired his imagination as because it freed God from blame for man's sinfulness. Typically, he embraced the belief more passionately than had Edward himself. Yet at the same time he rejected as presumptuous his brother's claim to a new version of God's government of the universe. He wrote:

I do not believe that "the system of God" has been revealed except in some partial details. . . . Nor that it is possible for your mind, however daring and however powerful, nor any other mind . . . to grasp that system and measure all the height and depth and length and breadth of the great theme [of] the origin of evil. And the very fact that any mind proposes to do such a thing . . . is enough to stamp discredit upon the whole of its proceedings.

Perhaps he sensed that Edward had been, after all, seduced by pride.

Charles also helped Harriet as she worked on *Uncle Tom's Cabin,* giving her his impressions of Southern life as he had seen it in Louisiana. It seemed natural, therefore, that when she was invited to visit Europe in 1853, Harriet should ask him to join her as secretary and escort. They had always been compatible; he was gentle and he had the face and air of an artist; he was a writer and had a gift for languages, and he loved good music. Weary in spirit as well as body, Charles welcomed the opportunity.

Once in Europe, he was kept busy writing letters for Harriet, accepting invitations here and there to deliver sermons, and acting as an interpreter in France. In her record of the tour, *Sunny Memories of Foreign Lands,* Harriet included entries from Charles's diary. Strangely, for one who had been an admirer of Byron and Rousseau, he was in some ways more prudish than his sister: he was shocked by the gin shops of London, deplored the social dancing, including the waltz, in the Jardin Mabille in Paris, and was offended in museums by the "salacious images of mythological abomination." Donning the Beecher mantle of moral reform, he lectured the British on the dangers of alcoholic drinks, including wine, and even claimed that no American family of his acquaintance drank wine. Generously, Harriet bought him a fine Amati violin in Geneva, and he diverted himself with the works of Beethoven and Mozart.

After the rich experience of Europe in Harriet's triumphal cortege, Charles returned to his church in Newark with mixed emotions. He welcomed a call to help prepare the music for Henry's *Plymouth Collection of Hymns* and contributed largely to its success. He also shared the interest in spiritualism—the furor over the spirit rappings of the Fox sisters in upstate New York was at its height—and made a report, called *A Review of the "Spiritual Manifestations,"* to the Congregational Association of New York and Brooklyn. In it he traces the "manifestations" of clairvoyants, mediums and their like to derangements produced by drugs or to "possession" by demons—wicked spirits that enter men and women and destroy them unless driven out. Once again we are reminded of Puritan charges against early New England's witches. No such manifestations are recognized in the Bible, he argues, and the mediums usurp Christ's function as Mediator. But such explorations should be received with respect, for "if they are in error, it is an honest one" and God, who "brings good out of evil, may bring benefit even out of this."

Critics asserted that Beecher's interpretations might well prove more dangerous than spiritualism itself because they revived a belief in demons. Undeterred, Charles continued to study "manifestations," becoming, as we shall see, more and more convinced of their validity.

In Galesburg, Edward now persuaded Knox College to offer Charles a post as teacher of rhetoric—that is, elocution—and, as it turned out, music. Although Charles was popular with the students, Edward's defeat in the struggle between the Presbyterian and Congregational factions over control of the school made Charles uncomfortable and he left after little more than a year. Once again he returned to the East. While he was biding his time in Andover, the family chose him to help prepare their father's autobiography. He occupied himself with that work on and off for the next few years. Almost from the first he was struck by Lyman's acute concern with saving the souls of his children. He wrote to Henry:

It is really one of the most solemn things I have attended to for a long time. It fills me with concern for my own children, and my own great Stupidity in regard to them, and above all, my unbelief in regard to their danger. *Is* eternal punishment a reality? Father thought so. He never doubted. Strike that idea out of his mind, and his whole career would be changed, his whole influence on us modified.

What would have happened, he asks, if their father had not believed in "future endless ruin"? Yet, he continues,

Isabella and Mary, I fear, reject father's belief on that point, and Hatty's mind is, I fear, shaken. . . . Do *you* really believe that the wicked will exist forever and continue forever in sin. . . . If they exist, I can conceive that they might be unchangeably wicked, and of course miserable. . . . How can we affect *our* children as Father did us, if we have not the same concern, the same sense of their awful danger.

Only Lyman's extraordinary influence can explain why a man who does not believe in the eternal punishment of sinners feels deep guilt because he has not challenged his children with such punishment.

Charles also bemoans the fact that he himself is failing to achieve communion with God: "My soul seems cold as death, and I have not strength enough to pray or strive." He yearns for the old days when there was a unity in the family, before their strong individual natures drew them apart. They must try, he pleads, to revive that spirit. "Above all," he concludes, just as he had when he left his exile in New Orleans to seek help from Henry in Indianapolis, "I wish you would write to me a good letter to help me in things spiritual."

A month later, still in the same mood, he sends Isabella a letter that is almost as troubled and groping as any he had written to her twenty years earlier from New Orleans. He is waiting desperately for a call from a church in Georgetown, Massachusetts, or—if Isabella can get their brother-in-law Thomas Perkins to help out—from one in Hartford. If he does not get such a summons, he will go somewhere west again. Fortunately he received a call from the Georgetown Congregational Church and began a stay there that would last for many years.

They were not his happiest years. A man of a sensitive and introspective nature, he found the life of a poorly paid small-town pastor a drudgery that drained him. Within two years he was once more pouring out his problems to his sister Belle. In one letter, after thanking her for money she had sent him, he told her that he was selling his once precious violin: since he had no time to practice to the point where he could play such music as Beethoven's sonatas, keeping the violin was like keeping a dead child in its coffin. With a seething, neurotic intensity, he described what he suffers as a village pastor:

To burn by a slow fire . . . to be ground on a great grindstone, to be bought and held as the slave of every darned fool in the village. . . . With nerves all raw, and sensitive to the slightest touch, to swim in a solution of weak vitriol and water would be a kind of refreshment. . . . Moreover, there is no release in death. No amount of thought, eloquence, talent, genius, effort makes any difference.

Thus I am crucified with Christ. The things I believe, nobody understands, nor wants to understand, nor believe. . . . But patience . . . I go on calmly explaining, expounding, instructing. . . . By and by the Lord will come and all will be over.

But these were all routine grievances; they scraped like sandpaper but they did not crush. The hard blow was still to come. It came because

Charles, borrowing some of Edward's more unorthodox ideas, persisted in preaching the theory of a suffering God and the preexistence of the soul. Even more disturbing to his fellow clergymen was his insistence, first expressed in Fort Wayne, that churches which substitute their sectarian creeds for the Bible are guilty of apostasy. He had doubtless escaped censure in Fort Wayne because he was a young preacher in an obscure western pastorate.

Now, fifteen years later, he was still proclaiming such rebellious doctrines. The orthodox churches, he asserted, are torn by feuds, debased by Mammon, and "debauched by slavery," and the religious press is full of lies and slander. Sinner, he cried, with a surge of Calvinist fervor his father would have applauded, if you do not feel you are distressing God, "you are ripening in sin. You are filling up with the cup of iniquity. . . . Away with orthodoxy if it come in as an obstacle in your salvation." What was needed, he declared in another sermon, was a new system of the universe.

He had clearly gone too far. Twenty-seven members of his congregation signed a petition declaring that his theories of preexistence, atonement, and the state of souls after death were not according to the faith accepted by the orthodox churches of New England. They asked that a council be called to investigate his views. The council met in the summer of 1863, not simply to investigate but to try him for heresy.

Even as the council was assembling, Charles received word that his eldest son, Frederick, had been seriously wounded—the first report said he had been killed—at Gettysburg. Charles would have turned from the trial and hurried to Gettysburg if his wife, Sarah, had not offered to go by herself. She found Fred lying in a barn with his wound abscessed; she had to nurse him for two months.

The Beechers closed ranks around Charles. Because his own theories were at issue, Edward came from Galesburg to defend his brother. Harriet, furious at such treatment of one of her favorite brothers, plunged into the battle, seeking help from high-placed churchmen. The persecution of Charles, she wrote to Dr. Leonard Bacon of Yale, is being conducted by "an unscrupulous minority in his church" and has proceeded to "a length that flesh and heart can no longer endure." Charles, she explained with true insight, is "full of imagination and loves to plunge and explore and revel in the celestial statistics and geography in years before the world was. . . . Now certain moles and bats pick up fragments of these things and pore over them as heresies."

Their efforts were of no avail. The council found Charles's teachings "fundamentally erroneous" and recommended that he be dismissed. It added that if he had held his theories but not preached them, the decision would have been different. In their hot reply, *The Result Tested,*

Edward and Charles seized on this admission and wrote: "The Council has no objection to heresy, however damnable, provided it is 'brought in privily.'" They went further, charging that the council had no authority to conduct a trial and that it was really a continuation of the Old School's relentless war against Lyman Beecher. Finally they declared the verdict a retaliation against Charles's insistence that the church back immediate abolition. He had gone even further: in December 1860, when President Buchanan, frightened by Southern belligerence, had proclaimed a day of fasting for the sin of opposing slavery and provoking Southern rebellion, Charles had persuaded a majority of his congregation to sign a resolution charging the President with a "treasonous conspiracy" and "an act of hypocrisy . . . in the highest degree insulting and detestable." It was these acts, *The Result Tested* said, that had led "the ecclesiastical copperheadism of New England" to bring him to trial.

Having made their countercharge with all possible force, the brothers took the position that they were the true conservatives: they held, in the "most orthodox sense, the doctrine of the native . . . depravity of the human race" and they believed that eternal punishment awaits the wicked. Privately, Charles characterized the verdict as slanderous, mean and a disgrace to all who accepted it.

The heresy trial of Charles Beecher was in fact an anachronism, an empty gesture betraying the helpless rigidity of the orthodoxy. Unable to deal with contemporary problems, it resorted to outworn ecclesiastical weapons to meet dissent. A few opponents in Charles's congregation withdrew and formed another church but the majority supported him. And in 1864 the citizens of Georgetown elected him to represent them in the Massachusetts legislature. A few years later another conference of Congregational ministers rescinded the council's verdict and restored him to good standing.

After the trial, Charles published his major work, *Redeemer and Redeemed: An Investigation of the Atonement and of Eternal Judgment.* Like a penitent with a votive offering for a saint, Charles dedicated his book "To her who gave me birth; consecrated me to the ministry; died before I knew her; whom next to my Redeemer, I most desire to meet in the Resurrection." Having proclaimed his adoration of his imagined mother, he devoted the preface to the influence of his very real father; that influence was so great, he admitted, that he had rebelled against him in order to survive as an individual.

As learnedly as any of Edward's books, *Redeemer and Redeemed* explores various theories, either tenuous or tortuous, of the Atonement. It presents a cosmic scenario in which Satan, who is, according to Charles, the firstborn and favorite son of God, seeks to rule the universe, and having failed, becomes the leader of fallen angels. Satan then charges that

God is a merciless despot and he manages by this and other strategies to seduce and corrupt mankind. At last Christ comes to suffer and die, proving God's capacity for sacrifice and selfless love.

The product of twenty years of study, published in the depths of a devastating civil war, it is the work of a brilliant mind but one that soon crosses the narrow line separating fertile speculation from fantasy. For all its learned Biblical analysis, its conclusion is as primitive as a nature myth. Although *Redeemer and Redeemed* is not unlike *Paradise Lost* in its aims and passion, Milton's work is epic poetry while Beecher's is a controversial thesis punctuated by mystic rhapsodies.

Reviewers acknowledged its erudition but found its theories bizarre and its rhapsodies at times unintelligible. They even saw it as dangerous in the power it attributed to Satan. But whatever Charles felt about this judgment, like Edward he never retreated from his position.

As in many families of the time, almost all Lyman's married sons and daughters suffered the loss of at least one child, and in several instances as many as five children. Charles's losses came late but in stunning succession. The two youngest of his children, twelve-year-old Hattie and fifteen-year-old Essie, went boating with their cousin George, Edward Beecher's twenty-year-old son, and all three were drowned. As Charles described it in a harrowing letter to his son, when a neighbor brought word that the three young people had disappeared, Charles and Sarah, dazed and uncomprehending, rushed to the pond. When they saw men desperately diving into the depths, Sarah "fell down as though dead." Charles insisted on diving, but in the depths it was like midnight—in every sense—and when he came up, neighbors made him leave. When the bodies were finally brought up, the two girls looked as though they were sleeping and at peace. Charles then saw, he said, that it was God's will and way.

When Isabella arrived for the funeral in Georgetown, she saw that "the Lord was in that household" and such an "atmosphere of heaven" pervaded it that it was good to be there; and when she came away she found it "hard to breathe earthly air at all."

Scarcely a year later Charles's son Frederick, who had remained in the army and was serving with the Forsyth Scouts in the West, died agonizingly while leading his men in a skirmish against Indians on the Colorado frontier. (The action became known as the Battle of Beecher Island and was marked by a monument where the young lieutenant fell.) In a letter to his sister Harriet, Charles poured out his heart, mixing anguish and pride with a tormenting sense of "the profitlessness of the fight, the miserable nature of the war." Writing to Henry of Charles's plight, Harriet cried out, "Annihilation reigns ... his hold on life is broken. . . . Poor Charley—he was so gay and so handsome and so full of life at twenty-two!" But Charles's grief was assuaged by a deep conviction that Frederick had joined his sisters in heaven. Although no one explained how the brutal death of the children could be considered blessed, the Beechers' belief in the reality of heaven once again proved priceless.

Indeed, Charles's belief in a spirit world increased with the years. But his view was unique: he endorsed a "Christian spiritualism" but thought psychic manifestations could be dangerous because the universe was full of "impure" and demonic as well as holy spirits.

In the spring of 1867, Harriet, returning from Florida full of enthusiasm for the easeful life she envisioned in Mandarin, urged Charles to buy a place next to hers. She also planned, she wrote, to establish a church there, especially for the Negroes of the area, and if he would enter the Episcopal Church, he would be just the minister they needed. Charles refused to change his church but he was tempted by the promise of peace and beauty as well as the possibility of working among the freedmen. After exploring various parts of Florida, he quit his comfortable post in Georgetown and in 1870, his surviving children all grown up, he bought a house and a few acres in Newport, in Florida's northwest panhandle. He would start a new life there, free at last from the dissensions of the church and the corruptions of society.

Throughout William Beecher's youth, as we have seen, the question in his family had been "What shall we do with William?" With his father's help he had managed to be ordained and to get church posts in Newport, Rhode Island; in Middletown, Connecticut; in Putnam, Ohio, where his sermons against slavery and intemperance had displeased some of his parishioners; in Batavia, New York, where he took over when his brother George left; in Toledo, where his opposition to a deacon's liquor bar caused the withholding of his salary until he sued for it; and, as his last station in the West, in Euclid, Ohio. So he had had six pastorates in less than twenty years and had left each one when the congregation would not pay what it owed him or what he desperately needed, or when some church members disapproved of his political and social principles or simply wanted a change. Which explains why, among the Beechers, he was called "William the Unlucky."

That name did suggest that his misfortunes were not necessarily his fault. Indeed, he was surely typical of many ministers who were simply not brilliant, aggressive or charismatic. Yet despite the lack of an education such as his brothers had had and his sense of inferiority in the face of their achievements, he appears to have been quite competent and as conscientious and pious as any of them. By the time he was forty he himself felt that his problems were mainly the fault of his congregations. In an address that he delivered at various installations of clergymen in the region around Batavia, he summed up the plight of many preachers, especially in the West. It was at once a protest, a warning and a cry of wounded pride.

Know, William begins, who your minister is. Remember that a pastor was considered an "angel of God" and a "gift of Christ." But he is also a "dying man," as liable to weariness and sickness, and as much in need of friendship, sympathy and love as anyone else. The ministry, William admits, "does not occupy as elevated a position as it did fifty or even twenty years since." But if the minister is treated with coldness, or neglect, or even undue familiarity, he loses the respect his work deserves. He is often compelled to "occupy the poorest tenement, some small, old brown house, in the back street, with fences, gates, windows, and out houses in a most dismal state of dilapidation. Or he is forced to board, with only one or two rooms for parlor, study, bedroom and kitchen."

No lawyer or physician, William continues, would work for so little pay. "If he is to have power to exhort, rebuke and warn successfully, and be the son of thunder and consolation, and his preaching be the fire and the hammer . . . then you must convince men that he is Christ's servant and very highly esteemed." The revolving system fills the minister with apprehension, breaks his spirit and his health, makes him timid and time-serving, ready to yield to every grievance. It keeps him from working with his people from birth to death and developing a "matured affection." He has no home, his children are born wanderers, and he descends to ever smaller churches. He finds that one or two influential church members can drive him out. Or he realizes that he is sent for as a revival preacher and will be replaced as soon as some parishioners grow tired of him, that churches look "to man rather than to God—more to talent than to piety—more to eloquence than to simple truth." You say you want your minister, William cries: "True, if he will submit to your terms—to be almost starved or naked—to be neglected and despised and loaded with contempt—without a house, a library, or an adequate salary—if he will come and be your drudge. . . . This," he concluded, "he can never do." And William never did. So he continued to go, as we have seen, from church to church.

While this address shows William as more or less resigned to an undistinguished career, it has the Beecher stamp in its aim of bringing light to the misguided and teaching people how to behave. His indictment of churchgoers was probably justified, but what he failed to realize—or accept—was that the old awe of ministers as beings apart was gone forever.

Like other members of the family, William developed an early interest in "animal magnetism," clairvoyance and phrenology, and was quite proud of his power to use mesmerism in healing. In an article in 1843 he told of visiting a Reverend Mr. Childs in the Genesee region of New York State and finding the minister with a ten-year-old boy in a cataleptic fit. The boy, subject to as many as half a dozen fits a day, had sore places on his head and spine from a fall some months before and had not spoken for several days. William "magnetized" the youth with a few passes. He then led him into a clairvoyant state in which the boy identified the taste of substances that Beecher, in another room, took into his mouth, and described the study in Beecher's home in Batavia. Using another favorite "science" of the Beechers, phrenology—William's article had originally appeared in *Fowler's Phrenological Journal*—he made the boy pray by putting his hand on the youth's "organ of Veneration" and then caused him to raise his fist threateningly by touching the "organ of Destructiveness."

The parents of the boy later claimed that he had been cured by William's treatment, and William himself noted that he had subsequently cured swellings, a tic, toothache and other ailments by means of mesmerism. He added that although he did not believe fully in clairvoyance, he did believe what he saw and knew. Let us give it a fair trial, he wrote, and if it is the work of the devil, as some say, let us learn his devices. It may be used by men for evil ends, he concluded, but so is everything else. Yet William was no rebel: When critics continued to charge that clairvoyance—and spiritualism in general—was a product of sorcery, he backed away not only from experimenting with the occult but also from magnetic healing.

Virtually starved out in Ohio, William followed the rest of his family east in the 1850s. His father being too old to help him, he found a place for himself in the Reading Bethesda Church, in eastern Pennsylvania. But soon he met the same old reactions—dissatisfied parishioners and dismissal. It solaced him little to know that a church council placed the blame on a faction in the congregation.

Now Harriet and Calvin Stowe had to come to his aid, getting him a pastorate in North Brookfield, Massachusetts. Because he also took on the duties of town postmaster, he was at last able to survive the trials of a pastorate—including an attempt to oust him from his postmastership— and stayed there until his wife died in 1870. Then, almost seventy years old, he retired and went to live with his daughters in Chicago.

When a reporter visited him in 1874 to get his opinion of the scandal surrounding his brother Henry, he described William as a patriarchal figure—tall, thin, white-haired, with a full white beard and, like Calvin Stowe, a black skullcap. Asked whether he thought Henry guilty, he answered as one not involved in the family passions: "Of course, it is possible, and I must confess that the statement of Tilton's is a tough thing to get around, but I believe that Henry can refute it, and that he will."

William Beecher was a dedicated minister, vigorous in some of his opinions, as in his early support of abolition, and not really as inept or contentious as his career might suggest. But unlike most of his brothers and sisters, he was not a writer, a scholar, a crusader or a magnetic personality. And he never got over a feeling of inadequacy. Nothing is more pathetic than the letter he wrote to Henry congratulating him on his triumphs in England during the war: I am as strong as ever in both mind and body, he writes, but

I don't think God *needs* me. I don't think all I've done or can do amounts to much. . . . Still I feel daily that there is a flood of emotion pent up in my heart . . . if I could only find a place where I could be allowed to preach the real gospel [and not] to please the rich and worldly and curry favor with the young.

So he alone of Lyman Beecher's sons fades into obscurity, dying in 1889, unrewarded and unsung.

Isabella Beecher, the first of Lyman Beecher's children by his second wife, in a portrait by Jared Flagg in 1852.

Harriet Beecher Stowe and Calvin E. Stowe, from a daguerreotype made shortly before the publication of *Uncle Tom's Cabin*.

Frederick Stowe, ill-fated son of Harriet and Calvin, poses in an oversized uniform as a recruit in the Union army.

James C. Beecher on his return from missionary work in China became the colonel and chaplain of one of the first black Union regiments recruited in the South and ended his Civil War service as a brevet brigadier general.

James and his second wife, Frances "Frankie" Johnson. After a tragic first marriage, his second appears to have been nearly ideal.

22

ISABELLA

In Search of an Identity

When John and Isabella Hooker bought a large wooded tract on the outskirts of Hartford in 1851 and put up an imposing home there, they would seem to have achieved an ideal frame for their lives. John was a successful and well-liked lawyer, Isabella was a charming and admired woman, both came from distinguished families and they had many friends in the best social circles. Although the Nook Farm area did not reach its heyday as a community of congenial and talented men and women until Harriet and Calvin Stowe and, later, Mark Twain and his wife, Olivia, joined it, it had by the mid-1850s half a dozen highly respected and remarkably compatible families. "We lived," John Hooker said, "like a little society by ourselves—each of us making free of the others' houses and each keeping open house."

Despite such an agreeable setting, an adoring husband and, by 1855, three cherished children, Isabella's letters, whenever John was away on business or she herself was visiting, complain constantly of her weaknesses, spiritual as well as physical. Even if we discount Catharine's observation, when Isabella was only eighteen, that her sister seemed to enjoy the effect on others of her illnesses, Isabella dwells in inordinate detail on her excessive menstrual flow, the leaden feeling of a displaced uterus (is she so candid about female ailments because they show what special handicaps a woman must face?), headaches, back pains, dyspepsia, constipation, nasal polyps that deadened her sense of taste and, most disturbing, a "diseased nervous system" and sometimes a sense of mental weakness and confusion. All this, we soon see, gives her a ready explanation for her failure to live up to expectations. A talented young woman, looked on as a leader, she finds herself, a dozen years after marriage, only someone's wife, without individual identity or recognition of her capacities. She is teased, too, by the increasing fame and productivity of her brothers and sisters: Harriet the noted author, Henry the celebrated preacher, Catharine the educator, Edward a college president . . . From a water cure in Florence, Massachusetts, to which she went in 1853, she writes to her husband: "I do believe I have less self-reliance . . . than I had six or eight years ago. You have more and I seem to lose as you gain." She tends to morbid exaggeration: "Disease has really worn upon my mental powers more than I realized. . . . You might live on to a good old age. . . . The question is, can you do it, with the burden of a family and the wife useless." Married at nineteen, with one child dead and two living by the time she is twenty-five, plagued by ailments real and imaginary (she would live to the age of eighty-five), she cries out in a panic when John, worn out by business cares, goes off to Europe for several months. She swings from a touching tenderness to a childlike fear that he will die: "I feel as if I must see or feel you this night—my arms seem almost to stretch themselves out into vacancy, with an imploring grasp, and I say, my husband . . . how could you leave me, thus—alone—how horrible it is to think, that this may be my portion for long years to come!" Despite or perhaps because of her dependence on him, she mocks his physical weakness: Give up your exercises and your dumbbells, she writes, and resign yourself to having a weak body. Although elsewhere she says that the physical aspect is not important compared to mental qualities—a proper feminist attitude—and his mental qualities are "exquisite," she wishes he were like Jervis Langdon, an older friend of the family, who was apparently admirable in all respects.

Isabella must also have been challenged by the evidence that her husband was achieving a measure of success and recognition. He was only twenty-four when a small group of antislavery voters who held the balance of power in Farmington elected him to a term in the Connecticut House of Representatives, and in 1858 he was appointed official reporter of the State Supreme Court. In *Some Reminiscences of a Long Life* he says he turned down a judgeship in 1861 because he did not feel ready for it (Isabella insisted that his health wouldn't allow it), but he may have been passed over because of his unorthodox views on abolition, woman suffrage and, perhaps, spiritualism. He retained throughout an idealistic commitment to reason and justice. (Something of a wag, he also enlivened boring court sessions and some of his letters with jokes and doggerel.) Perhaps it was this quality along with the impact of the war that turned him away from the old theology. As early as 1856, in an address at the Farmington Congregational Church, he declared: "The old pulpit is gone, with a good deal of the theology that was preached in it. Let them both go. The pulpit inspired me with awe, but some of the theology with a deadly fear; a fear which, thank God, has since given way to a more intelligent trust and to some measure of that love that casteth out fear." A man of delicate sensibilities ("I was made for the enjoyment of beautiful things. . . . I love everything that is exquisite"), he was often exhausted by his work and came to share Isabella's faith in water cure resorts.

For a host of middle-class women—and a few men—these resorts were, as we have seen, a refuge from both overwork and boredom. For a fee that almost all the Beechers seemed able to afford, a woman could throw off all responsibilities, be waited on hand and foot, and mingle intimately in a society of her equals. Thus when Isabella reached a physical and spiritual low point in 1860 she fled to Gleason's water cure in Elmira, New York, close to the home of her brother Tom and his wife Julia and their rich and generous friends the Langdons, and she used every excuse to remain there for month after month. She even held up the possibility that a coming crisis—obviously the menopause—could leave her an invalid for life.

The nearly one hundred letters that Isabella wrote to her husband during her four and a half months at the cure are a complete course in the conflicting loyalties of a middle-class Victorian wife who is approaching middle age and is increasingly challenged by her fate. She brooded constantly over her inadequacies: "I can't write a book—nor draw pictures—nor do any other productive work. I have always told you that you overestimated your wife." Isabella loved her family dearly and enjoyed her husband's flattery, but she craved independence and influence. Finding that even in faraway Elmira she is known only as the Reverend Tom Beecher's sister, she complains: "Everywhere I go, I have to run on the credit of my relations. Nowhere but at home can I lay claim to a particle of individuality, to any distinction of goodness, smartness or anything else whatever." But she takes heart when Mr. Langdon, whom she admires so greatly, tells her that she is the only one in her entire family who has "treated Tom just right" and has done him good rather than harm. Again confirmed in her conviction that she is born to guide people, she continues:

this is true. . . . It becomes more and more evident to me that I have great power of personal influence—family name goes a great way no doubt, but there is a magnetism of heart and eye and voice that is quite individual—oh how I wish I might exert this on a broad scale, to sweep people along on the right path. Approbativeness—real love of admiration is as strong as in the days of childhood and youth.

Perhaps aware that she is being vain, she adds: "but benevolence is uppermost, I am quite sure of that. I only wish I knew how much one might enjoy of the personal tribute that follows successful effort without becoming selfish or . . . vainglorious."

Although we have no references by Isabella to the women's rights movement of this period, she must have watched with fascination its progress from its beginnings in July 1848—year of revolutions and manifestos—at the Woman's Rights Convention in the little town of Seneca Falls, New York. Initiated and managed entirely by women, it was like a cry piercing the complacency of the mid-Victorian social scene. Led by Lucretia Mott, Elizabeth Cady Stanton and others, and abetted by a few men such as black abolitionist Frederick Douglass, it called for woman's equality with man in every direction—for her right to vote, own property, have a legal identity apart from a husband, and be given unrestricted opportunities for education and work. Many men and some women responded with utter indifference or ridicule, but a few women across the land, hearing those demands articulated, realized that they had always wanted such rights and would not rest until they had them. So year after year in national conventions and local meetings, with agents and tracts and petitions, they worked tirelessly for a place in the sun.

It was out of this ferment as much as her own experience that Isabella Beecher Hooker ventured in 1859 to sum up the arguments for and against woman suffrage in a brave if amateurish composition called "Shall Women Vote? A Matrimonial Dialogue." In it a wife answers her husband's objections to woman suffrage. When he asserts that women have too many family obligations, she answers that older as well as unmarried women do not have such obligations, and when he objects that women will simply vote as their husbands do, she retorts that women will soon learn to think for themselves. Unfortunately, too many of the answers digress or aim mainly to establish the wife's respectability. And when the husband asks at last whether she would grant women the vote immediately, she retreats into a modest: Not until public opinion demands it, and a pious: Let us do what we can and leave the rest to God.

Plainly trying to compete with all the Beechers and Stowes who were filling the columns of the *Independent,* she sent her squib to Thomas Wentworth Higginson, author of graceful essays, abolitionist and supporter of women's rights, in the hope that he would help her get it published. Higginson—later one of the first to recognize Emily Dickinson—praised its "fresh and vigorous thoughts" but suggested as gently as he could that it had "deficiencies of style." It was hard enough, he added, to earn money by one's writing, but far harder when one's views were radical.

The stay at the Elmira water cure seems to have opened new vistas for Isabella. Seeing how much Mrs. Gleason accomplished—among other things she had acquired a quick medical degree—and how well brother Tom served the Elmira community, Isabella sought desperately to find new purposes for her own life. Exposed to all sorts of treatments of women's ailments, she talked of becoming a water cure gynecologist. Despite her husband's gibes about straining her brain, she studied political economy. And she was one of the bold women who ventured outdoors with the costume—Turkish-style pantaloons and a knee-length overskirt—Amelia Bloomer had made famous (or notorious) in the early 1850s. But nothing came of these explorations, and as soon as she returned home she was again caught up in coping with a seven-year-old son and two teenage daughters.

But she was shaken out of herself by a meeting with Anna Dickinson, a reading of the feminist writings of Harriet Taylor Mill and John Stuart Mill and finally by the pressures of war. Miss Dickinson was a nineteen-year-old Quaker who had challenged propriety by campaigning publicly for the Republican party and abolition. With plain features but dark deep-set eyes, a radiant complexion and glossy black hair, she transfixed audiences everywhere with her youth, eloquence and fire. Newspapers were already describing her as an American Joan of Arc by the time she came to Hartford in her crusade against slavery. The Hookers were nevertheless apprehensive: she would be the first woman to speak in public in the city and she would face a conservative audience. But she was matchless. "The audience," Charles Dudley Warner's *Press* reported, "which began to listen in a quiet, half-critical manner, soon lost control of itself under the witchery of such a spell as a Hartford audience was never under before. . . . In certain powers as a speaker we have never heard her excelled."

Isabella was so enchanted that she insisted on bringing Miss Dickinson home with her. Anna was young enough to be her daughter, but they stayed up all night in heart-to-heart talk. Anna told her in particular about those two exciting leaders of the movement, Elizabeth Cady Stanton and Susan B. Anthony. But Isabella was not yet ready for such outspoken and militant women.

It was hardly surprising that fastidious John Hooker should have thought Abe Lincoln an "awkward creature" to put in the White House. He has, Hooker declared, "the manners of a Maine logger or a half-civilized back-woodsman, almost a boor, yet he is honest and fearless, and after all the corruption and subserviency that have prevailed I think we can get along with the want of courtly manners." Isabella shared this view but began, like other members of her family, to doubt the President's powers as a leader. Lincoln had been in the White House little more than half a year when she wrote to him, righteously urging him to resist the corrupting temptations of Washington and to proclaim emancipation as soon as military success allowed it. A month later she fired off an impassioned letter to Henry, criticizing him for asserting that the government had no constitutional right to declare emancipation. Since it is the South that has rebelled and broken the contract, she asserted, we are justified in using every weapon against it. Eager to share in the war effort, Isabella also began working with the Women's Sanitary Commission, that invaluable aid to the Union hospital and medical services, and proved particularly effective in writing circulars and drawing up resolutions. Then late in 1862, she joined Harriet in a trip to Washington, partly to see her brothers—James, a lieutenant colonel, Thomas, a chaplain, and Harriet's son Fred, a lieutenant—but even more, to meet with the President himself.

Of the glimpses she had of wartime Washington, there were several she would never forget. A day after dining—quite lavishly—in Thomas's tent in a camp outside Washington, Isabella and Harriet were resting in their boardinghouse in the city when they heard the sound of marching men. They rushed outside in time to see James wheel by at the head of his regiment. The women waved their handkerchiefs and the young lieutenant colonel saluted them with his sword. Later he came galloping back with several handsome captains. For James it was a shining moment; only a few months later, he suffered his first breakdown.

Equally memorable was the spectacle of a thousand freedmen lined up outside their barracks. Isabella was thrilled as the men hailed Harriet, then marched into a large, well-ordered dining room, and again when they sang "Go Down, Moses" and other spirituals—"a slow, solemn and plaintive music as wild as the free winds." It was a first lesson in what abolition might achieve.

They saw the President too, but it was a disappointing and in some ways—as Harriet also testified—a ludicrous experience. According to Isabella's version, they were ushered into a drab, poorly furnished chamber and waited there until "a rough, scrubby, black-brown, withered, dull-eyed object" entered. That was Abraham Lincoln. Harriet was momentarily speechless, leaving Isabella to make conversation. Harriet finally recovered and was soon exchanging stories with the President. The two women were repeatedly moved by Lincoln's sincerity and pathos, especially when he said that he was sure he would not, as Isabella described it, "last long after all this was over." But Isabella would recall most of all his "indifferent speech and rustic manners." (Curiously, just as no record of Harriet's version mentions Isabella, so Isabella does not mention the presence of Harriet's daughter Hattie and young son.)

Anna Dickinson was not only a revelation of the effectiveness of a woman in a role from which women had been barred but the source of an important intellectual experience: she introduced Isabella to an essay, "Enfranchisement of Women" by Harriet Taylor Mill, which had appeared in the *Westminster Review* in 1851. Mrs. Mill, wife of the great

English political philosopher John Stuart Mill, told how she had been inspired by the Woman's Rights Convention held in Worcester, Massachusetts, the year before. There a group of American women had taken the revolutionary step of carrying their cause into the political arena. They had declared that every human being is entitled to a voice in the enactment of laws and that the word "male" should be stricken from every state constitution. Mrs. Mill went on to argue that woman's inferior position, like every other basic human relationship, had been established by force, and that—borrowing another resolution from the Worcester convention—no part of the human race should decide the proper sphere of any other part. In a remarkable anticipation of modern views, she added that the differences in the capacities of women and men resulted not from differences in their mental powers but from their circumstances.

To the argument that involvement in politics would harden women—a typically Victorian insistence that women be pure and sweet—she retorted that many aspects of life already did that. Because men have set the standards, the paramount virtue in women is generally said to be loyalty to men. There are women today, she wrote, who are the intellectual equals of any man who ever lived, but such individuals will continue to be exceptional until every career is open to women. Marriage is corrupting to both men and women: in men it produces the vices of power; in women the vices of artifice. Some women do not desire emancipation because "custom hardens human beings to any kind of degradation"— especially if they are taught to regard their degradation as their honor. If some English literary women say they are quite satisfied with their place in society, they do so because they have such a low opinion of men that they believe that only one in ten thousand does not "dislike and fear strength, sincerity or high spirit in a woman." Now at last, she concluded, there are women who demand full equality.

That conclusion, written a dozen years earlier, must have given Isabella sharp pangs of conscience at her own inaction. Harriet Taylor Mill's arguments would become Isabella's woman's rights gospel.

At home, Isabella was the solicitous, and sometimes oversolicitous, mother. When Alice at eighteen had a personality crisis, longing to be rich and more desirable, to engage in all the stylish pastimes, have a smaller waistline, and so forth, she was sent off to the cure-all, Gleason's sanitarium in Elmira. Later she went regularly to Dr. Walker's fashionable "Movement Cure"—the doctor stressed "gymnastics"—in New York, and sometimes Isabella or John joined her there, making it a base for vacations in the big city. One of Isabella's letters to Alice as her daughter faced the long ride back to Hartford in midwinter seems charming until one recalls that it is addressed to a nineteen-year-old. You must wear, mother writes,

two pairs of underdrawers, and if you have a skirt, that can be worn under your hoops, just long enough to reach ankles. . . . Then you must have leggins or some thick pair of stockings down into your boot tops. . . . Fur cuffs and woolen gloves of course and something to put over your ears if needed, and a blanket shawl of course. Take a good lunch also. . . .

Craving an ideal family life, with herself as the center of affection, Isabella was not prepared for her daughters to marry. At first everything looked promising when Mary married Eugene Burton, younger brother of Nathaniel Burton, the Hookers' minister and old friend. But perhaps because the couple came to live with the Hookers, the unusual warmth and intimacy that had at first marked Isabella's relationship with "Gene" soon vanished. Or perhaps it was Isabella's very hunger to be worshiped and needed. In letter after letter to her husband and her daughter Alice she reveals how shattered she is because Gene doesn't cling to her or even respect her. In a five-page outpouring to Alice she writes:

One whole long year I have been waiting for the one blessed word mother from his lips and it has not come, and I am sobbing this moment as I write, with a grief that always takes hold of me past subduing when I allow myself to think how my heart has been set upon this son.

The hurt was doubled and redoubled when Alice became engaged to John Calvin Day, a lawyer of a socially prominent Hartford family, and he, too, failed to give Isabella the affection she required. When she disapproved of the marriage, young Day must have been even further alienated. Having two sons-in-law who did not cherish her was a blow not only to her passionate conception of family relationships but to her pride.

Such were the speculation fevers of the age that they even reached the Hookers. One of the more unusual enterprises in which Hartford citizens invested was the American Emigrant Company, which imported skilled labor from Eu.ope. For a time a sizable part of John Hooker's income came from investments in this company and from serving it as a lawyer. But when it did poorly after the war or during depressions, the Hookers felt the pinch and repeatedly had to rent their house to ease John's burden.

The women's rights movement languished during the war. In 1864 Isabella, while visiting South Carolina to see Eugene, who had been wounded, did manage to spend time with Caroline Severance, suffragist and abolitionist. A veteran reformer, Mrs. Severance gave her a glimpse of the factions that were already dividing the women's movement. Once the war began, almost all the feminists had given priority to the struggle against slavery. Stanton and Anthony opposed the complete abandonment of their cause but they nevertheless led in organizing the Woman's Loyal League and worked for fifteen months to collect 400,000 signatures of women in favor of the Thirteenth Amendment, which would abolish slavery.

The expectation of the suffragists was that the abolitionists would reciprocate once the war was over. But the problems of the freed blacks and of Reconstruction soon engrossed the abolitionists. They pointed out again and again that women were far better off than blacks and that their cause, in short, could wait. Stubbornly the suffragists kept asking such questions as "Do you believe the African race is composed entirely of males?" and arguing that the Constitution never mentions the word "male." But the abolitionists were unconvinced. When the Fourteenth Amendment was passed it granted the vote only to "male citizens"—a signal defeat for women.

That setback along with a young son and two unmarried daughters at home helps to explain why Isabella did not become fully active in the suffragist movement until a few years after the war. Her first step was a guarded one—an unsigned article, "A Mother's Letters to a Daughter on Woman Suffrage," in *Putnam's Monthly* late in 1868. (Two years later, grown bolder, and having organized the Connecticut Woman Suffrage Association, she signed it and had it published by the association.) The article mixed a few fresh arguments with some that she borrowed from the Mills, but it set them forth in the genteel terms of a Victorian mother talking to a daughter. If women can be tried for crimes, she wrote, they should be allowed to sit in judgment in criminal courts; wars will never cease until women have a voice in government; no training fit for young men should be closed to young women; the sexes should attend all schools together, thus encouraging the "gentle amenities," and the barring of women from legislatures should be abandoned as a relic of barbarism. Compared to the writings of Elizabeth Cady Stanton, Lucy Stone or Ernestine Rose, it was a tame effort, leaning too heavily on the theory that women would raise the moral level of politics and bring a motherly wisdom to the affairs of government.

A little less cautious was her joining in the formation in Boston of the New England Woman Suffrage Association. This step introduced her to the more conservative leaders of the movement, including Julia Ward Howe of "Battle Hymn of the Republic" fame, Paulina Wright Davis, and to their famous antislavery associates William Lloyd Garrison and Frederick Douglass.

Armed with the kind of dignity, elegance and piety that Isabella admired, Davis was able to persuade her to test her deep disapproval of the two primal feminists, Anthony and Stanton, in a personal meeting. Isabella consented, visited the Davises' "almost ducal estate" in Providence and met the two leaders there. Her capitulation was complete: "While I have been mourning in secret over the degradation of woman, you have been working through opposition and obloquy to raise her to self-respect and self-protection through enfranchisement, knowing that with *political rights* come equal social and industrial opportunities." Even though inspired by false hopes, it was a large-hearted acknowledgment.

After studying Miss Anthony—"the one really hoofed and horned demon of this movement"—for nearly a week, Isabella pronounced her a woman of "incorruptible integrity," without equal in "unselfishness and benevolence," and with tremendous energy and executive ability. As for Stanton, she is, Isabella told Mrs. Severance:

a magnificent woman and the truest, womanliest woman of us all.... I have now spent three days in her company and in the most intense heart-searching debate I ever undertook.... I have handled what seemed to me her errors, *without gloves,* and the result is that I love her also, just as I do you.... I have handed in my allegiance to you three women as the leaders and representatives of the cause dearer to me than any other in the world.

By contrast with Anthony and Stanton, Lucy Stone and her Boston associates seemed to Isabella guilty of a jealousy that hurt the cause and was, she thought, a "sign of moral weakness."

Stanton and Anthony complemented each other strikingly. Stanton at fifty-four was short, plump and rosy-cheeked—a matronly figure. She was the daughter of a judge in upper New York State who had determined her career, quite unwittingly, by never forgiving her for having been born a girl. She had married a lawyer with strong abolitionist sympathies and had borne seven children. Rich in wit and enthusiam, she was a forceful and outspoken writer, a very effective speaker and above all a bold-minded woman. She had begun her career as a reformer at the age of twenty-five, when she and her husband, just married, attended the World's Antislavery Convention in London in 1840. She had later joined Lucretia Mott in organizing the historic first Woman's Rights Convention in 1848 and had been a militant champion of women ever since.

Foes of the feminists encouraged the notion that Susan B. Anthony was a sour, angular old maid with a forbidding mien and manner. Although certainly an aggressive feminist, she was a lithe and vital woman with boundless nervous energy and immense strength of character. Brought up on a farm near Rochester, she was much influenced by her Quaker parents and their ardent support of the abolitionist and temperance movements. At the age of thirty she left schoolteaching to join the women's rights struggle and soon began her lifelong association with Elizabeth Cady Stanton. She never married—she did, however, like to take care of the Stantons' children whenever she stayed with them—and even more than Stanton, she poured her life into the women's movement for half a century. While Susan was the organizer and manager, arranging conventions, orienting delegates, circulating petitions and tracts, collecting money and testifying before legislatures, Elizabeth was the star performer, lecturer, writer of ringing manifestos and inspiring slogans—remarkable fusion of matron and rebel, homemaker and crusader.

When Garrison, Phillips and other antislavery leaders continued after the war to thrust aside women's claims, insisting, "It is the negro's hour," Stanton and Anthony raged. Consumed by frustration, Stanton resorted for once to disparaging other disfranchised groups, referring to the masses of "ignorant" foreigners and blacks who would win the vote before even the most distinguished native white woman. But this was after twenty years of mockery and insult and five years of subordinating their cause to that of the abolitionists.

That was why Stanton and Anthony exploited every possibility and accepted help from almost any source. Thus when word came that Kansans would be allowed to vote on an amendment to enfranchise women as well as Negroes, the pair went off to Kansas and for four exhausting months toured scores of prairie settlements and cities. And that was why, finding themselves running low on money and strength, they let George Francis Train join and finance them.

A fabulous character, with a fortune made in business ventures everywhere, Train was handsome and vigorous, a flamboyant figure in a blue coat with brass buttons, patent leather boots and lavender kid gloves. When he made a speech, he danced about and showered the audience with wit, jingles and bombast. He is, the Burlington *Sentinel* said, "one of the most wide-awake, rip-up-and-tear-to-pieces young Americans this country has ever produced." But the eastern suffragists, and especially the New England moderates, were shocked, describing Train as a crack-brained clown and a Copperhead guilty of derogatory remarks about blacks.

But Train rescued the two women, if not the campaign—both amendments were defeated—and then volunteered to finance a newspaper for the movement. The women were jubilant. The motto of *The Revolution* set its tone: "Principle, not policy: justice, not favors. —Men their rights, and nothing more; women their rights, and nothing less." It lasted only two and a half years but it summed up the resentment and anger of twenty years. In bristling editorials and articles, it covered not only the familiar women's rights themes but such controversial or even forbidden issues as unfair divorce laws, the unjust treatment of working women, lack of protection against rape, the dangers of legalized prostitution, the arrogance of the double standard, and compensation for housework. It was so far in advance of its time that some of its objectives have still not been completely achieved.

In an effort to bring the Negro and the women's rights factions together, the Equal Rights Association was formed in 1866, with Theodore Tilton acting as its leading organizer and Henry Ward Beecher as its first president. But it was soon apparent that neither group would compromise. The conflict broke into the open at the association's annual meeting in May 1869 in New York. Most inflammatory of all was the attack by radicals of the New York group on the Fifteenth Amendment because it guaranteed the vote only to male citizens, including blacks. Exasperated, Frederick Douglass, once a valiant supporter of the women, finally exclaimed:

When women because they are women, are hunted down through the cities of New York and New Orleans; when they are dragged from their houses and hung upon lamp-posts, when their children are torn from their arms . . . when they are in danger of having their homes burnt down over their heads . . . then they will have an urgency to obtain the ballot equal to our own.

There was, beyond that, much petty jealousy and personal animosity. Many in the Boston circle thought Susan Anthony autocratic and sharp-tongued and even charged that she never accounted for her use of association funds.

Impatient with the criticism and the bickering and convinced that men had once again betrayed them, the New York wing, led by Stanton, Anthony and Davis, in November 1869, organized the National Woman Suffrage Association, staffed entirely by women. The Boston group, marshaled by Julia Ward Howe, Thomas Wentworth Higginson, Lucy Stone and her husband, Henry Blackwell, responded by forming the American Woman Suffrage Association and made Henry Ward Beecher its president. The two groups would not come together again for almost twenty years.

Freed of most of her family obligations—her two daughters were married and her son was fourteen years old—ignited by association with Stanton and Anthony, and dreaming of leading on the widest front, Isabella threw in her lot with the New York group. She saw many roles for herself. She could serve as a mediator between the factions because she sympathized in certain ways with both of them. With such an enlightened and nationally admired minister as Horace Bushnell of Hartford's North Congregational Church opposing woman suffrage as "a reform against nature—an attempt to make trumpets out of flutes, and sun-flowers out of violets," Isabella felt that it was important to persuade the Boston group that the New York band was made up of ladylike women, many of them devoted wives and mothers. Offering the Beecher and Hooker names and her own reputation, she could contribute a guarantee of social esteem. In a postwar world seeking stability and security, belligerent reformers were hardly welcome, and Isabella decided that the suffragists must reassure the cautious and conservative. She was also able to make a strong religious appeal, often referring to her desire to preach the gospel of Christ.

Her own religious views continued to broaden. When the Hookers' highly respected minister Nathaniel Burton worked himself up into what Isabella decried as a "harsh and repulsive" series of "unadulterated" Calvinist sermons, she found them contrary to Scripture, common sense and human nature. So it was understandable that, like the rest of her family, she should turn more and more to Christ and invoke his aid in her effort.

Spurred by invitations to write for *The Revolution*, Isabella, trading on family prestige, proposed that she and Harriet become associate editors of the paper, and be paid accordingly. Even though Stanton and Anthony were not being paid and were soon drawing on their own resources to keep the publication going, Anthony saw in Isabella's proposal a priceless opportunity to get from Mrs. Stowe the women's rights equivalent of *Uncle Tom's Cabin*. She wrote Paulina Davis:

And if *cash* will bring Mrs. Stowe to the *Revolution*, with her *deepest holiest woman, wife and Mother Soul* struggle—clothed in her *inimitable story garb*— then *it is cash that must be*. Mrs. Stowe, even, has never yet given to the world *her very best*—for she nor any other woman can, until she writes direct out of *her own soul's experiences*— Oh how I long to see the *picture* as none but that one pencil can draw it.

But now Isabella came up with another demand: to satisfy Harriet and perhaps mollify the Boston group, the name of the paper must be softened. That was too much for Stanton:

A journal called "The Rosebud" might answer for those who come with kid gloves and perfumes to lay immortal wreaths on the monuments which in sweat and tears others have hewn and built; but for us and that great blacksmith [Parker Pillsbury, co-editor of *The Revolution*] who forges such red-hot thunderbolts for Pharisees, hypocrites and sinners, there is no name like *The Revolution*!

Realizing that she would have been held responsible if the change of name hurt the paper, Isabella was content to be a contributing editor. That would give her an opportunity, as she put it, to preach Christ and the Bible to an audience of five thousand readers.

Already distrustful of *The Revolution*, Harriet was completely alienated, and even Isabella was troubled, at the end of 1869, by the position of the paper on the Richardson-McFarland scandal. A Mrs. Daniel McFarland had divorced her husband because of his dissolute habits and was to marry Albert D. Richardson, a well-known journalist on the staff of the *Tribune*, when McFarland entered the *Tribune* office and shot Richardson. Mrs. McFarland married Richardson on his deathbed in a ceremony performed by the Reverend O. B. Frothingham and, supposedly because he had heard that McFarland was guilty of adultery, by Henry Ward Beecher. McFarland was acquitted and even given custody of his one child.

Stanton, in *The Revolution*, saw the affair as another example of society's contempt for women:

I rejoice over every slave that escapes from a discordant marriage. With the education . . . of women we shall have a mighty sundering of unholy ties that hold men and women together who loathe . . . each other. . . . One would really suppose that a man owned his wife as the master the slave, and that this was simply an affair between Richardson and McFarland, fighting like two dogs over one bone. . . . Suppose women should decide to shoot their husbands' mistresses, what a wholesale slaughter of innocents we should have of it!

When Isabella was challenged on Stanton's view of divorce, she described her as "a motherly hearted woman" who thought mainly of the suffering of children from "uncongenial and discordant parents." She would never condone, Isabella said, the "personal gratification" that motivated free lovers. My rule, Isabella added, is to listen to reformers if I am satisfied with their "life and conduct."

Henry Ward beat a hasty retreat from the whole affair, but his role in it would be held against him when the Tilton scandal erupted two years later.

Harriet was simply confirmed in her hostility to the radicals. In a piece in the *Woman's Journal*, the newspaper started by the American group to rival *The Revolution*, she struck out at George Sand as an evil influence. Provoked by this, Stanton, writing in *The Revolution*, declared:

George Sand has done a grander work for women . . . than any woman of her day, while Mrs. Stowe has been vacillating over every demand made for her sex, timidly watching the weathercock of public sentiment and ridiculing the advance guard. . . . When women first demanded suffrage in this country, where was Mrs. Stowe? While the thousands of wives of drunkards, licentious men, tyrants and criminals call aloud today for deliverance from all these degrading . . . relations, where is Mrs. Stowe?

Behold her, Bible in hand, proclaiming to these unhappy ones, "a woman hath not power over her own body, but the husband."

Harriet responded with an article attacking French novels and George Sand and sent it to Henry Ward for use as an editorial in the *Christian Union*. In the covering letter she added: "Susan Anthony and other honest old maids who know no more about evil than an old country minister's horse will suppose of course that [Sand's] *Lelia* is a woman's right tract." The remark not only ignored such suffragists as Stanton and Isabella, who presumably knew as much about evil as she did, but it supported the popular caricature of a women's rights follower.

Isabella's surge, at the age of forty-seven, into the vanguard of the women's movement must have seemed very surprising to those who did not know that she had been preparing for such a leap for twenty-five years. She emerged from the chrysalis ready for full flight.

Also contributing deeply to her confidence in her new role was a mystic sense of the significance of motherhood. When an article by a Reverend Todd blamed abortion (which he called foeticide) among married women—apparently a not uncommon practice—on women who wanted to live in ease, Isabella asserted, in a little book *Womanhood: Its Sanctities and Fidelities,* that the blame should fall on husbands who exercised no control over "animal passion" and wore out their wives with childbearing and child care. In a revealing passage she claimed that women were but feebly endowed with this passion (Stanton would have denied this: she once pointed out that Whitman was apparently ignorant of the great natural fact that a healthy woman had as much passion as a man) and that it was further reduced by maternity. Women submitted, Isabella said, only out of a wish to please their husbands or a fear that the men would be driven to a "moral aberration." In decorous but nonetheless daring terms she urged what amounted to birth control and pleaded with mothers to explain to their sons the nature of sexual activity and its consequences. Mingling extremes, *Womanhood* is Victorian in its conception of sexuality as an animal passion excessive in men and weak in women, yet quite modern in its support of sex instruction for boys and controlling the size of families. Although her views of sexual activity seem to reflect her own experience, it is hard to imagine John Hooker, who deplored desire in older men as well as "lust" in young men, as subject to "animal passion."

Two years later, in a letter thanking John Stuart Mill for sending her a copy of his latest book, *The Subjection of Women,* Isabella proclaimed her belief that a mother has a "moral advantage" over the father. She alone is, like God, a creator:

. . . a mother is the only being in this world who thus approximates the divine nature. So feeble in the comparison is the father's relation to her child . . . that it is within the experience of many a mother . . . that from the moment of blessed annunciation to heavenly birth, she, like the Virgin of old, has known no father to her child save the Holy Ghost.

Carried away by her visions, she concludes: "Cleaving the future, I see such honor and power coming to woman as makes me tremble."

What her husband thought of all this we do not know. Mill, obviously taken aback by this American Mother God, managed to accept the idea of a mother's closer physical relation to her child but brushed aside Isabella's other claims. But Isabella was in no way discouraged: her sense of her powers already bordered on the messianic.

Inspired by her vision and hoping to bring together the radicals and the moderates, Isabella within a few months had organized—and financed—Hartford's first national women's rights convention. So intent was she on insuring a decorous meeting that her instructions to the speakers evoked a typically mettlesome reply from Stanton: "Rest assured that our dress, manners and speech shall be worthy of . . . the Opera House of Hartford. I . . . will give my hair an extra curl, and wreathe my face in its sweetest smile, and keep my heart full of love and tenderness for all mankind." But it ended on a sharper note:

I for one am willing to grow into the grandest human proportions, to have every sharp angle and rough point rounded into lines of grace and beauty—but all the outgrowth of my own life. Each soul must be its own sculptor. . . . I can no more think, act, write as you do than you as I do. . . . When I demanded the right of suffrage twenty-five years ago all my friends were shocked and grieved—more so than the world is today when I protest against the present relations of the sexes. Twenty-five years hence perhaps you will see more than I do now. . . . "Let each mind one and the world will be mended."

The convention was a success. It did not bring the two factions together—Garrison created a particularly tense moment when he blasted *The Revolution*—but it did give the movement respectability and made clear that even proper Victorian ladies could resent their second-class status. And it established another Beecher as a formidable reformer. After Isabella had finished speaking, the Reverend Burton, who was serving as president of the newly formed Connecticut Woman Suffrage Association for the Study of Political Science, declared: "If such women don't vote before I die—well, I won't die till they do." As for the irrepressible Stanton, she reported:

I . . . appeared in a black velvet dress with real lace, and the most inoffensive speech I could produce; all those passages that would shock the most conservative were ruled out, while pathetic and aesthetic passages were substituted. . . . From what my friends said, I believe I succeeded in charming everyone but myself and

Susan, who said it was the weakest speech I ever made. I told her that was what it was intended to be.

Isabella had found a purpose and found it triumphantly. As far back as 1860 she had had intimations of a great and perhaps divine mission: she would be a champion of women, directed by Christ and spirits on high.

But her achievement would not be without severe trials and suffering. It was surely a result of the double standard and other Victorian sexual attitudes that at almost the same time as Harriet revived old charges of Byron's immorality and Henry Ward was mired in the Tilton adultery scandal, Isabella became a chief defender of Victoria Woodhull's purity of soul and her right to make love as she pleased.

23

THOMAS

Going His Own Way

Four years of facing the slum children of a Philadelphia grammar school and the lack of intellectual and spiritual challenge in a Hartford high school had convinced Thomas Beecher that schoolteaching was not for him. He had also learned from his brother Henry and the Reverend Horace Bushnell that a minister need not be a church functionary, a theologian or the captive of a sect; he could be simply a teacher, a friend and an inspiration.

So after another year of studying and working with his father, Thomas once again followed the other Beechers eastward. He was ordained in Williamsburgh, across the East River from New York City, in September 1851, with Bushnell delivering the sermon—Henry was not available—at the ceremony. He preached, then, in a few churches in Connecticut, and someone who heard him there reported that his voice was very fine and clear and his sermon somewhat eccentric, "with strange and sometimes undignified passages, but . . . full of feeling and genius and eloquence, not well balanced exactly but real. . . . Mr. Beecher is full of sensibility and enthusiasm and if he does not run wild entirely will make a noble preacher." At last he was called, on Henry's recommendation, to a newly formed Congregational church in Williamsburgh.

Just as important was the fact that while principal in the Hartford high school he had met and fallen in love with Olivia Day, a teacher and the daughter of Jeremiah Day, former president of Yale College. Although Thomas had not been infected by Byronism like Charles or swayed by emotions like Henry, he was no less in search of sympathy and love. And he had already experienced one disappointment, when Catherine Mussey had passed him by and married a well-established Cincinnati lawyer.

So "Livy" Day, pretty, highly intelligent, one in whom, as Harriet had said of some New Englanders, thinking had grown to be a disease, came to Thomas as heaven sent.

The unreachable goals of the old religion and the limitations Victorian standards had put on women had turned Olivia Day's gaze away from this world and, like several women of the Beecher circle and a few of Harriet's heroines, toward the imagined bliss of the next. The letters Livy wrote Tom during their courtship were so thoughtful and beguiling that, proud of having won such a treasure, he had to share them with someone. He chose the discriminating and finely tuned John Hooker. Bringing along almost a score of her letters, he spent hours reading them to Hooker. Hooker, much flattered, promptly reported to Isabella that the letters were "the most exquisite things" and that Livy had "the most graceful, classic, vivacious and richly furnished mind" he had ever met. Tom himself was so enchanted that he warned Livy to stop writing if she hoped to get married. He seems "perfectly contented," Hooker commented, with his "bird in the bush" and "more disposed to hear her warble and chatter from the spray than to hear her simply sing from her cage."

Livy for her part was fascinated by the unpredictable aspects of Tom's character. In her first word about him to her beloved cousin Julia Jones, she already has some remarkable insights into his protean nature.

He is a strange person. From what I have said you might easily fancy him more gentle, elegant and pleasing in his manners than he is. He can be the first at times but it is not his habitual manner. He has noble, generous traits of character. . . .

Do not be severe upon my absolute inability to describe Mr. Beecher. . . . He is said by some who ought to know, to be inconsistent and unreliable. I can only say that I do not find him so at school. I can also say truly and safely that he has extraordinary and wonderfully universal talents. He does everything vigorously and well, whether it be singing, teaching, carpentering or furnace tending, but especially planning.

Later she offered an even keener estimate:

He is very much in earnest about life. I find him kind and thoughtful . . . but I know he does say hateful things, does do rude things, amazing, unaccountable, unexpected things, and he is sometimes inconsistent. . . . He gives himself strongly to the mood of the moment, seeing things so vividly from one point of view and then from another and giving utterance to his thoughts freely and impetuously. . . . I believe that he is truly and earnestly religious, and I trust he will come out symmetrical sometime.

Her attachment to Thomas increases but she still clings to Julia: "He is the air I breathe but you are the blue sky." After Julia has been ill, she writes to Tom: "I am yours as I am not hers, but she is to me the loveliest human being on earth." Beecher agreed happily, declaring, "We shall celebrate a triple alliance," never dreaming how tragically this would come to pass.

Julia, outgoing, dynamic, life-loving, complemented Livy perfectly and Livy admitted freely that she lived the more vivid kind of experiences through her cousin. The Reverend Annis Ford Eastman, who worked with Beecher in his last years, said that Livy had "none of the iron joys in life itself." Endowed with a "superfine organization" that shrank from "contact with naked facts," Livy was not fitted, Mrs. Eastman wrote, "for the long road . . . and the daily battle with a melancholy temperament like Mr. Beecher's."

Livy truly feared marriage, believing it would put a "dead . . . stop to all the quiet little enjoyments of life." The prophecy was almost self-fulfilling, for at the beginning they were poor and soon Livy was pregnant and wretchedly ill. The illness was ominous, for Livy was unable—or unwilling—to fight it. When Thomas realized that she and the baby were doomed—she was having convulsions every hour—he wrote to Henry: "The opinion is that she may die at any moment . . . but if you can, do come down if only for an hour, and tell me that *you* love me." Faced by a devastating loss, he falls back on the thought that she will be better off out of this harsh world. So he adds, "You may come only in time to rejoice with us either way."

When he continued in this vein even after Livy's death, his family, and especially his sisters Mary and Isabella, were shocked. Mary, repelled by his behavior, declared, "Though I dislike . . . as he does the heathenish manner in which a Christian death and burial is generally regarded . . . I cannot conceive of anyone, be he a Christian or not—losing what has become dear and necessary as their own heart's blood, without suffering." Thomas answered firmly, as though it were they who were unchristian in their lack of faith in the blessing of death:

I cannot make you see—as I do without any effort—that for Livy to have lived and become a mother would have been as foul an incongruity as it would have been for Undine [a water nymph in a fairy romance by De La Motte] to have been transformed into a steady dutch vrow, nursing her children through the measles.

It was, had he thought about it, a rather unflattering observation to make to two mothers. He added:

I cannot make you see that God's providence culminated so appropriately and symmetrically in her death—I mean in preparing her to go and me to stay, that now I keep wondering why I did not prophesy it, and expect it as the only answer possible to all our prayers.

Hagridden by despair, he declares that not one of his plans has ended happily

till my crucifixion was completed as a teacher. No mortal but Livy . . . ever knew the agony I suffered when my *last* life's plan was cut off, and I a wreck . . . and many an hour have I wept in agony over my ruined hopes, my head upon her knee, while she would tell me "We love each other—that's real"—so we have lived and loved till she fell asleep.

Not only did they share, like other young lovers, their feelings about life, but "everyday since our betrothal, we have talked about death—as near to us."

Scorning the conventional responses, the "solemn sighing" and trite expressions, he had expected Isabella to be thankful that Livy had been released from tribulation. He concluded:

I am not anxious to compel men to feel as I do. I will not pronounce it exemplary or pious or even sane. It is simply *my* fact—that after twenty-six years of despair, Christ gave me Livy—and some mysterious elixir of *something*—so that when He took her I rejoiced and did not weep, and cannot.

Livy's death overwhelmingly confirmed his feeling that the world was a place of brief pleasures and much pain. Two years later he wrote to his brother James what was surely one of the most bitter and discouraging letters ever sent to someone who had just entered the ministry. He is ready to do anything that will make someone happy. "All else," he writes, "I steer away from."

I agree that slavery exhibits monstrous iniquity, but so does liberty. I agree that Popery is an awful delusion, but so is Protestantism. I agree that Theodore Parker curdles my blood with his blasphemy, but so does Edward Beecher. I agree that marriage is a blessed state, yet it is also a cursed condition for nine out of every ten. Were I a one-eyed reformer I should be a great, red-hot, zealous man. But I have looked and loved and longed and suffered. I see more things at a time than most men do. I give it up. We, as a race, are lost children in a mazy wilderness of life. Let us be gentle, humble, good, forgiving, patient, kind.

But the ordeal, coupled with his establishment in his Williamsburgh parish, increased his sense of independence in his personal relations as well as in his spiritual attitudes. For the rest of his life he would increasingly go his own way.

When Thomas Beecher first began his work in Williamsburgh, the congregation was building a large new church despite the fact that the Brooklyn-Williamsburgh area—called the "City of Churches"—was already said to have a church seat for every one of its population of ninety thousand. (Some felt that the church was only part of a real estate boom.)

Meanwhile Beecher held services in the Odeon, a shabby "opera house" redolent with the odors of countless theatrical performances. One visitor remembered Beecher as a slender young man with light-brown hair worn long, blue eyes and a pleasant smile who already expressed his individuality by wearing a coat of mixed materials instead of the conventional minister's coat and white tie. Before long he had a reputation as a preacher with stimulating and sometimes startling ideas. Emulating Henry, he also soon organized a Sunday school and all kinds of social and educational activities, especially for the young.

Thomas appealed particularly to the plain people, and after a while the more prosperous and money-minded began to criticize him because his sermons were not likely to attract the rich. They may also have been disappointed because the church had been organized—with Henry's help—by a group of abolitionists and they now saw that their young pastor did not share their strong opposition to slavery and slaveholders.

It is one of the curious inconsistencies in Beecher's views—or was it some kind of loose Whitmanic breadth of sympathies?—that while he would not take part in any crusade against slavery, he delivered a lecture, "The Unity of Reforms," in which he pointed out that the selfsame people espouse "Abolitionism, Socialism, Woman's Rights, Servants' Rights, People's Rights, Papists' Rights, Irish Rights, Everybody's Rights," and then added: "It is a good sign. Of such a freight man cannot take too much. The more he has, the lighter he steps. . . . Whoso begins as a Christian Abolitionist will surely walk in high places."

But the attacks of the malcontents increased, especially when he began to criticize the practices of certain businessmen in his congregation. With the same quixotic purpose that marked William when he denounced the deacon who owned a bar, or Henry when he bearded the whiskey distiller Comegys, Thomas threatened to expose the businessmen. Astonished at being challenged by their preacher, they called him before a church council, intending to dismiss him. Their questions seemed insulting to Beecher and he refused to answer them. If he did not respond, the council members said, he would not be given official notice of his separation and thus would not be able to get another congregation.

Young Beecher—he was not yet thirty years old—rose, bade the council good day and walked out of the room. For a moment it seemed as though his career as a minister was over. But, so one version goes, as he left the building he was met by a Mr. J. M. Robinson, deacon of the First Congregational Church of Elmira, in central New York State. The deacon had come to offer him the post of pastor there. Lyman Beecher would have said it was Divine Providence, but Thomas had in fact been recommended by a New York City relative of Robinson's who had heard the young man preach.

Having considered the invitation with great care, Thomas wrote the Elmira congregation a letter that was unique in its almost truculent independence and its unorthodox conception of a minister's role. Addressing a leading member of the church committee (who would become one of his closest friends), he wrote:

Mr. Jervis Langdon—and Dear Brethren:

I promised you a final response on Thursday of this week. Until that day I cannot . . . make a formal answer unless I hear yes or no from you to the following questions:

1. Although I owe nothing and can borrow unlimitedly yet I HAVE no money. . . . I ask, therefore, can you and will you pay at the rate of $1500 per annum, monthly and in advance? Yes or no.

2. Can you and will you make me a gift of $40 to pay expenses of moving self, library and furniture? Yes or no.

3. Do you fully understand that as you make me no promises . . . so I make you none, except to keep busy and preach for you as truly as I can. . . . We must owe nothing but to love one another. In brief do you fully understand that at the end of any month you may request me to leave without hurting my feelings, or I may leave you (of course, giving you my reason) without forfeiting your confidence? Do you understand this, yes or no?

4. Do you fully remember that I do not think that good can be done by a preacher's preaching? It must be by Christians working that good is done, if at all. Do you remember that MY choice is to work with my hands and do good on a small scale; and I come to you full of doubt as to whether it is possible for any church to be benefited by any services of mine as preacher and teacher? Do you remember this, yes or no?

5. Do you remember that while in good faith I profess to you that I am sound and evangelic in doctrine, yet I have no ambition to found or foster or preserve a church as such? My exclusive aim is to help men as individuals to be Christians. No church prosperity dazzles me; no church poverty or adversity troubles me. Do you remember this, yes or no?

You can answer all these questions by telegraph, by number, yes or no. . . . If you can answer all of them Yes I think the way is clear. . . . Pardon my plain speech. Truth is at the bottom of all enduring love. . . . For though I speak bold words, yet my heart is very tender and very tired and would fain rest in just some such place as Elmira.

I ask these questions not through suspicion—not from cautious bargain-driving, but because in my heart I am aching with the sight of the irregularity, superficiality and easy discontent which marks so many churches. As a CHURCH, I can do nothing for you; as individuals, I can love and work for you as long as you will let me, and I am not without hope that SOMEHOW, good may be done in Elmira. . . .

What was supposed to be a letter of negotiation was thus a radical manifesto. Had it not been so modest (yet so bold) and so informal (yet so intense), the people who received it might have realized that this young man, going far beyond Bushnell and brother Henry, was brushing aside doctrine and the trappings of worship and promising only to preach the words of Christ and try to be a Christian. That letter should have frightened the Elmira brethren into hasty withdrawal. But they were almost as high-principled as Beecher. Eight years earlier, forty-nine of them had braved the scorn of the community by breaking away from a local Presbyterian church because its pastor defended slavery.

A leader in the rebellion was Jervis Langdon, a onetime country storekeeper who had made a fortune in coal and lumber and had then opened his home and his purse not only to the great radicals of the age— Garrison, Phillips, Douglass, Gerrit Smith—but to every runaway slave. He and his wife now literally welcomed Thomas with open arms.

So Thomas came to little Elmira—it had only eight thousand inhabitants—and although he stayed forty-six years, he insisted on a month-to-month relationship in case either he or the church should want a change.

Since the original statement of principles of the church founders guaranteed freedom of opinion and speech to every member of the congregation, they could hardly reject a spiritual leader who asked such guarantees for himself. As for his position on slavery, perhaps they thought that a brother of Harriet Beecher Stowe and Henry Ward Beecher must at heart be a foe of slavery. But after his death a letter in the New York *Sun*, reprinted in an Elmira paper, quoted Thomas as having declared:

There are questions nearer home than slavery to occupy our attention. . . . I will make a five years' agreement with you. . . . During that period we will let the thing rest. If you can stand by my pro-slavery nonsense I can stand by your anti-slavery absurdities.

Either he was misquoted or it was a misjudgment that no one could explain away.

Although he did not share all their views, their integrity challenged and inspired him. "It was this little group of radical come-outers," he later said, "that saved me from misanthropy. . . . When bruised, broken and despairing of men entirely, I prayed, and they prayed with me, we came into unity and into declared love and peace based on God."

Although the congregation knew, of course, that most of the Beechers were unpredictable, if not eccentric, and Thomas's letter had given them warning enough that he was a maverick, they must at times have felt that they had got more than they had bargained for. A large man, almost six feet tall, with a brown beard and flowing hair, he went about town in plain, well-worn or even shabby clothes and a cap with a large visor such as railroad men wore. In cold weather he wrapped himself in a gray shawl. The church itself was old, dilapidated, and in winter, icy: once water in the tumbler at his side began to freeze and another time he revealed that he was wearing two pairs of trousers, arctic overshoes and a cardigan jacket under his overcoat, and said that anyone who was too cold should go home. When in a happy mood he would start skipping as he walked—shades of Lyman Beecher doing the double shuffle!—and in later years he rode briskly around Elmira in a splendid tricycle that he and a blacksmith had made out of iron, pine and leather. But there were periods when he would sink into a deep depression—mysterious moods that were as much a legacy from both his father and his mother as a reaction to the state of the world.

But he preached with a combination of insight, humor and originality that fascinated his listeners and after a while led some of them to say that he was as eloquent as his famous brother Henry. To be as accessible as possible, he rented two rooms in town and set them up as a "downtown office." His fellow ministers were shocked and some criticized him sharply, but in time most of them followed his lead. And the people loved it, coming to him with their hopes and fears. Within a decade Beecher's congregation increased many times over, he had a thriving Sunday school, various auxiliaries, and was well on the way to making his church the great community center it later became.

The variety of his abilities impressed everyone: he could run a lathe, take apart and reassemble a watch or a sewing machine, use a surveyor's transit and level, run a locomotive (the engineers on the Erie often let him take over the throttle), play an organ, lay out a building, mix the mortar, lay the brick, do the carpentry and hang the wallpaper. For forty years he checked the town clock daily against observations of the sun that he made on his own instruments. Always he exalted craftsmanship and the beauty of a job well done.

And the point was that he did such things for other people more often than for himself. Humbly he offered himself for almost any task:

I cannot make pastoral calls. . . . I am not constructed so that I can. But I am yours all times of the day and night. . . . If you are sick and need a watcher, I will watch with you. If you are poor and need someone to saw wood for you I will saw wood for you. I can read the paper for you if you need somebody to do that. I am yours, but you must call me the same as you would a physician.

But his congregation had to tolerate something more unorthodox than mere idiosyncrasies: Thomas's penchant for not quite respectable pleasures. In spite of their stated commitment to freedom of opinion, Elmira was still a rural community with many a vestige of Puritan prohibitions. At the founding the congregation had strictly forbidden the use of intoxicating liquors or attending theaters, balls or dancing parties. Now they had to live with a minister who liked to bowl, play billiards and whist, and, later on, join other older men in a game with the Lively Turtles Base Ball Club. Most wicked of all, he would not only stop in a saloon— it was actually a neighborhood place run by a very respectable German— for a glass of beer but have his own mug there.

He ignored, in short, the ministerial code and behaved like an average man. He had obviously learned much from the Henry who had scorned the idea that a minister must "*dress* minister, *walk* minister, *talk* minister, *eat* minister and wear his ministerial badge as a convict wears his stripes."

There was one person who mourned Olivia Day as much as Thomas did—Julia Jones. After Olivia's death, the two of them, yearning for what they had lost, drew closer and closer, and finally, in 1857, they were married. "We were made one first in love of Livy," he later said, "and then in grief for her." Julia had long loved him: when he had proposed to Olivia and she had helplessly asked Julia what she should do, Julia burst out, "If Tom Beecher ever asks me to marry him, I'll do it so quick he won't have a chance to change his mind." But as Julia acknowledged long afterward, Olivia would be not only the bond but also the shadow between them. Their coming together was uncannily like the way Harriet, becoming intimate with Calvin Stowe out of a shared love for his first wife, Eliza Tyler, married him after Eliza died. (Just as the Stowes had a painting made of Eliza Tyler and reminisced in front of it on each anniversary of her death, so Julia sculptured a bust of Livy and she and Thomas enshrined it next to their house.) For the men it was as if they were marrying a reminder of the wife who had gone.

Although from a New England home of great refinement and culture—her father was a minister, her grandfather the great lexicographer Noah Webster—Julia had been an athletic girl and was an energetic woman who entered into life with boundless enthusiasm. When the women of the church wondered whether she would fit into their crude little world, she put their fears to rest by joining in mopping and dusting the church and even—as she illustrated it in amusing little drawings— crawling into a ceiling ventilator to clean it out. In a typical gesture she cut off her long braids of soft brown hair to save time for more useful work. In later years, when asked how he was, Thomas would sometimes answer, "As well as can be expected for one who is hitched to a steam engine." In much the same vein, William Walter Phelps, later American ambassador to Germany, said one evening as he was having dinner at the Beechers', "Mrs. Beecher, I like to watch you pour coffee; you do it with such indiscriminate fury!" Despite what a friend described as their "warring temperaments" and "contradictory natures," Thomas and Julia Beecher would live together devotedly for forty-three years, Julia never giving up her efforts to shake or cajole him out of his recurring fits of despondency.

For a few years after they were married, the Beechers lived at Gleason's water cure, in those early days a rather bare, unfinished place, but Mrs. Gleason finally persuaded them that it was unhealthy for a newly married couple to live among ailing or disturbed people. So they built themselves—with Thomas doing much of the work himself—a comfortable home across the road on a hillside overlooking the town and the Chemung Valley.

Their charitable activities became a legend. Not waiting for the church to take action, one of them would set out in an old chaise—or in winter Thomas would haul a sled—with food and bundles of clothes for a family in need. Residents would long remember seeing Thomas trot down the street with a full-size sewing machine or even a sofa on his back. And he could never keep money in his pocket if he came upon someone in trouble; despite an increasing salary, he had no savings.

With Thomas and Julia living at the Gleasons' or close by, it became a favorite retreat for the Beechers. In 1857, as we have seen, Thomas brought young Fred Stowe there to help the youth quit drinking and smoking. Quite casually, in a little-noted letter to Calvin Stowe about Fred's condition, Thomas reveals that he himself had had a drinking habit that he broke only by subjecting himself to a vegetarian and water cure regimen in a secluded resort called Glen Haven, in the Finger Lakes region of New York.

A year or two later, when his younger brother James's first wife, Annie, returned from China with a mysterious problem, it was Thomas who arranged for her to stay at Gleason's and went through the harrowing experience of coping with her increasingly scandalous behavior. Through Thomas, too, Isabella retreated to Gleason's for the long stay in 1860 in which she began to search for a new function in life. Staying so near Tom and Julia's place, she saw them frequently and was much impressed by the way Julia dealt with Thomas:

Jule does well with him—wonderfully well—and she is growing herself into a more and more superior woman through intimacy with his truly great mind, and through a patient and pitying endurance of his weaknesses, which she fully understands and traces to their true source.

Isabella also noted that even though Thomas's congregation dissented from some of his views, his "best people" worshiped him. Almost grudgingly she conceded that he was completely dedicated to his high ideals. Although his cynical views depressed his family, with Isabella speaking of his "pernicious absurdities," "vagaries" and "hypochondria," Harriet referring to him as "Thomas the Doubter" and "the same odd stick he always was," and Henry saying, "I always get the blues when I go toward Elmira," they all recognized his selfless willingness to help them and everyone in any way he could.

Although he helped escaped slaves on their way to Canada, Thomas refused to join any action against the South and maintained—alone in his entire family—that slavery, despite some brutal exceptions, was not in itself evil. But once it became evident that the South was willing, if pressed, to dissolve the Union, he committed himself unreservedly to the Northern cause. He helped recruit a regiment of New York Volunteers, in which his brother James became a lieutenant colonel, and in 1862 he joined it as a chaplain.

Brief as his experience in the army was, he seems soon to have decided that it was riddled with corruption. He left it after only four months because he didn't relish his role as a chaplain and because his congregation urged him to return to Elmira. But a family biographer, Lyman Beecher Stowe, declares that Thomas had a far more disturbing reason for leaving the service: he had uncovered evidence, he believed, that Southern sympathizers—the so-called Copperheads—in General George McClellan's Army of the Potomac, then near Washington, were planning to seize Lincoln and his cabinet and set up McClellan as a dictator. Thomas secured an appointment with Lincoln, whom he had known in their Illinois days, and presented his evidence. The army, so the story goes, immediately took steps to crush the conspiracy.

In outline the story is doubtless true. What is misleading is the implication that Thomas was mainly responsible for exposing a formidable conspiracy. Actually almost everyone knew that McClellan was not opposed to slavery and that he considered abolitionists scoundrels, and some also knew that, deluded by his popularity among his troops, he flirted with the idea of displacing Lincoln and making himself dictator. What probably happened is that Beecher heard men talking of helping McClellan seize power, and since he knew Lincoln, he told the President what he had heard and thus contributed another detail to the many reasons that led Lincoln to replace McClellan in November 1862.

How very cynical Thomas was about antislavery feeling is made witheringly clear in a letter he wrote to Henry in August 1862:

I think you in error, and doing great harm by a most noble over-estimate of men and of public sentiment. After six weeks of ceaseless work raising soldiers, I am prepared to certify you that all appeals to the sentiments of justice, liberty and philanthropy toward the blacks are simply useless.

Observing that an army needs men of muscle rather than those with high ideals but feeble bodies, he adds:

You remember Indiana. Do you soberly think that those fighting Hoosiers would hurry to enlist for the sake of freeing the slave? Will negro-hating Illinois that *now* gives half her [men] to the war consent to fight to free the slaves she despises? I can answer for rural New York. The more emancipation you talk, the less recruits you can enlist.

His bitter conclusion was that the army "with one consent will say, 'We ain't going to fight for the niggers.' "

As personally generous as he was and as much as he loved his brother, Thomas's high tone here is one of almost contemptuous superiority. Although he had so little faith in the outcome, he continued to support the war effort vigorously. Through an old friend, Miss Ella Wolcott, who served as an army nurse and with whom he carried on an intimate correspondence, the Park Church—as it was known—contributed clothing and bandages to army hospitals throughout the war. But during the Reconstruction period he observed, it was said, that most blacks were worse off than they had been before the war.

Many years later, this gloomy view long forgotten, he wrote a glowing tribute to the courage and nobility of the Union soldiers and the Northern cause. But it is hardly surprising if Beecher's opinions in the dark days of 1862, when he tried to recruit men to fight against slavery, cannot be reconciled with his conclusions thirty years after the North had met the challenge and the slaves had long been free.

While Thomas was in the army, his letters were published in an Elmira newspaper and when he returned home he began contributing a column called "Saturday Miscellany" to the Elmira *Advertiser* and later to the *Weekly Gazette;* he would continue to do so for many years. A random mixture of editorials, lay sermons, anecdotes and impressions, it covered everything from politics, education and monetary policy to drinking, dancing, fishing and, insistently, the need to heed the words of Christ. The product of a wide-ranging mind, the columns, as we would call them, are often informative and amusing, at times daring—as when he defends suicide or cremation or discusses abortion—and only occasionally eccentric. Untroubled by possible inconsistencies, he is sometimes conservative, sometimes radical and sometimes, but more rarely, an advocate of compromise.

Considering himself a servant of the people, he often accepted public service: he was on the board of education and active in the building of several schools; he was the most effective member of a commission supervising the building of iron bridges across the Chemung River, and he constantly allowed himself to be drawn into politics. He made a few speeches in 1856 for Frémont, the first Republican presidential candidate; and his eloquence and popularity soon brought him invitations to run for office himself. He never turned such invitations down and over the years he ran for various offices under the labels of the Democratic, Republican, Greenback and Prohibition parties. Viewing such activities as an opportunity to teach, he showed no interest in winning ("I neither accept nor decline but anyone who wants to vote for me may do so") and sometimes even rebuked his own party. Not surprisingly, he never won. Members of his congregation, it is said, voted against him to prevent him from winning an office and leaving them.

Thomas's interest in the sciences, which Julia shared, continued as strong as ever. Together with his good friend Charles Samuel Farrar, a professor at Elmira College, he founded the Elmira Academy of Sciences. It was unusual enough for a minister, especially in a rural area, to take such an active interest in science, but when he also carried on a correspondence with such leading proponents of evolution as Darwin, Huxley and Tyndall, he was ignoring all the fears and warnings of proper churchmen everywhere. But in this he was not quite alone, even among churchmen: his brother Henry was reconciling mankind's spiritual with its evolutionary ascent. And before long it was evident that religion and the sciences would have to learn to live with each other.

Like his father and other members of the family, he had to rest from "brain work" by taking a vacation or even a leave of absence involving manual labor. Verging on a breakdown in 1867, he implored Henry to send him money and then, with aid from Jervis Langdon, went off alone on a voyage around Cape Horn. He made stops in Brazil and California and helped to earn his way by working on building construction and other odd jobs.

Both Thomas and Julia loved children. But never able to have any of their own, they became deeply attached to the four daughters of the Farrars, and when the professor and his wife died they adopted the girls. One of them was physically handicapped and the Beechers characteristically went out of their way to give her both attention and responsibilities.

Another young woman, Alice Hooker, Isabella's nineteen-year-old daughter, once stayed with Julia while Thomas was away. After a week she gave her mother a vivid glimpse of Aunt Julia and the Beechers' household. It was so different, she reported, from "any kind of life I knew before—so honest, so unaffected, unselfish and religious." Alice tried to be helpful, she said, but everyone awoke so early and did the housework so efficiently that "a sensibly sleepy mortal like myself doesn't get much of a chance to be useful." She felt that if she spent the winter there she would learn more not only practically but intellectually, morally and Christianly than anywhere else. I am delighted with Aunt Julie. She is too splendid, odd, funny, absurd, and good for anything. . . . I look with almost awe at her for some lovely Christian thought she may have uttered, most likely while washing the dishes, and the next scream with laughter at some funny and eccentric "Aunt Julie" idea.

Probably for her mother's benefit, Alice added that Julia kept saying, "We get on splendidly, don't we, Alice, for we are both good natured and keep praising one another. I believe in praise, don't you!"

Thomas Beecher's scorn for religious prejudice and sectarian rivalry was deep. When a rather naive young man asked him what the best path to heaven was, Beecher answered:

My boy, you can go to New York from Elmira by the Erie, the Lehigh Valley, the Lackawanna or the Northern Central. You can walk, ride horseback, or you can go by boat. One way may be somewhat more roundabout than the other but you will get there all right if you follow the sign posts. You can reach heaven by the Catholic church, or by the Synagogue, Universalist or Baptist, and you can even reach it through the Park Church—but, whatever you do, do it unto the Lord.

Along with Beecher's lack of prejudice went a distaste for pomp and ceremony. Within a few years after the war, when the audiences for his Sunday evening services became too large for the old church, he decided to hold the services in the new opera house in town. In an effort to further what he called church unity—we now term it "ecumenicism"— he invited the other ministers in the area to join him at the opera house. Scandalized, they cried out that it was a sacrilege. They called him the "opera house preacher" and even circulated a vile story about him.

But the people of Elmira cheered him on and the opera house services grew more and more popular. The outrage—and jealousy—of his fellow ministers continued and they finally expelled him from the local ministerial union. Turning the other cheek, he treated them most courteously and continued to attend their meetings, saying he would leave the opera house whenever they gave him a good reason for not using it. Exasperated, they thereafter held their meetings in secret. So Thomas maintained the family tradition of shocking fellow clergymen and being harshly criticized by them.

Instead of being chastened, Thomas outraged the ministerial brethren even more by holding Sunday morning services, in good weather, in the pleasant surroundings of Eldridge Park, on the edge of town. Worse still, he helped the street railway get permission to break the law by bringing people out to the park on Sunday. And he himself turned out in a white duck suit and white felt hat! While the other ministers fumed and fulminated in their pulpits, the crowds flocked to Eldridge Park.

In all these actions Jervis Langdon supported Beecher wholeheartedly. "My purse is always open to you," he declared. "You can do more with it than I can," and he even offered to buy shares in the opera house to ensure its availability. When Langdon's daughter Olivia prepared to marry Samuel Clemens, a young western humorist who wrote under the name Mark Twain, they all agreed that Thomas Beecher should perform the ceremony. And when Clemens heard of the ousting of Beecher from the ministerial union, he wrote to the Elmira *Advertiser:*

Happy, happy world that knows at last that a little congress of congregationless clergymen, of whom it had never heard before, have crushed a famous Beecher and reduced his audiences from fifteen hundred down to fourteen hundred and seventy-five at one fell blow!

Beecher used the opera house for ten years. By the time he left it, he had persuaded almost every preacher in the area to conduct Sunday evening services there.

But it became evident that a new church was needed. Beecher wanted it not as a monument to his achievement or simply as a place to preach but—scandalous thought—for education and recreation and for the whole family. Not just a shrine for Sunday worship, but a part of the stream of life.

24

JAMES
The Odd One

The last of Lyman Beecher's children, born only a few years before his mother's death, James Chaplin Beecher was brought up by a stepmother—she had six children of her own—and knew his older brothers and sisters only as visitors from far-off places. So he went his own way, as we have seen, flouting the rules at Dartmouth, challenging the professors, drinking, going off to Boston to do as he pleased, and excelling his college friends—so his brother Thomas claimed—only in "wit (low) and wickedness." Suspended in his junior year, he was taken back only because he was Lyman Beecher's son. It was Tom's theory that Jim was "combative" and resistant to authority because he had been brought up by a stepmother and one of her sons.

Whatever the explanation of James's waywardness, once out of college he dreamed youth's old dream of escape from parents, school and prim neighbors: the sea. His father feared the plan and Tom distrusted it. But Henry, to whom all the younger brothers now turned and who had once had a similar dream himself, arranged it: first a run on a coastal vessel carrying hay, cheese and such to Charleston, and then, in 1848, on a great clipper ship to exotic Canton.

It worked. Initially as a common seaman but after a while as a first mate, James spent a full five years in the East India trade. When the prodigal returned, he was a handsome, blue-eyed youth with golden brown hair, a bronzed complexion and a tremendous store of experience. One story he liked to tell was the way an entire crew in San Francisco in 1849 ran off to join the Gold Rush, leaving only the captain and himself on board.

For a short while he tried being a businessman in Boston, living under the wing of his brother Edward, but not surprisingly, that way was not for James Beecher. After spending time with him, Isabella reported to her husband that her youngest brother was an "odd fish" who troubled her persistently. She wrote:

I wish I could forget him. . . . I can't tell where the fault is, but somehow I don't love him much, or anybody else who is always ridiculing everybody and everything. . . . It seems impossible that Jim should settle down into a good, *rational* man. . . . If it were not for our mother, I could shirk him entirely. . . . But I am haunted with the thought of her anxieties for us, and the responsibility that she laid on me in regard to my brothers.

Although James would always retain a passion for outdoor life and physical activity, he was in the end ruled, as every Beecher child had been, by his father's love and prayers. The capitulation was not as sudden as it seemed. He had known for years that when the time came to choose a career, the example as well as the influence of his father—not to mention all his brothers—would be overwhelming. He was half relieved, half rueful when he declared on returning from a voyage to China, "Oh, I shall be a minister. That's my fate. Father will pray me into it!" He began to feel—it amounted to a Beecher instinct—an obligation to guide other people and serve God.

So he was dispatched to Andover Theological Seminary. He had been there less than two years when a call came for a missionary to manage a seamen's bethel in Canton. James seemed so well suited to the post that he left the seminary, was hurriedly ordained and departed for Canton. With him went his wife, Ann Morse, a widow from Newburyport, Massachusetts. She was several years older than he and had a child.

Confronted by every kind of obstacle, James Beecher in his five years of mission work in Canton and Hong Kong showed a dedication and fortitude not surpassed by any Beecher. He promptly set up a "floating chapel" among the docks and boats at Whampoa and then, utilizing his experience as a seaman, supplemented it with services held in the forecastles of visiting ships. He even succeeded in getting a melodeon for the chapel and soon had his congregation singing with him. But the clearest indication of his change of heart since his college days was his anguish at the drunkenness and profanity among the sailors.

James was at Whampoa only five months when a new outbreak of hostilities between the English—in their effort to "open up" China—and the Chinese forced him and his wife to abandon their chapel home and flee to Hong Kong. They had to make their way through waters swarming with pirate and Mandarin boats. In Hong Kong, James promptly set up another floating chapel. The sailors' quarter of the city was crowded with prostitutes and brothels and for well over four years James contended with the "intemperance and lust," as he phrased it, that flourished among the seamen. "China is," he writes, "a moral Golgotha for sailors," one in which they are "robbed, diseased and murdered." Agreeing with the prevailing Western view of the Chinese, he describes them as a "cowardly, cunning, crafty set of scoundrels, who will win your confidence by devotion and faithfulness one day and poison your breakfast or fire your house the next."

He managed to collect five thousand dollars, mainly from board-inghouse keepers, for a new chapel, but the war had spread, creating "famine prices," and the attendance at his services was poor. Welcoming work, he added to his duties the role of chaplain in the English Seaman's Hospital. Voyages in the surrounding waters grew more and more dan-gerous: while James was on a trip to Shanghai as chaplain on a coastal vessel, it was wrecked on the sandy, barren Peata Shoals. The stranded passengers were threatened by pirates and saved themselves only by con-vincing the attackers that it would be more profitable to hold them for ransom than to kill them.

As a preacher James was, his wife said, more like his father than were any of Lyman's other sons. When he won a good response and thought he had started a revival he was ecstatic: "My soul has been half way to heaven all this week. . . . Oh, my heart is full, my cup runneth over!" But he became more and more discouraged, especially by the rapid turnover in his congregation. After a while, seeing how often sailors were out of work and how endless their hardships, he could no longer under-stand why anyone should want to spend his life at sea.

Annie, harboring an ambition to be a writer, tried to start a newspa-per. Then in 1859, supposedly for reasons of health, she returned to America. With the help of Tom—James would always consider Tom and Isabella his only true brother and sister—she entered Gleason's sani-tarium in Elmira.

James now began to supplement his income with editorial work on a local newspaper. (He was later offered three thousand dollars a year to stay on as a regular editor and writer but he refused to abandon the ministry.) The problems of the mission continued. Finally a typhoon wrecked his chapel. He raised almost ten thousand dollars to rebuild it, but he was increasingly depressed by his situation and by Annie's absence.

Annie had failed to return to Hong Kong for other reasons than health. From a very confidential letter to Isabella Beecher Hooker from Edward's wife, the other Isabella, we learn a horrendous secret: Annie, whom she has known for many years, is addicted to drink. But, she adds at once, Annie is "worth saving." Later Fred Stowe's alcoholism would shake the Beechers, but that was as nothing to this story of a young woman with the same dread affliction. Since Tom was managing Annie's affairs, Isabella Beecher Hooker wrote to him immediately. Tom's an-swer was a complete rejection of the rumors: Annie, he says, is cheerful, affectionate and a welcome companion; she appears to be well except for her "chronic cough"; she writes, sings and seems to be a "good, pure and lovable woman—volatile yes—childishly impulsive," but not, so far as he knows, "addicted to any fatal or disreputable habits." He mocks the rumors circulated by "brawling women" and points out that Jim has never uttered a syllable of "doubt or uneasiness" concerning his wife. Annie's plan, Tom adds, is to "complete some writing, publish, get the cash and then sail for Hong Kong."

The rumors spread by the "brawling women" were, however, well founded. In January 1860 James is still telling Isabella that he expects Annie to return shortly. But he is in a state of depression, opposed by sailing captains whose "gross wickedness" he has exposed and surrounded by millions of heathens who wonder at his stupidity in not "burning joss paper and fire crackers before praying."

When, however, Isabella, in her role of mother surrogate, confronts him with reports on Annie's condition, he admits he is not surprised. But he defends Annie doggedly:

Whatever may have taken place in the last three years, of sorrow and hopelessness, yet I testfify to the love and devotion of my dear wife, and never has my love changed. . . . If I have suffered, she has suffered more, for it was the thought that her fearful weaknesss was breaking my heart which gave her greater agony than even her own danger of destruction.

Although he misses her, James concedes that Annie is probably better off away from this "half-civilized country."

Now, too, Tom has begun talking of Annie as not responsible for what she does. Although her doctor considers her safe enough to go to the city "unattended" and she may soon leave the sanitarium, Tom fears that when she begins to write again, she will require "stimulation as of old."

By June of 1860 Annie has been committed to an asylum. Isabella, sending her husband a copy of one of Jim's letters to Tom, reveals again a view of life as a drama that she is helping to direct. Have daughter Mary, she writes, read the first page aloud to you in a low pathetic voice,

and see if the style does not remind you of Dickens. . . . This letter is touching, but it is nothing compared to those Tom read me. . . . He [Jim] told of the first time when the thought flashed upon him. It was after a picnic and she [Annie] lay insensible before him. He wondered that he did not go mad with the suddenness of the blow. . . . There followed agonized efforts to prevent her ever obtaining stimulants of any kind.

Despite this, she adds, James is "a noble man. The years of suffering . . . have only drawn him closer and closer to Christ." Betraying the conflict between a proper Victorian's instincts and Christian duty, Isabella says that although Annie is probably deranged and although Isabella herself cannot think of her without aversion, the family must still try to love her.

To add to Annie's agony, her favorite brother, Stephen, a sailor, was stabbed on the street in New York and died before she could reach him. The bloom is gone from her cheeks, Julia, Tom's wife, reports, and Jim is due home momentarily.

James Beecher returned to the United States early in 1861 and promptly enlisted in the army. Through Henry's influence he got a post as chaplain in the First Long Island Regiment, called the "Brooklyn phalanx," but impatient at the lack of action, he requested active duty. An able soldier, he became the senior captain of the regiment and was soon appointed lieutenant colonel of the 141st New York Volunteers, in which brother Tom was chaplain. It was at this point that Isabella and Harriet visited him in Washington and proudly watched him, the handsomest of the Beechers, pass by at the head of his regiment. But when Isabella tried to discuss politics with him, she found him infected, she said, with Tom's "pernicious absurdities," meaning no doubt Tom's misanthropic views. She quickly dropped the whole subject.

But Jim had good reason to be bitter: Annie had slid into hopeless alcoholism; and in his regiment he himself had had to cope not only with increasing responsibilities but with regimental politics. He was now also deeply attracted to Frances Johnson, a young woman from Guilford, Connecticut. In sharp contrast to Annie, "Frankie," as everyone called her, was a stable and religious woman—she had attended Mount Holyoke Seminary in Massachusetts—whom the Beechers immediately respected and liked.

Guilt-ridden and overburdened, Jim began breaking down. Tom, having had to cope with Annie's problems and then Jim's anxieties, was also at the end of his resources. Characteristically he did everything he could for them but criticized them unsparingly. Dramatizing their plight, he writes to his friend Ella Wolcott of the "long delayed retribution" that is overtaking them, including possible court-martial for James. His brother, he declares, is being driven to madness: "To hear of his suicide would not surprise me at any time. Annie is a shirt of Nessus clinging to him."

A few weeks later he tells Isabella that Jim has been saved from court-martial only because the colonel of his regiment was ousted. But he himself, Tom adds, has been barely able to "stave off insanity." He is only too glad to turn Jim over to her care but warns her not to pet or "carry" him. If she is about to suggest a divorce she should wait another year, when, he is sure, Annie will have sunk so low that there will be no resistance. Tom then gave Isabella as mortifying a piece of news as any Beecher had ever heard: Annie was drunk in Elmira's streets on Monday and disappeared from her room on Tuesday night. "I know not where," he concludes. "But ere long she will be somebody's mistress—or everybody's."

But a week later, when Isabella advises pressing for a divorce at once, Tom answers that neither he nor Jim has any evidence that warrants such a step. "Be careful not to subpoena me as a witness," he writes, "for while I loathe the woman, I cannot in truth and honor think Jim entitled to divorce." Separation, yes, but not divorce. With Puritan severity, he concludes: "If his courage fail, I'll still pity him but never . . . love him as I like to love the patient ones who bear their crosses well—till all is finished."

In still another week Tom admits that after every one of Annie's "breakaways" he thinks that she will truly sink into infamy, for he knows "the perils that yawn around an unprotected woman"; yet each time she comes through. After she disappeared from her room, he reports, it was thought that she had gone to Haights Hotel—"a house where many girls have been seduced—if common fame be true." But she turned up at a respectable private house. Swinging between righteous condemnation and an effort at objectivity, he adds:

"Bad woman" I think her. But I have not supposed that "bad" and adulterous were interchangeable terms. I repeat to you what I said to Henry—Annie loves Jim in every fibre of her being. She is coarse, amorous, sensual, in her love—but I verily believe and so does Jim—*faithful*. She has adulterous thoughts and I have been sorely tempted to declare her an overt sinner. But I cannot in honor.

Meanwhile Isabella had assumed the role of Jim's mother confessor and guide. From Jim's room in New York, where he has come for medical help, Isabella reports that he is at times terribly despondent and that his head is "sore and crazy." He is too "excitable" to remain in the army and they must find something for him to do. Differing with Tom, she thinks Jim must be loved and petted.

With impressive confidence, Isabella went to Washington and persuaded Secretary of War Stanton, an old friend of the Stowes and the Beechers, to give James an honorable discharge. Jim has apparently done nothing wrong, she reports to her husband,

simply been overworked and worried by the regimental troubles, which are terrible . . . then took chloroform to try to sleep, was drugged with morphine by the surgeon, and finally sent into the hospital here, utterly broken down and out of his head. But he is recovering. . . . The coming of Annie to the hospital . . . and a room provided for them together, capped the whole. Jim loathes her—her breath is pestilence itself, and he could not endure it, so he came here, after sending her back to Elmira.

Isabella brought Jim back to New York and left him at Dr. Taylor's sanitarium. He was now ready to seek a divorce but feared not only what Annie might do but also Tom's condemnation. Now Henry wanted to go to Elmira but, Isabella claimed, Tom was in such "a fearfully excited state, and so entirely misjudged Jim that it would only arouse Henry's indignation against Tom, who after all must be dealt with gently." The impression Isabella gives is that only she knows how to cope with her brothers. Quite conscious of the drama in which she is playing a part, she concludes: "The complications of Jim's troubles is beyond anything that novels relate."

Solving Jim's problems and ending the Beechers' mortification, Annie Morse Beecher died of delirium tremens in April 1863. So at last James was free: free of shame, free of guilt, and free to marry Frances Johnson. I am, he announced, on "the threshold of a new life."

At thirty-five he had been given another chance; he would make the most of it.

James was readmitted to the service but given a staggering task: recruiting a black regiment—the First North Carolina Volunteers—in the South. Another New England minister and a famous abolitionist, Thomas Wentworth Higginson, had already raised such a unit but it had not yet served in a major action. And a young Bostonian, Robert Gould Shaw, was on his way to Charleston with the first black regiment in the United States, but it came from a free state—nor did anyone know how it would perform. (A few months later it acquitted itself admirably in a desperate attack on Fort Wagner, but Shaw, while leading his men, was killed.) The prevailing opinion was that former slaves were lazy, ignorant and unreliable, and could never be turned into effective soldiers. "The nigger," the saying was, "won't fight."

But James Beecher, whether because of his experiences at sea or the antislavery faith of his brothers and sisters, had no such doubts. He opened a recruiting office in New Bern, North Carolina, and not only raised a regiment but equipped, trained and led it. He also served as its chaplain.

When he assembled his men for one of the first Sunday evening services, he was filled with exultation at the transformation that had been wrought in these former slaves in only a few weeks. He formed them in close columns and then gave out a hymn. He wrote:

6 or 700 good, pleasant voices came in grandly. . . . I felt like preaching. I told them of the common ground where all met. They had known themselves as slaves, contraband and what not. They should know themselves as God beloved, God begotten and, purifying themselves bodily and spiritually, commence their new manhood. I never enjoyed speaking so intensely. I never preached to so

appreciative an audience. Then I prayed with them. All knelt in the ranks with uncovered heads.

Amazed at how readily the men took to training, he added:

I wish doubtful people at home could see my three-weeks regiment. They would talk less nonsense about negro inferiority. Our discipline is better than any regiment I know of. . . . I think the government can't growl at a regiment enlisted, organized, uniformed, armed, equipped and handsomely encamped in *six weeks.*

Just as significant about James Beecher the man as well as the officer is his boast a little later: "I do not know of a commanding officer whose relations with his men are more intimate and to whom his men go with more unrestrained freedom." Far from shirking responsibility, he is happier, he tells Frankie, than he has been in many months because, aside from having her, he has an "unbounded liberty to work without let or hindrance."

The regiment joined the siege of Charleston in the fall and remained dug in around the city until the end of the year. His description of drilling on the beach before dawn reminds us that he has the Beecher gift with words:

There is to me something peculiar about military movements by moonlight. It is low tide and we have a parade nearly 100 yards wide and as smooth and hard as an oak floor. The sea is calm, just breathing and no noise, while the moonlight overhead is so clear that I can dress the whole line as accurately as at noon day, and when in columns . . . the effect is fine, clear black lines on the white sand . . . and so still that every time I give a command it seems to float all around through the air . . . and then as I order "fix bayonets," bright sparklings flash along the line . . . and at "shoulder arms" my long low cloud becomes silver edged . . . and the quiet, solemn old moon looking down as much as to say, "Do it well and soberly, boys, I'm watching you."

There was another, sardonic side to James Beecher and it was manifested in this letter in scathing references to the stupidity of the generals, especially in the way they were giving the enemy every opportunity to strengthen the defenses of Charleston. The work of these officers, which will be praised by the government, James wrote, and win the thanks of the poor folks at home has been puffed up by newspaper correspondents, who "deserve hanging" for their lies.

James's responsibilities continued to mount until he realized that he was heading toward the same kind of crisis that had shattered him the previous winter. That breakdown, he had thought, was the result of his use of "stimulants." But he knew now that he had turned to stimulants because he had reached the limit of his nervous energies. So this time he dropped everything, saying to himself, "I've done my best."

Meanwhile the skeptics were still waiting to see how the regiment would fare under fire. That test came when the unit was moved to Florida and committed to action at a crucial point in the battle of Olustee. To his everlasting regret, Colonel Beecher happened to be in the North trying to get better arms for his men. But all reports were full of praise for the black contingent. The *Herald* correspondent wrote:

The First North Carolina and the 54th Massachusetts of the colored troops did admirably. The former held . . . with the greatest tenacity, and inflicted heavy loss on the enemy. It was cool and steady and never flinched. . . . The two colored regiments had stood in the gap and saved the army.

The casualties among the black units were great: one company lost fifty-two out of eighty-six men. But the battle helped to end another myth about Negroes.

Although both James and his betrothed had been trying to meet in order to get married, it was not until July 1864, when James was in Jacksonville, Florida, that Frankie won permission from the secretary of war to join her fiancé. At last, attended by officers in full-dress uniform, they were married in the old Jacksonville house that was being used as headquarters.

As conscientious as her husband, Frankie was appalled by the number of soldiers who could not even sign their names. Soon she was spending much of her time teaching them to read and write. Sometimes, when James was not away on a raid, the couple would manage to ride out into the countryside.

In November, units of the regiment, now called the 35th U.S. Colored Troops, were sent into South Carolina. There they were thrust into a battle at Honey Hill in an effort to break the Southern line along the Charleston and Savannah Railroad. Beecher led five separate charges until his horse was shot out from under him and he was seriously wounded in the thigh. But he refused to leave the field before nightfall. He spent months in a hospital in Beaufort and then convalescing in the North, always with Frankie at his side.

He returned to active duty in time to join the drive on Charleston. In one letter he reports that he has been in the saddle from 6 A.M. to 6 P.M.—raiding, burning, taking horses and carts as needed. It grieves him, he writes, to burn a splendid house, but the "planters have lived most luxuriously" and they "have got to rough it now." Caught up in the fever of the drive, he exults in their victories. The great fires that light up the horizon at night are "splendid," and he adds:

I have only stolen 3 horses, one cart and a Methodist minister—who begged hard for the horses, but I told him he and his brother ministers had forced me to leave the pulpit and take to fighting and I'd not only take his horses but burn his house if it came in my line of march.

Then at last the fighting was over, and as March flowered in the high-walled gardens of Charleston, Colonel Beecher and his men entered the ruined and desolate city. Soon Beecher was put in charge of the northern part of the city. In his almost unique capacity of soldier-priest, he celebrated the capture of the city with an address to an audience of freedmen in the largest church in the city. "He entered the pulpit," Dr. Marcy, the regimental surgeon and his close friend, later wrote,

in full uniform . . . followed by members of his staff. Unbuckling his sword and laying it tenderly on the desk, he took for his text, "The liberty wherewith Christ has made us free." His impassioned oratory at times swayed the vast audience as a mighty wind the tree-tops . . . recounting God's care for his children . . . and there was not a dry eye in the house, and when at the close all bent in prayer, broken sobs and utterances of, "Thanks to God we's free," attested to his power.

It was another triumphant moment for the Beechers. Even as word came that James had been made a brevet brigadier general, Henry, invited by President Lincoln, arrived at Charleston to give the address at the raising of the United States flag over Fort Sumter. For a few days, Henry and his party were the guests of James and Frankie at the headquarters opposite the Citadel.

In the midst of the celebration word came of the assassination of the President.

For the people of the region, peace was hardly joyous. The mixture of ironies was rich: having destroyed, the chaplain/general must now help to reconstruct. James was put in charge of a ninety-square-mile section of the Charleston military district, including six hundred plantations, two good-sized towns and the Sea Islands. It was a damaged land, stripped by waves of soldiers and bushwhackers, and each military official had to make his own rules. With Frankie helping to examine applicants, they fed and clothed the needy, including poor blacks, "white trash" with their "bloodless faces and mournful eyes," and planters' wives "reared in luxury." Beecher set about making contracts with both planters and freedmen for tilling the fields and dividing the produce. He faced problems bravely. When it was rumored that violence had broken out in Edisto Island, south of Charleston, he went there at once. He found that the freedmen who had begun to work the land had been notified that all plantations would be returned to their original owners. They simply refused to work. James reported that the rumors of violence and anarchy were not only false but malicious. And he sturdily declared, in a letter to Senator Charles Sumner, that the government would be guilty of bad faith if it did not give the freedmen an opportunity to lease or buy the land they were working. His suggestions were widely adopted, but they were abandoned soon after the government troops were withdrawn. Weighing Beecher's work, a newspaper declared that he was "honest, bold and uncompromising," doing everything in his power to secure justice for all.

So the black sheep, the irresponsible youth who had leaned on any available brother or sister, had become first an able commander, liked and admired by his men, and then a just and compassionate administrator in a troubled land.

Having completed its enlistment, Beecher's regiment was disbanded in June 1866. After five rugged years in the army, Beecher faced another trial—return to civilian life.

Welcoming it as a helpful transition, James served for nine months in Tom's church in Elmira while his brother was on leave seeking spiritual renewal on a trip around Cape Horn. James and his family lodged at Gleason's water cure, across the way from the parsonage. While they were there, Alice, Isabella's nineteen-year-old daughter, came, as we have seen, for a long visit to her aunt Julia. She was as perceptive about her uncle Jim as about Julia, noting that he was "blue" because he thought the congregation missed Tom and only tolerated his brother. But Alice said they really liked both Uncle Jim's preaching and his lectures. Jim had also taken on a small church in a rural community called Christian Hollow. Once again making her contribution, Frankie conducted a Sunday school and held prayer meetings there. It was a labor of love and the poor people of the Hollow, Alice reported, were deeply grateful to both of them. Perhaps because of Jim's experience with Annie, Alice also let her mother know how devoted Frankie was, kissing her husband constantly, while Jim was as "handsome and as unresponsive and monosyllabic as ever."

In May of 1867 James became the pastor of the Congregational church in Owego, a town in central New York State scarcely thirty miles from Tom's church in Elmira. He would remain there four years and then go on to serve five years in the Hudson River town of Poughkeepsie. After the excitement of the clipper ships and the teeming streets of Hong Kong, after the nightmarish last years with Annie and the horrors of war, life as a pastor in the country towns of New York must have seemed like a blessed refuge, balm for a man wounded in body and spirit. In both towns he became known for his interest in his parishioners, and he and

Frankie formed close ties with a number of them. James, friends later recalled, had a tendency to be melancholy and to undervalue his work and his worth.

James and Frankie had been married half a dozen years and already had one adopted daughter, Kathie, when the mother of a large family in Owego died, leaving twin infant girls; charmed by little Margie and Mary (called May), the Beechers promptly adopted them. James Beecher was now at last surrounded by love, respect and security—he was earning three thousand dollars a year—and he should have been content. But he and Tom had repeatedly vacationed in the Catskill Mountain wilderness in the eastern part of the state and the more he saw of that lovely untouched country, the more he longed to live there.

So in 1876, a self-appointed missionary to the lumbermen, small farmers and rustics of the region, he moved his family to the Hardenberg area of Ulster County. There he bought a densely wooded tract, one mile square, with a clear pond which he named Beecher Lake. It was many miles from any town and there was no road to his place until a few neighbors helped him cut one through the woods.

At first the family lived in a large hospital tent with a board floor and did their cooking and dining in a wooden shanty nearby. Before long, James hand-built a rough but comfortable cottage and cleared ground for a farm that eventually covered twenty acres. Like his half brother Charles in Florida in those same years, he was his own carpenter, blacksmith, glazier and handyman. The family had trout from the lake, geese, partridge, woodchuck, rabbits, berries and honey from the woods, milk and butter from three cows, sugar from the maple trees and a wide variety of garden vegetables. Tom and Julia visited them regularly and enjoyed the place as much as they did.

Soon some of the settlers invited James to preach in the nearest schoolhouse, four miles away, and then in another schoolhouse twice as far off. In time the Sunday services developed into a combination of "sociable," picnic and, with the aid of an old organ, theater.

The local schools, open only six months of the year, were so poor that the children could neither read nor write. So Frankie again organized a school, with desks, books and writing materials contributed by Poughkeepsie friends, and carried it on for several years. Both the preaching and the school won the Beechers the friendship of the settlers and there was much visiting to and fro, in winter using horse-drawn box sleighs or even oxen yoked to wooden sleds.

Ned Buntline, popular writer of countless dime novels, visited the "hermit preacher"—as did more and more newspaper interviewers and curious travelers—and described the setting as one of the most picturesque in the Catskills:

... there is every reason to believe that there is no earthly inducement which could induce James Beecher to enter again on his old-time career. The few neighbors who have gathered about his lake fully appreciate him. "He is queer," they admit, but for all that they love him.

But after more than six years he did allow himself to be lured away. Perhaps he did so because he was now in his fifties and because he was increasingly haunted by fears of madness in his heritage. He was as skeptical as the other Beechers about Isabella's spiritualist activities and even distrustful of her obsessive concern with women's rights. Not long before he left the Catskills he wrote:

I think sister Belle would have done far better to come here this winter than to be browsing around Brooklyn and Elmira where she will only make a nuisance of herself. She might have my pulpit every Sunday. . . . She could explain her spiritual systems to Mr. Dibbles and her higher life woman's rights to Mr. Nelson Kelly.

With a lucidity that almost belies what he is saying, he continues:

I am sure that there runs a streak of insanity in our mother's three children—or rather a monomania, assuming diverse forms. I recognize it in Tom and myself. The only advantage I have is in being thoroughly conscious of the fact. Tom is partially so. Belle is absolutely unconscious and is therefore the craziest of the three.

He concludes on an amusingly cynical note:

However, she is almost sixty. If she got well, she couldn't do much good, and if she grows worse, she cannot do much harm—and a very few years will clear us all out, and in a dozen years or so if any body should ask who were those Beechers anyhow, there will be nobody able to answer the question.

He was lured away by brother Henry, who asked him to take charge of the Plymouth Church bethel. So, late in 1881, James left the Catskill woods to work with the poor of Brooklyn. It was probably the worst step he could have taken: he was simply not ready to cope with the wretched of the world. Dormant anxieties were awakened and would not go away. By the fall of 1882 his behavior had become so erratic that he had to be persuaded to commit himself to an institution. The letterhead of his first letters home cruelly proclaimed that he was in the State Homoeopathic Asylum for the Insane in Middletown, New York.

That was the beginning of James Beecher's descent into hell, into four interminable years of wandering from institution to institution: Middletown . . . Elmira . . . Winchendon . . . Elmira again . . . round and round in a maze of blind alleys, in a spirit-shriveling search for a cure of his swings from manic elation to bottomless depression, from hallucinations and paranoid fears to complete lucidity and a self-knowledge that was worst of all. . . . Four years of humiliation in which the former commander of clipper ships and army regiments suffered the nameless indignities of asylums and attendants—in which a man who had come through tragedy and violence to love and peace now helplessly watched them slip away forever, as he begged his wife to save him. . . .

How his wife could bear to read his letters, so full of love and longing, so terrible and moving in their awareness of his condition, is almost beyond understanding. After one of her visits, he writes:

Why it was I let you go without me I cannot tell. . . . I seemed to be moved by a spirit other than my own. . . . I want to go this moment but dread to start alone lest I should get to vacillating as I have done before. I am as clear-headed now as I ever was but what shall I do when the cloud comes down. . . . I want a friend whom I can trust and lean on, to go with me. . . . I will get home—I will break through the strange paralysis which has come upon me. . . .

Elsewhere, out of the memory of half a lifetime spent at sea or in the wilderness, he cries: "I want to be in the open air. Confinement is death to me—worse than death." Explaining why he does not write more often, he reveals wild fears:

I shrink from having my heart sorrow and heart love fouled by the dirty, cowardly brutes who tamper with our letters. . . . Every day is a longing for congenial companions for though I keep myself from resenting discourtesies and treat with courtesy those who are doing all in their power to annoy, yet God help me, I have not a friend whom I can trust.

From the Elmira water cure he writes:

There was company here last night. One old lady telling about a funeral sermon I preached in Elmira fifteen years ago says she should "never forget it," etc. etc. Another one (a man) telling of something in my former ministry here, and so it goes. Oh my wife, it is terrible to compare the humiliation and the helplessness and the forsaken uselessness of the present with even the narrow life I thought I was living while it passed.

In desperate defiance of his condition, he writes:

My precious, my beloved, I won't reiterate, because it does no good. Only this, don't let man or devil, on appearances make you doubt even for a moment the tenderness and faith of my love for you and the dear children.

I want to write to Tom but my hands seem tied fast. . . . Tell him that excepting my wife only, I love him better than anything in Heaven or on earth, that I long for him with longing unutterable. Somehow I feel as though if he would take me by the hand, I could walk and even hope. . . .

And then, in ultimate despair:

You shall have this line of love faithful and enduring if nothing more. But remember, my dear, I can only write one thing—*you must help me to come home.* . . . I cannot endure it any longer. It makes me sick in body, heart and mind. . . . And the worst of it all is that it is the tenderness of your love that is killing me by inches. So come, my dearest, before it is too late.

In one of her last letters to him, Frankie responds in kind:

But do not think for a moment of any one trying, even, to separate us, for they cannot do it, and must know there is no use in trying. I am sure we love each other all the better in many ways for the sorrow we share, as well as the years of joy we have had. Never doubt my heart and my love which is yours only forever.

Perhaps because confinement for four years had obviously not helped him—he still had delusions of persecution—James was released in the fall of 1886 in the custody of a nephew. One day he came to Elmira to visit Gleason's sanitarium and to see his brother Tom. While there he went out with several other men to Dr. Gleason's private rifle range. An experienced marksman, he made an excellent score. That evening after supper, as the company sat talking in the piazza, he went into the house. A few minutes later those outside heard a shot. Rushing into a rear room they found him dead, shot through the mouth . . . like his half brother George forty-three years before.

Edward wrote a notice for the newspapers in which he pointed out that his brother had long been mentally ill and was not responsible for his act. That was undoubtedly the proper and Christian thing to say—an obeisance to the prohibition against taking one's own life. But it was not entirely true or just, for the suicide was the act of a man strong enough to refuse to live a useless life or inflict further pain on those who loved him.

In judging James Beecher we have relatively few of his views to guide us—he published no books or articles—but we have his acts and deeds. After a youth that was a classic of sowing wild oats, and despite a tendency to eccentricity, he was as devoted to the communities he served as any of his family in a similar position. And if we consider those he served—the plain, the neglected and the poor—he was as earnest, unassuming and genuinely self-sacrificing as any other Beecher.

If his ten-year marriage to Annie Morse was a tragic error, his twenty-one-year union with Frances Johnson was a triumph. It surely proved that Thomas was wrong in his righteous charge at the time of Annie's troubles that James was not fit for marriage. As for the taint of madness, it seems, if anything, to have made him humble and did not in any way prevent him from understanding himself, from helping others, or from loving.

In the matter of human rights and needs, James Beecher expressed himself as effectively in actions as others did in words. His commitment to the seamen on the waterfront of Hong Kong, the fellowship he and his wife established with the people of small towns and the Catskill woods, his organizing, leading and inspiring a regiment of newly freed slaves, and his compassion as a governor of a broken land distinguish him as another remarkable Beecher and perhaps the most neglected of all.

IV
❦

SUNSET OF A DYNASTY
1870-1900

25

HENRY WARD BEECHER

Trial by Fire

The Beecher-Tilton scandal shook prudish Victorian America to its roots. Yet it was only another sign of the shift from self-denial to self-indulgence. After the sacrifice and suffering of the war, after the destruction and the profiteers, the loss of innocence and the fading of utopian hopes, came a surging desire to enjoy life. The Puritan bonds were broken, the pioneer struggle was receding, and the seasonal rhythm of farm and village was giving way to the hectic pace of the cities.

The evidence of corruption and of the relaxation of standards was everywhere. In Washington, lobbyists, who had learned their business during the war, moved more boldly than ever in a world of bribes, favors, subsidies and grants. Among the moneyed, lavish entertainment was common, the jets in the crystal chandeliers burning far into the night. Gambling houses and brothels flourished, in Washington thirty luxurious ones closing down when Congress adjourned for the summer of 1869. The Credit Mobilier scandal, in which a railroad construction company swindled the government out of millions of dollars, tarred Vice-President Colfax, a future President—Garfield—and a covey of congressmen. Another fraud, the "Whiskey Ring," involved leading distillers, treasury officials and Grant's favorite secretary, Babcock, who was paid off with a thousand-dollar bill, a diamond pin, and the services of a "gay sylph."

Jay Gould, master manipulator of stocks, and "Commodore" Vanderbilt, former ferryboat captain, plundered the railroads and lived like barons. Prostitution had spread so rapidly that a Methodist Episcopal bishop in New York asserted in 1866 that there were as many prostitutes as Methodists in the city. Almost a hundred "houses of assignation" allowed men and women of polite society to spend a clandestine afternoon together. Jim Fisk, the blowsy, roistering peddler who became a railroad president, milked the Erie of millions, put its offices in a New York opera house because he liked show girls, and flaunted the fanciest mistress in town. "As to the World, the Flesh, and the Devil," he proclaimed, "I'm on good terms with all three. If God Almighty is going to damn us men because we love the women, then let him go ahead and do it." When he was shot to death by a rival lover, many people mourned his passing—either because his candor was so refreshing amidst so much moral sham or because he afforded vicarious release from rigid conformity. But the preachers, and chief among them Henry Ward Beecher, seized on his life and death as an object lesson. Summoning all his powers of condemnation, Beecher cried:

And that supreme mountebank of fortune . . . that man of some smartness in business but absolutely without moral sense, and as absolutely devoid of shame as the desert of Sahara is of grass—that this man, with one leap, should have vaulted to the very summit of power in New York, and . . . rode out to this hour in glaring and magnificent prosperity—shameless, vicious, abominable in his lusts . . . and yet in an instant, by the hand of a fellow-culprit, God's providence struck him to the ground!

Fisk was an unvarnished rogue, but what should be said of the Reverend Isaac Kalloch. The talented son of a Maine clergyman, Kalloch was called to the largest church in Boston, the Tremont Temple, and became an immensely popular minister there. A red-haired giant of a man, he was fiery in the pulpit but outside the church was a genial companion who enjoyed a cigar, a glass of whiskey and the adoration of the ladies.

Kalloch was already well known when he was accused, in 1857, of committing adultery with the wife of a respected citizen. He admitted taking her to a Cambridge inn but denied the charge and was exonerated. An unaccountably restless man, he moved briefly to the fashionable Laight Street Baptist Church in New York, thence to a congregation and a college presidency in Lawrence, Kansas, and finally to San Francisco. Although he was everywhere attended by rumors of dissipation and of a loose way with women, the truth and other people's money, and although he accepted Darwinism and questioned the infallibility of the Bible, rich parishioners in San Francisco built him the largest Baptist church in the United States, the city elected him mayor, and he died rich.

Isaac Kalloch was a profligate, an opportunist and probably an embezzler. Yet he became a famous preacher in four American cities, president of a college as well as of a railroad, and mayor of San Francisco. This record was so similar to Henry Ward Beecher's that Tilton's lawyer in Henry's adultery trial mentioned it as a comparable instance of "clerical depravity," and Kalloch himself wrote Henry at the height of the trial, declaring that he and the people of Kansas loved Henry and believed in him. Kalloch's extraordinary career was partly the result of his dynamic personality. But it also reflected the temper of the time and place: the decadence of Puritanism in Boston, the admiration of masculinity and rugged individualism in Kansas, and the tolerance of flamboyant characters in early San Francisco. Kalloch was of course exceptional, but his career would have been unthinkable only half a century before.

When Henry Ward Beecher, struggling with the early chapters of his novel, *Norwood,* turned to Elizabeth Tilton for help and encouragement, she was thirty-three and the mother of five children, three of them still alive. She was a tiny woman, dark-haired, dark-eyed, an appealing creature in the eyes of men, and easily dominated. She had been a devout member of Henry's congregation since her childhood, taught faithfully in the Plymouth Church Sunday school and was active in help for the poor. An avid reader of the popular novels of Charles Reade and E. D. E. N. Southworth and the poetry of Elizabeth Barrett Browning, she mixed a turbid romanticism with religious fervor. In her, as in Henry, feeling was paramount; when she listened to him preach she was at times gripped by something like ecstasy. That is why when aroused she so easily fused the religious and the erotic.

When Henry visited the Tilton home he found not only distinguished and stimulating visitors—Greeley, Whittier, Sumner and such leading feminists as Elizabeth Cady Stanton and Susan B. Anthony—but a heady zeal for lofty causes. He also found warmth. He was welcomed by Lib Tilton, all aglow at the sight of the great Reverend Beecher—whom she had so long worshiped from a distance—as a dear friend in her home.

To Henry the contrast with the cold and sterile respectability of his own home was overwhelming. "O Theodore," he confessed, "I dread to go back to my own house." The Tiltons' style was a revelation and it drew him irresistibly. "God might strip all other gifts from me," he told Tilton, "if he would only give me a wife like Elizabeth and a home like yours." Flattered that he should be master of so enviable a household, Tilton pressed Henry to come more often. With a freedom reminiscent of attitudes in some communal experiments of the time, he added, "There is one little woman down at my house who loves you more than you can have any idea of."

Plainly the word "love" was here used loosely. The Tiltons—and especially Theodore—were, like Henry himself, moving away from the dark old religion of guilt into a bright new religion of love, and along the way love, or more accurately sentiment, seeped into other human relationships, such as those between a man and a woman or between a man and his friends' wives. Henry accepted Tilton's invitation and was almost a daily visitor. He became a part of the family circle, warming himself freely in the glow of Elizabeth Tilton's affection. "During these years of intimacy in Mr. Tilton's family," he later recalled, "I was treated as a father or elder brother. Children were born, children died. They learned to love me, and to frolic with me as if I were one of themselves." He spoke of Mrs. Tilton as turning to him with "artless familiarity and with entire confidence. Childish in appearance, she was childish in nature, and I would as soon have misconceived the confidence of her little girls as the unstudied affection she showed me."

Other forces were having a softening effect on the rigid code governing the relations between the sexes. One of these was the women's rights movement. The leading suffragists were frequent visitors at the Tilton salon and Henry became familiar with all of them. Although these women were still very much a radical fringe, in circles like the Tiltons' their demand for greater freedom in social relations as well as equality in politics, education and employment had its effect. (Eunice cordially disliked such women and their ideas and never visited the Tiltons with her husband.) The most daring of them all, Victoria Woodhull, called for equal rights in love as well. She outraged most Victorians, but a few, like Theodore Tilton, were unsettled by her. He in turn unsettled his wife. His growing skepticism in religious matters had already upset her. Originally a strict Calvinist, he had taken to questioning basic doctrine, including the Godhead of Christ, and ignoring many of the conventional religious observances. Although Elizabeth had tried to share his attitudes, skepticism did not come naturally to her and she found it much easier to fall back on Beecher's firm and reassuring faith.

The first accusation against Henry in connection with the adoring women around him in his church was, as we have seen, Henry Bowen's dreadful story of his wife's deathbed confession, which Bowen had revealed, in strict confidence, to Tilton in 1862. Shortly after that, in a letter to Tilton, Bowen declared that he had other, equally horrid secrets: "I sometimes feel that I *must break silence,* that I *must* no longer suffer as a *dumb man.* . . . One word from me would make a *revolution* throughout Christendom. . . . You have just a little of the evidence in my possession. . . . I am not pursuing a phantom, but solemnly brooding over an awful reality." Biographers who accept Bowen's story believe he did not make it public because he feared it would ruin Plymouth Church, which he had fathered and financed. Defenders of Henry assert that Bowen was simply lying in order to injure Henry for having withdrawn from the *Independent* in protest against the paper's "radical" views and dubious advertising. They point out that at the trial Bowen admitted that he had named no names and produced no evidence for his charges. Of course, the imputation that he had invented the story about his wife makes him out to be a monster.

When Henry returned from Europe in 1863, he was hailed as a hero, but he was still alienated from Bowen and the *Independent*. Tilton, however, was ready to resume where he had left off. He had apparently put out of mind Bowen's stories, especially after Bowen remarried. Perhaps when Tilton saw Henry, now in his fifties, with a paunch and loose jowls, but still craving affection, he felt pity for him. Or perhaps he had become tolerant of other men's desires because he himself had begun to take love wherever he could find it.

Whatever the reason, he welcomed Henry back into the old intimacy. And Elizabeth Tilton welcomed him even more cordially, for now she was troubled not only by her husband's increasingly unorthodox religious views but by his support of more liberal divorce laws. She yearned for guidance and sympathy and these Henry gave her in full measure, out of a lifetime of practice. He visited her more and more often, even when Tilton was away, and he flattered her tremendously by telling her of his own problems. He gave her gifts of books and pictures; as her pastor he may have been able to justify these, but when he sent her huge bouquets of flowers he was being either very naive or very careless.

That Tilton was not unconcerned about his wife's relation to Henry seems evident in a letter he wrote to Elizabeth from Iowa during a lecture tour. Referring to a plan for her to meet him in Chicago, he writes:

Now that the *other* man has gone off lecturing . . . you can afford to come to *me*. . . . Leave home, children, kith and kin, and cleave unto him to whom you originally promised to cleave. You promised the *other* man to cleave to *me*, and yet you leave *me all alone* and cleave to *him*. "O Frailty! Thy name is woman."

The impeachment is direct even though the teasing tone robs it of some of its sting.

The political truce between Tilton and Henry did not, as we have seen, last long. When Henry in the fall of 1866 endorsed proposals made by a Cleveland convention of soldiers and sailors for a soft treatment of the South, Tilton, in the *Independent*, pounded him until he reeled. When Henry retreated, Tilton wrote to his wife: "I believe he is not as morally great as he once was. I do not refer at all to his political views. . . . But there was an older virtue which has since gone out of him—an influence which used to brighten my life . . . an influence which became gradually quenched like a vanishing sunbeam."

Was it so? If it was, Elizabeth seems not to have noticed it, or if she had, it evoked only sympathy.

As though candor would justify her behavior, Elizabeth makes completely clear to her husband how dear Henry is to her and how troubled she is by her attachment to this other man. She writes:

My beloved, I have been thinking of my love for Mr. B. considerably of late, and these thoughts you shall have. . . . Now, I think I have lived a richer, happier life since I have known him. And have you not loved me more ardently since you saw another high nature appreciated me? . . . During these early years, the mention of his name, to meet him, or better still, a visit from him, my cheek would flush with pleasure. . . . It is not strange, then, darling, that on a more intimate acquaintance my delight and pleasure should increase. Of course, I realize what attracts you both to me is a supposed purity of soul you find in me. Therefore it is that never before have I had such wrestlings with God. . . . I live in an agony of soul daily; nevertheless, I am profoundly happy in my privileges, opportunities and blessings.

Another letter, several months later, seems astonishingly transparent in its forbidden longings:

Oh how my soul yearns over you two dear men! . . . Why I was so mysteriously brought in as actor in this friendship, I know not, yet no experience of all my life has made my soul ache so verily as the apparent lack of Christian manliness in this beloved man. . . . I do love him very dearly, and I do love you supremely, utterly, believe it. Perhaps if I by God's grace keep myself white, I may bless you both. I am striving. God bless this trinity!

Her confusion of values is evident in the way she applies the sacred term "trinity" to a relationship verging on infidelity. God, pastor and husband are all dipped in the same simmering syrup of "love" and all come out looking alike. Early in 1868 the guilt that has so far been unconscious forces itself to the surface and she begins to protest the innocence of her behavior:

About eleven o'clock today, Mr. B. called. Now, beloved, let not even the shadow of a *shadow* fall on your dear heart because of this now, henceforth or forever. He cannot by *any possibility* be much to me, since I have known *you*. . . . Do not think it audacious in me to say I am to him a good deal. . . . You once told me you did not believe that I gave a correct account of his visits, and you always felt that I repressed much. Sweet, do you still believe this? . . . It would be my supreme wish . . . to have you *always with me*. This trinity of friendship I pray for always.

The Tilton household was not so tranquil or idyllic as Henry thought. Tilton was temperamental and moody. According to testimony given at Henry's trial by Bessie Turner, who had come to the Tiltons as a serving girl and after eight years had become a member of the family, Mrs. Tilton was sweet and kind whereas Tilton was willful and cruel. He stalked about in the middle of the night, she said, trying everyone's bed to find one that suited him. He scolded his wife for hours at a time and even locked her in her room. When he was upset, Elizabeth would try desperately to calm him down, submitting abjectly to his wishes. Even in company he would correct her English or deplore her small size. She once said to Bessie, "I would have cut off my right arm to be five inches taller." Beyond that—and this seriously damaged Tilton's reputation—Bessie claimed that he repeatedly forced his attentions on her and tried to convince her that caresses and physical expressions of love were not improper between those who had an "affinity"—Goethe's notion of "elective affinities" was still in vogue—for each other. Tilton denied all these charges, but Bessie's account was so naively frank and circumstantial that she was generally believed.

More than one friend of the Tiltons was fully aware of how often the pastor was making calls at their house. Not only did Susan B. Anthony know of it but she stoutly justified it: "The Tiltons' was the second home of Mr. Beecher, and scarcely a day passed that he did not visit it. He found here the brightness, congeniality, sympathy and loving trust which every human being longs for."

In August 1868 the Tiltons' little son Paul died of cholera. It was the third child Elizabeth had lost. Since Tilton had gone on a lecture tour, Elizabeth was left alone with her grief—except for Henry, who came down from his summer place in Peekskill to preach at the funeral.

Early in October there was an election rally for General Grant, and Henry, who admired Grant unreservedly, was the orator. Elizabeth Tilton decided to attend. Afterward she was glad she had gone because Henry outdid himself and the applause was long and glorious. The following day she hurried over to his home to tell him how exciting it had been. He was alone, writing a sermon, his family still in Peekskill. Lib was overflowing with emotion, deeply stirred by both Henry's triumph and her child's death.

On what happened that evening, according to Theodore Tilton, was based the charge—made by Tilton in City Court, Brooklyn, six years later—that Henry,

on or about the tenth day of October, 1868, and on diverse other days and times, at the house of the defendant, 124 Columbia Street . . . and at the house of the plaintiff, 174 Livingston Street, wrongfully and wickedly and without the privity and connivance of the plaintiff, debauched and carnally knew the said Elizabeth . . . by means whereof the affection of the said Elizabeth for the said plaintiff was wholly alienated and destroyed. . . .

At the time there was of course no reference anywhere to such an incident, but Susan B. Anthony later reported that she had seen this brief but extraordinary entry for October 10 in Elizabeth Tilton's diary: "A Day Memorable."

As we have seen, part of Henry's effectiveness in the pulpit was the way he used his sermons to unburden himself. A few months later the following passage leaps from the midst of a sermon on sin:

The man who has been wallowing in lust, the man who has been on fire in his passions, and who by God's great goodness has been brought to an hour and a moment when . . . his monstrous wickedness stands disclosed in him—that man ought not to wait so long as the drawing of his breath. Wherever he is . . . if he does the thing that is safest and best he will rise in his place and make confession. . . . he will stand up and say, "Here I am, a sinner, and I confess my sin, and I call on God to witness my determination from this hour to turn away from it." That is the wise course, and you would think so, if it was anybody but yourself.

If he was guilty as charged, such a passage indicates how he was able, without too much agony of spirit, to explain forbidden behavior. Nor is there a whisper of the punishment that might follow the failure to do what he said was right. Perhaps he salved his conscience with the thought that he had not branded such weakness a fearful sin. Outwardly at least, no punishment did follow, and according to Tilton, the pastor and his parishioner were intimate again and again in the months that followed.

Henry now found other outlets for his writing: he and his friends the Howards bought a minor religious weekly, changed its name to the *Christian Union,* and made Henry its editor. Although it was successful and many in the Beecher clan contributed to it, including Eunice, Harriet, Edward and Thomas, Elizabeth Cady Stanton thought it remained a dull paper without a new thought in morals, religion or politics. But it did put Henry in a position to seek a reconciliation with Bowen. So one night at a friend's house, encountering Bowen, he cried, "We must be friends. There must be no break between us; it would kill me!" Bowen agreed and at the next Plymouth prayer meeting, Henry happily announced that he, Bowen and Tilton had returned to their "old relations of love, respect and reliance." On the following Fourth of July, when President Grant was a guest at Bowen's place in Woodstock, Connecticut, Henry made the speech of the day and even ran a footrace with Bowen. He did not of course know what had taken place in the Tilton household the night before.

Henry continued to see Elizabeth Tilton fairly often during 1869 and the early part of 1870. He took her driving and bought her gifts although, she later told her husband, she had increasing qualms about her relationship with her pastor and had often to resist his persistent advances. In the late spring of 1870, deeply troubled and ill, she went to Schoharie, New York, for the summer.

But on the night of July 3, she returned suddenly to Brooklyn, and apparently deeply disturbed, went directly to her bedroom. There, according to her husband's testimony at the trial, she made a full confession of the relationship that had developed between her and Henry Ward Beecher. Tilton declared that his wife made him promise not to use her confession against Henry. Then, he testified with startling frankness, she went on to say that her friendship with Henry

had been in later years more than friendship, it had been sexual intimacy; that this sexual intimacy had begun shortly after the death of her son Paul; that she had been in a tender frame of mind, consequent upon her bereavement; that she had received much consolation ... from her pastor; that she had made a visit to his house ... and that there, on the 10th of October, 1868, she had surrendered her body to him in sexual embrace ... that she had repeated such acts at various times ... and at other places ... from the Fall of 1868 to the Spring of 1870.

She then told him that she had been persuaded by Henry that

as their love was proper and not wrong, therefore it followed that any expression of that love, whether by the shake of the hand or the kiss of the lips, or even bodily intercourse ... was not wrong; that Mr. Beecher had professed to her a greater love than he had shown to any woman in his life ... that he wished to find in her ... the solace of life which had been denied to him by the unfortunate marriage at home.

Although Tilton had had his suspicions, he was left, he later told a friend, "just blasted" by the confession. After days of soul-searching, he said, he found an excuse for his wife in the thought that she had been "trapped up in her teacher and guide" and had followed him blindly. Tilton had finally said to himself: "That man is growing old, I will punish him only to this extent—Elizabeth shall go and tell him that I know from her own lips what pattern of Godliness he is, and that I am a living, suffering sacrifice for his children as well as my own."

This decision gave him such a feeling of magnanimity and sacrifice as to raise him for weeks into a kind of ecstasy. It is hard to imagine a more romantic delusion. During this period he was moved to publish in the *Independent* an editorial, "The Wreck of a Life," obviously about Henry.

When a man of unusually fine organization, with high-strung nerves, with a supersensitive conscience, with a tremendous sensibility to reputation, and with a boundless ambition, suddenly, by one act, sacrifices the slow honors of a lifetime, there is something in his self-destruction to excite the pity of mankind.

To such a man the agony is that there is no restoration. ... if any human creature deserves sympathy, this is the man.

All these letters, editorials, sermons and statements, all so feverishly intense and overwrought, can hardly be understood except as the emotional forces that accumulate in an age of sexual repression. Under the Victorian lid, this cauldron had come to a boil.

But Tilton could not keep the story to himself. Although he was busier than ever as editor of the Brooklyn *Union* (also owned by Bowen) as well as the *Independent,* president of the radical suffragists group, lecturer, and active opponent of the Grant administration, he could not help brooding over Elizabeth's confession. He revealed it to two friends at Plymouth Church; then one night, while Susan B. Anthony kept his ailing wife company at home, he went to dinner with Elizabeth Cady Stanton and another leading suffragist, Laura Curtis Bullard, and blurted out his secret to them. Mrs. Stanton described his outburst as the most extreme "manifestation of mental agony" she had ever seen. "Oh, that the damned lecherous scoundrel should have defiled my bed..." he cried, "and at the same time professed to be my best friend." No character in a Victorian melodrama would have expressed it otherwise.

When he returned home, a violent quarrel—such as had become frequent in the Tilton household—broke out between Tilton and his wife, with Miss Anthony trying to protect Elizabeth from her husband's fury. Miss Anthony, loyal and kind, never gave any account of the incident, but Mrs. Stanton did. According to the latter, Miss Anthony stayed with Elizabeth all night and Elizabeth told her the whole story of "her own faithlessness, of Mr. Beecher's course, of her deception, and of her anguish." Mrs. Stanton added that it corresponded completely to the disclosures Tilton had made to her at dinner.

That was in 1870; Mrs. Stanton would not reveal what she had heard until four years later. It was Elizabeth Tilton who committed the greatest indiscretion: she told her mother the tale. According to almost everyone who knew Mrs. Morse, she was subject to manias and frenzies. After she had almost choked her second husband to death, he had separated from her. There had even been talk of committing her to an asylum. Because she was ordinarily capable of kindliness and affection, the Tiltons had let her live with them, but about a year earlier she had suddenly come at Theodore with a carving knife. They had then made her leave, and she had moved to a house nearby.

Now she developed the delusion that if she could eliminate Tilton, the Reverend Beecher would somehow take his place. So she spread lurid stories of Tilton's infidelities and cruelties, sent Tilton himself vile letters and even wrote to Henry as "My dear Son."

To escape from her troubles, Elizabeth went to visit friends in Ohio. From there in November 1870 she wrote her husband one of her more agonized and incriminating letters:

When, by your threats, my mother cried out to me, "Why, what have you done,

Elizabeth, my child?" her worst suspicions were aroused, and I laid bare my heart then, that from my lips, and not yours, she might receive the dagger into her heart. . . . For the agony which the revelation has caused *you*, my cries ascend to Heaven night and day that upon mine own head all the anguish may fall. . . . Even so, every word, look, or intimation against Mr. B. though I in no wise be brought in, is an agony beyond the piercing of myself a hundred times. . . . Once again I implore you, for your children's sake . . . that *my past* be buried—left with me and my god.

When Elizabeth returned to Brooklyn, a bitter quarrel broke out, according to Bessie, with Tilton pointing to a red couch and saying that it had been "consecrated to sexual intercourse" between his wife and Henry. Elizabeth and Bessie packed up and went to Mrs. Morse's place but Tilton came after them and persuaded them to return. A few days later Mrs. Morse asked Henry for help. For once, Henry thought his wife's advice was needed—or perhaps he wanted to show her that he made no secret of his relationship to Elizabeth Tilton—and the next day he brought Eunice to Mrs. Morse's house. Mrs. Beecher, who had always disliked Tilton himself, detested his ideas, and begrudged her husband's friendship with him, was scandalized. While she conferred in one room with Elizabeth's mother, Henry went upstairs with Elizabeth and talked and prayed with her. The following day the Reverend and Mrs. Beecher solemnly advised Elizabeth to seek "a separation and *a settlement of support*."

Elizabeth Tilton did not follow their advice, but for weeks thereafter Tilton slept at the house of his friend Francis Moulton. On December 24, Mrs. Tilton suffered a miscarriage. In a letter to a friend the following summer she said of this: "A *love-babe*, it promised, you know."

It was, as Moulton later observed, a very curious expression for a woman nearly forty years old, who had borne six children, to use about a baby, especially when she has admitted that she and her husband have been quarreling bitterly for months.

Discord now developed between Tilton and Bowen. Bowen had been annoyed by Tilton's refusal to give editorial support to Grant—with whose friend, the collector of the Port of New York, Bowen was involved in various "deals." Bowen was also disturbed by rumors of Tilton's promiscuity. It did not help matters that Tilton now published an editorial in the *Independent* entitled "Love, Marriage and Divorce," which contained such statements as: "Marriage without love is a sin against God" and "Marriage, if broken, whether broken by the body or the soul, is divorce." For much the same kind of statement, that notorious defender of free love Victoria Woodhull was being branded a daughter of the devil.

Bowen had already begun to feel that as the editor of a religious newspaper Tilton was a dangerous person. So he relieved him of his post on the *Independent* and offered him a substantial salary if he would carry on with Bowen's other paper, the Brooklyn *Union*. Tilton agreed and Bowen inserted a fulsome tribute to him in the *Independent*, praising him as a bold and uncompromising person and a brilliant, imaginative and poetic writer. Then late in December, Bowen heard a rumor that Tilton was about to run off with another woman. He confronted Tilton with this story and in the heat of the exchange that followed, Tilton revealed his wife's confession.

Some say Bowen at once saw an opportunity to get back at Henry for the pastor's alleged affair with Lucy Bowen without involving Lucy, himself or his second wife. They say he also hoped to oust Henry before the rumors about the preacher brought ruin to Plymouth Church. Henry's defenders said Bowen wanted only to revenge himself on Henry for fostering the *Christian Union*, the *Independent*'s chief competitor. Whatever his motives, Bowen cried out that Henry must not be permitted to stay another week in his pulpit. Promising that he would back Tilton and "furnish the proof," he persuaded Tilton to give him a note to Henry. Fired by Bowen's indignation, Tilton wrote to Henry: "I demand that, for reasons which you explicitly understand, you immediately cease from the ministry of Plymouth Church, and that you quit the City of Brooklyn as a residence."

It was an adolescent gesture, melodramatic and rash: when Tilton told his friend Moulton what he had done, the worldly Moulton at once pronounced him a ruined man and a fool to boot. Moulton was sure that Bowen would use the letter without assuming any responsibility for it. And so it was. Beyond that, it was the beginning of an endless tangle of charges and countercharges, evasions and concealments, of bitterness and remorse, of secret pacts and public trials that would drag on for five years until all the world knew every sad and sordid detail of the whole affair.

The next day Bowen delivered the letter to Henry. Henry immediately declared: "I think the man is crazy." He sat silent for a moment and then began to tell Bowen all the derogatory things he, too, had heard about Tilton. Whether Bowen was persuaded by Henry's confidence or simply decided to remain uncommitted, he agreed with Henry, revealed that he had already eased Tilton off the *Independent,* and even added three adulteries to the catalog of Tilton's delinquencies.

Elizabeth, distraught at her husband's rage, gave him a letter to Henry that declared she had told Theodore everything and she still loved her husband dearly. Armed with this, Tilton let Bowen know that he had decided to confront Henry. Bowen, furious, threatened that if Tilton disclosed what he had said against Henry, he would fire Tilton instantly. Tilton again turned to Francis Moulton and they decided that Henry should be summoned to a meeting at Moulton's house. Moulton went straight to Plymouth Church, where Henry was about to conduct his weekly prayer meeting. Moulton reported that Tilton wanted to see Henry at once. Henry protested, but when Moulton indicated, ominously, that it concerned Henry's relations with the Tilton family, Henry followed him. Outside, a snowstorm raged and as they struggled through it Henry cried, "What can I do? What can I do?"

"I don't know," Moulton answered. "I am not a Christian; I am a heathen; but I will try to show you how well a heathen can serve you. . . . I will try to help you."

Henry, with a dark premonition and always aware of the dramatic, muttered, "This is a terrible night. There is an appropriateness in this storm."

From this point on, Francis Moulton was to act as the "Mutual Friend," the tireless witness of all meetings, and the messenger in all communications. In his early thirties, Moulton was already a junior partner in the export house of Woodruff & Robinson. A well-built man with red hair and great mustaches, he apparently inspired confidence through his self-possession and his patience. Henry's critics characterized Moulton as a man of conscience who was determined to see truth prevail and justice done. Henry's defenders, on the other hand, described him as a shrewd manipulator who renewed a college friendship with Tilton (they had attended the New York Free Academy, later the City College) because Tilton was an influential editor. In his business, they said, he was that new kind of agent, the "contact man," who did the "dirty work" of getting favors from the government. He had married his boss Jeremiah Robinson's niece, a level-headed young woman who had long been a member of Henry's congregation.

Whether justifiably or not, Moulton won the trust of Beecher as well as of both the Tiltons and held it during the long years he spent as the go-between in the quarrel. He served so perseveringly, he claimed, because he believed that if the story became public it would be a national calamity and "lay low a beneficent power for good." He did not, of course, know how sensational the charges against Henry would become.

When Henry and Moulton reached the latter's house, Henry went upstairs with Tilton. What the two men said to each other in that meeting would become one of the central issues of the case. Tilton testified that he declared that, for his wife's sake, he would not make the matter public. He then read Henry her note, which, he later claimed, confessed "sexual intimacy."

According to Henry, Tilton charged that

I had not only injured him in his business relations and prospects but that I had also insinuated myself into his family and . . . in a sense superseded him there . . . that I had corrupted Elizabeth, teaching her to lie, to deceive him, and hide under fair appearances her friendship to me . . . that I had made overtures to her of an improper character.

The last phrase was crucial, for at the trial Henry and all his defenders behaved as though he were being charged not with adultery but with some vague and innocuous kind of impropriety. When Tilton finished reading, Henry grew red in the face and cried, "This is a dream. I don't believe Elizabeth could have made charges so untrue against me."

Tilton urged him to have Elizabeth verify the letter. According to Tilton, as Henry went down the stairs he staggered, and Moulton said he moaned, "This will kill me."

It did not kill him, but for three and a half years more he would live with the knowledge that the "secret" had not been kept and was spreading, and for two years after that he would run an unheard-of gauntlet of church and civil trials and more publicity than had been given to any other such scandal in the nation's history.

As Henry and Moulton started for the Tilton home, the storm outside began to abate. "I went forth like a sleep-walker . . ." Henry said, as though creating a setting in a novel. "The winds were out and whistling through the leafless trees, but all this was peace compared to my mood within."

Henry went up to Elizabeth's room alone and, as in a scene in a poem by William Morris or a painting by Holman Hunt, found her lying on her bed (she was still ill from her miscarriage), "white as marble . . . and with her hands upon her bosom, palm to palm, like one in prayer." On the witness stand he wept freely as he recalled the scene. He told her, he said, all the terrible charges her husband had made, and he asked her why she had become a party to such falsehoods. With tears in her eyes, she said that Tilton had worn her down and made her believe that if she confessed her love for Henry, "it would help him confess his alien affections." She then conceded, Henry testified, that the charges were untrue and gave him what he claimed was a voluntary statement: "Wearied with importunities, and weakened by sickness, I gave a letter inculpating my friend, Henry Ward Beecher, under assurances that that would remove all difficulties between me and my husband. That letter I now revoke. . . . I regret it, and I recall all its statements." When Tilton returned home, after midnight, he went up to his wife's room; and after a while he emerged with a letter that read:

Dec. 30, 1870—Midnight

My Dear Husband:

I desire to leave with you . . . a statement that Mr. Henry Ward Beecher called upon me this evening, asked me if I would defend him against any accusation in a *council of ministers,* and I replied solemnly that I would in case the accuser was any other but my husband. He (H.W.B.) dictated a letter, which I copied as my own, to be used by him as against any other accuser except my husband. . . . I was ready to give him this letter because he said with pain that my letter in your hands addressed to him, dated December 29, "had struck him dead and ended his usefulness."

Elizabeth Tilton's second retraction in a few hours, it was the beginning of such a bewildering series of recantations and contradictory statements that in the end nothing she said was fully believed. Her fault was simply that she yielded to anyone who put pressure on her. And yet it is hard to understand how she could have been persuaded to confess to the cardinal sin of adultery if she was not guilty.

At Elizabeth's request, Moulton went to Henry the next day, told him of the second retraction, and insisted that he return Elizabeth's letter. Henry understandably protested that it was his only evidence against false charges. But he did return the letter, asserting that it was an act of conciliation. Then, according to Moulton, Henry confessed, with much weeping, that he "had loved Elizabeth Tilton very much; that . . . the sexual expression of that love was just as natural in his opinion . . . as the language that he used to her." He also said, "My life is ended. When to me should now come honor and rest, I find myself upon the brink of a moral Niagara, with no power to save myself, and I call upon you to save me."

Henry emphatically denied all this, asserting that the sexual question had never even come up, and adding, "Such language is simply impossible to me." No one denied, however, that Frank Moulton labored increasingly to keep the affair quiet and that Henry consulted him— generally at Moulton's house to avoid any questions by Mrs. Beecher—at all hours of the day and night.

No sooner had Moulton returned from Henry's place than Tilton met him with more bad news. As the New Year's chimes rang out, Tilton told him he had been fired by Bowen and was jobless. The next day, for the first time in seven years Bowen went to a New Year's reception at the Beechers' and promptly let Henry know that he had let Tilton go. Henry approved. But as the day wore on, his premonitions of trouble and his remorse increased rapidly. Finally he called Moulton into his study and, spurred by the younger man's defense of Tilton, admitted he was "ashamed and mortified" at the part he had played. The more he talked, the more he condemned and abased himself. Moulton calmly wrote down the gist of what he said and then had him sign it. I was the experienced one, it read, and she the child; if she did not know that the tendrils of affection were creeping up on me, I ought to have known it. His admirers were to consider this not an admission of sin but evidence of his compassion for a poor buffeted woman. Although Henry testified that he did not read what Moulton had written and that the language was Moulton's, it became known as the "Letter of Contrition." It read:

January 1, 1871

My Dear Friend Moulton:

I ask through you Theodore Tilton's forgiveness, and I humble myself before him as I do before my God. He would have been a better man in my circumstances than I have been. . . . I will not plead for myself; I even wish that I were dead; but others must live and suffer. I will die before anyone but myself shall be inculpated. All my thoughts are running toward my friends, toward the poor child lying there with her folded hands. She is guiltless, sinned against, bearing the transgressions of another. Her forgiveness I have. I humbly pray to God that he may put it into the heart of her husband to forgive me.

I have trusted this to *Moulton* in confidence.

H. W. Beecher

Henry would always maintain that he was referring only to having advised Elizabeth to leave her husband, and to having disparaged Tilton and thus encouraged Bowen to dismiss him. To have damned himself so completely for such minor offenses seems excessive even if we realize that Henry and his coterie had developed a language and a code in which everything was made to seem ten times as agonizing, or blissful, as it actually was.

Moulton considered the letter a complete confession. Henry, acting as though he were compensating only for Tilton's loss of his editorial posts, helped finance a literary weekly, *The Golden Age,* for Tilton to edit. He also contributed to the expense of shipping Bessie Turner off to an Ohio boarding school. Henry's critics have considered these acts an effort to hush up the charges; his admirers saw them as evidence of his softheartedness and an almost pathetic desire not to hurt Tilton.

Moulton seemed at last to have the fire under control, and Henry, eternally resilient, repeatedly met with the Tiltons in an effort at a full reconciliation. Once, Tilton declared, he called in Henry to remove any doubt concerning the paternity of little Ralph Tilton, born June 20, 1869, almost nine months after the alleged seduction. Henry branded this "a monstrous and absolute falsehood."

Nonetheless he tells of his attempts to mend the friendship. Once the

two men came upon each other in Moulton's parlor and Henry impetuously clasped Tilton's face and kissed him on the mouth. Henry himself
later testified that on one occasion, after he and Tilton had patched up a
quarrel, they momentarily resumed their old cordiality: when Mrs. Tilton entered the room she found Henry sitting on Tilton's knee! At still
another meeting, this one in Mrs. Tilton's bedroom, Henry reported, "I
kissed him and he kissed me, and I kissed his wife and she kissed me, and
I believe they kissed each other." It was plainly such a statement that
caused George Templeton Strong, prominent New York lawyer and
Trinity Church comptroller, a man of rocklike integrity and acerb
tongue, to declare in his diary:

Plymouth Church is a nest of "psychological phenomena," *vulgo vocato* lunatics,
and its chief Brahmin is as moonstruck as his devotees. Verily they are a peculiar people. They all call each other by their first names and perpetually kiss one
another. The Rev. Beecher seduces Mrs. Tilton and then kisses her husband,
and he seems to acquiesce in the osculation. ... They all seem, on their own
showing, to have been afflicted with both moral and mental insanity.

Henry was surely not so foolish as his words may make him seem. He
would hardly have described such a scene without some hope that it
would make all gestures of affection between him and the Tiltons seem
harmless and even silly. He may also have hoped that it would show that
Tilton had forgiven everything.

Along with the meetings came a resumption in the spate of letters;
after they had been read, they were all turned over to Moulton, now
Henry's most trusted friend. But then, with an unbelievable lack of dis-
cretion, Henry and Elizabeth began to write each other without benefit
of Moulton's antiseptic supervision. In one of these "Clandestine Letters," as they came to be known, he closed with the information that his
wife had taken the boat for Florida, and in another he said: "If I don't
see you tomorrow night, I will next Friday, for I shall be gone all the
fore part of next week."

Elizabeth was as emotional as ever, writing in one letter: "Does
your heart bound *towards all* as it used? So does mine! I am myself again.
I did not dare to tell you until I was sure; but the bird has sung in my
heart these *four* weeks, and he has covenanted with me never again to
leave. 'Spring has come!' "

In another she wrote: "In all the sad complications of the past years,
my endeavor was entirely to keep from you all suffering, to bear myself
alone. ... My weapons were love, a large untiring generosity and *nest-
hiding!*" The italicized ending, containing an allusion to the way a woman in Henry's *Norwood* conceals her love for a man, lent itself, during
the trial, to coarse jests. No one reading their letters would have guessed

that they were not carefree young lovers but a fifty-eight-year-old preacher and a thirty-seven-year-old Sunday school teacher, each married and with a family.

The illusion that their difficulties were over was soon shattered. But nothing could have been more unexpected than that the person who would do the shattering would be Victoria Woodhull.

Sober-sided historians almost never mention "The Woodhull," as she was known, yet in her life and loves as well as her views she was one of the most emancipated and uninhibited women of that or any other American time. The daughter of a river gambler named Claflin, she had grown up as one of ten neglected children in an Ohio hillside shack. The Claflins were caught up in the vogue of spiritualism and in their early teens Victoria and her sister Tennessee were already wandering the Midwest as faith healers selling a "Magnetic Life Elixir" at two dollars a bottle. By the time she was fifteen, Victoria was married to a Dr. Woodhull, a dandy and, as it turned out, an alcoholic. They had a son who was retarded, and a daughter. Later she shed Woodhull and acquired Colonel James Blood, a spiritualist and a philosophical anarchist who furnished her with a framework for her views on the free life. With him she roved the countryside as a clairvoyant whose "spirit-guide" was Demosthenes, the great orator and champion of Greek liberties.

At thirty, pert, vibrant, wearing bold ankle-length skirts and charming Alpine hats, she turned up with Tennessee in New York and the sisters soon had old and ailing Commodore Vanderbilt so infatuated with their amiable ways and their technique of healing by the "laying on of hands" that he set them up as brokers on Wall Street. Aided by tips from him, the "Bewitching Brokers" made a small fortune and became the talk of the town. Victoria established herself in a Murray Hill mansion along with Colonel Blood, Dr. Woodhull (he had been readmitted to the fold), numerous Claflins and a crew of servants. Perhaps the strangest figure in this bizarre household was a learned visionary, Stephen Pearl Andrews, the tall, great-bearded, sixty-year-old "Pantarch" of an imagined system of world government called the Pantarchy.

Vanderbilt also helped the sisters establish *Woodhull & Claflin's Weekly,* a sixteen-page newspaper. It flaunted the motto "Progress! Free Thought! Untrammeled Lives!" and proceeded to bombard everything from financial fraud to prostitution. It printed Marx's Communist Manifesto and it crusaded for such causes as birth control, public housing, spiritualism, a universal language called "Alwato" and—inspired by a prophecy from Andrews—Victoria Woodhull for President. That she borrowed her ideas from her associates does not detract from her ability to assimilate their views and challenge the world with them.

Joining the struggle for women's rights, Victoria Woodhull went to

Washington during the third annual convention of the National Woman Suffrage Association in January 1871, and to the astonishment of everyone became the first woman to appear before the Judiciary Committee of the House of Representatives. An attractive woman with a musical voice, she created a sensation with a learned memorial on women's rights. Disregarding her disreputable background and more extravagant views, the leaders of the radical suffragists, Susan B. Anthony, Elizabeth Cady Stanton and Isabella Beecher Hooker, welcomed her enthusiastically. The following day, introduced by Isabella, she captured the woman's rights convention itself.

Returning to New York, Victoria was busily engaged in puncturing the pretenses of Victorian respectability when her mother went into court, charging that Colonel Blood was mistreating her. Nothing came of the charge, but it caused the whole outlandish ménage on Thirty-eighth Street to be exposed to merciless, hot-eyed publicity. Mrs. Stanton stoutly defended Victoria Woodhull's right to live as she pleased, but the suffragists in general disavowed her, recognizing that The Woodhull was not interested in any movement but her own.

Conspicuous among the women who began to attack her were Catharine Beecher and Harriet Beecher Stowe. Unfortunately for them, Mrs. Stanton had told Victoria Woodhull—perhaps because of Woodhull's attacks on prominent men who frequented "public houses"—the "secret" of Elizabeth Tilton and Henry Ward Beecher. Victoria Woodhull was now fully equipped to document her charge of male hypocrisy. On May 22, 1871, there appeared in the New York *World* and the New York *Times* an open letter—or "card" as such a communication was called—to the editor:

Sir: Because I am a woman and because I conscientiously hold opinions somewhat different from the self-elected orthodoxy . . . and because I think it . . . my absolute right . . . to advocate them with my whole strength, self-elected orthodoxy . . . endeavors to cover my life with ridicule and dishonor. . . . I do not intend to be . . . offered up as a victim to society by those who cover over the foulness of their lives and the feculence of their thoughts with a hypocritical mantle of fair professions. . . . I advocate free love in its highest, purest sense as the only cure for the immorality . . . by which men corrupt and disfigure God's most holy institution of sexual relation. My judges preach against "free love" openly, and practice it secretly. . . . For example, I know of one man, a public teacher of eminence, who lives in concubinage with the wife of another public teacher of almost equal eminence. All three concur in denouncing offenses against morality. . . . I shall make it my business to analyze some of these lives, and will take my chances in the matter of libel suits. . . .

The god of irony must have laughed gleefully at the spectacle of Henry Ward Beecher threatened with exposure not by a pillar of conventional morality but by a champion of free love urging him to admit his adherence to her beliefs.

Hastily Tilton, Moulton and Henry met, and decided that Tilton—perhaps because his views were closest to Mrs. Woodhull's—should attempt to placate her. Tilton did so with such enthusiasm, describing her in *The Golden Age* as the Joan of Arc of the women's movement and writing so flattering a biographical sketch of her for her Presidential campaign (one of "the most divinely gifted of human souls," he chanted, her energies are "mad and magnificent") that it was assumed that he not only admired her theories but practiced them with her. On one occasion, as she was leaving Chicago for New York, she gave a reporter something he was itching to hear when she blithely told him that Tilton had been her "devoted lover for half a year"—but in New York she just as casually denied the story!

When Mrs. Stowe and Catharine Beecher persisted in criticizing her, Mrs. Woodhull finally wrote Henry that if they did not stop she would strike back devastatingly at him, and she summoned him to an interview. He came but, he later said, refused to support her views or activities. Mrs. Woodhull's version of the interview was that he agreed with her on such subjects as divorce and free love but admitted, with tears, that he was too much of a moral coward to proclaim the fact.

Henry meanwhile continued to write to Elizabeth Tilton and even to have brief meetings with her. But the threats suspended over him by Victoria Woodhull and by Mrs. Morse, who was now writing letters asking for money, were telling on him, and he wrote Moulton despairing letters. In one that came to be known as the "Ragged Edge Letter," he even offered to resign from Plymouth Church, saying in part:

Nothing can possibly be so bad as the horror of great darkness in which I spend much of my time. I look upon death as sweeter-faced than any friend. . . . But to live on the sharp and ragged edge of anxiety, remorse, fear, despair, and yet to put on all the appearance of serenity and happiness, cannot be endured much longer.

Critics found it hard to believe that such terms as "anxiety," "fear," and "despair" were the result of remorse over minor improprieties.

Ironically, this period was in other ways a high point in Henry's career: he was the first Lyman Beecher Lecturer in Preaching at Yale Divinity School and during his three-year tenure (1872–1875) he delivered some of his most instructive lectures. He encouraged an approach that was immensely reassuring and certain to prove popular. The overwhelming majority of people, he declared, respond to preaching that appeals to the emotions rather than to reason. "They are," he declared, "fed by their hearts."

On the twenty-fifth anniversary of his reign at Plymouth Church he triumphantly announced that where the old theology had depended on fear, he emphasized "divine love." Some critics called it the "religion of sentiment" and the "Gospel of Gush." One of the more cynical comments came from his half brother Thomas in Elmira. "In my judgment Henry is following his slippery doctrines of expedience and, in the cry of progress and the nobleness of human nature, has sacrificed clear, exact, ideal integrity." Thomas went even further. "Mrs. Woodhull," he said, "only carries out Henry's philosophy, against which I recorded my protest twenty years ago, and parted (lovingly and achingly) from him. . . . Of the two, Woodhull is my hero, Henry my coward."

The suffragists had become increasingly critical of Victoria Woodhull and she of them, and in May 1872 they prevented her, in an open clash, from taking part in one of their conventions. At the same time, Tilton, angered by her attacks on his old suffragist friends, broke violently with her. Finally Vanderbilt, who had been lumped by her with other rapacious money men, withdrew his support. Her brokerage business crumbling, beleaguered by critics, The Woodhull struck back: at a meeting of spiritualists in Boston, she told the entire Beecher-Tilton story. When the exposé was ignored by the newspapers, she devoted the whole of the November 2 issue of *Woodhull & Claflin's Weekly* to the case, intending it to fall "like a bombshell into the . . . moralistic social camp."

It succeeded beyond her wildest expectations. One hundred thousand copies of the issue were sold, some at ten and even twenty dollars for a secondhand copy; and the case became overnight the greatest domestic scandal of the century. In her account, Victoria gave Beecher the kiss of death, writing:

The immense physical potency of Mr. Beecher, and the indomitable urgency of his great nature for the intimacy and embraces of the noble and cultured women about him, instead of being a bad thing as the world thinks . . . is one of the noblest . . . endowments of this truly great and representative man. Plymouth Church has lived and fed, and the healthy vigor of public opinion for the last quarter of a century has been . . . strengthened from the physical amativeness of Rev. Henry Ward Beecher.

Beneath the flourishes and the touch of sarcasm in the reference to "noble," the passage contained a most remarkable insight into the sources of Henry Ward Beecher's power. Mrs. Woodhull went on to declare that Henry was at heart an "ultra-socialist reformer," but "a poltroon, a coward and a sneak" in failing to own up to his beliefs.

Within a few hours Anthony Comstock, vice hunter for the Young Men's Christian Association and later the most fanatic censor of morals of his time, had the sisters thrown into jail for sending obscene matter through the mails. (After a month of hearings in which the sisters were repeatedly in and out of jail, they were acquitted.)

Once again Tilton, Henry and Moulton met in panic, but all they could agree on was a counsel of despair, to wit: silence. But this was like recommending nonchalance in the eye of a hurricane. The Beecher clan itself was torn apart by the scandal, with the children of Roxana Foote—all in their sixties and seventies—shocked and furious, closing ranks with Henry, while at least two of Harriet Porter's children, Isabella and Thomas, challenged him sharply. The issue was drawn when Isabella, by then an outspoken feminist, wrote to Henry demanding "the truth," and he answered, "I tread the falsehoods into the dirt from whence they spring." But he thoughtlessly added: ". . . think of the barbarity of dragging a poor dear child of a woman into this slough!" Whereupon Isabella wrote to her brother Thomas: "So far as I can see it is he who has dragged the dear child into the slough—and left her there." She even threatened to go to Plymouth Church and expose him, and for several tense weeks Harriet waited during services in the church, ready to intervene in case Isabella turned up.

When Isabella explained to her half brother Edward that she wanted Henry to confess for his own salvation, Edward answered her like an authority on Christ's standards, God's justice and Henry's morals: "if he is guilty, confession will not save him. He will fall in all the Christian world, as [did] Lucifer son of the morning. . . . His own people will not forgive him." Christ, he added, "condemns divorce except for one cause, and denounces even looking at a woman to lust after her as adultery. Mrs. Woodhull's movement will sink in perdition all who indorse it." Piously he concluded: "I fully believe he is innocent and pure . . . and I do not believe that God would thus sustain a liar, a hypocrite and a libertine, and he is all that if he is guilty."

When Henry declared that the entire story was a fraud, Susan Anthony exclaimed, "Wouldn't you think if God ever did strike any one dead for telling a lie, He would have struck then?" Victoria Woodhull was less polite. Forced from her home and hounded from hotel to hotel, she vowed that she would make it hotter than hell for Henry Ward Beecher. Raking up the scandal week after week in her paper and daring Henry to sue her for libel, she nearly succeeded.

A number of newspapers began at last to express disgust with Henry as well as with Mrs. Woodhull and Tilton. In despair, Henry gave Moulton his written resignation from the pastorate of Plymouth Church, but added that he could no longer "save from shame a certain household." When Tilton heard this postscript he declared that he would shoot Henry on sight. Henry did not resign. Instead, in another fit of despair

Theodore Tilton, brilliant protégé and close friend of Henry Ward Beecher. He later charged Beecher with seducing his wife.

Elizabeth, Theodore Tilton's wife, a devout but overly pliant woman who changed her allegiance so many times during the Beecher-Tilton affair that she lost all credibility.

"GET THEE BEHIND ME, (MRS.) SATAN!"—[SEE PAGE 145.]

WIFE (with heavy burden). "I'D RATHER TRAVEL THE HARDEST PATH OF MATRIMONY THAN FOLLOW YOUR FOOTSTEPS."

Thomas Nast's cartoon of Victoria
Woodhull as "Mrs. Satan" leading
the way to sin and doom.

Victoria Woodhull shocked Victorian America as "the lady broker of Wall Street," editor of the radical *Woodhull & Claflin's Weekly*, feminist, spiritualist, defender of free love and exploder of the greatest sexual scandal of the century, the Beecher-Tilton affair. Below, the front page of the issue of her *Weekly* in which she nominated herself for the Presidency.

WOODHULL & CLA[
WEEKLY.

PROGRESS! FREE THOUGHT! UNTRAMME[

BREAKING THE WAY FOR FUTURE GENERATIONS.

VOL. 2.—No. 23.—WHOLE No. 49.   NEW YORK, APRIL 22, 1871.   PRICE TEN CENTS.

VICTORIA C. WOODHULL & TENNIE C. CLAFLIN
EDITORS AND PROPRIETORS.

THE FIRST WOMAN BALLOT.

The Fourteenth Amendment has Begun its Work.

WHO WILL STOP IT?

The pioneer woman voter is Mrs. Nannette B. Gardner, and she lives in Detroit, Mich. She succeeded in registering her name week before last, and on Tuesday, the 4th of April, she cast the first vote for a State officer deposited in an American ballot-box by a woman for the last half century. Some time since, by the way, a number of ladies, of St. John, Mich., succeeded in getting themselves registered, but they were not permitted to vote. Why was this? However, as to the pioneer. We quote at length from the Detroit *Post* :

"Mrs. Gardner arrived at the polls of the First Precinct of the Ninth Ward at about half-past 10 o'clock, in a carriage accompanied by her son, a lad of ten years, Mrs. Starring and Mrs. Giles H. Stebbins. Barely a dozen bystanders were present at the voting place, and the larger part of these were laboring men." No demonstration, whatever followed the appearance of the ladies, the men remaining quiet and civil, and contenting themselves with comments *sotto voce* on this last political development, and with speculations as to how the newly enfranchised would vote. Mrs. Gardner presented herself at the polls with a vote of flowers and also a prepared ballot, which she had decorated with various appropriate devices. The inspectors asked the questions in regard to name and residence usually put to all applicants, and her name being found duly registered her ballot was received and deposited in the box without any further proceedings whatever. There was no argument, no challenging no variation from the routine traversed by each masculine exerciser of the elective franchise. Mrs. Gardner voted, as we understand, for the Republican candidates generally, with one Democrat and one lady. After the vote was deposited she presented the vase of flowers to the inspectors, and also handed them a large picture representing a large crowd of women in darkness just entering the portrait of an arch inscribed " Liberty," and upon which an eagle was perched. The gates were held open by Columbia and the Goddess of Justice. The foremost woman held in her hands a scroll inscribed " The Fourteenth Amendment." To the right were imps of darkness fleeing away, some with barrels of whisky. On the left was pictured the Capitol of Washington, with men crowding its steps, cheering, etc. Streams of light flowed upon them, while, with the exception of this and the foreground, the picture was darkness intensified. The following lines appeared underneath :

"We come, free America, five millions strong,
In darkness and bondage for many years long;
We've marched in deep silence, but now we unroll,
The Fourteenth Amendment, which gives us a soul!
Glory, Glory, Hallelujah, glory, etc.
As we go marching on!

COLUMBIA—" Welcome, beloved daughters.
Take your places beside my sons."

After the vote had reached its resting-place there was a faint attempt at hurrah among some of those present, but this was frowned down by the others as tending to interfere with the solemnity of the occasion. The ladies then left the voting places and matters resumed their usual appearance thereabouts.

THE COSMO-POLITICAL PARTY.

NOMINATION FOR PRESIDENT OF THE U.S., IN 1872.

VICTORIA C. WOODHULL

SUBJECT TO

RATIFICATION BY THE NATIONAL CONVENTION.

WEDDING PRESENTS OF THE PRINCESS LOUISE.

EMERALDS AND DIAMONDS IN PROFUSION.

THE BRIDEGROOM'S PRESENTS.

HER TROUSSEAU.

The following presents were given to her Royal Highness the Princess Louise on the occasion of her marriage to the Marquis of Lorne :

FROM HER MOTHER, QUEEN VICTORIA.

A very large and fine emerald, set with brilliants as a centre of bracelet ; another as centre of necklace ; a very fine opal and brilliant necklace, with five large opals, set round with brilliants and connected by a diamond chain ; a large drop brooch, with two very fine opals, set round with brilliants ; a pair of opal and diamond earrings to correspond ; a richly-chased, silver-gilt dessert service, consisting of one centre, two sides and four corner ornaments.

FROM THEIR ROYAL HIGHNESS THE PRINCE AND PRINCESS CHRISTIAN.

A beautifully-chased silver-gilt tea and coffee service, containing the following pieces : Coffee-pot, two tea-pots, one sugar basin, one hot milk jug, one cream ewer, in case.

FROM THEIR ROYAL HIGHNESSES, PRINCE ARTHUR, PRINCE LEOPOLD AND PRINCESS BEATRICE.

Two diamond daisy flowers mounted as hair-pins.

FROM HER ROYAL HIGHNESS THE DUCHESS OF CAMBRIDGE.

A silver-gilt ink-stand in the shape of a shell.

FROM HIS ROYAL HIGHNESS THE DUKE OF CAMBRIDGE.

A richly-engraved silver salver.

FROM THE DUKE AND DUCHESS OF ARGYLE.

A tiara formed of a band of emeralds and diamonds, surmounted by a scroll-work also of emeralds and diamonds.

FROM THE MARQUIS OF LORNE.

A beautiful pendant ornament, with a large and fine sapphire, mounted with brilliants and pearls and pearl-drop; the centre formed a bracelet.

FROM THE CLAN CAMPBELL.

A necklace composed of pearls and diamonds, from which is suspended a locket of oval form, with pendant. The centre of the locket is formed by a large and extremely beautiful Oriental pearl, surrounded by a closely-set row of diamonds of large size and great brilliancy. The outer border also consists of large diamonds, but set in such a manner as to give an appearance of lightness very seldom obtained

in ornaments of a similar description. The pendant, the characteristic portion of the jewel, is suspended by an emerald sprig of bog myrtle (the Campbell badge), and bears in the centre the galley of Lorne, composed of sapphires on a *pavé* of diamonds ; the border, also of sapphires and diamonds, bears the inscription, "*Ne obliviscaris.*"

FROM THE LADIES AND GENTLEMEN OF HER MAJESTY'S HOUSEHOLD.

One large single candelabrum for five lights ; four smaller ditto for three lights each ; a very complete toilet service in silver-gilt, with the cipher and coronet engraved on each article.

FROM THE QUEEN'S HOUSEHOLD.

A silver tea and coffee service, with table mounted in silver.

FROM THE BRIDESMAIDS.

A very handsome gold bracelet, with rubies and diamonds.

FROM THE DUKE OF ROXBURGH.

A silver-gilt tea-kettle to correspond with the service presented by their Royal Highnesses Prince and Princess Christian.

FROM THE DUCHESS OF BUCCLEUCH.

A richly chased antique pattern silver toilet casket.

FROM THE COUNTESS OF MACCLESFIELD.

A case of silver-gilt coffee-spoons.

OTHER PRESENTS.

In addition to the above, and numerous other presents, a very large and handsome silver tankard has been presented to Lord Lorne by Eton. It is richly chased all over with battle subjects, after LeBrun; the handle formed of satyrs. The black base on which it stands has two inscription plates. On one are engraved the Arms of Eton College, and on the other " Presented to the Marquis of Lorne on his marriage, by the present Members of his old School—Eton, 1871."

His Highness the Maharajah Duleep Singh's gift was a very fine specimen of a Lahore pendant, with 13 large emerald drops, and composed of Indian bosque diamonds from the collection of the renowned Runjeet Singh, once the mighty ruler of the Punjaub. It was arranged with a massive gold chain, and inclosed in a white velvet casket bearing the coronet and letter L.

Earl Russell's gift was a very beautiful pearl and torquoise bracelet, of Abyssinian design. The Countess's present to the Marquis of Lorne was a beautiful cornelian and pearl handkerchief ring; the Hon. E. F. Leveson Gower, M.P., giving his lordship an elegant gold spring cigar-cutter of novel design.

Not the least interesting item of this happy event are three beautiful *souvenirs de mariage*, yclept in English bridesmaids' gifts. Her Royal Highness's talent as an artist is well known, and upon this occasion she has brought to bear her excellent good taste in a design at once simple, pure and ele-

The Beecher-Tilton adultery case as pictured in a spread in *Leslie's Illustrated Weekly*. Top row: the Tilton residence; Mrs. Tilton; Henry Ward Beecher; Mr. Tilton; the Storrs residence where the investigating committee met. Center row: reporters at the Storrs home; Beecher with newsboys; Beecher's summer home; Beecher on his farm; New Yorkers reading Tilton's latest statement. Bottom row: Plymouth Church; ladies he threatened, in a letter to Moulton, an even more drastic step:

My mind is clear. . . . I shall write for the public a statement that will bear the light of judgment day. God will take care of me and mine. . . . Your noble wife . . . has been to me one of God's comforters. . . . I have a strong feeling . . . that I am spending my *last Sunday* and preaching my last sermon.

The pain of life is but a moment; the glory of everlasting emancipation is wordless, inconceivable, full of beckoning glory. Oh! my beloved Frank, I shall know you there, and forever hold fellowship with you.

The next day, Mrs. Moulton later testified, Henry told her he had a powder in his library table that would put him to sleep forever. But Henry Ward Beecher had no intention of going to sleep forever.

If anything, he became even more active. Great crowds poured into Brooklyn to hear him preach. Sixty years old, gray-haired and corpulent—he weighed over two hundred pounds—he nevertheless performed without diminution of zest or power. For some he had acquired the glamour of the superior individual who lives the way others would like to live, a genius who cannot be held to the laws that bind other men. The great majority of those who supported him refused even to consider the possibility that the model of all their moral values might be a seducer of other men's wives.

At last, to silence members of his congregation who were beginning to clamor for Tilton's expulsion, Henry wrote two letters to the Brooklyn *Eagle*. One asserted that Tilton was not responsible for certain calumnies against Henry. The other declared that the stories and rumors circulated about Henry himself were "utterly false."

But it was too late; the stories had been circulating for years. Members of the church now forced a vote on the charge that Tilton had slandered his pastor. Although Henry refused to testify against him, Tilton was expelled. Each Congregational church was an independent body, but the Reverend Richard Storrs, prominent pastor of another Brooklyn Congregational church, was so disturbed by the treatment of Tilton that he called an "Advisory Council" of sister churches to consider the case. A veteran—from the days of his father's trials—at coping with church bodies, Henry ignored the council and unconcernedly threw himself into the annual sale of Plymouth pews.

The council emerged with only a mild rebuke of Plymouth Church, but its moderator, the distinguished Dr. Leonard Bacon of Yale, once a staunch friend of Lyman Beecher, criticized Henry for not striking back at his accusers. And he referred to Tilton as a knave and a dog. Only a short while before a popular lecturer all over America, Tilton now found himself scorned as though he, not Henry, were the accused. Furious, he immediately published a long reply and then followed it with the release of that most damaging of Henry's outpourings, the "Letter of Contrition."

Victoria Woodhull's efforts were bearing fruit.

Henry hurried back from his country place in Peekskill that summer of 1874 and turned to his legal advisers: General William Tracy, a veteran politician, and General Ben Butler, a lawyer and Massachusetts congressman known for his ironhanded occupation of New Orleans during and after the war. Tracy first tried threatening Tilton and Moulton as blackmailers and then offered to send the Tilton family for a long stay abroad. Tilton scorned these proposals. Butler, declaring that he didn't care who was right or wrong, advised avoiding any public confrontation.

But Henry, haunted by Dr. Bacon's challenge and hoping to avoid a civil court, decided that his own church should try him. He himself picked the six members who were to look into "the rumors, insinuations, or charges respecting my conduct." A vindication was assured when his followers persuaded poor Lib Tilton to quit her husband and take up a place at Henry's side. Speaking of the adultery charge, she said pathetically to Mrs. Moulton, "For the sake of Mr. Beecher, for the sake of the influence on the world, for my own position, for my children, I think it is my duty to deny it."

The one reason that is conspicuously lacking is that the charge was a lie.

As the first witness before the committee, Mrs. Tilton declared that Henry had never made an improper proposal to her but had in fact shown her the kind of respect and appreciation she had failed to get from her husband. Tilton was, she said, madly jealous of Henry, himself guilty of "free love," and godless to boot.

After that there were frantic, last-minute efforts to get Tilton to moderate his charge, but all in vain. On July 20 he came before the committee, swore to the charge of "criminal seduction," and reviewed the seven-year-old affair at length. He added such details as that he himself had seen Henry touch Elizabeth's lower limbs as he looked at engravings on the library floor and once, having returned home unexpectedly, found his wife and Henry locked in her bedroom. He nevertheless defended his wife as pure-souled but living in a cloud. The committee betrayed its prejudices when it insinuated that Tilton's relations with Elizabeth Cady Stanton and Susan B. Anthony had been something less than proper.

It was at this time that Mrs. Beecher wrote to Anne B. Scoville that Henry's eyes were at last opened:

he sees both Tilton and Moulton in their naked depravity and baseness. It has been hard work to convince the dear guiltless simple-hearted man that such baseness and treachery could exist. . . . For a week he suffered terribly. . . . But at last . . . the noble old Lion roused himself . . . and holds back nothing. Many things that is very hard for him to expose—as they show . . . how weakly he has trusted—how fearfully he has been muted or blackmailed—not through *fear* but through *kindness and sympathy.*

These highly charged words must be read in the light of Eunice's deep dislike of her husband's friends and of course her need to deny that he had been in any way unfaithful.

At last Henry himself testified. Now he spared no one, using all those dramatic postures and appeals that had made him famous. He spoke of Elizabeth Tilton as having "thrust her affections on me unsought," and he explained all his acts of contrition and self-denunciation as attempts to protect his life work from ruin. Tilton he described as guilty of "promiscuous immoralities," a reckless schemer who was motivated by hatred and greed and had succumbed to disreputable associates and doctrines. Woodhull, he asserted, was a collector of loathsome scandals, a woman with an appetite for all that was vile. Was not any personal sacrifice warranted, he concluded, to prevent the morals of an entire community from being corrupted by "the filthy details of scandalous falsehoods." It is time, he thundered, "that this abomination be buried below all touch or power of resurrection."

The committee's report, read to the jubilant brethren of Plymouth Church by Rossiter Raymond, a professional elocutionist, described Theodore Tilton as malicious and revengeful, Elizabeth Tilton as guilty of "inordinate affection," and Henry Ward Beecher as completely innocent but just too trusting. In the middle of the reading, Francis Moulton, elegant in olive coat, white vest and white pantaloons, entered and sat down. Almost at once Raymond assailed him. When he charged that Moulton had "poisoned the public with his infernal lies," Moulton leaped to his feet and shouted, "You are a liar, sir."

In the near riot that followed, men were heard crying, "Put him out!" and others, it was said, waved pistols. Several policemen had to escort Moulton from the church. As he left, accompanied by jeers and threats, the triumphant worshipers in the holy place were giving Henry Ward Beecher a vote of unmeasured love and confidence.

Tilton, convinced that he simply had been used, now instituted suit in City Court against the Reverend Henry Ward Beecher for willful alienation of his wife's affections.

Meanwhile the nation's newspapers, which during the war had come into their own as purveyors—or creators—of sensational news, had begun a preoccupation with the case that lasted two years and was unparalleled in journalism. Everyone even remotely connected with the case was interviewed, trailed and hounded. After the Plymouth Church "trial," most New York newspapers still sided with Henry, apparently feeling it was more important to save "the most famous pulpit . . . since Paul preached on the Hill of Mars"—as the *Tribune* described it—than to arrive at the truth. Using the fact that Tilton's brother had died in an insane asylum, the Brooklyn *Eagle* came up with the sensational story reproduced on the facing page.

But elsewhere, and especially in the Midwest, editors were just as brutal about Henry Ward Beecher. The Chicago *Tribune* published a devastating analysis by Elizabeth Cady Stanton that underscored Henry's cruelty, especially in describing Mrs. Tilton as having thrust her affections on him "unsought." It also boldly exposed the various church-connected "rings" that would do anything to protect Henry's name. Chief among these were the bondholders of Plymouth Church, whose investment depended on Henry's reputation, and the publishers of the *Christian Union*, of Henry's unfinished *Life of Christ* and other books. It all smelled to high heaven, and there were years of it still to come.

During the church investigation and in the months that followed, the newspapers pawed and sifted every aspect of the case. The Chicago *Times* spread out the details of what it claimed was Henry's affair with Lucy Maria Bowen, and the Chicago *Inter-Ocean* dug up the tale of the lovely Indianapolis lass Betty Bates. Rude cartoons and lurid pamphlets exploited the scandal mercilessly. Tilton even released more than one hundred of the most intimate letters that had passed between him and his wife from 1866 to 1870. Intended, he later testified, to counter the charge that they were forged but also to show how close their relationship had been, they revealed even more strikingly Mrs. Tilton's sexual submissiveness and her mystical mixing of love and religion. Scattered throughout were such statements as: "Do you wonder that I couple your love . . . and relation to me, with the Saviour's?"

After all this, the trial of Tilton versus Beecher, which opened in the dreary halls of the City Court, Brooklyn, on January 11, 1875, should have proved an anticlimax. But like the parade before a circus, it had only whetted the appetite. The trial was of course not a circus at all but an uncensored performance of a sex drama. It was especially titillating in that it featured a spiritual leader and a devout matron, the one pictured by the plaintiff as a sly lecher and the other as a willing victim. In a time when even nudity in art was banned, when authors censored their novels down to milk-and-water sentimentality, and women did not dare show their ankles in public, this was a free exhibition, revealing—or so the prosecution declared—how a famous clergyman cuckolded an old friend. The public, respectable Victorians all, responded with passionate interest.

tiemen, that is yours. They are at liberty to make that public or not, just as they please. Of course I have kept a copy of that sworn statement, which I reserve to myself the right to publish or not, just as I please.

Reporter—Then I suppose that your action in regard to publishing this will in a great measure depend on the action of the Committee in that respect?

Mr. Tilton—On what do you base your supposition?

Reporter—On your own answer to me that I should first go to the Committee before asking you for a text of your statement.

Mr. Tilton—It all rests with them. If they want to publish the statement now it is their property, and they have the right to publish it if they please.

Reporter—Then it is useless to ask you for that statement at present?

Mr. Tilton—Yes, it is.

Reporter—May I ask what is the nature of the statement?

Mr. Tilton—

IT IS A LONG STATEMENT,

It would occupy about four columns of a newspaper. It took me three-quarters of an hour to read it for the Investigating Committee It is a history of events extending over a lengthened period. It gives evidences and dates, and corroborative testimonies.

Reporter—Now, Mr. Tilton, I want to ask you one question in all seriousness, and I presume you will consider it your duty to answer it. It has been publicly stated in the newspapers and elsewhere that this sworn statement of yours would involve the honor of some women who are now in their graves. It was stated that the spectres of these women would be dragged before the Investigating Committee of Plymouth Church by you. It was even asserted that your statement would deeply concern the honor of a young lady moving in high circles in Brooklyn at present. I wish to ask you positively if your statement goes outside your own grievance or family troubles?

Mr. Tilton turned quickly in his chair, and looking the reporter full in the face, said: "Do you think any gentleman would go into any other family's affairs in such a connection?"

Reporter—It has been so stated, Mr. Tilton, and I wish to have your positive statement on that head if possible.

Mr. Tilton (emphatically)—No, sir. My statement does not, directly or indirectly; it remotely concerns

NO OTHER FAMILY.

Reporter—Then the statement merely touches your own family troubles and marital relations, and the reports mentioned are false?

Mr. Tilton—Only the troubles of my own family has my statement anything to do with. The statement was in manuscript form, and it took me a long time to read it; but it concerns my family affairs alone, and goes over a long interval.

Reporter—That sets at rest a very important question, Mr. Tilton. May I ask you if in your opinion your statement is of such a nature as to leave the Investigating Committee only one alternative in the premises?

Mr. Tilton—That is for them to say?

Reporter—I asked you in your own opinion?

Mr. Tilton—I cannot be drawn into any statement on that head. I have done my duty by the Investigating Committee. I told them I should give them a sworn statement, and I have done so. There my duty to them ends. My allegations are made on oath, and if they are false I can be prosecuted for perjury. They are succinct, and if they be wrong I can be punished. What the committee may think of them it is for them to say.

Reporter—Mr. Tilton, how did the Investigating Committee receive you?

Mr. Tilton—Oh, I knew nearly all these gentlemen personally for a long time, and they received me pleasantly. It was nearly nine o'clock before I commenced to read my statement, and it was nearly ten o'clock before I got through. Before I commenced I made it

AN EXPRESS CONDITION

that no questions should be asked of me while I was reading. I requested that if there were any to be put they should be asked at the end. During the reading there were little or no interruptions. Once some one asked a question as to the date of certain occurrence mentioned in my statement. At another time there was a question of veracity, but on the whole no interruption. Questions were then asked from ten until twelve o'clock on the different points involved in the statement. All these questions I answered.

Reporter—Mr. Tilton, you will pardon me for asking you one more question, as I assure you there is no impertinence intended. It has been said that

You have been offered large sums of money if you would consent to seal your lips on this painful matter. In this connection it has been said that John Russell Young has approached you with a ...

SOLVED.

Is Insanity the Key to the Beecher Scandal?

Startling Revelations Concerning Mrs. Tilton's Mental Condition—His Brother, an Uncle and Three Cousin's Insane—The Testimony of Facts and the Testimony of Experts.

MR. BEECHER'S STATEMENT.

A Summary of What He Will Say Next Week in Detail—The Letters to Moulton and Mrs. Tilton's Confession Put in Their Proper Relation—Light that Brings the Great Preacher's Innocence Into Relief.

ANOTHER STATEMENT BY MRS. TILTON.

The Lid Lifted from a Domestic Hell—One of the Most Heart Rending Pictures Ever Painted—A Wife Compelled to Call Upon the Police to Remove Her Husband's Harlots from the House.

A Remarkable Letter from Mr. Beecher in Relation to the Woodhull Scandal.

The readers of the EAGLE cannot fail to have noticed the suggestions which have recently been thrown out by some of our exchanges and correspondents as to the propriety of looking into the mental condition of Mr. Tilton. Thousands of people who, while confident of Mr. Beecher's innocence, were yet unwilling to believe Mr. Tilton capable of deliberate and malicious lying in the premises, have in their charity asked whether the key to the scandal was not to be found in some delusion of Mr. Tilton's brain. In other words, these people who knew Mr. Tilton years ago only

to admire, have shown a disposition to consider him mentally unfortunate rather than morally bad—as a person to be sympathized with rather than ruthlessly condemned. In this spirit the EAGLE presents the subjoined statement, for the care and truthfulness of which we vouch to our readers.

Is Theodore Tilton Crazy?

This is a question that many people are asking to-day. It is a question that very intimately concerns the happiness of thousands of others in this distracted community. It is a question, the solution of which would go far to settle one of the most perplexing social difficulties that ever divided and exasperated a people. It is a question that possibly involves the personal safety, if not the lives, of two members of this community, and upon it the EAGLE attempts to throw some light.

THE CAUSE OF THE INVESTIGATION.

It is a matter of public notoriety that a brother of Theodore Tilton was for some time an inmate of the Flatbush Lunatic Asylum, and that he died insane. This fact, the unaccountable performances of Theodore Tilton in relation to the all-absorbing investigation now going on, and the following letter, which explains itself and which was recently received at this office, were the moving causes of the inquiries instituted by the EAGLE, the results of which are here given:

JERSEY CITY, July 25, 1874.
To the Editor of the Brooklyn Eagle:

If the people of your city cannot reconcile the insincerities, the fickleness, the cunning, the polish, the apparent openness, the frankness and the duplicity of Mr. Theodore Tilton, perhaps if you could see Dr. ——, of Trenton, he could tell you something of Mr. Tilton's family's mental history. I refer you also to ex-Judge ——, of ——, who knows the whole of the Tilton family and can relate incidents of their aberrations. I knew T. T.'s poor book peddling brother in Keyport. This poor creature had a softening of the mind that often betrayed itself. He died with loss of faculties. If you go to Keyport, where Tilton's father now lives, you will find but one belief among the people there, and that is that Theodore Tilton is *suffering under strong delusion.* They will tell you that it takes but a little spark to fire the timbers of the Tilton house.

I write this merely in charity to Mr. Tilton, believing that it bears directly upon and in the end will account for the mystery that now agitates and divides your community. In strict confidence,
[References.]   [Signed.]

ON THE WING.

On Wednesday last, armed with letters of introduction to responsible parties, the reporter of the EAGLE went to Keyport. This place, a beautiful village of three or four thousand inhabitants, is in Monmouth County, and is situated on the Raritan Bay. It is reached by a delightful sail of two hours by steamer from New York. Making his headquarters at the Pavilion, a seaside hotel kept by an old resident of Brooklyn, the reporter soon put himself in communication with reliable sources of information and went to work.

STATEMENT OF THE FIRST PARTY.

The first party of whom inquiries were made is an old and respectable inhabitant of the town, a gentleman of some scientific and of good intellectual acquirements, and related, not very distantly, to a New York municipal officer of high rank. The desired information was freely given, the only condition made being the omission of the informant's name, a condition made in every instance by the kind hearted people who deprecated equally public notoriety in the Beecher-Tilton case and any possibly arising differences from this cause among themselves.

From this gentleman the following facts were learned: The father and mother of Theodore Tilton and several of his uncles, live in Keyport and vicinity. They have always been considered a "queer" set. Theodore's father was originally a shoemaker, and was in the business in Greenwich street, New York, acquired some means, increased his property by a life insurance on the life of the lunatic son who was treated at Flatbush, and now is quite well to do in the world. The family originated near Middletown, a few miles from Keyport, and was considered an old one. The grandfather of Theodore on his father's side died many years ago, and nothing was known in Keyport, or at least could be learned on brief inquiry, of his mental peculiarities. Of his sons—Theodore's father and uncles—Theodore's father was considered to be the "soundest" one, mentally, of the number. One of his uncles traveled about, shoemaking a little and playing on the fiddle a great deal. Another was a carpenter. Another, "Zickel," as he was familiarly termed, now dead, had two sons, George and Benjamin, by one wife, and a daughter, Mary, by another. Benjamin now lives in New York, and is janitor of the Irving Bank Building. George now lives in Keyport. Before going to New York Benjamin got in a "queer" way. He went there at the instance of the present cashier of the bank who took an interest in him. The cashier lives in Keyport. It is believed that Benjamin's mind is right now. George has been "in a queer way for years back." He was a carpenter. He would get discouraged and give up business without assignable cause, as he was well to do and had a nice place. His wife got him off to Virginia six or seven weeks last Winter on account of his mental condition. He is still "in a queer way," has, apparently, a species of hypochondria. He would quit work for no reason, say

The trial lasted almost six months and put on record well over a million words of testimony. The verbatim record fills almost three thousand pages and was printed and sold in installments as the trial progressed. Political and social leaders fought for tickets, sometimes paying five dollars apiece for them, and ate their lunch in their seats. The crowds came as though to a fair, and often thousands were turned away in a single day. The trial was given more space in newspapers than any event since the Civil War. As far as the participants were concerned, the vaunted sanctity of Victorian private life was invaded with fiendish ingenuity and obscene curiosity.

Tilton retained three lawyers but his case was presented by only a few witnesses, principally Moulton and his wife. Henry used William Maxwell Evarts, an excellent lawyer and later secretary of state under Hayes, as well as five other attorneys and almost one hundred witnesses. Henry's own testimony was often vague, irrelevant or so flippant that the New York *Herald* declared that he presented to "scientific men a psychological problem which they must despair of solving." Otherwise a master of the brilliant retort, Henry resorted almost nine hundred times to such phrases as "I can't recollect" or "I don't know." At times he would sniff the violets that he kept on the floor at his side.

In the role of spectator, Henry was his familiar genial self, Tilton was grave, and Mrs. Tilton melancholy. For Mrs. Beecher, who did not miss a day and looked on with stony impassivity, it was surely the kind of injustice she always expected from life. At first Henry and the two women chatted when they met in court and Henry received great bouquets of flowers, as though he were about to preach. But this practice was soon abandoned.

The court trial brought out little that was not already known. Henry denied the adultery charge and the claim—sworn to by Tilton, Moulton and Mrs. Moulton—that he had admitted it. He continued to insist that his oft-repeated *mea culpa*s concerned only his failure to discourage Mrs. Tilton's affections and his role in the firing of Tilton. But he did not satisfactorily explain why he had endured such a long-drawn-out agony for such inconsequential reasons. Nor why he had poured seven thousand dollars into Tilton's magazine, *The Golden Age*. And all his aplomb did not save him from being repeatedly led into awkward admissions or contradictions by the sharp cross-examination of Tilton's lawyer Fullerton. Yet he never lost his self-assurance; it was this that persuaded several of his critics, including one of Tilton's attorneys, William A. Beach, that he was innocent. "I felt and feel now," Beach said years later, "that we were a pack of hounds trying in vain to drag down a noble lion."

Henry denied even any undue familiarity with Elizabeth Tilton, but two witnesses contradicted this: one, a wet nurse, declared she had seen Elizabeth sitting on Henry's knee, and Joseph Richards, Elizabeth's brother, testified that he had come upon the pair in Tilton's parlor and seen Elizabeth, her face "highly flushed," drawing hastily away from Henry.

Tilton came off little better than Henry. It was his personality that told against him. He had obviously been a domineering and unfaithful husband. He was intellectually brilliant but emotionally adolescent, especially in his tendency to dramatize himself and make romantic gestures. As General Tracy said, the world would never forgive him for having condoned what he himself declared were his wife's transgressions. Nor was it possible to defend his agreeing to keep the affair secret and then blabbing about it to half a dozen persons, or his accepting money and aid from Henry.

It also did not help his cause when members of Victoria Woodhull's household testified that they had seen him embracing her or entering her bedroom with her. And it did him little credit when he admitted, like a child caught in a naughty act, that the relationship with Victoria Woodhull had been "wrong." Thereafter Mrs. Woodhull understandably referred to him with scorn: "Mr. Tilton would make quite a man if he should live to grow up." And even his old friend Mrs. Stanton took him publicly to task for his sudden retreat.

Francis Moulton was a more effective witness. Although on the stand for eleven days, he maintained his air of cool detachment. Neither Elizabeth Tilton nor Victoria Woodhull was, for obvious reasons, called by either side, but Mrs. Tilton did provide one of the more dramatic moments of the trial when near the close she rose and asked the judge to read a letter she had written. He consented; it declared in her usual overwrought manner that having been released from the "will" whose power had made her incriminate herself, she wanted again to assert her innocence. Even though it was apparent that she was ready to swear to anything to gain Henry's acquittal and thus save her own name, the defense lawyers did not call her. They were wise: three years later she reversed herself once again and forever.

One of the most interesting witnesses was Moulton's wife, Emma, a soft-voiced woman in her middle thirties. Henry himself repeatedly referred to her in letters to Moulton as one of his dearest friends even though her "clear truthfulness" laid him "pretty flat." Her account of a meeting with Henry in June 1873 was one of the highlights of the trial:

He expressed to me his love for Elizabeth, and his great remorse and sorrow that she should ever have confessed to her husband . . . that it would bring only ruin in the end to all. . . .

He walked up and down the room in a very excited manner, with tears streaming down his cheeks, and said that he thought it was very hard, after a life of usefulness, that he should be brought to this fearful end. . . . he sat down in a chair. I stood behind him and put my hand on his shoulder, and I said: "I will always be your friend if you will only go down to the church and confess, because that is the only way out for you. . . ."

And he said: "You are always to me like a section of the Day of Judgment.". . . And I said: "I have never heard you preach since I knew the truth that I haven't felt that I was standing by an open grave. I cannot express to you the anguish and the sorrow it has caused me to know what I have of your life. I believed in you since I was a girl—believed you were the only good man in this world. Now it has destroyed my faith in human nature. I don't believe in anybody.

She then quoted Henry as saying that he particularly feared that if the affair came to light his wife and children would despise him. Mrs. Moulton tried to tell him that he could retire to his farm and spend his time writing, but he answered: ". . . if I cannot continue as a moral and spiritual leader, why there is nothing left for me to do." He was deeply disturbed, Mrs. Moulton testified, and told her very positively he would take his life, whereupon she tried to calm him down.

Henry denied all this, but the account was so circumstantial, with every detail so characteristic of Henry, that his lawyers could do little besides claim that it never took place at all. Against anyone except Henry Ward Beecher, Emma Moulton's testimony would have proved devastating. But the pastor of Plymouth Church had become an idol, the kind of public figure that battens on all publicity, good or bad. Proving him a fake and a sham would presumably undermine confidence in all spiritual leaders.

Evarts astutely based much of his summation for the defense on just that. Henry, he said, was a pillar of decency and tearing him down would result only in a victory for the cynical and the evil-minded. He argued that it was inconceivable that a man of Henry's nobility and loving-kindness should be guilty of such a crime. Tilton's counsel countered this by arguing that Henry's illustrious name and the wealth and power of Plymouth Church must not be allowed to exempt him from punishment for his sin.

In the midst of a prostrating late-June heat wave, the jury retired to deliberate. They stayed out for eight days, with reporters watching them through spyglasses from the windows of nearby buildings. At last, after fifty-two ballots, they brought in their verdict: nine to three against Theodore Tilton.

That evening, when Henry arrived at Plymouth Church, a group of cheering worshipers awaited him, and on Sunday a great throng crowded the streets around the church in the hope of seeing or hearing him. For them the idol was untouched, and his reputation had become, if anything, more fabulous.

Henry soon left for Twin Mountain House, New Hampshire, his "summer parish." And there, to amuse those who had not been present at the courthouse, he and a few of his followers staged a parody of the trial.

But not everyone thought the trial had been amusing, or even that the split decision established Henry's innocence. Some reactions were scathing. In England George Meredith wrote: "Guilty or not, there is a sickly snuffiness about the religious fry that makes the tale of their fornications absolutely repulsive to read of." Typical of the religious press was the view of the *Advance:* "On his own showing . . . he has exhibited a degree of moral weakness and cowardice almost incredible were it not proved sadly true." Tom Appleton, a wit, world traveler and patron of the arts, put it a good deal less politely: "Mankind fell in Adam, and has been falling ever since, but never touched bottom till it got to Henry Ward Beecher."

Plymouth Church nevertheless raised the huge sum of $100,000 to help pay Henry's legal expenses. By contrast, Theodore Tilton was financially ruined. But Francis Moulton was unshaken. Although the curtain had apparently been rung down, he began to play his part even more aggressively than before. During the church investigation, Henry had unthinkingly sworn out a complaint against Moulton for criminal libel. The last thing Henry wanted now was another trial, with the prospect that Moulton, unlike Tilton, would not hesitate to call Mrs. Tilton to testify. Henry hastily dropped the suit. Moulton thereupon published a letter to the district attorney in which he declared: "I am indicted of criminal libel in charging Rev. Henry Ward Beecher with criminal intercourse with a female member of his congregation. The charge is true; he knows it to be true; and whatever the imperfections of man's tribunals, the Supreme Ruler will some day reveal the truth." He then dared Henry to sue him for libel. When Beecher did not respond, Moulton, crying, "Pulpit or prison!" sued the preacher for malicious prosecution, but the court dismissed the case.

That fall the brethren of Plymouth Church retaliated by dropping Emma Moulton from the church rolls. She immediately requested a council like the one that had reviewed the expulsion of Theodore Tilton. Henry, once again sure of his judges, complied; he called together more than two hundred prominent Congregationalists and welcomed them cordially. A friendly spirit reigned and Henry was given a vote of complete confidence and Christian fellowship. Exultant, but his patience exhausted, Henry now spoke out with all his characteristic vibrancy:

I am questioned, and questioned, and questioned . . . through months and years, on the supposition that the truth has not been got out. And I suppose it will be so to the end of my life. . . . I think there is hope in the grave, and beyond; but for me I expect to walk with a clouded head, not understood, until I go to heaven.

And at another session:

as long as God knows, and my mother, how it is . . . I don't care for you or anybody else. Well . . . I do care and I don't . . . just as I happen to feel. . . . I am tired of you; I am tired of the world.

Once again dramatizing himself, he asked, "Is it possible for a man to live as long as I have . . . and to have acted upon so large a theatre, and been agitated by such world-shaking events, and be so utterly misconceived?" Wearily he added, "Tomorrow morning it will be said in the local journals: 'Well, Mr. Beecher—how rhetorically he managed the matter!' And it will be put in the religious papers: 'Oh! yes; that was a very plausible statement . . . but—but—' "

After the vote, he spoke again, crying: "I have not been pursued as a lion is pursued; I have not been pursued even as wolves and foxes. I have been pursued as if I were a maggot in a rotten corpse"; and: "When you shall find a heart to rebuke the twining morning-glory, or any other plant that holds on to that which is next to it . . . you may rebuke me for loving where I should not love. It is not my choice; it is my necessity." It was always Henry's gift that before an audience he could speak from the heart, confess—confess anything—and inspire his followers to believe in him more than ever.

No one can say for sure why at this point Henry Bowen was moved to face the challenge he had avoided since what he described as the death-bed confession of his wife fourteen years before. Perhaps he felt that Henry was about to escape retribution forever and this was his own last chance to speak, or perhaps he could not contain himself any longer. A painfully thin figure with sunken eyes in a pallid face, he went before a special Plymouth Church committee and recalled how he had helped establish the church almost thirty years before, labored to bring Henry Ward Beecher to it as its first pastor, and then aided him in countless ways over the years. "At last," Bowen said, "there came to my knowledge evidence of his guilt which astounded and overwhelmed me. . . . I received from a lady whom, under the circumstances, I was compelled to believe . . . full and explicit confession of adultery with Mr. Beecher." The lady, Bowen continued, had a key to Henry's study in Plymouth Church and had "frequent intercourse" with him there—until she saw another woman enter with a similar key. She never got over the shock,

Bowen said, and died shortly afterward. Almost everyone knew he was talking of his first wife, Lucy.

"If you carry out what I believe is your pre-arranged plan," Bowen declared, "and expel me from the church of which I am the oldest member . . . God will hold you to account." But if God was listening, he was surely not edified by either side. Ostensibly because Bowen had offered no proof, Plymouth Church responded to his charges by expelling him. He would be worthy of pity if there were not so many stories of his shady business practices and the gap between his life and his religion.

With some misgivings, Henry now resumed his career as lecturer. Occasionally at first there was the jeer, the coarse remark, the audience waiting coldly. He was in his sixties now, his hair stringy and thin, the skin flabby under the chin and hanging loosely from the throat. But he was the same old Henry, lavish of his gifts, the superb actor of a hundred parts, needing only an audience; and after a while he was as successful as ever. Under the management of a leading agent, Major James B. Pond, he delivered one hundred thirty-two lectures in one hundred thirty-five days to a total of almost half a million persons. The admission fee was one dollar in cities and fifty cents in towns. Before long he was being guaranteed from six hundred to a thousand dollars a night. He could boast after a Boston lecture that "ten thousand people couldn't get in" and that when he entered a meeting of Congregationalist ministers he was cheered, asked to address it, and had everyone weeping so that "it broke up like a revival meeting." Because Henry Watterson, editor of the Louisville *Courier-Journal*, had described the scandal as a "dunghill covered with flowers," Henry gloatingly reported that when he came to Louisville to lecture, Watterson sent for tickets for his family. "I was in good trim," he added, "and avenged myself on that audience." Even in his late sixties Henry continued to enjoy the lecture tours: "It is a pleasant sort of intellectual gypsy life—respectable vagabondage!" The crowd, as Henry knew, after a while forgets and forgives; more than that, it often interprets notoriety as fame.

But the embers of the scandal were not all dead. In April 1878, Elizabeth Tilton, now living with her mother, and still as tormented as ever a decade after the events, had her legal adviser publish the following letter in the New York *Times*:

A few weeks since, after long months of mental anguish I told . . . a few friends whom I bitterly deceived, that the charge brought by my husband, of adultery between myself and the Reverend Henry Ward Beecher, was true, and that the lie I had lived so well the last four years had become intolerable to me. That statement I now solemnly reaffirm and leave the truth to God, to whom also I commit myself, my children, and all who must suffer.

I know full well the explanations that will be sought for this acknowledgement: desire to return to my husband, insanity, malice—everything save the true one—my quickened conscience, and the sense of what is due the cause of truth and justice. . . .

It was the only statement she ever made free of pressure, and it had the ring of truth, but it came too late.

In northern New York, where he was lecturing, Henry found a new way of characterizing—and stigmatizing—Elizabeth Tilton. She is a clairvoyant, he said, subject to trances in which "she would grovel in the dust . . . even kissing the feet of those to whom she most felt herself under obligation."

The *Times*, however, took solemn note of the statement, and its verdict was:

On the evidence submitted at the trial of Henry Ward Beecher, *The Times* reached the conclusion that he was guilty of the charge brought against him. Since that time we have seen no reason to change the opinion then recorded. . . . *The Times* proclaimed the guilt of Mr. Beecher on other grounds than the confession and retraction of Mrs. Tilton. The card from her which we publish today does not, therefore, strengthen the case against him as it has been regarded in these columns. It is worthless as legal evidence, however strongly it may confirm the moral presumption of Mr. Beecher's guilt. This weak and erring woman has so hopelessly forsworn herself as to forfeit all claim to attention or credence. Her letter will, however, be effectual . . . in lending to the odious gang who traded on their knowledge of Mr. Beecher's guilt a species of vindication. . . . As for Mr. Beecher, he remains the impure and perjured man which any rational construction of his own letters proved him to be.

Even discounting the sensational name-calling that was the stock-in-trade of the journalism of the time, the editorial has a crushing force.

Tilton, who was also on a lecture tour, said nothing. He continued to support his children, but after a few years the lecturing opportunities dwindled. He would never be forgiven for having defiled the great name of Beecher. Shorn of wife, causes and spirit, he drifted to Paris. There he lived in an attic room on the Île Saint-Louis. When not writing poetry or romantic novels, he could be seen in the Café de la Régence playing chess with another expatriate, Judah P. Benjamin—onetime secretary of state in the Confederacy—or, later, with Jules Grévy, twice president of France. He died, quite forgotten, in 1907.

Having made her final confession, Elizabeth Tilton faded into obscurity. She went to live with one of her daughters and steadfastly shunned the world until her death in 1897. She was the main victim of the scandal.

By contrast, Victoria Woodhull flourished—but only at the expense of her greatest distinction: her nonconformity. Finding herself penniless and ill after the Beecher trial, she renounced free love, "divorced" Colonel Blood, and began to see virtues in conventional marriage and motherhood. On a trip to England she captivated the son of a banker and, after establishing her respectability to the satisfaction of his family, married him. Even though Victoria Woodhull Martin over the years toyed with eccentric causes, returned to spiritualism, and in her last years had herself driven in big automobiles at furious speeds across the English countryside, she was, when she died in 1927, merely another rich, somewhat quaint old woman.

Only Henry Ward Beecher did not change. Once on a tour in 1878 he wrote to Eunice that he had seen Frank Moulton near him on a train. He spoke of Moulton as of an old lover who brought back precious memories. "Could I be happier?" he continues. "Oh yes, if another were only here—if only my T. T. could complete this Trinity! It was a comfort to see on Moulton's wrists a pair of noble jasper medallion sleeve buttons which I gave him. It shows how tenderly he cherishes my memory. If only it were possible," he concludes, "for us to be friends again...." Amativeness was still all.

26

HENRY WARD BEECHER

Changing Gods

The need for applause lay deep in Henry Ward Beecher's psyche and it grew with the years. Surely speaking from self-knowledge, he declared in 1872:

A minister says: "I am very sensitive to the praise and opinion of men.". . . What is such a man to do? Can he change his own temperament? . . .

Well in a sense he cannot change at all. One can make just as many prayers, write just as many resolutions . . . and when you are screwed down in your coffin, you will have been no less a praise-loving man than when you were taken out of the cradle. . . . You will find that men get over some things in time . . . but if vanity is a part of their composition . . . they grow worse and worse as they grow in years.

That is why Henry went back so promptly to lecture tours. But he had also fought for his right to political activity and to express himself on controversial social issues—a right that the clergy had more or less lost early in the century. So now, needing more than ever the wine of approval, he spoke out on political issues and candidates.

But his instincts were not always trustworthy: a resurgence of his old self-confidence along with a deep-rooted faith in the Protestant work ethic led him at least once into a singularly callous statement. Reacting to strikes that swept the East after the financial crises of 1873–1876 had thrown a million people out of work, Henry declared that although labor had a right to organize, foreign socialistic elements in the unions were stirring up a dangerous discontent. Strangely oblivious of the desperate and hungry families in every city, he added:

It is said that a dollar a day is not enough for a wife and five or six children. No, not if the man smokes or drinks beer. . . . But is not a dollar a day enough to buy bread with? Water costs nothing and a man who cannot live on bread and water is not fit to live.

Unhappily for Henry, cartoonists and critics, ruthless all, knew that he had an income of at least forty thousand dollars a year. The cries of outrage that went up made him modify the statement but not withdraw it. He did not intend, he said, to belittle the working classes, but God had meant that the "great shall be great and that the little shall be little ... and no equalizing process will take place till you can make men equal in productive forces." So predestination still defied a democratic faith in the unlimited potential of everyman.

Paradoxically, it was a belief in the freedom of the individual and free competition in the labor market that led Henry to oppose the rising labor unions. At one point, jarred by the violence of strikes and the destruction of property, Henry along with other clergymen urged that troops be called out to end the disorder. But almost in the same breath he attacked the captains of great corporations. Thus once again he took advantage of his position above the battle to call down a plague on both houses. It did not matter that he offended the more radical unionists or the more arrogant employers—as long as he struck a responsive chord in hundreds of thousands of Americans. They flocked to his lectures and came away idolizing him.

Equally inconsistent was his attitude toward the common people. Repeatedly he expresses a Jacksonian faith in the average American, and he made this the theme of one of his most popular lectures in the middle and late 1870s, "The Reign of the Common People." But elsewhere he reveals a fear that the lower classes can be a source of dangerous unrest unless they are properly instructed. Although he was out of sympathy with such intellectual critics of American society as E. L. Godkin, editor of *The Nation,* and the Adams brothers, Henry, Charles Francis Jr. and Brooks, he assumed that leadership would come from those with naturally superior mental and moral endowments. His critics have branded his various positions as arrant opportunism while his admirers have seen them as evidence of his lofty standards and his honesty. There were both aspects in Beecher, but the very emotionalism with which he announced his positions has tended to polarize his critics. Only recently have they perceived that on social issues Beecher often simply reflected the crosscurrents of his age: he was elitist in some matters, democratic in others, at one and the same time a believer in individualism and in the wisdom of the people, in rural values and the attractions of the city, informal in manners and dress but with a leaning toward the sumptuous in his home.

Yet in at least one respect he exhibited an admirable freedom from common prejudices. He continued to criticize arrogant attitudes toward Mexico and he was unsparing in his condemnation of the treatment of Indians. At the height of the Civil War he raged at the sins of this nation against the Indian, who . . . unlike the slave, has almost none . . . to speak of his wrongs. . . . We have wasted their substance; we have provoked their hostility and then chastised them for their wars . . . we have formed treaties with them only to be broken; we have filched their possessions. . . . A heathen people have experienced at the hands of a Christian nation almost every evil which one people can commit against another.

His courage as well as his compassion was displayed just as strongly in his friendship for the Jews. When Czarist pogroms drove many Jews out of Russia, Henry called on Americans to welcome them. But his most impressive assault on anti-Semitism was a sermon "Gentile and Jew" that he preached in June 1877. It was provoked by the action of business baron A. T. Stewart and Judge Henry Hilton, one of "Boss" Tweed's supporters in New York, in having the palatial Grand Union Hotel in Saratoga Springs turn away Joseph Seligman and his family because they were Jewish. Seligman was not only a prominent banker but a friend of presidents and cabinet members and a leader of New York's proud German Jewish clan. Henry made clear that although he had come to know and love the Seligmans during summer vacations at Twin Mountain House in Vermont, he was speaking for a principle, not simply for friends.

In his long and impassioned sermon, Henry pointed out that from the Jews, still persecuted everywhere, the world had received "a treasure of benefits such as no other people had ever conferred upon mankind": they had established the first true commonwealth; they respected women far more than did other eastern peoples or even the Greeks; they gave their children love, an excellent education and an ideal home life; and they had created an ethical religion. The Greeks had built better temples but the Jews, Henry declared, had built men, and they had developed a moral sense which Christianity had borrowed freely. They are an industrious people, he concluded, and if they are shrewd bargainers in business, Yankees were hardly the ones to cast the first stone. The incident drew nationwide attention, but in many resort hotels and clubs Henry's plea fell on deaf ears.

At Henry Ward Beecher's death, rabbis eulogized him unstintingly.

The Beechers' house on Columbia Street was spacious, but when their son Henry and his family moved in with them for reasons of economy, Eunice, ailing and now in her middle sixties, felt displaced as mistress of the household. This feeling increased when Henry Ward began urging her to go to Florida for the winter months for her health. At first she responded as though she were being sent into exile, but after several winters in the South she liked it well enough to publish a book on her impressions. The tiny volume, *Letters from Florida,* could have been, like Harriet's earlier *Palmetto Leaves,* a charming account of Florida life in the 1870s, but admitting that she had no feeling for the romantic or the exotic, she contented herself with a perfunctory report on the opportunities for farming and fruit growing. Rather stiffly she warns off those who do not like hard labor. Plainly, none of her husband's zest had rubbed off on her.

Hoping to cheer her up, Henry took her on one of his lecture tours. Instead of relaxing and enjoying the experience, she spent her time—or so Henry said—complaining to almost everyone about her troubles and Henry's extravagances. Convinced that she had a "morbid craving for sympathy over fictitious woes," Henry never again took her with him.

Partly to accommodate the growing families of his children—a daughter and two of his three sons lived near enough to visit him and Eunice in summer—but also because he shared Harriet's love of elegant homes, Henry decided to replace the farmhouse on his Peekskill acres with a new summer home. Much like Harriet when she was building Oakholm in Hartford, he went enthusiastically at the task ("a house is the shape which a man's thought takes when he imagines how he would like to live") and achieved a three-story neo-Gothic building with stone walls, oak beams, great porches, handsome fireplaces and carved oak paneling. The interior, as in his town house, was loaded with massive furniture and rank on rank of ceramics (the auction catalog of his artworks after his death listed 345 of these pieces)—all in all, a model of substance, comfort and Victorian refinement.

To escape the hay fever season, Henry would generally spend the last weeks of August with his sister Harriet at Twin Mountain House in New Hampshire. Calling it his summer parish, he conducted services in the hotel on Sundays. During the week the favorite pastime of both Henry and his sister was croquet; they played it with characteristic Beecher intensity, sometimes into the dusk, using lanterns to light the wickets.

Proud of his position in the Republican party since its birth in 1855, Henry returned to the political scene when General Grant was nominated in 1868 and ran against Seymour. "I have liked Grant from the first," he declared. "Solid, unpretentious, straightforward . . . wise in discerning men, skilful in using them . . . I confidently anticipate that . . . he will hereafter be known even more favorably for the wisdom of his civil administration." As a principal orator at a campaign meeting, his enthusiasm carried him even further; confronting the stories of Grant's weakness for drink, he cried, "I had rather have General Grant a drunkard than Horatio Seymour sober!"

But Grant, completely unqualified for battlefields where men fought with words and ideas, was a failure in the White House. As scandal after scandal broke around his administration, he remained his stolid self, his command post becoming an ivory tower. Yet Henry supported him for a second term and would have done so again in 1876; and at Grant's death he condoned the general's shortcomings and declared him a man without vices.

But Henry hankered for more political influence. Thus when Rutherford B. Hayes became President in 1877 and chose as his secretary of state William Maxwell Evarts, who had been Henry's chief counselor during his trial for adultery, Henry seized the opportunity to press for Brooklyn patronage. He succeeded in keeping a worthy man in the important office of Collector of Revenues in Brooklyn. But he also supported spoilsmen, such as Senator Roscoe Conkling of New York, against the party's efforts to jettison them. When Hayes, weary of the burdens of office, refused to run again, Henry switched to Grant. But when James A. Garfield was nominated, Henry backed the Ohio congressman, declaring at a major rally that party loyalty was of paramount importance. With his usual facility he came up with a glib slogan, "For God and Garfield," and called on all Republicans to unite for party, country and humanity. Personally gratified by Garfield's election, he was doubly shocked by the assassination of the President only a few months later. When the administration of Garfield's successor, Chester A. Arthur, ignored him he was piqued and exasperated, and only after Arthur invited him to the White House did he agree to support him.

But Henry had still to learn how treacherous politics could be. Although Arthur was an excellent administrator, he was cruelly thrust aside in the Republican presidential convention of 1884 in favor of the speaker of the house, James G. Blaine. Because Blaine put pressure on Henry to back him—even asking Harriet to use her influence on his behalf—but also because it was widely said that Blaine had profited from land grants to railroads, Henry scorned him. Similarly disillusioned, such highly respected Republican independents and reformers as Carl Schurz began shifting to the Democratic nominee, Grover Cleveland, who had served creditably as governor of New York.

Then came a sensational disclosure: Cleveland had once fathered a child out of wedlock. When the independents persisted in backing Cleveland, Henry demanded of Schurz how reformers could recommend such a "grossly dissipated man." The answer, that the episode had taken place fourteen years before and that Cleveland had supported the child, melted Henry's objections. The campaign was bitterly personal, with the Republicans making use of such ditties as:

Ma! Ma! Where's my pa?
Gone to the White House,
Ha! Ha! Ha!

But when Henry's friends at Plymouth Church warned him to steer clear of the Cleveland affair he was offended. He began to campaign ever more vigorously, perhaps seeking a vicarious triumph over ugly charges. The climax of his efforts came in a huge rally at the Brooklyn Rink in October 1884. After denouncing the Republican party for failing to deal with such urgent issues as civil service reform and the rights of labor, he turned to his favorite mode, the dramatic personal appeal:

When in the gloomy night of my own suffering . . . I vowed that if God would bring the day star of hope, I would never suffer brother, friend, or neighbor to go unfriended, should a like serpent seek to crush him. That oath I will regard now. . . . Men counsel me to prudence lest I stir again my own griefs. No! I will not be prudent. If I refuse to interpose a shield of well-placed confidence between Governor Cleveland and the swarm of liars that nuzzle in the mud . . . may my tongue cleave to the roof of my mouth. . . . I will imitate the noble example set me by Plymouth Church in the day of my own calamity. They stood by me with God-sent loyalty. . . .

It was a bold move, linking Cleveland and himself as victims of similar vicious attacks. How could anyone believe that he would dare to bring up the whole wretched affair again if he had been guilty? Sure that he had at last exorcised the scandal, he cast all prudence aside, and addressing a youthful audience at a YMCA, he declared: "If every man in New York State tonight, who has broken the seventh commandment, voted for Cleveland, he would be elected by 200,000 majority." Having thus insolently assumed that adulterers were common, he added a jibe: "There are men in Brooklyn who will say, 'I have been bumming with Cleveland at night.' I say to any such man: 'You were bumming on your own hook, and were so drunk that you couldn't see who was bumming with you!'" No wonder a distinguished reformer and fellow campaigner, Thomas Wentworth Higginson, spoke of "the coarse jauntiness in his [Beecher's] way of treating the attack on Cleveland" and the *Tribune* referred to his "buffoonery." More than one American must also have asked whether he would have made so light of adultery if he had not been guilty of it himself. And what had happened to the lurid warnings against the "scarlet woman" that had filled his *Lectures to Young Men?*

When Cleveland won, it was in its way a vindication of Henry Ward Beecher: an admitted adulterer had been awarded the highest honor in the land. But it also suggested once again that Henry's influence in politics, as elsewhere, was based on personality and emotions rather than social issues.

Over the years Henry had been hammering away at the more fearful aspects of Calvinism. He had cheered his audiences by dismissing innate depravity, election and the orthodox view of conversion and a vengeful God. Then in 1877, he discarded hell. As always in such matters, he knew that his audience was ready for it. In fact, hell had already been declared obsolete by no less an authority than the canon of Westminster Abbey. In Henry's gospel of hope for all sinners, what place could there be for the threat of hellfire and damnation? So just before Christmas, with all his old sense of the dramatic, he said, speaking of all peoples who had lived before Christianity:

If . . . you say that they went to hell, then you make an infidel of me; for I do swear, by the Lord Jesus Christ, by his groans, by his tears, and by the wounds in his hands and in his side, that I will never let go of the truth that the nature of God is to suffer for others rather than to make others suffer. . . . To tell me that back of Christ is a God who for unnumbered centuries has gone on creating men and sweeping them like dead flies—nay, like living ones—into hell, is to ask me to worship a being . . . much worse than the conception of any medieval devil. . . . But I will not worship the devil. . . . I will *not* worship cruelty, I *will* worship Love—that sacrifices itself for the good of those who err.

It was not a philosophical or theological concept but only an attitude born of his own deep need of freedom from fear. Still, it came as a miraculous act of liberation for his listeners, a general amnesty from eternal damnation. It is not surprising that they adored him.

In exploding the concept of hell, Henry was marching with the times. But in his sweeping acceptance of the theory of evolution he was a step ahead of his time, and especially of those orthodox clergymen who were denouncing evolution because it dethroned God, denied the divine inspiration of the Bible and degraded humankind by describing it as descended from monkeys. Accepting evolution was not really a radical step for Henry because he had long held a view of God, original sin and the future of mankind that was, as far as he could see, simply reinforced by the findings of the biologists and the geologists. As early as his *Star Papers* and his novel, *Norwood,* he had seen God as manifest in the workings of nature rather than in the Bible or in churches. Thus when a dinner was given in Delmonico's in 1882 in honor of Herbert Spencer after the eminent evolutionist had made a three-month tour of America, Henry was one of the speakers. "I began to read Mr. Spencer's works more than twenty years ago," he declared. "They have been meat and bread to me." He proceeded to poke fun at some of the Bible stories and amused the audience with such quips as "I would just as lief have descended from a monkey as from anything else—if I had descended far enough."

A few months later, in a letter to a fellow minister, Dr. Kinnard, he defined his position more seriously:

I am a cordial Christian evolutionist. I would not agree by any means with all of Spencer, nor all of Huxley, Tyndall and their school. They are agnostic. I am not—emphatically. But I am an evolutionist and that strikes at the root of all medieval and orthodox modern theology. Men have not fallen as a race. Men have come up.

Seventy years old and a law unto himself, he now resigned from the Brooklyn Association of Congregational Ministers, grandly explaining that he wanted no one to be embarrassed by his views:

I am not worthy to be related in the hundred-thousandth degree to those more happy men who never make a mistake in the pulpit. I make a great many. I am impetuous . . . I know very well I do not give crystalline views nor thoroughly guarded views; there is often an error on this side and an error on that, and I cannot stop to correct them. . . . Let them go. . . . The average and general influence of a man's teaching will be more mighty than any single misconception.

It was a lenient but shrewd self-estimate. He could always make an admission of his faults seem like an admirable largeness of spirit. He spoke out freely now, liberated by age and by a record of challenges met and overcome. In 1885, in a group of sermons published under the title *Evolution and Religion,* he summed up his antipathy to the old doctrines and his hopes for the new.

His attack was bitter. The old theory of sin, he said, is "repulsive, unreasonable, immoral and demoralizing." As Catharine had a few years before, he scoffed at the Bible story of how God had created Adam and Eve, subjected them to the temptations of the devil, thrust them out of the Garden of Eden and then transmitted their "corruption" down through countless ages. "I hate it," he cried, "because I love God," and, "It is hideous . . . it is turning creation into a shambles and God into a slaughterer, and the human race into a condition worse a thousandfold than that of beasts." The idea that the flesh is corrupt in and of itself is a "wild heathenism" that still lurks in the blood of the Church but will be purged away by evolution. Boldly he denied the divine inspiration of the Bible. Geology, he asserted, has refuted Genesis. Eden must now be looked on as a poem from a childlike age of history. And once again he translated abstractions into the most personal terms:

I cannot content myself with a sitting down in a sweet little parish where everything is regulated by the highest morality . . . and where a sweet, loving people fan me with affection, trust and praise, and then cipher out a doctrine of the sinfulness of man and the reasonableness of eternal punishment. When I think about the condition of men after death, I think . . . of that vast sweep of creation, illimitable, uncountable, of human beings that have been created in conditions that . . . necessitate imperfection, and ask myself . . . Are they wailing in immitigable torment? If that is so, never let me mention the name of God again.

Henry declared that when people said to him, "It is generally understood you are not a Calvinist," he answered, "John Calvin can take care of himself. But I am a preacher of righteousness. I am a lover of mankind." We are still sinful creatures, he says, but our sins are weaknesses—infirmities not bred in the bone.

Now, too, he saw Jehovah in the same warm light as he had long seen Christ: God's indignation at what is despicable is, he said, like a passing summer storm, while "his lovingkindness and tender mercies surpass in expression all that is known . . . of love among men." God, he says again, can be found in nature, but this is not pantheism, which is a darker and more mysterious belief than what it attempts to explain.

Everywhere in these pages there is an acceptance of the new social role of the church and what we now recognize as the secularization of religion. Only fifty years before, he pointed out, ministers behaved like superior beings; children hid when they came in sight; Sunday was a day of gloom, and to ride out was a deadly heresy. Today, he said, churches have parlors, flowers on the platform, hymn books with tunes to be sung, cheerful Sunday schools and festivals for the children. The platform of Plymouth Church has seen things "that would have made John Knox shiver," and the Sunday school picnics would have caused Calvin to cry, "Horror, Horror!" The "ascetic soot that went through the flues of the Church is being swept out" and along with it the belief that Christians must be "unhappy here, with the hope of being happier in heaven." And having abolished hell, he did not hesitate to scorn the fear of death and the somberness of funerals.

The old doctrines such as foreordination and election may in time, Henry observes, become beautiful, "like old castles when they are no longer inhabited, and when vines and ivy have grown all over them." What remains is a living spiritual guide. And the ablest defender of that core, Henry boldly declares, is Herbert Spencer: "he will be found to have given more truth in one lifetime than any man who has lived in the schools of philosophy in this world." The theory of evolution, Henry concludes, has shown us that there is an "unfolding process that is carrying creation up to higher planes . . . with systematic and harmonious results, so that the whole physical creation is organizing itself for a sublime march toward perfectness." So once again the world is seen as advancing toward the millennium—this time by virtue not of God but of evolution, with Herbert Spencer as the chief apostle.

In 1886, after an interval of twenty-three years, Henry visited England again. His tour was cordial and profitable, if not triumphant, and all the more because at seventy-three he was venerable and yet still amply and passionately alive. He met audience after audience with a flow of words and images as fresh, as humorously extravagant, and as unforced as ever.

In the winter, after his return to Brooklyn, he agreed to try to complete the second volume of his life of Christ, now a dozen years overdue. But on March 3, 1887, without warning, he suffered a stroke and died a few days later. His body lay in state amid a sea of flowers, and some fifty thousand mourners, most of them women, passed the bier.

He would have thought that the warmth and admiration in the tributes that came from everywhere were answer enough to all his critics.

The history of Henry Ward Beecher's reputation is a lesson in changing standards and tastes. In the decade after his death there were four full-scale biographies, almost all of them idolatrous, along with collections of his wit and humor, his prayers, patriotic addresses, lectures, and selections from his sermons. Such volumes continued to appear as late as 1913. They attest beyond question to his immense personal influence.

But the period after World War I, marked by disillusion and a rebellion against both Puritan and Victorian values, brought a wave of iconoclastic biographies and harsh reappraisals. One of these, by Paxton Hibben, uncovered enough damaging information about Henry to convince many readers, including some influential critics, that although Henry was a gifted minister and a magnetic personality, he was hypocritical, self-serving and a master at sailing with the wind.

We today, not mesmerized by Henry's personality or obliged, like the critics of the 1920s, to demonstrate a freedom from Puritan and Victorian taboos, can see grounds for both interpretations. It is plain that Henry was neither saint nor charlatan, neither the greatest preacher since Paul nor a fraud.

The gravest charge against him, hypocrisy, rests of course on the fact that he was a minister and, unlike the average citizen, could be held responsible for any gap between his preaching and his practice. And although he performed enough of a service as a foe of slavery to be signally honored by Lincoln, critics argue that he came late to the struggle, vacillated, and was stronger in words than in actions.

Politically he was a moderate but also something of an opportunist, with a craving for influence. On social issues, despite his praise of the common people, he still thought, like many of his New England ancestors, that poverty resulted from a lack of application and industry. He frequently attacked the big corporations and the increasingly feverish pursuit of success, but he condoned the extravagance of the rich and he rationalized his own and others' indulgence in luxuries.

Whether Henry was guilty as charged in the adultery trial is not crucial. (Tipping the scales against him is the fact that the jury in the end was divided and that Elizabeth Tilton's last confession, which she had good reason not to make, admitted her guilt.) It was that exceedingly worldly wise observer Mark Twain who after Henry's death declared it a pity "that so insignificant a matter as the chastity or unchastity of an Elizabeth Tilton could clip the locks of this Samson and make him as other men, in the estimation of a nation of Lilliputians creeping and climbing about his shoe-soles." But it was the effect of the trial that is important. Among the conservatives it was clear evidence that the gospel of love led to erotic license, disrespect for traditional Christian standards, and a breakdown in family ties. For the ever increasing group who wanted, consciously or not, release from Puritan bonds, the scandal was a confirmation that the old prohibitions were unnaturally repressive.

What the trial certainly demonstrated was that Henry was a creature of emotions and that the paramount emotion was what he called love, what today might be termed libido and what Victoria Woodhull labeled amativeness. He expressed this emotion in a religion of love: not Platonic or ideal love but personal love. This he generated in almost palpable waves whenever he addressed an audience, mingling—especially in his revival efforts—amatory and religious appeals in one torrent of ardor. In his abandonment to impulse and instinct he was a great force in the drift away from every vestige of Puritan discipline and self-denial.

From early childhood Henry had been, as he said, "enthusiastic and outgushing." As a youth he fled from the dark message of Calvinism and found in the world of nature—God's world—a well of joy and inspiration. In the Litchfield hills, on the banks of the Ohio, in the mountains of New Hampshire, in the rolling country overlooking the Hudson, he discovered the works of a God he could adore. Ironically, of all those who paid tribute to Henry after his death, no one marked this more clearly than that sworn enemy of all the old religions Robert G. Ingersoll. After the withering indictment, quoted earlier in these pages, of Lyman Beecher as the warden of "rayless, hopeless and measureless dungeons of the damned" in which the "loving hearts" of children "were stained and scarred with the religion of John Calvin," Ingersoll describes, with an eloquence for which he was famous, how young Beecher found in meadow and stream, in flower, forest, hill and sky, escape from the prison of Calvinist doctrine.

Nor did Ingersoll praise Henry because he might be helping to undermine religion. Beecher, he said, had been a great positive force: "No one can overestimate the good accomplished by this marvellous, many-sided man . . . [who] tried to put the star of hope in every sky."

But just as Henry's powers derived from his fervor, so did his weaknesses. There was a fatal softness in him, something molten at the core. In a crisis he dissolved in tears; in his affairs with women affection smothered common sense; and with young men such as Constantine Fondolaik and Theodore Tilton he was immaturely romantic, verging, we would say, on the homosexual. His subjection to emotion manifested itself in all manner of ways: the indiscriminate kissing, the melodramatic auctioning of slave girls, the perfervid passages in his sermons, the urge to wring tears as well as laughter from his congregation, the caressing of gems, the changes of heart on great issues.

But none of these hurt him in the public eye. That he was as much the victim as the master of his emotions did not seem to matter; his surrender to his feelings simply testified to their strength. People may not have reverenced him but they were fascinated by him and deeply drawn to him. In his excesses they found release.

Henry Ward Beecher acted out of his own inexorable needs. But he also satisfied a deep hunger in the America of his time.

EDWARD AND CHARLES BEECHER

Echoes of Another Age

When Edward Beecher returned east in 1871 after his long second foray into the West, he was still committed to the theory of preexistence that he had conceived in 1827. The rejection of *The Conflict of Ages* in 1853 had simply convinced him that the nation needed his message more than ever.

Arriving in the East, he settled in Brooklyn partly because he expected to serve as an assistant editor of the *Christian Union* and partly because he wanted medical attention for his son George, who was crippled by rheumatism. He also planned to work with Henry Ward, now at the zenith of his career.

Although Edward dealt with social issues in some of his articles for the *Christian Union,* his conclusion in most of them was that the problems would be solved only by the moral and religious reform of mankind. In other articles he continued to rattle the bones of such dead controversies as whether punishment of sinners is eternal. Backward-looking in theme as well as method, his book *History of Opinions on the Scriptural Doctrine of Retribution* fully justified Elizabeth Cady Stanton's observation that he was a dealer in "theological antiquities."

When a new owner took over the *Christian Union* Edward was eased out of his post. He began now to serve as an adviser to Henry at Plymouth Church. Despite a gap of ten years between them and one or two occasions when they had clashed over the editorial policies of the *Independent,* the two brothers had long had a genuine respect for each other, with Henry often calling on Edward's remarkable knowledge of religious thought and Edward admiring Henry's power to teach and inspire.

That may be why Edward stood fast at Henry's side when the Tilton scandal broke open in 1872. But his attitude toward Henry's possible guilt is so ambivalent as to suggest that he did not want to know the truth. A letter from his sister Isabella, already a militant feminist, refers to a conversation in which she had said that if Henry was guilty he should confess, whereupon Edward retorted that if Henry was guilty he should, on the contrary, not confess. That was, Isabella declared, not only hypocritical but unjust to the woman. If Edward also meant that he must defend Henry regardless of guilt, that, as even a sympathetic critic has said, was inexcusable.

Aside from writing reviews and giving addresses to church associations, Edward seems to have been busy during the early 1880s in writing a novel. If this seems quite out of character, considering his scholarly bent and his opinion of fiction as a waste of time, it must be that Harriet's novels and Henry's *Norwood* had persuaded him that fiction could be morally and spiritually useful as well as entertaining. The novel, called *Cornelia, A Tale of the Second Century under the Reign of Marcus Aurelius* (it was never published), is set in Rome at a time when its moral standards were giving way to a worldliness and corruption resembling, Edward felt, that of post–Civil War America.

When Cornelia, the nobly born heroine, faces a crisis, she appeals to Marcus Aurelius but finds his stoic philosophy of no help to her, much as Catharine Beecher after Fisher's death found her father's Calvinist credo deeply disappointing. Cornelia turns to skepticism and finally, guided by a slave woman, to a new religion, Christianity. In its sympathetic picture of Jesus and its faith in love, she finds what she seeks. So Edward in his later years may be said to have turned, like Henry and Harriet, to a religion of love.

But this did not prevent him, in an address on the fiftieth anniversary of the founding of Boston's Park Street Church, from assailing the "apostasy" of those who had in the past allowed the unregenerate into the church or had questioned the doctrine of human depravity or the divinity of Christ. As with most of the Beechers, there were contradictions in Edward's attitudes that he never resolved.

As energetic as ever, Edward began at eighty-two to serve part time at the Parkville Congregational Church on Eighteenth Avenue in Brooklyn. About twenty families attended the services. Paid a small salary, mainly by the Home Missionary Society, he needed financial help from other sources. He still tried to keep abreast of contemporary thought, his occasional letters to Charles ranging from Henry George's proposals for community land use to the claim by evolutionists—which Edward rejected—that man had ascended from a savage state. Almost to the end he lamented that he was not sufficiently free of financial cares to write one or two more books on religious doctrines.

In answer to a publisher's request, he wrote a highly sympathetic appraisal of Henry Ward's religious principles. He declared that in many ways Henry was quite orthodox and that in others he was simply doing God's work most effectively in his own fashion. In his unpublished biography of Edward, Charles, moved by this token of the bond between his brothers, sums them up thus:

Henry was a Beecher; Edward a Foote; Henry followed his father; Edward his mother; Henry was naturally exuberantly expressive; Edward both by nature and the stress of circumstances reserved and reticent. . . . Henry had, in the world's view, unbounded success; and the trials which every Christian must pass through . . . were not conspicuous. Edward had apparent professional failure and almost no popularity or applause. Yet there was never the least superciliousness on the one side nor jealousy on the other.

With typical Beecher enthusiasm, Charles concludes that in their "utter mutual confidence, their perfect loves, there was something heavenly."

Edward was still serving the Parkville community in 1889 when a horrible accident ended his active career. As he was returning one night from a church meeting, his leg was crushed by a train when he fell from the platform of a crowded station. Accepting suffering as a test of faith, he was able to joke with Charles as to whether his brother's loss of hearing was worse than his own loss of a leg. Because of his athletic activities he managed to move about quite freely with an artificial leg and a cane. In time his wife reported that he seemed happy but still longed for something to do. Gradually his faculties failed. "He thinks every day is Sunday," she wrote. "He wonders why we do not go to church." Because only two of their eleven children survived, the couple adopted a young woman, Voice Adams. She took care of them in their last years, giving Edward much pleasure each evening by singing hymns and playing a mandolin.

Although Edward's theory of preexistence would seem to have made life on earth only one stage in the life of the spirit, he had long deplored spiritualism as a work of the devil. But in their last years he and his wife, both of them almost helpless, turned to spirit communication. They attended séances, usually with those dedicated spiritualists Isabella Beecher Hooker and her husband, John, and when Edward's wife developed cancer and was given up as incurable, Edward in desperation called in a clairvoyant to help heal her.

When Edward died, at the age of ninety-one, his brother Tom delivered the eulogy at the funeral, but the most remarkable tribute was the book-length biography of him by his eighty-one-year-old brother Charles. It was a culminating act of homage and affection—a history of bygone spiritual dreams and controversies. Edward Beecher was above all a scholar and theorist. A firstborn son, he was aware at an early age that he had been dedicated to God and Congregationalism and he never rebelled against his father or questioned his fate. Although he may have been, as Charles said, like his mother in temperament, he was deeply influenced by his father's creed; whatever changes he did propose were essentially theoretical. He attacked the "cursed doctrine of the fallen Adam" but accepted the dogma of man's inherited depravity and the role of Satan. He insisted that God was suffering and compassionate, but he never gave up the belief that some sinners were doomed to eternal punishment. He deplored Unitarianism, thundered against Catholicism, was not tempted, like several of his brothers and sisters, by Episcopalianism, and resisted spiritualism until his dotage.

Edward's strength lay in his intellectual powers and his learning, but his most memorable work, *Narrative of Riots at Alton,* was a product of passion. He was concerned with social reform and he held what could be called a modern view of the community's responsibility for social evil. But he saw reform mainly as a moral matter and he was sure that the deterioration in American life could be arrested only by a new view of God. To the end he believed that his enduring contribution was his "revelation" of man's preexistence, even though *The Conflict of Ages* was battered when it was published and quite forgotten by the time Edward died. Little as he realized it, his great moment was when Elijah Lovejoy, facing a heart-shaking crisis in his struggle for abolition and freedom of the press, turned to him for advice, and he said: "The time for silence has gone by. . . . I say go on."

For Charles Beecher, the 1860s had been a time of frustration and tragedy. First the war, and his son Fred, a strong and loving youth, going off to the front. Then a council of ministers finding him guilty of heresy, and, without respite, stunning word that Fred had been badly wounded at Gettysburg. Scorning the council's verdict, he had proclaimed his love of God and Christ in his *Redeemer and Redeemed,* but the book had been little read or, if read, dismissed. Finally, the drowning of his two youngest daughters, and soon afterward, the death of Fred in a wretched war against Indians. All that sustained Charles Beecher in his grief was the conviction that his three beloved children were in heaven, freed from the trials of this world.

Freed from the trials of this world—that was what Charles must have envisioned when Harriet in 1870 began reporting the serenity of Mandarin, the jessamine blooming there in February and the opportunity to help freed blacks. So at the age of fifty-three he had left Georgetown and the harsh New England winters and settled in Florida, south of Tallahassee. For a time he tried to help the blacks, free but abandoned and confused. He had some success until they somehow learned that he was "unsound," which may have meant to them that he was not quite sane.

A carpetbag government from the North held power in Tallahassee, capital of the state, and it appointed Charles, perhaps on the recommendation of Harriet, Superintendent of Public Instruction for Florida. Soon, just like Harriet, he was giving poor "besnowed" friends and relatives in the North "a taste of Eden," describing how in his two-and-a-half-acre front yard he had pomegranates, figs, bananas, pecans, dates, peaches, a grapevine arbor measuring sixty by forty feet, and *"Roses Roses Roses!!"* To Isabella he wrote:

We consider ourselves about the most quiet, sequestered, comfortable couple anywhere. . . . We have the best mule and best mare in the county; make our own butter, eggs, syrup, sugar, potatoes, corn, and meat. . . . I can file and set a saw, grind an axe, sharpen a plane or chisel; shingle a roof, hang a door, put in a window, repair a cart or plow . . . with anybody in Wakulla.

Since Charles's jurisdiction as state superintendent included agriculture, he performed some interesting plant experiments on his little plantation. Most impressive was his demonstration that potato plants failed when planted in warm spring weather but flourished if planted in the fall and harvested in January or February.

He even hammered cold iron on his anvil and felt the blood of his blacksmith ancestors in his veins. Betweentimes he served as a voluntary weather observer for the government, carved animal heads in wood, read Bulwer-Lytton's novels to his wife, and occasionally played a game of euchre or whist.

The sharp edge of news from the outside world was usually blunted by the time it reached Newport, but at least once an ugly story intruded on this Florida paradise: late in 1872 Charles heard rumors of the Beecher-Tilton scandal and of Isabella's connection with Henry Ward's accuser, Victoria Woodhull. We know you are conscientious, he wrote to Isabella, but we "could not approve your course toward Henry, even supposing the charge were true, a supposition we never for a moment admit as possible." A few months later, when the church council in Brooklyn began its hearings, Charles, remembering his own experience with such groups, was as contemptuous of the council as of the charges. While on a visit to Eunice, Henry's wife, in her winter place in Mandarin, he wrote to Henry describing the council as "an old Bourbon Hunker element" that becomes "more and more cantankerous as it grows more narrow and impotent," and he predicted that if the decision went against Henry, it would divide the churches of the nation. He would never waver in his faith.

Meanwhile, the interest in spiritualism, already widespread when Charles had made his preliminary report in *A Review of "Spiritual Manifestations"* in 1863, was by the end of 1870 a kind of underground religious movement in America and England. Because of the charlatans and cranks who were associated with it on its lower levels, its more respectable devotees dissembled their interest. How popular it truly was is reflected in such novels as Howells's *The Undiscovered Country*, James's *The Bostonians*, Hawthorne's *Blithedale Romance* and sundry lesser works, not to speak of the vogue of books by such leading spiritualists as Andrew Jackson Davis and Robert Dale Owen. Full of promise of a blissful afterlife, spiritualism moved into niches left by the retreat of Calvinism.

Convinced that Christian Spiritualism, as he called it, could be a valuable religious force, Charles put together in *Spiritual Manifestations*, in 1879, a most elaborate case for its significance. He had a variety of justifications for his position: like many other Americans after the Civil War, he welcomed the assurance that he would be reunited with his dead children and other kin. With his deep faith in the preexistence of man, he saw life on earth as only one stage in the eternal life of the spirit. He also valued spiritualism as a movement that could operate outside the orthodox church and its tight hierarchy. Finally, as we have seen, he thought it confirmed a belief in heaven and hell that was essential in disciplining wayward mankind.

As passionate as ever in his convictions, Charles made clear in *Spiritual Manifestations* that he had never doubted the existence of spirits. All the religions of the world embraced this view, he pointed out, and apparitions and ghosts occurred in the folklore of every culture. That is why spiritualism has become, he asserts, "a household religion" and is "rapidly extending throughout Christendom." Unfortunately, the examples he gives of psychic phenomena—such as an Andover professor's report of a house in which spoons flew about and turnips dropped from the ceiling—reveal a naiveté that quite undercuts his lofty claims for the movement. He is somewhat more impressive when he returns to the cosmic view and writes such passages as "Man is a celestial race, exiled from his native skies. . . . He is abroad on his pilgrimage—not as a felon incarcerate; not expiating guilt; but for a remedial purpose . . . not merely for individual restoration, but with reference to the political regeneration of the moral universe." Even on this level there is too much that is vaporous and high-flown. In its vision of Satan and demonic spirits wrestling with Christ over the souls of men, it reads like a Greek myth of the wars of the Titans before the beginning of time. Spun out of a hundred threads from the Bible, it vanishes as soon as the reader closes the book.

The years at Newport passed as serenely as Charles could have wished. It was of course a pity for a man who loved music so much that his hearing should now begin to fail and that in his last years he would lose it entirely. But he had his inner world and out of it at intervals came sundry articles and a book, *The Eden Tableau,* another highly imaginative interpretation of a Bible story.

Making up for his youthful rebellion against father and family, he clung in later years to the hope that the clan would return to its old intimacy. As late at 1884, in a letter to Henry, he tried to pick up where they had left off at Lane Seminary and on the Indiana frontier long years before. Anything would be better, he wrote, than almost no communication at all:

I inferred from some remarks you made when I last saw you, that you had some slight differences of opinion in matters theologic from me and Edward. . . . We think man a fallen being, you think him a risen being,—but that need not prevent our writing letters to each other. . . . It seems to me that a belief in the fall of man may be tolerated in this era of liberty and liberality.

But Henry, impatient with the whole doctrinal approach, treated Charles's phrase "the fall of man" as referring to the fall of Adam, although he surely knew that both Charles and Edward had repudiated that doctrine. Or perhaps he simply thought the entire concept of inherent depravity was stultifying regardless of how it was explained. He answered:

I am annoyed that you go back to Adam for an adequate supply of sin to furnish the needs of the world. About here, we can have it fresh, first class, too, manufactured on the spot. . . . The fact is Adam's sin is like stale yeast, not fit to rise. . . .

In all sobriety—just now among thinking unchurchly men, and among many ministers, the choice is between Evolution and Infidelity. I prefer the former. The whole force of organized religion has been directed to *Fear and Conscience.* In a low and barbarous condition this works well. It is time that as much *power* upon the soul should be developed from the higher religious sentiments, hope, trust, faith, Love, as from its basilar powers.

Written when Henry was seventy-one, it sums up both his views and his nature. It was a sweeping rejection of all the Puritan remnants in Charles's view; but it was also the kind of attitude that would lead, some fifty or sixty years later, to such ministerial best-sellers as Norman Vincent Peale's *The Power of Positive Thinking.*

But Charles was too deep in his own visions to be converted. In 1885, turning seventy himself, he came back to New England, stayed briefly in Georgetown again, and then for a number of years served in a Scotch-Irish community in Wysox, Pennsylvania. Finally, in 1893, he returned to Georgetown and the home of one of his daughters. For a time he worked on the spiritual biography of his brother Edward. It was a lofty, mystically sympathetic account, so attuned to Edward's thinking that one hardly knows what is Edward's and what is Charles's. But America, rushing forward to wealth and power, had no time for a brother's homage to an almost forgotten preacher, and he never tried to publish it.

In his retirement, even as he watched the strange and wonderful developments of the 1890s and read widely in the literature of the period, his own thought-world flowed on, as uncurbed as ever. His last work, *Patmos; or, the Unveiling,* is an interpretation of the book of Revelation, that tantalizingly mysterious section of the New Testament written, it is said, by Saint John on the Greek island of Patmos. In its use of cryptic symbols—Dragon, Lamb, Harlot, Tiger—to describe the conflict between Satan, said to represent the pagan Roman world of Saint John's day, and God, it was the perfect fuel for Charles's imagination. Borrowing Biblical tone and imagery, Beecher's book is at times a blend of abstruse analysis and mystical prophecy, ending in a vision of heaven at once Byzantine and Victorian:

Cloudland above cloudland, thick sown with incandescent angel-forms, like fireflies in a tropic night! No frost in that electric city, even to the surface of the atmospheric sea. . . . The delicate network walls of filmy gold, the diamond panes, shut out frost and shut in millions of spirit song-birds. . . . The posts and bars and sash of that aviary intangible but infrangible; geometric lines without thickness, mathematical points of force without magnitude; planes of electric magnetic action, the continental cube ethereal, yet stronger than steel or adamant, sparkling, flashing, blazing, phosphorescent . . . and in the center the cherub-borne throne, with thunder-voice, saying, "Holy, holy, holy!" and throned elders responding, "Thou has redeemed us by thy blood, and we are reigning on the earth!"

Mixed incongruously with these outpourings are comments on contemporary life, ranging from the marvels of science to the anti-Christian attitudes of the foremost thinkers and writers of the English-speaking world, including Arnold, Browning, Carlyle, Darwin and Hardy in England, and Emerson, Whitman and Henry James in America. Most prophetic is his conviction that both evolution and socialism will rob religion of its moral force. Evolution, he writes, takes away "deep conviction of sin, and thus seems to shield the mind from . . . the displeasure of God. The human race, according to this philosophy, is not a fallen race but a risen or rising race. Guilt is simply undeveloped growth. The devil is arrested development. Man is not blameworthy; he is the victim of environment." Marxist determinism, he declares, has much the same effect: it asserts that the causes of man's woe are

external—society, nature, environment; not internal, not innate guilt. . . . There is no inborn sin. The soul enters life pure, and is corrupted by the general system . . . hence it is our duty to reorganize society in all its parts, so that it will not corrupt the soul. This is socialism.

At the same time Sigmund Freud in Vienna was pursuing the studies that would lead him to at least one strikingly parallel conclusion: that instinctual urges and desires, not external forces, that the psyche, not society, is the key to human behavior.

Charles Beecher died in 1900, fully prepared to enter the realm he had come to know so well in his visions.

Beginning as an idealistic youth who yearned to be a musician and a poet but was made into a minister through the influence of his entire family, Charles Beecher emerged, not surprisingly, as an individualistic, sometimes inspired and sometimes embattled clergyman. Caught between his native impulses and the standards of his church and time, he was a passionate disciple of Christ yet an "unsound" minister, a rejecter of dogma yet a believer in demons, a cosmic visionary yet a narrow moralist, a prophet of doom and yet a herald of the millennium. "In every soul," he wrote, "there is an invisible realm, a heavens and earth of thought. . . . This, if one can see it, is his home, his inner world." Charles Beecher had a fantastically rich inner world. Even more than his adored brother Edward, he led two lives: in one he was a barely appreciated pastor in Fort Wayne, Newark, Georgetown, Newport and Wysox; in the other he was an artist manqué, sailor of celestial seas, explorer of the primal origins of sin, mythmaker dreaming of a new God.

28

HARRIET BEECHER STOWE

"And now I rest me, like a moored boat"

More than one of their contemporaries thought that the Beechers some-times failed to distinguish between helping others and meddling. Certain-ly one of Lyman Beecher's legacies to his children was the habit of telling other people how to behave. It helped make his seven sons preachers and three of his daughters reformers. For the sons it became a profession; for the daughers it was an avocation but one that they pursued like a sworn duty.

That explains in part why Harriet Beecher Stowe thrust herself into the Byron affair—which, in the opinion of many, tarnished her reputa-tion forever. It began inconspicuously enough when the aged Countess Guiccioli, who in the 1820s had been Byron's last mistress, published in 1868 a book, *My Recollections of Lord Byron*. A dull work, it would have been promptly forgotten if it had not revived the story that Lady Byron's cold and prudish nature had driven the poet into exile, bitterness and death. Harriet read the British reviews and then the book itself and raged: it was unbearable that a debauched woman should exalt her licen-tious lover and besmirch the saintly woman, now dead almost ten years, whom Harriet had come to know and adore. When no one protested, she could not contain her fury: the result was an article, "The True Story of Lady Byron's Life."

She began by recalling Byron's glorious reputation even in the small towns of America in the 1820s. She told of the dismay caused by his separation from his wife and how his verses on their parting—

> Fare thee well and if forever,
>   Still forever, fare thee well,
> Even though unforgiving, never
>   'Gainst thee shall my heart rebel. . . .

were put to music and were sung by weeping schoolgirls. The truth, Harriet went on, was that from the very day of their wedding, Byron's treatment of his young bride was fiendish in its cruelty and culminated in his revealing to her his love affair with a "blood relation"—his married half sister, Augusta Leigh. Although heart-stricken, Lady Byron hoped still to live with Byron. But Byron, according to Harriet, was simply infuriated by his wife's patience and goodness and, with Augusta at his side, ordered his wife and their infant daughter out of the house. He then left England forever.

Lady Byron, trying desperately to find some excuse for his behavior—so Harriet claimed—spoke of the strain of insanity in his family. She also believed that his Scottish Calvinist upbringing had proved, "as it often does in sensitive minds, a subtle poison," leaving Byron permanently hostile to Christianity.

In the next few years, Harriet claimed, Byron indulged in every kind of vice, shamelessly wrote poems on incestuous unions, as in *Manfred,* and pictured his wife as a marble-hearted woman. Meanwhile Lady Byron selflessly devoted herself to their daughter and even befriended Augusta Leigh and the "unfortunate child of sin" whom Augusta bore.

But then, Harriet wrote, Byron's death in the war for Greek independence made him a hero throughout Europe, and not one of his friends who knew the "secret" would disclose it, especially while Byron's daughter by Lady Byron was still alive. For her part, Lady Byron bore her humiliation in a noble silence. She never revealed her secret because she still loved Byron and because, she explained to Harriet, "There was the angel in him." She also nurtured a pious hope that his soul had been redeemed. According to Harriet, Lady Byron filled the rest of her days with acts of charity—until that moment, ten years before, when a new edition of Byron's works threatened to revive the old stories. Then, meeting Mrs. Stowe and feeling at once an almost mystical communion with her, she made the visitor from America the trustee of her secret.

Such was Harriet's sensational story. Calvin and others, perceiving the shock and anger her charges would cause, warned her against publishing it. But it had already become a sacred mission, and in the fall of 1869, overriding all objections, she placed it in the *Atlantic Monthly* and, in London, in *Macmillan's Magazine.* Calvin was right. The reception given the article on both sides of the Atlantic was, with some notable exceptions, nothing less than ferocious, consisting entirely, her son Charley said, of pitiless criticism and brutal insults. Typical was a cartoon showing a witchlike crone scrambling up the legs of a noble statue of Byron, leaving marks of filth wherever she touched it. A review in the *Independent,* where she had so often appeared herself, called the article revolting, obscene, garbage. Some said it was merely scandal-mongering gossip; others declared it was in keeping with Mrs. Stowe's well-known adulation of English nobility, a vicious attack on a great poet who could not defend himself, a gullible acceptance of the delusions of a rejected wife, and inexcusable because utterly without proof.

The reaction, and especially the charge that it was Harriet who was being obscene, reflected a characteristic Victorian wish to keep any evidence of aggressive sexuality out of sight. Behind the British response was also resentment that an American should presume to indict the morals of an English genius. The result was a twofold prudery: Harriet denouncing Byron's licentiousness and the critics denouncing her for dragging the affair into print.

In an editorial, the *Independent* announced:

It is with regret that we employ the columns of a journal in which Mrs. Stowe has been a familiar contributor . . . to utter a protest against her . . . horrible tale concerning Lord Byron. Startling in accusation, barren in proof, inaccurate in dates [Harriet had said the Byrons were married two years; it was one year], infelicitous in style, and altogether ill-advised . . . her strange article will . . . everywhere evoke against its author the spontaneous disapprobation of her life-long friends.

The *Atlantic* was shaken almost to the point of collapse by the number of readers who canceled their subscriptions. Driven frantic, especially by the clamor for proof, Harriet finally refused to read any more criticism of her article. "I thought," she wrote to Susan Howard, "the world's people must have all lost their senses—or I. . . ."

Then came a letter from her old friend and faithful admirer Oliver Wendell Holmes, quietly pointing out that besides Lady Byron's testimony, there was the evidence of Byron's shocking behavior, the revealing passages in his poems, his self-accusations, and the fact that the story had not been contradicted by those most likely to know the truth.

That was all Harriet needed; she was once again the crusading author of *Uncle Tom's Cabin*, doing battle for truth and justice, a woman, as she told Annie Fields, with a message from the Most High. Remarkably like Catharine defending Delia Bacon, she became the champion of wronged womanhood, the one friend who dared to speak out, come what might.

She had other motives. At last she could pay back Byron for having seduced her into adoring him and then leaving her ashamed of herself when she learned that he was a libertine. It never occurred to her that even if Lady Byron was not the rigid prude she was reputed to be, she had no public significance except as Byron's wife, that Byron's vices were well known and in the long run of little importance, and that it was pointless for a stranger, forty-five years after the event, to make such a fuss about a marital relationship.

Again like Catharine in the Bacon imbroglio, Harriet, now more militant than ever, decided to write a book about the affair. With the help of husband Calvin, sister Isabella and a crew of lawyers and literary advisers, she put together *Lady Byron Vindicated* (1869), intending it, she said, to fall like a bombshell among her critics. But the book proved to be little more than an expansion of the article and underscored the lack of proportion between her aim and the effort to achieve it. She had used a bomb to kill a fly.

If the affair merited any notice from Harriet, it should have been a letter to a paper simply recounting what Lady Byron had told her. Instead, puffed up at the thought that a highborn Englishwoman had entrusted to her, and her alone, the secret of a heinous sin, she could not resist climbing into the Beecher pulpit and telling the world about it. Some modern biographers of Byron believe that he did have a love affair with his half sister and may even have married to cover his tracks, but the evidence remains inconclusive.

If we judge Harriet's effort by its effect, it was a fiasco, leaving Lady Byron as unimportant as ever and Byron the unregenerate spirit he was always known to be. The episode would in time be forgotten and Harriet's books would continue to sell, but her reputation would never be the same. Even among those who had never heard of the Lady Byron affair, Harriet Beecher Stowe's name acquired overtones of righteousness and Mrs. Grundy. Convinced that she had done what she had to do in the eyes of God, Harriet insisted to the end of her life that she regretted not a word of *Lady Byron Vindicated*.

Barely six years after the Stowes had moved into Oakholm, Harriet conceded that the house had been a mistake. Not only had it given them endless trouble and expense, but the neighborhood had deteriorated woefully, with slums and factories closing in around the house and the once beautiful Park River becoming so filthy that it was called Hog River. So Harriet put the house up for sale and early in 1870 left for Florida.

The home in Mandarin became a precious sanctuary for both Harriet and Calvin, and from 1866 to 1884 they spent as much as six months a year there. Calvin with his great white beard, black skullcap and gold-headed cane would settle his huge bulk—his tailor told him he measured almost four feet in circumference—into his rocking chair on the veranda and, with a basket of books in sundry ancient languages at his side, move as little as possible.

After a while, tourists in droves were brought up the river from Jacksonville to see the home of the celebrated Mrs. Harriet Beecher Stowe. When the visitors were congenial Calvin enjoyed talking to them. But sometimes one of them was an oaf. Such a one broke a branch off an orange tree in front of the house. "You ruthless little varlet," Calvin roared, "get off this place as fast as you can travel!" When the man muttered, "I thought this was Harriet Beecher Stowe's place," Calvin shouted, "So it is, and I'll have you know I'm the proprietor of Harriet Beecher Stowe and of this place!" One woman ventured up on the veranda; when she realized that Calvin was sitting there, she said, "But I would have preferred to meet Mrs. Stowe." "So would I," Calvin answered. "So would I—a thousand times."

Often there were guests from the North, but with one of the twins, Hattie, doing the housekeeping—Eliza did the same in Hartford—and three black servant girls, Harriet was usually free to go on rambles, or on excursions up the river in a neighbor's boat, or to paint, or to work on sketches for another book, *Oldtown Fireside Stories*. As often as ever she slipped into reveries so deep that she forgot where she was. A daughter of the Cranes, the Stowes' neighbors in Mandarin, recalled that Mrs. Stowe sometimes wandered through their house and out again without uttering a word.

For this easy way of life Harriet salved her Puritan conscience by doing a little missionary work: she persuaded the Freedman's Bureau to put up a building that would serve as a school on weekdays and an Episcopal church on Sundays, and she boasted in her letters about Calvin's sermons and the pleasure that she was sure the services gave to both blacks and whites of the neighborhood.

Only rarely did an unfriendly recollection of *Uncle Tom's Cabin* intrude. Amanda M. Brooks, a popular writer of the day, tells of attending in 1878 a church in Jacksonville where Calvin was to preach. When "Mr. and Mrs. Uncle Tom" entered, a few people immediately walked out, even though, as Mrs. Brooks reported, Mrs. Stowe looked quite harmless: "Three snowy curls on each side of her face gave her a matronly look, and her stout-built frame . . . a substantial appearance." Calvin preached and, Mrs. Brooks noted, Mrs. Stowe fell asleep. Meanwhile, each year Harriet's superintendent shipped thousands of oranges north in crates emblazoned: "ORANGES from Harriet Beecher Stowe, Mandarin, Florida." She would learn too late that northern Florida was unsuitable for raising frost-sensitive fruit.

Along with Henry Ward, Harriet now invested in the *Christian Union* and began to contribute to it together with other members of the clan. From a series of "letters" she sent to the paper in the next two years she assembled *Palmetto Leaves,* a chatty little book on living and farming in northeastern Florida. (One of the earliest pieces of publicity from Florida, it will come as a surprise to those who think of the state as *terra incognita* before the land boom of the 1920s.) Harriet would never get over the "rugged savageness of beauty" around Mandarin and wrote shamelessly to sleet-and-ice-bound Northerners of yellow jessamine in January, moss-hung live oaks, mockingbirds, the radiance of orange trees in full fruit and giant magnolias in flower. With missionary enthusiasm she dismissed the drawbacks: fierce midday heat for many months, swamps, malaria, insects. More and more each fall, she and Calvin could hardly wait to go south. Moving was always a trial, with Calvin invariably packing as many books and as few clothes as possible and Harriet so absentminded that once, as the carriages drew up to the door, Hattie found her mother in the back garden absorbed in painting.

Mandarin was lotus land, what Harriet called her "calm isle of Patmos"—escape not only from New England weather but from obligations, appeals and the proddings of conscience. To her brother Charles, who had settled in the northwestern part of the state, near Tallahassee, she said after a beautiful spring in Mandarin: "It is enough to make a saint out of the toughest old Calvinist. . . . How do you think New England theology would have fared if our fathers had been landed here instead of on Plymouth Rock?" She never seems to have noted how easily she succumbed to this untamed Eden or the irony of her having become its most famous citizen; here even the wartime rancors seemed far away in time and space.

When they went back north in June—only because they had a house in Hartford that must be lived in—they again left son Fred behind. Despite all his parents' prayers and the influence of May Osborne, a young women to whom he was engaged, Fred had no more control than ever over his addiction. He would be sober for a week or two or three, raising the family's hopes, then would vanish and come back blind drunk. By 1871, life, he wrote to his mother, had become unbearable:

I cannot live on shore and did I only think of my own comfort I would kill myself and end it all but I know that you and all the family would feel the disgrace such an end would bring upon you and the talk and scandal it would give rise to. . . . I am willing to serve . . . the rest of my life in the navy rather than to live on shore subject to this continual torment and fear of falling into a sin I hate and despise but before which I seem to be powerless. . . . I know it will be said that I have not tried but I do not care what they say.

Finally, early in the summer of 1871, after a visit to Charleston, Fred announced that he had signed on for a voyage around Cape Horn to Chile and San Francisco. Months later his companions reported that he stayed with the ship until San Francisco but sought out liquor there. They tried to get him to a hotel but he slipped away and was never seen again. The police could find no trace of him. As he had hoped, he created no scandal and no shame. Even sorrow was postponed in case he should turn up. There was only pity and, for his mother and father, an emptiness that nothing would ever fill. Harriet never gave up the hope that he would someday return.

In *My Wife and I* and its sequel, *We and Our Neighbors,* Harriet created a character named Bolton who is altogether admirable except for dread bouts of drunkenness; but there Harriet described his intemperance as a sickness, not a sin.

When Edward Everett Hale, editor of the magazine *Old and New,* asked Harriet to do a novel of "domestic life," she soon consented. She did so partly because it was a new direction for her—an opportunity to deal with life in the big city as seen by a daughter of New England, a relatively contented wife and mother and a faithful Christian. Whether she liked the work or the money, or both, she wrote not one but three novels of New York society. Although they do display her versatility, they remain minor works, with two of them, *Pink and White Tyranny* and *We and Our Neighbors,* hardly more than potboilers. She obviously used the novel form only because it was popular and because she felt free—too free—to manipulate it to suit her purposes.

She proclaimed her motives: speaking of *Pink and White Tyranny,* she wrote to Hale: "I design to show the domestic oppression practiced by a gentle pretty pink and white doll on a strong-minded generous gentle-man who has married her in a fit of poetical romance . . . and being to some extent a woman's rights woman . . . I shall have a right to say a word or two on the other side." As though candor would make the novel's shortcomings—and excesses—acceptable, the introduction announces it as a story with a moral. "It will send you off," she wrote, "as edified as if you had been hearing a sermon."

The two central characters serve mainly to point the moral. John Seymour, a high-minded, straitlaced lawyer from a rich New England family, marries Lillie Hess, a "pink and white doll," pampered by her middle-class parents, devoted to parties, clothes and flirtations, all of which Harriet deplores but describes in zestful detail. Having titillated her loyal women readers with glimpses of the life of a pleasure-loving, sexually glamorous woman, Harriet consoles them by showing that Lillie is vain, lazy and deceitful. Even worse, she dislikes babies, hates home-making and tries to win back an old suitor who has neglected her. She is in short the embodiment of any number of qualities that both the Puritan and the genteel tradition abhorred. She is also, by the same tokens, too naughty to be true.

The husband, constantly brought to heel by his wife's sulking and tears, continues to forgive her faults until, when his business fails, she suggests that he should ignore his creditors. This is evidently the last straw; he admits to his sister Grace, a model of wholesome, serious-minded New England womanhood, his dreadful mistake. She, surely speaking for Harriet, takes a kind of reverse women's rights position, saying that it is men who spoil the Lillies and turn them into selfish creatures, "perpetual children," and "everybody's toy." Lillie, Grace says, is simply a moral invalid who must be cared for like any sick person. Here Harriet makes one point of her parable: reformers are unwise to clamor for easy divorce because women like Lillie, once cast off, are "broken-winged butterflies" that inevitably "sink into the mud of the streets." That is why Christ, weak woman's great protector, made the law of marriage irrevocable. So Harriet condemns Lillie but denies John Seymour the right to a divorce. Once again she converts a social issue into a matter of sin. The main victim is her novel.

Of course John remains with Lillie and is rewarded when, after bearing him three children, she dies repentant. With John as the Christian Gentleman and Lillie as the Heartless Coquette, *Pink and White Tyranny* is a Victorian morality play. It weighs the mores and manners of the big city in the scales of Harriet's native New England and finds them sadly wanting. In Lillie Hess in particular Harriet summed up her disapproval of the liberties young women were taking with the Christian virtues.

In one of Harriet's New York novels, a magazine writer declares: "We talk to a *blasé,* hurried, unreflecting, indolent generation, who want emotion and don't care for reason. Something sharp and spicy, something pungent and stinging—no matter what or whence." Convinced that she was catering to just such an audience, Harriet plunged into another novel of New York society, *My Wife and I; or, Harry Henderson's History.* Sprinkling her pages with the slangy, bantering dialogue of young journalists, and the gossip and smart talk at New York parties, she sought to capture the excitement as well as the pitfalls and pressures of the upper crust of the postwar metropolis. And since the "new woman" was the talk of the town, at least in sophisticated circles, with Mrs. Stanton and Miss Anthony lighting fireworks in their journal *The Revolution,* The Woodhull tossing bombs in her *Weekly,* and sister Isabella issuing her historic "Declaration and Pledge" on behalf of woman suffrage, Harriet made the position of women a central theme.

Harriet was actually of two minds on the women's rights movement and its leaders. As the most successful professional woman in America, she was, like Catharine, a supporter of a woman's right to an independent career and to equality with men in education and work. But as a woman who had achieved success without sacrificing femininity, respectability or piety, she was nettled and shocked by the "ultra" feminists who tolerated or even advocated free love and campaigned militantly for their rights.

Saucily she opened *My Wife and I* with a challenge, making Harry, the narrator, declare: "I trust that Miss Anthony and Mrs. Stanton, and all the prophetesses of our day, will remark the humility and propriety of my title. It is not *I and My Wife*—Oh no! It is *My Wife and I*. What am I, and what is my father's house, that I should go before my wife in anything?" I will deal, Harry continues, with the oldest and sweetest form of Christian union—marriage. He is aware that it had lately been treated as a far from sacred or indissoluble partnership, one in which the parties have "the liberty of giving three months notice, and starting off to a new firm.... It is not thus," he concludes, "that we understand the matter."

Harry is a minister's son from the mountains of New Hampshire— just as Harriet was a minister's daughter from the hills of Litchfield— who comes to New York to make his way as a journalist. He is a Horatio Alger hero, honest, ambitious, pure-minded and so attached to his mother that he describes himself—as no young man would dream of doing—as "a mother's boy." Even before he leaves for New York he gets a taste of the new way of the world: an attractive girl rejects him because he is poor. He gets another shock when his cousin Caroline, an intelligent and independent young woman, envying his freedom of action, exclaims, "A woman's lot! and what is that, pray? to sit with folded hands and see life drifting by—to be a mere nullity, and endure to have my good friends pat me on the back, and think I am a bright and shining light of contentment in woman's sphere?" As for marriage, her fate is to be put up on exhibition, she says, for the eligible men of the neighborhood—"men who want wives as they do cooking stoves." She would rather scrub floors for a living. So, she concludes, "you are sure to find me ten or twenty years hence a fixture in this neighborhood, spoken of familiarly as 'old Miss Caroline Simmons,' a cross-pious old maid.... She held her head too high and said 'No' a little too often." If you get to be a prosperous editor, she tells Harry, "speak for the dumb, for us whose lives burn themselves out into white ashes in silence and repression." Unfortunately Harriet does not sustain the brave thrust of this passage: she allows Caroline to free herself, go off to study medicine in Paris and eventually unite with a man she respects and loves. Even this was less a triumph of women's rights than the happy ending favored by magazine fiction.

Harry's first experiences as a journalist give Harriet a chance to deplore the commercialism and rivalries of the magazine world. A rather wooden character, Harry soon loses his naive illusions about publishers but is consoled when he accidentally falls in with Eva Van Arsdel, the charming and beautiful daughter (all Harriet's heroines, unlike Harriet herself, are divinely pretty, just as all her heroes are, unlike Calvin, handsome) of the wealthy Van Arsdels.

Mr. and Mrs. Van Arsdel and their four daughters represent different views of the rights of women. Eva realizes that as a rich young woman she is part of the "only aristocracy privileged to live in idleness"; compared to Lillie Hess she is an angel, but an angel without duties or functions. Eva's older sister Ida, perhaps because she is the plainest of the daughters, is a purposeful young woman who goes on living a simple life devoted to serious study. ". . . there's the old Puritan broken loose in Ida," Eva observes. "She don't believe any of their doctrines, but she goes on their track." Ida is, much like Harriet herself, of the "moderate party," wanting equality in work but opposed to giving women the vote until they are "educated" for it.

Mr. Van Arsdel, anticipating by a dozen years Howells's classic portrait, in *The Rise of Silas Lapham,* of the self-made American, is a farm boy who has become a successful businessman. Characteristically, his reaction to "woman's rights" is that "good women" are not meant to govern in this wicked world and certainly not to enter politics, lest they be "covered with dirt" and "torn to shreds." Only a "brazen tramp" could survive that. You don't let a baby, he concludes, play with matches and gunpowder. Although he thinks that all the show and luxury around him is "humbug," he indulges his womenfolk without qualms. He fulfills the American dream—from farmhouse to Fifth Avenue in one generation—but he has also gone, Harriet seems to say, from frugality to waste, from women who ran their homes with faculty to daughters who are, with the exception of Ida, cage birds.

Much as she may frown on idle young women, Harriet reserves her harshest thrusts for the Woman's Rights extremists. Because he has written a few articles on the "modern woman," Harry is invited to the salon of Stella Cerulean. Modeled, according to some, on Elizabeth Cady Stanton but in various way more like Harriet's half sister, Isabella, Mrs. Cerulean is a handsome, brilliant woman, full of enthusiasm and charm. She is convinced that women are gifted—as all men have told her she is—with divine inspiration: her whole set is filled with "the spirit of martyrdom, without any precise idea of how to get martyred effectually." Many of them depend on spiritualist communications to guide them, but each brings a different message. All agree that in the good times to come "nobody was ever to do anything he did not want to do." Warming to the attack, Harry compares the radical feminists to the Illuminati who helped foster the French Revolution, except that the French were elegant and cultured whereas the Americans are gross, poorly educated and lacking in common decency.

But Stella Cerulean is only a flute compared to the clarion that is Audacia Dangyereyes (pronounced, we assume, either "Danger-eyes" or "Dang-yer-eyes"). Without warning, a dashing young woman in a "wicked-looking cap with nodding cock's-feather set askew on her head" bursts into Harry's room one day as he is writing and seats herself on his desk. As he gazes in dumb amazement, she introduces herself, announces that she has read his articles on women, and then, "stroking [his] shoulder caressingly," she adds, "you go for the emancipation of woman; but bless you, boy, you haven't the least idea what it means—not a bit of it, sonny, have you now? Confess!" While he stutters helplessly, she goes on:

"You've been asserting, in your blind way ... the rights of women ... to do anything that men do. Well, here comes a woman to your room who *takes* her rights.... I claim my right to smoke, if I please, to come up into your room ... and have a good time with you, if I please, and tell you that I like your looks, as I do. Furthermore to invite you to come to call on me at my room.... I've got the nicest little chamber that ever you saw.... Say, will you come round?"

So shocked is he that "Dacia" even gets him to subscribe to her paper, *The Emancipated Woman.* If there was any doubt that she was modeled on Victoria Woodhull with a bit of Victoria's sister Tennessee thrown in, the fact that she published such a paper quite settled the matter. Actually the portrait is a caricature. Harriet not only described a single scene of an obviously shocking kind but endowed Dacia with a coarseness and vulgarity that was sure to make her offensive to *Christian Union* readers. Long afterward, Benjamin Tucker, publisher of libertarian journals, recalled the first meeting in his love affair with Victoria Woodhull; she did take the initiative but she was so charming that he was enchanted. He soon wearied of the Bohemian disorder of her life but he remained deeply grateful to her. So Harriet was guilty of distortion not only in the portrait of Dangyereyes, but in making her foil, Harry, a priggish "mother's boy."

To mitigate her attack on such moderate radicals as Mrs. Stanton and Isabella, who were after all as cultured as Harriet herself, she has a worldly-wise colleague of Harry's picture them as dupes of Dacia Dangyereyes. Jim Fellows says:

"Mrs. Cerulean don't see anything in Dacia's paper that, properly interpreted, need make any trouble; because you see, as she says, *everything ought to be love,* everywhere, above and below, under and over, up and down, top and side and bottom, ought to be *love,* LOVE. And then when there's general all-overness and all-throughness, and an entire mixed-up-ativeness, then the infinite will come down into the finite, and the finite will overflow into the infinite, and, in short, Miss Dacia's cock's feathers will sail right straight up into heaven and we shall see her cheek by jowl with the angel Gabriel, promenading the streets of the new Jerusalem."

It was a wicked mocking not only of the visionaries and romantic reformers who filled the communal utopias of the period but also of the "love" litany of the Tilton-Beecher circle.

Harry Henderson not only climbs quickly to the top as an editor but wins Eva Van Arsdel—just the reward Horatio Alger's novels would soon be promising every poor but upright and industrious American youth. Harriet also sought to teach rich girls a lesson by making Eva decide to have a modest wedding and live in a small house on an "unfashionable street." All these amiable examples of virtuous behavior made *My Wife and I* so popular that it doubled the circulation of the *Christian Union* and then quickly sold fifty thousand copies in book form.

As a full-time novelist, Harriet was now constantly seeking material for her stories. After a meeting with Thomas Bailey Aldrich, then a young magazine editor, and his wife, she decided that Mrs. Aldrich was someone she might use in a novel. So she announced to Aldrich that she would like to visit his wife. The prospect of being weighed and tested by the famous Mrs. Stowe left Mrs. Aldrich somewhat unnerved. When the author arrived at the Aldrich summer cottage in Portsmouth, New Hampshire, hot and thirsty from a ride on a crowded train, Mrs. Aldrich mixed her a pitcher of ice-cold claret cup. Soon—too soon perhaps—the pitcher was empty and Mrs. Stowe, complaining that the room was tilting and bobbing dizzily, had to lie down on a couch. In a moment she was sound asleep. As Mrs. Aldrich recalled years later:

Women still wore hoops or reeds in their skirts; and, in lying on the sofa, Mrs. Stowe's skirts . . . "flew up," revealing very slender ankles and feet encased in prunella boots, the elastic V at the sides no longer elastic but worn and loose. The stockings were white, and the flowery ribbon of the garter knot was unabashed by the sunlight.

After a few hours, Mrs. Aldrich, expecting her husband at any moment, tried to drape a scarf over Mrs. Stowe's skirt. Startled, Mrs. Stowe cried, "Why did you do it? I am weak, weary and warm. . . . Let me sleep." When Mrs. Aldrich called attention to her skirt, Harriet declared: "I won't be any properer than I have a mind to be." But she finally rose and adjusted her clothes. The following morning as she kissed Mrs. Aldrich goodbye, she indicated that she probably would not model a character on her hostess after all.

Harriet allowed herself no rest. In her sixtieth year she published two of her "society novels," as well as the collection of *Oldtown Fireside*

Stories, and several long stories for holiday issues of the *Christian Union*. It is hardly surprising that at the end of the year, while on a trip to New York, she wrote to her daughers that she felt like the poor woman

> Who always was tired
> 'Cause she lived in a house
> Where help wasn't hired,

And as she lay dying,

> She folded her hands
> With her latest endeavor,
> Saying nothing, dear nothing,
> Sweet nothing forever.

But far more tiring spiritually was the need, more and more often, to face the sickening rumors concerning Henry Ward. When she met with him during her regular late-summer vacation at the Twin Mountain House she poured out her anger at the rumormongers and urged him to confront them with a shattering denial. But he insisted, puzzlingly, that the best policy was to ignore them. His attitude even persuaded her to preface the book version of *My Wife and I* with a disclaimer—perhaps the first of its kind—declaring, not very convincingly, that none of the characters in it was based on any living person.

Then at the end of the year word came that Isabella, believing herself inspired by God through the medium of Victoria Woodhull, was threatening to go to Plymouth Church and expose Henry in order to save him from himself. As the most influential sister, Harriet was called on to stand guard at services in the church. Isabella did not carry out her threat, but it was the beginning of a painful rift between her and her older brothers and sisters.

Encouraged by the success of *My Wife and I*, Harriet undertook a sequel, *We and Our Neighbors; or, The Records of an Unfashionable Street*. The story of how Harry and Eva set up house on New York's lower West Side, it is a kind of middle-class counterpart of the earlier society novels. Once again, it appeals to an audience of women in its chatty details of household arrangements, clothes, and the courtship of Eva's sisters, and in its complete neglect of all male activities. In a rather forced attempt to present the ethnic variety of the city, the novel samples the problems of two old Dutch women, relics of New York's past, and of the Hendersons' Irish cook. The cook's daughter, Maggie, following the classic Victorian fate of young women who sin, has been seduced, abandoned and thrust into a "house of evil." Everyone is baffled by this tragedy except Eva, who single-handedly rescues Maggie with kind treatment and Christ-like compassion. The only male given much attention in *We and Our Neighbors* is St. John, the local Episcopal minister. A delicate young man, he had been driven into "agonized convulsions" by the "sterile chillness" of Calvinism in his native New Hampshire village. "To such a one the cool shades of the Episcopal Church, with its orderly ways, its poetic liturgy, its artistic ceremonies were as the shadows of a great rock in a weary land." He obviously reflects the path being taken by Harriet, her daughters, and other upper-middle-class men and women, especially in eastern cities. To some of them, such as Eva Van Arsdel, Episcopalianism served as a token observance, a fashionable halfway house in the secularizing of religion. St. John is drifting toward Catholicism when Harriet has him fall in love with Angelique, one of Eva's younger sisters. Given St. John's monkish tendencies, his capitulation to the dainty Angelique might seem rather improbable except that every man in Harriet's New York novels is the willing victim or, perhaps, beneficiary of the woman who sets her cap for him. Even the veteran journalist Bolton is saved from his enslavement to alcohol by Caroline Simmons.

This pattern has been taken as evidence of Harriet's scorn for men and, beyond that, the feminization of American life. Although this seems to be borne out by the assertion of Eva's domineering Aunt Maria that women do not need special rights because a woman can easily lead a man by the nose, it is a question how much of this was simply Harriet's flattery of her women readers.

Compared to the New England novels, which were the distillation of a lifetime, the New York novels are mainly evidence of Harriet's ability as a professional novelist to create popularly acceptable characters and scenes on the basis of scattered observations. The novels are best when Harriet turns her sharp eye and droll humor on everyday life, but they are fuzzy or thin when it comes to other than New England types or to unfashionable city people. With its loose structure, wandering focus, and its chapters on such themes as pet dogs and decorating a church for Christmas—authors were paid, after all, by the installment—*We and Our Neighbors* is plainly a book to be taken lightly and soon forgotten. In the *Nation*, a fastidious young critic named Henry James found it shapeless and full of vulgarisms as well as characters who do little but talk.

As the installments of *My Wife and I* in the *Christian Union* continued to flaunt Harriet's mockery of the Woman's Rights leaders, Victoria Woodhull began to boil and steam. First she invited Catharine Beecher for a carriage ride in Central Park (Catharine was an old foe of the suffragists but she had once told Isabella that Mrs. Woodhull was "a pure woman, holding a wrong theory") and relayed what she had heard

LORD BYRON

In 1869 Harriet Beecher Stowe's attack on Byron as a libertine—forty years after the poet's death—stirred a storm of criticism, including this savage cartoon in *Fun Magazine* depicting her as besmirching the poet's image.

THE ADVANCED WOMAN OF THE PERIOD.

"' You go for the emancipation of woman; but bless you, boy, you haven't the least idea what it means—not a bit of it, sonny, have you now? Confess?' she said, stroking my whiskers coaxingly."

A sketch from *My Wife and I* (1871), one of Harriet Beecher Stowe's New York society novels, illustrates the brazen behavior of an "advanced woman." Based on the notorious Victoria Woodhull, this characterization helped goad "The Woodhull" into her sensational charges against Henry Ward Beecher.

BEECHER'S THEORY AND PRACTICE

H.W.B.—"The man who can't live on bread and water is not fit to live!"

When in a thoughtless moment Henry Ward Beecher said that any man ought to be able to live on bread and water alone, the scandal sheets of the period pilloried him mercilessly.

Henry Ward Beecher's last summer home, built in 1878, was a formidable, many-gabled house on the Hudson near Peekskill.

Critical of her husband and strict with her children, Henry Ward Beecher's wife, Eunice, came to be known as "The Griffin."

In her later years Harriet Beecher Stowe continued to write tirelessly and sometimes memorably, especially about the New England types she knew so well.

Calvin Stowe in his seventies, rich in Biblical scholarship and stories of his New England boyhood, justified Harriet's references to him as "my old Rabbi."

The Stowes at their winter home in Mandarin in northeast Florida where they spent as much as six months a year from 1867 to 1884. From left to right: Eliza (one of the twin daughters), Harriet Beecher Stowe, Charles (a son), Calvin Stowe, Eunice Beecher, and Hattie (the other twin).

Amateur scientist and expert mechanic as well as a pioneer in building a community center church, "Father Tom" Beecher checked time by the sun, using his own instruments, and rode a splendid tricycle of his own devising.

of the relationship between Henry Ward and Lib Tilton. Catharine rejected the story instantly and angrily. The second warning from Woodhull was her open letter in May 1872 declaring that she would not be anyone's scapegoat and referring to "a public teacher of eminence" who was living in "concubinage" with the wife of another equally eminent teacher. Exasperated, Harriet continued to make unflattering references to "ultra" reformers.

A new kind of excitement entered Harriet's life late in 1872: a Boston lecture bureau proposed that she go on tour with readings from her books. Still influenced by the Biblical tradition that forbade women to speak in public, even in a church, she was frightened by the challenge. But she was also flattered and tempted. Serving as actors and entertainers as well as teachers, many lecturers—as Harriet surely knew from Henry's experience—won great popularity and earned large fees. Torn between fear and desire, Harriet wrote to Annie Fields: "My state . . . may be described by the phrase, 'Kind a'—love to—hate to—wish I didn't—want ter.' " But she finally succumbed and was soon scheduled to give readings in forty New England towns and cities at a rate of about three a week.

Her debut in Springfield, Massachusetts, was a failure. Gripped by stage fright, her voice weak, she gave a feeble performance. But she recovered quickly. Always an excellent mimic, she began to draw on her memories of her father's manner. In the Fieldses' house before a crucial reading in Boston's Tremont Temple, she called Annie into her room, brushed her hair straight back into a pompadour, struck a pose and said, "Look here, my dear . . . now I am exactly like my father when he was going to preach." Mrs. Fields added: "That reading was a great success. . . . It was the last leap of the flame which had burned out a great wrong." Harriet was soon vividly recreating scenes not only from *Uncle Tom's Cabin* but from *The Pearl of Orr's Island* and even episodes in rural dialect from Oldtown "fireside stories." When her voice failed to carry, the audience would come as close as possible, and afterward they would crowd forward to thank her and touch her and show her the children they had named after her. Once, from Portland, Maine, she wrote movingly to Calvin of a deaf woman who said to her, "I came jist to see you. I'd rather see you than the Queen." Each performance left her exhilarated but exhausted.

The tours became even more trying when Calvin fell ill. Conscience-stricken, Harriet began to look for another permanent home. She found it on Forest Street in the pleasant Nook Farm area of Hartford. This time she bought a house built a few years earlier, a modest place but comfortable enough, with high-ceilinged rooms, mahogany woodwork and a strip of garden roundabout. An additional attraction was a young neighbor, Mark Twain, whose first book, *Innocents Abroad*, had been a great success. Harriet had another link to Samuel Clemens and his wife, Olivia: they had been married by the popular Reverend Thomas K. Beecher in his church in Elmira, New York, where Olivia Langdon had grown up. Riding high, Clemens had built himself a splendid home, sparing no expense. Because an essayist-editor, Charles Dudley Warner, was also a neighbor, Hartford people were soon calling it the "Nook Farm Literary Colony." And nearby were Harriet's sisters Mary Perkins and Isabella Hooker. The Stowes would remain there for the rest of their lives.

Pleased by Mrs. Stowe's success, the lecture bureau asked her to make a western tour the following year. She agreed and worked her way through Illinois and Ohio, welcomed everywhere by sympathetic audiences. But she was so drained by the rides in crowded trains, the poor food, the dreariness of hotel rooms, and the readings themselves in great gaslit halls that in the end she wanted only to get back home. After an appearance in Washington, D.C., she went off to Mandarin and never lectured again.

She had another and far more disturbing reason for retreating to the South: in the November 2 issue of her *Weekly*, Victoria Woodhull had delivered the blow against Beecher and Tilton that she had long promised. For Harriet, with her acute sense of sin and her deep love of her brother, that newspaper article would mean years of helpless rage and humiliation. The idea that Henry of all people—trusting, loving, pure-souled Henry, America's model of the man of God—should be charged with secret lechery, and with a married woman, a mother and the wife of a friend, was intolerable. Her conviction that it was a wicked plot devised by jealous men and a vile woman did not console her when the trials began and the proud name of Beecher was dragged through the lurid headlines of scores of newspapers day after day. Even though she herself had told a friend several years before that many people hated Henry because of his popularity and hoped to see him brought low, she was totally unprepared for the degrading way it came about.

Frustrated by her inability to silence Henry's accusers, Harriet grew spiteful: When she heard that Victoria Woodhull and her sister had been released from jail on bail but had been prevented from renting an auditorium in Boston, she wrote to Annie Fields, "I am delighted that Boston has fought the good fight with those obscene birds so manfully." She added:

Did I tell you that here in Framingham lives the wife of that Colonel Blood whom this wretched woman has seduced and infatuated to be her tool and slave? Mrs. Blood is a lovely, dignified, accomplished woman. . . . Her husband, she tells me, was a young man of one of the best families in St. Louis . . . perfectly correct in all his habits and devoted to her and her child. This Woodhull woman set up in St. Louis as clairvoyant physician and Blood consulted her as to his wife's health. Immediately this wretch set her eye on him and never left practicing every diabolical art till she really got him to give up his family . . . to follow her in a life of infamy. . . . I do hope this pending trial will land The W. in the penitentiary.

Just as disturbing to Harriet was Isabella's support of Victoria Woodhull and the radical women's rights position. Pain and bitterness mingle in a letter to her daughter Eliza. Isabella and her children had so deeply wounded her, she wrote, that if Eliza had not reestablished relations with them, she herself would not have done so. Like many "monomaniacs," Harriet wrote, Isabella was all right until the wrong string was struck. She was not easily offended, she went on,

but there are things which strike my very *life* and these accusations against my brother are among them. I cannot hear that subject discussed as a possibility opened for inquiry without such an intense uprising of indignation and scorn and anger as very few have ever seen in me . . . but if ever I should hear those who ought to know better maundering out insinuations and doubts about him I think there will be the eruption of a volcano that has for years been supposed to be extinct.

It was an empty threat; the eruption would come from the enemy.

George Eliot's first book, *Scenes of Clerical Life,* had revealed a novelist with a grasp of the deepest springs of character. Sensing a kindred spirit, Harriet started a correspondence with her in 1869 and sent her a copy of *Oldtown Folks.* The parallels between the two women are worth noting: both came from intensely religious homes, both turned, belatedly, to writing novels—novels that often involved moral values— and both chose men who were noted scholars. The differences were equally marked: Eliot rejected conventional religion and became a rationalist and, disregarding public opinion, she went to live with a man, G. H. Lewes, who already had a wife and children.

Haunted by memories of her dead children, Harriet tried to share with Eliot her belief that spiritualism could make contact with the "spirit world." Repeatedly she offered the Englishwoman fragments of evidence, such as the story of a friend who, using a planchette, received long messages from Charlotte Brontë, and whose hand, presumably controlled by a literary spirit, wrote a sonnet while she was talking to Harriet's daughter. Evidently trying to convince herself as well as Eliot, she added:

To me this perfect wave that is going over the land, surging toward the other life is something inexpressibly affecting. . . . We have had a war that has put almost every family into mourning—and hence this sudden increase of spiritualism. It is the throbbing of the severed soul to the part of itself that has gone within the veil.

In her answer George Eliot complimented Harriet on her sympathetic treatment, in *Oldtown Folks,* of different attitudes toward religion, but she again dismissed the spirit-rapping aspect of spiritualism as "degrading folly." As early as 1860 Harriet had secretly corresponded with Robert Dale Owen after his *Footfalls on the Boundary of Another World* had created a stir among spiritualists. Now she greeted his second book, *The Debatable Land Between This World and the Next,* with an article in the *Christian Union.* A son of Robert Owen, the English socialist, Owen had begun his career as a reformer in utopian communities in the West and on radical journals in New York and had even published a daring book on contraception. He had then turned conservative and eventually served as a congressman from Indiana and as United States ambassador to Italy. Writing to Eliot after a lapse of two years, Harriet devoted most of her letter to recommending Owen's books. She also gave an account of a séance with one of the famous Fox sisters, complete with glowing lights and floating hands.

"In regard to all this class of subjects," she wrote, "I am of the opinion of Goethe that it is just as absurd now to deny the facts of spiritualism as it was in the middle ages to ascribe them to the Devil." Eliot agreed to read Owen's books even though the reports that she had had of spirit communication had come to her "in the painful form of the lowest charlatanerie." But she added that "apart from personal contact with people who get money by public exhibitions as mediums, or with semi-idiots such as those who make a court for a Mrs. _____ . . . I would not willingly place any barrier between my mind and any possible channel of truth affecting the human lot."

Calvin now joined the exchange. His own visions were as vivid as ever. Once when he thought that Harriet had gone away but he saw her moving about his study, he ignored her, thinking she was an apparition, until she startled him by speaking. At another time, the devil, apparently having heard how heartsick Calvin had been at the loss of three of his sons, came to him night after night in the guise of a horseman and tested his faith in God by shouting that his surviving son, Charley, then studying in Germany, was dead. "But I was ready for him last night," Calvin reported to a clergyman friend. "I had fortified myself with passages of Scripture . . . and when he came last night . . . I hurled them at him. I tell you it made him bark like a dog, and he took himself off. He won't trouble me again."

Thus when George Eliot spoke of her disgust at the sensation created in London by the American medium Daniel Hume, Calvin answered her. Harriet introduced him, writing: "My poor Rabbi sends you some Arabic [a reference to his handwriting] which I fear you cannot read. On *diablerie* he is up to his ears in knowledge, having read all things in all tongues, from the Talmud down." Calvin wrote: "I fully sympathize with you in your disgust with Hume and the professing mediums generally. Hume spent his boyhood in my father's native town ... and he was a disagreeable nasty boy. But he certainly has qualities which science has not yet explained and some of his doings are as real as they are strange."

More tolerant than Harriet, he went on: "I think you are a better Christian without church and theology than most people are with both, though I am ... a Calvinist of the Jonathan Edwards school." He added that he had "a warm side for Mr. Lewes on account of his Goethe labors," and concluded with a quaint vignette: "In 1830 I got hold of his *Faust* and for two gloomy, dreary November days, while riding through the woods of New Hampshire ... to enter upon a professorship in Dartmouth College, I was perfectly dissolved by it."

George Eliot replied gently but firmly that she still thought that such visions as Calvin's were of subjective origin—which remains just about the most sensible explanation of his peculiar faculty.

Perhaps because Eliot had deferred to her as a famous older woman with a rich experience of family life, Harriet was somewhat more critical of Eliot's novels than Eliot was of Harriet's work. Thus Harriet wrote of *Middlemarch:* "As art it is perfect, but art as an end, not instrument, has little to interest me." Coming from an author whose latest work was *Pink and White Tyranny,* it was a peculiarly patronizing comment. Maintaining the tone of mother confessor, she added: "I seem to feel that you exhaust yourself with too constant giving of your life forces to others and that you need a more positive communion with Him who is immortal youth, health, strength, and vitality."

An equally interesting exchange came after Harriet had read Eliot's *Daniel Deronda,* a novel of an adopted son of a titled English family who discovers that he is Jewish. Unlike Calvin, who, with his intimate knowledge of Jewish tradition and his friendship with a leading rabbi, was fascinated by the novel, Harriet found the emotions of Jews a "morass" (as a friend described it) through which she could not wade. Eliot's response was a scathing indictment of English racial prejudices. She had long been appalled, she said, by the coarse and shameful way the English made fun of Jews, forgetting that Christ, as well as many aspects of Christianity, was Jewish. Perhaps she was including Harriet when she said that this deadness to any kind of life not "clad in the same coat tails and flounces as our own lies very close to the worst kind of irreligion."

Meanwhile, like a plague, the Beecher-Tilton affair had spread into the courts, and the rumors, sickening as they had been to Harriet, were as nothing to the actual charges. Once again, in late August, Harriet, along with her sister Mary, communed with Henry at Twin Mountain House. In his humiliation, he wept. They talked and talked, but in the end the sisters knew little more than they had before, in part because Henry, typically, had stopped reading the newspapers, saying that if he read them he would not be able to carry on his work.

Harriet left for Mandarin in October, the earliest she had ever gone south. She was there when the climactic civil trial started in Brooklyn in January 1875. Unable to tolerate the prurience, the shameless suggestiveness of much of the newspaper reporting, she relied on her friend Susan Howard's letters. When Susan neglected to write for a few days, Harriet cried out in agony: "Faithful friend, cease not to write, for your letters are as cold water to a thirsty soul." She seems never to have doubted that Henry was innocent, but while the trial was in progress she held it up to Charley as a lesson in the dangers of worldly success. After a fierce attack on Bowen as "a consummate villain and hypocrite," too powerful and dangerous for Plymouth Church to expel, she wrote:

Dreadful as this trial is, I can see blessed fruits already. Your uncle has had a degree of worldly success. He has had power and wealth and worldly strength, so that a rabble was following him for loaves and fishes, using his name to sell quack medicines and him as a speculation. The Lord has lopped away all this worldly growth. None cling to him now but the really good. As to him, he was in danger of over self-confidence and of wandering into a naturalistic philosophy. . . . I do believe that this . . . crucifixion has so entirely subdued his will to God's that he is now in that blessed state of *rest* which comes from having given up self altogether.

It was of course only a pious hope; if Henry had changed, the change was only temporary.

It was not until a year later that Harriet was able to disclose what a frightful ordeal the trial had been for her. "This has drawn on my life— my heart's blood," she wrote to George Eliot. "He is myself; I know that you are the kind of woman to understand me when I say that I felt a blow at him more than at myself." Seeking to justify her faith in Henry, she added:

He is of a nature so sweet and perfect that, though I have seen him thunderously indignant at moments, I never saw him fretful or irritable—a man who continuously . . . is thinking of others . . . and that every sorrowful, weak, or distressed person looks to as a natural helper. . . . In all his long history there has been no circumstance of his relation to any woman that has not been worthy of himself—pure, delicate, and proper—and I know all sides of it.

Once more it was purely wishful thinking. Not having lived with Henry since their youth, she hardly knew "all sides of it."

Harriet's letters to her children had always been saturated with moral advice and pious exhortation. But when Charley returned from his theological studies at Bonn and found a pastorate in Saco, Maine, in 1878, Harriet came into her own as an evangelist—a preacher in all but the name. For years, in letters from ten to twenty pages long, all reminiscent of her father's, she discussed religious issues, sometimes with Biblical citations and often with feverish intensity. Whenever Charley voiced what Harriet called, with child-scaring imagery, the "bats wings" of "Rationalistic doubtings," she would assail him with all the ardor of a camp-meeting exhorter. Once he shocked her to her Calvinist roots by declaring that he despised "orthodoxy for its slovenly inconsistency and its dishonesty" and was thinking of becoming a Unitarian. Every vestige of her father's prejudices aroused in her, she cried out that nothing could be more dangerous for him than to fall into the hands of a "denomination of skeptics and rationalists," some of whom were barely Christians. Even Charley protested that her letters seemed to be written in a constant state of nervous excitement. Which stirred her to an even more heated reply.

Her evangelizing urge still not satisfied, she published *Women of Sacred History,* an ornate volume of biographical sketches padded out with sentimental verse by popular poets and saccharine chromolithographs. Somewhat more creditable was a collection of interpretations of the stages of Christ's life. It reveals a curious reason for her faith in the Virgin Birth: she sees Jesus as exclusively the child of a woman and thus capable of a sympathy with women that no ordinary man could achieve. The most appropriate image of Jesus, she said, surely thinking of the chromos she was fond of, was "one of those loving, saintly mothers . . . leading along their little flock."

Daughter Georgie, who had always been so spirited and gay, was now beset by such severe depressions as well as sleeplessness that she could not be left alone. A doctor prescribed morphine to quiet her down, and as often happened in such cases, she became addicted to the drug. So Harriet had a second dark secret to keep. Later, when Georgie and her husband moved to Boston, Georgie continued—apparently in spite of her nervous disorder—to enjoy late parties, wine and the company of actors and actresses.

Although they still troubled their mother by their lack of piety and active benevolence, the twins, now in their forties, continued to be a comfort. Confirmed spinsters, deprived, as twins, women and the daughters of a famous mother, of any distinct identity, they had resigned themselves to the shadow role of caretakers of the two Stowe households.

Harriet had long since ceased to close her letters on some such doleful note as: "If I live out the year," but she now often dwelt on images of death approaching. "I feel myself at last as one who has been playing and picnicking on the shores of life," she wrote to George Eliot, "and waked from a dream late in the afternoon to find that everybody, almost, has gone over to the beyond. And the rest are sorting their things and packing their trunks, and waiting for the boat to come and take them." It was a much more serene attitude than the earlier one, but almost as premature: she would live for another twenty years.

But the fountain of creativity was at last showing signs of drying up. *Poganuc People*, Harriet's last book of any consequence, is, even more than *Oldtown Folks*, an exercise in nostalgia. It apparently took all her strength to finish it, but she was still eager to please her audience. "Your mother is an old woman, Charley mine," she wrote to her son, "and it is best that she should give up writing before people are tired of reading her . . . but all, even the religious papers, are gone mad on serials . . . and I thought, since this generation will listen to nothing but stories, why not tell them?"

In *Poganuc People* she once again exploited the experiences of her Litchfield childhood, this time as seen through the eyes of little Dolly, one of the ten children of Parson Cushing. Dolly is a sentimentalized version of Harriet herself and the parson is a rather tame copy of Lyman Beecher. All the furrows and blemishes of life in New England are smoothed away or overlaid with recollections of Fourth of July celebrations, community apple bees and passages of country humor. As a wistful touch there is the now familiar episode in which the little girl longs to share the Christmas festivities of the Episcopalian children down the road.

But the book lacks the conflict and tension of *The Minister's Wooing* and, like Henry's *Norwood*, ignores the darker side of New England life. The result is a pleasant, relaxed piece of "regional fiction." The only challenging character is a farmer, another variation of Uncle Lot, so independent and contrary that he antagonizes even those who agree with him. (When he proposes moving the schoolhouse from a bare and windy hilltop, and no one takes action, he hitches his oxen to the building and drags it down the hill all by himself.) But even the farmer is almost a caricature; after his infinitely patient wife dies a holy death, he allows himself to be converted, with a large admixture of sentimentality, by little

Dolly—and promptly turns, like other crusty old codgers in Harriet's books, mellow and indulgent.

In one way *Poganuc People* does differ from Harriet's earlier New England novels: although the parson is treated with respect for the rigor of his principles, his daughter, as she grows up, turns to the Episcopal service as a gentler, more humane approach to God. So the novel reflects not only Harriet's own change of heart but the ebb of the entire Calvinist tide.

In May of that year Catharine died at brother Tom's home in Elmira. Harriet, in Mandarin, was perhaps not sorry that she could not be at the funeral, for there was still a coolness between her and Tom. And even though Catharine had been the "big sister" of her childhood and her collaborator on homemaking books, those were all fading memories, some of them not altogether happy.

When Harriet herself reached seventy, the *Atlantic Monthly* gave her a splendid party—she was the first woman to be so honored—in the garden of the summer home of William Claflin, former governor of Massachusetts. Holmes and Whittier and Aldrich and Howells and Bronson Alcott and other stars in New England's literary galaxy, as well as most of the Beechers were there. It was a memorable assemblage, the women in long dresses with bustles, the men in silk hats and high-buttoned tail coats, with the colored parasols and the stripes of the canvas marquee making a vivid pattern on the green of the broad lawn. Holmes, Whittier and others read poetic tributes, Henry Ward made a little speech, and finally Harriet said a few words, describing the happiness she had seen among some of the more independent blacks of Mandarin. She closed on a note that sounded curiously like the old Calvinist doctrine of predestination: "Let us never doubt. Everything that ought to happen is going to happen."

Harriet's fits of abstraction continued to embarrass her friends. Once when she and her son's wife, Susie, were visiting the Claflins, their hosts invited a distinguished group to meet her. But when the guests arrived Harriet was nowhere to be seen. Going to her room, Susie found her in bed. When Susie implored her to dress and come downstairs, Harriet declared that she had a headache and that, anyway, such important people really wouldn't miss her. She never did join the party.

But visitors with a mission, such as Frances E. Willard, a leader of the Women's Christian Temperance Union, found her kind and courteous. Miss Willard left a cameo-like portrait of her:

A little woman entered, seventy-five years old, decidedly under-size. . . . She was very simply attired in a dress of black-and-white check, with linen collar and small brooch; her hair . . . hung fluffily upon a broad brow and was bound by a black ribbon in front and gathered in a low knot behind. Her nose is long and straight, eyes dimmed by years, mouth large and with the long Beecher lip. . . . This is what time has left of the immortal Harriet Beecher Stowe.

Time had also mellowed her, allowing her at last to achieve a goal that she had long before—in a letter to Georgiana May—set for herself: "I love everybody," she told Miss Willard.

Not long afterward, Calvin, almost eighty, after a lifetime of complaining about imaginary ailments, fell ill: it was Bright's disease and incurable. The Stowes managed to get to Mandarin again that year, but it was the last time. Calvin lingered for two years, remaining as competent as ever to explain a Biblical text or tell a droll story. Harriet was at his side much of the time. "I think," she wrote to a friend, "we have never enjoyed each other's society more than this winter." Calvin died in August 1886 and was borne to the cemetery in Andover where their beloved Henry had been buried long years before.

In his ineptness and hypochondria, his visions and roly-poly bulk, Calvin Stowe cuts a rather quaint figure. But he was in fact a man of vigorous opinions and shrewd judgments, much sounder than Harriet in such matters as dealing with hostile British audiences during the war or in estimating the effect of her defense of Lady Byron. As the husband of a world-famous wife, he filled a difficult role admirably. In a time when such an attitude was rare, he encouraged her wholeheartedly in her career as a writer and he was a source of rich and colorful stories of New England life. He strongly influenced both Harriet and Henry Ward with his warm personal view of God and his scorn for theological controversy. And as a scholar and teacher he lived a life of his own.

Now death was truly taking over Harriet's circle, Henry Ward dying the following year and then Georgie losing, at forty-four, her struggle with illness and opiates. Fortunately Charley moved down from Maine to become the pastor—probably as arranged by Harriet—at a Hartford church. Among other tasks, he took over the preparation of an autobiography that Harriet had planned—and intended to call *Pebbles from the Shores of a Past Life*—but no longer had the will or the power to carry through. Once, as she was reading the letters she had assembled, she said to Charley:

It is affecting to me to recall things that strongly moved me years ago . . . when the occasion and the emotion have wholly vanished from my mind . . . those days when my mind only lived in *emotion*, and when my letters never were dated because they were only histories of the *internal*, but now that I am no more and never can be young in this world, now that the friends of those days are almost all in eternity, what remains?

Sad to say, the biography, too closely monitored by Harriet, is a spiritless collection of letters, dates, names and impersonal comments. It appeared in the fall of 1889 and her signature on the preface may be said to have marked the end of her life as others had known her. She was shortly afterward laid low, as though by a stroke, and although she recovered, she was never herself again.

It was just as well that she was out of touch with reality, for on her eightieth birthday only a few papers noted the occasion and some of them were condescending. To America of the 1890s she was a relic of the prewar world, a writer whose most famous book, now forty years old, seemed to be tied to a moment and to circumstances gone forever. Some felt that she had accidentally struck the right notes at the right time, and nothing more. It did not help her reputation that many of her other books were about a New England and a religion that seemed more and more local to a nation filling out with people from other cultures and other faiths. Finally, Americans had been exposed not only to such writers as Hawthorne, James, Emerson, Howells and Twain but to a dazzling constellation of European novelists from Dickens and Thackeray to Tolstoy, Dostoyevsky and Zola.

Harriet now sank into a kind of second childhood. Leaving behind all the works and challenges of a lifetime, including seven children and thirty-three books, she picked wildflowers (and sometimes the flowers in Mark Twain's greenhouse), played at random on an old piano, sang snatches of songs, and more than once ran out of the house to greet a stranger in uniform as her lost son Fred. At another time, when a delegation of ministers came to read a tribute to her, she grew restless and like an impatient child ran around behind the august reader and drummed on his back. Or, as Mark Twain reported, she would steal up behind some unsuspecting stranger and let out "a war whoop that would jump that person out of his clothes." A strong Irish woman was called in to attend her constantly but Harriet managed sometimes to steal away from her and might later be found wandering through a neighbor's house.

But occasionally she had completely lucid moments and on one of these in 1893 she wrote a luminous and remarkably self-aware letter to her old friend—himself eighty-four—Oliver Wendell Holmes. After declaring that she was always cheerful, she added:

My mental condition might be called nomadic. . . . I wander at will from one subject to another. In pleasant summer weather I am out of doors most of my time, rambling about the neighborhood, calling upon my friends. . . . Now and then I dip into a book much as a humming-bird, poised in air on whirring wing, darts into the heart of a flower, now here, now there, and away. Pictures delight me and afford me infinite diversion. . . . Of *music* I am also very fond. I could not have too much of it, and I never *do* have as much of it as I should like.

I make no mental effort of any sort; my brain is tired out. It was a woman's brain and not a man's. . . . And now I rest me, like a moored boat, rising and falling on the water, with loosened cordage and flapping sail.

With only her Irish nurse at her bedside, she died, simply worn out, on July 1, 1896, and was buried in the Andover cemetery between Calvin and Henry. Among the flowers on the casket was a wreath from Boston with a card that read: "From the children of Uncle Tom."

Henry's wife, Eunice, eighty-five, and Isabella Beecher Hooker, seventy-five, were at the funeral, but they did not speak to each other. Charles came, but Thomas could not make it. Edward had just died, William had gone seven years before, and Catharine, Henry and James were dead a decade or more. . . .

Mary was not there either. Major J. P. Pond, who had managed the lecture tours of Harriet and Henry as well as Mark Twain and had been a frequent visitor to Nook Farm in its golden days, was saddened to see what time had done to so gifted and shining a company. Hearing that Mary was still living close by, he visited her and reported that although ninety-one years old and an invalid, she was "bright and sparkling." The only Beecher without a special calling, talent or urge to change mankind, she had led an even-keeled and unsensational life. Was she sorry that she had been the only private member of a public family? Our only clue is her saying in her later years:

When I was a young woman I was known as the daughter of Lyman Beecher. In my middle age I was introduced as the sister of Harriet Beecher Stowe and Henry Ward Beecher. Now in my old age I am identified as the mother-in-law of Edward Everett Hale.

But she seems to have said this as much with pride as with regret; she still had no greater ambition than to live to be one hundred years old.

Harriet had started life with two disadvantages: she was the sixth of eleven children and she was a girl. In *My Wife and I* she describes the reception given Harry Henderson as the tenth child of a poor parson in New Hampshire. The neighbors said, "Poor Mrs. Henderson—another boy!" and his father said, "God bless him," and "returned to an important treatise which was to reconcile the decrees of God with the free agency of man and which [Harry's] entrance into the world had interrupted for some hours."

That she was a girl was inevitably disappointing to her father. All seven of her brothers were given the best available education and primed for an important place in the community; Harriet and her sisters received only a token education and were prepared mainly for housekeeping. Seeing no place for herself anywhere, Harriet turned to books and inward to dreams.

Equally important in those early years was her father himself. Despite his relentless efforts to save their souls, he won his children's love and respect, and as a leading preacher he was both a formidable father figure and God's surrogate. Handing down heaven's word from his exalted pulpit, he was as close to God as a child could get. But there was a rub. Although he pressured Harriet along with her brothers to confess her sinfulness, she was barred from following in his footsteps. So she turned more and more to two other figures: Jesus, who would forgive and redeem her, and her mother—or the idealized image of her mother—who was all tenderness and sympathy. Women, she decided, were made of finer clay than men, and mothers were an inexhaustible source of love. In her later life, as we have seen, she sometimes merged her two idols, envisioning Christ as a mother leading her flock.

With her father a high priest and all her brothers joining him in his holy guild, it is not surprising that Harriet wanted to be, like them, a messenger of God. Frustrated in that ambition, she married a clergyman and she shepherded her one surviving son into the church and even tried to preach through him. She scattered homilies throughout her books and she retained, like her father, a faith in the Bible and in the belief that sin is punished, if not in hell, then certainly on earth. Again like her father, but in an instinctive, less conscious way, she was a reformer of morals; once, in *Uncle Tom's Cabin*, she took on a social issue larger than any he had dared, but she generally kept, like him, to such petty matters as the theater, liquor and popular novels.

Her experiences, and especially her marriage and her success as a writer, convinced her that women were as intelligent and, if given a chance, as capable as men. She also found that men—for example, her husband—could be quite as unworldly as women were supposed to be. Although she did not, as far as we know, see faithlessness in men at first hand, she evidently concluded that in the love relationship some men took unscrupulous advantage of their greater freedom of behavior. In the face of such an array of injustices most women, she felt, led lives rich in courage and self-sacrifice.

Such attitudes are reflected in almost everything she wrote. In novel after novel the heroines are generally pure and pious, often beautiful and charming, and sometimes saintly. Of the women that are less than admirable, only Audacia Dangyereyes is made to seem truly wicked. By contrast, all the men at the center of her novels have vital shortcomings, with several of them, such as Horace Holyoke, the narrator of *Oldtown Folks*, so colorless as to leave no impression whatever. The towering male figures in her two antislavery novels, Uncle Tom and Dred, are both more myths than men. Finally, the most attractive men in her fiction, Burr, Ellery Davenport and St. Clare, are cynics, and in matters of love the first two are cruel deceivers.

But there were aspects of Harriet's life and work that were the result not so much of her personal history as of the spirit of the time. Above all there was Calvinism and what we call, for lack of a better term, Romanticism. The influence of both of these is pervasive: she wrote an essay, "Can the Immortality of the Soul Be Proved by the Light of Nature?" for a school competition but she composed a Byronic verse romance, *Cleon*, in secret. She taught Butler's *The Analogy of Religion* in Catharine's Hartford seminary but she devoured Madame de Staël's *Corinne* in her spare time. She married the Reverend Calvin Stowe but mooned over Lord Byron. She was fascinated by Byronic types but deplored their sinfulness. And what could be more of a fusion of fantasy and faith than her claim concerning several of her books that they were inspired by God? Like Henry Ward, Harriet wanted to wring laughter and tears from her audience and yet send them away feeling virtuous.

There was even something Romantic in the way she remodeled Calvinism. Again like Henry, she shifted from a remote and unfeeling deity to a loving Jesus. Alienated by the bareness and chill of Congregationalism, she eventually turned to Episcopalianism and from time to time she was entranced by the mystery and fervor of Catholicism. Religious and romantic impulses were combined in her hope that spiritualism could prove that the soul was eternal, and she never could resist mediums, spirit rappers and other masters of wish fulfillment. Although her own experience as a mother was fraught with tragedy, she insisted on idealizing motherhood. Despite the death by plague of her baby in Cincinnati and the twofold trauma of Henry's drowning and Fred's disappearance, she persistently sentimentalized death, converting it into a blessed event for the survivors as well as the dying. Her romantic illusions about Lady Byron and her puritanic disillusion with Lord Byron led her into the most quixotic gesture of her career.

The romantic impulse even stirred her into challenging Puritan attitudes toward the arts. She came, in particular, to resent the way New Englanders were deprived of things of beauty. In Europe she was seduced by the masterpieces in great collections and especially by the sensual vitality of a Rubens, and she ranked Mozart with Shakespeare among the givers of great delight.

Whatever her limitations, Harriet Beecher Stowe had gifts that were on occasion touched with genius. They included a matchless understanding of that seedbed of American character, New England, an abiding love of the natural world—remarkably like her brother Henry's—an almost mystical sympathy with black slaves (which, curiously, did not extend to any other minority), a wry Yankee wit, and an ear not simply for New England speech but for New England ways of thinking.

When, however, we compare her work with that of the master novelists of her time, we sense a lack of depth and subtlety in her characterizations, a carelessness in her craftsmanship and, most troubling, a blindness to the ambiguities of both good and evil.

And yet, at her most effective, Harriet's combination of feeling and moral conviction served her well. Guided by her heart, she felt the horror of slavery long before she arrived at the arguments against it, and that is why *Uncle Tom's Cabin* continues to move us. And she forsook her ancestral religion not so much because of its doctrines as because it lacked mercy and warmth. Indeed, the culmination of her mingling of religious faith and romantic feeling was her rapturous worship of what she described as "the inconceivable loveliness of Christ." The older she grew, the more she turned to that as hope, refuge, stimulant and, at last, the path to the peace that passeth understanding.

29

THOMAS K. BEECHER

"I wait—singing songs in the night"

When a child of the Reverend Samuel Scoville, Henry Ward Beecher's son-in-law, died in 1870, Thomas Beecher wrote Scoville a letter that was a cry of anger against the cruelty and injustice of life:

> To me the death of your little boy chimes in with a unison of evil. I say it was bad . . . It was of the devil, who has the power of death. I hate him. I hate his works, and I hate this world. It is a world where Jesus could not live, my Livy couldn't nor your boy. They all died too soon. 99 in every 100 die too soon. Death has passed upon all. This is a gloomy world. I give it up. I have no part of it. I won't plan. I won't hope. I won't fear. I will only endeavor to keep from its evil, bind up its gashes, shine into its darkness, prophesy heaven and wait—wait—wait—singing songs in the night.

Here night stands for the evil and pain of the world, and the songs he sings and his binding up of the gashes of the world are his work as teacher, servant and bringer of solace. The statement is electrifying in its intensity but there is something petulant in its indiscriminate rage, in the way it blames the world for the death of Scoville's child and of Livy and finds a parallel between their deaths and Christ's.

And yet, even as he is writing this message of frustration and gloom, he is—in his other ego—thinking of the great new church he must build. Even as he broods and weeps, he is making plans to give his people a home for the spirit and the flesh—for pleasure as well as prayer.

He approached the task in his characteristically candid fashion. A newspaper article, "A New Beecher Church," by Mark Twain, who spent his summers on Quarry Hill, in Elmira, not far from the mansion of his wife's family, the Langdons, has Thomas present it thus:

> When I came to Elmira, the First Congregational Church was perhaps the worst church building in Elmira. That was 20 years ago. I think the building has held its own ever since. I do not think it will fall down for some time yet. . . .
> Several times since I have been here the question of a new church has been

advocated. I have always opposed the idea, because I knew that you were not ready. I did not wish you to get subscription on the brain, and run races to see who should put down the largest sum. . . . A new church is not necessary to me. I can preach in the park in the warm weather and in a hall in winter; or I can do as the Lord himself did—preach from house to house. . . .

"Still," Thomas continued, "there are advantages in a suitable building." It would cost, he estimated, about $50,000. So he put it to a vote to see how much each member could contribute. The vote in favor of a new church was overwhelming; $65,000 was pledged, and the Langdons volunteered to match that sum. So Thomas, a builder at heart, drew up rough plans and got himself a splendid church, one of the largest in the region. When his brother Henry saw it he said, "Tom, when I go, I shall leave behind me no such great monument to my life's work."

More significant was the way Thomas made it into a "people's church": besides the standard facilities it had a gymnasium, hospital services, a "Romp Room" with a stage, parlors in which members could entertain their friends, a kitchen equipped to serve over two hundred people, a public library—the first in Elmira—billiard and pool tables. It put on exhibitions of the decorative arts, presented plays, had a Shakespeare club and of course a sewing circle. Once a week there was a "picnic supper" and in the rapidly growing Sunday school, children marched to their rooms to organ music that ranged from "Onward, Christian Soldiers" to "There'll Be a Hot Time in the Old Town Tonight."

All the original strictures against dancing and theaters were forgotten. Far from protesting, the congregation responded joyously; at first local pastors were critical, but soon similar churches were springing up all over America. Such "institutional churches" flourished until, as a later churchman in the Beecher family pointed out, the auxiliary functions began to be filled by YMCAs, YWCAs, settlement houses, the Boy Scouts and similar groups.

As Thomas's reputation spread, he received impressive offers, including one for ten thousand dollars a year, from churches in various cities. But he rejected all of them, feeling that he could do as much good in Elmira as anywhere else; he contented himself with a salary of $3,500—along with many gifts—from the church. Since he eventually became the most beloved figure in the region, his decision was probably wise.

Perhaps, too, he suspected that his idiosyncrasies would not be tolerated so readily in a metropolitan church. Once when he was considering a particularly attractive offer, his brother Henry wrote: "Don't leave the Park Church—they can appreciate you and endure you!" Indeed, his people became so embarrassed by, among other things, the shabby look of his old brown coat that Jervis Langdon insisted on taking him to a tailor and having a fine new one made for him. But when Langdon met him a few weeks later he was still wearing the old coat. Shamefacedly, Thomas explained that he had met a man with no coat at all and had given him the new one because the old one was too poor a gift.

Thomas's simple, almost ascetic habits, it seems, were far from in-born; they took a strenuous act of self-denial. One old friend later recalled that he had "a princely relish for the elegances, the refinements and luxuries of life; a discriminating taste for the dainties of the table; a love for the soft raiment, the art, and luxurious furnishings of wealth," and that in living so modestly he had "crucified his strong natural bents." He had also organized a luncheon and discussion group known as "Our Club," in which he revealed not only "the daring range of his specula-tion . . . fertility in vivid illustration, and his vast accumulation of practi-cal knowledge" but his "flashing wit and Rabelaisian wealth of humor."

With our psychoanalytically suspicious views of motives, we might find ungenerous interpretations of Thomas Beecher's random personal acts of charity, but altogether extraordinary were his efforts to root out that vice of almost all religions—sectarianism and prejudice. Most spec-tacular was a series of lectures, later published in a book, *Our Seven Churches*. "Charity between churches," he asserted, "is too often a mere sentiment, a transient thing smiling out now and then at some . . . meet-ing, and each one is careful to say nothing in particular, and all go home . . . thankful that the meeting 'went off well,' without a quarrel or any scandal." In the old days, he noted, the established church considered itself magnanimous if it tolerated dissent as a kind of "remediless evil," but in America, where there is no established church or privileged class, "he who talks of *tolerating* his fellow-citizens insults them and becomes himself intolerable in his conceit." I do not find, he added, "that the people whom I serve are any less content with our own faith and order because of my repeated efforts to show them that other churches excel us in some particulars." He devoted one lecture to the virtues of each church, from the Catholic—the largest in town—on the right to the Uni-tarian and the Universalist on the left:

I have walked in them as in gardens of the Lord; their beauties have filled my eye, and the air is fragrant roundabout.
    Every church can teach every other church something. . . . There are many churches but one religion.

Yet he did not urge a merging of all churches, believing that "every man has his own horizon."

Thomas may be excused if Congregationalism, described by him as the earliest, simplest and purest form, without "church machinery" or "church lawyers," comes off as somewhat more appealing than the others. Although insignificant in size, he says, "it seems to me extremely attractive, a very pleasant little tabernacle in which two or three pilgrim saints bound for the Holy City may meet and rest."

With a broad-mindedness that must have been a wonder to everyone, he declares that it hardly matters what brings people to a particular church, whether parents, wife or husband, its social status, its pastor (but they should not mistake "pleasant excitement for sound doctrine") or even "honest secular or pecuniary considerations," as long as they believe in the sect. Each church will serve. Joining those who, like Emerson, saw special virtues in the American experience, he added that churches should adapt to "the democracy and voluntaryism of the American atmosphere." He walks a thin line between pragmatism and mere expediency when he declares that "a man does well not to run a tilt against the inexorable stratifying of society." But he is brave indeed and clarifies some of his own seeming inconsistencies when he asserts that people should feel free to shift their allegiances because their "perception of truth may change." "The church of one's boyhood," he declares, "cannot be the church of one's manhood." He concludes that it is a fallacy to think that what is old is true.

Our Seven Churches is a mind-opening little book and perhaps Thomas Beecher's most precious legacy. It would have astonished and confounded Lyman Beecher.

Thomas's newspaper columns continued occasionally to explore controversial subjects. Once he declared that suicide was defensible when an individual felt that he could no longer do good in the world. But when this pronouncement stirred up a great hue and cry, he compromised by adding that the individual should first get the consent of all his relatives. At another time he advocated cremation—fire being a purification—as in every way preferable to the loathsome practice of burial. (He himself would be cremated.)

Thomas returned again and again to the temperance issue, not only because people felt so strongly about it or because Lyman Beecher had helped to start the temperance movement but because he himself loved wine and beer and knew what it was to be addicted. His addiction had clearly made him a student of liquors, and several of his columns are expert explanations of the differences between pure and fermented wines (including deceptive labeling), beers, ale, porter and "ardent spirits." One of his favorite hobbies was making various wines, and a letter to his old friend Ella Wolcott gleefully reports: "There's a temperance revival here. And there's ale in my cellar."

At first he advocated temperance as against total abstinence, observing that liquor has always been "nature's readiest and almost universal stimulus," and at one point he outraged his fellow clergymen by defending liquor dealers. But in time he became convinced that most drinkers could not remain temperate and that the tragedies resulting from addiction to drink could be met only by total prohibition. Considering his own independence of thought and action, it is strange that he should have come to favor such interference with individual behavior.

In such controversies, Thomas sometimes ruffled the feathers of friends as well as foes. The Reverend Annis Ford Eastman, who, along with her husband, succeeded Thomas at the Park Church, saw this simply as a result of his honesty and candor:

He who denies all human authority over his conscience, who fearlessly examines all religious systems and social conventions, taking what is good for him and rejecting what is bad . . . who can see both sides of every question, and bravely state them—he must often be a sore trial to the average sense of propriety in a community.

Excessive drinking was an old problem; a fresh problem was the conflict between workingmen and their employers in the great new industries. The prevailing attitude was that poverty was the result of laziness and that any man who was, as Isabella's husband, John Hooker, put it, "temperate, virtuous and industrious" could secure all reasonable comforts. One might express, as the Hookers did, a humanitarian concern for the poor and be active in charity, and even dare—as Isabella had done during the Haymarket riots in Chicago in 1886—to denounce Carnegie for his brutal treatment of strikers. But few people thought of workingmen as having "rights." Unfettered capitalism, it was felt, would spread the wealth to all classes: those who were poor today could be rich tomorrow.

On such issues Thomas had a deep sympathy with workingmen and an equally deep distrust of industrialists. That was in great part why he accepted an invitation to run for Congress on the Greenback party ticket in 1880. Although the party originally aimed mainly at getting more paper currency so that debtors in particular could take advantage of "cheap money," it increasingly backed other legislation to help workingmen and farmers. Thomas knew of course that many in Hartford had a deep-rooted prejudice against immigrants, and especially the Irish, who were coming to work in local factories, and a conviction that political corruption, particularly in the big cities, resulted from the votes of ignorant workingmen. When Joseph Twichell, his Nook Farm friend and fellow clergyman, chided him for allowing himself to be drawn onto the

Greenback ticket, Thomas explained his position in typically personal terms:

I wish you had any social convictions as to the welfare of the masses. . . . I enclose the green-back platform—which with trifling exceptions I cannot gainsay. Read it and think, that's all. Dear Joe Twichell whom I loved from the word go—as the healthiest and heartiest minister that lets me call him friend—this very mail brings me two letters, one from a widow—the other from a man of fifty in Idaho—whose struggles I have known for 20 years. Whatever you and I have felt in days by gone as the scared fugitives from slavery came shivering to us by night showing cracked pit scars, and in rags, until we could endure *slavery* no longer—the same I feel daily and hourly as the unending procession of my neighbors files by me—anxious, heartbroken, or worse, with eyes of hate and envy, as they know themselves the bleeding grist of our great financial mill—that in defiance of Scripture and the testimony of the ages insists that to lend money—exact interest . . . and grow rich while brother men and partners are *cleaned out*—is honest christian enterprise.

No—Joe—praise me for my patience. These twenty five years I have been of intenser convictions than Garrison ever was. . . . You know I am not a party man—nor a blasphemous Kearny—nor a . . . communist. I am only Jeremiah *redivivus*.

—There, I love you and so I write as I never wrote other.

So, privately, he was Jeremiah reborn—a radical Jeremiah. But in one of his newspaper columns of the same period, writing of a railway strike in Buffalo, he took a rather more neutral position. There he concluded that both sides had justifications but that they must restrain their passions, listen to authority and let the government regulate such "fierce competitions."

Guided in part by Christian doctrine, Thomas was well ahead of his time in his sympathy with those who worked for the new lords of society.

If any of Thomas Beecher's views are difficult to understand, it is his feeling that women were just as well off without the vote. With such a wife as Julia and such sisters as Isabella, Catharine and Harriet, it is strange that he should have considered women's housework as something to cherish because, like Christ's work, it is "remedial" and done for love. That, too, is why he said that women were better able to appreciate Christ. Enfranchisement would perhaps give woman equality with man and gain more money for her, but it would make her, like man, "thin, shrewd, dry, exacting," and cause her to lose her way to God. The only explanation of this attitude is Thomas's scorn for many aspects of man's role that women might envy.

The story of how Thomas rescued a prostitute has repeatedly been told as an example of the breadth of his sympathies. His daring to take a notorious "fallen woman" into his home—defying his neighbors to think the worst—until she had been restored to respectability was certainly a brave, if somewhat self-conscious, gesture.

When the Beecher-Tilton scandal exploded in 1872, Thomas was the only Beecher who found his sister Isabella not unjustified in believing that Henry was guilty or had at least laid himself open to such shameful charges. The day after Victoria Woodhull published her exposé, Isabella wrote to Thomas:

> The blow has fallen, and I hope you are better prepared for it than you might have been but for our interview. I wrote H. a single line last week thus, "Can I help you?" and here is his reply, "If you still believe in that woman [Woodhull] you cannot help me. . . . I tread the falsehoods into the dust from whence they spring, and go on my way rejoicing. . . . I trust you give neither countenance nor credence to the abominable coinage that has been put afloat. The specks of truth are mere spangles upon a garment of falsehood. . . ."

She also sent Tom a copy of the letter in which Woodhull spoke of herself as one resigned to martyrdom and predicts that Isabella will play a blessed role in "the grandest revelation the world has yet known." Finally Isabella enclosed the letter in which Henry adjured her to keep silent on the entire subject. Isabella added that she would be silent for the present but if Henry did not soon "confess all," she could not "stand as consenting to a lie."

Tom's answer, typically brusque and unsparing, is a vivid statement of the differences between him and Henry:

> To allow the Devil himself to be crushed for speaking the truth is unspeakably cowardly and contemptible. I respect, *as at present advised,* Mrs. Woodhull, while I abhor her philosophy. She only carries out Henry's philosophy, against which I recorded my protest twenty years ago, and parted (lovingly and achingly) from him, saying "We cannot work together." He has drifted, and I have hardened like a crystal till I am sharp-cornered and exacting. . . . In my judgment Henry is following his slippery doctrines of expediency, and, in his cry of progress and the nobleness of human nature, has sacrificed clear, exact, ideal integrity. Hands off, until he is down, and then my pulpit, my home, my church, and my purse and heart are at his service. Of the two, Woodhull is my hero, and Henry my coward, *as at present advised.*
>
> I return the papers. *You* cannot help Henry. You must be true to Woodhull.

Deeply disturbed, he added one postscript after another. In the first he intimates that the affair confirms his distrust of Henry's and Isabella's hopeful view of human nature and society:

You are in a tight place. But having chosen your principles I can only counsel you to be true and take the consequences. For years, you know, I have been apart from all of you except in love. I think you all in the wrong as to anthropology and social science.

In another postscript he adds: "You have no *proof* as yet of any offence on Henry's part. . . . remember that you are standing on uncertain information, and we shall not probably ever get the facts, and I'm glad of it."

What was unendurably humiliating for all those proud men and women in the Beecher tribe was that these letters would be displayed during the trial with all their revelations of family dissension and shame. . . . Even Henry's acquittal did not heal the wounds.

For a while Thomas's relationship with Henry remained ambivalent. Once he told a friend that being a son of Lyman Beecher and a brother of Henry Ward Beecher had been one of the great handicaps of his life. At another time, called on to deliver a sermon in Plymouth Church, he noted as he rose to speak that some who had come to hear Henry were preparing to depart. Nettled, Thomas announced: "All those who came here to worship Henry Ward Beecher may now leave—all who came to worship God may remain."

Thomas's relationship with James, his only full brother, remained very close, especially after James's first wife, Annie, died and James married Frances Johnson. Like their father and most of their brothers, both Thomas and James loved the outdoor life and physical work. Summers, as we have seen, they explored the Catskill wilderness and fell in love with a lake in the woods of Ulster County. James and his wife and children settled there permanently. Thomas and Julia were content to spend six or eight weeks of each summer on "Beecher Lake"—farming, fishing, boating, hunting grouse. Julia worked as hard as the men, pitching tents, cutting a path through the woods, and building a "dining cabin" and an outdoor fireplace. She also continued to be a fountain of kindness, good humor and creative energy. She stuffed old stockings and turned them into such charming rag dolls that she was able to sell a great many of them, with the proceeds going to charity. Using the roots of trees, she made grotesque carvings of birds and beasts, and also auctioned these off for charity. Mark Twain, spending his summers on nearby Quarry Hill and seeing the Beechers whenever they visited Hartford, was fascinated by these bizarre figures:

I have arranged your jobberwocks [his name for the carvings] and other devils in procession . . . on the piano in the drawing room and in that subdued light they take to themselves added atrocities of form and expression and so make a body's flesh crawl with pleasure. . . . Make more; don't leave a root unutilized in Chemung County. But . . . don't breathe the breath of life into them, for I know (if there is anything in physiognomy and general appearance) that they would all vote the Democratic ticket, every devil of them.

There were no gaps or withholdings in Julia's generous nature. When Catharine Beecher at the age of seventy-seven came in her wanderings to Gleason's water cure, and Thomas—only a half brother and twenty-four years younger—raised with Julia the possibility of taking her into their home, Julia responded unhesitatingly:

I think there are worse afflictions in the world than the care of an old Christian woman who has at least tried to do good all her life and needs someone's kind attentions till the Lord calls her home. I am not going to worry about that.

Catharine came, and died peacefully in their home a year later.

Julia was as vital intellectually as physically and broke through conventions almost as readily as her husband. Along with the Reverend Annis Ford Eastman, Thomas's associate in the Park Church in later years, Julia was as aware as if she were in "advanced" circles in New York. While some biographers of Mark Twain picture the Elmira in which Twain spent much time—he wrote *Tom Sawyer* there—as a provincial and culturally stifling world, Julia and Annis shared a strong interest in such writers as Emerson, Whitman and William Morris, with Julia reading aloud the sensual "Calamus" poems from Whitman's *Leaves of Grass*. Annis also reported how eager Julia was to "assimilate the results of scientific research in every field." Although she—and Thomas—believed in the eternal life of the spirit, and she followed psychic research eagerly, a streak of common sense kept Julia from putting any stock in the claims of mediums and clairvoyants. A popular teacher in the Sunday school, she was so completely sure of herself that she could say of a doctrine that she herself had discarded: "But it was necessary in its time." She loved beautiful objects and constantly criticized the jumble of small pictures crowded onto the walls of typical Victorian parlors. "Don't you see," she would say, "how much better one big simple picture would look?" "To the end," her friend Annis writes—in a little book called *A Flower of Puritanism: Julia Jones Beecher*—"she was Puritan and Greek."

Thomas knew how much he owed to Julia and in later years he referred to her as "my strong, courageous, energetic Julia" and gave her credit for "nine-tenths of the achievement of our long life in Elmira."

It is easy to lose sight of the fact that only one generation separated Lyman Beecher and Harriet Porter from Thomas Beecher and Julia.

By the time Henry died, in 1887, he and Thomas had been reconciled, and of the hundreds of tributes to the pastor of Plymouth Church none was more touching than that of his half brother. Thomas recalled the glorious days when his big brother Henry was the hero of his childhood, and then how Henry, as a young preacher on the Indiana frontier, "astride his long-boned, fast-walking sorrel, with well-worn and ill-filled saddle-bags, rode hundreds of miles, as courageous as Paul, as gentle as John."

Having long since forgotten, or blocked out, his severe reaction when he had first heard, from Isabella, of the Beecher-Tilton affair, he now said:

In those sad days when his good name was besmirched . . . my brother Henry— solemnly asseverated his innocence and his purity. Knowing him I believed him and read no further. . . . He cared as little for logic and consistency as an apple-tree that blossoms bountifully in the sunshine to the song of robins and bluebirds.

His summary of Henry's role was as sensitive as anything written about his brother:

He was a watchman and, seeing the first turn of the tide, shouted discovery. Men thought him the cause of great movements. He never so esteemed himself. "The man that sees the streak in the east is not the cause of the sunrise," he said.

Thomas came to Henry's home in Brooklyn for the funeral, but treasuring his loving memories of his brother, he refused to enter the carriage going to the cemetery. Forever the rebel against empty gestures, he said, with tears in his eyes, "I'm not going to traipse all over Brooklyn behind a corpse."

The growth of the Park Church was spectacular, the membership increasing from fifty in 1854 to seven hundred by 1900—Elmira was by then a city of almost forty thousand—and the Sunday school reaching a thousand students, many of them adults. On Sundays fifteen hundred people crowded the church, including many from other churches, or from no church at all. He was a legend now, "Father Tom," his head still handsome but his beard streaked with gray. His preaching still hewed to a wisdom outside dogma and doctrine, combining common sense, old-fashioned ideals, imagination. Imagination took over completely in a sermon called "A Vision of Creation." He pictured himself as dreaming that he was witness to the six days in which God created the universe. On the first day he finds himself amidst nothingness:

There was silence and there was space, and I alone remained. No more land. No more sea. No more twinkling stars, nor paling moon, nor rising sun. . . . Around me darkness, emptiness. I felt that I was stationary, yet fancied myself rushing like a falling star. Where was I? . . . I alone in silence and in space.

The darkness began to lighten, redden, glow. Commandment seemed to fill all space. Words without voice . . . seemed to start the glowing particles: "Light is coming. Let light be!" Warmer and warmer grew a presence breathing on every side. With the warmth came rosiness, shining. More than I could bear grew the heat. I shot through it as fishes dart through water. Vast spaces, up or down, I stabbed like a rocket in my flight, but everywhere was stir, and light, and strange, resistless motion. Escape I could not, and with an outcry I awoke. So the first scene began and ended.

At the other extreme was his bitter side, his newspaper columns scourging graft, corruption, the greed of the moneymen. Periods of depression still overwhelmed him, aggravated by poor health and failing eyesight. When Isabella visited the Beechers in Elmira in 1891, she found their home charming and Julia still tireless but her brother "a hypochondriac and as queer as ever." But Thomas had his own resentments. A few months later, writing to Isabella and her husband to explain why he could not attend their fiftieth wedding anniversary, he said, with mingled sorrow and bitterness, that he would have liked to look once more on "the visions of love and fidelity—as it was before the tornado struck us scattering the Beecher fleet along lines of notoriety toward will o' the wisps of reform, over restless waters of 'agitations.'" Perhaps Isabella with her incessant crusading brought out that side of him. There were other women, such as his mother, his aunt Esther, the "three Olivias"—his Livy, Olivia Langdon and Olivia Langdon Clemens—whom he worshiped as saints. Gentle women, with a healing grace, and no sharp edges or militancy. . . .

A few years later, no longer able to carry on, he called on the Reverend Samuel E. Eastman and his wife, the Reverend Annis Ford Eastman, to serve as associate pastors, and was thereafter relatively inactive. When he was stricken with paralysis on March 9, 1900, the city seemed to hold its breath; he died a few days later. That he should die only after the new century opened seemed appropriate, for in some ways he belonged to the new age more than did any of his brothers or sisters.

Memorial tributes to popular public figures too often slip into unctuous adulation: the dead become saints, their faults charming, their weaknesses virtues. But the outpouring of homage after Thomas Beecher's death was one of love as well as reverence. Everyone vied in telling stories of his selflessness, independence and humor. Ministers, priests and a rabbi joined in trying to define his nature and his spirit. A statue was set up in the park. Forty years later a well-known editor and author, Max Eastman, who, as the son of the Eastmans, had known Thomas in his last decade, said in a sketch called "Mark Twain's Elmira":

The central figure in that Elmira, the dominant and molding intellectual and spiritual force, not only to Olivia Langdon but in large measure to Mark Twain himself, was this same eloquent and great Beecher . . . a man of more than Mark Twain's stature, you must realize, in the minds of those around him. He called himself "Teacher of the Park Church" and a whole rebel character and thought of life lay behind that choice. His thought was to live and be helpful in the community as a modern Jesus would, a downright, realistic, iconoclastic, life-loving Jesus with a scientific training and a sense of humor and a fund of common sense. He was, in fact . . . more eloquent to a lucid listener [Washington Gladden, a noted preacher] than his famous brother, Henry Ward.

Despite all this, many knew that Thomas Beecher was never a happy man. And no one knew it better than Julia. Ruefully she would say in her last years: "When I get to heaven I will find Tom and take him to Livy and say, 'Here he is, Livy, I have done my best, but I could not make him happy, now take him.' "

It is impossible to classify Thomas Beecher because he was guided not by doctrine or theory but by compassion. Although he had left behind his father's Calvinism, he came to see the world as a place of pain and defeat. It was an outlook colored by a hypochondria that surely stemmed from his mother's melancholia as well as what the Beechers called "dyspepsia," "blues" or "nerves." It was fixed indelibly in him when his beloved Livy, carrying their baby, died in the second year of their marriage.

But instead of trying, like some of his brothers and sisters, to reform mankind, undertake great crusades, invent new systems of the universe, or tell his parishioners they were like gods, he sought simply to give aid and comfort. So he chose a country town rather than a mixed metropolitan community, believing he would find in an Elmira a more peaceful way of life as well as freedom from conflicting demands.

Although he adored Henry and learned much from his brother's beliefs and behavior, including a supreme devotion to Jesus, a rejection of dogma and sectarianism, and a large indifference to ministerial conventions—including manner and garb—he never shared Henry's ebullient faith in human nature or the future of the race. Thus, where people turned to Plymouth Church for a thrilling emotional experience, they came to Thomas Beecher for instruction, sympathy and practical help.

Responding separately to each person and situation, Beecher paid no attention to consistency, surely agreeing with Emerson that it was the hobgoblin of little minds. In an age famous for conformity, he was uncompromisingly independent—the complete individualist. He not only believed that everyone had a right to a change of heart and mind but he expected growth to bring about such changes.

So his views abound in paradoxes: he was opposed to "church machinery," yet he built an elaborate church organization; he was ready to help any suffering individual but not, with one or two exceptions, to join a movement on behalf of a suffering minority; his wife Julia and his sisters Catharine, Harriet and Isabella were remarkable by any measure, yet he thought that granting women the vote would rob them of precious qualities; he was conspicuously self-denying, yet some who knew him said he loved luxuries and elegances; he had a scientist's sense of structure and precision, but his ministry, he admitted, moved without plan or design; he treasured wines and liquors but eventually advocated strict prohibition. Often his inconsistencies were the product of fresh insights and experience, but sometimes they were merely the result of eccentric impulses or plain misjudgment.

The greatest irony was that although he became an immensely popular preacher, he wanted often to be something else. Repeatedly he expressed a nagging discontent ("I'm sick of ministerial nonsense") with his role as a minister, yearning, as he once said, "to be at some absorbing work, such as the age calls for." Since he had wanted in his youth to be a scientist or an engineer, was he in part another sad result of Lyman Beecher's misguided zeal?

In his awareness of evil and sinfulness, Thomas Beecher retained a remnant of his father's religion. For the rest, he imitated Jesus as well as he could and did his best to ease the trials of those in his care. And although he thought the prospect bleak and the path full of pitfalls, he continued—as he once said to Samuel Scoville—to bind up gashes, prophesy heaven and sing songs in the night.

Loved and respected for his quirky
independence, his scorn of
sectarianism and his compassion,
Thomas K. Beecher became a
legend in the Elmira region and
was, some said, the greatest of
the Beechers.

Respected members of what
remained of Hartford's
distinguished Nook Farm "literary
colony," Isabella Beecher Hooker
and her husband, John, on their
golden wedding anniversary
in 1891.

Isabella Beecher Hooker (center) with her daughter Alice (left) and her granddaughter Katharine Seymour Day (right).

ISABELLA BEECHER HOOKER

An Identity Achieved

With all four of the Beecher daughters living there, Hartford in the 1870s became for the Beechers what Cincinnati had been in the 1830s and Litchfield in an earlier day. When Harriet returned there she found it a very different city from the one she had known during her stay at Catharine's Hartford Female Seminary in the 1820s. "... old Hartford," she wrote, "seems fat, rich and cosy—stocks higher than ever, business plenty—everything as tranquil as possible."

A few years later, a young newspaperman from the boom towns of California and Nevada saw the city—he was thinking chiefly of the Nook Farm section—in an even more attractive light. Mark Twain, visiting Hartford for two weeks and staying with the Hookers, friends of his future wife, Olivia Langdon, described the town as the most handsome he had ever seen. As wide-eyed as any country boy, he reported in a letter to the *Alta California* in 1868:

This is the center of Connecticut wealth. Hartford dollars have a place in half the great moneyed enterprises of the union. All these Phoenix and Charter Oak Insurance Companies, whose gorgeous chromo-lithographic show cards it has been my delight to study in far-away cities, are located here.

Hardly less impressive evidences of growing industrial power were the factories that made Pratt and Whitney machinery, Colt revolvers and Sharps rifles.

Of his hosts the Hookers, Mark was only half jesting when he wrote:

I tell you I have to walk mighty straight. I desire to have the respect of this sterling old Puritan community, for their respect is well worth having—and so ... I don't dare do *anything* that's comfortable or natural. It comes a little hard to lead such a sinless life.

The reference to Puritans was of course joking; he admired the city and its people so much that he returned in 1871 to build a mansion for himself in Nook Farm.

All the families in Nook Farm had indeed come from Calvinist homes, but almost all had slipped the shackles and were embracing a bland and secularized religion centering on a benign Christ. Several were already toying with an improvised parlor religion called spiritualism. The plain old churches of Puritan days were giving way to community centers made attractive with charity bazaars, Sunday sociables and cultural lectures. Puritanism was being routed not by skepticism or atheism but by complacency and affluence. Faith in the Lord had to compete with faith in progress. (The leading Hartford divine, Horace Bushnell, had said in 1847: "Prosperity is our duty." Hartford responded by achieving the highest per capita income in the United States.) Prayer was reserved for Sundays, and property commanded as much respect as piety. Conscience had made way for social acceptability.

With prosperity came new pleasures. Nook Farm families toured Europe regularly and sometimes stayed for several months or went on to the Holy Land and Egypt. They kept a carriage, usually with a driver, followed the fashions in clothes and architecture, adorned their homes with costly bric-a-brac, dared to go to the theater—where they saw and applauded Edwin Booth, Ellen Terry, Henry Irving and Joseph Jefferson—and boasted of a corps of women, following in the footsteps of Lydia Sigourney, who made best-sellers out of sentimental verse.

Croquet on well-kept lawns, whist in the evening, horseback riding—and later bicycling—in fine weather, concerts and even private theatricals contributed to the sense of bonhomie and good living. For a while, too, the intellectual flame burned bright. Distinguished visitors came to Nook Farm regularly, some to be lavishly entertained at the home of Charles Dudley Warner or of Mark Twain, others to pay tribute to Mrs. Stowe, and still others to discuss feminism and spiritualism at the Hookers'. Between the travel abroad, the visitors, and the freedom that affluence allows, old prejudices and prohibitions dissolved almost imperceptibly. So, for a time, Hartford was second only to Boston as a cultural center in New England.

As the influence of the clergy, their eyes still partly fixed on the next world, waned, a breed called humanitarians drew attention to the ills and injustices of this world. In Hartford, Isabella would become a leader of this group.

The story of how Isabella Beecher Hooker rose in little more than a year from an apprenticeship in the suffragist movement to organizing a national convention in Washington, and how the notorious Victoria

Woodhull captured the convention and, for a moment, the suffragist movement, is one of the most dramatic in the history of women's rights in America.

Isabella's success in Hartford had completely confirmed her belief in her special powers. So she moved forward on two fronts. Assisted by her husband, with his knowledge of laws and lawmakers, she drafted and introduced at the 1870 meeting of the Connecticut legislature a bill giving married women the same property rights as their husbands. (It was turned down, but she reintroduced it at every session until it was finally passed in 1877.) At the same time she sent out a call for a suffrage convention that would be held in Washington early in 1871 and would put pressure on the legislators.

Although Elizabeth Cady Stanton was rattled by Isabella's cocky assertion that she expected to accomplish "far more by a convention devoted to the purely political aspect of the woman question than by a woman's rights convention," she and Susan B. Anthony were quite willing to let Isabella see what she could do. "You are," Stanton wrote, "younger [Isabella was seven years younger than Stanton but only two years younger than Anthony] and have more time, leisure, freshness and enthusiasm," and then added with characteristic bluntness: "Moreover, I perceive in all your letters a healthy fear . . . of contact with my innumerable idiosyncrasies, and so, in all tenderness and pity, I would stand from between you and the sun. I have no doubt the coming conventions will be as successful under your leadership as they have ever been in Washington."

Isabella now joined Anthony in a speaking tour of the West, exchanging enthusiasm and advice with supporters in half a dozen states. Although she borrowed some of her platform manner from Henry and her father, she had developed a very effective style of her own, mingling common sense, witty thrusts and emotional appeal. In Chicago she addressed the second convention of the National Woman Suffrage Association; she was well received and returned to Hartford a national figure in the movement and fully prepared to manage a national convention.

But a stunning surprise awaited the delegates when they arrived in Washington: the Judiciary Committee of the House of Representatives announced that on the morning of the convention it would hold a special meeting to hear a memorial on women's rights by Victoria Woodhull—a recognition never before accorded a woman. To the delegates Victoria Woodhull was an adventuress: the "Lady Broker of Wall Street," publisher of a sensational weekly, a leading spiritualist, exponent of free love, and a self-nominated candidate for the Presidency. The mystery of her appearance before a congressional committee on the very morning of the convention was later explained by the disclosure that her good friend Representative Benjamin Butler, shrewd politician, lawyer and Civil War general, was a member of the committee.

There was no containing the delegates; the convention was postponed until afternoon and the women crowded the committee hearing. Mrs. Woodhull surprised everyone by appearing in dark, conservative clothes with only a rose as ornament—a model of propriety and womanly appeal. Speaking firmly but with increasing passion, she presented a well-ordered series of arguments—probably prepared with help from Butler—calculated to show that the Fourteenth and Fifteenth amendments as well as the Constitution referred to women no less than men.

It was a masterly performance and as soon as Woodhull was finished, the delegates, including Isabella and Anthony (Stanton had stayed away), crowded around her, glowing with excitement and admiration. They carried her off to the convention hall and, introduced by Isabella, she once again entranced her audience. Both the hearing and the convention made headlines across the nation. So a meeting intended to demonstrate the respectability of the suffragist movement became a triumph for the most outrageous woman of the age.

Excited by these developments, Isabella now drew up a "Declaration and Pledge of the Women of the United States Concerning their Right to . . . the Elective Franchise" and collected thousands of signatures for it. The Senate Judiciary Committee, duly impressed, invited her to testify before it. She performed admirably and came away tremendously exhilarated. "I was perfectly infused with it and inspired by it—" she wrote to her husband, "it flowed out of my inner consciousness as if it were part of my very being. . . . I dare not tell you all that I see in the future. . . . God knows it and that is enough." Her confidence soared when Senator Charles Sumner called her presentation "able, lucid and powerful" and Susan Anthony hailed her as "the soundest Constitutional lawyer in the country."

In the months that followed, the praise was overshadowed by letters and editorials protesting against the alliance with Woodhull. It was possible to ignore criticism that came from people plainly hostile to the entire movement. Far more disturbing was the reaction from her family (all three of her sisters, she reported, had nearly "crazed" her with letters imploring her to have nothing to do with Woodhull) and from active supporters of the cause.

Phebe Hanaford of New Haven, an author and a Universalist preacher—the Universalists believed that all human beings were eligible to be saved—resigned from the executive committee of the association and wrote to Isabella: "why do you countenance illegal prostitution thinly veiled with the term soul marriage! . . . in our State especially, you are a leader, of natural right, a born Queen in the moral realm . . . and I cannot help regretting your acceptance of Mrs. W. as an associate leader."

A month later Mrs. Hanaford, completely out of patience, added:

as neither the trustees of my church nor myself owe any sort of allegiance to your "darling Queen," the notorious mistress of Col. Blood's affections . . . it will not be agreeable to us to invite you to speak in our church.

For you, personally, we have great admiration and respect, mingled with the deepest regret that you should place yourself before the world as the loving subject of such a Cleopatra. New Haven reverences the Beecher blood in you . . . but I fear your influence is wrecked by this unholy alliance.

If you wish my pulpit to repudiate the claims of that "darling Queen" to your allegiance . . . then it may be obtained, but not while you appear to sanction free love or free-lovers.

Isabella's reaction to Woodhull was a mixture of generous impulses and mystic convictions. She saw in her an inspired woman who grasped certain truths about the relationship between the sexes both intuitively and as a result of a marriage to a profligate who had abandoned her with two children. Insofar as Woodhull had sinned, Isabella felt called upon to help and redeem her. She believed, moreover, that like Woodhull, she herself was guided by heavenly spirits. Perhaps she also felt ashamed at having scorned the woman before she knew her and at abandoning her after embracing her.

Much of this was expressed, sometimes confusingly, in Isabella's letters. She insists that she has not heard "one word of criticism from any who have *seen her for themselves*." She does admit that she was never so perplexed in forming a judgment, adding:

My prevailing belief is in her innocence and purity. I have seldom been so drawn to any woman. . . . I knew she had visions and was inspired by *spiritual* influences she thought, but her inspiration seemed very like my own. . . . I shall always love her, and in private shall work for her redemption if she is ensnared, for I never saw more possible nobilities in a human being than in her. If she is leading souls to death through this wonderful magnetism of hers, of course we shall not . . . make her a leader in any way . . . but we will not denounce her publicly, however guilty, till the time when men guilty of the same crimes are avoided and denounced.

Especially challenging were the protests of Mary Rice Livermore, a leader of the American Woman Suffrage Association and the editor of its paper, the *Woman's Journal*. Isabella, busy lobbying in Washington, responds that she has made a vow to "stand by all suspected women as if they were my own sisters, and when they were proved guilty I would stand by harder than ever." She reports that Woodhull is in Washington working "for womanhood twelve hours a day with quiet dignity and sweetness."

Replying to the complaints of a suffragist from Minnesota, Isabella falls back on the Bible: "the whole New Testament is luminous with the idea of fraternizing with sinners in all their righteous work and full of denunciations of the 'I am holier than thou' spirit." She does agree that Mrs. Woodhull should refuse to have any official connection with the coming convention in New York. But she asserts in the next breath that "no cry of free love will keep me from thoroughly investigating the whole subject [of marriage and divorce] when the time comes. . . . I believe . . . that unchastity and sensuality are as possible in marriage as out of it."

The National Association leaders bravely allowed Victoria Woodhull to speak at their New York convention in May 1871, and again she electrified her audience, this time with an incendiary call to action. If Congress refuses women the full rights of citizenship, she will, she said, call a convention to establish a new government. In the conclusion of what the press called the "Great Secession Speech"—doubtless composed mainly by her anarchist associates—she cried: "We mean treason; we mean secession. We are plotting a revolution; we will overthrow this bogus Republic and plant a government of righteousness in its place!"

By the fall of 1871 Isabella was defending Woodhull with the intensity of desperation. In a revealing letter to a western acquaintance, Anna Savery, she mingled turbid spiritualist visions with Biblical prophecy. At her first meeting with Woodhull, she said, she was convinced that this woman was

heaven sent for the rescue of woman from the pit of subjection. She has ever since appeared to me as then—as a womanly woman, yet less a woman than an embodiment of pure thought, soul and reason—a prophetess, full of visions and messages . . . which it would be woe unto her to refrain from proclaiming, even though martyrdom were sure to follow.

She explained how unselfishly Woodhull had been taking care of her first husband, a helpless victim of drink and drugs, and her children, one of them a retarded boy whose condition, Isabella said, was the result of his father's vices. This woman, she added, is a "born Queen,"

and I owe her the allegiance of my heart. . . . She is a mystery to me, but so is every forerunner of the people of his or her day. . . . I verily believe that the *hour* of woman approaches and is even upon us . . . and as prophets were raised up unto men in the olden time full of human imperfections to be sure . . . so we may look for holy women to prepare the way of the Lord and announce his second coming. . . . Whether this woman is of that sort time will show. . . . I simply wait, saying—Come Lord Jesus—come quickly.

In her zeal Isabella enclosed a letter addressed by Woodhull to spiritualists. Her comment on it verged on delusion; it tells, she said, of the spirit world "waiting to pour itself upon this in a purifying flood—let it come I say and let those who fear the baptism stand from under—for me if I can but see the heavens opened my heart will exult with joy unspeakable."

If in their excited communings Woodhull hailed Isabella as destined in the coming millennium to be a God-appointed leader, it came to Isabella not as a revelation but as a confirmation. Her conversion into a self-reliant activist was now complete. She went regularly to Washington and in her capacity as president of the Central Woman's Suffrage Committee she met with senators, held receptions, collected money, sent out tracts and even inveigled congressmen into letting her use their franking privilege. The burden of work, she told a friend, is killing. Yet, almost perversely, she takes on more and more. The reason for this is not entirely noble: as she later admits, she must escape from the agony of being shunned by her sons-in-law and kept at a distance from her daughters and grandchildren.

She is oppressed, moreover, by the "bigotry and phariseeism" around her and by criticism from family and friends. Her husband, abhorring all that is discordant, disapproves of her connection with Victoria Woodhull more strongly than of anything that has ever come between them. The fact that he stands by her publicly makes it all the harder for her. And his sleepless nights, she adds, drive her frantic.

Catharine is even more difficult. Over seventy years old, she is challenged, as we have seen, by these aggressive younger women who make public speeches—as she never dared—and demand political rights, which she still thinks are of little importance. Obviously feeling that she, as a pioneer in the struggle for women's independence, has been carelessly passed by, she writes to the Hartford *Courant* when her name appears in print as an advocate of woman's suffrage:

This is not true of myself or of a large majority of my family and personal friends, most of whom would regard such a measure as *an act of injustice and oppression,* forcing conscientious women to assume the responsibilities of the civil state, when they can so imperfectly meet the many and more important duties of the family state. . . .

So I have, Isabella writes to Anna Savery, a foe in my own family. "If you can escape that," she adds, "you can live."

Hearing the stories about Henry and Elizabeth Tilton, Harriet and Catharine scorned them as the vile inventions of envious people. When Henry, spurred by threats from Woodhull, urged his sisters to stop criti-

COMMITTEE.

Pres., I B. HOOKER, Hartford, Conn.
Sec., J. S. GRIFFING, Wash., D. C.
Tr., M. B. BOWEN, Wash D. C.
P. W. DAVIS, Prov., R. I.
S. B. ANTHONY, N.Y. City.

Central Woman Suffrage Committee,

ROOM, CAPITOL,

R. C. Jerison Wash.

Washington, D. C., Feb. 11 , 1871

Dear friend Susan.

I have longed to see & talk
no less than you - but have been too feeble to write so
to think of it even - but now you must be treated as
to everything - so here begins.   We know as well as
you two desirable lecturing is - but we have no money
as yet, have just enough for current small expences of
2 Mrs Griffing's salary.   This is to be paid & part of
at . $100. a month - her daughter takes the charge of
autograph Pledge Book & keeps a great deal at
every way - so that a that is each salary are answer . /

cizing the woman, Harriet was puzzled—Woodhull was a snake, she said, who should be clipped with a shovel—and gave way only reluctantly.

Catharine was, as always, less tractable. When Woodhull arranged to lecture in Hartford, Catharine wrote to the *Courant,* urging the community to keep her out. Woodhull came and after a restrained plea for woman suffrage, noted that Catharine Beecher had once promised to strike her—and had now done so. Her response, she said grandly, would be to turn the other cheek.

But Isabella, knowing that those stories about Henry came from Anthony and Stanton and that they had heard them from Mrs. Tilton herself, could not dismiss them. So as early as April 1872 she mentioned them in a letter to Henry. His answer was cryptic:

I do not want you to *take any ground this year except upon suffrage.* You know my sympathy with you. Probably you and I are nearer together than any of our family. I cannot give reasons now. . . . Of some things *I neither talk, nor will I be talked with.* . . . The only help that can be grateful to me, or useful is, *silence.* . . . A day may come for converse. It is not *now.* Living or dead, my dear sister Belle, *love me,* and do not talk about me or suffer others to in your presence.

Isabella later said: "It looks as if he hoped to buy my silence with my love. At present, of course, I shall keep silence, but truth is dearer than all things else, and . . . I cannot always stand as consenting to a lie."

If defending Victoria Woodhull was forcing Isabella to wishful visions and disturbing her cherished relations with her husband, what must have been her feelings when Woodhull gave a lecture in New York entitled "Social Freedom," which was climaxed by the boldest public declaration of sexual liberty ever uttered by a woman in the United States. Provoked by a question shouted by a man in the audience, she cried:

Yes, I am a Free Lover. I have an *inalienable constitutional and natural* right to love whom I may, to love as *long* or as *short* a period as I can; to change that love *every day* if I please, and with *that* right neither *you* nor any *law* you can frame have any right to interfere . . . for I mean just that, and nothing less!

The attacks on Woodhull and her few remaining champions now mounted sharply. By early 1872 Isabella was admitting that the pressure in her home had become so acute that she had agreed not to draw Woodhull into the campaign the suffragists were planning for the Presidential race between Grant and Greeley. But to Stanton she pointed out that Woodhull had poured more than an immense amount of energy into the cause: "I verily believe she has sunk a hundred thousand dollars in Woman's Suffrage, besides enduring tortures of soul innumerable—let us never forget this." Stanton had not forgotten, and it was she who expressed the most fierce indignation at the attacks on Woodhull.

We have had women enough sacrificed to this sentimental, hypocritical prating about purity [she wrote to Lucretia Mott]. This is one of man's most effective engines for our division and subjugation. He creates the public sentiment, builds the gallows, and then makes us hangman for our sex. Women have crucified the Mary Wollstonecrafts, the Fanny Wrights, the George Sands, the Lucretia Motts of all ages, and now men mock us with the fact and say we are ever cruel to each other. Let us end this ignoble record. . . . If Victoria Woodhull must be crucified, let men drive the spikes and plait the crown of thorns.

But Anthony was now convinced that Woodhull, supported by a motley crowd of spiritualists, political extremists and disaffected hangers-on, was intent on taking over the movement for her own ends. The result was an ugly confrontation at the May 1872 convention of the National group. Soon after it opened, Woodhull marched onto the platform and urged the audience to join the campaign for her "People's Party." Anthony tried to cut her off but Woodhull pressed on, and Anthony finally had the lights turned out.

That was the beginning of the end for Victoria Woodhull. Deeply in debt, evicted from boardinghouses and hotels, she overflowed with anger against her foes, and particularly against Harriet and Catharine Beecher. So in September she converted her closing address as president of the National Association of Spiritualists into a revelation of all that she had heard of the Beecher-Tilton affair. A Memphis delegate reported that her words "poured out like a stream of flame." The Boston papers virtually ignored the speech or reported only that it had slandered a prominent clergyman. Frustrated beyond control, Woodhull, as we have seen, devoted an entire issue of her *Weekly* to her exposé.

No one in Nook Farm other than Isabella believed Woodhull's story. It was simply unthinkable that the spokesman for their spiritual ideals, he who had filled their religion with drama, poetry and hope, had been a lecher and a hypocrite. Who could credit such charges coming from such a source?

The answer was—Isabella Beecher Hooker. Soon after Woodhull's first public disclosure, Isabella had written to Henry offering to help. He had responded, with characteristic jauntiness, that he trod such "falsehoods into the dirt from whence they spring, and go on my way rejoicing." When, however, he referred to the "barbarity of dragging a poor dear child of a woman into the slough," Isabella, passing the letter along to her brother Thomas, remarked, as we have seen, that it seemed to be Henry who had not only dragged the woman into the mire but left her there. She added that he was now sending to prison another woman, Victoria Woodhull—a reference to Comstock's arrest of Woodhull for mailing obscene matter—"innocent of all crime but a fanaticism for the truth."

Isabella now gave Henry a detailed account of her mounting anxieties since first hearing the Tilton story from Stanton. She could not even share her fears with her husband, she said, "because he was already overburdened and alarmingly affected brain-wise." She declared that if the story was true,

you had a philosophy of the relation of the sexes so far ahead of the times that you dared not announce it, though you consented to live by it. That this was in my judgment wrong, and God would bring all secret things to light in his own time and fashion. . . .

Perhaps to persuade him that she was open-minded and could be confided in, she added:

I had come to see that human laws were an impertinence, but could get no further, though I could see glimpses of a possible new science of life that at present was revolting to my feelings and my judgment; that I should keep myself open to conviction, however . . . and as fast as I *knew* the truth I should stand by it, with no attempt at concealment.

Characteristically dramatizing her own sacrifice and her husband's weakness, she concluded:

. . . you can imagine, knowing what my husband is to me, that it was no common love I have for you . . . when I decided to nearly break his heart, already lacerated by the course I had been compelled to pursue, by sending him away to die, perhaps, without me at his side.

It is hard to say how much of her concern for Henry was genuine and how much another of her self-appointed roles in a moral drama. She was certainly aware that she was the only one who was intimate with both Victoria Woodhull and Henry Ward Beecher, and she quickly advertised this by sending her brother Tom copies of the letters she had received from both. In her last letter Woodhull had declared that Isabella still had a great mission, and she concluded portentously: "I see the near approach of the grandest revelation the world has yet known, and for the part you shall play in it thousands will rise up and call you blessed. It was not for nothing that you and I met so singularly."

Seduced by such flattering prophecies, Isabella reiterated her belief that Woodhull was "pure and unselfish and absolutely driven by some power" to speak out for the outcast and against only "the hypocrites in high places." Tom gave her little comfort. He had to respect Woodhull, he said, for speaking the truth but he abhorred her philosophy, and he loved Henry but had predicted the dangers in his drift into "slippery doctrines of expediency."

John Hooker's reaction was even more unsettling. He was so agitated by his wife's involvement in the Beecher-Tilton affair as well as her intimacy with Woodhull that he went off to Europe alone when Isabella decided not to accompany him. Despite Isabella's alarm, he was in no danger of dying (he lived for another thirty years); but he did write a desperate letter from Florence in an effort to save not only his wife's reputation but his own amidst all these bewildering entanglements. Convinced of Henry's guilt, he could imagine only one excuse for his brother-in-law's continued concealment of his role—that he had agreed to spare the Tiltons: "This would take off somewhat from the hypocrisy of the thing, but leaves the original crime as open to condemnation as ever." Reduced to a deviousness he had always abhorred, he adds:

Can you not let the report get out . . . that you have kept up friendship with Mrs. W. in the hope of influencing her not to publish the story, you having learned its truth . . . and that you gave up going to Europe with me so as to be at home and comfort H. when the truth came out. . . . This will give the appearance of self-sacrifice to your affiliation with her, and will explain your not coming abroad with me—a fact which has a very unwife-like look. I know that you will otherwise be regarded as holding Mrs. W.'s views, and that we shall be regarded as living in some discord, and probably (by many people) as practising her principles. It would be a great relief to me to have your relations to Mrs. W. explained in this way. . . . There is not half the untruth in it that there has been all along in my pretended approval of Mrs. Woodhull's course, and yet people think me an honest man. . . . I have lied enough about that to ruin the character of an average man.

Deacon and honored lawyer though he is, his chief concern is his reputation for respectability. Isabella brooded over her duties and responsibilities until the questions raised by an editorial in the Hartford *Times* spurred her into a desperate ultimatum. "I can endure no longer," she wrote to Henry. "I must see you and persuade you to write a paper which I will read, going alone to your pulpit, and taking sole charge of the services. . . ." Writing as one "commissioned from on high," she adds, once again directing a drama: "Do not fail me, I pray you; meet me at noon on Friday as you hope to meet your own mother in heaven."

Moulton later testified that Isabella did not carry out her threat because Tilton met with her and threatened to "reveal" that she herself had been guilty of adultery in Washington. Whether Tilton actually did this or invented the incident to besmirch Isabella, it was an ugly story— and unconvincing to boot. Isabella was now ostracized by all her brothers and sisters except Catharine and by most of her Nook Farm neighbors.

Although the Hookers had been the first in Hartford to extend hospitality to Mark Twain and had rented their house to him while he was building a mansion nearby, he forbade his wife ever to cross the Hooker threshold again.

But the harshest reaction came from Harriet. Shortly after she had stood guard against Isabella's invasion of Plymouth Church, she declared in a letter to a friend that it was Victoria Woodhull who was responsible for Isabella's delusions:

No one could understand the secret of her influence over my poor sister—an incredible infatuation continuing even now. I trust that God will in some way deliver her for she was and is a lovely good woman and before this witch took [possession] of her we were all so happy together.

When Isabella persisted in her stand, Harriet, as we have seen, described her as one of those monomaniacs who are "all right if the wrong string is not jarred." She made this remark in a letter to her daughter Eliza, but others were surely aware of her opinion.

On his return from Europe, John Hooker, tormented by his own as well as his wife's sullied reputation, kept trying to convince his friends and neighbors—to the point of annoying a few of them—that Isabella had acted out of love in urging Henry to tell the whole truth before it was too late. The implication, of course, was that Henry was guilty. Their Hartford neighbor the Reverend Joseph Twichell, a forthright, down-to-earth clergyman, reported to his close friend Mark Twain that Hooker was beginning to make some converts. Just then, the final church council on the Beecher affair absolved Henry of everything except a foolish trust in his enemies. Twichell went along with this conclusion and ever after spoke of Isabella with evident disdain.

Although Isabella continued to labor for women's rights, much of her energies and emotions were drained off into defending her alliance with Woodhull and into her conflict with her famous brother. She clung to her position with a combination of reasonable arguments, emotional assertions and characteristic Beecher righteousness. But finally, early in the summer of 1874, she and John retreated to Europe. She did not return for a year and a half, staying away until the flood of sickening rumors and headlines had begun to recede. Not that she was allowed to escape from all the charges and countercharges. One story, apparently circulated by both Woodhull and Stanton, was that Isabella had known all along of Henry's sexual philosophy and conduct and did not disapprove of it. Isabella now denied this heatedly. She explained that she had not done so sooner because she had been reluctant to contribute to the widespread view that Woodhull had no regard for the truth.

The trip to Europe was a serious interruption in Isabella's career. In the previous four years she had pushed into the vanguard of the women's rights movement and seemed about to reach the very front rank. Now her stubborn attachment to Woodhull and her hounding of Henry—not to mention her faith in spiritualism—called into question her reliability as a setter of standards and a model of behavior. This was still the Victorian era: respectability and propriety were still watchwords and certainly as important as showing Christian sympathy for a woman like Victoria Woodhull or condemning a brother for the sake of a principle.

Where others might have been overwhelmed by the waves of disapproval, Isabella found both refuge and support in spiritualism. Alone in a hotel room in Paris, many weeks away from the scene of the scandal, she had a vision in which her mother—dead for forty years—appeared to her and promised to guide her toward her divine role. Later she referred to this apparition as the Angel of Annunciation—an unabashed comparison between herself and the Virgin Mary.

Isabella returned to America in the fall of 1875. Although she resumed her work in the women's movement, her true solace for the frustrations in her family life came from her spiritualist activities. Far from being thought eccentric, she found that her interest was shared, sometimes fanatically, by men and women everywhere. In December she wrote to her son Ned, who was studying medicine in Boston, that she might be "called away" before Christmas. I want you, she wrote, "to pray that I be not overwhelmed by the magnitude of the work" before me. She was, of course, not called away. Undiscouraged, she wrote to Ned again several months later, "The abundance of the revelation and the fullness of my inner life shut me off from everything else at present."

Her inner life bursting with such great secrets, Isabella poured her hopes and anxieties into a journal that she began when she and her husband moved back into their home—a severe economic depression forced them to share the house with tenants—in May of 1876. The diaries are not so much a daily record as almost obsessive ruminations on a few themes. But they do reveal more than we know about the inner life of any other member of the family. The dominant subjects are her estrangement from her daughters' families, her communication with the spirit world, her messianic role, and her husband's alleged infringement on her individuality.

What is astonishing about her relationship to Mary and Alice and their families is that a woman who worshiped motherhood and craved a loving family should have aroused such hostility in her sons-in-law. Her smothering love of her daughters along with her belief in the unimportance of fathers in relation to children could hardly have endeared her to these men. Her views on feminism and spiritualism also contributed to the alienation. She herself accepted a face-saving explanation offered by Mary to the effect that Eugene feared Isabella would come between him and his child. So Eugene barred her from his home. She notes that she has never in eight years spent a Thanksgiving or a Christmas day with her grandchildren. When she does meet them for an hour or an afternoon she is ecstatic, and when people tell her how delightful they are, she writhes and could weep. A score of entries tell of her deep conviction that Eugene will one day be overcome by remorse and call her "mother" again. (He never did.) Ironically, a remarkable number of other young men and women see her just as she desires—as a wonderfully wise and sympathetic mother: the famous Anna Dickinson, a Robert Allen, whom she calls her adopted son, a young feminist, Kate Trimble, who addresses her as "Mama," the Gillettes' son Will—later an actor famous for his role as Sherlock Holmes—who comes to her for healing and help.

Although in her daily activities a self-possessed and charming woman, Isabella admits that her family problems sometimes leave her "crazy with pain and confusion." And this in turn leads to another theme: her escape into spiritualism. It was a peculiarly satisfying experience: unlike the traditional religions, it made no demands and used no threats. Instead it promised divine guidance, spiritual healing, and eternal life to the spirit. Isabella soon set aside an upstairs room as a sanctum for messages from the spirit world and for healing by the laying on of hands. She adorned it under the supervision of her dead child, Thomas, who had apparently developed artistic gifts in the other world. Over the years she held sessions there with mediums from near and far, meeting with them as often as several times a week and, with a few, for a period of years. Indeed, Hartford seemed to be alive with otherwise commonplace women who had suddenly acquired a miraculous power to communicate with the dead and foretell the future. Magical as well as dramatic, spiritualism was a fascinating replacement for older churches that had lost some of their influence and much of their mystery.

Isabella found that she herself could sink into a trance and with her very considerable gifts of voice and gesture "impersonate" the spirits that were invoked. Or she could allow a spirit control to use her hand for messages from the beyond. Her husband later estimated that they had communicated with 450 spirits, ranging from old friends and relatives to Napoleon (she tried to lead him into constructive ways), Byron, Jeanne d'Arc (assumed to be her otherworld counterpart), Harriet Martineau (who wanted to teach her economics), Dickens and, reflecting her love of music, Paganini, Haydn and Beethoven. Indian maidens and warriors were common "controls" and Isabella's favorite among these was King

Philip. When she made contact with Harriet's vanished son, Fred, he sounded as though he were being scalped, and Isabella's unkind conclusion was that he had delirium tremens.

She was only briefly disturbed when some of her principal prophecies proved false. One of these was the prediction that Alice and Eugene's little Kathie would die within a year. It may be cruel to say that she passed along this harrowing augury because she wished unconsciously to punish Alice for keeping her grandchildren away from her, but the only excuse she herself offers is that it was meant to prepare Alice for the blow. Kathie lived on until 1923. That episode alone would have been enough to embitter any son-in-law.

At another time Isabella, neurotically fearful of burglars and hoping for a reconciliation with Eugene, came out of a trance with a prediction that an armed robber will invade Eugene's house and wound him and that she, John and Ned will rescue him. Somehow, she persuades her husband and son to prepare for the event, including a tourniquet and stimulants for the wounded man, and then mounts a vigil. Nothing happens. Undaunted, she comes up with a specific date for the deed. Despite his skepticism, John gets two policemen in plain clothes—perhaps through his influence as a Supreme Court officer—to join them on the appointed night.

Throughout the night, Isabella waits tensely at the window—Eugene's house is within sight—ready to rush to the rescue. It is a mad incident conducted with utmost care and decorum. It is also a fiasco. And this time, when Isabella tries to offer an excuse, John rejects it indignantly. For a few days Isabella's humiliation is unbearable, but that soon fades.

Perhaps the most absurd episode of all results from her anticipation of a divine mission. Waiting with increasing anxiety for the great moment, Isabella decides that it will come, appropriately, on the eve of the new year. Once again she sees the event as a drama: "The play moves on and actors seem to me to have been preparing for years past for the grand drama that is already silently upon the stage. When the curtain rises, what shall we see?"

We see guests arriving on New Year's Eve at the big Hooker house and gathering in the parlor. Among them is Sam Clemens and his wife and the Warners, who will stay briefly before going on to the Warners' place. Then the tragicomedy begins. Mrs. Roberts, one of Isabella's favorite mediums, comes in a common housedress. Isabella gives her one of her own dresses and then deposits her in an upstairs bedroom. Now little Miss Perry, another medium, arrives dressed in an ordinary wrapper—with her mother in tow. This is almost paralyzing, and John is frantic. When Mrs. Perry begins talking loudly, Isabella hastily shunts her and her mother upstairs. As Isabella turns back toward the crowded parlor, she is aghast to see Dr. Williams, another and a somewhat less agreeable medium, standing in the hall. She grasps him by the arm and hurries him upstairs and into the bedroom. Alice, coming down the stairs, bursts out, "Why, what is going on in your room, mother? There is the queerest looking lot up there." Isabella quickly hushes her up. The assemblage of contacts with the next world is by now overwhelming, but instead of embarrassing Isabella, it convinces her that something momentous is about to take place.

Instead Dr. Williams, evidently unhappy at having been stowed away in a roomful of rival prophets, comes down the stairs just as the Clemenses and Warners decide to leave. Fortunately they ignore him. Then the Perrys descend, and tiny Miss Perry, apparently endowed with some of the strength of the Indian warrior who is her control, pounds John vigorously—to the vast amusement of Sophie the maid. But the other guests have apparently not noticed anything amiss. As they leave, several remark how beautifully Isabella manages such affairs, Susie Warner exclaiming that it was just like old times.

That was good enough for Isabella. Avoiding her husband, she sat up all night in the study, already dreaming a new dream: she would continue to hold such Sunday gatherings until they would at last become a source of immense spiritual power—"the beginning of the church on Nook Farm which I have seen so distinctly in vision over and over again."

In the morning, compelled to face her husband, she insisted that she had not "consciously planned the events of the evening without consulting him." He retorted that she was a "monomaniac, thinking intently on only one thing and therefore not to be trusted," and that she should always consult him. Son Ned intervened, loyally declaring that Isabella was not "crazy nor in any way disturbed in her mind."

Thus supported, Isabella defended herself vigorously. She asserted that far from dwelling only on spiritualism, she read widely in politics, science and art, enjoyed music, whist and entertaining company, devoted herself to John day and night, and was as helpful in his work as she could be. Growing more aggressive, she pointed out that he himself had lately confessed that he had been a hypochondriac from birth and feared that his tendency to melancholia would leave him quite insane in his old age. Now, she wrote,

Simply because I am investigating phenomena that claim the attention of the whole scientific world today—no less than the religious, guided by a peculiar experience of my own ... *you dare to call me insane.* I think this is the pot calling the kettle black—and so we ended—and not a word has he said since, either of recrimination or apology.

She had not intended to say anything more. But she found herself compelled, out of wounded pride, to tell the two men that she had become the "Comforter" whom Jesus said would recall all his words and deeds. (Apparently it did not matter that the passage in John 14 refers to the Comforter as a man.) She sees herself as bringing love and wisdom to a "*maternal government* of this great nation" and introducing "the great millennial period, toward which aching hearts have so long turned their weary longings." Elsewhere she refers to herself as "*the* inspired one who is to reign as the vicegerent of this blessed Christ [and] with him to usher in the millennial day." And finally, in other statements, she speaks of herself as no less than the sister of Jesus.

As unworldly as she seems in such moments, at other times she reveals the not so noble aim of becoming the envy of men, and especially churchmen: she sees the spirit of Horace Bushnell returning to apologize for his opposition, Joseph Twichell stunned by her glorification, and brother Henry literally kneeling before her. . . . Also less than heaven-inspired is her mother's concern with Isabella's clothes or where she places her furniture and pictures. Getting support on such matters was evidently an effort to fortify herself against her husband's criticism on everyday as well as astral levels. Another step down from her loftier sentiments is the way she finds occult significance in every rap and knock around the house. At her most gullible, she climbs out on the tin roof below her bedroom window and while sitting in the sun hears messages in the popping sounds that come through her silk parasol.

Like many of those who have thought of themselves as chosen by God, she has moments—but only moments—of heart-shaking doubt. It is evidence of her underlying sanity that she keeps on planning for a life outside her promised divinity so that she will not be "utterly wrecked" if it should not come to pass. Occasionally she feels "like one drowning or clinging to a stray plank in mid-ocean," and in her darkest hours her visions, she writes, seem like a "delusion and a mockery and I groan inwardly, being burdened." Physically she has days when she is so tired—especially because of a limp resulting from an ankle broken long before—that her body and will seem paralyzed.

Life of course went on outside her revelations. She visited the Philadelphia Centennial, and, annoyed at its failure to recognize the role of women, went about spreading the suffragist gospel. A great victory came in 1877 when the bill to give women property rights, which she and John had been presenting since 1870, was passed by the Connecticut legislature. But even more spectacular was the special hearing, on Washington's birthday, 1878, before the Senate Committee on Privileges and Elections granted to Isabella at the request of a score of senators. The Washington *Post* reported that she spoke with Beecher fervor and eloquence. "Wire-pulling politicians," she charged, may well fear to have women enfranchised because women will not be easily duped. Attacking the government's Indian policy, she declared that if Lucretia Mott could have led in councils of the nation, the Indian problem would have been settled peacefully long before and the millions spent on fighting Indians might have been used in kindergartens for the poor. When women come to vote, she asserted, they will say, "Down with the army, down with appropriation bills to repair the consequences of wrong-doing." To some who heard her she may have seemed presumptuous when she went on to review the Chinese question, the labor problem, compulsory education, police regulations, the "social evil" and other topics, but they would not have known that she had constantly heard equally weighty issues debated at the family table forty years before.

Now, too, there was the beginning of a reconciliation with the family and old friends. Catharine, staying with the Stowes, visited Isabella regularly and heartened her by agreeing that there were some occurrences that only spiritualism seemed able to explain. Harriet invited her to play croquet, and learning of the Hookers' financial distress, impulsively sent her sister fifty dollars, which Isabella promptly interpreted as a kind of "reparation." But brother Tom was not so pliable. When he visited her, she brought him into her sanctum and solemnly told him of the message she had received from their mother in Paris. Taking his hand, she sank into a trance and, acting as Livy, his beloved first wife, she sobbed and talked and caressed his hand. But when she recovered, she was saddened to discover that he was not convinced.

Even her old admirer, brother Charles, was not as receptive as she expected.

Uncle Charles who left here last Friday [she wrote to her daughter Mary] told me he was looking daily for the coming of Christ, and though cautioning me kindly against spiritualism as of the devil probably, I found . . . that our views were very similar as to the interpretation of the Bible and life generally. And when he told me he was sure there was a conspiracy against Henry—he being utterly innocent—*which was of the devil surely,* my confidence in his judgment of Spiritualism was weakened, especially as he acknowledged the phenomena to be largely true.

It was surely a curious confrontation: a Beecher who claimed to be in touch with the spirit world dismissing another who believed in the devil.

It was during this visit that Charles also reported to Isabella that sister Mary loved her as much as ever but would not "fellowship" her until she conceded that Henry was innocent. Isabella explained, quite firmly, that she could not do so because Henry had never answered her own or her husband's questions on the subject. As he was leaving, she added:

Well, Charley, we have spent many hours together in the happiest manner, without a thought of this subject coming between us, and we could live together year in and year out . . . just as we used to do—why not Mary?— He laughed that little sweet cheery laugh I remember so well . . . and went out without saying a word. . . . So that is settled for the present. I shall not go there any more and it is better so.

Seeking to reestablish her social position, Isabella began by entertaining a score of women for lunch—fried oysters, cold chicken and celery salad, followed by Susie Warner playing Beethoven on the piano. It was, everyone agreed, like the old days. Since women who dared to be suffragists were often receptive to other unorthodox ideas, Isabella later gave luncheons in which the guests were both suffragists and spiritualists.

But she was not quite so successful with Sam Clemens. When she took a friend to see his home—it was already a Nook Farm showplace—she had a disconcerting encounter with him. Jokingly she remarked that he apparently no longer liked a pretty lamp shade after learning that it came cheap. He seemed vexed that the story was being circulated and declared that he knew nothing about such things, so that when an established shop said an article was good and charged a good price for it, he could feel that it was worthy of his Livy. Isabella observed that one might sometimes pay a high price for a homely article in such circumstances, a remark that Clemens also seemed to resent. When Isabella added that it was all a joke and that "one so given to joking as himself mustn't mind it, etc. . . . his eyes flashed and he looked really angry." Mrs. Clemens came in just then and, hearing Sam assert that cheap things were not worth giving, said that no matter how small the gift, it was the thoughtfulness that made it valuable. Clemens obviously did not relish this either and Isabella, becoming more and more uncomfortable, moved on.

She also met Bret Harte in the house and later, when she passed through the billiard room, the two men were there, with "bottles of spirit" at hand. As socially sophisticated as she might be, her reaction was: "I felt a new distrust of such companionship and ever since the thought has haunted me that perhaps I have something to do there by way of warning." Fortunately her Beecherian moral urge was tempered by prudence, so she adds: "I dread to lose the friendship of that house which is but a slender thread already."

Isabella's commitment to spiritualism seems to have had more effect on her son Ned than on her daughters. Soon after becoming a doctor, he revealed that he was trying, in emulation of Christ, to heal by a laying on of hands and by prayer. Convinced that he had great "magnetic" powers, Isabella encouraged him, telling him that his birth was as pure as Christ's. It is clear, as she had told John Stuart Mill, that she considered herself the only true creator of her children—with her husband simply an accessory. (She was much pleased to learn from one of her heavenly informants that in the other world one's sex did not matter at all.)

It therefore troubled her that her husband discussed large issues with her but showed no confidence in her capacity to cope with daily affairs. He believed that she was fitted for "positions of universal scope" but not for writing a note or hiring a horse. And he still harped on her failure to follow his advice concerning Victoria Woodhull and the Beecher-Tilton case.

Much of the friction with her husband was part of a general resentment against male domination. But sometimes it was only the familiar kind of domestic discord in which a minor irritant sets off a major clash. This occurred when John saw a photograph Isabella was sending to one of her many admirers among the feminists. It looks, he said with uncharacteristic bluntness, like "one of those dancing girls." She answered that she was vain enough to enjoy looking young and beautiful rather than solemn, and that he was, as so often before, trespassing on her individuality. When he insisted that it was he who usually gave in to her, she replied sharply but tried to blunt the effect by adding that she was only quoting Catharine: "You have ridden me as Balaam the ass . . . but it was the ass who saw the angel, and not Balaam." All these years, she added, "you have wished to guide me by the bridle, with a bit in my mouth . . . but this is all over now."

To her journal she confides that her husband mistook fastidiousness of taste for reason and judgment. He puts her, she says, under a magnifying glass, concentrates the eyes of the world upon her, and says, "See what a figure you cut," whereas she, knowing that she is pure and unselfish, doesn't care what the world thinks. She shifts bewilderingly between disparaging him and praising him, saying that he underestimates his "exquisite spiritual nature," which, she adds, is "all there is of him to me, and it is this which holds me to him as to no other man I have ever seen." Perhaps to avoid responsibility for stronger criticism of her husband, she here allows Catharine—who had died only a few months earlier—and then another strongly opinionated person, the editor Samuel Bowles, who had also died that year, to take control of her pen. As Catharine takes over, Isabella's handwriting in her journal changes radically, and after a few lines, as Bowles begins to communicate, it changes again. Catharine insists—ironically, Isabella still resents her officious tone—that Hooker should stop "molesting" his wife with unreasonable criticisms. Bowles then urges him not to yield to his lower, or masculine,

nature. Here visitors interrupt Isabella and she resumes her own character and handwriting. From our ground it is easy to see the episode as a
demonstration not of occult communication but of autosuggestion. When
she recovers, Isabella herself realizes that John will not believe that such
messages come from anyone but her.

As the 1878 journal draws to a close, Isabella, still convinced of her
divine mission, lists the twelve men and women who will become her
disciples, including not only such favorites as Anna Dickinson, Will Gil-
lette, Robert Allen and her daughters, but also her son-in-law Eugene
Burton, presumably in the expectation that he will eventually come back
into the fold.

In such a community of professional and literary people as made up
Nook Farm in the 1880s, the old religion seemed more and more the
creed of an outworn time. There are frequent references in Isabella's
letters to Calvinism even in its moderate form as hideous and to the
theological quarrels that still beset the Presbyterian Church as absurd—
almost enough to make one prefer Catholicism. The Bible is a wonderful
book, she says, and she wishes she could believe in it, but it no longer
matters as evidence concerning the next life because the new "scientific"—by which she means "spiritualist"—evidence has taken its place.

But profound shifts in faith are not easy. Like Matthew Arnold, she
found herself between two worlds, the old one gone and the new one not
yet come. She had managed to read *Pilgrim's Progress* to her children;
but she could not read it to her grandchildren. ". . . that is another sorrowful thing about life—" she wrote to Alice, "this giving up old beliefs
and not finding anything to take their place."

Socially she was not as straitlaced as Harriet or even Charles. She
saw no harm in drinking wine, especially in view of Christ's tolerance of
it, and she thought temperance a far more sensible goal than total abstinence. The women who now began to appear at parties with bare shoulders troubled her, but they bothered her prudish husband much more.
And during her visits to Europe there is none of the moral disapproval
that had marked Charles's and Harriet's travel reports.

Isabella's difficulties with her family continued. Perhaps the most
painful episode in that shattered relationship came when Henry lay dying in 1887. In an agony made up of guilt, love, grief and a desire for
vindication, she hurried to Brooklyn. But she was barred from the
house—Eunice was as unforgiving as ever—and stirred up ugly old stories by lingering on the street outside. She was convinced that even after
his death Henry would somehow apologize to her. So late at night she
joined the end of the line moving slowly past the coffin in Plymouth
Church, desperately hoping for a sign. . . .

Despite the humiliating situations in which spiritualism had sometimes entangled her, it proved invaluable in the great tragedy of her later life, the death, from tuberculosis, of her daughter Mary at the age of thirty-nine. Even though the Hookers did not realize until a year or so before she died how serious were Mary's bronchial attacks and constant coughing, her last years were a torment to them because of her bitter estrangement from her husband. He lived apart from her, and communicated with her only on business matters and by postal card. After her father spent a vacation with her in the summer of 1884, he reported that she was admired by everyone for her beauty and wit and that those who knew of her plight sympathized with her. But for John Hooker all this was poisoned by the fact that she was "bound to a brutal husband who cares nothing for her and . . . probably wishes she was dead." Her husband's behavior had long since left Mary callous—or so she said—but her father reached a point where, temperate and amiable as he might be, he declared, "It seems as if I could shoot the scoundrel even if I had to be hung for it."

In the years after Mary's death the Hookers found their greatest solace in the conviction that they could communicate with her almost at will. In an upstairs room Isabella fixed up a little shrine in Mary's memory and never ceased to believe that her daughter was hovering nearby. Her devotion was not without a trace of guilt: involuntarily in those last months she had shrunk from Mary's embrace—from the very affection she had always craved. . . .

When Isabella thought of her dominant interests, she put spiritualism first and women's rights second. Her third interest, she wrote, was Jews, which seems strange until we learn that she had been much impressed by a visit from Emma Lazarus, poet and impassioned defender of Judaism, and had also become increasingly curious about Christ's Jewish heritage.

Not that she neglected the rights of women. She carried on a correspondence with suffragists everywhere and went about New England setting up women's clubs for the study of political science. Having won property rights for her sex in Connecticut, in 1878 she submitted to the state legislature a bill that would give the vote to women in the state. It failed to pass, but she presented it annually for the remaining twenty years of her life. She attended almost every national women's rights convention and was often a principal speaker. In an address, "The Constitutional Rights of the Women of the U.S.," before the International Council of Women, which she helped to convene in Washington in 1887, she gave her broadest interpretation of the responsibilities as well as the rights that women needed if they were to grow in stature. With ever widening social sympathies, she declared that we must let the poor and every newcomer to our shores share our obligations as well as our liberties. "If all the advocates were as cultivated, refined and convincing as Mrs. Hooker," the Washington *Post* declared, "one might almost be tempted to surrender." She had, the article added, "a rare magnetic influence," and Isabella herself wrote:

Sometimes I feel such a sense of power within me that nothing seems impossible—in fact, I have been conscious of something of this sort from childhood, but there have been years and years . . . when it was all crushed out of me by opposition of my nearest and dearest . . . but I have never resigned the hope that sometimes and somewhere I should be allowed to work for righteousness according to my impulse and the clear vision of great possibilities.

As time passed and she became more and more convinced of the superior mental and moral power of womankind, she could hardly contain her anger at men. After appealing to Connecticut legislators to introduce a bill permitting women to vote on school matters and the sale of liquor, she noted that she appears good-natured outwardly; but all the time, she adds, "my soul is indignant and I keep wondering how a gentleman can look me in the face and declare that he was born to rule and I to obey— he a sovereign, I a subject, from the cradle to the grave." So, too, when she hears that women are not being included in the plans for the great World's Columbian Exposition in Chicago in 1892, her exasperation is uncontrollable:

I have never been so moved in my life. The Philadelphia Centennial, the neglect and insults of it, sank deep into my soul, but this one stirs me to the very depths. A male oligarchy has called itself a republic for a hundred years, and during forty of them good men and women have patiently protested against the misnomer and asked for justice. . . . Yet today the national junketings are to be paid for by women equally with men and *never* an acknowledgment of their existence as political entities.

Her conclusion was a cry of pure anguish: "What shall we do to be saved?"

But the women's rights movement had lost its novelty and even its power to arouse opposition; it was simply ignored. When Connecticut held a constitutional convention in 1892, Isabella prepared a memorial from the Connecticut Woman Suffrage Society asking that the word "male" be stricken from the article granting citizens the right to vote. The managers of the convention not only refused to let her read the memorial at the convention or appear before the appropriate committee, but even prevented her from submitting printed copies of arguments for the measure. Mrs. Hooker had buttonholed and besieged them for twenty-three years and they were simply tired of her petitions.

Her chagrin at her defeat was assuaged by her appointment in 1890 as the Connecticut representative on the Board of Lady Managers of the Chicago exposition. The 150 buildings going up on the shore of Lake Michigan was America bursting with power and pride, confidently comparing itself to the great empires of the past. . . . She was active in the planning stages and by the fall of 1891 had earned a tribute in the Chicago *Herald* that was little short of adulation. She is, the reporter said, the "character" of the Woman's Board and, like all Beechers, incomparable. Beautifully dressed, vivacious and frank, she blends, the article continued, acute perception, relentless logic and an almost childlike playfulness. It was the latter quality she displayed when she announced: "I want the Fair gates opened early on Sunday and let everybody in, but I want somebody else to get up to open them." The power of this striking woman, the article concludes, "her drollery, her picturesqueness, her very faults . . . have turned the Woman's Board . . . into an Isabella society."

But perhaps Isabella's greatest contribution was the "universal litany" which she wove together out of passages from the scriptures of the ancient Egyptians, the Hebrews, Buddhists, Chinese, Hindus, Muslims and Christians, and read at a huge international religious service. In its reach and open-mindedness, it was light-years away from her father's Calvinism and even the position of most of her brothers and sisters.

The similarities between spiritualism and Christian Science seem apparent. Both sprang from a widespread discontent with the threats and warnings, the dark view of human nature, and the rigid structure of the Calvinist churches. And both held out the promise of eternal life of the spirit and the power of mental healing. Emerging in the 1880s, Christian Science attracted Alice Hooker just as spiritualism had captured her parents in the 1860s and '70s. When she revealed her interest—in letters from London, where she had been living with her husband since 1887— her father was truly pleased. He felt that she was going in the same direction as he and Isabella. Self-effacingly, he hailed her as the heir to her mother's great mind and heart. Turned into a true believer in Isabella's grand mission, he added that Alice would now be able to write the memoir that her mother's life deserved—for "she will be looked upon by coming generations as one of the great prophetic souls of the world's history."

But Isabella was not so sympathetic. Whether she was jealous of a woman who was achieving the kind of messiahship she herself dreamed of or genuinely felt that Mary Baker Eddy, founder of Christian Science, was too self-serving, she belittled her. She had read Mrs. Eddy's writings, learned her history from a friend and was dubious about both. She declared that Mrs. Eddy had not given credit to her spiritualist teachers, was egotistical and inconsistent and lived elegantly on the profits from her teachings. When Alice asserted that Mrs. Eddy had been a physician and spiritualist but had outgrown both, Isabella retorted that she was a superior mental healer but as "bigoted as any old Calvinist that sends all to hell who do not agree with his 'plan of salvation.' " As strong-minded in some ways as her mother, Alice was not persuaded.

It seems surprising that Isabella's affinity for young women with feminist leanings should not have brought her closer to the most radical and emancipated member of the next two generations of Beechers, Charlotte Perkins Gilman. It will seem equally surprising that Charlotte, born in 1860, was the granddaughter not of Isabella but of Mary, the most proper and conforming of all Isabella's siblings. It may be that Isabella and her grandniece remained distant because Charlotte was the daughter of Mary's intellectually gifted but highly individualistic son Frederick, who shocked Hartford circles in the late 1860s by leaving his wife and children. It could not have helped matters when Charlotte, some twenty years later, left her husband and child.

Victim of a broken home, Charlotte developed a deep resentment against male dominance, female dependence and the obligations of a wife and mother. This explains in great part why in her late twenties she separated from her husband and daughter in order to concentrate on her career as a writer and reformer. But these acts left her with a recurring sense of guilt and failure so that, much like her great-aunt Catharine and not unlike Isabella and Harriet, she went from periods of buoyant activity to bouts of depression and nervous breakdown.

In her periods of productivity, beginning in the 1890s, she turned out a large number of bold and mordant articles, books, lectures and—in a feminist periodical, the *Forerunner,* which she edited for seven years—radical editorials on the frustrations of women and on social and political problems. Mixing an imposing grasp of economics and social history with a theory—borrowed from sociologist Lester Ward—that woman was the primary sex, she pictured woman as the age-old victim of gender, imbued with a "slave mentality."

Charlotte also wrote poetry and fiction, and one of her most impressive performances is "The Yellow Wallpaper," a haunting short story of a housewife and mother driven slowly insane through the stifling of her individuality, mainly by her physician husband. Based on Charlotte's own experience, "The Yellow Wallpaper" is an unforgettable glimpse of the situation of a woman in late-Victorian America. The manner is Poesque fantasy; the substance is chilling case history.

The clearest clue to Isabella's attitude toward her grandniece is a letter she wrote in 1901 to her old suffragist associate Olympia Brown.

Evidently feeling, ironically enough, that Charlotte's personal life unfitted her for active suffragist campaigning, Isabella declared:

As to Mrs. Perkins Gilman she is all right—a noble woman of large gifts who has had a history that can't be put into print. . . . She was divorced from Mr. Stetson—for reasons satisfactory to them. . . . But I doubt if she can do much but write books—the world will not pardon peculiarities—and you may not be able to carry her without injuring your own usefulness.

The progress from Catharine Beecher's early campaigns for women's education and financial independence to Isabella's work for women's rights, and thence to Charlotte's efforts to live as a liberated woman in the 1890s, is perhaps the most striking example of the persistence in the Beecher family of commitment to a social ideal.

In Charlotte Perkins Gilman's later years—she lived until 1935—she was looked on as a relic of nineteenth-century suffragism, but she now seems as relevant in many respects as though she wrote yesterday.

Progress brought its own problems. The movement from country to city and from farm to factory had produced a new class—factory workers. Although she conformed on many minor matters, Isabella had her own convictions on such large issues. Far removed socially and spiritually from the world of factory workers, she was nonetheless shocked by the inhumanity of certain industrialists in the labor unrest of the 1890s. Although motivated by humanitarian sentimentality rather than social justice, her response to the outrages in the Homestead strike of 1892 was unequivocal: "Only think of Carnegie with his 30-odd millions grudging his faithful workmen the trifle that would help them to lay by a mite for a rainy day, and preparing hot steam and rifles to protect his works."

John Hooker never achieved a judgeship and he acknowledged that he had spent his life in a "subordinate and unnoticed position," but he was an intimate of many justices and occasionally wrote opinions for those who were too lazy or incompetent to do so. Enjoying his work, he did not retire until he was seventy-eight years old. A man of wide reading and an open mind, he grew less and less rigid in his religious views. He came to feel that a man's chief accountability for his sins was to himself, not God, that the Old Testament was full of stories of an "age of brutality," and that the idea of eternal punishment was nonsense. Declaring that a man was saved by his own character, not by Christ's sacrifice, he noted that "fine Jews such as our rabbis do not accept the atonement of Christ and yet there are no more godly men." In the end he put his faith in a "liberal Christianity," saying, "I do not believe in creeds" but only in "the Fatherhood of God and the Brotherhood of Man."

As a Connecticut Supreme Court official and a church deacon, Hooker in some ways commanded more respect than his wife. (On their golden wedding anniversary in 1891, a grand affair attended by notables from all over New England, the newspapers made as much of Hooker's services and his distinguished ancestry as of his wife's achievements.) And yet in his *Some Reminiscences of a Long Life,* his social and political opinions repeatedly challenge our conception of well-placed Victorians as complacent and conformist. He accepted Darwinism and natural selection, had an almost Marxist sympathy for the laboring classes, and believed that absolute social equality for women was not far off.

If he also capitulated to spiritualism, that was a concession a man might make to a woman he admired and hoped to rejoin in the hereafter. But insofar as he did share that interest with his wife, he was subjected to the distrust of his neighbors. The Twichells were never reconciled to the Hookers. And Mrs. Annie Fields, Harriet's old friend, seeking signatures for a Harriet Beecher Stowe memorial in the late 1890s, wrote to the Warners: "*Must* we ask Mr. Hooker to sign or any of that bad, bad, mad, company?"

But it hardly mattered anymore. Nook Farm had become just another Hartford residential area. The bright company of the early years had faded forever. Its two luminaries were gone: Clemens, beset by financial worries and increasingly cynical, had moved away in 1891 and Harriet had died in 1896. His hypochondria proving quite unfounded, Hooker lived to the age of eighty-five. Such was Isabella's conviction that he would be far better off in the next life than ill in this one that she was disappointed when he recovered from a sinking spell a week before he died. As with her daughter Mary, she was soon communicating with him as though he had not died at all.

With something of her father's energy, Isabella went on as busily as ever. And she expected everyone else to do the same. "I don't ask you to keep the Ten Commandments—" she said to one of her granddaughters, "you probably will anyway—but if I ever catch you being bored I'll disown you." But the new century brought a few changes that saddened her: when another granddaughter began using the telephone instead of letters, Isabella mourned the passing of a great Beecher tradition.

On her eightieth birthday she invited to her home all the preachers and teachers in the city as well as her friends. As a Beecher biographer, Lyman Beecher Stowe, reported, they responded overwhelmingly—blacks and whites, the local Catholic bishop, Jewish rabbis, the Irish mayor, suffragists and spiritualists, the cranks along with the pillars of society. Borrowing a leaf from Thomas Paine, she had taken as her motto: "The world is my country; to do good is my religion."

Along with Anthony and Stanton, she became a venerated figure at meetings of the National-American Suffrage Association. In 1898 Anthony asked her to prepare a written address for a national convention. With her cameo features and her silvery hair she was a beautiful presence, but unaccustomed to reading a speech, she could not make herself heard. When the audience grew restless, Anthony came forward and chided the delegates, declaring that they should be content just to look at Mrs. Hooker. Isabella promptly put aside her manuscript and spoke with all her old-time power. Afterwards, as the audience cheered, Anthony cried:

To think that such a woman, belonging by birth and marriage to the most distinguished families in our country's history, should be held as a subject and have set over her all classes of men. . . . Shame on a government that permits such an outrage.

If anything, Isabella's exasperation increased with the years. In 1905 she wrote: "The degradation of my political classification with minors, criminals, and idiots is harder to bear than ever before and rouses within me a storm of indignation that shakes my very soul of souls."

Spiritualism remained her one unfailing refuge. She set aside a period every morning for communing with dead friends, relatives and such eminent figures as her mediums called up. Sometimes the spirits came in a throng—Beechers, Hookers, Footes and others, crowding the great stage of her imagination. She still believed she was destined for a divine role but she was reconciled to the idea that it would not come about until she herself was in heaven. I am, she writes in her diary, "the last of the original Beecher tribe and have a message second to no other from the sphere invisible. Oh how I long to make it known—not heard but *known*."

At last, early in 1907, she too passed, we presume, to the heaven she had so long envisioned, there to recline, as she put it, "on mossy couches with angels bending over you . . . and wiping away the cobwebs of time and the bewildering dreams of earth."

Although Isabella Beecher Hooker finally achieved, at the age of forty-seven, an identity besides that of wife and mother, it was a patchwork put together beneath the silken straitjacket that Victorian America imposed on women. Outwardly a proper New England matron, inwardly she became a rebel, striving for a place in the sun.

The conflict drew her into strange contradictions. It made her shuttle between vigorous political action against sexual inequalities and mystical revelations of a heavenly role. It left her a worshiper of motherhood and family love who was alienated from her daughters, and a model wife who challenged her husband and championed the most flagrant free-lover of the age. And it caused her, alone in her family, to believe her brother Henry guilty of adultery.

Once released from the years of repression, she compensated by asserting herself on two levels—on a worldly plane as a feminist and on a spiritual plane as divinely inspired. In public she was a field general in the suffragist wars; in private, a visionary guided by spirits. Although persuaded in her youth that she had a magnetic power to lead people, Isabella spent almost twenty-five years—lulled by a happy marriage and cherished children—groping for relief from frustrations and an outlet for ambitions. Then various influences, ranging from the writings of the Mills to the evangelistic spirit of her family, ignited her. Throughout the long remainder of her life she continued to be driven to right the world's wrongs.

Unquestionably, Isabella Beecher Hooker suffered from delusions—such as that mothers were, in their childbearing, like God, that woman was the superior sex, and that she herself was destined to become Christ's deputy on earth. She also believed she could communicate with the dead, but that notion she shared with many people everywhere. Yet any suggestion that she was insane—as her brother James implied—ignores the crucial fact that she kept her chief delusion secret, never let any really unacceptable beliefs intrude on her public activities, and even allowed for the possibility that her revelations might not come true.

After her death a lawsuit challenging her will exposed her secret obsessions to ridicule. The public, wearied by sixty years of suffragist propaganda, dismissed her, along with other militant feminists, as something of a crank. Only recently has it become plain how far ahead of their time were such early leaders of the women's movement. It is not too much to declare that almost everything now said in favor of women's liberation was said, and often as convincingly, over a hundred years ago by Isabella Beecher Hooker and her associates.

of that creed—and we may not of course apply our standards in judging its worth to them—it gave them and their ancestors a stable and complete view of the world, one that served them for two hundred years. They knew their roles and duties, their loyalties and goals and, above all, their ultimate reward.

However oppressive it might seem, their creed also prepared them to cope with death and catastrophe. But their children, like the children of our time, sought release from such rule. Led by Henry Ward Beecher and his successors, they sloughed off the Puritan code. They were freeing themselves, they felt, from psychic bondage, from a dark spell. Encouraged by democracy, social reformers, smug interpretations of evolution and material rewards, they were persuaded that mankind was making shining progress from beast to god, from barbarism to civilization.

So in time the pendulum swung from discipline, repression and self-denial to indulgence, permissiveness, self-realization and the conviction that society, not the individual, is responsible for crime, cruelty and hatred. Having dismissed the contention of the Lyman Beechers that mankind is weak and sinful and that evil is mighty and lies in wait everywhere, their descendants were quite unprepared for such enormities as the Holocaust, Hiroshima, gulags and genocidal wars. Far more than Arnold, they seemed to be wandering between two worlds, one dying and the other powerless to be born.

If in the end Lyman Beecher failed to make his children accept the sterner aspects of his code, it was chiefly the changing world that defeated him. But he did instill in almost all of them a sense of their individuality and the value of their opinions. It was this that encouraged them to set forth their beliefs in countless sermons, lectures, letters and one hundred and twenty books. One has only to think of Catharine as the militant educator bristling with convictions, Harriet as the antislavery crusader, Isabella as the embattled feminist, Edward and Charles with their heretical theories of the universe, Tom as maverick pastor of his unique church in Elmira, and Henry outfacing English audiences during the war, to see some of the more positive effects of Lyman's way.

That training may also help to explain why all the Beechers were so marvelously articulate and why a few of them were among the most eloquent—whether in speech or in print—of their time. Inadvertently, perhaps, it also left three of the daughters, Catharine, Harriet and Isabella, with a persistent sense of the right to speak out and to assume whatever roles they chose, regardless of their sex. By contrast, the three wives of Lyman and the wives of almost all his sons remain figures in the background—supporting characters in the cast of life.

CODA

As he handed down the laws of the universe from his pulpit on high, Lyman Beecher was, in the eyes of his children, God. And mother Roxana, shepherding them and caring for them lovingly, was Christ. Although their Father/God brought them dire warnings and applied stern pressures, he was also movingly concerned about them and could even weep over them. With such images in their hearts, the children, once grown, insisted that their God, unlike John Calvin's, sorrowed over their sins and perhaps even wept over their weaknesses. At the same time they turned more and more to a Christ who was tender and forgiving and, in Harriet's and Henry's eyes, as much a woman as a man.

But they also changed their views because America had changed— transformed from a theocracy ruled by austere churchmen, guilt, fear and the hope of heaven, from a string of colonies ruled by a far-off monarch, from a land of farmers, craftsmen and penny-saving tradesmen—from all these to a confident, continent-spanning democracy governed by lawyers, generals and empire-builders, and dedicated to progress, profit and success.

So where Lyman was a priest and prophet, his children were social servants and reformers; where he was intent on saving men's souls and fixing their thoughts on the life to come, his children sought to change men's ways here and now; where he was occupied with man's attitude toward God, his children struggled with man's inhumanity to man, as in the enslavement of blacks and the subjection of women. Where Lyman Beecher in church wrestled with doctrine and dogma, his sons increasingly turned their churches into centers of social service and good works.

The virtue of Lyman and Roxana's faith is that it enabled them to answer with supreme assurance the great questions of life and death. (The measure of their certainty is that Lyman and his colleagues quarreled only over almost invisible differences.) Whatever the shortcomings

Lyman fostered in his children not only a sense of individuality but the belief—sometimes a delusion—that they knew what was best for almost everyone else. They persisted in such patterns even when their efforts earned them only criticism and contempt, as in Harriet's defense of Lady Byron, Catharine's support of Delia Bacon, and Isabella's championing of Victoria Woodhull. And just as Lyman believed he had a commission from on high to save the West for Protestantism, so Harriet claimed that she was simply God's scribe when she wrote *Uncle Tom's Cabin,* Isabella believed she would be Christ's vicegerent in the world to come, and Edward described his theory of the universe as a divine revelation.

In at least one direction, the struggle against slavery, their convictions concerning other people's behavior made them effective on every front—Harriet as writer, Henry as preacher and agitator, Edward as alter ego of Lovejoy, James as leader of one of the first freedmen's regiments in the South, Charles in his sermons, and Isabella and her husband in a variety of ways.

Amidst all the threats and hazards of his religion, Lyman maintained his hope that the millennium was not far off. In the optimism of the young Republic, of an America full of shining promises, it was hard to doubt that great climaxes were in the offing. Utopian communities had sprung up everywhere and in the early years great revivals still served to fan the flames of faith. But as Lyman's hopes for the West faded and the revivals came at greater intervals and Calvinism seemed a bleak and increasingly backward-looking creed, some of the Beechers turned to Episcopalianism or even Unitarianism and at least five of them responded to spiritualism for the hope it gave them in the face of death. Henry, distrusting spiritualism as a pale substitute for the mediation offered by Christ and his ministers, found in evolution all the additional evidence he needed that man was forever ascending from ape to angel.

Lyman's open affection for his sons as well as his daughters and for men like Nathaniel Taylor—all part of the sentiment sanctioned by the age—fostered in his children the precious capacity to love each other, the power to express for this brother or that sister passionate attachment: Harriet and Henry for each other, Charles for Isabella and Edward, Thomas for Henry, James and Thomas for each other, and all the children for their mother and father. And it was surely the dream of continuing or resuming such a relationship in an afterlife that helped to draw so many of them to spiritualism.

The question that remains is what happened when the children of Lyman and Roxana and Harriet Porter found themselves in a world in which the old standards were being challenged, relaxed or even discarded. Obviously there is no simple answer. If graft and corruption were infecting government and business, and the new rich were beginning to flaunt their wealth, who shall say how much of this was due to the war, to the temptations offered by a superabundance of natural resources and to the explosive growth of industry. As clergymen, all Lyman's sons except Henry had meager or at best modest incomes and lived within their means. Harriet sank a small fortune in her first Hartford home and another fortune in growing oranges in a Florida area that was not frost free, but the Stowes themselves lived rather simply and without show.

The belief that the Protestant work ethic inevitably encouraged materialism and the pursuit of wealth simply does not apply to the Beechers. Almost all of them labored long and hard but not one of them made wealth a goal and none of them except Henry accumulated any property worth mentioning. Even if we concede that Henry was guilty of adultery and that his rationalization of opulent living and his paid testimonials for soap and trusses were less than admirable, he remained, judging from the testimony of his contemporaries, one of the most inspiring figures of his time.

After the turbulence and tensions of the war, and as the younger generation of Beechers grew older, some of them did retreat from the challenges and the confrontations, seeking a measure of peace and repose. Harriet and Charles withdrew for long periods to back-country Florida, James stole away from society into the Catskill wilderness, Henry refreshed himself with gentleman farming and horticulture, and others fled periodically into various kinds of cures.

But none of them ever really gave up their missions, each guiding some group through uncharted waters well out from the shores on which their ancestors had stood. Henry and Isabella remained in the public eye, he with his plea for love and she with her plea for women. Harriet in Mandarin started a church and a school for blacks, James and his wife served their wilderness neighbors with their preaching and teaching, William doubled as a postmaster in order to continue as a pastor, Charles was over seventy when he left Florida and took on a parish in Pennsylvania, and Edward at eighty-five was still riding the "cars" to a tiny congregation on the outskirts of Brooklyn when he lost his leg.

Young Lyman Beecher, preaching in the tradition of Jonathan Edwards, had begun his service to God in an East Hampton church in 1800. One hundred and five years later, Isabella Beecher Hooker ended her service to women because she could face the suffering of the world only as long as she could do something about it. "Now that I can no longer help," she declared, "I can't stand it!"

In the shift from Calvinism to the gospel of social service, from Jehovah to Christ, in the freeing of the slaves and the restoration of their humanity, in the effort to make women independent and win for them their rights—in all these, the Beechers were among the pilots as well as the passengers, the movers and shakers as well as the moved and the shaken.

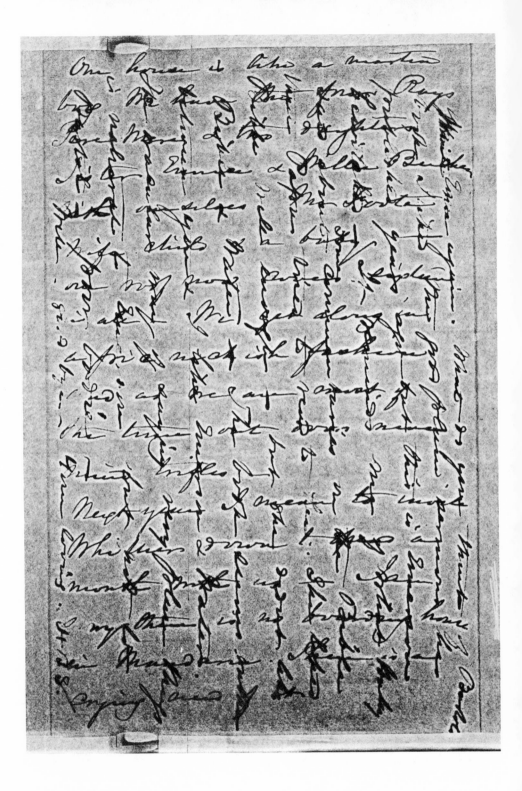

A Note on Letter Writing in the Nineteenth Century

Almost no one today can fully appreciate the role of letters in American life before the coming of the telephone and modern transportation. Up to the Civil War, every child learned that the only regular communication it would have with relatives and friends at a distance would be by mail. Proximity did not matter: hundreds of letters passed between Isabella Beecher Hooker and her husband, John, when one of them was staying in Hartford and the other was in Farmington—his parents' home—only four or five miles away.

Letters were used not only for personal and business news but as an outlet for emotions and all kinds of intimate details. Beecher family letters were rarely less than four pages long, commonly ran to eight or ten pages, and occasionally to twenty pages. In the first half of the century, mail, carried mainly by stagecoach, was extremely expensive. In 1830 a single sheet cost 6 cents for only 30 miles, 10 cents for 30–50 miles, 12½ cents for 80–150 miles, 18¾ cents for 150–400 miles, and 25 cents for over 400 miles. So every conceivable device was used to get as much as possible into each letter: in the earlier period the Beechers usually wrote in tiny script across every inch of the paper front and back, and did not hesitate to write perpendicularly across a page already covered horizontally. Since the cost was based on the number of sheets, writers often used large sheets or conveniently forgot how many sheets they had used. The Beechers also wrote cumulative letters over the course of a week or more, and they sometimes resorted to round-robin letters that might go to as many as eight members of the family. When John Hooker in Hartford was engaged to Isabella Beecher while she was still in Cincinnati, the two letters he wrote to her each week cost him the huge sum of 50 cents. The cost dropped rapidly after 1850; Hooker pointed out that in the late 1890s those same letters would have cost only 2 cents each.

The effect of all this was that families often treasured letters because they reflected so much of their lives. There are at least 2,500 extant letters by Harriet Beecher Stowe, probably even more by Henry Ward Beecher, and several thousand by such a less well known member of the family as Isabella Beecher Hooker. The beneficiaries of this custom have been the students of the private as well as the public lives of Americans before 1900.

Notes and Sources

These notes are intended mainly to give the sources of key quotations and occasionally of matters covered more extensively in other books. Each note is preceded by the page and line to which it refers; thus, 12/14 refers to page 12 and the quotation (or group of quotations) or statement that ends on line 14.

The name Beecher is abbreviated "B." In chapters devoted to one member of the family, only the first name of that person is given. *The Autobiography of Lyman Beecher* is referred to as *The Autobiography*.

Abbreviations of Sources

Abeles	Collection of Margaret Beecher Abeles and Alfred T. Abeles
Amherst	Amherst College Library
Boston Pub. Lib.	Boston Public Library
Cincinnati	Cincinnati Historical Society
Connecticut	Connecticut Historical Society
Harvard	Houghton Library, Harvard University
Huntington	Henry E. Huntington Library
Hayes	Rutherford B. Hayes Library
Indiana	Indiana Historical Society
Lib. Congress	Library of Congress
Mass.	Massachusetts Historical Society
Michigan	Clement Library, University of Michigan
Mt. Holyoke	Williston Memorial Library, Mount Holyoke College
N.Y. Pub. Lib.	New York Public Library, Research Libraries and Berg Collection
Radcliffe	Schlesinger Library on the History of Women in America, Radcliffe College
Stowe-Day	Library of the Stowe-Day Foundation
Virginia	University of Virginia Library
Yale	Yale University, Sterling Memorial Library
Yale, Beinecke	Yale University, Beinecke Rare Book and Manuscript Library

Chapter 1. Lyman Beecher: Belated Puritan

4/25 *The Autobiography of Lyman Beecher,* ed. Barbara M. Cross, 2 vols. (Cambridge, Mass., 1961), I, p. 9. First published in 1863.

5/8 Calvin E. Stowe. "Sketches and Recollections of Dr. Lyman Beecher," *The Congregational Quarterly,* vol. 6, July 1864, pp. 221–35.

5/27 *The Autobiography,* I, p. 12.

5/38 Henry Ward Beecher, *Eyes and Ears* (Boston, 1862), p. 223.

6/10 *The Autobiography,* I, p. 19.

6/29 Lyman Beecher Stowe, *Saints, Sinners and Beechers* (Indianapolis, 1934), pp. 22–23.

7/37 Constance Rourke, *Trumpets of Jubilee* (New York, 1927), p. 6.

8/31 Ibid., pp. 11–12.

9/10 Ibid.

9/18 Marie Caskey, *Chariot of Fire* (Cambridge, Mass., 1978), pp. 40–42.

10/3   *The Autobiography*, I, pp. 46, 27.
10/15   Ibid., p. 28.
11/34   Ibid., p. 46.
13/18   William C. Beecher and Rev. Samuel Scoville, *A Biography of Henry Ward Beecher* (New York, 1888), p. 24.
14/1   *The Autobiography*, I, p. 51.
14/14   Ibid., pp. 53–54.
14/32   Ibid., pp. 55, 57.
15/36   Ibid., II, p. 384.
16/26   Ibid., I, p. 68.
16/35   Ibid., p. 71.
16/40   p. 71. Lyman B. to Roxana Foote, 23 February 1799. A generation later, Theodore Weld, who would lead student abolitionists in a rebellion at Lane Seminary when Lyman Beecher was its president, wrote to his betrothed, Angelina Grimké, who also became a well-known abolitionist, in exactly the same terms. I love you, he said, but "not supremely. . . . I do love the Lord . . . *better* than I love *you*. And it is because I love him *better* that I love you as I do." Not quite so divided in her feelings, Angelina answered: "ought God to be *all in all* to us *on earth?* I tho't so, and I am frightened to find He is not." See *Letters of Theodore Dwight Weld, Angelina Grimké Weld and Sarah Grimké, 1822–24,* ed. G. H. Barnes and D. L. Dumond (New York, 1934), II, p. 533.
17/24   Ibid., pp. 83–84.
18/3   Ibid., p. 93.
19/12   Ibid., pp. 96–97.
19/21   Ibid., p. 159. See also Catharine Beecher, *Educational Reminiscences and Suggestions* (New York, 1874), p. 15.
20/10   *The Autobiography*, I, pp. 85–86.
20/35   Ibid., p. 113.
21/19   Ibid., pp. 107–8.
21/40   Ibid., pp. 113–17.
22/25   Ibid.
22/42   Stuart C. Henry, *Unvanquished Puritan: A Portrait of Lyman Beecher* (Grand Rapids, Mich., 1973), p. 78.

Chapter 2. A Parsonage in Litchfield

26/40   Edward D. Mansfield, *Personal Memories, 1803–43* (Cincinnati, 1879), pp. 122, 136.
27/7   *The Autobiography*, I, p. 164.
27/20   Rourke, op. cit., p. 17.
27/43   Roxana B. (Mrs. Lyman Beecher) to Esther B., 13 January 1811. *The Autobiography*, I, pp. 168–69.
28/27   *The Autobiography*, I, p. 179.
28/41   Ibid., pp. 180–81.
29/13   So called because in signing the pledge to abstain they added the word "Total" with a large "T" after their name.
30/21   *The Autobiography*, I, p. 193.
31/9   Ibid., p. 190.
31/16   Lyman B. Stowe, op. cit., 42.
31/34   *The Autobiography*, I, pp. 252–53.
32/11   Roxana B. to Samuel Foote, 6 November 1814. *The Autobiography*, I, p. 208.
32/17   *The Autobiography*, I, p. 195.
32/35   Lyman B. to the Rev. Thomas Davies, 21 December 1821. *The Autobiography*, I, p. 347.
33/17   *The Autobiography*, I, pp. 215, 219.

34/5   Ibid., pp. 220–22. See also Mrs. Tapping Reeves to Mrs. Sally Tomlinson, 27 September 1816. *The Autobiography,* I, p. 217.
34/29   Catharine B. to Harriet Foote, 1 February 1817. *The Autobiography,* I, p. 244.
35/2   Lyman B. to Harriet Porter, 9, 11, 16, 21, 25 September and 3 October 1817 (Stowe-Day).
35/17   Catharine Gilbertson, *Harriet Beecher Stowe* (New York, 1937), p. 15.
35/27   Harriet Porter to Lyman B., 22 September 1817 (Stowe-Day).
35/40   *The Autobiography,* I, pp. 267–68.
36/21   Ibid., p. 273.
37/17   Ibid., pp. 257–58.
38/14   Ibid., p. 333.
39/27   Lyman B. Stowe, op. cit., pp. 45–46.
40/8   Lyman B. to William B., 6 February 1819. *The Autobiography,* I, pp. 288–89.
40/19   Lyman B. to Edward B., 25 August 1820, 7 April 1821. *The Autobiography,* I, pp. 320, 341.
41/6   *The Autobiography,* I, p. 354.

Chapter 3. Catharine: The Test of Faith

42/16   *The Autobiography,* I, p. 104.
43/17   Catherine Beecher, *Educational Reminiscences,* p. 26.
43/40   Emily Noyes Vanderpoel, *Chronicles of a Pioneer School,* ed. E. C. B. Buel (Cambridge, Mass., 1903), p. 147.
44/18   *The Autobiography,* I, pp. 264–65.
44/27   Catharine to Louisia Wait, [1819] (Radcliffe).
44/29   Lyman B. to Catharine, 26 May 1819 (Radcliffe).
45/7   Catharine Beecher, *Common Sense Applied to Religion* (New York, 1857), pp. xvi–xvii.
46/14   Catharine to Lyman B., 5 June 1821 (Radcliffe).
46/26   Horace Mann to Lydia Mann, 11 April 1822 (Mass.).
46/41   Catharine to Louisa Wait, 28 January 1822 (Radcliffe).
47/15   Lyman B. to Edward B., *The Autobiography,* I, p. 341.
47/23   Edward B. to Catharine, 29 March 1822 (Radcliffe).
47/31   Lyman B. to Edward B., *The Autobiography,* I, p. 353.
48/2   Catharine to Louisa Wait, 25 March 1822 (Radcliffe).
48/42   Lyman B. to Catharine, 30 May 1822. *The Autobiography,* I, pp. 355–56.
49/27   Isabella B. to John Hooker, 2 July 1841 (Stowe-Day).
50/2   Catharine to Edward B., 4 June 1822. *The Autobiography,* I, pp. 356–57.
50/13   Edward B. to Catharine, 27 October 1822 (Radcliffe).
50/35   Catharine to Edward B., July 1822. *The Autobiography,* I, pp. 359–360.
51/5   Catharine to Lyman B., and Lyman B. to Catharine, [August] 1822. *The Autobiography,* I, pp. 360–61.
51/26   Lyman B. to Catharine, 25 September 1822. *The Autobiography,* I, p. 364.
51/40   Lyman B. to Edward B., March 1822. *The Autobiography,* I, p. 353.
52/32   Entry 24 May 1817 in Fisher's "Notebook" and 1 August [1819?] in his "Religious Diary" (Yale, Beinecke).
53/5   Catharine to Lyman B., 15 February 1823, New Year 1823. *The Autobiography,* I, pp. 377–78, 368.
54/25   Lyman B. Stowe, op. cit., p. 106. See also Catharine Beecher, *The True Remedy for the Wrongs of Women* (Boston, 1851), pp. 63–64.
55/17   Catharine to Edward B., 18 July 1874. *The Autobiography,* II, pp. 8, 16.
55/42   10 October 1823 (Radcliffe).
57/35   Catharine to Edward B., 23 August 1828 (Mt. Holyoke).
58/32   Harriet B. to Elizabeth Phoenix, 21 August [1830] (Michigan).
60/31   Lyman B. Stowe, op. cit., p. 116.

61/7   Catharine to Mary Dutton, 8 February 1830 (American Literature Collection, Yale, Beinecke).
62/6   Kathryn Kish Sklar, *Catharine Beecher: A Study in Domesticity* (New Haven, 1973), pp. 98–99.

Chapter 4. The Boston Years

64/13   Barbara Cross, Introduction to *The Autobiography*, p. xxvii.
64/28   James C. White, *Personal Reminiscences of Lyman Beecher* (New York, 1882), pp. 4, 5, 25.
66/20   Stuart C. Henry, op. cit., pp. 151–55.
67/22   William B. to Edward B., 11 April 1826. *The Autobiography*, II, p. 39.
67/35   Harriet Porter B. to _____ , 25 June 1826. *The Autobiography*, II, p. 43.
68/15   Barbara Cross, op. cit., p. xiv.
70/36   *The Autobiography*, II, p. 103.
71/30   Ibid., pp. 119–41.
72/26   Theodore Parker, *Autobiography, Poems and Prayers* (Boston: Unitarian Association, n.d.), p. 296.
73/2   *The Autobiography*, II, p. 55.
74/23   Ibid., pp. 75 ff.
74/32   *Letters of the Rev. Dr. Beecher and Rev. Nettleton on the "New Measures"* (New York, 1828), pp. 90–93.
76/2   Harriet B. Stowe, in *The Autobiography*, II, pp. 81–86.
77/29   Calvin E. Stowe, op. cit., p. 231.
78/31   *The Autobiography*, II, p. 167.
79/21   Ibid., pp. 181, 184.
80/40   Ibid., p. 204.
82/15   Harriet B. Stowe, in *The Autobiography*, II, pp. 207–8.
82/31   Charles Fenno Hoffman, *A Winter in the West* (New York, 1835), I, pp. 30–35.

Chapter 5. Enter, a New Generation

84/18   Lyman B. Stowe, op. cit., p. 138.
85/13   *The Autobiography*, I, p. 310.
85/38   Lyman B. Stowe, op. cit., p. 140.
87/7   *The Autobiography*, I, pp. 318, 320, 341, 353.
87/39   Edward B. to Catharine B., 14 February 1822 (Radcliffe).
88/9   Edward B. to Catharine B., 16 September 1822 (Radcliffe).
88/43   Lyman B. to Edward B., 2 August, 5 September 1826 (Yale).
89/24   Edward B. to Lyman B., 15 October 1828 (Mt. Holyoke).
90/2   Charles Beecher, *Life of Edward Beecher* (unpublished manuscript), pp. 62–63 (Illinois College Library).
90/16   H. C. Englizian, *Brimstone Corner* (Chicago: Moody Press, 1968), pp. 108–110.
90/38   Charles Beecher, *Life of Edward Beecher*, pp. 102–5.
91/33   Mary B. to Edward B., 5 April 1826, February 1826 (Mt. Holyoke).

Chapter 6. Hattie: "She went owling about"

94/28   *The Autobiography*, I, p. 234.
96/2   Ibid., p. 391.
97/29   Ibid., pp. 393 ff.
98/13   Edward Mansfield, op. cit., pp. 139–40.
99/4   Lyman B. Stowe, op. cit., p. 154.

99/11   *The Autobiography,* II, p. 340.
99/37   Charles E. Stowe, *Life of Harriet Beecher Stowe* (Boston/New York, 1889), pp. 15–21. Contains the entire essay.
100/7   Lyman B. Stowe, op. cit., p. 159.
100/15 *The Autobiography,* I, p. 94.
101/4   Charles E. Stowe, op. cit., p. 152.
102/17 Ibid., p. 30.
103/38 Ibid., p. 32.
104/24 Ibid., pp. 33–34.
105/17 Ibid., pp. 36–37.
105/20 Forrest Wilson, *Crusader in Crinoline: The Life of Harriet Beecher Stowe* (Philadelphia, 1941), p. 78. See also J. C. Derby, *Fifty Years Among Authors, Books and Publishers* (New York, 1884), p. 459.
106/5   Charles E. Stowe, op. cit., pp. 36–37. Harriet to Catharine B., February 1827.
106/22 Ibid., p. 44. Harriet to Edward B., April 1828.
107/5   Ibid., pp. 47–48. Harriet to Edward B., Winter 1829.
108/29 Harriet to Mary Dutton [1803?]. Wilson, op. cit., pp. 80–82.
108/36 Harriet to Edward B. Charles E. Stowe, op. cit., p. 48.
110/1   Paxton Hibben, *Henry Ward Beecher: An American Portrait* (New York, 1927; Readers Club Edition, 1942), p. 47.
111/25 Harriet to Georgiana May [Summer 1832]. Charles E. Stowe, op. cit., p. 50.
111/42 Ibid., p. 51.

Chapter 7. Henry: "My nature was enthusiastic and outgushing"

114/11 Harriet Beecher Stowe, *Men of Our Times* (Hartford, 1869), p. 510.
115/2   Henry Ward Beecher, *Star Papers* (New York, 1855), pp. 189–93.
115/38 Beecher and Scoville, op. cit., p. 62.
116/5   *The Christian Union,* 3 January 1872.
116/33 Beecher and Scoville, op. cit., p. 66.
117/10 Ibid., pp. 66–67.
117/30 Ibid., p. 67.
118/41 Ibid., p. 80.
119/35 Henry Ward Beecher, *Norwood; or, Village Life in New England* (New York, 1867), p. 159.
120/34 Beecher and Scoville, op. cit., p. 90.
121/14 Henry to Eunice (Mrs. Henry Ward B.), 17 May 1849 (Yale).
121/37 Beecher and Scoville, op. cit., pp. 94–95.
123/9   Ibid., pp. 98–99.
123/23 *The Christian Union,* 8 October 1870.
124/18 Quoted by Paxton Hibben, op. cit., p. 31.
124/35 Beecher and Scoville, op. cit., p. 105.
124/42 James Thome, a young music teacher at Oberlin, who had become a passionate disciple of abolitionist Theodore Weld, wrote to his idol in 1832: "often when the gushings of my soul have prompted me to throw my arms around your neck and kiss you, I have violently quelled these impulses and affected a manly bearing." From *Letters of Weld-Grimké,* II, p. 642.
126/17 Lyman B. to Heman Humphrey, 30 September 1830 (Amherst).
127/31 Beecher and Scoville, op. cit., pp. 119–21.
127/28 Henry Ward Beecher, *Yale Lectures on Preaching* (New York, 1873), Second Series, p. 241.
129/18 Mrs. Henry Ward Beecher, "Mr. Beecher As I Knew Him," *Ladies' Home Journal,* October 1891.
130/3   Henry to Harriet B., 8 March 1832 (Yale).
130/20 Henry Ward Beecher, *Eyes and Ears,* p. 25.

131/4   Beecher and Scoville, op. cit., p. 119.
131/26 Henry to Harriet B., 28 March 1833 (Amherst).

Chapter 8. Cincinnati: Rebellion at Lane

136/9   Hoffman, op. cit., p. 131.
137/35 Frances Trollope, *Domestic Manners of the Americans* (1832; reprinted New York, 1949), pp. 75 ff.
139/23 *The Autobiography*, II, p. 231; Thomas K. Beecher, *Notable Sermons* (Elmira, N.Y., 1914), p. 7.
140/38 *The Autobiography*, II, p. 233.
141/9   Benjamin Thomas, *Theodore Weld: Crusader for Freedom* (New Brunswick, N.J., 1950), pp. 15 et seq.
142/6   *Letters of Weld-Grimké*, I, p. 298n. See also Thomas, op. cit., pp. 100-1.
142/26 Ibid., p. 59.
143/9   *The Autobiography*, II, p. 241.
143/41 Ibid., pp. 237-39.
145/24 Calvin E. Stowe, op. cit., p. 232.
145/37 *Letters of Weld-Grimké*, I, p. 273.
146/38 *The Autobiography*, II, p. 244.
147/4   *Letters of Weld-Grimké*, I, p. 138.
147/38 *The Autobiography*, II, p. 246.
148/3   *Letters of Weld-Grimké*, I, pp. 142-43.
148/17 Ibid., p. 171, Lyman B. to Theodore Weld, 8 October 1834.
148/33 Ibid., I, pp. 172-73.
149/15 *The Autobiography*, II, p. 248.
150/21 Thomas K. Beecher, op. cit., p. 114.
150/34 *The Autobiography*, II, p. 241.
151/28 Ibid., pp. 259-60.

Chapter 9. Lyman Beecher: Trials and Tribulation

153/30 Lyman Beecher, *A Plea for the West,* pp. 166, 179; *The Autobiography*, II, pp. 251-52.
154/17 Harriet Martineau, *Retrospective of Western Travel* (London, 1838), II, p. 55.
154/41 Raymond L. Hightower, "Joshua L. Wilson, Frontier Controversialist," *Church History,* 1933-34, pp. 306, 315.
155/32 Stuart Henry, op. cit., p. 214.
157/11 *The Autobiography*, II, pp. 265-66.
157/17 Quoted by Stuart Henry, op. cit., p. 221.
158/17 *The Autobiography*, II, pp. 267-68.
158/39 Ibid., pp. 268-69.
159/35 Ibid., pp. 99, 289, 303.
160/37 Lyman to Harriet Porter, 25 September 1817 (Stowe-Day).
162/34 Rev. James White, *Personal Reminiscences of Lyman Beecher* (New York, 1882), p. 42. See also manuscript of 29 January 1860 from Lucy Jackson White recording Lyman Beecher's reminiscences of his courting her mother Lydia (Stowe-Day).
162/41 Catharine B. to Mary Cogswell, 29 May 1837 (Radcliffe).
163/33 *The Autobiography*, II, p. 322.
164/3   Ibid., p. 323.
165/13 Gerda Lerner, *The Grimké Sisters from South Carolina* (Boston, 1967), p. 249.
166/21 *The Autobiography*, II, p. 308.
167/3   Ibid., p. 331.

168/1   Lyman to N. Wright, 4 January 1840, and Wright to Lyman, 14 January 1840 (Lib. Congress).
168/23 Rev. James White, op. cit., pp. 36–37.
169/25 *The Autobiography,* II, p. 406.
169/31 Catharine B. to Eunice (Mrs. Henry Ward B.), 15 January 1851 (Yale).
170/7   Lydia (Mrs. Lyman B.) to Lyman, 1852 (Stowe-Day).

Chapter 10. Catharine: A Dream for Women and the West

172/36 Catharine to Mary Dutton, 3 February 1833 (Yale, Beinecke).
175/6   Edward King to his wife, 24 December 1834 (Cincinnati).
175/25 Edward King to his wife, 12 August 1835 (Cincinnati).
175/37 Ibid.
176/6   Catharine Beecher, *Letters on the Difficulties of Religion* (Hartford, 1836), p. 32.
176/21 Lyman B. Stowe, op. cit., pp. 96–97.
176/31 Catharine Beecher, *Letters on the Difficulties of Religion,* p. 231.
177/10 Mae Elizabeth Harveson, *Catharine Esther Beecher: Pioneer Educator* (Philadelphia, 1932), p. 71.
177/24 Forrest Wilson, op. cit., p. 113.
181/32 Angelina Grimké, *Letters to Catharine E. Beecher in Reply to an Essay on Slavery and Abolitionism* (Boston, 1838), pp. 104, 114, 119.
182/21 Harriet B. Stowe to Catharine, 27 August 1858 (Radcliffe).
182/37 Charles B. to Lyman B., 27 September 1840 (Radcliffe).
183/2   Lyman B. to Henry Ward B., 8 December 1842 (Yale).
184/39 Charles Dudley Warner, *As We Go* (New York: Harper & Bros, 1894). See also Ann Douglas, *The Femininization of American Culture* (New York, 1977).
185/5   Catharine Beecher, *A Treatise on Domestic Economy* (New York, 1841), p. 38.
186/39 Catharine Beecher, *An Address to the Protestant Clergy of the United States* (New York, 1846).
187/8   Catharine B., *Educational Reminiscences,* pp. 119 et seq. See also Calvin E. Stowe to Harriet B. Stowe, 8 August 1848 (Stowe-Day).
188/10 Ibid. pp. 122–23.
188/24 Catharine Beecher, *The True Remedy for the Wrongs of Women,* p. 241.
189/20 Catharine Beecher, *Letters to the People on Health and Happiness* (New York, 1855), pp. 117–18.
190/8   Vivian C. Hopkins, *Prodigal Puritan: A Life of Delia Bacon* (Cambridge, Mass., 1959), pp. 71–78.
190/37 Catharine Beecher, *Truth Stranger Than Fiction* (New York, 1850), p. 216.
191/6   Ibid., pp. 206 et seq.
191/33 Ibid., pp. 281–84.
192/1   *Diary of James Hadley,* ed. Laura H. Moseley (New Haven; Yale University Press, 1951), p. 84.
192/39 Sklar, op. cit., pp. 200 ff.

Chapter 11. A Father and Four Sons

196/16 Quoted by Robert Merideth, *The Politics of the Universe: Edward Beecher, Abolition and Orthodoxy* (Nashville, 1968), p. 81.
196/25 Charles H. Rammelkamp, *Illinois College: A Centennial History* (New Haven, Conn., 1928), p. 65.
196/42 Charles Beecher, *Life of Edward Beecher* (unpublished), p. 128 (Illinois College Library).
197/26 Joseph C. and Owen Lovejoy, *Memoir of the Rev. Elijah P. Lovejoy* (New York, 1838), p. 142.

197/30 Merideth, op. cit. p. 95; John Gill, *Tide Without Turning: Elijah P. Lovejoy and Freedom of the Press* (Boston, 1958), p. 59.
198/5   Charles Beecher, op. cit., pp. 121–22.
199/7   Edward Beecher, *Narrative of Riots at Alton* (Alton, Ill., 1838), p. 55.
201/23 *The Autobiography*, II, p. 18; 12 and 6 November 1825.
201/26 *Biographical Remains of George Beecher*, ed. Catharine Beecher (New York, 1844), p. 83.
202/19 *The Autobiography*, II, pp. 216–19.
203/43 Ibid., p. 345.
204/8   Ibid., p. 371.
204/16 *Biographical Remains of George Beecher*, p. 109.
205/6   Charles Beecher, *Redeemer and Redeemed* (Boston, 1864), Preface, pp. vi–vii.
205/40 Charles Beecher, *The Incarnation; or, Pictures of the Virgin and Her Son* (New York, 1849), p. 21; Charles B. to Lyman B., 4 December 1833 (Radcliffe).
206/13 Thomas Beecher, "My Brother Henry," *Notable Sermons*, p. 6.
207/2   Lyman B. Stowe, op. cit., p. 336. But Caskey, op. cit., p. 216, attributes this statement to Henry Ward B.
207/11 Charles B. to Nathaniel Wright, December 1838 (Lib. Congress).
207/20 *The Autobiography*, II, p. 350.
207/38 Charles B. to Isabella B., 12 April, 12 September, 18 November 1839 (Stowe-Day).
208/11 *The Autobiography*, II, p. 351, and Charles B. to Isabella B., 1 June 1840 (Radcliffe).
208/23 Charles B. to Lyman B., 10 November 1839; Charles B. to Isabella B., 18 November 1839 (both Stowe-Day).
209/40 Quoted in Jane Shaffer Elsmere, *Henry Ward Beecher: The Indiana Years* (Indianapolis, 1973), p. 153.
210/22 Henry Ward B. to Lyman B., 18 March 1843 (Radcliffe).
211/21 Charles B. to Milton Badger, 16 September 1844. Quoted in Elsmere, op. cit., p. 211.
211/30 Henry Ward B. to Lyman B., 13 September 1844 (Radcliffe).
212/2   Hugh McCulloch, *Men and Measures of Half a Century* (New York, 1888), p. 149, also tells this story.
212/16 Charles B. to Amelia Ogden, 20 May 1845 (Radcliffe).
212/29 Julia Merrill to Jane Anderson Merrill, 20 September 1845 (Indiana).
212/42 Quoted in Lyman B. Stowe, op. cit., p. 337.

Chapter 12. Harriet and Calvin Stowe: "As domestic as any pair of tame fowl"

216/32 Quoted in Forrest Wilson, op. cit., p. 95.
219/39 Charles H. Foster, *The Rungless Ladder: Harriet Beecher Stowe and New England Puritanism* (Durham, N.C., 1954), Chapter 1.
222/23 Charles E. Stowe, op. cit., pp. 432–33.
223/27 Ibid., pp. 433–36.
224/37 E. Bruce Kirkham, *The Building of Uncle Tom's Cabin* (Knoxville, Tenn., 1977), pp. 105–9.
226/7   Charles E. Stowe, op. cit., pp. 76–77.
227/23 Ibid., pp. 80–81.

Chapter 13. Harriet: "I have six children and cares endless"

230/27 Harriet to Calvin Stowe, in her "Journal," 1836 (Yale).
231/19 Charles E. Stowe, op. cit., pp. 86–87.
233/17 Ibid., pp. 87–88.

235/3   Charles E. Stowe, op. cit., pp. 90–92.
235/32 Forrest Wilson, op. cit., p. 204.
236/36 Charles E. Stowe, op. cit., pp. 96–98.
237/10 Catharine B. to Mary Beecher Perkins, 22 October 1837 (Radcliffe).
237/19 Catharine B. to Mary Dutton. Quoted in Forrest Wilson, op. cit., p. 206.
238/39 Calvin Stowe to Harriet, 30 April 1842 (Stowe-Day).
239/9   Charles E. Stowe, op. cit., p. 104.
239/21 Ibid., p. 105.
239/35 Ibid., p. 106.
241/41 *The Autobiography*, II, pp. 371–74.
242/13 Charles B. to Isabella B., 14 July 1839 (Stowe-Day).
242/31 Harriet to Calvin Stowe, 21 and 8 May 1844 (Radcliffe).
242/39 Quoted in Edward Wagenknecht, *Harriet Beecher Stowe: The Known and the Unknown* (New York, 1965) p. 51.
243/24 Calvin Stowe to Harriet, 30 June 1844 (Radcliffe).
243/32 Calvin Stowe to Lyman B., 17 July 1844 (Radcliffe).
244/14 Harriet to Calvin Stowe, 19 July 1844 (Radcliffe).
244/25 Harriet to Calvin Stowe, 3 September 1844 (Radcliffe).
244/36 Calvin Stowe to Harriet, 29 September 1844 (Radcliffe).
245/31 Harriet to Calvin Stowe, 16 June 1845. Quoted in Charles E. Stowe, op. cit., pp. 111–12.
246/9   Forrest Wilson, op. cit., p. 222.
246/41 Charles E. Stowe, op. cit., pp. 116–17.
248/5   Calvin Stowe to Harriet, 8 August 1848 (Stowe-Day).
248/23 Charles E. Stowe, op. cit., p. 124.

Chapter 14. Henry: Frontier Interlude

250/27 Henry Ward Beecher's "Journal," 29 October, 27 June 1835 (Yale).
251/19 Beecher and Scoville, op. cit., pp. 148–49.
251/26 Hibben, op. cit., pp. 57–58.
252/13 Beecher and Scoville, op. cit., p. 137.
252/41 Ibid., pp. 154–55.
253/30 Mrs. Henry Ward Beecher, in *Ladies' Home Journal*, November 1891.
254/18 Elsmere, op. cit., pp. 17–19.
254/23 Lyman Abbott, *Henry Ward Beecher* (Boston, 1903), pp. 46–47.
255/19 Mrs. Henry Ward Beecher, *From Dawn to Daylight* (New York, 1861), pp. 80, 73, 126–29.
255/31 Beecher and Scoville, op. cit., p. 167.
255/42 Henry to George B., September 1838 (Yale).
256/6   Beecher and Scoville, op. cit., pp. 166–67.
256/20 *The Autobiography*, II, p. 359.
257/8   Eunice (Mrs. Henry Ward B.) to George and Sarah B., June 1838 (Yale).
258/33 Beecher and Scoville, op. cit., p. 178.
260/35 Elsmere, op. cit., pp. 90–91; and Mrs. H. W. Beecher, in *Ladies' Home Journal*, December 1891.
261/31 Henry Ward Beecher, *Yale Lectures on Preaching* (New York, 1872), First Series, pp. 11–12.
262/6   Isabella B. to John Hooker, 2 December 1839 (Stowe-Day).
262/26 Elsmere, op. cit., p. 121.
262/42 *A Tour Through Indiana in 1840: The Diary of John Parsons of Petersburg, Va.* (New York, Robert M. McBride & Co., 1920), pp. 156–57.
263/23 George S. Merriam, *Life and Times of Samuel Bowles* (New York, 1885), II, p. 49.
265/19 Beecher and Scoville, op. cit., pp. 191–92.

266/8   Milton Rugoff, *Prudery and Passion: Sexuality in Victorian America* (New York: G. P. Putnam's Sons, 1971), pp. 336–37.

266/22 Henry Ward Beecher, *Yale Lectures on Preaching,* Second Series, p. 294.

267/29 Clifford E. Clark, Jr., *Henry Ward Beecher* (Urbana, Ill., 1978), p. 62.

267/41 Harriet B. Stowe to Calvin Stowe, 15 July 1844 (Radcliffe).

268/11 Marie Caskey, op. cit., p. 308.

270/6   Henry Ward Beecher, *Twelve Lectures to Young Men* (New York, 1879), pp. 117–18.

271/39 *Lectures and Orations of Henry Ward Beecher,* ed. N. D. Hillis (New York, 1913), p. 190. See also Henry's *Autobiographical Reminiscences,* ed. T. J. Ellinwood (New York, 1898), pp. 56, 66–67.

272/6   Henry Ward Beecher, *Yale Lectures on Preaching,* First Series, p. 166.

272/34 Henry Ward Beecher, *Twelve Lectures to Young Men,* p. 47.

273/1   Elsmere, op. cit., pp. 176–77.

273/11 Lewis Tappan, *Life of Arthur Tappan* (New York, 1870), p. 233.

274/3   Hugh McCulloch, op. cit., p. 145.

274/27 *Indiana State Journal,* 14 January 1846. Quoted in Elsmere, op. cit., p. 247.

274/42 Ibid., 4 March 1846. See also Hibben, op. cit., p. 97.

275/6   Henry Ward Beecher, *Royal Truths* (Boston, 1866), p. 213.

275/35 Eunice (Mrs. Henry Ward B.) to Harriet Beecher Stowe, 27 December 1846 (Yale).

277/4   Elsmere, op. cit., pp. 285, 293.

277/14 John L. Ketcham to Rev. David Merrill, 12 and 18 August 1847 (Indiana).

277/20 J. C. Derby, *Fifty Years Among Authors, Books and Publishers* (New York, 1884), p. 475.

277/29 Samuel Merrill to Rev. David Merrill, 5 September 1847 (Indiana).

277/36 John L. Ketcham to Rev. David Merrill, 18 August 1847. See also John R. Howard, *Remembrance of Things Past* (New York, 1925), p. 146.

278/2   John L. Ketcham to Rev. David Merrill, 29 September 1847 (Indiana).

278/21 Henry to Julia Merrill, 5 June 1847 (Indiana).

Chapter 15. Children of a Later Time

280/19 Isabella Beecher Hooker, "The Last of the Beechers," *Connecticut Magazine,* 1905, p. 289.

280/33 Harriet B. Stowe to Lyman B. and Lydia (Mrs. Lyman B.), 3 July 1837 (Stowe-Day).

281/18 Lyman B. to Isabella, 3 March 1838, January 1839 (Stowe-Day).

281/35 Isabella B. Hooker, op. cit., p. 289.

282/8   Isabella to John Hooker, 21 October, 9 November 1839 (Stowe-Day).

282/32 Catharine B. to John Hooker, 27 November 1839 (Stowe-Day).

283/25 Isabella, op. cit., p. 293.

283/42 Isabella to John Hooker, 30 December 1842 (Stowe-Day).

284/14 John Hooker to Isabella, 3 January 1843, 20 October 1844 (Stowe-Day), and John Hooker, *Some Reminiscences of a Long Life* (Hartford, 1899), p. 342.

284/23 John Hooker to Isabella, 22 December 1844 (Stowe-Day).

285/12 Isabella to John Hooker, 10 January 1849 (Stowe-Day).

286/16 Thomas B. to Isabella, 5 October 1839, 9 January 1843 (Stowe-Day).

286/41 Clipping in Beecher Family Papers (Yale).

287/21 Thomas B. to Isabella, 9 January 1843 (Stowe-Day).

288/2   Thomas Beecher, "My Brother Henry," *Notable Sermons,* pp. 8–9.

288/26 *The Autobiography,* II, p. 366.

289/16 Ibid., pp. 381, 377–78.

289/36 Thomas B. to Isabella, 5 November 1846 (Stowe-Day).

290/13 Thomas B. to Isabella, 10 February 1847 (Stowe-Day).

290/26 Thomas B. to Harriet B. Stowe, 30 July 1846 (Radcliffe).
291/9   Thomas B. to Henry Ward B. [1848–1850] (Yale).
291/34 Nathan Lord to Lyman B., 6 June 1845, 10 July 1847 (Radcliffe). See also
        Thomas B. to Henry Ward B., 6 November 1848 (Yale).

Chapter 16. Lyman Beecher: Death of a Patriarch

293/25 Lyman B. Stowe, op. cit., p. 70.
295/22 *The Autobiography*, II, pp. 414–17.
296/15 Lyman Beecher, *Views in Theology* (Cincinnati, 1836), p. 195.
296/33 "Tribute to Henry Ward Beecher," 26 June 1887. *Works of Robert G. Ingersoll*
        (New York, 1912), XII, pp. 419–24.
297/6   G. A. Hubbell, *Horace Mann* (Philadelphia, 1910), pp. 7–8.
297/20 Catharine Beecher, *Religious Training of Children* (New York, 1864), pp. 340–
        45.
297/41 Lyman Abbott, op cit., p. 12.

Chapter 17. Catharine: The End of Many Beginnings

301/26 Catharine to Lydia (Mrs. Lyman Beecher), 30 April 1851 (Stowe-Day).
303/11 Catharine Beecher, *Letters to the People on Health and Happiness* (New York,
        1855), pp. 7, 9, 126.
305/9   Catharine Beecher, *The Elements of Mental and Moral Philosophy* (1831), p.
        xxiv.
306/6   Catharine Beecher, *Common Sense Applied to Religion* (New York, 1857), pp.
        304–5. See also Lyman B. Stowe, op. cit., pp. 99–102.
307/38 William Wight, *Annals of Milwaukee College, 1848–1891* (Milwaukee, 1891),
        p. 80.
308/17 Lyman B. Stowe, op. cit., pp. 129–30, 121.
309/6   Isabella B. Hooker to Catharine [1869] (Stowe-Day).
310/7   Catharine to Henry Ward, 27 February 1860 (Yale).
311/3   Harriet B. Stowe to Lyman and Henry Ward B. [19 September 1851](Yale).
311/27 Catharine Beecher, *Miss Beecher's Housekeeper and Healthkeeper* (New York,
        1873), p. 423.
311/41 Catharine Beecher, *Woman Suffrage and Woman's Profession* (Hartford, Conn.,
        1871), pp. 86–87.
312/12 Catharine to John R. Howard, 19 August 1870 (Stowe-Day).
312/34 Lyman B. Stowe, op. cit., pp. 133–34.
314/12 Catharine to Leonard Bacon, 9 March 1872 (Yale, Beinecke).
315/12 Harriet B. Stowe to Catharine [1877?] (Radcliffe).
315/18 Lyman B. Stowe, op. cit., p. 136.
315/26 Thomas and Edward B. to Mary B. Perkins, 10 and 12 May 1878 (Stowe-Day).

Chapter 18. Harriet: Days of Glory

317/21 Harriet Beecher Stowe, *Men of Our Times*, pp. 226, 227.
319/18 Harriet Beecher Stowe, *The Key to Uncle Tom's Cabin* (Boston, 1854), pp. 42–
        44. See also Josiah Henson, *Truth Stranger Than Fiction: Father Henson's Story
        of His Own Life*. Introduction by Harriet Beecher Stowe (Boston, 1858).
319/21 Foster, op. cit., pp. 30–31.
319/36 Charles E. Stowe, op. cit., p. 145.
320/6   Ibid., p. 476. See also Harriet to George Eliot, 18 March 1876 (Berg Coll., N.Y.
        Pub. Lib.).
320/34 Harriet to Dr. Gamaliel Bailey, 9 March 1851 (1888 copy in Garrison's Letters,
        Boston Pub. Lib.).

321/15 Forrest Wilson, op. cit., p. 272.

322/41 Fredrika Bremer, *The Homes of the New World* (New York, 1854), II, pp. 108–9. Quoted by Foster, op. cit., p. 57.

324/17 Charles E. Stowe, op. cit., p. 153.

324/24 Henry James, *A Small Boy and Others* (New York: Scribner's & Co., 1913), pp. 158–60.

324/32 Annie Fields, *Authors and Friends* (Boston, 1897), p. 194.

325/16 Harriet Beecher Stowe, *Uncle Tom's Cabin* (Boston, 1852), II, p. 75.

326/4   James Baldwin, "Everybody's Protest Novel," *Partisan Review,* June 1949. A white critic who shared the same hostile view, J. C. Furnas, revived, in *Goodbye to Uncle Tom* (1956), the old Southern contention that Mrs. Stowe knew little about slaves and he added that she merely gave whites a new set of black stereotypes. Like Baldwin, he allowed her no credit for crystallizing antislavery sentiment and he held her to blame for almost every antiblack prejudice since her time.

326/10 The episode was aggravated by the fact that Parker was not only an eminent churchman, formerly president of Union Theological Seminary, and a friend of Lyman Beecher's, but had been a pro-slavery opponent of Edward Beecher and Elijah Lovejoy during the riots in Alton, Illinois.

327/29 Harriet to Calvin Stowe, 29 May 1852. Quoted in Charles E. Stowe, op. cit., p. 181.

328/16 Forrest Wilson, op. cit., pp. 294–95.

331/31 She gave a similar description of herself in 1852 in a letter to the Reverend Charles Kingsley, the English novelist, and expressed a fear that she would disappoint her European admirers (Berg Coll., N.Y. Pub. Lib.).

332/3   Harriet to Eliza Follen. Kirkham, op. cit., p. 137, dates this letter December 1852.

332/43 Harriet Beecher Stowe, *Sunny Memories of Foreign Lands* (Boston and New York, 1854), I, p. 54.

333/14 Ibid., p. 76.

334/6   Forrest Wilson, op. cit., p. 379.

335/11 *Sunny Memories of Foreign Lands,* I, pp. 223–24, II, 161–63, 386–92.

Chapter 19. Harriet: "The little lady who made this big war"

339/34 Harriet Beecher Stowe, *Dred: A Tale of the Great Dismal Swamp* (Boston, 1856), II, pp. 178–79.

341/2   Harriet to Calvin Stowe, 6 September, 10 October 1856. Charles E. Stowe, op. cit., pp. 273, 279.

341/28 Forrest Wilson, op. cit,. p. 428.

342/16 Ibid., p. 429.

342/26 Harriet to Lady Byron, 2 June 1857 (Radcliffe).

343/12 Harriet to Catharine B., 17 August 1858 (Radcliffe).

343/34 Harriet to her daughter Georgie, 12 February 1859. Charles E. Stowe, op. cit., pp. 341–42.

344/10 *Independent,* 3 September 1857.

345/37 Harriet Beecher Stowe, *The Minister's Wooing* (New York, 1859), pp. 71–72, 261.

346/24 Ibid., pp. 252–58, 385.

347/36 Ibid., pp. 245, 258.

348/31 Merriam, op. cit., II, p. 165.

349/43 Forrest Wilson, op. cit., pp. 450–51.

352/9   Harriet to her daughter Hattie, 2 May 1861 (Radcliffe).

352/18 Wilson, op. cit., p. 468; Harriet to Charles Sumner, 13 April 1866 (Sumner Papers, Harvard).

353/15 Harriet to James Fields [early 1861] (Huntington).
356/1   Forrest Wilson, op. cit., p. 480.
356/7   Harriet to the Duchess of Argyll, 31 July 1862 (Viginia).
356/22 Harriet to James Fields, 13 November 1862 (Huntington).
357/6   Hattie Stowe to her sister Eliza, 3 December 1862 (Radcliffe).
358/13 Harriet to her son Fred, 11 July 1863 (Stowe-Day).
359/1   Harriet to James Fields, 3 November 1863 (Huntington).
359/36 Harriet Beecher Stowe, *Oldtown Folks* (Boston, 1869), p. 316.
360/18 Harriet Beecher Stowe, "Chimney Corner" column in *Atlantic Monthly*, May
        1865, and Wagenknecht, op. cit., p. 175.
360/27 Harriet to James Fields, 18 May 1865 (Huntington). See also Harriet Beecher
        Stowe, *The Chimney Corner* (Boston, 1868), pp. 303–7.
362/25 Annie Fields, *Life and Letters of Harriet Beecher Stowe* (Boston, 1898), p. 314,
        and Harriet to Annie Fields, 13 March 1868 (Huntington).
365/41 Harriet to James Fields, 28 December 1868 (Huntington).

Chapter 20. Henry: The Great Spellbinder

368/20 Eunice (Mrs. Henry Ward B.), *Ladies' Home Journal*, December 1891.
368/40 Beecher and Scoville, op. cit., p. 219.
369/14 Robert Shaplen, *Free Love and Heavenly Sinners* (New York, 1954), p. 24.
369/23 Henry Ward Beecher, *Yale Lectures on Preaching*, pp. 73–74.
369/37 John R. Howard, op. cit., p. 48.
370/4   Oliver H. Smith, *Early Indiana Trials and Sketches* (Cincinnati: Moore, Wil-
        stach, Keys & Co., 1858), pp. 94–95.
370/36 Henry Ward Beecher, *Patriotic Addresses*, ed. John R. Howard (New York,
        1887), p. 74.
370/39 Theodore Parker, in *Christian Union*, 24 April 1872.
371/22 Thomas B. to Harriet B. Stowe, 3 September 1848 (Radcliffe).
371/32 Sermon by Henry Ward Beecher, October 1849. Quoted by Clifford E. Clark,
        Jr., op. cit., p. 85.
372/18 Henry Ward Beecher, *Star Papers*, pp. 94, 304.
372/21 Rourke, op. cit., p. 135. See also Henry Seidel Canby, *Thoreau* (Boston:
        Houghton Mifflin, 1939), p. 413.
372/31 Theodore Parker, "Henry Ward Beecher," *Atlantic Monthly*, May 1858.
373/5   Bremer, op. cit., I, pp. 240–44.
373/30 Clark, op. cit., pp. 86–87.
374/4   New York *Tribune*, 24 October 1848. See also Beecher and Scoville, op. cit., p.
        293.
375/6   *Independent*, 21 February, 23 May 1850.
375/18 Quoted in Hibben, op. cit., pp. 119–20.
376/2   Henry Ward Beecher, *Star Papers*, pp. 14, 16, 25, 69, 85. Also Henry to Eunice,
        16 August 1850 (Yale).
376/18 One story, probably apocryphal, has it that although Henry promised to spread
        Harriet's novel far and wide, he did not read it until it had become the talk of the
        world.
376/36 New York *Tribune*, 2 June 1853.
377/2   Beecher and Scoville, op. cit., p. 270.
378/5   Henry Ward Beecher, *Star Papers*, p. 305.
378/17 Henry Ward Beecher, *Royal Truths*, pp. 40–41.
379/21 Ibid., p. 139.
381/11 Beecher and Scoville, op. cit., pp. 284–85; Hibben, op. cit., p. 135.
381/32 Henry Ward Beecher, *Freedom and War* (Boston, 1863), p. 10.
382/9   Beecher and Scoville, op. cit., pp. 297–98; Hibben, op. cit., p. 136.
383/26 *Independent*, 26 June 1856; Henry Ward Beecher, *Freedom and War*, pp. 64, 71.

383/36 *Independent,* 3 November 1859.
384/13 Henry Ward Beecher, *Freedom and War,* p. 23.
384/21 William G. McLoughlin, *The Meaning of Henry Ward Beecher* (New York, 1970), p. 198.
384/42 Henry Ward Beecher, *Freedom and War,* pp. 15–17, 63–65, 71.
386/25 *Theodore Tilton vs. Henry Ward Beecher. Action for Criminal Conversation.* Verbatim Report (New York, 1875) II, p. 11.
386/36 *Independent,* 27 October 1859.
387/11 Ibid., 8 December 1859. See also Heny Ward Beecher, *Norwood,* p. 278.
387/42 Henry Ward Beecher, *Woman's Duty to Vote* (New York, 1867). A speech at the eleventh National Woman's Rights Convention.
389/2   *Independent,* 7 August and 11 September 1862.
389/16 Henry Ward Beecher, *Freedom and War,* pp. 102–3.
389/28 *Independent,* 16 January 1862.
391/2   Ibid., 7 August 1862.
391/15 *Independent,* 11 September 1862; Harriet Beecher Stowe to Henry, 2 November 1862 (Yale).
392/5   Henry to Harriet Beecher Stowe, 28 July 1863 (Yale).
393/25 Henry Ward Beecher, *Patriotic Addresses,* p. 422.
394/28 Henry Ward Beecher, *Lectures and Orations,* p. 268.
395/14 Hibben, op. cit., p. 171.
395/29 Henry Ward Beecher, *Patriotic Addresses,* p. 741.
396/7   Hibben, op cit., p. 173; New York *Tribune,* 3 September 1866.
396/38 From a clipping of an advertisement (Stowe-Day).
397/19 Henry Ward Beecher, *Freedom and War,* p. 415.
398/34 Henry Ward Beecher, *Norwood,* pp. 133, 26.
399/2   Ibid., p. 308.
400/12 *Independent,* 21 November 1867.

Chapter 21. Sons in a Time of Transition

402/5   Isabella B. Hooker to John Hooker, 18 July 1852 (Stowe-Day).
402/11 G. W. Bungay, *Off-hand Takings* (New York, 1854), pp. 342–3.
402/42 Charles Beecher, *Life of Edward Beecher* (unpublished), pp. 182–83.
404/20 Ibid., pp. 205, 410, 509, 210–22.
405/40 Edward B. to Henry Ward B., 4 October, 13 November 1855 (Yale).
406/13 Hermann R. Muelder, *Fighers for Freedom* (New York, 1859), pp. 386–87, and Earnest Elmo Calkins, *They Broke the Prairie* (New York, 1937), pp. 191–93.
406/34 Edward Beecher, *The Concord of Ages* (New York, 1860), pp. 559–60, and Robert Merideth, op. cit., pp. 204–5.
408/27 Isabella B. Hooker to John Hooker, 26 June 1852 (Stowe-Day).
409/3   Charles B. to Isabella B. Hooker, 1 May 1848 (Radcliffe).
409/18 Charles B. to Edward B., 16 June 1846 (Radcliffe).
411/13 Charles B. to Henry Ward B., 12 April 1857 (Yale).
411/39 Charles B. to Isabella B. Hooker, 12 June 1859 (Stowe-Day).
412/16 Charles Beecher, *The Divine Sorrow* and "The Antichrist of New England," (both 1860).
412/39 Harriet B. Stowe to Leonard Bacon, 19 October 1863 (Yale, Beinecke), and Lyman B. Stowe, op. cit., p. 339.
414/29 Charles B. to his son Charles McCulloch B. Enclosed in a letter from Harriet B. Stowe to Henry Ward B., August 1867 (Yale).
414/41 "Stand at the Arikare," *Colorado Magazine of the State Historical Society of Colorado,* Fall 1964, and Charles B. to Harriet B. Stowe, 30 September 1868 (Stowe-Day).
415/1   Harriet B. Stowe to Henry Ward B., n.d. (Yale).

416/33 William H. Beecher, *The Duty of the Church to Her Ministry,* as delivered at Attica, N.Y., October 1839 (New York, 1841).
417/11 Reprinted as an appendix in Henry Jones, *Magnetism Repudiated* (New York, 1846).
418/1 *Chicago Post and Mail,* 24 July 1874. In scrapbooks assembled by Henry Bowen (N.Y. Pub. Lib.).
418/13 William B. to Henry Ward B., 23 December 1863 (Yale).

Chapter 22. Isabella: In Search of an Identity

419/12 John Hooker, *Some Reminiscences of a Long Life,* p. 170.
420/22 Isabella to John Hooker, 16 October 1853, 23 April 1857 (Stowe-Day).
421/1 Hooker, op. cit., p. 117; John Hooker to Isabella, 27 May 1854 (Stowe-Day).
421/21 Caskey, op. cit., p. 112.
421/31 Isabella to John Hooker, 24 June 1860 (Stowe-Day).
424/25 John Hooker to Isabella, 21 May 1860 (Stowe-Day).
424/25 Isabella to John Hooker, 25 and 26 November 1862 (Stowe-Day).
424/36 Isabella to John Hooker, 2 December 1862 (Stowe-Day).
426/21 Isabella to her daughter Alice, 17 January 1866, 22 September 1867 (Stowe-Day).
428/7 "The Last of the Beechers," *Connecticut Magazine,* 1905.
428/20 Isabella to Caroline Severance, 27 August 1869 (Stowe-Day).
428/23 Isabella to Mary Livermore, 15 November 1869 (Stowe-Day).
430/19 E. C. Stanton, S. B. Anthony and M. J. Gage, *History of Woman Suffrage* (Rochester, 1883–1900), II, pp. 380–92.
431/1 Horace Bushnell, *Women's Suffrage, The Reform Against Nature* (New York: Charles Scribner's & Co., 1869), pp. 166–67, 177.
431/29 Susan B. Anthony to Paulina Davis, July or August 1869. See also *Portraits of a Nineteenth Century Family,* eds. Earl A. French and Diana Royce (Hartford, 1976), p. 88.
431/37 *Elizabeth Cady Stanton as Revealed in Her Letters, Diaries and Reminiscences,* ed. Theodore Stanton and Harriot Stanton Blatch (New York, Harper & Bros., 1922), II, p. 124.
432/19 Ibid., p. 190, and Stanton to Isabella, 29 May 1870 (Stowe-Day).
432/42 *The Revolution,* 15 September 1870, and Judith Papachristou, *Women Together* (New York, 1976), p. 69.
433/6 Harriet B. Stowe to Henry Ward B., in late 1870 (Yale).
433/20 Isabella Beecher Hooker, *Womanhood: Its Sanctities and Fidelities* (Boston, 1873), pp. 13–15.
434/5 Ibid., p. 35.
434/27 E. C. Stanton to Isabella, 23 September 1869 (Stowe-Day).
435/2 Lutz, op. cit., pp. 182–83.

Chapter 23. Thomas: Going His Own Way

436/18 John Pitkin Norton diary, 28 September 1851 (Yale, Beinecke).
437/17 John Hooker to Isabella B. Hooker, 26 March 1850 (Stowe-Day).
437/38 Annis Ford Eastman, *A Flower of Puritanism: Julia Jones Beecher* (Elmira, N.Y. [1910]), p. 21.
438/11 Ibid., pp. 24–29.
438/22 Thomas to Henry Ward B. [1853] (Yale).
438/29 Mary B. Perkins to Isabella B. Hooker (Stowe-Day). See Caskey, op. cit., p. 276.

439/17 Thomas to Isabella B. Hooker, 16 September 1853 (Stowe-Day).

439/31 Annis Ford Eastman, "Thomas K. Beecher and the Park Church," *Christian Register,* 26 April 1900.

440/24 Memorial pamphlet in scrapbooks on Thomas K. Beecher (Stowe-Day).

441/42 Thomas to Jervis Langdon and the First Congregational Church of Elmira, 18 September 1854. Clipping in scrapbooks on Thomas K. Beecher (Stowe-Day).

442/29 Clipping in scrapbooks on Thomas K. Beecher (Stowe-Day).

442/36 Lyman B. Stowe, op. cit., p. 362.

443/37 Max Eastman, *Heroes I Have Known* (New York, 1942), p. 115.

444/16 Annis F. Eastman, *A Flower of Puritanism,* p. 35.

444/19 Clipping in scrapbooks on Thomas K. Beecher (Stowe-Day).

445/1 Lyman B. Stowe, op. cit., p. 365.

445/26 Thomas to Calvin Stowe, 14 February 1857 (Stowe-Day).

445/38 Isabella to John Hooker, 26 May 1860 (Stowe-Day).

446/18 Lyman B. Stowe, op. cit., pp. 367–69.

446/35 Joseph S. Van Why, in *Portraits of a Nineteenth Century Family,* eds. French and Royce, pp. 123–24.

447/9 Thomas to Henry Ward B., 30 August 1862 (Yale).

449/9 Alice Hooker to her mother, Isabella, 31 January 1867 (Stowe-Day).

449/19 Clipping in scrapbooks on Thomas K. Beecher (Stowe-Day).

450/14 Lyman B. Stowe, op. cit., p. 369.

Chapter 24. James: The Odd One

452/6 Isabella B. Hooker to John Hooker, 18 July 1852 (Stowe-Day).

453/3 See letters and articles by James Beecher in *Sailor's Magazine,* vols. 29–30, 1856–57.

453/18 Ibid., vols. 30–32, 1857–59.

453/21 James to Isabella B. Hooker, 11 January 1860 (Stowe-Day).

453/33 *Sailor's Magazine,* vol. 33, 1860–61.

453/38 Isabella Jones B. to Isabella B. Hooker, 30 April 1859 (Stowe-Day).

454/7 Thomas B. to Isabella B. Hooker, 30 April 1859 (Stowe-Day).

454/23 James to Isabella B. Hooker, 20 December 1859, 11 January, 28 March 1860 (Stowe-Day).

454/27 Thomas B. to Isabella B. Hooker [early 1860] (Stowe-Day).

454/39 Isabella B. Hooker to John Hooker, 5 June 1860 (Stowe-Day).

455/16 Isabella B. Hooker to John Hooker, 30 November 1862 (Stowe-Day).

455/33 Thomas B. to Ella Wolcott, 27 February 1863 (Stowe-Day).

456/23 Thomas B. to Isabella B. Hooker, 12, 19, 26 March 1863 (Stowe-Day).

457/9 Isabella B. Hooker to John Hooker, letters of late February, early March and 10 March 1863. (Stowe-Day).

457/13 James to Frances Johnson B., 26 June 1863 (Radcliffe).

458/7 James to Frances Johnson B., 15 June 1863 (Abeles).

458/28 James to Frances Johnson B., 3 October 1863 (Abeles).

458/41 James to Frances Johnson B., 23 December 1863 (Radcliffe).

459/10 Frances [Johnson] Beecher Perkins, "Two Years with a Colored Regiment," *New England Magazine,* January 1898.

460/2 James to Frances Johnson B., 19 February 1865 (Abeles).

460/34 Frances Beecher Perkins, "Two Years with a Colored Regiment."

461/5 James to Charles Sumner, 7 December 1865 (Radcliffe).

461/32 Alice Hooker to Isabella B. Hooker, 31 January [1867?] (Stowe-Day).

462/3 Leroy W. Kingman, *Early Owego* (Tioga County Historical Society, n.d.), pp. 602–5, and Memorial Address [1886] (Abeles).

463/4 Lyman B. Stowe, op. cit., p. 388.

463/26 James to [his wife], 1879 or 1880 (Radcliffe).

464/24   James to his wife, undated letters (Abeles).
464/31   James to his wife, 1882 or 1883 (Abeles).
464/39   James to his wife, 18 October [1885?] (Abeles).
465/5   James to his wife, [1885] (Abeles).
465/10   Frances Johnson B. to James, 31 January 1886 (Abeles).

Chapter 25. Henry Ward Beecher: Trial by Fire

470/15   Rugoff, op. cit., pp. 252, 280.
470/41   *Tilton vs. Beecher, Action for Criminal Conversation.* Verbatim Report by the Official Stenographer (New York, 1875), III, pp. 844–46. Also Isaac Kalloch to Henry Ward B., 14 April 1874 (Yale).
471/28   Charles F. Marshall, *The True History of the Brooklyn Scandal* (Philadelphia [1874]), p. 568.
472/8   *Tilton vs. Beecher,* II, p. 742. See also Marshall, op. cit., p. 257.
472/35   Ibid., I, p. 68, 16 June 1873.
473/36   Ibid., p. 496, 27 December 1866; p. 503, 2 December 1866.
474/33   Ibid., p. 493, 28 December 1866; p. 499, 25 January 1867; p. 490, 1 February 1868.
475/15   Ida H. Harper, *Life of Susan B. Anthony* (Indianapolis, 1898), I, p. 464.
475/40   Brooklyn *Daily Union,* 26 August 1874. But one source (Marshall, op. cit., p. 253) says it was Tilton who claimed that when his wife revealed the episode to him she showed him the entry.
476/10   *Tilton vs. Beecher,* III, p. 960, 20 December 1868.
477/20   Ibid., p. 819.
477/28   Shaplen, op. cit., p. 63.
477/39   *Independent,* 14 July 1870.
478/14   Shaplen, op. cit., p. 66.
479/8   Brooklyn *Argus,* 18 September 1874.
479/27   New York *Sun,* 22 August 1874.
480/22   *Tilton vs. Beecher,* I, pp. 75, 515, 26 December 1870.
481/15   Ibid., I, p. 61.
482/11   Ibid., II, p. 761, III, p. 28.
482/29   New York *Sun,* 14 August 1874.
483/10   *Tilton vs. Beecher,* I, p. 75.
483/27   Ibid., p. 188.
484/21   Ibid., pp. 65, 94.
485/8   *Tilton vs. Beecher,* III, p. 72.
485/17   *Diary of George Templeton Strong,* eds. Nevins and Thomas (New York: Macmillan, 1952), IV, p. 552.
485/40   *Tilton vs. Beecher,* I, pp. 87, 83, 84.
488/9   Theodore Tilton, *Victoria Woodhull: A Biographical Sketch* (New York, 1871), p. 35.
488/32   *Tilton vs. Beecher,* I, pp. 86–87.
489/11   Thomas B. to Isabella B. Hooker, 2 November 1872, in New York *Sun,* 22 August 1874.
489/34   *Woodhull & Claflin's Weekly,* 2 November 1872.
490/14   Henry to Isabella B. Hooker [25 October 1872] (Yale).
490/33   Brooklyn *Eagle,* 16 December 1872; Brooklyn *Argus,* 18 September 1874.
491/8   *Tilton vs. Beecher,* I, p. 100.
492/20   Ibid., p. 722.
493/5   Mrs. Henry Ward B. to Anne B. Scoville, 9 August 1874 (Yale).
494/16   Chicago *Tribune,* 1 October 1874.
496/42   Lyman B. Stowe, op. cit., p. 321.
498/13   *Tilton vs. Beecher,* I, pp. 721, 740–41.

499/17　Robert Shaplen, op. cit., p. 258; scrapbooks kept by Henry Bowen (N.Y. Pub. Lib.); Hibben, op. cit., p. 282, quoting from Tom Appleton's *More Uncensored Recollections.*
499/31　New York *Times,* 15 September 1875.
500/22　Beecher and Scoville, op. cit., pp. 545–48 and 552–54.
501/1　New York *Sun,* 2 and 3 March 1876.
502/4　New York *Times,* 16 April 1878.
502/26　Ibid.
503/19　Henry to his wife, 6 December 1878 (Yale).

Chapter 26. Henry Ward Beecher: Changing Gods

504/11　Hibben, op. cit., p. 254.
505/7　Henry Ward Beecher, *The Strike and Its Lessons* (N.Y., 1877) pp. 18–19. Quoted in Clark, op. cit., pp. 236–37.
506/6　Henry Ward Beecher, *Freedom and War,* pp. 63–64.
506/34　Henry Ward Beecher, "Gentile and Jew," a sermon reprinted in *The Carolina Israelite,* August 1945, vol. 2, no. 7. See also his editorial in *The Christian Union,* 17 September 1873, and Stephen Birmingham, *Our Crowd* (N.Y.: Harper & Row, 1967), pp. 141–47.
507/12　Clark, op. cit., p. 245.
507/20　Henry Ward Beecher, *Star Papers,* p. 285.
507/41　New York *Times,* 11 July 1868.
508/38　Henry to Carl Schurz, 29 July 1884 (Yale).
509/19　Henry Ward Beecher, *Lectures and Orations,* p. 311.
509/30　New York *Sun,* 29 October 1884.
510/21　Henry Ward Beecher, *Evolution and Religion,* enlarged ed. (New York, 1886), p. 166.
511/11　Henry Ward Beecher, *Lectures and Orations,* pp. 323, 318; *Congregationalist,* 27 July 1901.
511/20　Henry Ward Beecher, *Statement Before the Congregational Association of New York* (New York, 1883).
512/7　Henry Ward Beecher, *Evolution and Religion,* 1885, pp. 88–90.
513/2　Ibid., pp. 141, 115.
514/15　Kenneth R. Andrews, *Nook Farm: Mark Twain's Hartford Circle* (Cambridge, 1950), p. 52, from a letter in Joseph H. Twichell's *Journal,* V, p. 121 (Yale, Beinecke).
515/6　"A Tribute to Henry Ward Beecher," 26 June 1887. *Works of Robert G. Ingersoll* (New York, 1912), XII, pp. 419–24.

Chapter 27. Edward and Charles Beecher: Echoes of Another Age

517/5　Merideth, op. cit., p. 229.
517/23　Ibid., pp. 233–38.
518/9　Charles Beecher, *Life of Edward Beecher* (unpublished), pp. 394–95, 399–400, 483–84.
520/12　Charles to Isabella B. Hooker, 27 November 1873 (Stowe-Day).
520/38　Charles to Henry Ward B., 31 March 1874 (Yale).
521/35　Charles Beecher, *Spiritual Manifestations* (Boston, 1879), p. 94.
522/14　Charles to Henry Ward B., 14 January 1884 (Yale).
522/30　Henry Ward B. to Charles, 19 January 1884 (Yale).
523/27　Charles Beecher, *Patmos; or, the Unveiling* (Boston, 1896), pp. 312–13.
524/2　Ibid., pp. 193–94, 221.
524/18　Charles Beecher, *Spiritual Manifestations,* p. 9.

Chapter 28. Harriet Beecher Stowe: "And now I rest me, like a moored boat"

527/17 *Independent,* 26 August 1869.
527/22 Annie Fields, *Life and Letters of Harriet Beecher Stowe,* p. 323.
529/31 Mary B. Graff, *Mandarin on the St. Johns* (Gainesville, Fla., 1953), p. 67.
530/17 Harriet to Charles B., 19 May 1873. Quoted in Charles E. Stowe, op. cit., p. 406.
530/34 Isabella B. Hooker to Robert Allen, 4 January 1870 (Stowe-Day); Fred Stowe to Harriet, 5 February 1871 (Radcliffe).
531/23 Harriet to E. E. Hale, 14 April 1869 (Stowe-Day).
532/24 Harriet Beecher Stowe, *My Wife and I* (New York, 1871), p. 334.
536/31 Mrs. Thomas Bailey Aldrich, *Crowding Memories* (Boston/N.Y., Houghton Mifflin, 1920), pp. 120-7.
538/7 Harriet Beecher Stowe, *We and Our Neighbors* (New York, 1873), pp. 94, 335.
538/36 Henry James, in *The Nation,* 1875, XXI, p. 61.
539/17 Harriet to Annie Fields, 6 February 1872 (Huntington).
539/29 Annie Fields, *Authors and Friends,* pp. 220-21.
541/7 Harriet to Annie Fields, 25 December 1872 (Huntington).
541/21 Harriet to her daughter Eliza, 11 May 1873 (Radcliffe).
542/22 Harriet to George Eliot, 25 May 1869, 8 February 1872 (Berg Coll., N.Y. Pub. Lib.).
542/29 George Eliot to Harriet, 4 March 1872 (Racliffe); Wilson, op. cit., pp. 575-76.
543/18 Charles E. Stowe, op. cit., pp. 420-21.
543/31 Harriet to George Eliot, 20 April 1873 (Berg Coll., N.Y. Pub. Lib.).
543/43 Harriet to George Eliot, 25 September 1876 (Berg Coll., N.Y. Pub. Lib.) and George Eliot to Harriet, 29 October 1876 (Radcliffe).
544/28 Harriet to her son Charles, 23 May 1875 (Radcliffe).
545/2 Harriet to George Eliot, 18 March 1876 (Berg Coll., N.Y. Pub. Lib.).
545/21 Harriet to her son Charles, [4] and 16 February 1881 (Radcliffe).
545/31 John R. Adams, *Harriet Beecher Stowe* (New York, 1963), pp. 81-82.
546/11 Harriet to George Eliot, 18 March 1876 (Berg Coll., N.Y. Pub. Lib.).
546/22 Charles E. Stowe, op. cit., pp. 413-14.
548/4 Forrest Wilson, op. cit., p. 628.
548/42 Charles E. Stowe, op. cit., pp. 507-8.
549/30 *Mark Twain's Autobiography* (N.Y./London: Harper & Bros., 1924), II, p. 243.
550/3 5 February 1893 (Lib. Congress).
550/18 Kenneth R. Andrews, op. cit., p. 219.
550/26 Joseph S. Van Why, in *Portraits of a Nineteenth Century Family,* eds. French and Royce, p. 111.

Chapter 29. Thomas K. Beecher: "I wait—singing songs in the night"

554/11 Thomas to Rev. Scoville, 7 February 1870 (Yale).
555/31 Lyman B. Stowe, op. cit., pp. 370-73.
556/12 Rev. Edson Rogers, in memorial volume, *Teacher of the Park Church* (Elmira, N.Y., 1900), pp. 21, 24.
556/16 Elmira *Advertiser,* 15 March 1900. Reprinted in *Teacher of Park Church.*
557/5 Thomas K. Beecher, *Our Seven Churches* (New York, 1870), pp. vi-vii, 93-97.
557/42 Thomas to Ella L. Wolcott, 24 January 1865 (Stowe-Day).
558/17 Lyman B. Stowe, op. cit., p. 373.
559/21 Andrews, op. cit., p. 133, from Joseph Twichell, *Journal,* IV, p. 54, November 13-16, 1880 (Yale, Beinecke).
559/38 Newspaper clippings in scrapbooks on Thomas K. Beecher (Stowe-Day).
560/16 Isabella B. Hooker to Thomas, 3 November 1872, in Marshall, op. cit., p. 333.

561/7 Thomas to Isabella B. Hooker, 5 November 1872, in Marshall, op. cit., pp. 335–36.
562/3 Quoted in Max Eastman, *Heroes I Have Known,* pp. 124–25.
562/11 Julia B. to Olivia Langdon, 28 April 1877 (Stowe-Day).
562/29 Max Eastman, op. cit., p. 127.
563/19 Thomas Beecher, "My Brother Henry," *Notable Sermons,* pp. 10, 13–14.
564/8 Thomas Beecher, *Notable Sermons,* Addendum.
564/20 Thomas to Isabella and John Hooker, 4 August 1891 (Stowe-Day).
565/10 Max Eastman, op. cit., p. 112.
565/15 Annis Ford Eastman, *A Flower of Puritanism,* p. 38.
566/20 Thomas to Isabella B. Hooker, 25 August 1863 (Stowe-Day).

Chapter 30. Isabella Beecher Hooker: An Identity Achieved

567/7 Annie Fields, *Life and Letters of Harriet Beecher Stowe,* p. 294.
567/27 Twain to Mrs. Fairbanks, *Mark Twain to Mrs. Fairbanks,* ed. Dixon Wecter (San Marino, Cal., Huntington Library, 1949), p. 15.
569/25 E. C. Stanton to Isabella, 28 December 1870, 3 January 1871 (Stowe-Day).
570/31 Lyman B. Stowe, op. cit., pp. 348–49.
571/14 Phebe Hanaford to Isabella, 9 August, 15 September 1871 (Stowe-Day).
571/36 Isabella to Susan B. Anthony, 11 March 1871 (Stowe-Day).
572/3 Isabella to Mary Livermore, 15 March 1871 (Stowe-Day).
572/12 Isabella to Sarah Stearns [Spring 1871] (Stowe-Day).
572/21 Johanna Johnston, *Mrs. Satan* (New York, 1967), p. 102.
572/42 Isabella to Anna Savery, 12 November 1871 (Stowe-Day).
573/35 Catharine B. to the Hartford *Courant,* 1 February 1871.
575/19 Henry Ward B. to Isabella, 25 April 1872, from a copy made by Henry E. Burton, Isabella's son-in-law (Yale).
575/22 Isabella to Thomas B., 3 November 1872, in Marshall, op. cit., 334.
575/32 18 November 1871. As published in *Woodhull & Claflin's Weekly,* 16 August 1873.
576/10 Lutz, op. cit., p. 218.
577/26 Isabella to Henry Ward B., 1 November 1872, in New York *Sun,* 22 August 1874.
577/36 Victoria Woodhull to Isabella, 8 August 1871, in New York *Sun,* 22 August 1874.
578/37 John Hooker to Isabella, 3 November 1872, and Isabella to Henry Ward B., 27 November 1872, in New York *Sun,* 22 August 1874.
579/12 Harriet B. Stowe to Mary B. Claflin, 24 December 1872 (Hayes).
580/27 Isabella to her son Edward, 14 December 1875, 20 February 1876 (Stowe-Day).
581/18 Isabella's Diaries, 1878, p. 109 (Connecticut). Of the parts of her diaries that have been located (some were found in a waste pile in a Hartford barn in 1934), the 1876–1877 and 1901 segments are at the Stowe-Day Foundation and the 1878 segment at the Connecticut Historical Society. Most of them are reproduced on microfiche in *The Isabella Beecher Project.*
582/27 Isabella's Diaries, 1876, pp. 128–30 (Stowe-Day).
583/18 Ibid., pp. 187, 250–53.
583/43 Ibid., pp. 254–57.
584/34 Ibid., pp. 41, 53, 94, 72, 87.
585/8 Stanton, Anthony and Gage, op. cit., III, 104–6.
586/8 Isabella to her daughter Mary, 26 July 1877 (Stowe-Day).
586/38 Isabella's Diaries, 1876, pp. 193–94.
587/26 Isabella's Diaries, 1878, pp. 89, 92, 93–94.
588/26 Isabella to her daughter Alice, 11 December 1889, 7 January 1890, 9 December 1892, 4 February 1892, 29 October 1891 (all Stowe-Day).

589/17 John Hooker to Isabella, 23 September 1884 (Stowe-Day).

590/12 Stanton, Anthony and Gage, op. cit., IV, p. 116, and III, p. 99n; Isabella to [John Hooker?], 5 March 1889 (Stowe-Day).

590/32 Isabella to her daughter Alice, 2 June 1889 (Stowe-Day).; Isabella to a Hartford newspaper, 23 March 1889, included in a letter to Alice dated 10 July 1889 (Stowe-Day).

591/15 Chicago *Herald,* reprinted in the Hartford *Times,* 23 September 1891.

591/36 Isabella and John Hooker to Alice, 12 October 1893 (Stowe-Day).

592/6 Isabella to Alice, 28 November 1893, 4 January 1894 (Stowe-Day).

593/7 25 April 1901 (Radcliffe). See also Mary A. Hill, *Charlotte Perkins Gilman: The Making of a Radical Feminist* (Philadelphia: Temple University Press, 1980).

593/26 Isabella to Alice, 25 July 1892 (Stowe-Day).

594/18 Andrews, op cit., p. 268, note 12.

594/33 Lyman B. Stowe, op. cit., p. 352.

595/13 Stanton, Anthony and Gage, op. cit., IV, p. 296.

595/17 "The Last of the Beechers," *Connecticut Magazine,* 1905, p. 295.

595/21 Isabella's Diaries, 1901, pp. 11, 68 (Stowe-Day).

Selected Bibliography

Books of only incidental reference are not included in this list but are identified in the Notes.

Adams, John R. *Harriet Beecher Stowe*. New York: D. Appleton-Century Co., 1963.

Abbott, Lyman. *Henry Ward Beecher*. Boston: Houghton Mifflin Co., 1903.

Abbott, Lyman, and Halliday, S. B. *Henry Ward Beecher: A Sketch of His Career*. Hartford, Conn.: American Publishing Co., 1887.

Andrews, Kenneth R. *Nook Farm: Mark Twain's Hartford Circle*. Cambridge, Mass.: Harvard University Press, 1950.

Baldwin, James. "Everybody's Protest Novel." *Partisan Review*, June 1949.

Banner, Lois W. *Elizabeth Cady Stanton: A Radical for Woman's Rights*. Boston: Little, Brown & Co., 1980.

Beecher, Catharine. *An Address to the Protestant Clergy of the United States*. New York: Harper & Bros., 1846.

———. *An Appeal to the People on Behalf of Their Rights as Authorized Interpreters of the Bible*. New York: Harper & Bros., 1860.

———. *Common Sense Applied to Religion; or, The Bible and the People*. New York: Harper & Bros., 1857.

———. *Educational Reminiscences and Suggestions*. New York: J. B. Ford & Co., 1874.

———. *The Elements of Mental and Moral Philosophy, Founded upon Experience, Reason and the Bible*. Privately printed, 1831.

———. *An Essay on the Education of Female Teachers*. New York: Van Nostrand and Dwight, 1835.

———. *An Essay on Slavery and Abolitionism with Reference to the Duty of American Females*. Philadelphia: Henry Perkins, 1837.

———. *The Evils Suffered by American Women and American Children: The Causes and the Remedy*. New York: Harper & Bros., 1846.

———. *Letters on the Difficulties of Religion*. Hartford, Conn.: Belknap and Hamersley, 1836.

———. *Letters to the People on Health and Happiness*. New York: Harper & Bros., 1855.

———. *Miss Beecher's Housekeeper and Healthkeeper*. New York: Harper & Bros., 1873.

———. *The Moral Instructor for Schools and Families*. Cincinnati: Truman and Smith, 1838.

———. *Physiology and Calisthenics for Schools and Families*. New York: Harper & Bros., 1856.

———. *Religious Training of Children in the School, the Family, and the Church*. New York: Harper & Bros., 1864.

———. *Suggestions Respecting Improvements in Education*. Hartford, Conn.: Packard & Butler, 1829.

———. *A Treatise on Domestic Economy, for the Use of Young Ladies at Home and at School*. New York: Harper & Bros., 1841. Revised edition, 1851.

———. *The True Remedy for the Wrongs of Women*. Boston: Phillips, Sampson & Co., 1851.

———. *Truth Stranger Than Fiction: A Narrative of Recent Transactions, Involving Inquiries in Regard to the Principles of Honor, Truth, and Justice, Which Obtain in a Distinguished American University*. New York: Privately printed, 1850.

————. *Woman Suffrage and Woman's Profession*. Hartford, Conn.: Brown & Gross, 1871.

Beecher, Charles. *The Divine Sorrow: A Sermon*. Andover, Mass., 1860.

————. *The Duty of Disobedience to Wicked Laws: A Sermon on the Fugitive Slave Law*. Newark, N.J., 1851.

————. *The Eden Tableau*. Boston: Lee & Shepard, 1880.

————. "Eoline; or, The Wind-Spirit." *Godey's Lady's Book*, September 1840.

————. *The Incarnation; or, Pictures of the Virgin and Her Son*. With an Introductory Essay by Harriet Beecher Stowe. New York: Harper & Bros., 1849.

————. *Life of Edward Beecher*. Unpublished. Illinois College Library.

————. *Patmos; or, the Unveiling*. Boston: Lee & Shepard, 1896.

————. *A Plea for the Maine Law*. A Sermon. London: National Temperance Society, 1853.

————. *Redeemer and Redeemed: An Investigation of the Atonement and of Eternal Judgment*. Boston: Lee & Shepard, 1864.

————. *A Review of "Spiritual Manifestations."* New York: G. P. Putnam & Co., 1853.

————. *Spiritual Manifestations*. Boston: Lee & Shepard, 1879.

Beecher, Edward. *The Concord of Ages*. New York: Derby & Jackson, 1860.

————. *The Conflict of Ages; or, the Great Debate on the Moral Relations of God and Man*. Boston: Phillips, Sampson & Co., 1853.

————. *Narrative of Riots at Alton*. Alton, Ill.: George Holton, 1838. Paperback edition with Introduction by Robert Merideth. New York: E. P. Dutton, 1965.

————. *The Papal Conspiracy Exposed, and Protestantism Defended*. Boston: Stearns & Co., 1855.

Beecher, Edward, and Beecher, Charles. *The Result Tested: A Review of the Proceedings of a Council*. Boston: Wright & Potter, 1863.

Beecher, George. *The Autobiographical Remains of Rev. George Beecher*. Edited by Catharine Beecher. New York: Leavitt, Trow & Co., 1844.

Beecher, Harriet. *See* Harriet Beecher Stowe.

Beecher, Henry Ward. *Autobiographical Reminiscences*. Edited by T. J. Ellinwood. New York: Frederick A. Stokes & Co., 1898.

————. *Evolution and Religion*. Enlarged edition. New York: Fords, Howard & Hulbert, 1886.

————. *Eyes and Ears*. Boston: Ticknor & Fields, 1862.

————. *Freedom and War*. Boston: Ticknor & Fields, 1863.

————. *Lectures and Orations*. Edited by N. D. Hillis. New York: Fleming H. Revell & Co., 1913. Reprinted by AMS Press, 1970.

————. *New Star Papers; or, Views and Experiences of Religious Subjects*. New York: Derby & Jackson, 1859.

————. *Norwood; or, Village Life in New England*. New York: J. B. Ford & Co., 1867.

————. *Patriotic Addresses*. Edited by John Raymond Howard. New York: Fords, Howard & Hulbert, 1887.

————. *Royal Truths*. Boston: Ticknor & Fields, 1866.

————. *The Sermons of Henry Ward Beecher*. 8 vols. New York: J. B. Ford & Co., 1869-73.

————. *Star Papers; or, Experiences of Art and Nature*. New York: J. C. Derby, 1855.

————. *A Summer in England with Henry Ward Beecher*. With an Account of the Tour by James B. Pond. New York: Fords, Howard & Hulbert, 1887.

————. *Twelve Lectures to Young Men*. New York: D. Appleton & Co., 1879. An enlarged edition of *Seven Lectures to Young Men*. Indianapolis: Thomas B. Cutler, 1844.

————. *Yale Lectures on Preaching*. New York: J. B. Ford & Co., 1872-73.

Beecher, Mrs. Henry Ward. *From Dawn to Daylight; or, The Simple Story of a Western Home*. By a Minister's Wife. New York: Derby & Jackson, 1861.

————. *Letters from Florida.* New York: D. Appleton & Co., 1879.

————. "Mr. Beecher As I Knew Him." *Ladies' Home Journal,* October 1891–August 1892.

Beecher, Isabella. *See* Isabella Beecher Hooker.

Beecher, James. Letters and articles in *The Sailor's Magazine.* Vols. 29–33. New York: The American Seamen's Friend Society, 1856–61.

Beecher, Lyman. *The Autobiography of Lyman Beecher.* Edited by Barbara M. Cross. Cambridge, Mass.: The Belknap Press of Harvard University Press, 1961.

————. *Letters of the Rev. Dr. Beecher and Rev. Mr. Nettleton on the "New Measures."* New York: G. & C. Carvil, 1828.

————. *A Plea for the West.* Cincinnati: Truman & Smith, 1835.

————. *Six Sermons on . . . Intemperance,* 2nd ed. Boston: Marvin, 1827.

————. *Views in Theology.* Cincinnati: Truman & Smith, 1836.

————. *Works.* Boston: J. P. Jewett & Co., 1852–53.

Beecher, Thomas K. *Notable Sermons.* Elmira, N.Y.: Osborne Press, 1914.

————. *Our Seven Churches.* New York: J. B. Ford & Co., 1870.

————. Scrapbooks Relating to Thomas K. Beecher. Hartford, Conn.: Stowe-Day Foundation.

————. *Thomas K. Beecher: Teacher of the Park Street Church.* Memorial Addresses and Editorials. Elmira, N.Y., 1900.

Beecher, William C., and Scoville, Samuel, assisted by Mrs. Henry Ward Beecher. *A Biography of Henry Ward Beecher.* New York: Charles L. Webster & Co., 1888.

Beecher, William H. *The Duty of the Church to Her Ministry.* As delivered at Attica, N.Y., October 1839. Batavia, N.Y., 1841.

————. "The Phenomena of Mesmerism." An appendix in *Animal Magnetism Repudiated as Sorcery,* by Henry Jones. New York: J. S. Redfield, 1846.

Bremer, Fredrika. *The Homes of the New World: Impressions of America.* New York: Harper & Bros., 1854.

Bungay, George W. *Off-hand Takings; or, Crayon Sketches of Notable Men of Our Age.* New York: DeWitt & Davenport, 1854.

Calkins, Earnest Elmo. *They Broke the Prairie, Being Some Account of the Settlement of the Upper Mississippi Valley.* New York: Charles Scribner's Sons, 1937.

Caskey, Marie. *Chariot of Fire: Religion and the Beecher Family.* New Haven: Yale University Press, 1978.

Chester, Giraud. *Embattled Maiden: The Life of Anna Dickinson.* New York: G. P. Putnam's Sons, 1951.

Christian Union, The. A weekly issued in New York. See especially 1871–75.

Clark, Clifford E., Jr. *Henry Ward Beecher: Spokesman for a Middle-Class America.* Urbana: University of Illinois Press, 1978.

Corning, James Leonard. *Personal Recollections of Henry Ward Beecher.* An address at Plymouth Church, March 1, 1903. Brooklyn: Brooklyn Eagle Press, n.d.

Derby, J. C. *Fifty Years Among Authors, Books and Publishers.* New York: G. W. Carleton & Co., 1884.

Detty, Victor Charles. *History of the Presbyterian Church of Wysox, Pa.* Privately printed, 1939.

Douglas, Ann. *The Feminization of American Culture.* New York: Alfred A. Knopf, 1977.

Eastman, Annis Ford. *A Flower of Puritanism: Julia Jones Beecher, 1826–1905.* Elmira, N.Y.: Snyder Bros. [1910].

————. "Thomas K. Beecher and the Park Church." *The Christian Register,* 26 April 1900.

Eastman, Max. *Heroes I Have Known: Twelve Who Lived Great Lives.* New York: Simon & Schuster, 1942.

Elsmere, Jane Shaffer. *Henry Ward Beecher: The Indiana Years.* Indianapolis: Indiana Historical Society, 1973.

Fields, Annie. *Authors and Friends.* Boston: Houghton Mifflin Co., 1897.

————. *Life and Letters of Harriet Beecher Stowe*. Boston: Houghton Mifflin Co., 1898.

Flexner, Eleanor. *Century of Struggle: The Woman's Rights Movement in the United States*. Cambridge, Mass.: Harvard University Press, 1959.

Foster, Charles H. *The Rungless Ladder: Harriet Beecher Stowe and New England Puritanism*. Durham, N.C.: Duke University Press, 1954.

French, Earl A., and Royce, Diana, eds. *Portraits of a Nineteenth Century Family*. Hartford, Conn.: Stowe-Day Foundation, 1976.

Furnas, J. C. *Goodbye to Uncle Tom*. New York: William Sloane Associates, 1956.

Gilbertson, Catherine. *Harriet Beecher Stowe*. New York: D. Appleton-Century Co., 1937.

Gill, John. *Tide Without Turning: Elijah P. Lovejoy and Freedom of the Press*. Boston: Starr King Press, 1958.

Graff, Mary B. *Mandarin on the St. Johns*. Gainesville: University of Florida Press, 1953.

Grimké, Angelina E. *Letters to Catherine E. Beecher in Reply to an Essay on Slavery and Abolitionism*. Boston: Isaac Knapp, 1838.

————. *See* Weld. *Letters of Theodore Dwight Weld, Angelina Grimké Weld and Sarah Grimké*.

Harlow, Alvin F. *The Serene Cincinnatians*. New York: E. P. Dutton & Co., 1950.

Harveson, Mae Elizabeth. *Catharine Esther Beecher: Pioneer Educator*. Philadelphia: University of Pennsylvania Press, 1932.

Hatch, Rebecca Taylor. *Personal Reminiscences and Memorials*. New York: Privately printed, 1905.

Hayward, Edward F. *Lyman Beecher*. Boston, 1904.

Henry, Stuart C. *Unvanquished Puritan: A Portrait of Lyman Beecher*. Grand Rapids, Mich.: William B. Eerdmans Publishing Co., 1973.

Henson, Josiah. *Truth Stranger Than Fiction. Father Henson's Story of His Own Life*. With an Introduction by Harriet Beecher Stowe. Boston: J. P. Jewett, 1858.

Hibben, Paxton. *Henry Ward Beecher: An American Portrait*. New York: George H. Doran Co., 1927. Readers Club edition, with a Foreword by Sinclair Lewis, 1942.

Hightower, Raymond L. "Joshua L. Wilson, Frontier Controversialist." *Church History*, vols. 2–3, 1933–34.

Hill, Mary A. *Charlotte Perkins Gilman: The Making of a Radical Feminist*. Philadelphia: Temple University Press, 1980.

[Hoffman, Charles Fenno.] *A Winter in the West*. New York: Harper & Bros., 1835.

Holmes, Oliver Wendell, "The Minister Plenipotentiary." *Atlantic Monthly*, vol. 13, 1864. On Henry Ward Beecher.

Hooker, Isabella Beecher. *The Isabella Beecher Hooker Project*. A Microfiche Edition of Her Papers. Millwood, N.Y.: KTO Microform, 1979. Guide/Index published by Stowe-Day Foundation, Hartford, 1979.

————. "The Last of the Beechers: Memories of My Eighty-third Birthday." *Connecticut Magazine*, vol. 9, 1905.

————. *A Mother's Letters to Her Daughter on Woman's Suffrage*. Hartford: Connecticut Woman Suffrage Association, 1870. Tracts 2 and 4. First published anonymously in *Putnam's Monthly*, November, December 1868.

————. *Womanhood: Its Sanctities and Fidelities*. Boston: Lee & Shepard, 1873.

Hooker, John. *The Bible and Woman Suffrage*. Hartford: Connecticut Woman Suffrage Association, 1870. Tract 1.

————. *Some Reminiscences of a Long Life*. Hartford, Conn.: Belknap & Warfield, 1899.

Hopkins, Vivian C. *Prodigal Puritan: A Life of Delia Bacon*. Cambridge, Mass.: Belknap Press of Harvard University Press, 1959.

Howard, John Raymond. *Remembrance of Things Past*. New York: Thomas Y. Crowell, 1925.

Independent, The. A weekly issued in New York. See especially 1848–70.

Johnston, Johanna. *Mrs. Satan: The Incredible Saga of Victoria C. Woodhull.* New York: G. P. Putnam's Sons, 1967.

———. *Runaway to Heaven: The Story of Harriet Beecher Stowe.* New York: Doubleday & Co., 1963.

Kirkham, E. Bruce. *The Building of Uncle Tom's Cabin.* Knoxville: University of Tennessee Press, 1977.

Knox, Thomas W. *Life and Work of Henry Ward Beecher.* New York: Wilson & Ellis, 1887.

Leary, Edward A. *Indianapolis: The Story of a City.* Indianapolis/New York, Bobbs-Merrill Co., 1971.

Lerner, Gerda. *The Grimké Sisters from South Carolina: Rebels Against Slavery.* Boston: Houghton Mifflin Co., 1967.

Lovejoy, Joseph C. and Owen. *Memoir of the Rev. Elijah P. Lovejoy.* New York: John S. Taylor, 1838.

Lutz, Alma. *Created Equal: A Biography of Elizabeth Cady Stanton.* New York: John Day Co., 1940.

Mahan, Asa. *Autobiography: Intellectual, Moral, Spiritual.* London: Published privately, 1882.

Mansfield, Edward D. *Personal Memories, 1803–43.* Cincinnati: Robert Clarke & Co., 1879.

Marshall, Charles F. *The True History of the Brooklyn Scandal.* Philadelphia: National Publishing Co., 1874.

Mathews, W. S. B. "A Remarkable Personality: Thomas K. Beecher." *The Outlook,* vol. 82, 10 March 1906.

McCray, Florine Thayer. *The Life-Work of the Author of Uncle Tom's Cabin.* New York: Funk & Wagnalls, 1889.

McCulloch, Hugh. *Men and Measures of Half a Century.* New York: Charles Scribner's Sons, 1888.

McLoughlin, William G. *The Meaning of Henry Ward Beecher: An Essay on the Shifting Values of Mid-Victorian America.* New York: Alfred A. Knopf, 1970.

Merideth, Robert. *The Politics of the Universe: Edward Beecher, Abolition and Orthodoxy.* Nashville: Vanderbilt University Press, 1968.

Mill, John Stuart, and Mill, Harriet Taylor. *Essays in Sex Equality.* Edited with an Introduction by Alice S. Rossi. Chicago: University of Chicago Press, 1970.

Papachristou, Judith. *Women Together: A History in Documents of the Women's Movement in the United States.* New York: Alfred A. Knopf, 1976.

Parker, Theodore. "Henry Ward Beecher." *Atlantic Monthly,* May 1858.

Perkins, Frances Johnson Beecher. "A Seven-Years' Outing." *New England Magazine.* N.S. 22, June 1900.

———. "Two Years with a Colored Regiment: A Woman's Experience." *New England Magazine,* vol. 17, January 1898.

Rammelkamp, Charles Henry. *Illinois College: A Centennial History, 1829–1929.* New Haven: Yale University Press, 1928.

Randall, Randolph C. *James Hall, Spokesman of the Midwest.* Columbus: Ohio State University Press, 1964.

Rourke, Constance Mayfield. *Trumpets of Jubilee.* New York: Harcourt, Brace & Co., 1927. Reprinted as Harbinger Book, 1963.

Sailor's Magazine, The. Vols. 29–33, 1856–61. *See* letters and articles by James Beecher.

Shaplen, Robert. *Free Love and Heavenly Sinners: The Great Henry Ward Beecher Scandal.* New York: Alfred A. Knopf, 1954.

Sklar, Kathryn Kish. *Catharine Beecher: A Study in Domesticity.* New Haven: Yale University Press, 1973.

Smith, Henry Nash. *Democracy and the Novel.* New York: Oxford University Press, 1978.

Stanton, E. C., Anthony, S. B., and Gage, M. J. *History of Woman Suffrage.* 4 vols. Rochester, N.Y., 1887–1922.

Stowe, Calvin E. "Sketches and Recollections of Dr. Lyman Beecher." *Congregational Quarterly,* vol. 6, July 1864.

Stowe, Charles Edward. *Life of Harriet Beecher Stowe.* Boston/New York: Houghton Mifflin Co., 1889.

Stowe, Harriet Beecher. *Agnes of Sorrento.* Boston: Ticknor & Fields, 1862.

———. (Pseudonym: Christopher Crowfield.) *The Chimney Corner.* Boston: Ticknor & Fields, 1868.

———. *Dred: A Tale of the Great Dismal Swamp.* Boston: Charles R. Osgood & Co., 1856. Later issued as *Nina Gordon.*

———. *The Key to Uncle Tom's Cabin.* Boston: John P. Jewett & Co., 1854.

———. *Lady Byron Vindicated.* Boston: Fields, Osgood & Co., 1870.

———. (Pseudonym: Christopher Crowfield.) *Little Foxes.* Boston: Houghton Mifflin Co., 1865.

———. *The Mayflower; or, Sketches of Scenes and Characters Among the Descendants of the Pilgrims.* New York: Harper & Bros., 1843.

———. *Men of Our Times; or, Leading Patriots of the Day.* Hartford, Conn.: Hartford Publishing Co., 1869.

———. *The Minister's Wooing.* New York: Derby & Jackson, 1859.

———. *My Wife and I; or, Harry Henderson's History.* New York: J. B. Ford & Co., 1871.

———. *Oldtown Folks.* Boston: Fields, Osgood & Co., 1869.

———. *Palmetto Leaves.* Boston: James R. Osgood & Co., 1873.

———. *The Pearl of Orr's Island.* Boston: Ticknor & Fields, 1862.

———. *Pink and White Tyranny: A Society Novel.* Boston: Roberts Bros., 1871.

———. *Poganuc People.* New York: Fords, Howard & Hulbert, 1878.

———. *Sunny Memories of Foreign Lands.* 2 vols. Boston: Phillips, Sampson & Co.; New York: J. C. Derby, 1854.

———. *Uncle Sam's Emancipation and Other Sketches.* Philadelphia: Willis P. Hazard, 1853.

———. *Uncle Tom's Cabin; or, Life Among the Lowly.* Boston: John P. Jewett, 1852.

———. *We and Our Neighbors; or, The Records of an Unfashionable Street.* New York: J. B. Ford & Co., 1873.

———. *Women in Sacred History.* New York: J. B. Ford & Co., 1873.

Stowe, Lyman Beecher. *Saints, Sinners and Beechers.* Indianapolis: Bobbs-Merrill Co., 1934.

Thomas, Benjamin P. *Theodore Weld: Crusader for Freedom.* New Brunswick, N.J.: Rutgers University Press, 1950.

Tilton, Theodore. *Victoria Woodhull: A Biographical Sketch.* New York, 1871.

Tilton vs. Beecher. Action for Criminal Conversation. Verbatim Report by the Official Stenographer. 3 vols. New York: McDivitt, Campbell & Co., 1875.

Trollope, Frances. *Domestic Manners of the Americans.* Edited by Donald Smalley. New York: Alfred A. Knopf, 1949. First published in 1832.

Wagenknecht, Edward. *Harriet Beecher Stowe: The Known and the Unknown.* New York: Oxford University Press, 1965.

Weisberger, Bernard A. *They Gathered at the River: The Story of the Great Revivalists and Their Impact upon Religion in America.* Boston: Little Brown & Co., 1958.

Weiss, Harry B., and Kemble, Howard R. *The Great American Water-Craze.* Trenton, N.J.: Past Times Press, 1967.

Weld. *Letters of Theodore Dwight Weld, Angelina Grimké Weld and Sarah Grimké.* Edited by G. H. Barnes and D. L. Dumond. 2 vols. New York, D. Appleton-Century, 1934.

White, James C. *Personal Reminiscences of Lyman Beecher.* New York: Funk & Wagnalls, 1882.

Wight, William. *Annals of Milwaukee College, 1848–1891*. Milwaukee, 1891.
Wilson, Edmund. *Patriotic Gore: Studies of the Literature of the American Civil War*. New York: Oxford University Press, 1962.
Wilson, Forrest. *Crusader in Crinoline: The Life of Harriet Beecher Stowe*. Philadelphia: J. B. Lippincott Co., 1941.

Index

BELMONT COLLEGE LIBRARY